❖

The Invisible Woman

Gender, Crime, and Justice

THIRD EDITION

JOANNE BELKNAP
University of Colorado, Boulder

THOMSON
™
WADSWORTH

Australia • Brazil • Canada • Mexico • Singapore • Spain
United Kingdom • United States

THOMSON
WADSWORTH

The Invisible Woman: Gender, Crime, and Justice, **Third Edition**
Joanne Belknap

Senior Acquisitions Editor, Criminal Justice: Carolyn Henderson Meier
Assistant Editor: Rebecca Johnson
Technology Project Manager: Amanda Kaufmann
Marketing Manager: Terra Schultz
Marketing Assistant: Jaren Boland
Marketing Communications Manager: Linda Yip
Project Manager, Editorial Production: Jennie Redwitz
Creative Director: Rob Hugel

Art Director: Vernon Boes
Print Buyer: Becky Cross
Permissions Editor: Sarah D'Stair
Production Service: Sara Dovre Wudali, Buuji, Inc.
Copy Editor: Kristina Rose McComas
Cover Designer: Yvo
Cover Image: Scott Cunningham/Getty Images
Compositor: Integra Software Services
Text and Cover Printer: West Group

Library of Congress Control Number: 2006924575

ISBN 0-495-09055-7

Thomson Higher Education
10 Davis Drive
Belmont, CA 94002-3098
USA

For more information about our products, contact us at:
Thomson Learning Academic Resource Center
1-800-423-0563

For permission to use material from this text or product, submit a request online at
http://www.thomsonrights.com.
Any additional questions about permissions can be submitted by e-mail to
thomsonrights@thomson.com.

This book is dedicated with the deepest admiration to fourteen young women who refused to be invisible and spoke up and out to force changes in responses to campus sexual assault and sexual harassment reports:

Pasha Cowan
Monique Gillaspie
Anne Gilmore
Sara Hering
Katie Hnida
Gretchen Hume
Megan Irby
Stacy Raye Kellogg
Candice Lopez
Dana Ruehlman
Georgina Salomon
Charlene Schmoker
Lisa Simpson
Shalini Swaroop

About the Author

Joanne Belknap received a Ph.D. in Criminal Justice and Criminology from Michigan State University in 1986. She is Professor of Sociology and Women's Studies at the University of Colorado. Dr. Belknap has written numerous scholarly publications, most of which involve the topics of violence against women and girls and female offenders. She has secured almost a million dollars in grant money to conduct research on women, girls, and crime (as a principal or co-principal investigator). Recent and forthcoming empirical publications investigate college campus fraternity rapes; the court processing of woman battering cases; delinquent girls transferred to adult court; and a gender comparison of delinquent girls' and boys' trauma histories. She has served on state advisory boards for female offenders and women in prison, as well as on U.S. Attorney General Janet Reno's Violence Against Women Committee, and she gave expert testimony to the Warren Christopher Commission investigating the Rodney King police brutality incident in Los Angeles. Dr. Belknap is the recipient of the 1997 national Distinguished Scholar of the Division on Women and Crime award from the American Society of Criminology and won the Student-Nominated University of Colorado Teaching Award in 2001 for her class "Violence Against Women and Girls." She is the past Chair of the Division on Women and Crime of the American Society of Criminology. Finally, Dr. Belknap is the 2004 recipient of the Boulder Faculty Assembly Teaching Award, the most prestigious teaching award at the University of Colorado, and the 2004 Inconvenient Woman Award from the American Society of Criminology for speaking out on behalf of college women reporting rapes by football players.

Brief Contents

❖

Contents

Foreword

It is common knowledge that the criminal justice system has been growing for over three decades. Most people also know that women make up a minority of felony offenders—about 20 percent of felons, and about 9 percent of prisoners. What is not well known is that for more than a decade, the growth rate of female offenders has been higher than that of males. And among victims, women are more numerous than they are among offenders: About 40 percent of the victims of violent crime are women.

Despite these figures, criminal justice practices—and most books that study them—are geared toward men, not women. When state and federal legislatures establish their penal codes, they tend to do so with male offenders in mind, and when courts establish their sentencing guidelines, they base them upon men. Correctional programs in prison and supervision policies in the community are also developed with men in mind. In this way, women—as clients of the criminal justice system—are truly invisible: When laws are passed and policies are established, it is typically the case that nobody will ask how they will eventually affect the women offenders who are coming through the criminal justice system in increasing numbers and increasing proportions.

That is why, as editor of the *Wadsworth Contemporary Issues on Crime and Justice Series,* I am delighted to announce the publication of the third edition of *The Invisible Woman: Gender, Crime, and Justice,* by Joanne Belknap. The *Contemporary Issues Series* is devoted to furthering our understanding of important issues in crime and justice by providing in-depth treatment of topics that are neglected or insufficiently discussed in today's textbooks. *The Invisible Woman* is an excellent example of the kind of work the series was designed to promote.

The void in criminology filled by this book is a basic one. The traditional theories of the causes of crime have been developed largely on studies of men, mainly with male offenders in mind, and have been tested by studies predominantly of men. But the factors that may explain why a 15-year-old young man runs afoul of the law may not apply very well to a 15-year-old young woman, and the factors that influence adult male offenders into and out of their criminal careers may not apply in the same way to adult women.

Women are also invisible as victims. In recent years, great strides have been made to include victims as people of standing in the criminal justice process. But when women are victimized, especially by men, a host of special circumstances often apply that the criminal justice system has been slow to recognize. Women are often victimized by intimates, and when a woman becomes a victim, it often leads to later criminal behavior as one natural consequence of the circumstances of her victimization.

As the criminal justice system has grown, it has become more open to the special circumstances of women. In part, this has been a result of increasing employment of women in professional roles that previously had been domi-nated by men: police, prosecutors, correctional officers, and others. As women have been more active in the professions of criminal justice, there has been an emergence of interest in the special problems facing women as clients and victims. Just as important, women who joined the justice professions have blazed new professional trails for those who will follow, fighting open and covert job discrimination and facing intolerant thinking from those who think men, not women, deserve certain types of positions. And the slow opening of doors to women as professionals has magnified the human face of the field. Among law enforcement employees, one-fourth are women, but only 10 percent of uniformed officers are women. In corrections, almost 30 percent of employees are women, but only about 20 percent of the line correctional officers are women.

Complex questions arise, however, regarding women and criminal justice policy. On the one hand, the criminal justice system needs to find ways to recognize the special circumstances faced by women as offenders, the special needs among women victims, and the unique opportunity for advancing the profession that comes from opening doors to women. But these new policies face a tough standard because the most significant tradition of the criminal law is "equal treatment under law." The argument that women have unique needs and circumstances has for many years been used as a rationale to treat women unfairly under the law, to apply misogynistic legal and program practices, and to justify paternalistic justice strategies—to the disadvantage of the very women who were being given "special" treatment. The contemporary challenge is not whether to recognize the differences represented by women as clients and workers but how to incorporate policies that are fair and effective when considering the relevant differences regarding women in these roles and circumstances.

That is why I am delighted with the way *The Invisible Woman* has been received as a book in this series. The book has received widespread critical acclaim and is being used in numerous college classrooms. The third edition includes more information on how racism intersects with sexism to the disad-vantage of women and develops themes about global/international issues for women as victims, offenders, and workers in the criminal legal system. It also provides a more detailed and separate account of the various types of women as workers in criminal justice.

No other book on the market today is as effective in its analysis of the special issues regarding women in the network of crime and justice. Professor Belknap, a lifelong advocate for women's issues and a talented analyst of the criminal justice system, has written a superb book. Those readers who are inclined to think about women and criminal justice from a reform perspective will find much to support their views and will obtain a wealth of important analysis that will shape how they see the tasks ahead. For those of you who have never really thought about women in crime and justice—for those to whom these women have been for too long invisible—this book will change forever your understanding of this essential aspect of crime and justice.

Todd R. Clear
Series Editor

Preface

For as long as anyone has recorded offending rates and behaviors, it has been abundantly clear that breaking the law is "gendered": Males are far more likely than females to break the law. While this is not necessarily the case for some of the more-minor offenses, in general, the more serious the offense, the larger the gender gap in offending. In fact, the gendered nature of offending has been given as one of the reasons why girls' and women's offending has remained so invisible and why convicted girls and women have received such limited programing and treatment until recent years. For the most part, until the 1970s, research on offenders either left girls and women out of the samples or, if including them, portrayed them in highly sexist manners. This bias continues; for example, a significant amount of media press and some scholarly work in the past decade claim that women and girls are getting "meaner" and more violent.

The nature of abuse and violent victimization is also gendered. For sexual and intimate partner abuse and violence, girls and women are more likely to be the victims and boys and men the perpetrators. However, these offenses have been so ensconced in stigma, particularly a victim-blaming approach, that sexual and intimate partner abuse victims were also largely invisible until the 1970s.

Despite the gendered nature of offending and victimization, women as arbiters of justice was also highly uncommon until the 1970s. Women working in law enforcement, policing, jails, prisons, and courts was a rarity until Title VII, a 1972 amendment to the Civil Rights Act requiring that terms of employment (e.g., hiring, firing, and promoting) not be made (in most cases) by an applicant's or worker's sex/gender.

Removing the cloak of invisibility from women's and girls' offending and victimization and from women's access to working in the criminal legal system were very much a result of the second wave of the women's movement in the 1970s. For the first time, women (1) were more empowered to speak out about victimizations by strangers, acquaintances, and intimates; (2) had significantly greater access to jobs and education in the criminal legal system (e.g., as police, guards, lawyers); and (3) were obtaining the research backgrounds and education to study women's and girls' offending through a less sexist lens than had been used in the limited existing studies of girls and/or women.

As in the previous editions of this book, this third edition attempts to explain the historical and current issues regarding women's and girls' victimization and offending, as well as women's entry into the professions of and current-day experiences as judges, lawyers, police officers, and guards. One of the most powerful aspects of the research in recent years is accounting for the significant link between victimization and offending for women and girls. The book also addresses the complexities of many of these issues, such as a need to carefully examine the recent reports claiming girls are becoming more violent.

ORGANIZATION

This book is divided into twelve chapters and organized into five parts. Part I is comprised of one chapter, an introduction to the topic of women/girls and crime. Part II, which includes Chapters 2–5, focuses most heavily on women's and girls' offending. The chapters are about criminological theories, the rates of offending, the gendered nature of processing those charged with offenses, and the prison system. Part III is a detailed account of women and girls as victims, particularly sexual, intimate partner, and stalking abuse victimizations. Part IV covers women as workers in the criminal legal system, specifically as police officers, prison/jail guards, and lawyers and judges. Part V is a conclusion to the book and offers some changes that have occurred in the areas of women's and girls offending and victimization as well as women's work in the criminal legal system.

NEW TO THIS EDITION

This edition is different from the last in a number of respects. First, whereas the last edition had two chapters devoted to women working in the criminal legal system, grouping the professions of police, guard, and attorney together, this edition has separate chapters devoted to women working in each area of the system. Second, an effort was made to make this edition more global in nature. To this end, every chapter has a boxed insert reporting studies from a country other than the United States or reporting a comparative study (comparing two or more countries). Third, as the scholarship on race/ethnicity has grown, this edition has correspondingly included a greater amount of analysis combining racism with sexism, and for the first time, the theory section includes critical race feminism. Fourth, particularly in the victim section of the book (Part III), there is additional information on women and girls who are more marginalized by age, race, disability, and sexual orientation. The chapter on sexual victimization now includes information on "date-rape" drugs. Finally, this edition provides more information on biosocial and evolutionary theories, as they have been gaining acceptance in recent years and have profound ramifications regarding the gendered nature of crime.

ACKNOWLEDGMENTS

It is definitely good news about the state of research on women and crime that the revisions for this third edition of the book took so long. There has been an explosion in the rate of research on women and crime since I wrote the first edition. This book is almost like a child to me; every edition has felt like a rebirthing. I'm anxious about whether I'm getting it all in and all right and eventually have to let go, knowing that something is going to be missing, so I apologize in advance for that. I'm very grateful to the many scholars I e-mailed, called, and asked to look at portions of this book (usually about their own research). They made this process far more interactive and enjoyable.

I would like to thank my many peers who use my book and provide me with feedback. The feedback has come from both them and their students and has helped me realize some of the changes that were needed in this new edition. I would also like to thank the many colleagues and mentors who provided guidance during both the initial stages of this project and the revisions that produced the third edition:

Nawal Ammar, Kent State University

Dana Britton, Kansas State University

Cathleen A. Cameron, Pittsburg State University, Kansas

Kathleen Contrino, Buffalo State College

Nanette Davis, Western Washington State University

Charles Dean, University of North Carolina at Charlotte

M. George Eichenberg, Sam Houston State University

Helen Eigenberg, University of Tennessee, Chattanooga

Edna Erez, Kent State University

Venessa Garcia, Kean University

Angel Geoghagan, University of Tennessee, Chattanooga

Marie Griffin, Arizona State University

Donna Hale, Shippensburg University

Violet Hall, University of Cincinnati

Michael Hallett, University of North Florida

Penelope Hanke, Auburn University

Barbara Hart, University of Texas at Tyler

Vickie Jensen, California State University, Northridge

Christina Johns, Florida A&M University

Teresa Madden, California State University, Northridge

Jacquelyn McClure, San Jose State University

Michelle Meloy, Rutgers University, Camden

Molly Merriman, Kent State University

Susan Miller, University of Delaware

Roslyn Muraskin, University of Cincinnati

Joycelyn Pollock, Southwest Texas State University

Kaylene Richards-Ekeh, California State University, Sacramento

Jill Rosenbaum, California State University, Fullerton

Kristine Thomas, Methodist College

Patricia Van Voorhis, University of Cincinnati

I am grateful to two of Wadsworth's wonderful group. First, my editor, Carolyn Henderson Meier, encouraged me when I thought there was too much information to possibly incorporate into this edition and when the revisions were feeling overwhelming. Second, Rebecca Johnson was a cautious and caring assistant in the development process.

I am very indebted to all my friends and family members who have really been there for me through all of this. There are a few people whom I must mention by name because they went out of their way: First, the best librarian ever, Lindy Shultz, hunted down citations high and low. Second, thanks to my partners in crime (read: the other "feminist big mouths" who held the banner with me as I worked with the women to whom this book is dedicated), Claudia Bayliff, Regina Cowles, and Janine D'Anniballe. Third, thanks to my friends Bonnie Berry, Helen Eigenberg, Lori Fear, Dora-Lee Larson, E. Gail McGarry, Joanne Meyerowitz, Jane Pampel, Cris Sullivan, Pat Swope, and Patti Witte for regularly checking in on me. Fourth, muchas gracias to my supporters on campus: Janet Jacobs, Polly McLean, Jane Menken, Hillary Potter, Rick Rogers, and Louise Silvern. Fifth, I'd like to thank the students who laughed at my jokes. Finally, I am so very grateful for my wonderful sister, Sandra Dangler, my partner, R. S. Summers, and our wonderful son, Casey Belknap-Summers, for inspiration and support (and the last for asking with great enthusiasm over the last couple of months, "Mom, are you done with your book yet?").

In addition to the state of the research on women and crime changing drastically since the last edition, I was diagnosed with breast cancer. I must say that I was given the gift of a huge amount of strength and support from my friends in the Division on Women and Crime (particularly Kim Cook, Helen Eigenberg, and Susan Sharp), from former students, and many others. When

I was at the depths of my despair, I often thought about some of the girls convicted as adults that Emily Gaarder and I interviewed in an adult prison. They will likely never know this, but meeting them gave me a significant amount of power and armor: I reflected on their courage, optimism, and passion for life as I was struggling the hardest.

Joanne Belknap

1

❖

The Emergence of Gender in Criminology

> The need for feminism arises from the desire to create a world in which women are not oppressed. If there is no term or focus, no movement which incorporates the struggle against sexism, women run the risk of becoming invisible.
>
> JOHNSON-ODIM, 1991, 319

This book presents the current state of women and girls in criminology (the study of crime) and criminal justice (the processing of victims and offenders). Whereas criminology is concerned with developing theories on what causes crime, criminal justice focuses on workers in the criminal justice system and the ways decisions are made about victims and offenders. To understand the current state of women and girls and the way in which gender relates to crime and criminal justice, it is first necessary to comprehend the historical evolution of the status of women and girls in the home, society, and the workplace. Therefore, this book includes relevant historical factors that have affected the status of women and girls in crime today. Finally, this book examines successes in effecting change for women and girls as victims, offenders, and professionals in the criminal justice system.

The term *criminal justice* is most often used to describe the practices of workers in the system (such as police, judges, and prison staff), as well as the formal processing and treatment of crime victims and offenders. This book replaces the term *criminal justice* with the terms *crime processing*, *criminal processing*, and *criminal legal system*, given that much of this book reports on studies that indicate the processing of victims and offenders as anything but "just." Indeed, the lack of justice for women and girls, especially the more marginalized, is the focus of this book.

The purpose of this chapter is to expose readers to an overall view of the important concepts behind women (and girls) and crime. These significant concepts include a presentation of women's invisibility in criminology and crime-processing

1

studies, relevant concepts and definitions, and an understanding of how the images of women and girls in society have affected their experiences as victims, offenders, and professionals in society and in the crime-processing system.

INVISIBILITY OF WOMEN AND GIRLS IN CRIME

The title of this book was chosen to reflect the strong theme of invisibility in the three major areas covered in the book: (1) women and girls as offenders, (2) women and girls as victims, and (3) women professionals working in the crime-processing system. This section briefly explains how women's experiences have been denied or ignored. Moreover, this section discusses how women and girls do not always fit neatly into one of the three categories: offenders, victims, and professionals in the crime-processing system. Rather, a great deal of overlap exists. For example, many times when I have interviewed women police officers, they have spoken about being abused by their husbands or ex-husbands. One jail guard I interviewed told me she was an incest survivor. Many of the delinquent girls and women in prison that I have met report astounding rates of victimization including incest, date rape, stranger rape, and intimate partner abuse. When I interviewed an incarcerated girl once and asked whether she believed any childhood events had led to her offending, she reported that she just didn't cope the same after she saw her uncle shoot her father and he died with his head in her lap. Thus, my own and many other researchers' work (covered in this book) reports a significant blurring between the victim and offender categories in women's and girls' lives, and many women working in the crime-processing system have histories of victimization.

Any discussion on the invisibility of women and girls in the study of crime must address the current resistance to this topic in academic research as well as in the classroom. Historically, women and girls as both victims and offenders were usually left out of the studies or, if included, were typically done so in sexist and stereotypic ways. In conducting the research for this book, I often found it frustrating to search through mainstream journals (and some books) to find out whether women and/or girls were included in the research questions or samples. For example, studies with male-only samples rarely identified this in the title, whereas studies with female-only or female and male samples consistently reflected this in their titles. If women were excluded from the study, then most authors perceived no need to include "male" in the title. Similarly, Naffine (1996, 20) notes with some alarm that "it is still possible to study criminal men scientifically without referring to their sex" in mainstream U.S. and British criminology texts. A recent study of U.S. and British criminology publications from 1895 to 1997 found "a glaring and persistent deficiency" in the representation of women and girls in criminology studies and that this was partly related to the underrepresentation of women criminologists (Hughes, 2005, 21). (That is, women are more likely than men to include women/girls in their research.)

On a more positive note, it is clear that significant pro-feminist changes are occurring. Not only are "women and crime" courses more routinely offered and required but academia is also producing more feminist scholars (women and men), and for the past decade, criminal justice and sociology departments have increasingly recruited "feminist criminologists." The advances in research on women offenders in recent years are unprecedented. Although we still have much to learn, this book describes the historical as well as the more recent research in and the great contributions to understanding both the risks for offending and also the gender differences and similarities in the processing, treating, and punishing of offenders. Research on violence against women and girls has also increased exponentially in recent years. This is in part due to the increased number of women and feminists in academia but has been greatly aided by the implementation of the federal Violence Against Women Act (VAWA) of 1994. Congress passed this act, which in 1994 was signed into law by President Clinton and established the Office on Violence against Women in 1995 to implement VAWA. Due to VAWA, research on violence against women (e.g., domestic violence, sexual assault, and stalking) has been funded, and programs in a variety of agencies (e.g., police, courts, Native American communities) regarding violence against women have been implemented and funded at unprecedented rates (see Stuart, 2005). On October 4, 2005, VAWA was reauthorized through strong bipartisan support from the U.S. House and Senate.

Another example of the "boom" of research in the area of violence against women and girls is the development of the quarterly journal *Violence Against Women* in 1995. The editor, Claire Renzetti, was soon so overwhelmed and impressed with the large number of high-quality manuscripts submitted to the journal that in 1999 she increased the number of issues published per year to twelve (monthly) which is almost unheard of in social science scholarly journals. Unfortunately, the research on women working in the criminal-processing field has not experienced such a significant increase in research and attention. However, this newer research on women workers provides important insight and is reported in this book.

Women and Girls as Offenders

Most criminology theories are concerned with what "causes" crime and thus focus on factors related to offending, primarily male juvenile offending. Until the late 1970s, it was highly unusual for these studies to include girls (or women) in their samples. Although gender is the strongest factor indicating a person's likelihood to break the law, these (almost exclusively male) researchers rarely thought it necessary to include women or girls in their samples. The irony is that "sex, the most powerful variable regarding crime has been virtually ignored" (Leonard, 1982, xi). Criminology theories were constructed "by men, about men" and explain male behavior rather than human behavior (ibid.). Stated alteratively, studying why women and girls offend less frequently than men and boys "could arguably provide clues for dealing with men's criminality" (Morris, 1987, 2).

When the researchers did include girls in their samples, it was typically to see how girls fit into boys' equations. That is, rather than include in the study a means of assessing how girls' lives might be different from boys' lives, girls' delinquency has typically been viewed as peripheral and unnecessary to understanding juvenile offending and processing. Thus, these theories failed to address gender differences in criminal behavior (Leonard, 1982; Morris, 1987). Whereas social class, access to opportunities to learn crime, and area of residence in a city have been used to explain boys' likelihood of turning to crime, the causes of girls' criminality were rarely examined until more recent years. Additionally, criminological theory historically tended to view women as "driven" to crime because of biological influences, whereas men were viewed as turning to crime due to economic or sociological forces. For instance, Shaw and McKay's (1969, 365) book *Juvenile Delinquency and Urban Areas* devotes only a few pages to girls' delinquency and then implies it is mostly sexual—associated with the "hunting ground" these girls live in, which is composed of dance halls, massage establishments, movie theaters, and so on. Chapter 2 in this book discusses how the early criminologists (such as Cesare Lombroso, Otto Pollack, W. I. Thomas, and even Sigmund Freud) emphasized biology to explain women's criminality.

Thus, girls' delinquency was seen as neither interesting nor important until the past couple of decades. Similarly, theory has traditionally placed boys in the center. Feminist theories not only attempt to focus women and girls more centrally but they include how the inequalities between the sexes can differentially affect male and female experiences and behaviors. Furthermore, feminist theory has been increasingly committed to examining how factors such as racism, classism, and heterosexism, in addition to or in conjunction with sexism, are useful for understanding gender differences and discrimination dynamics. Fortunately, particularly in the last fifteen years, research assessing the "causes" of women's and girls' criminality has grown rapidly. This research, presented mostly in the next chapter, offers new and exciting (although sometimes depressing) ways of understanding women's and girls' offending. Moreover, the feminist research contributing to the understanding of why some girls commit crimes is making a significant impact on understanding why some *boys* commit crimes. For example, traditional strain theory never measured incest as a source of strain that might lead to delinquency for either girls or boys. In the late 1970s and early 1980s, three studies were published on the high rates of victimizations in offending girls' and women's lives (Chesney-Lind and Rodriguez, 1983; James and Meyerding, 1977; Silbert and Pines, 1981). Since then, many other studies report that incest and other childhood victimizations increase the likelihood of subsequent offending not only for girls and women (e.g., Arnold, 1990; Browne, Miller, and Maguin, 1999; Chesney-Lind and Shelden, 1992; Coker et al., 1998; Gilfus, 1992; Klein and Chao, 1995; Lake, 1993; Owen, 1998; Singer et al., 1995) but also for boys and men (e.g., Belknap and Holsinger, 2006; Dembo et al., 1992; Dodge, Bates, and Pettit, 1990; Widom, 1989a, 1989b).

Another aspect of the invisibility of female offenders is the "correctional" institutions provided for women and girls. The prisons and delinquent institutions for women and girls, both historically and presently, vary drastically from those for boys and men, mostly to the disadvantage of girls. Moreover, historically, treatment and punishment issues/opportunities differed vastly for women based on race (Freedman, 1981; Rafter, 1985). The excuse for the lack of research on institutions housing women offenders, as well as the lack of training, vocational, educational, and counseling programs available to incarcerated women, is that women make up a small percentage of offenders. This lack of interest in and opportunities for women and girls is particularly disturbing given that since the 1970s their incarceration rate is growing much faster than men's (e.g., Immarigeon and Chesney-Lind, 1992; Kline, 1993; Mumola and Beck, 1997; Sokoloff, 2005).

Women and Girls as Victims

"Feminist criminology has perhaps made its greatest impact on mainstream criminology in the area of women's victimization" (Britton, 2000, 64). The crimes that women and girls are most likely to experience—sexual victimization (rape) and woman battering (domestic violence)—not only are the most under-reported but also are abusive, fear-inducing, humiliating, and often violent and dangerous. Moreover, most young women and girls grow up with strong messages about dangerous men lurking in alleys and behind bushes; thus, in a sense, women are trained to fear crime (see Madriz, 1997).

Another "gendered" form of victimization that is rarely recognized is "corporate" or "organizational" victimization. Gerber and Weeks's (1992) overview of this topic highlights a number of examples. First, they note that sweatshops and other factory-type jobs have numerous instances of "accidents" from poor working conditions and that the victims of these accidents are predominantly women. Second, they discuss the intrauterine birth-control device called the "Dalkon Shield," which was proved to be linked to "illness, sterility, spontaneous abortions, birth defects, and deaths" (ibid., 333). Notably, although a considerable amount has been written about this as "white-collar" and "corporate" crime, the fact that women were the primary victims was rarely recognized. Furthermore, Gerber and Weeks (ibid.) point out that some oral contraceptives (e.g., Depo-Provera and Ovulen) for women are related to breast and uterine cancer, yet the manufacturers fail to inform the consumers, or if the U.S. Food and Drug Administration (FDA) does not allow them to distribute certain drugs in the United States, they do so in other, usually Third World, countries. Third, Gerber and Weeks (ibid.) discuss how some on-the-job hazards, such as carpal tunnel syndrome and over-exposure to video display terminals, are disproportionately experienced by women workers given their prominence in clerical and factory work. Finally, they note that although a gender analysis of "brown lung" disease has not been conducted, this affliction appears to be disproportionately experienced by women.

Another example of corporate violence against women is silicone breast implants. Rynbrandt and Kramer (1995) identify Dow Corning (the largest supplier of silicone breast implants), plastic surgeons, and "an apparently indifferent government" as the key players in allowing this dangerous procedure, which has been used in over 2 million women in the United States since 1964. These scholars document that the FDA approved these implants despite inadequate research assessing their safety. In 1991, rather than recalling the procedure until adequate safety testing could be conducted, they simply called for more testing. "The committee argued that they chose not to end or restrict silicone implants—despite the suspected risks—because they were a public health necessity both after cancer surgery and simply to enlarge breasts" (ibid., 209). (In actuality, 75–85 percent of breast implants were for cosmetic reasons rather than for reconstructive surgery after breast cancer.) Despite the FDA's significant lack of concern for examining the safety of breast implants before approving them, the encouraging aspect of this battle is the role of the media and individual women who came forward to file lawsuits against Dow Corning and other companies. More specifically, when the government did not act responsibly, fortunately some journalists did by reporting what was really happening to women. For example, internal memos from Dow Corning regarding some of their staff who feared the implants were unsafe were "leaked" to the press. This was followed by Dow Corning releasing documents in 1992 indicating that they had known for more than two decades "that the implants could leak and that the gel could cause health problems" (ibid., 212). In March 1994, implant manufacturers agreed to a $4 billion class action settlement (ibid.). Thus, the press and individual women banding together to sue these companies in civil court resulted in actions taken against these irresponsible corporations. Croall's (1995, 233) overview of women's victimization in the corporate world in England addresses most of the types of abuses noted earlier, but she also includes two more types: (1) the "big business" of the "slimming industry" (questionable and often inadequately tested weight-loss products), and (2) the high rates of sexual abuse and sexual exploitation women workers face from coworkers.

Finally, a current practice that may well end up being classified as a form of organizational crime is the practice of paying women to undergo drug treatment in order to harvest their eggs for infertile couples. The women most sought after for their eggs are young, White college women (indicating racist and classist assumptions of the "best" genes). To date, little is known about the long-term effects of this intrusive medical procedure of "harvesting" eggs. Indeed, it may be that the heavy drug treatment used to produce numerous eggs, temporarily "throwing" these women into hyperovulation, may increase these "donors'" chances not only of ovarian cancer but also of infertility problems themselves later on (Mead, 1999).

Women as Professionals in the Crime-Processing System

The final major area of women and crime covered in this book is women's employment in the crime-processing system. The three major types of employment opportunities in crime processing include prisons and jails, policing, and the law. Part IV of this book examines historical and current issues for women correctional officers, policewomen, and women lawyers and judges. In all of these jobs, women faced considerable resistance to employment. This resistance was based primarily on the attitude that women are unsuitable because working with male offenders requires "manly" men. Title VII, a 1972 amendment to the 1964 Civil Rights Act, proved crucial for women's professional entrance to the crime-processing system. Unfortunately, women's advancement in both numbers and rank has been slow. Despite current efforts by law schools and police departments to hire more women, the numbers of women in these occupations are still quite low, as are the number of women working in men's penal institutions (the majority of incarceration facilities). As reported later in this book, even today some women working in these fields (policing, prisons/jails, and courts) still face some resistance and hostility from male administrators and coworkers. Finally, it has been noted that not only are women working in the crime-processing system "invisible" in these systems and in the research until recently but women criminologists have also been invisible, with historical accounts of criminology often ignoring women scholars' contributions to the field (Laub and Smith, 1995).

Blurring of Boundaries of Women's Experiences in Crime

In addition to acknowledging the invisibility of women offenders, women victims, and women working in the crime-processing system, it is important to recognize the overlapping of these categories in many women's experiences. As was stated earlier, my research on women working as police officers and in jails included numerous disclosures by these workers of having survived incest, extrafamilial child sexual abuse, stranger rape, and woman battering in intimate relationships. (A number of the women police officers discussed battering perpetrated by their police officer husbands.) Moreover, given the high rates of women in general who experience male violence (some statistics suggest as many as half of all women in the United States; see Chapters 6 through 8), it would be difficult to have women working in the crime-processing system who had not been victimized. Although this has not been empirically studied, women's victimization experiences may be related to their desire to work in the crime-processing system.

There is growing documentation that delinquent girls and women prisoners have disproportionately high records of victimization, usually incest, rape, and battering, preceding their offending behaviors (e.g., Acoca, 1998; American Correctional Association, 1990; Arnold, 1990; Belknap and Holsinger, 1998, 2006; Browne, Miller, and Maguin, 1999; Carlen, 1983; Chesney-Lind and Rodriguez, 1983; Coker et al., 1998; Daly, 1992; Fletcher and Moon, 1993; Fox and Sugar, 1990; Gaarder and Belknap, 2002; Gilfus, 1992; Gray, Mays, and Stohr, 1995; Greenfeld and Snell, 1999; Immarigeon, 1987a, 1987b; Lake, 1993; Mullings, Marquart, and Brewer, 2000; Sable et al., 1999; Sargent, Marcus-Mendoza, and Yu, 1993; Singer et al., 1995). Many of these accounts suggest that the likelihood that prior victimization, offending (especially prostitution, running away, and drug offenses), and subsequent incarceration are interrelated (Arnold, 1990; Browne, Miller, and Maguin, 1999; Carlen, 1983; Chesney-Lind and Rodriguez, 1983; Daly, 1992; Gilfus, 1992; Lake, 1993; Owen, 1998; Singer et al., 1995). Recent research has identified running away from home and drug use as women's and girls' means of coping with and surviving abuse in their homes. Thus, the "escape" options open to women and girls who are being sexually and/or physically victimized are often illegal.

Although no actual count exists, U.S. prisons house many battered women survivors who killed their batterers as a last resort (e.g., Browne, 1987; Richie, 1996). Historically, the crime-processing system that chronically failed to respond to battered women as victims responded harshly to them as "offenders." However, these women rarely have any criminal record before the murder, they are usually the ones who notify the police of the murder, and the murder almost always occurs during a battering incident in which the victim is acting in self-defense (see Maguigan, 1991). In the past, these women typically received longer sentences than men who killed their wives (Schneider and Jordan, 1981). In the late 1980s and early 1990s, governors from Ohio, Illinois, Maryland, and Texas received considerable press for commuting the sentences of women who had served time after killing their abusive partners in self-defense. Furthermore, allowing expert witnesses to testify on the dynamics of intimate partner abuse became far more prevalent in the 1990s and has helped with fairer processing of women who killed abusive mates in self-defense. A more recent study documents how girls tried and convicted at the deepest end of the system, those tried and convicted as adults and serving time in adult prisons, often experience extreme victimizations ignored by the same systems that treat their offending at the most serious levels (Gaarder and Belknap, 2002).

As discussed earlier, women victims, offenders, and professionals in the crime-processing system have historically remained invisible. Because of the shame associated with sexual abuse and battering, these crimes are not routinely reported to crime-processing authorities, research interviewers, or even family members and health care officials. Similarly, offending women have remained invisible because, until recently, they made up less than 5 percent of the prison population. Finally, roles for women professionals were largely nonexistent until the 1970s. The goal of this book is to make issues surrounding women and crime more visible, to trace the changes in society and the crime-processing system that have occurred, and to propose changes that still need to occur. But first, to understand these issues, it is important to have an understanding of feminism and the difference between sex and gender.

SEX VERSUS GENDER

Differences between men and women have been divided into two categories: sex differences and gender differences. Sex differences are biological differences, including differences in reproductive organs, body size, muscle development, and hormones. Gender differences, on the other hand, are those that are ascribed by society and that relate to expected social roles. Examples of gender differences include clothing, wages, child-care responsibilities, and professions. Most differences between men and women are gender differences, which are determined by society; they are not biologically determined. Moreover, socially based differences are rooted largely in inequality (MacKinnon, 1990). Because society creates these inequalities, society must also be the solution to restructuring the images and opportunities of women and men (and girls and boys) in order to achieve equality.

Women's and men's different roles historically have been viewed as "biologically based and unalterable." More recently, however, feminists assert that "women's roles are learned and socially determined" (Klein, 1984, 3). Thus, it is important to examine and acknowledge how sex differences (and sexism) influence gender differences. For instance, when only boys are allowed to take part in sports programs, girls are prevented from exercising their bodies and becoming strong. It is necessary to acknowledge that even in the traditional sense, some women are stronger than some men. Also, the relative differences in men's and women's times for running marathons, shorter running events, and swimming have significantly decreased since the 1930s, possibly due to girls' and women's increased access to exercise and training for sports (Fausto-Sterling, 1985). In fact, between 1964 and 1984, women's marathon times decreased by more than one and a half hours, whereas men's times decreased by only a few minutes (ibid.). In addition to women holding the records in marathon swimming, the first woman ever "allowed" to swim the English Channel (in 1926) "not only astounded the world by succeeding at all, but she broke the men's record by two hours!" (ibid., 218).

West and Zimmerman (1987), in a classic article called "Sex and Gender," call for the need to understand three phenomena: *sex, sex category,* and *gender.* They define *sex* as "a determination made through the application of socially agreed upon biological criteria for classifying persons as males or females" (ibid., 127). Thus, they point out that even sex is not immutable and that it is socially agreed-upon biological criteria. It is useful to have this discussion in terms of intersexed individuals (also known as hermaphrodites, those born with ambiguous genitalia and other than XX or XY chromosomal make-up). That is, even biologically it is not always clear what sex someone is; 1 in 2,000 births are intersexed individuals, and the pattern has been to have the doctor decide the sex at birth in these "questionable" cases (see Kessler, 2004). *Sex categorization* involves how people within a society establish and maintain whether an individual is female or male. One does not need a chromosomal test to assume one's sex; rather, we assume that someone's sex is what it appears to be "unless we have a special reason to doubt" it (ibid., 133). Similar to sex category, *gender* refers to the ways individuals manage the activities and attitudes prescribed for their sex category. "Gender activities emerge from and bolster claims to membership in a sex category" (ibid., 127). Thus, West and Zimmerman (ibid., 129) examine the construction of gender as not only individual but also heavily "socially organized." Gender is not simply an individual attribute but rather is accomplished through interactions with others. In later work, West and Fenstermaker (1995) attempt to examine "doing difference" by examining how race and class fit in with "doing gender." They point out the vast complexities in this endeavor, particularly in terms of attempting to determine how people are perceived and how they experience situations based on where they "fit" in the categories of race, sex, and class. Their approach, however, has been criticized for "treating gender as the most fundamental, theoretical category and then 'adding' on race and class. They lay out their theoretical argument within a gender-only framework and then generalize this argument to race and class" (Collins et al., 1995, 493).

Acker's (1990) focus is on how organizational structure is gendered. Specifically, a *gendered organization* is one in which control, identity, meaning, actions, emotions, and advantage are patterned by distinguishing between male and female (and masculine and feminine). Acker (ibid.) notes some interacting processes by which gendering occurs, including (1) the construction of divisions along gender lines (e.g., allowed behaviors, power, and office space); (2) the construction of images and symbols that reinforce these gender divisions (e.g., dress, the media, and technical skills); and (3) interactions among workers that portray submission or

EXHIBIT 1.1   The Five Elements That Distinguish Feminist Thought from Other Types of Social and Political Thought

1.   Gender is not a natural fact but a complex social, historical, and cultural product; it is related to, but not simply derived from, biological sex differences and reproductive capacities.

2.   Gender and gender relations order social life and social institutions in fundamental ways.

3.   Gender relations and constructs of masculinity and femininity are not symmetrical but are based on an organizing principle of men's superiority and social and political—economic dominance over women.

4.   Systems of knowledge reflect men's views of the natural and social world; the production of knowledge is gendered.

5.   Women should be at the center of intellectual inquiry, not peripheral, invisible, or appendages to men.

SOURCE: Kathleen Daly and Meda Chesney-Lind. 1988. "Feminism and Criminology." *Justice Quarterly* 5:504.

dominance (e.g., men taking more "turns," asking questions, making comments, and interrupting more). This approach is useful for examining many of the jobs, such as policing, law, and jail and prison work, described in more detail later in this book.

Court cases on sex discrimination have historically confused sex and gender differences, often ruling to the disadvantage of women on the basis that cultural/societal (or gender) differences are "immutable" (Rhode, 1989, 3). That is, legal discourse has historically failed to distinguish sex from gender differences, viewing both as inherent and not recognizing the role society plays in perpetuating gender inequalities. In fact, some scholars believe that most societies, including the United States, have invested in perpetuating gender distinctions (Epstein, 1988, 120). Daly and Chesney-Lind (1988, 504) clearly delineate the importance of gender and a feminist approach (see Exhibit 1.1).

Inherent in this distinction between sex and gender are the concepts of sexism and patriarchy. *Sexism* refers to oppressive attitudes and behaviors directed at either sex; that is, sexism is discrimination or prejudice based on gender. In practice, the discrimination, prejudice, and negative attitudes and behaviors based on sex and gender are directed primarily at women (that is, women are not as "good" as men, women exist for the sexual pleasure of men, women are defined by their beauty, and so on).

Patriarchy, on the other hand, refers to a social, legal, and political climate that values male dominance and hierarchy. Central to the patriarchal ideology is the belief that women's nature is biologically, not culturally, determined (Edwards, 1987) and that laws are from men's standpoint, consistent with men's experiences (MacKinnon, 1989). What feminists identify as gender differences (for example, the ability to nurture children), therefore, are often defined as sex differences by the patriarchy. Patriarchy and its privileges, then, remain as part of the defining quality of the culture and thus of criminology and crime processing. Starting in the 1970s, some feminists advocated for "feminist or woman's law" in order to "describe, explain and understand women's legal position, especially for the purpose of improving women's position in the law and society" (Dahl, 1986, 240). Jurisprudence, which is the philosophy or science of law, was employed by feminist legal scholars to develop *feminist jurisprudence*, consistent with radical and critical race approaches, to understand the law "as an institution of male dominance" (Haney, 2000, 644). But feminist legal scholar Carol Smart (1989) questions whether feminist jurisprudence can "de-center" the legal system when patriarchy is so ingrained in it.

It is often assumed that changes made to advance gender equality will result in unfairness to men. This view not only is used to justify opposition toward equality but also ignores the fact that changes may benefit men. For instance, Cincinnati Bell Telephone was brought to court for failure to hire women to work on telephone poles. The court upheld that such a practice was discriminatory, which caused Cincinnati Bell to devise new and improved equipment so that women could more easily perform the job. Such innovations included making lighter ladders and tools with improved torque that required less muscle power. The male workers responded, "Why didn't you do this a long time ago?" Such changes made the job open to a wider range of male workers as well as female workers. This is similar to the point made earlier that the feminist research on the causes of women's criminality has helped us to better understand male criminality as well (e.g., the risk of childhood victimization as a precursor to delinquency).

As stated earlier, some women are physically stronger than some men. Even so, exceptionally strong women historically have been denied access to "men's" jobs that require physical strength. Unfortunately, such dedication to exclusively male occupations is not restricted to jobs associated with high use of physical strength. Traditionally, women have faced obstacles in their efforts to enter fields associated with strong mental abilities, such as science, engineering, law, and medicine. Ironically, women's so-called tender susceptibility has barred them from prestigious professions "but not from grueling and indelicate occupations like factory and field labor" (Rhode, 1990, 200). Only in the past couple of decades has women's access to traditionally male jobs become more commonplace.

Understanding the distinction between sex and gender informs us that most differences between men and women and boys and girls are societally based (gender), not biologically determined (sex). Although this is encouraging in that we are more likely to be able to change society than we are to alter biology (and the ethics of biological changes are daunting), this book examines how gender differences are strongly entrenched in tradition and have negatively affected the lives of women and girls, including in the crime-processing system. Furthermore, sex differences, such as the ability to become pregnant, have also worked to women's disadvantage in many law cases.

WHAT IS FEMINISM?

Feminism and feminists recognize that gender inequalities exist in society, and they value change that enhances gender equality. While the perspectives of feminism are numerous, the approach has been to attempt to answer the "woman question(s)," where "partial and provisional answers intersect, joining together both to lament the ways in which women have been oppressed, repressed, and suppressed and to celebrate the ways in which so many women have 'beaten the system,' taken charge of their own destinies, and encouraged each other" (Tong, 1989, 1–2). Although the first "unmistakably feminist voices were heard in England in the seventeenth century," feminist philosopher Alison Jaggar states:

> In a sense, feminism has always existed. Certainly, as long as women have been subordinated, they have resisted that subordination. Sometimes the resistance has been collective and conscious; at other times it has been solitary and only half-conscious, as when women have sought escape from their socially prescribed roles through illness, drug and alcohol addiction, and even madness. (1983, 1)

African American feminist bell hooks defines feminism simply as "the struggle to end sexist oppression" (1984, 26). She compares patriarchy to racism and other forms of oppression and points out that for sexism to end, racism and other forms of oppression cannot remain intact. Feminism, therefore, is part of the larger movement to end domination in all of its forms (hooks, 1990). "The aim of feminism is not to benefit solely any specific group of women, any particular race or class of women. It [feminism] does not privilege women over men. It has the power to transform in a meaningful way all our lives" (hooks, 1984, 26).

Unfortunately, a number of myths have damaged the concept of feminism as a legitimate issue and approach. Journalist Susan Faludi (1991) documents in her book *Backlash* how the media and politicians sometimes exaggerate or manipulate statistics and incidences in order to condemn feminism and keep women in gender-specified roles. Daly and Chesney-Lind (1988) identify three myths about feminism: (1) Feminism lacks objectivity; (2) feminist analysis narrowly focuses on women; and (3) there is only one feminist perspective. Regarding charges that feminism lacks objectivity, Daly and Chesney-Lind (ibid.) point out that men and nonfeminists are no more objective about gender issues than are women and feminists. The problem is that too often "men's experiences are taken as the norm and are generalized to the population" (ibid., 500). With regard to the criticism that feminism focuses too narrowly on women, in fact, feminist analysis does not ignore men and masculinity; rather, men are included in—but are not the center of—the analysis. Obviously, it is necessary to examine masculinity and men's lives and viewpoints in order to fully understand women's lives (ibid.). "The irony is that feminist scholarship is characterized as being only about women or as hopelessly biased toward women, when in fact the project is to describe and change both men's and women's lives" (ibid., 501).

Feminist theory, overall, "is a woman-centered description and explanation of human experience and the social world. It asserts that gender governs every aspect of personal and social life (Danner, 1989, 51). Similar to the *praxis* aspect of Marxism, feminist theory and research is expected to be buttressed with *activism* to help stop women's oppression (Britton, 2000; Danner, 1989). While many people think there is a single "feminism," an examination of feminist analysis quickly establishes that there are many feminist perspectives. The five major strains of feminist theory are liberal, Marxist, socialist, radical, and postmodernist feminism.

The origins of *liberal feminism* can be traced back to the late eighteenth century with Mary Wollstonecraft's publication, *A Vindication of the Rights of Women*, and later John Stuart Mill's article, "The Subjection of Women." Fundamentally, liberal feminists argue that women's access to equality in education and employment, or the "public world" in general, is blocked by customary and legal constraints (Tong, 1989). Gender justice, therefore, requires that the rules to the "game" are fair and that no one's civil rights and economic opportunities are disadvantaged in playing the "game" (ibid.). The goal "is to achieve just practices and bias-free beliefs by eliminating sexist and andocentric assumptions" (Harding, 2004a, 180). Liberal feminist criminology has been criticized for posing "men as the criminal yardstick" and equating justice with equality without examining injustices of the system and taking sex, race, and class as "givens" without recognizing the construction of their meanings (Britton, 2000). For example, prison reform for women would not be nearly as effective in achieving equality with men's prisons if the only goal was to allow the same access to health care, vocational, educational, legal, and treatment programs. While these would be significant advances, it is also necessary to request reforms that address women prisoners' experiences, needs, and histories that differ from male prisoners, "particularly in relation to violence, their lack of control and power over their own lives, and the importance of a woman-centered approach to justice" (Shaw, 1993, 52). Chesney-Lind (1993, 10) describes the response by the system as "vengeful equity," because while incarcerated women still lack in many areas relative to incarcerated men, they have become more "equal" in terms of their rising numbers, the implementation of boot camps and chain gangs, and so on. Additionally, some feminists also criticize liberal feminist criminology for failing to examine girls' and women's *agency* (self-determination) and for falling into the trap of seeing women as strictly victims (see Britton, 2000; Maher, 1997).

Marxist feminists, on the other hand, are most concerned with inequalities set up in a capitalist society. It was "formulated to deal with the conditions of working-class women during the heyday of European and U.S. industrialization in the late nineteenth and early twentieth centuries" (Harding, 2004a, 183). Marxist feminists believe that abolition of a class society, where the means of production are shared and wealth is not owned by a few, will liberate women because they will not be economically dependent on men. Marxist feminists do not view women's oppression as a result of individuals' intentional actions but rather as due to the political, economic, and social structures of capitalism (ibid.). Marxist feminism is most concerned with work-related inequities and has advanced understanding of the trivialization of women's work in the home (especially raising children) and the boring, poorly paid jobs women have predominantly occupied (ibid.).

The socialist and radical feminist theories are largely reactions to Marxist feminism. In particular, *socialist feminism* purports that class alone fails to explain women's subjugation; thus, both class and the patriarchy must be examined as dual systems of domination (ibid.). "Without overthrowing the economic system of capitalism, as socialists and communists organize to do, we cannot liberate women and everybody else who is oppressed" (Wong, 1991, 290). Gender and class play equal roles in explaining women's oppression (Tong, 1989). Socialist feminists criticize Marxist feminists for implying that the abuse women suffer from men is inconsequential compared with what the proletariat (worker) endures from the bourgeoisie (the production managers and owners) (ibid.).

Radical feminists, also disillusioned with Marxist feminism, first organized in the 1960s and 1970s. Radical feminism was also a result of women who were active in the "New Left" antiwar and civil rights movements being treated as "second-class" citizens within these movements (Donovan, 1985). Unlike Marxist feminists, radical feminists believe that patriarchy is central to women's oppression. Radical feminism points out that Marxist feminism's focus on work-related concerns has left little room to address other feminist issues, particularly reproductive freedom and violence against women (Tong, 1989). Radical feminism is also more apt than the other strains of feminism to hold individual men, rather than society, responsible for oppressing women (ibid.).

Postmodernist feminism argues against socialist feminism's "unrealistic" goal to synthesize feminism and find one theory to explain women's oppression (ibid.). Rather, postmodernists propose that because women's experiences differ based on class, race, sexual, and cultural lines, feminist theory should reflect this (Gagnier, 1990). For example, legal scholar Angela P. Harris (1990, 588) warns against the practice of gender essentialism: "[t]he notion that there is a monolithic 'women's experience' that can be described independent of other facets of experience like race, class, and sexual orientation. . . ." Furthermore, Harris (ibid., 589) states that "feminist essentialism paves the way for unconscious racism." She reports on the harm in essentialism:

> In my view, however, as long as feminists, like theorists in the dominant culture, continue to search for gender and racial essences, black women will never be anything more than a crossroads between two kinds of domination, or at the bottom of a hierarchy of oppressions; we will always be required to choose pieces of ourselves to present as wholeness. (ibid.)

Crenshaw (1989) elaborates on this approach, arguing that there is a tendency to treat race and gender as mutually exclusive categories of experience and analysis, with the result that lawsuits addressing discrimination are defined "by [W]hite women's and Black men's experiences" (p.143).

> Black women sometimes experience discrimination in ways similar to [W]hite women's experiences; sometimes they share very similar experiences with Black men. Yet often they experience double-discrimination— the combined effects of practices which discriminate on the basis of race, and on the basis of sex. And sometimes, they experience discrimination as Black women—not the sum of race and sex discrimination, but as Black women. (ibid., 149)

Johnson-Odim (1991) discusses the necessity of addressing Third World women's needs in defining feminist and women's needs. She exams women living in the Third World as well as what she refers to as "Third World women living in the Western World." She therefore defines the former as residents of "'underdeveloped'/

overexploited geopolitical entities" and the latter as "oppressed nationalities from these world areas who are now resident in 'developed' First World countries" (ibid., 314). Regardless of whether these Third World women are living in the Third World or are residents in the First World, Johnson-Odim argues that their needs for change are far greater than simply gender equality:

> The point is that factors other than gender figure integrally in the oppression of Third World women and that, even regarding patriarchy, many Third World women labor under indigenous inequitable gender relationships exacerbated by Western patriarchy, racism, and exploitation. For Third World women resident in the West, race and class, along with gender, have been indivisible elements in their oppression. (ibid., 321)

In an analysis of "lesbians and the law" in Canada, Eaton (1990) effectively highlights some of the additional legal (as well as social) forms of discrimination experienced by lesbians, compared to their heterosexual sisters. Moreover, Eaton's overview is applicable to "lesbians and the law" in most Western countries, and much of the legal and social homophobic responses to lesbians are also experienced by gay men. Some of the examples of additional oppression experienced by lesbian (relative to "straight") women are as follows: (1) they cannot legally marry nor can they reap the social and legal benefits from this institution (e.g., health benefits, legal rights, and so on); (2) lesbians are more at risk of being labeled as "sexual aggressors" (particularly in terms of sexual relationships with "straight" women); (3) women who divorce husbands and identify themselves as lesbians risk losing the custody of their children (a significant reason to keep women with young children "closeted"); and (4) lesbians have less legal protection for basic human rights (e.g., in acquiring and maintaining housing, employment, and services).

Rosemarie Tong concludes her book on feminist thought by relating that although these various approaches to feminism are at times confusing and splintered, "feminist thought permits each woman to think her own thoughts. Apparently, not the truth but the truths are setting women free" (1989, 238). Despite the various frameworks of feminist thought presented in this section, it appears that all of the feminist perspectives presented here are increasingly adopting the need for inclusion of many women's experiences and recognizing that gender intersects with race/ethnicity, class, sexuality, national identity, religion, and other forms of oppression. This is certainly true of socialist feminism (Danner, 1989, 51). Or, as Naffine (1996, 29) states in her book on feminism and criminology, it is "apparent that none of the divisions between the different styles of feminism stand firmly." Postmodernism markedly shifted feminist jurisprudence by using the law as a framing discourse to examine how legal language is the site of power struggles (see Frug, 1992; Haney, 2000; Smart, 2003). In short, the goal is to view how the power of gender, race, and class are bigger than individual experiences, that is, where legal feminism is more "sociologically inspired" (Haney, 2000, 648).

For the purposes of this book, I describe these various types of feminism to clarify that "not all feminists think alike." On the other hand, there is a common thread among feminists: Men (and boys) and women (and girls) should be treated equally but frequently are not. Although many find the word feminist too

---

Comparative Perspectives: Global Feminism

- Transnational mobilization, organization, and advocacy on women's/feminist issues
- Decolonizing the representational matrix of women, gender, and nation
- Examination of women/gender in the context of:
  - power
  - marginality
  - commodification
  - resistance
- Broadening of feminism beyond a Western perspective
- Resistance of the pattern of Western feminists controlling or patronizing the feminist agenda

---

SOURCE: Valerie Sperling, Myra Marx Ferree, and Barbara Risman. 2001. Constructing Global Feminism. *Signs: Journal of Women in Culture and Society* 24:1155–1186; Kasic, Biljana. 2004. Feminist Cross-Mainstreaming within "East–West" Mapping: A Postsocialist Perspective. *European Journal of Women's Studies* 11:473–485.

"political," the tendency is to wrongly reduce it to mean "man hating." It is hoped that readers of this book who fall into that category were enlightened by this section documenting what feminism is, the ways it has grown (particularly in becoming more inclusive regarding race, class, and sexuality), and the overview of "feminist" problems that this book addresses. Naffine notes that despite the differences between some of the "feminisms," they all have one thing in common:

> The animating force of their scholarship is both political and intellectual. It is to think about women's lives in new ways, and so improve the lives of women. All of these feminist criminologies have therefore helped us to see crime differently—with greater intellectual rigour and with a sharpened sense of the political significance of the purposes and methods of criminology. (1996, 29)

It is also hoped that readers will see ways that feminist changes potentially help men and boys, too.

WHAT IS FEMINIST METHOD?

It is useful to recognize that not only does feminist theory distinguish itself from many theories (other than Marxist and radical theories) in its efforts to be applied and actually result in changes in society, but that in many senses, feminist theory purports a variety of means of collecting data, particularly in terms of hearing women's voices. For example, Maher (1997) writes in her book on women crack users that she was partially motivated to conduct her research because of the ways these women were presented as "monsters" in the media: "I want to present the accounts of a group of women we hear much about but little from ..." (ibid., x). Additionally, it is important to address the idea that feminist theory and methods are not designed to understand women exclusively. Notably, to fully address male offending, it appears useful to use feminist theory and applications of masculinity to explain males' likelihood of offending. Instead, it appears that research on crime has attempted to design theories to explain boys' and men's criminality and then tried to "fit" them to girls and women (also known as "the add-women-and-stir approach" and "the generalizability problem") (see Daly and Chesney-Lind, 1988; Naffine, 1996).

> The maleness of crimes is true of the United States of America, of Britain, of Australia and indeed of all Western countries. Men are the vast majority of violent and non-violent offenders. ... In view of this remarkable sex bias in crime, it is surprising that gender has not become the central preoccupation of the criminologist, rather than an after-thought. Surely it would be natural to ask the "man question": what is it about men that makes them offend and what is it about women that makes them law-abiding? (Maher, 1997, 6)

The focus on method in criminology has been "empirical criminology," or rather, how can we scientifically understand such important criminological and criminal processing questions as "Why do (some) people commit crimes?" "What policies best deter offenders from future offending?" "How are decisions made by the police, prosecutors, judges, parole review boards, and others?" "How frequently do different types of crimes occur?" "What increases people's chances of victim-ization?" and "How can victims of crimes best recover?" We can approach answers to these research questions empirically (scientifically) through a number of means. Feminist methods might mean coming up with more sensitive questions to quantify a rate or determining how best to interview women and girls about the questions that need to be asked. Concerning the issue of more sensitive questions, for example, it was common before the 1980s to measure rape occurrence as the number of rapes reported to the police. Feminist researchers later began asking women, knowing that many rape victims do not report their victimizations to the police. Next, it became apparent that asking women whether they have been raped "lost" a number of rapes, given that many women and girls do not define their experiences as "fitting" the legal definition of *rape*. Now it is known that the best method to capture rape rates is to ask women whether they have been "forced to have sex" rather than simply to ask, "Have you been raped?" The former wording captures a far more accurate measure of rape.

An important aspect of the research on gender and crime in the past twenty-five years is that, given the relative newness of research in this area, particularly from a feminist perspective, much of this research is exploratory in nature. That is, the researcher may not have a formed hypothesis but may instead be trying to determine what questions need to be asked. Exploratory research is more consistent with qualitative methods than quantitative methods. At the same time, many scholars minimize or decry qualitative findings as "unscientific" and "ungeneralizable."

Although quantitative data collection and analysis are preferred to determine rates of particular phenomena and ways in which various phenomena may or may not be related to each other, without collecting extensive qualitative data we may not even know which variables to include in quantitative surveys and models.

Finally, feminist research methods, perhaps more than any other method, have attempted to focus on the relationship between the researcher and those studied:

> Insofar as women's perspectives and experiences are subordinated in scientific inquiries and the larger culture, feminist researchers seek to eliminate hierarchies of knowledge construction. We are sensitive to our place in such hierarchies, so we disclose the multiple, historically specific positions we hold in relation to both study questions and participants. (Presser, 2005, 2067)

Presser's (2005) study of males convicted of violent crimes (including rape) is a prime example of *reflexivity*, where she consistently addresses the manner in which power relations between the interviewees and her became part of the data. For example, the ways some of these men mildly coerced and threatened her during data collection not only influenced the method but also the findings. *Standpoint theory* is a starting point for many feminist studies. Standpoint theory starts with the acknowledgement that "one's social situation enables and sets limits on what one can know" and thus must be taken into account when starting a research design (Harding, 2004b). "Standpoint epistemology sets the relationship between knowledge and politics at the center of its account in the sense that it tries to provide causal accounts of—to explain—the effects that different kinds of politics have on the production of knowledge" (ibid, 44). Criminological feminist research methodology, then, involves the choice of research topics, means of collecting and interpreting data, understanding the researcher's relationship with the participants, *reflexivity* (the critical examination of the research process itself), and a commitment to policy and action (it is not enough to collect the data and publish it, but we have an obligation to use our findings to improve awareness of women's and girls' [and men's and boys'] lives and experiences) (Flavin, 2001).

EFFECT OF SOCIETAL IMAGES
ON WOMEN IN CRIME

It is difficult to understand how women victims, offenders, and professionals are viewed and treated in the crime-processing system without first understanding the images of women in society. Rafter and Stanko (1982) identified six images of women that influence how they are perceived in the crime-processing system and in society as a whole when they offend, are victimized, or work in crime-processing jobs. Rafter and Stanko's (ibid.) first image is woman as the *pawn of biology*, where women are viewed as "gripped by biological forces beyond [their] control" (ibid., 3). For example, when Walter Mondale selected Geraldine Ferraro as his running mate during the 1984 presidential election, numerous journalists and others made observations such as "What if he dies and she becomes president? She might go through menopause and get us involved in a nuclear war." Similarly, women's menstruation and premenstrual syndrome have often been inappropriately used to explain women's behavior or even used as reasons why women should not be allowed to be astronauts. Regarding the practice, both historically and currently, to limit women's opportunities due to their "unpredictable mood swings," Karlene Faith (1993, 46) points out the irony of this given the "overwhelming evidence that male anger and mood swings present significantly more danger to other people."

The second image of women offered by Rafter and Stanko (1982) is woman as *impulsive and nonanalytical*, where women are perceived to act illogically and intuitively. A person with these perceived characteristics is unlikely to be hired as a professional, particularly to deal with crime or important court cases. The third image, women as *passive and weak*, implies that women are easy prey for victimization, will blindly follow criminal men into a life of crime, and as professionals are incapable of assuming authority. Rafter and Stanko's (ibid., 3) fourth image, woman as *impressionable and in need of protection*, implies that women are "gullible and easily led astray." Again, this stereotype makes women appear inadequate for crime-processing jobs. Furthermore, it is less likely to be available as a "loophole" for a lesser sentence if the offender is of color than if she is White. Rafter and Stanko's (ibid.) fifth image, *the active woman as masculine*, views any women who break from stereotypical passive roles as deviant and likely to be criminal. These women are also likely to be viewed as lesbian (whether they are or not); thus, they are prey to the hostility and discrimination associated with homophobia in society. *The active woman as masculine* is consistent with two of the images Karlene Faith (1993) identified of "unruly women" in films and movies. Specifically, Faith discusses how strong women in movies are depicted as "masculine" and how lesbian characters are often presented as "villains." Rafter and Stanko's (1982) final image, *the criminal woman as purely evil*, implies that it is worse for women than for men to be criminal because women not only are breaking out of law-abiding boundaries but, perhaps more importantly, are stepping out of stereotypical gender role boundaries. One of Faith's (1993) categories of depictions of women in popular film, "devil woman," is analogous to Rafter and Stanko's (1982) *criminal woman as purely evil*. The films Faith (1993) describes as "devil woman" films are those where offending girls and women have close links with the devil (e.g., *Rosemary's Baby* [1968], *The Exorcist* [1973]) or are simply evil (e.g., *The Bad Seed* [1956]).

Criminology research has also helped to reinforce stereotypes of women and girls, which affects their assessment in society and the crime-processing system. For instance, the concept of "victim precipitation," used by Hans Von Hentig (1948), Menachem Amir (1971), and Marvin E. Wolfgang (1958), has largely been used to see how women (and men) "attract" victimization. Whether it is to reinforce myths that women who wear certain clothes are "asking to be raped" or that women who stay in battering relationships are "masochistic," victim precipitation models have often been used to deny women's real risk of victimization while at the same time blaming them for this victimization.

Feminist research on other images includes acknowledgment that women have been dichotomized into either "Madonnas" or "whores" (Feinman, 1986). This model asserts that women are often assigned to either a Madonna category, where they are sweet and passive and produce children, or to a whore category, which includes any women who do not follow the prescribed societal role defined by the Madonna category (ibid.). The source of this Madonna/whore dichotomy was recently attributed to a comparison of Adam's two wives in the Bible: "Lilith is the independent seductress, refusing to lie beneath Adam, but later sneaking into the tents of men and sleeping with them. Sexuality is central to the evil in both Eve and Lilith, dooming Eve to the pains of childbirth and subservience, and Lilith to the death of her demon children" (McDermott and Blackstone, 2001, 89). Racist insinuations abide, with Lilith shown as "dark and beautiful from the waist up, but hairy and ugly below the waist. She thus has power to seduce men, and they never know her true nature until it is too late" (ibid.) Although both women are "flawed" by their use of sexuality, Eve's more virginal and maternal image makes her "good" while Lilith's sexual independence and failure to be a good mother make her "bad." McDermott and Blackstone (2001) argue that these sexuality-driven images of women persevered through the twentieth century in the societal and formal processing of women and girls as offenders, particularly regarding their sexuality.

Young (1986) challenges the Madonna/whore typology to the extent that it may apply only to White women. She claims that whereas the Madonna/whore dichotomy implies a good girl/bad girl dichotomy, categories for women of color include no "good girl" categories. Instead, she views women of color as falling into four categories, all of which are negative. The *amazon* is seen as inherently violent and capable of protecting herself; the *sinister sapphire* is vindictive, provocative, and not credible; the *mammy* is viewed as stupid, passive, and bothersome; and the *seductress* is sexually driven and noncredible as a victim or professional (ibid.). DeFour (1990) discusses the additional ramifications for women and girls of color regarding sexual harassment. She argues that these women may be more at risk of sexual harassment victimization yet receive the least serious responses due to societal portrayals of them as "very sexual" and "desiring sexual attention" more than their White sisters. She points to cultural myths portraying Latinas as "hot-blooded," Asian women as "exotic sexpots," and American women as "devoted to male elders" (ibid., 49). Thus, not only are women and girls treated differently than men and boys for identical sexual behaviors, but *among* women there is often discrimination in expectations due to damaging myths.

It is useful to examine the images of women and crime in the popular media using specific examples. One example is two movies (released about the same time) about women offenders that the public and the media reviewed very differently. Specifically, the movie *Pretty Woman* received numerous accolades as a romance and a "fun" movie. The movie portrayed a sex worker who married one of her patrons. One could argue that the effect of this "feel-good" movie on girls would be, "Wow! Prostituting results in finding handsome, wonderful husbands!"—hardly the message mainstream U.S. culture supports. The second movie, *Thelma and Louise*, depicted women taking a road trip where one shoots and kills a man trying to rape the other in a parking lot. The woman who shoots fears (it would seem legitimately, given information provided later in this book) that she is going to receive serious prison time for killing this would-be rapist. This results in the two women trying to evade the police. Despite public acclaim for this film, a significant number of people, including journalists, portrayed this as a "bad" message for girls. Notably, the reviews for *Pretty Woman* never came to that conclusion. One could argue that the overall message is that sex work is fun and rewarding, but do not shoot a man trying to rape your friend.

A final example of images of criminal as gendered and raced is the way the recent "school shootings" have been portrayed in the media. These shootings have been committed primarily by White boys, and the targets have disproportionately been girls; the media has ignored these strong gender and race patterns (Steinem, 1999). After the Columbine High School shootings in Colorado in 1999, journalists asked, "What's wrong with our children?" (ibid). It seems better questions would include: "What's wrong with how we're raising our boys?" "Why do we have so many of these school shootings?" "Why are girls the main targets?" "Why are these mostly White boys?" Danner and Carmody (2001) document how, in addition to the media, scholarly studies of school violence ignore and "discount the role of masculinities, bullying, and male violence against girls and women, and few of the policy recommendations address these concerns" (2001, 87). The reports focus on guns or individual psychology rather than on reporting what witnesses know:

> Those closest to the suspects and victims in the [school shooting] incidents—their classmates—were most likely to report that the violence was a response to bullying or retaliation against a girlfriend in those cases where this was a likely explanation; they recognized the interpersonal and gendered dynamics behind the attacks. In contrast, "experts" such as academics, professionals, and law enforcement officials rarely identified the violence in this manner. (ibid., 107)

Other research affirms the gendered nature of bullying: A British study of secondary students found boys far more likely than girls to act as bystanders when witnessing bullying, while girls are more likely than boys to report the bullying behaviors to school officials (Cowie, 2000).

Finally, in our discussion of popular images of women and girls, it is useful to remember that girls and women who merely fail to adhere to stereotyped gender norms, regardless of whether their appearance or actions are in fact criminal, are often viewed as offensive simply for violating the gender norm. Karlene Faith (1993, 1) refers to such women as "unruly":

> The unruly woman is the undisciplined woman. She is renegade from the disciplinary practices which would mold her as a gendered being. She is the defiant woman who rejects authority which would subjugate her and render her docile. She is the offensive woman who acts in her own interests. She is the unmanageable woman who claims her own body, the whore, the wanton woman, the wild woman out of control. She is the woman who cannot be silenced. She is a rebel. She is trouble.

DIVERSITY AMONG WOMEN

In the search for the role of gender and themes of sexism in victimization, offending, and working in the crime-processing system, it is important to remember the significant amount of diversity among women and girls (Daly and Chesney-Lind, 1988). The gender role stereotypes differ for women and girls of different classes and races/ethnicities (Brennan, 2002). Historically, feminist scholarship has focused too strongly on the lives and experiences of White, middle-class women and girls, failing adequate discussions of race and racism and class and classism.

Feminist legal theorists have proposed the concept of *multiple consciousness*: that we are often born with more than one identity (Harris, 1990; Matsuda, 1989). Multiple consciousness is a "process in which propositions are constantly put forth, challenged, and subverted" (Harris, 1990). A reason for this challenge and subversion, according to Harris (ibid., 585), is the phenomenon (discussed previously) referred to as "gender essentialism," in which women's experiences are "isolated and described independently of race, class, sexual orientation, and other realities of experience." Similarly, Asian American legal scholar Mari J. Matsuda (1989, 7) describes how legal training in most law schools includes "training the students out of the muddle-headed world where everything is relevant and into the lawyer's world where the few critical facts prevail." Matsuda describes how this training results in bifurcated thinking, separating what one believes is relevant from what one's legal training has taught is relevant. This involves "shifting back and forth between consciousness as a Third World person and the White consciousness required for survival in elite educational institutions" (ibid., 8). Further, a woman of color may feel more able to bring up issues of male violence in a law or criminal justice class where the professor is a White woman instead of a White man, but she may not feel that she can safely bring up issues of racism as well as male violence. Or a woman of color attorney may feel able to bring up her client's racism experiences before a man of color judge but feel less comfortable discussing her client's sexism experiences relevant to the case. Hence, multiple consciousness is the result. However, multiple consciousness as a method "encompasses more than consciousness-shifting as skilled advocacy. It encompasses as well the search for the pathway to a just world" (ibid., 9). Matsuda closes with this information:

> I cannot pretend that I, as a Japanese American, truly know the pain of, say, my Native American sister. But I can pledge to educate myself so that I do not receive her pain in ignorance. And I can say as an American, I am choosing as my heritage the 200 years of struggle by poor and working people, by Native Americans, by women, by people of color, for dignified lives in this nation. I can claim as my own the Constitution my father fought for at Anzio, the Constitution that I swore to uphold and defend when I was admitted to the bar. It was not written for me, but I can make it my own, using my chosen consciousness as a woman and person of color to give substance to those tantalizing words "equality" and "liberty." (ibid., 10)

Finally, Ruth Chigwada-Bailey (1997, 25) notes: "The various intersections between race, gender, and class oppression—and other differentiating characteristics—affect how and when all women experience sexism."

In the same vein, this book hopes to make women and girls visible as victims, as offenders, and as professionals in the crime-processing system, while acknowledging that women's and girls' experiences may differ based on their race, class, sexual preference, national origin, and other personal characteristics. It is important to note the more recent identification of hate crimes as a social problem and the subsequent studies on this. There is some debate by both scholars and activists as to whether "sex/gender" should be one of the target-group categories of hate-crime victimizations, under the assumption that women and girls are battered and raped because they are female. Regardless of one's feelings about which groups should be legally protected in hate-crime legislation (e.g., racial minorities, lesbian/gay/bisexual/transgendered persons, persons with disabilities, religious minorities, and so on), it seems clear that women in these proposed subgroups are at more risk of hate-crime victimization (including rape and murder) than women who do not fit into these categories (e.g., Brenner, 1995; Ferber, 1998; Jenness and Broad, 1997; Levin and McDevitt, 1997). A particularly chilling account is Claudia Brenner's (1995) autobiography about her experiences of being shot and witnessing her partner's murder while camping because a male camper who saw them from a distance was angry they were lesbians. In addition to physical victimization, another significant form of hate crimes in most hate-crime legislation is the destruction of property (e.g., painting swastikas on synagogues, painting racial or homophobic slurs on people's homes or businesses). In 1994, some students at the University of New Mexico took, hid, and defaced with offensive slogans and symbols over 100 books from the Gender and Gay Studies section of the library (Hood and Rollins, 1995).

Finally, with our shrinking world and the globalization of the economy and politics, important differences among women and girls likely can be accounted for by comparing countries. While I report on some research in other countries, unfortunately, it is beyond the scope and page limit of this book for me to adequately report on the existing research on gender, women, and girls in crime across the globe. This book's focus is on the United States, with minimal references to Canada, Mexico, England, and a few other countries. But to try to allow the reader a greater exposure to other countries, boxed inserts in most of the chapters describe comparative studies of various countries or report on a study in a country other than the United States.

SUMMARY

Sadly, despite the significant contributions of feminist research (explained in detail in the next chapter) highlighting the role of gender in delinquency and offending risks, current studies still often leave out women and girls or only address them fleetingly. The same can be said for abuse and trauma, also highlighted by feminist research as important risk factors for offending (e.g., Arnold, 1990; Chesney-Lind and Rodriguez, 1983; Daly, 1992; Gaarder and Belknap, 2002; Gilfus, 1992; Owen, 1998; Richie, 1996; Silbert and Pines, 1981). Examples abound in recent theory books. In Warr's (2002) book on the effects of peers on delinquency, 10 out of 140 pages of text mention girls/gender, and neither abuse nor trauma is in the index. Agnew's (2005) *Why do Criminals Offend?: A General Theory of Crime and Delinquency* promises to incorporate previous theories and research on crime, yet only 12 of 214 pages discuss girls and/or gender, and the book scarcely addresses abuse or trauma. Notably, when abuse is mentioned in the one section on girls, the discussion is placed in parentheses: "(It is, however, important to note that girls are more likely to be sexually abused than boys, and such sexual abuse may play an important role in much female crime....)" (ibid., 163–164). In yet another recent book on crime over the life course, out of almost 300 pages, gender appears on 2 pages (to explain why girls/women were not included in the sample), and abuse appears on only 3 pages (Ezell and Cohen, 2005). Thus, not only are girls and women still invisible in far too much of the research and programming, but abuse and trauma, which can likely help explain male criminality as well (e.g., Belknap and Holsinger, 2006; Dembo et al., 1992; Dodge, Bates, and Pettit, 1990; Harlow, 1999; Widom 1989a, 1989b), are often ignored or discounted.

Given the history of criminology as "one of the most thoroughly masculinized of all social science fields...the phrase 'feminist criminology' may well seem something of an oxymoron" (Britton, 2000, 58). Yet feminist criminology has been growing since the 1970s and is having an increasingly strong impact on this male-dominated field: "Feminist criminologists have been at the forefront in pointing out that when women and other marginalized groups are ignored, devalued, or misrepresented, society in general and the understanding of crime and justice in particular suffer as a result" (Flavin, 2001, 271). This chapter presented the numerous ways that women's and girls' experiences as victims, offenders, and professionals in the crime-processing system have been made invisible. The concepts of sex, gender, feminism, and patriarchy were explored. Finally, this chapter discussed the importance of not assuming a monolithic experience for women and girls and the reasons why race, class, sexual preference, and other variables must be considered when discussing and researching women's and girls' experiences and behaviors.

REFERENCES

Acker, Joan. 1990. Hierarchies, Jobs, Bodies: A Theory of Gendered Organizations. *Gender and Society* 4:139–158.

Acoca, Leslie. 1998. Outside/Inside: The Violation of American Girls at Home, on the Streets, and in the Juvenile Justice System. *Crime and Delinquency* 44:561–589.

Agnew, Robert S. 2005. *Why do Criminals Offend? A General Theory of Crime and Delinquency*. Los Angeles: Roxbury Publishing.

American Correctional Association. 1990. *The Female Offender: What Does the Future Hold?* Arlington, VA: Kirby Lithographic Company.

Amir, Menachem. 1971. *Patterns in Forcible Rape.* Chicago: University of Chicago Press.

Arnold, Regina. 1990. Processes of Victimization and Criminalization of Black Women. *Social Justice* 17:153–166.

Belknap, Joanne, and Kristi Holsinger. 1998. An Overview of Delinquent Girls: How Theory and Practice Have Failed and the Need for Innovative Changes. Pp. 31–64 in *Female Crime and Delinquency: Critical Perspectives and Effective Interventions,* edited by R. T. Zaplin. Gaithersburg, MD: Aspen Publishing, Inc.

———. 2006. The Gendered Nature of Risk Factors for Delinquency. *Feminist Criminology* 1:48–71.

Brennan, Pauline K. 2002. *Women Sentenced to Jail in New York City.* New York: LFB Scholarly Publishing.

Brenner, Claudia. 1995. *Eight Bullets.* Ithaca, NY: Firebrand Press.

Britton, Dana M. 2000. Feminism in Criminology: Engendering the Law. *Annals of the American Academy of Political and Social Science* 571:5–76.

Browne, Angela. 1987. *When Battered Women Kill.* New York: Free Press.

Browne, Angela, Brenda Miller, and Eugene Maguin. 1999. Prevalence and severity of lifetime physical and sexual victimization among incarcerated women. *International Journal of Law and Psychiatry* 22:301–322.

Carlen, Pat. 1983. *Women's Imprisonment: A Study in Social Control.* London: Routledge and Kegan Paul.

Chesney-Lind, M., and R. G. Shelden. 1992. *Girls, Delinquency and Juvenile Justice.* Pacific Grove, CA: Brooks/Cole.

Chesney-Lind, Meda. 1993. Reinventing Women's Corrections. Pp. 3–13 in *The Incarcerated Woman,* edited by S. F. Sharp. Upper Saddle River, NJ: Prentice Hall.

Chesney-Lind, Meda, and Noelie Rodriguez. 1983. Women under Lock and Key. *Prison Journal* 53:47–65.

Chigwada-Bailey, Ruth. 1997. *Black Women's Experiences of Criminal Justice.* Winchester, England: Waterside Press.

Coker, Ann L., Nilam J. Patel, Shanthi Krishnaswami, Wendy Schmidt, and Donna I. Richter. 1998. Childhood Forced Sex and Cervical Dysplasia among Women Prison Inmates. *Violence against Women* 4:595–608.

Collins, Patricia Hill, Lionel A. Maldonado, Dana Y. Takagi, Barrie Thorne, Lynn Wever, and Howard Winant. 1995. On Fenstermaker's "Doing Difference." *Gender and Society* 9:491–505.

Cowie, Helen. 2000. Bystanding or Standing By: Gender Issues in Coping with Bullying in English Schools. *Aggressive Behavior* 26:85–97.

Crenshaw, Kimberle. 1989. Demarginalizing the Intersection of Race and Sex: A Black Feminist Critique of Antidiscrimination Doctrine, Feminist Theory, and Antiracist Politics. *University of Chicago Legal Forum* 14:139–167.

Croall, Hazel. 1995. Women's Victimization and White-Collar Crime. Pp. 227–245 in *Gender and Crime,* edited by R. E. Dobash, R. P. Dobash, and L. Noaks. Cardiff: University of Wales Press.

Dahl, Tove Stang. 1986. Taking Women as a Starting Point: Building Women's Law. *International Journal of the Sociology of Law* 14:239–247.

Daly, Kathleen. 1992. Women's Pathways to Felony Court. *Review of Law and Women's Studies* 2:11–52.

Daly, Kathleen, and Meda Chesney-Lind. 1988. Feminism and Criminology. *Justice Quarterly* 5:497–538.

Danner, Mona J. E. 1989. Socialist Feminism: A Brief Introduction. Pp. 51–54 in *New Directions in Critical Criminology*, edited by B. D. MacLean and D. Milovanovic. Vancouver: The Collective Press.

Danner, Mona J. E., and Dianne C. Carmody. 2001. Missing Gender in Cases of Infamous School Violence. *Justice Quarterly* 18:87–114.

DeFour, Darlene C. 1990. The Interface of Racism and Sexism on College Campuses. Pp.45–52 in *Ivory Power: Sexual Harassment on Campus*, edited by M. A. Pauludi. Albany: State University of New York Press.

Dembo, R., L. Williams, W. Wothke, J. Schmeidler, and C. H. Brown. 1992. The Role of Family Factors, Physical Abuse, and Sexual Victimization Experiences in High-Risk Youths' Alcohol and Other Drug Use and Delinquency: A Longitudinal Model. *Violence and Victims* 7:245–266.

Dodge, Kenneth A., John E. Bates, and Gregory S. Pettit. 1990. Mechanisms in the Cycle of Violence. *Science* 250:1678–1683.

Donovan, Josephine. 1985. *Feminist Theory*. New York: Frederick Ungar.

Eaton, Mary. 1990. Lesbians and the Law. Pp.109–131 in *Lesbians in Canada*, edited by S. D. Stone. Toronto: Between the Lines.

Edwards, Anne. 1987. Male Violence in Feminist Theory: An Analysis of the Changing Conception of Sex/ Gender Violence and Male Dominance. Pp. 13–29 in *Women, Violence, and Social Control*, edited by J. Hanmer and M. Maynard. Atlantic Highlands, NJ: Humanities Press International.

Epstein, Cynthia F. 1988. *Deceptive Distinctions: Sex, Gender, and Social Order*. New Haven, CT: Yale University Press.

Ezell, Michael E., and Lawrence E. Cohen. 2005. *Desisting from Crime*. Oxford, England: Oxford University Press.

Faith, Karlene. 1993. *Unruly Women: The Politics of Confinement and Resistance*. Vancouver: Press Gang Publishers.

Faludi, Susan. 1991. *Backlash: The Undeclared War against Women*. New York: Doubleday.

Fausto-Sterling, Anne. 1985. *Myths of Gender: Biological Theories about Women and Men*, 2nd ed. New York: Basic Books.

Feinman, Clarice. 1986. *Women in the Criminal Justice System*, 2nd ed. New York: Praeger.

Ferber, Abby L. 1998. *White Man Falling: Race, Gender, and White Supremacy*. Lanham, MD: Rowman & Littlefield.

Flavin, Jeanne. 2001. Feminism for the Mainstream Criminologist. *Journal of Criminal Justice* 29: 271–285.

Fletcher, Beverly R., and Dreama G. Moon. 1993. Introduction. Pp.5–14 in *Women Prisoners: A Forgotten Population*, edited by B. R. Fletcher, L. D. Shaver, and D. G. Moon. Westport, CT: Praeger.

Fox, Lana, and Fran Sugar. 1990. Survey of Federally Sentenced Aboriginal Women in the Community. Canada: Correctional Service of Canada, 16pp. (or available at http:// www.csc-scc.gc.ca/text/prgrm/fsw/ nativesurvey/toce_e.shtml).

Freedman, Estelle. 1981. *Their Sisters' Keepers: Women's Prison Reform in America, 1830–1930*. Ann Arbor: University of Michigan Press.

Frug, Mary Joe. 1992. *Postmodern Legal Feminism*. New York: Routledge.

Gaarder, Emily, and Joanne Belknap. (2002). Tenuous Borders: Girls Transferred to Adult Court. *Criminology* 40:481–517.

Gagnier, Regenia. 1990. Feminist Post-modernism: The End of Feminism or the Ends of Theory? Pp. 21–32 in *Theoretical Perspectives on Sexual Difference*, edited by D. L. Rhode. New Haven, CT: Yale University Press.

Gerber, Jurg, and Susan L. Weeks. 1992. Women as Victims of Corporate Crime. *Deviant Behavior* 13:325–347.

Gilfus, Mary E. 1992. From Victims to Survivors to Offenders: Women's Routes of Entry and Immersion into Street Crime. *Women & Criminal Justice* 4:63–90.

Gray, Tara, G. Larry Mays, and Mary K. Stohr. 1995. Inmate Needs and Programming in Exclusively Women's Jails. *The Prison Journal* 75:186–202.

Greenfeld, Lawrence A., and Tracy L. Snell. 1999. Women Offenders. Bureau of Justice Statistics: Special Report. U.S. Department of Justice, December, 14pp.

Haney, Lynne A. 2000. Feminist State Theory. *Annual Review of Sociology* 26:641–666.

Harding, Sandra. 2004a. Can Men Be Subjects of Feminist Thought? Pp. 177–197 in *Feminist Perspectives on Social Research*, edited by Sharlene Nagy Hesse-Biber and Michelle L. Yaiser. New York: Oxford University Press.

———. 2004b. Rethinking Standpoint Epistemology. Pp. 39–64 in *Feminist Perspectives on Social Research*, edited by Sharlene Nagy Hesse-Biber and Michelle L. Yaiser. New York: Oxford University Press.

Harlow, Caroline Wolf. 1999. Prior Abuse Reported by Inmates and Probationers. Selected Findings, Bureau of Justice Statistics., 4pp.

Harris, Angela. 1990. Race and Essentialism in Feminist Legal Theory. *Stanford Law Review* 42:581–615.

Hood, Jane C., and Stephen Rollins. 1995. Some Didn't Call It Hate. *Violence Against Women* 1:228–240.

hooks, bell. 1984. *Feminist Theory: From Margin to Center*. Boston: South End Press.

———. 1990. Feminism: A Transformational Politic. Pp. 185–196 in *Theoretical Perspectives on Sexual Difference*, edited by D. L. Rhode. New Haven, CT: Yale University Press.

Hughes, Lorine A. 2005. The Representation of Females in Criminological Research. *Women & Criminal Justice* 16:1–27.

Immarigeon, Russ. 1987a. Women in Prison. *Journal of the National Prison Project* 11:1–5.

———. 1987b. Few Diversion Programs Are Offered Female Offenders. *Journal of the National Prison Project* 12:9–11.

Immarigeon, Russ, and Meda Chesney-Lind. 1992. *Women's Prisons: Overcrowded and Overused*. San Francisco. National Council on Crime and Delinquency.

Jaggar, Alison M. 1983. *Feminist Politics and Human Nature*. Totowa, NJ: Rowman & Allanheld.

James, Jennifer, and Jane Meyerding. 1977. Early Sexual Experiences and Prostitution. *American Journal of Psychiatry* 134:1381–1385.

Jenness, Valerie, and Kendal Broad. 1997. *Hate Crimes: New Social Movements and the Politics of Violence*. Hawthorne, NY: Walter de Gruyter.

Johnson-Odim, Cheryl. 1991. Common Themes, Different Contexts: Third World Women and Feminism. Pp. 314–327 in *Third World Women and the Politics of Feminism*, edited by C. T. Mohanty, A. Russo, and L. Torres. Bloomington, IN: Indiana University Press.

Kessler, Suzanne. 2004. The Medical Construction of Gender. Pp. 51–66 in *Feminist Frontiers*, 6th edition edited by L. Richardson, V. Taylor, and N. Whittier. Boston: McGraw Hill.

Klein, Ethel. 1984. *Gender Politics*. Cambridge, MA: Harvard University Press.

Klein, Hugh, and Betty S. Chao. 1995. Sexual Abuse during Childhood and Adolescence as Predictors of HIV-Related Sexual Risk during Adult-hood among Female Sexual Partners of Drug Users. *Violence Against Women* 1:55–76.

Kline, S. 1993. A Profile of Female Offenders in State and Federal Prisons. *Female Offenders: Meeting the Needs of a Neglected Population* (pp. 1–6). Laurel, MD: American Correctional Association.

Lake, E. S. 1993. An exploration of the violent victim experiences of female offenders. *Violence and Victims* 8:41–51.

Laub, John H., and Jinney S. Smith. 1995. Eleanor Touroff Glueck: An Unsung Pioneer in Criminology. *Women & Criminal Justice* 6:1–22.

Leonard, Eileen B. 1982. *Women, Crime, and Society*. New York: Longman.

Levin, Jack, and Jack McDevitt. 1997. *Hate Crimes: Rising Tide of Bigotry and Bloodshed*. New York: Plenum Press.

MacKinnon, Catherine. 1989. *Toward a Feminist Theory of State*. Cambridge: Harvard University Press.

———. 1990. Legal Perspectives on Sexual Difference. Pp. 213–225 in *Theoretical Perspectives on Sexual Difference*, edited by D. L. Rhode. New Haven, CT: Yale University Press.

Madriz, Esther. 1997. *Nothing Bad Hap-pens to Good Girls*. Berkeley, CA: University of California Press.

Maguigan, Holly. 1991. Battered Women and Self-Defense: Myths and Misconceptions in Current Reform Proposals. *University of Pennsylvania Law Review* 140:379–486.

Maher, Lisa. 1997. *Sexed Work: Gender, Race and Resistance in a Brooklyn Drug Market*. Oxford, England: Clarendon Press.

Matsuda, Mari J. 1989. When the First Quail Calls: Multiple Consciousness as Jurisprudential Method. *Women's Rights Law Reporter* 2:7–10.

McDermott, M. Joan, and Sarah J. Blackstone. 2001. Lilith in Myth, Melodrama, and Criminology. *Women & Criminal Justice* 9:85–98.

Mead, Rebecca. 1999. Eggs for Sale: Annals of Reproduction. *The New Yorker Magazine* (August 9):56–65.

Morris, Allison. 1987. *Women, Crime, and Criminal Justice*. Oxford, England: Basil Blackwell.

Mullings, Janet L., James W. Marquart, and Victoria E. Brewer. 2000. Assessing the Relationship between Child Sexual Abuse and Marginal Living Conditions on HIV/AIDS Related Risk Behavior among Women Prisoners. *Child Abuse and Neglect* 24:677–688.

Mumola, Christopher J., and Allen J. Beck. 1997. Prisoners in 1996. Bureau of Justice Statistics, 15pp.

Naffine, Ngaire. 1996. *Feminism and Criminology*. Philadelphia: Temple University Press.

Owen, Barbara. 1998. *In the Mix: Struggle and Survival in a Women's Prison*. Albany: State University of New York Press.

Presser, Lois. 2005. Negotiating Power and Narrative in Research: Implica-tions for Feminist Methodology. *Signs: Journal of Women in Culture and Society* 30:2067–2090.

Rafter, Nicole H. 1985. *Partial Justice: Women in State Prisons 1800–1935*. Boston: Northeaster Press.

Rafter, Nicole H., and Elizabeth A. Stanko. 1982. Introduction. Pp. 1–28 in *Judge, Lawyer, Victim, Thief: Women, Gender Roles and Criminal Justice*, edited by N. H. Rafter and E. A. Stanko. Stoughton, MA: Northeastern University Press.

Rhode, Deborah L. 1989. *Justice and Gender: Sex Discrimination and the Law*. Cambridge, MA: Harvard University Press.

———. 1990. Definitions of Difference. Pp. 197–212 in *Theoretical Perspectives on Sexual Difference*, edited by D. L. Rhode. New Haven, CT: Yale University Press.

Richie, Beth E. 1996. *Compelled to Crime: The Gender Entrapment of Black Battered Women*. New York: Routledge.

Rynbrandt, Linda J., and Ronald C. Kramer. 1995. Hybrid Nonwomen and Corporate Violence. *Violence Against Women* 1:206–227.

Sable, Marjorie R., John R. Fieberg, Sandra L. Martin, and Lawrence L. Kupper. 1999. Violence Victimization Experiences of Pregnant Prisoners. *American Journal of Orthopsychiatry* 69:392–397.

Sargent, Elizabeth, Susan Marcus-Mendoza, and Chong Ho Yu. 1993. Abuse and the Woman Prisoner. Pp. 55–64 in *Woman Prisoners: A Forgotten Population*, edited by B. R. Fletcher, L. D. Shaver, and D. B. Moon. Westport, CT: Praeger.

Schneider, E. M., and S. B. Jordon. 1981. Representation of Women Who Defend Themselves in Response to Physical or Sexual Assault. Pp. 1–39 in *Women's Self-Defense Cases: Theory and Practice*, edited by E. Bochnak. Charlottesville, VA: Michie Company Law Publishers.

Shaw, C., and H. McKay. 1969. *Juvenile Delinquency and Urban Areas*. Chicago: University of Chicago Press.

Shaw, Margaret. 1993. Reforming Federal Women's Imprisonment, Pp. 50–75 in *Conflict with the Law: Women and the Canadian Justice System*, edited by E. Edelberg and C. Currie. Vancouver, Canada: Press Gang Publishers.

Silbert, Mimi H., and Ayala M. Pines. 1981. Sexual Child Abuse as an Antecedent to Prostitution. *Child Abuse and Neglect* 5:407–411.

Singer, Mark I., Janet Bussey, Li-Yu Song, and Lisa Lunghofer. 1995. The Psychosocial Issues of Women Serving Time in Jail. *Social Work* 40:103–113.

Smart, Carol. 1989. *Feminism and the Power of Law*. London: Routledge & Kegan Paul.

———. 1993. Proscription, Prescription and the Desire for Certainty? *Feminist Theory in the Field of Law Studies in Law, Politics, and Society* 13:37–54.

Sokoloff, Natalie J. 2005. Women Prisoners at the Dawn of the 21st Century. *Women & Criminal Justice* 16:127–137.

Steinem, Gloria. 1999. Supremacy Crimes. *MS. Magazine* (August/September): 45–47.

Stuart, Diane M. 2005. Statement before the United States Senate Concerning the Reauthorization of the Violence Against Women Act. Presented on July 19, 2005. http://www.ojp. usdoj.gov/vawo/docs/testimony 07192005.pdf.

Tong, Rosemarie. 1989. *Feminist Thought*. Boulder, CO: Westview Press.

Von Hentig, Hans. 1948. *The Criminal and His Victim*. New Haven, CT: Yale University Press.

Warr, Mark. 2002. *Companions in Crime*. Cambridge, England: The Cambridge University Press.

West, Candace, and Sarah Fenstermaker. 1995. Doing Difference. *Gender and Society* 9:8–37.

West, Candace, and Don H. Zimmerman. 1987. Doing Gender. *Gender and Society* 1:125–151.

Widom, Cathy S. 1989a. Child Abuse, Neglect, and Adult Behavior: Research Design and Findings on Criminality, Violence, and Child Abuse. *American Journal of Ortho-psychiatry* 59:355–367.

———. 1989b. The Cycle of Violence. *Science* 244:160–166.

Wolfgang, Marvin E. 1958. *Patterns in Criminal Homicide.* Philadelphia: University of Pennsylvania Press.

Wong, Nellie. 1991. Socialist Feminism: Our Bridge to Freedom. Pp. 288–296 in *Third World Women and the Politics of Feminism,* edited by C. T. Mohanty, A. Russo, and L. Torres. Bloomington: Indiana University Press.

Young, Vernetta D. 1986. Gender Expectations and Their Impact on Black Female Offenders and Victims. *Justice Quarterly* 3:305–327.

2

❖

Critiquing Criminological Theories

> Returning to a less judgmental perspective may help us see female delinquents in a fuller and more sympathetic light and let us incorporate gender as the complex, meaningful, and power-laden social process that it really is.... the intertwining processes of gender and delinquency provide some theoretical insights for the study of crime and delinquency in general. ... [C]rime is fundamentally about power relations and survival.
>
> BOTTCHER, 2001, 925

Criminology is not unique among academic disciplines in its historical exclusion of females from most research questions (see Fausto-Sterling, 1985; Morris, 1987; Smart, 1976; Spender, 1981). Most criminological theories explain why some males, but not females, break the law. This occurs despite the fact that over time "the sex ratio of offending is remarkably consistent," with males exhibiting significantly greater offending levels (Britton, 2000, 60). For every age group, including young children, females are far more law-abiding (Loeber and Farrington, 2000). But given that theoretical criminology was largely constructed by men and about men (Leonard, 1982; Messerschmidt, 1993; Naffine, 1996), perhaps it is not surprising that female offending and the significant role of gender were largely invisible until recently. There are two important implications of focusing solely on males' experiences: (1) The theories and findings are really theories and findings about male crime, and (2) we must question the validity of any "general" theory if it does not also apply to women (Morris, 1987, 2).

Rasche's (1975) offers three explanations for the historical neglect of female offending: (1) Women make up a small percentage of prisoners (approximately 7 percent, currently); (2) prison authorities are more likely to oppose research on women (than on men) prisoners; (3) women have been deemed insignificant compared to the more "deserving" offenders: men. Smart (1976) reported that when female offenders were acknowledged in criminology research, it was in terms of their deviations from the stereotypical aspects of women's lives, such as maternal deprivation. Further, female lawbreakers historically (and to some degree today) have been viewed as "abnormal" and as "worse" than male law-breakers—not only for breaking the law but also for stepping outside of pre-scribed gender roles of femininity and passivity.

Rashe's (1975) and Smart's (1976) charges still prevail to some extent, although there has been a huge increase in research on women prisoners and girl delinquents since 1975, particularly from a feminist perspective that goes way beyond judging female offenders for their failure to abide by gender stereotypes. One reason is that the number of women in prison has increased at an unprece-dented rate—indeed, at a pace much greater than male imprisonment. (Data on the explosion in women's incarceration in the United States since 1980 is detailed in Chapter 5.) Feminists and the women's movement have also helped at least some scholars redefine criminological research as pertaining to females as well as males. Although there still exists a tendency for studies on offenders to be conducted solely on males (Hughes, 2005), grant-giving institutions and journal editors are more likely to request a legitimate explanation as to why a sample would be all male. In short, although there is a great deal of catching up to do in order to understand, respond to, and explain female criminality, important strides have been made in recent years.

This chapter discusses the various schools of criminological theories developed since the late 1800s: traditional, strain and subcultural, differential association, labeling, social control, Marxist/radical/critical, women's liberation/emancipation, biosocial/evolutionary, and life-course approaches. During the periods in which these theories developed, studies often either routinely ignored women or viewed them through a stereotypical lens. The more recent pathways approach offers a less sexist approach that increases the likelihood of identifying not only females' but also males' childhood experiences and traumas related to subsequent offending.

THE TRADITIONAL POSITIVIST STUDIES

The traditional, or original, studies of female criminality were conducted between the end of the nineteenth century and the middle of the twentieth century. The most prominent researchers included Cesare Lombroso and William Ferrero (1895), W. I. Thomas (1923, 1967), Sigmund Freud (1933), and Otto Pollak (1950, 1961). These studies were grounded in the belief that biological determin-ism accounts for female criminality: Whereas men are rational, women are driven by their biological constitutions. Also referred to as the classical or positivist studies, these traditional approaches were informed by four main assumptions: (1) Individual characteristics, not society, are responsible for criminal behavior; (2) there is an identifiable biological nature inherent in all women; (3) offending women are "masculine," which makes them incompetent as women and thus prone to break the law; and (4) the differences between male and female criminality are due to sex, not gender, differences. The classical theorists, not surprisingly, have been accused of viewing women as turning to crime because of their "perversion of or rebellion against their natural feminine roles" (Klein, 1980, 72). In addition to the sexist nature of the classical studies, they have been classist, racist, and hetero-sexist, focusing on wealthy, White, married women as the "feminine" standard. These theorists' works are reviewed in the following sections.

The Atavistic Female Offender

Cesare Lombroso, a physician, psychiatrist and criminal anthropologist who studied both incarcerated men and women in nineteenth-century Italy, is often referred to as the "father" of criminology. In forging a legacy of scientific studies of crime, his positivist method unfortunately set the stage for sexist, racist, and classist approaches to studying the causes of crime. For example in *Criminal Man* (originally published in Italian in 1876, with two partial translations in English in 1911), he proposed a racial hierarchy with Black Africans at the bottom and White Europeans at the top, identifying people of color as "savages" with physiological and psychological anomalies (Rafter and Gibson, 2004). By focusing exclusively on the physical and psychological makeup of the individual in determining criminal behavior, he dismissed the effects of socialization or social-structural constraints as important determinants of criminal behavior or the labeling of behavior as criminal.

Lombroso and (his son-in-law) Ferrero's book *The Female Offender* (first published in Italian in 1893 and translated into English in 1895) explains female criminality through atavism. *Atavism* is a concept that views some deviant behavior as a "throwback" to an earlier evolutionary stage in human development. Thus, in his theorizing, "Lombroso firmly maintained that deviants are less highly evolved than 'normal' law abiding citizens" (Smart, 1976, 31). Lombroso and Ferrero concluded that women offenders showed less degeneration than men simply because women had not evolved as much as men. Despite their perceived slower evolution, however, women were viewed as less likely than men to be criminal. Lombroso frequently distinguished prostitutes from other female offenders, explaining why these sex workers were the true atavists and why the other offending women did not fit well with his theory. Rafter and Gibson (2004) report the devastating effects of Lombroso and Ferror's work on the Italian women's movement at this time (providing "proof" that women are biologically inferior to men, thus unworthy of demands for equality in education, work, and the home), but they also point out that *The Female Offender* had a longer lasting impact (and a more negative one) on the study of female crime than *Criminal Man* had on male crime.

As noted in the last chapter, Lombroso and Ferraro provided two simplistic categories available to women, both of which they considered inferior to men: (1) bad, primitive, and masculine women; and (2) law-abiding, civilized, and feminine women (Rafter and Gibson, 2004, 10). Feinman (1986, 4) identified this as a biologically driven Madonna/whore duality, where women are either good or bad:

> Implicit in the madonna/whore duality is women's subservience to men, who assumed the role of protectors of the madonna and punishers of the whore....A good woman is a loyal, submissive wife who serves her husband, and for this she is honored and protected. The evil woman, on the other hand, destroys man and brings pain and ruin.

In their search for degeneration and atavism, Lombroso and Ferrero measured and documented incarcerated women's craniums, heights, weights, hair color (and baldness), moles, tattoos, and genitalia. Lombroso and Ferrero also assumed that criminal behavior was a sex, not a gender, trait. Racism surfaces here in the description of how women of color "resemble men in their strength, intelligence, and sexual promiscuity" (Rafter and Gibson, 2004, 18). Another troubling impact of Lombroso and Ferrero's (1895, translation in 2004, 185) work is their association between women's and girls' sexuality and their offending:

> We saw how sexuality can be exaggerated in female born criminals; this is one of the traits that makes them similar to men. Due to it, all women born criminals are prostitutes. While prostitution may be their least significant offense, it is never absent. Eroticism is the nucleus around which their other characteristics revolve. This exaggerated eroticism, which is abnormal in most women, forms the starting point for vices and crimes. It turns female born criminals into unsociable beings, preoccupied entirely with the satisfaction of their own desires, like lustful savages whose sexuality has not been tamed by civilization and necessity.

Given this context, it is hardly surprising that kleptomania, a biological "explanation" of middle-class, White women's shoplifting, was identified in the late nineteenth century as a "uterine ailment" (Abelson, 1989). More recently, in the 1970s and 1980s, PMS (premenstrual syndrome) was often characterized as a biological problem of all women. This reinforced cultural stereotypes and implications about women's "place" and was even used as a defense in trials of women accused of murder (see Rittenhouse, 1991). As this and the next two chapters document, the marks of biologism and female sexuality and offending continue.

The Unadjusted Girl

W. I. Thomas's work, published in the books *Sex and Society* (1907) and *The Unadjusted Girl* (1923, 1967), was heavily influenced by Lombroso, although Thomas was more liberal. Thomas advanced Lombroso's work to define criminality as "a socially induced pathology rather than a biological abnormality" (Smart, 1976, 37). Similar to Lombroso and Ferrero, however, Thomas viewed differences in males' and females' likelihood to become "politicians, great artists, and intellectual giants" as a result of sex rather than gender, thus overlooking the strong societal restrictions of women during that era (ibid.). An example of a "sex" difference that Thomas attributed to women was the inclusion of more varieties of love in their nervous systems:

> [Thomas] argued that it was this additional and intense need to give and
> feel love that leads women into crime, particularly sexual offenses like
> prostitution. The prostitute, he argued, is merely looking for the love
> and tenderness which all women need, but the means by which she seeks
> satisfaction are not socially approved. (ibid., 39)

Again, these assumptions completely deny the socialization of women and girls
and the very real constraints on their opportunities. The reality is very different
from what Thomas suggests, given that most sex workers are driven into this
occupation due to the lack of well-paying legitimate occupations. This relates to
the film *Pretty Woman* (discussed in Chapter 1), that is, that sex workers are
simply "looking for love." It also, like the film, suggests that women find "love
and tenderness" in sex work, which could not be further from the truth.

Further, Thomas "equated female delinquency with sexual delinquency,"
confusing "promiscuity" with crime; notably, this kind of logic never occurs in
studies of male crime (Heidensohn, 1985, 117). The disadvantaged position of
women and girls in society was of little importance to Thomas in his accounting
of male and female differences. His later work, however, acknowledged that
women were property of men, and he departed from social Darwinism to
examine the complexity of the interaction between society and the individual
(Klein, 1980).

Thomas's analyses of class and sexuality are overly simplistic concerning the
links between gender, sexuality, class, and crime. According to Thomas, middle-
class women are invested in protecting their chastity and thus commit few crimes;
poor women, on the other hand, long for crime in the manner of a new
experience. In fact, he believed that delinquent girls manipulate males into sex
as a means of achieving their own goals. Thus, Thomas favors psychological over
economic motivations to explain female criminality. Given that Thomas was
writing in an era of mass illness and starvation, the choice to ignore economic
deprivation as a potential cause of female crime is rather remarkable (ibid.).

Anatomy as Destiny

Psychiatrist Sigmund Freud's attempts to explain female behavior center around
the belief that women are anatomically inferior to men—hence, Freud's infamous
"penis envy" approach to explaining female behavior. To Freud, the healthy
woman experiences heterosexual sex as a receptor, where sexual pleasure consists
of pain, while the sexually healthy man is heterosexual and aggressive and inflicts
pain (Klein, 1980).

Thus, the deviant woman is a woman who wants to be a man, and she will
only end up neurotic in her fruitless search for her own penis. "Women may be
viewed," says Klein (ibid., 72) of this psychological explanation, "as turning to
crime as a perversion of or rebellion against their natural feminine roles." Included
in this analysis is a glorification of women's duties as wives and mothers, and, in
turn, the view that treatment involves "helping" deviant women adjust to their
"proper" traditional gender roles (ibid.). Again, in addition to the obvious sexism,

Freud's theories are fraught with racism, classism, and heterosexism: "Only upper- and middle-class women could possibly enjoy lives as sheltered darlings. Freud sets hegemonic standards of femininity for poor and Third World women" (ibid., 89).

Behind the Mask

Although Otto Pollak's (1950, 1961) study of female criminality, *The Criminality of Women*, was published more than a half century after Lombroso and Ferrero's work, it has been closely linked with their approach. Like Thomas, Pollak believed that sociological factors, in addition to biological factors, have some relevance in crime determination. To Pollak, however, the fundamental influences on female criminality are biology and physiology; he thus repeats many of the assumptions and prejudices encountered in Lombroso and Ferrero's and Thomas's works (Smart, 1976).

The major emphasis of Pollak's analysis is the "masked" nature of female criminality. He assumes that male and female crime rates are similar. In part, claims Pollak, female crime is "masked" by the supposedly chivalrous or lenient treatment of women in the crime-processing system. But Pollak's main point is that women are better at hiding their crimes. He emphasizes the "deceitful" nature of women, using as supporting evidence females' ability to hide the fact that they are menstruating or having orgasms and their inactive role during sexual intercourse. One has to wonder what would happen to women who did *not* "hide" the fact that they were menstruating. Second, Pollak fails to consider that women's inactive role during heterosexual sex (where it existed or exists) may be culturally rather than biologically determined. Further, women's training in acquiescence to men, particularly during sex, could account for the fact that women were not hiding orgasms but rather were not experiencing them. Smart compares Pollak's analysis to Eve's deceit with Adam (in the Bible), where women are viewed as evil and cunning: "It is Pollak's contention that women are the masterminds behind criminal organizations; that they are the instigators of crime rather than the perpetrators; that they can and in fact do manipulate men into committing offenses whilst remaining immune from arrest themselves" (Smart, 1976, 47)

Thus, similar to the other positivist theorists, Pollak's analysis fails to account for the power imbalance between men and women. His discussion is based purely on speculation, with no empirical evidence. Rather, he made sweeping assumptions in arriving at his conclusion that a great deal of female criminality is undetected and thus unreported.

LEGACY OF THE POSITIVIST THEORISTS

The enduring effects of the positivists can be viewed in the research on female criminality that was published in the 1960s and 1970s. Similar to Pollak, Gisela Konopka (1966) portrays women in her book, *The Adolescent Girl in Conflict*, as the instigators of crime. Her main point is that women and girls are driven to crime because of emotional problems, specifically loneliness and sexuality (Klein,

1980). Economic and social explanations are ignored at the expense of explaining female criminality through physiology and psychology.

Similarly, Vedder and Somerville (1970) stress the importance of the female as criminal instigator in *The Delinquent Girl*. Not only do they claim that female delinquency is simply a result of maladjustment to the "normal" female role but they also ignore the causal importance of social and economic factors. Most disquieting, they attribute high rates of delinquency among African American girls to "their lack of 'healthy' feminine narcissism"—an explanation with racist overtones (Klein, 1980, 99). Following this logic, they see psychotherapy as the solution to female delinquency and ignore the need to address the potentially criminogenic social and economic constraints in which many delinquent girls are enmeshed. Finally, in their book *Delinquency in Girls*, Cowie, Cowie, and Slater (1968) use masculinity, femininity, and chromosomes to explain female criminality. "In this perspective, the female offender is different physiologically and psychologically from the 'normal' girl," in that she is too masculine; she is rebelling against her femininity (ibid., 101).

Thus, in the positivist school, because women's behavior was believed to be largely biologically determined, the complexity of women's criminal behavior was reduced to a challenge of the traditional gender role—a role not rooted in nature but societally specified. The positivists assumed that the girl or woman who defied the prescribed gender role had a problem, and thus they were blind to the possibility that there was a problem with the prescribed role that women, regardless of resources or situation, are expected to fulfill. Indeed, it has been recognized more recently that there is not one societally prescribed role for all women but that "appropriate" gender roles vary depending on a woman's race and class and that a dominant patriarchy does not affect all women in the same way (Rice, 1990). As we will see in the following three chapters, women's and girls' offending is often still interpreted through a positivist lens, and the responses to female offending are too often practiced with vestiges of the traditional or positivist approach.

STRAIN AND SUBCULTURAL THEORIES

Drawing on Durkheim's anomie (state of normlessness) theory, Robert Merton (1938, 1949) has been credited with developing *strain theory*. A refreshing departure from biological determinism, Merton's premise is that strain and frustration occur when individuals are taught the same goals in their culture but are denied equal access to legitimately attain these goals. For example, the values of educational success and upward mobility are ingrained in U.S. culture, but not all citizens have the means of achieving these shared values. There are a number of criticisms of strain theory, but the most important—and the one that applies most to girls—is that this framework measured strains primarily in terms of class inequalities, comparing the strains of the working class to the middle class, and then only of boys. Approaches that focus on poverty as an explanation of criminal behavior, while preferable to biological explanations, frequently ignore that "[f]emales constitute the most impoverished group of every Western society, yet females commit by far the least crime" (Faith, 1993, 107).

Strain Theory

In his book *Delinquent Boys*, Albert Cohen (1955) adapted Merton's strain theory to explain the development of delinquent gangs among working-class boys in the United States. In Cohen's analysis, boys have broad and varied goals and ambitions, whereas girls' narrow ambitions center around males: dating, dancing, attractiveness, and, generally, acquiring a boyfriend or husband. Thus, men "are the rational doers and achievers" in American culture while women exist solely to be the helpmates and companions of men (Naffine, 1987).

A strength of Cohen's (1955) is addressing the construction of gender for boys, in that his work vividly depicts the masculinity of boy delinquents. That is, he is likely the first theorist to actually pay attention to the construction of masculinity (he drew on Freud to do so). In contrast, however, he devotes only four pages of his book to girl delinquents. He portrays girls as boring and only capable of expressing their delinquency through sexual promiscuity (Mann, 1984; Naffine, 1987). In Cohen's prime, and still today, the term *promiscuity* is rarely if ever applied to boys and men, and Cohen joined the disturbing tendency in criminological theory to link inextricably girls' criminality and sexuality, while ignoring or implicitly applauding the identical sexual conduct of boys.

In short, Cohen believes that boys have the "real" strains of employment and income in their lives, whereas girls' only strain is to marry well. Cohen was so confident of the accuracy of this stance on girls that he saw no need to confirm his hypothesis through data collection. However, the earliest tests of strain theory conducted on girls and women rebuff Cohen's contention of their sexually driven offending. Campbell's (1987) study of Puerto Rican female gang members claims that gang membership for females, like males, is a means of fulfilling their identities in an environment plagued with classism, racism, and sexism. Another exception is a study by Joe and Chesney-Lind (1995) of racially diverse gang members in Hawaii. They found that both girls and boys join gangs primarily to resolve boredom and for the sense of social solidarity it provides in an otherwise hostile environment. Similar to Campbell (1987), they note that these youths live in communities "racked by poverty, racism, and rapid population growth" (Joe and Chesney-Lind, 1995, 427). Indeed, Joe and Chesney-Lind report that, for both boys and girls, gang membership serves as an "alternative family" for these youths who are often neglected and/or abused in their homes. Notably, the strains of neglect and abuse in one's family and daily experiences with poverty, racism, and sexism are ignored in the traditional theories.

Delinquency and Opportunity

Cohen's (mis)portrayal of female delinquents was reaffirmed in Cloward and Ohlin's (1960) book *Delinquency and Opportunity*. Cloward and Ohlin, however, took a different twist in their version of strain theory, which is known as *opportunity theory*. In Cloward and Ohlin's opportunity theory, boys were viewed as having legitimate struggles to attain the "American dream," whereas girls encounter only frivolous concerns, such as finding boyfriends. In this version, the focus was to explain that delinquent subcultural values and gangs served as a collective solution to the frustrations that lower-class urban males experienced in schools and in terms of bleak job prospects. Again, females were left out of the model.

The subculture, often represented by gangs, not only gave juveniles a sense of belonging but also provided them with opportunities to learn illegal means to achieve success. (Subcultural theories have been criticized for implying that crime occurs exclusively among the poor [Leonard, 1982].) Cloward and Ohlin's approach is almost identical to Cohen's, concerning male versus female delinquency:

> The delinquent subculture is therefore a male solution to an exclusively male problem. Females are neither pressured to achieve the major success goals of their society nor offered a delinquent outlet for their frustrations. The horizons of the female are confined to the family. The limited nature of their offending, its predominantly sexual nature, reflects this narrow set of concerns with personal relationships. (Naffine, 1987, 15)

Cloward and Ohlin, as well as other strain theorists, failed to recognize that females also experience unequal opportunities. "Indeed, logically, one might expect women to have a higher crime rate than men since their opportunities are more limited" (Morris, 1987, 76). At the same time, females generally have less access than males to illegal means (a less delinquent subculture than males, for example), which would account for their lower crime rates (Harris, 1977). Bottcher's (1995, 2001) data on the siblings of incarcerated boys provide some support for opportunity theory, mostly concerning boys' greater opportunities to commit crimes. As expected, she found that many of the girls and boys in the study were barred by their class from legal means to reach social and economic success. However, despite their similar class restrictions, other structures were more gendered. For example, girls' freedom was limited relative to boys' in their demands to care for younger children. Without the child-care responsibilities, boys could take part in more activities, meet more people, and cover wider geographical areas. However, due to this freedom, the boys were more likely than the girls were to report risks of accidents, and more likely to face conflict, peer pressure, and delinquency at younger ages, when they were lacking in more mature judgment (Bottcher, 1995, 53–54). Bottcher's (1995) study provides information relevant to many theories, and thus a summary of this work is presented in Exhibit 2.1.

General Strain Theory (GST)

Robert Agnew (1985, 1992) is responsible for a revision of traditional strain theory into what he calls *general strain theory* (GST). This theory posits that negative events (strains or frustrations) create pressure for delinquent or criminal behavior. GST advances and expands on earlier strain theories by broadening the sources of and types of adaptations to strains and acknowledging that goals may vary depending on an individual's race, class, and gender. Rather than simply focusing on structural factors limiting financial success (like traditional strain theory does), GST includes three psychosocial strain sources: (1) the presence of negative stimuli, (2) the loss of

E X H I B I T 2.1   Jean Bottcher's (1995) Study of the Gendered Nature
of Youths' Activities, Definitions, and Social Controls

Activities
- **Range**: Boys typically operate in a wider arena and spend more time away from home, largely due to fewer home responsibilities than their sisters.
- **Timing**: Boys are more able than girls to be out of their homes late at night.
- **Pace**: Boys move faster, farther, and more freely and engage in more activities than girls.
- **Focus**: Girls have more focused activities, particularly social activities, than boys; girls tend to have a smaller circle of friends than boys; boys are more able to avoid parental responsibilities than girls; and girls' focus on their children and a single boyfriend (at least at one time) seemed to shield them from delinquency.

Definitions
- **Self-Definitions**: Boys are more self-centered, and competitive, are bolder and more macho than girls.
- **Peer Pressure**: Most youth spend most of their time in sex-segregated leisure time, and boys are more responsive to peer pressure in committing crimes.
- **Societal Definitions**: Boys are more likely labeled by the police than girls, and some crimes are more acceptable when committed by one sex than another (e.g., a boy stealing a car).
- **Physical Differences**: Boys' greater strength and running speed make them better able to commit crimes; parents are stricter with daughters than sons because of fear of pregnant daughters.
- **Meanings of Crime**: Girls commit fewer crimes than boys because they are smarter than the boys; boys are more bold and "showy" in the commission of their crimes.

SOURCE: Jean Bottcher. 1995. "Gender as Social Control." *Justice Quarterly* 12(1):33–58.

positive stimuli, and (3) the failure to achieve positive goals. According to GST, whether responses to strain and frustrations are law–abiding or delinquent depends on an individual youth's personality, self–esteem, social support system, and so on (e.g., if anger is the response, the coping strategy is more likely to be delinquent) (Agnew, 1992). Additionally, GST addresses the importance of allowing for varied goals due to individuals' gender, race, and class differences (Broidy, 2001). Stated another way, GST suggests that both strains and the responses to these strains may be gendered (or "raced" or "classed").

In the previous edition of this book (Belknap, 2001), strain theory was criticized for failing to address the very real strains of experiencing abuse and other childhood traumas and for focusing on blocked economic opportunities without measuring the daily injustices and strain of experiencing racism, sexism, and classism. In that same year, Bottcher (2001, 894) criticized GST for failing to consider gender as "a product of individual and interpersonal action," and Agnew (2001) himself published concerns with the tests of GST, specifically that many key strains outlined in GST were not included in the tests and that most GST tests focused on a single, cumulative measure of strain. For example, he (finally) noted that child abuse (including sexual abuse) and criminal victimization were important to account for as stressors for delinquent behavior (ibid.). Additionally, Agnew (ibid.) pointed out that it is necessary to look at the severity, injustice, duration, recency, and centrality of the strain: The more severe, unjust, lasting, and central to the individual's life the strain is, the more likely it will result in anger and thus criminal behavior. Moreover, he recognized that abuse and criminal victimization are often perceived as unjust and serious, and thus could result in stronger feelings of anger and injustice than other strains. Thus, victims of abuse may engage in delinquent/criminal behavior in efforts to compensate for the serious injustices they experienced (Agnew, 2001, 2002).

Tests of (Traditional) Strain and General Strain Theories

In 1964, Ruth Morris was the first scholar to focus strain theory on girls as well as boys. She viewed girls as slightly more dimensional than did her predecessors: Girls were not interested just in husband hunting but were also concerned with other affective relationships, such as with family members. Morris found that girls, delinquent and not, were faced with less subcultural support and more disapproval for delinquency than boys, and she believed this might explain girls' lower delinquency rates. Furthermore, delinquent girls were more likely than delinquent boys to describe their families as unhappy.

It is instructive that studies in the late 1960s and 1970s found that girls' efforts to find mates were not related to their delinquency rates (Sandhu and Allen, 1969) and that the patterns of boys' and girls' delinquent behavior were quite similar, except that boys' rates were higher (see Naffine, 1987, 18). Research on gender differences in the role of youth subcultures (often measured as gangs) tends to confirm that boys' subcultures are more prone to delinquency than girls' subcultures (Esbensen and Huizinga, 1993; Joe and Chesney-Lind, 1995; Lerman, 1966; Morash, 1983, 1986; Morris, 1964, 1965; Rahav, 1984; Thompson, Mitchell, and Dodder, 1984). However, research findings have been inconsistent regarding whether the traditional strain theory frustration, "blocked opportunity," is more, less, or equally related to boys' and girls' delinquency rates. Some studies report that strain is more relevant in predicting girls' delinquency than boys' (Datesman, Scarpitti, and Stephenson, 1975; Segrave and Hastad, 1983); another study notes that strain is more influential in predicting boys' delinquency than girls' (Simons, Miller, and Aigner, 1980); and still others claim that strain similarly influences girls' and boys' delinquency rates (Cernkovich and Giordano, 1979; Figueira-McDonough and Selo, 1980; Smith, 1979). Yet another study reported that traditional strain variables were related in the opposite direction as expected for White females but in the expected direction for African American females (Hill and Crawford, 1990). Overall, the findings are quite mixed regarding whether strain, as it is traditionally defined, affects boys' and girls' delinquency similarly or differently.

Given the more recent research (discussed in the prior chapter and in more detail later in this one) assessing the strain of child abuse (e.g., nonsexual physical, sexual, and neglect) that is related to boys' and girls' subsequent offending, it seems the traditional measures of strain were grossly lacking when not including child abuse and neglect as means of strain. Moreover, the traditional strain theories appeared to be more invested in addressing blocked legal economic opportunities, while ignoring the strain of experiencing poverty, racism, and sexism on a daily basis. General strain theory promised a broadening of strain measures and to account for individual strain experiences and responses to these strains as tempered by individuals' race, gender, and class (Agnew, 2001, 2002). Two studies testing GST that reported few gender differences in stressful life events, astonishingly, did not measure abuse victimizations (Hoffman and Su, 1997; Mazerolle, 1998). Broidy's (2001) test of GST reported that while strain causes *anger* in both sexes, females were more likely to report other negative emotions (e.g., guilt, worthlessness, disappointment, depression, worry, fear, and insecurity). Broidy and Agnew (1997) found that both strain and the responses to strain explain gender differences in offending. For example, compared to boys, girls report more restrictions on their lives and behaviors and greater family caretaking expectations, and are more likely to report all types of abuse (emotional, physical, and sexual). While girls felt more stress surrounding close relationships with friends and family, boys felt more strain about external achievement such as material success. Another study found, as predicted by GST, that anger was a significant predictor of violent, property, and drug crimes, and criminal behavior was related to sexual abuse, homelessness, relative deprivation, and more deviant peers (Baron, 2004). Although this study reported that gender "was a significant predictor of crime" (ibid., 474), it did not explain how. Another study of GST found that although stressful life events increase the likelihood of delinquency, this relationship was the same regardless of a youth's sex/gender, socioeconomic status, self-esteem, or perceived control over her/his environment (Hoffman and Cerbone, 1999). Finally, though not tests of GST but related to these findings, other studies conclude that boys report significantly more delinquent behavior than girls do at the same time that girls report more negative self-feelings (e.g., depression and anxiety) than boys do (Kaplan and Lin, 2000; Luthar and D'Avanzo, 1999).

DIFFERENTIAL ASSOCIATION THEORY (DAT)

Edwin Sutherland, first alone and then in collaboration with Donald Cressey, developed the *theory of differential association* (DAT) in the classic text *Principles of Criminology* (1939, 1966). Sutherland's attempt was to move away from poverty as the major explanation of crime. The basic tenet of DAT is that *criminal behavior is learned*, just as any other behavior is learned. Thus, one's peer group association is instrumental in determining whether or not one becomes delinquent.

Although Sutherland and Cressey agreed with Cohen's contention that there is unequal access to success in the United States, they departed from Cohen's belief that all classes have internalized the same definition of success (that is, the goals of middle-class males). Further, Sutherland and Cressey claimed that criminal subcultures are not unique to frustrated working-class male youths; people of all classes, including white-collar workers, can and do partake in criminal behavior. Similarly, whereas Cohen defined a U.S. culture that excludes women and girls, Sutherland and Cressey's perspective is not so exclusively male in theory and is presented as a general non–sex-specific theory (Naffine, 1987).

Despite Sutherland and Cressey's promise of a non–sex-specific theory, they rarely addressed girls. And where girls are briefly mentioned, they are seen as uniform and homogeneous. Again, girls are treated as peripheral and insignificant to the mainstream culture. Thus, Sutherland and Cressey's gender-neutral approach exists only in words, not in content. What is additionally disturbing is the easy acceptance of Sutherland and Cressey's view of males as "free to engage in a range of behaviors" and the view of girls as belonging in the family (Naffine, 1987). Further, girls' perceived tendency toward abiding the law is portrayed as dull, rather than as positive and moral (ibid.).

Feminist criticisms of DAT centered mainly on Sutherland and Cressey's decision to avoid discussing females in any meaningful way (see Leonard, 1982; Naffine, 1987). Some feminists have suggested, however, that DAT is a useful way of examining male and female delinquency rates and of explaining gender differences. Two points are important. First, girls' relatively lower crime rates may largely be a result of the constraints they experience compared to boys. For example, at least traditionally, girls have been expected to stay closer to home, are more likely to have curfews, are more likely to be disciplined (particularly for minor infractions and sexual experimentation), and are generally provided less freedom than their brothers and other boys. The differential socialization of girls and boys, then, is believed to result in different or gendered behaviors of girls and boys (see Hoffman–Bustamante, 1973; Leonard, 1982; Lorber, 1994; Messner, 2000; Morris, 1987; Ridgeway and Correll, 2004; Risman, 2004). The second point is that the increase in girls' delinquency rates in the last couple of decades might be explained by females' increased freedom. Even Cressey (1964) asserted that where there is greater equality between the sexes, the crime-sex ratio is likely to be lower.

Although Sutherland and Cressey failed to examine the relevance of DAT for an explanation of girls' criminality, others did so. An early test found that girls were similar to boys in both their frequency of delinquent behaviors and their connections with delinquent companions (Clark, 1964). In contrast, while finding support for DAT and a strong relationship between delinquent friends and delinquent behavior for both girls and boys, Hindelang (1971) reported that girls had fewer delinquent friends and less delinquent behavior than boys did. Another study of delinquent girls found they were significantly influenced by their peers and in fact were more influenced by other *girls* than they were by boys who were their peers (Giordano, 1978).

More recent studies support DAT. Luthar and D'Avanzo (1999) reported that substance use was linked with peer *acceptance* for suburban boys but linked with peer *rejection* by delinquent girls. Thus, differential association results in substance use seeming "unfeminine" and more censured for girls. Mears, Ploeger, and Warr (1998) found that while girls report greater moral disapproval of all types of offenses, this could not solely explain boys' higher rates of offending. Rather, it was this greater moral disapproval combined with the ability or desire to better *block* their delinquent peers' influence that accounted for girls' lower offense rates.

Heimer and De Coster (1999) found that emotional bonds to families resulted in less attachment to violent behavior for girls (but not boys), traditional views of gender decreased girls' (but not boys') violence, and boys (but not girls) learned violence from aggressive friends and coercive parental discipline. Alarid and her colleagues (2000) studied an adult population of incarcerated felons and found significant support for DAT (also for social control theory, but not as strong). Indeed, when social control and differential association variables were in the models, there was no gender difference in the prisoners' drug and crime rates, although men had higher property crime rates than women did, even when controlling for these variables (Alarid, Burton, and Cullen, 2000). Another study of school youths and street (homeless) youths found that despite the recent media attention on "bad girls," "girlfriends matter" in decreasing property crimes: Female-dominated networks were related to less property crime for schoolgirls, street girls, and to a lesser extent, schoolboys. Only for street boys was there no correlation between female-domination networks and property crimes (McCarthy, Felmlee, and Hagan, 2004). In conclusion, although Sutherland and Cressey ignored females in their research, their theory potentially provides insight into gender differences and similarities in delinquent involvement.

LABELING THEORY

Labeling theory is concerned with the process by which deviant labels are applied and received. Specifically, labeling theory speculates about how people are "marked" (or labeled) as deviant, delinquent, or criminal, and the effect of the label on future behavior. It has been suggested that being treated as deviant may relate more to "the kind of person" one is than to her or his particular behavior (Schur, 1984). Labeling theory has two tenets. First, it proposes that some people are more likely to be labeled criminal because of their race, sex, class, and so on. Second, labeling theory posits that once someone is labeled delinquent or criminal, she or he may accept or resign her/himself to this label and continue on in crime as a *result* of the labeling. This has also been referred to as "the revitalized labeling theory," where structural disadvantage is viewed as key in labeling. Stated alternatively, official intervention (e.g., by the police) is disproportionately practiced among disadvantaged youths, thus more negatively impacting their education, employment, and criminal behavior (Bernburg and Krohn, 2003).

While many scholars advanced the concepts behind labeling theory (see Erikson, 1962; Kitsuse, 1962; Lemert, 1951), the most famous is by Howard Becker (1963) in his research on jazz musicians, in the book *Outsiders*. Becker's work is admirable in many ways, particularly his efforts "to enter the world of the deviant to find out how it worked by seeing it from the vantage point of those who lived there, from the viewpoint of those labeled deviant" (Naffine, 1996, 40). He collected his data through participant observation, playing the piano professionally with his subjects. Consistent with the theorists discussed thus far, however, Becker devotes his analysis almost exclusively to male musicians. When women are examined in Becker's work, it is most frequently as the wives of the men, and in these instances, these women are portrayed as boring, laughable, and "square." Thus, while Becker used innovative and in-depth methods to really get to know and understand the male musicians, his approach to studying the women "remained highly orthodox" (Naffine, 1996, 41). The women are seen only through the lens of the male musicians and are depicted as nags who threaten the livelihood of the band by trying to convince their husbands to get "real" jobs. When women musicians are given any attention in Becker's analysis, it is only as sex objects, not as legitimate musicians—an all-too-familiar approach to studying nonconforming and criminal women (Naffine, 1987). In the work of Becker and many others, conforming women are portrayed as boring and spineless, whereas criminal men are seen as creative and exciting.

Thus, the key question in the application of labeling theory to girls and women is determining whether there are gender differences in how offenders are labeled. For example, the possibility that girls are less likely than boys to be labeled or viewed as delinquent might help explain their lower arrest rates. On the other hand, perhaps before the second wave of the women's movement, women were more protected by chivalry (addressed in greater detail in Chapter 4), and the growing incarceration rate of women in the United States reflects a harsher labeling of girls and women in recent decades (Leonard, 1982). Still another possibility is that women and girls are labeled more harshly for some crimes, while men and boys are discriminated against for others.

Research on these issues has revealed inconsistent findings regarding police and court actions. Some studies found no gender differences, some found preferential treatment for men and boys, others found preferential treatment for women and girls, and still others found that women and girls were treated more harshly for some crimes, and men and boys were treated more harshly for others. Controlling for the amount of delinquency, one study showed that children, especially girls from mother-only homes, were more likely to be officially labeled delinquent than those from two-parent homes (Johnson, 1986). A unique study examined the impact of gender of labeled persons aged 15 to 23 on their subsequent job attainment and job stability and on their income when aged 29 to 37 years old (Davies and Tanner, 2003). Although the strongest predictor of employment variables for both females and males was their incarceration histories, only women's and girls' future employment status was negatively impacted by having been expelled or suspended from school as a youth. This is particularly noteworthy given a study that found no gender differences in adult probationers' educational achievements, yet the women were significantly more likely to be both poor and unemployed (Olson, Lurigio, and Seng, 2000). Another study found that when their parents labeled them as "rule violators," boys were more likely to start viewing themselves as delinquents and further violating the law, whereas the girls were more likely to want to please their parents and stop the delinquent behavior (Bartusch and Matsueda, 1996).

Another interesting point in examining gender differences in labeling is N (1987) contention that women are more likely than men to be labeled "me and men are more likely than women to be labeled "criminal." A "mental illness is presented as both an alternative to and an explana (ibid., 55). Similarly, whereas men may be more likely to be labeled "criminal," women are more likely to be labeled "deviant" or labeled in general (for example, they are called "nags" and "bitches" and are described as "promiscuous" and "hysterical"). Indeed, Schur (1984, 190) reported that historically (and perhaps still) women "do not really have to engage in specific acts in order to be defined and responded to as deviant. Physical appearance—and in a sense perhaps even the mere condition of 'being' a woman—can lead to stigmatization."

In a historical overview of how women's "madness" has been related to crime, Frigon (1995, 29) summarizes: "The female offenders, of course, were the antithesis of ideal femininity." Punishing females (and to some degree, males) for not conforming to their "appropriate" gender roles has a long history. Frigon (ibid.) traces the historical manifestations of this, for example the execution of hundreds of thousands of lesbians and thousands of gays for heresy in fifteenth- and sixteenth-century France during the Roman Catholic Inquisition. Other examples include the long history of executing women charged as "witches." Thus, a distinction for the criminal female appears to falls into "mad" (mentally ill, including the rejection of culturally prescribed gender roles) and "bad" (just pure evil) (see Frigon, 1995).

A final aspect of the gendered nature of labeling is the willingness to accept a deviant label. Although there is limited research on this, what exists suggests that women are more likely to accept others' labels of them as mentally ill (Horwitz, 1977) or as having a problem (addiction to) spending money in an out-of-control manner (Hayes, 2000). Part of this process is the finding that women are more likely to take on feelings of shame when they themselves or others identify deviant behavior (Hayes, 2000). This has strong implications for restorative justice models.

SOCIAL CONTROL THEORY (SCT)

The theories discussed thus far have focused on what makes people break the law. Taking a different approach, the social control theories are more concerned with explaining what compels most of society to abide by the law. This section discusses such theories.

Social Bond Theory

in his book *Causes of Delinquency*, focuses on what motivates

eory, *social bond* or *control theory* (SCT), examines four

that prevent people from acting on their criminal

ent, involvement, and belief. A person's likelihood to

or his ties to (1) conventional people, especially

utions and behaviors in her or his employment

of society. Although the theory was described as

s application. Thus, to test his hypotheses, Hirschi

White schoolboys. He found that, indeed, the boys

s were less likely to report delinquency.

Given that Hirschi switched the approach of studying crime from "Why do people offend?" to "Why *don't* people offend?" it has been suggested that studying females—or, at least, including females in the sample—would have made more sense given that research overwhelmingly reports that girls and women are generally far more law-abiding than boys and men (Naffine, 1987). Interestingly, Hirschi began his study with males and females. Similar to Sutherland and Cressey, Hirschi (1) promised a non–sex-specific theory, (2) started with girls and boys in the study, and (3) for no apparent reason left out the girls (Naffine, 1987). Or, as Mann (1984, 263) points out:

> Travis Hirschi stratified his samples by race, sex, school, and grade. He included 1,076 black girls and 846 nonblack girls; but in the analysis of his data Hirschi admits "the girls disappear," and he adds, "Since girls have been neglected for too long by students of delinquency, the exclusion of them is difficult to justify. I hope I return to them soon." He didn't.

Additionally, where delinquent boys were often celebrated and revered in prior theory focusing on why some people (boys) commit crimes, in Hirschi's approach the conforming (law-abiding) boy becomes ennobled. This is particularly noteworthy given the image of conforming girls in research testing the other theories; they are depicted as lifeless, boring, and dependent. In the prior studies asking, "Why do people offend?" the criminal boy was portrayed as exciting, instrumental, and masculine. In Hirschi's approach, the noncriminal boy becomes lauded as responsible. In fact, it has been pointed out that men who conform are labeled "successful," whereas there is little or no reward for conforming women (Schur, 1984). "What all this seems to indicate is a profound criminological tendency to devalue the female and value the male even when they are doing precisely the same things" (Naffine, 1987, 67).

SCT was advanced by Michael Gottfredson and Travis Hirschi in *A General Theory of Crime* (1990). A *general theory of crime* (GTC) attempts to "bridge" classical and positivist traditions, where "low self-control is an individual-level attribute that causes crime at all ages, when combined with appropriate opportunities and attractive targets" (Taylor, 2001, 373). Moving the emphasis from social to *self-control*, GTC purports that self-control interacts with criminal opportunity to explain criminal/delinquent behavior: Individuals with low self-control and access to opportunities to commit offenses are more prone to offend. GTC suggests that gender, race, age, and class differences in delinquency are due to how these characteristics are related to self-control especially but also social control. GTC has been criticized, however, for (1) ignoring gender (Bottcher, 2001; Miller and Burack, 1993); (2) dismissing and misrepresenting male violence against women (Flavin, 2001; Miller and Burack, 1993); (3) ignoring feminist research on gender divisions within families (Flavin, 2001; Miller and Burack, 1993); (4) ignoring the role of power in crime (i.e., crime is the logical result when it is an available and desirable resource when resources are limited) (Bottcher, 2001); and (5) not clearly stipulating what constitutes both social and self-control and how they might relate and interact ("rather than setting them up as contradictory concepts") (Taylor, 2001, 383). Recent tests of GTC found, as expected, that girls exhibit greater self-control than boys (LaGrange and Silverman, 1999; Li, 2004; Nakhaie, Silverman, and LaGrange, 2000) and have less access to delinquent opportunities than boys, mostly because they are monitored more by their parents (LaGrange and Silverman, 1999). However, this research also found that even after controlling for self-control and access to delinquent opportunities, boys are still more delinquent/criminal than girls are (LaGrange and Silverman, 1999; Li, 2004; Nakhaie, Silverman, and LaGrange, 2000). *Self*-control was a better predictor of delinquency than *social* control, and the interaction of social and self-controls was the best predictor (Li, 2004; Nakhaie, Silverman, and LaGrange, 2000). One study designed specifically to test whether GTC could explain intimate partner abuse, in the form of dating aggression, found that lower self-control, greater opportunity to commit the abuse (more frequent private access to one's partner), and the perception of rewards from committing the abuse (e.g., more control over a partner and satisfaction from committing the abuse) all increased the likelihood of committing this abuse (Sellers, 1999).

Research on Social Control Theory

Numerous studies have tested social control theory. A study of African American and White girls and boys in California found that although introducing social control variables (measuring attachment to conventional people) greatly decreased the gender differences in reported delinquency rates, these social ties did not completely eliminate or explain boys' higher offending rates (Jensen and Eve, 1976). Another test of SCT found that although conventional ties predicted both girls' and boys' offending, this relationship was stronger for boys (Hindelang 1973). A study of girl delinquents measuring social bonding as attachment to school and education found that, although these factors played a role in determining delinquency rates, their effect was minimal (Torstensson, 1990). Another study of high school students found that similar "bond variables" influenced both girls and boys (Figueira-McDonough, Barton, and Sarri, 1981). A study of men and women (adults), on the other hand, found that even women with weak conventional ties were more law abiding than men, thus implying that conventional ties alone do not explain women's greater conformity (Smith, 1979). One study identified how heroin addiction weakened women's ties to conventional people and jobs, and propelled them into lives made up of criminal people and activities (Rosenbaum, 1981).

A number of more recent SCT studies attempted to determine social control within the family, such as the effects of parental and sibling interactions and behaviors. A study following female delinquents over time found strong evidence that dysfunctional family of origin places girls at increased risk of proceeding from status offenses[1] as youths to committing criminal offenses as adults (Rosenbaum, 1989). A study comparing parents' and their children's drug use

---

1. Status offenses, discussed in more depth in the next chapter, are offenses charged only to juveniles, not adults (e.g., drinking alcohol, running away from home, truancy from school).

found, for both daughters and sons, more support for social learning theory (that is, modeling and evaluating behaviors of significant others) than for SCT (Dembo et al., 1986). Another family study found that SCT better explained female delinquency than male delinquency. The study also found that some parental behaviors influenced daughters' delinquency, while other parental behaviors influenced sons' delinquency (Cernkovich and Giordano, 1987). Notably, another study found that the number of sisters a girl or boy has exerts no impact on her or his delinquency rate; however, the more brothers a boy has, the greater the likelihood that he will become delinquent, and the more brothers a girl has, the less the likelihood that she will become delinquent (Lauritsen, 1993). A longitudinal study of youths found that while stressful events increased both girls' and boys' depression as well as their offending, girls were more likely than boys to respond to stressful events by being upset or distressed, and boys were more likely than girls to respond by breaking the law (De Coster and Heimer, 2001). A recent study on gender as social control to explain gender differences in delinquency reported gender-related life conditions that contributed to these differences. Specifically, Bottcher's (1995) substantial study of the siblings of incarcerated boys (see Exhibit 2.1) reports that social structure of gender is a major form of social control, specifically through activities and definitions of the youths. Similarly, a study of urban African American youths found that parents monitor their daughters' more than their sons' activities, and the greater parental monitoring, the less problem behavior by the youths (Rankin and Quane, 2000). However, another study reported that girls' lower offending levels (relative to boys) is *not* due to weaker parental controls and supervision (Heimer and De Coster, 1999).

A study of Asian American youth subgroups' drug and alcohol use found some support for social control variables but showed that peer influence was a better predictor (Nagasawa, Qian, and Wong, 2000). After controlling for age, social control, and peer influence variables, there were no gender differences regarding drug and alcohol use among Japanese-, Chinese-, Korean-, Asian-, Indian-, and Pacific Islander American youths. However, even after controlling for these variables, among Filipino/a Americans, girls were more likely than boys to use drugs and alcohol, and among Southeast Asian Americans, boys were more likely than girls to use drugs and alcohol (Nagasawa, Qian, and Wong, 2000). Finally, a longitudinal study of about 800 youths from ages 10 to 18 in Seattle found a significant direct effect of gender on violence by 18-year-olds, even after controlling for social control variables: males were still more violent (Huang et al., 2001).

Notably, politicians, the popular media, and some researchers blame women's work outside the home as a cause of delinquency. However, careful research in this area finds no link between mothers' employment and their children's delinquency (Broidy, 1995; Vander Ven, 2003). A study using an extensive longitudinal data set of youths found the only instances where women's work could be linked in any fashion to their children's delinquency was when their work was coercive, they relied on welfare, and the family income was low, suggesting that "more children will be better off as women gain increased access to educational advancement, job training, and opportunities for stable, well-paying employment" (Vander Ven, 2003, 133).

Power Control Theory (PCT)

Hagan and his colleagues (1985, 1987) built on social control theory with the development of power control theory (PCT). One of the few theories to explicitly include gender, this theory joins class theory with research on gender and family relationships:

> Central to our extension of power–control theory is a conceptualization of class and family that focuses on power relations in the workplace and the home. A key premise of our extended theory is that positions of power in the workplace are translated into power relations in the household and that the latter, in turn, influence the gender-determined control of adolescents, their preferences for risk taking, and the patterning of gender and delinquency. (Hagan, Simpson, and Gillis, 1987, 813)

Hagan and colleagues (ibid.) found a greater gender difference in delinquency rates in patriarchal homes, where the mother had a lower status than the father, than in egalitarian homes, where parents had equivalent status or the mother was the only parent. Thus, this approach asserts that the gender-power makeup in the parents' relationship influences their daughters' subsequent delinquent behavior. Or rather, in a home where there is less sexism in the parents' roles, there should theoretically be fewer gender differences between sons' and daughters' behaviors. An assumption of this theory is that daughters from egalitarian homes are socialized, like their brothers, to engage in risk-taking behaviors, and because risk-taking behavior is associated with delinquency, girls from the more egalitarian homes will be more delinquent than their "sisters" from traditional, patriarchal homes. A clear limitation of this theory is the significant number of families that are single parent or where the mother's employment status is higher than the father's or the father is unemployed (Uggen, 2000).

The research by Hagan and his colleagues confirmed this belief, as did the research in a similar study (Singer and Levine, 1988). Another study found, however, that although both maternal and paternal support were effective in reducing delinquency, girls were more affected by maternal support and boys were more affected by paternal support (Hill and Atkinson, 1988). A related study reported that although girls' delinquency rates were more influenced than boys' by family risk factors—such as marital discord, marital instability, and discipline—the gender stereotypes did not always fit (Dornfeld and Kruttschnitt, 1992). Yet another study with a more detailed measure of parents' power structure did not find that parents' relative equality affected the sons' or daughters' delinquency rates; rather, these rates were related to the family's social class and the negative sanctions from the father (Morash and Chesney-Lind, 1991). Finally, another replication found no class-gender variations, yet gender differences by race were consistent with the theory: Gender differences were greater for Whites than for African Americans (Jensen and Thompson, 1990). The explanation offered for this difference was that "white families may be more 'patriarchal' than black families" (ibid., 1016).

Notably, a recent test of PCT found overall support, but while girls from more egalitarian homes were more delinquent than girls from more patriarchal homes (as hypothesized), boys from more egalitarian homes were *less delinquent* than boys from more patriarchal homes (McCarthy, Hagan, and Woodward, 1999). Blackwell (2000) incorporated perceived threats of the informal sanctions of shame and embarrassment into the PCT model and found, as expected, that gender differences in the perceived threat of legal sanctions were greater for those raised in more patriarchal homes, with females perceiving a higher threat from legal sanctions than males did. Another study reported that PCT variables (e.g., mothers' monitoring of youths) do not help explain gender differences in youths' self-reported victimizations, but these variables do help explain gender differences in youths' self-reported delinquency in the more patriarchal households, but the power-control variables mediate the gender-delinquency relationship in the less patriarchal households (Blackwell, Sellers, and Schlapitz, 2002). Reviews of tests of PCT are less than stunning, finding the support to be "inconsistent" (Kruttschnitt, 1996) or "modest" (Bottcher, 2001). Bottcher (ibid., 896) further criticizes PCT for "the unsubstantiated assumption that parental power structures and control practices are key sites for the reproduction of gender as it relates to delinquency."

Still other studies have tried to integrate sex, social bonds (conventional ties), and masculinity/femininity. Generally, "masculine" girls did not have weakened conventional ties (Norland, Wessel, and Shover, 1981; Thornton and James, 1979). Although one study found that males reported more delinquency than females in four types of crimes (violent, property, drugs, and status), controlling for "masculinity" reduced the effect of gender on delinquency rates. Further, although scoring high on "masculinity" was related to both sexes' increased reported delinquency, this was particularly true for males (Cullen, Golden, and Cullen, 1979). Notably, another study found that girls who were neither "masculine" nor "feminine" had the weakest conventional ties and the highest delinquency rates (Loy and Norland, 1981). Blackwell (2003) tested both social bond theory and PCT and found that (1) only in more patriarchal households do girls report higher levels of maternal control than boys, and in these homes, White youths reported lower levels of maternal control than youths of color; (2) there were no gender differences in either maternal or paternal controls in the less patriarchal homes; (3) there were no gender differences in youths reporting being emotionally attached to their parents; (4) regardless of the type of home (more or less patriarchal), girls were no more committed than boys to conventional norms; and (5) in more patriarchal homes, girls are more involved than boys in conventional activities (but there is no such gender difference in less patriarchal homes). A study that did not set out to test Hagan's (1988) PCT reported that the findings were consistent in a general way with this theory. Bottcher's (1995) interviews with sisters and brothers of incarcerated boys suggest that girls have stronger informal social controls than boys in their families and are more aggressively controlled by social service and law enforcement professionals. She points out that in contrast to Hagan's theory, both the girls and the boys in her study reported that the increased familial control of girls was due to the effort to monitor the girls' (and not the boys') sexual activities. She concludes that, for the high-risk youths in her study, the parental control cited by Hagan "is a very limited component of the social control that gender encompasses" (ibid., 53). Similarly, a longitudinal study of 1,000 Minnesota youths

---

Comparative Perspective: Vazsonyi (2001) and Colleagues' Empirical Test of a General Theory of Crime: A Study of Four Nations on Self-Control and the Prediction of Deviance

The Study
- Nations studied: Hungary, the Netherlands, Switzerland, and the United States
- Sample: Over 8,000 youths from 15 to 19 years old

The Findings
- The self-control measure was tenable across gender (and ages and nations).
- Self-control variables accounted for the most deviance (20 to 25 percent), followed by gender (9 percent), age (8 percent), and country/nation (less than 1 percent).
- Self-control accounted for 21 percent of male and 26 percent of female deviance.

Conclusion: The data are consistent with Gottfredson and Hirschi's (2001, 120) general theory of crime: "Self-control predicts deviance in males and females in members of different cultural or national groups."

SOURCE: Alexander T. Vazsonyi, Lloyd E. Pickering, Marianne Junger, and Dick Hessing. 2001. An Empirical Test of a General Theory of Crime: A Four-Nation Comparative Study of Self-Control and the Prediction of Deviance. *Journal of Research in Crime & Delinquency* 38:91–131.

---

collected data not only on parents' employment but also on the youths' employment under the assumption that boys who are given more freedom to work outside the home are also provided more access to offending (Uggen, 2000). This study reported that fathers' authority positions in the workplace increased the likelihood of arrests for sons but decreased it for daughters, while mothers' workplace authority increased the arrest likelihood for daughters while it decreased it for sons. Additionally, regarding the youths' own employment in the workforce, having more workplace power and control increased boys' but decreased girls' likelihood of arrest (Uggen, 2000).

Although not specifically a test of SCT or PCT, Jang and Krohn (1995) attempted to determine whether the role of gender for delinquents varies over youthful development. They were interested in testing two contradictory models. First, Gottfredson and Hirschi's (1990) "sex–invariant model" assumes that gender differences are predisposed at young ages and do not change over a youth's childhood; thus, gender differences in delinquency are stable over adolescence. Second, the "sex-variant model" assumes that "the causes of behaviors change over time and that the development pace at which boys and girls are socialized can vary"; thus, "differences in male and female delinquency can vary substantially over adolescence" (ibid., 196–197). Jang and Krohn (ibid., 195) tested these models using a sample of urban African American youths and reported: "[S]ex differences in delinquency tend to vary as the subjects grow older, rather than remain constant as the invariance thesis posits. Specifically, sex differences in delinquency peak at the age of 15 and thereafter decline with age. We also find that parental supervision significantly explains sex differences in delinquency for younger adolescence, but not for older adolescence."

In summary, SCT applied to women and girls offers inconsistent findings, as does PCT. Although women and girls tend to have stronger conventional ties and lower offending rates than men and boys, the social ties are generally insufficient to explain the gender differences in criminal behavior. Furthermore, women's increased attachment to conventional ties and decreased delinquency rates cannot be explained simply by their "femininity" or "masculinity."

MARXIST, RADICAL, AND CRITICAL THEORIES

In the late 1960s in the United States and early 1970s in Britain, a more radical perspective entered the ring of criminological theories (Naffine, 1996). "Conflict theory" is grounded in Marxism. Although Marx himself wrote very little about crime, his perspective on class struggle and on social relations under capitalism are the basis for conflict or Marxist criminology.

Conflict theory proposes that rather than looking at the offender, we should focus on society, particularly lawmakers and powerful interests. This approach assumes that laws are biased, reflecting the needs of the upper class, and thus enforcement of these laws is inevitably unjust. Crime itself is politicized and defined by the powerful elite. The key to solving the crime problem, then, is changing the economic system (Bonger, 1969), and this is highly political in nature.

The Marxist or radical perspective on criminology was crystallized and even renamed the "new criminology" and "critical criminology" with the publication of Ian Taylor, Paul Walton, and Jock Young's books of the same names (*The New Criminology* [1973] and *Critical Criminology* [1975]). Other criminologists have also helped develop this perspective (see Gordon, 1973; Platt, 1975; Quinney, 1972, 1975; Schwendinger and Schwendinger, 1970). The "new criminologists" viewed society as two-tiered—with harmful wealthy capitalist men beyond the arm of the law and working-class men offenders who should be regarded as "resistors" to the "real criminals" (the capitalists) and thus should be viewed with appreciation and sympathy (Naffine, 1996, 44). The most common criticism of the "new criminology" is that it is overly simplified and generalized (Leonard, 1982, 161). In addition to ignoring gender in general, and female offenders specifically, another feminist criticism of the "new criminologists" has been that they either outright overlook rape and domestic violence or document them uncritically (Naffine, 1996, 45).

Marx and his early followers rarely addressed the topics of crime and women, and the "new criminologists" were roundly criticized for ignoring women (Heidensohn, 1985; Howe, 1994; Klein and Kress, 1976; Leonard, 1982; Morris, 1987; Naffine, 1996). The same charge was made regarding Marxist legal scholars (Rhode, 1990). Indeed, in her 1987 book on the construction of women in criminology, Naffine only mentioned the Marxist approach in a footnote, claiming there was too little accounting of female crime by Marxists to include Marxist criminology in the book. Similarly, Morris (1987, 11) criticized Taylor, Walton, and Young for failing to "notice the relevance or applicability to women of the theories reviewed."

The "new criminologists" also often fail to recognize that economic factors alone cannot explain gender differences in criminal behavior; they require a political analysis as well (Leonard, 1982). In a refreshing departure from the numerous accounts of critical criminology that fail to address the "woman question," Dorie Klein and June Kress (1976) wrote an insightful article discussing how the status of women and sexist oppression were relevant to radical criminology. Other Marxist-feminist accounts declare that sexism is directly tied to capitalism, governing economic, social, and legal aspects of our lives (Messerschmidt, 1988; Rafter and Natalizia, 1981).

A book on radical criminology published in the late 1980s, however, devoted only five pages to women and gender (Lynch and Groves, 1989). In the late 1980s, some of the radical criminologists attempted to return to the "realism" of empirical criminology and to accept the claims of feminists and some working-class people that, indeed, much of the crime is harmful (Naffine, 1996, 63). These "left idealists" then transformed and renamed themselves "left realists" (ibid.). However, while the left realists claim to be sensitive to feminist accounts of crime, Naffine (ibid., 64) describes their approach as "naïve." Naffine (ibid.) cites work by Young and Rush (1994) pointing out that the left realists are concerned with crime in the public arena (read: street crime committed by men against men), reducing the frequently hidden crimes against women (e.g., rape and domestic violence). In her book on political economies and punishment, Adrian Howe (1994, 41) stated: "This is not the place to consider feminist theoretical encounters with unrepentant, unreconstructed, vulgar masculinist Marxism." On an encouraging note, some more recent evaluations state that radical criminologists are finally "getting it" regarding their history of ignoring gender and feminism (see Britton, 2000; DeKeseredy, 1996).

In the 1970s, *critical legal studies* (CLS) emerged from a radical group of predominantly White male legal academics (see Crenshaw, 2002; Wing, 1997). The CLS scholars questioned the objectivity of laws that they claimed for centuries had inherently oppressed the poor, people of color, and women, either outright or in their applications (Crenshaw, 2002; Seiler 2003). Some people of color and women who were scholars in the radical left worried that however well-meaning and radical the CLS component was, they seemed unable to promote an analysis beyond the White male elite lens through which they viewed the world (Wing, 1997, 2). These scholars, led by Derrick Bell, started *critical race theory* (CRT) in the mid-1970s, and it fully emerged in the late 1980s (Wing, 1997). Bell's (1973) book, *Race, Racism, and American Law*, is an amazing and comprehensive treatise of the many ways U.S. law discriminates by race. The originators of CRT believed that the Civil Rights movement had stalled and that the old approaches of marches, *amicus* briefs, and litigation were increasingly ineffective in combating de facto discrimination (Wing, 1997, 2). Instead they emphasized that recognizing and accounting for White privilege and power are core to understanding racism in the systemic discrimination and civil rights violations of people of color (see Bell, 1973; Crenshaw, 2002; Seiler, 2003). CRT identifies three beliefs accepted by mainstream society as myths: (1) ignoring race eliminates racism; (2) racism is caused by individuals, not systems; and (3) racism can be fought alone, without

**EXHIBIT 2.2   Tony Brown's Five Fundamental Tenets
of Critical Race Theory**

1.   Racial stratification is ordinary, ubiquitous, and reproduced in mundane and extraordinary customs and experience, and critically impacts the quality of lifestyles and life changes of racial groups.

2.   The race problem is difficult to comprehend and possibly impossible to remedy because claims of objectivity and meritocracy camouflage the self-interest, power, and privilege of whites.

3.   Races are categories that society invents, manipulates, and recreates.

4.   Blacks and other subordinated groups are competently able to communicate and explain the meaning and consequences of racial stratification because they are oppressed; thus, experiential knowledge is legitimate and appropriate.

5.   More than academic or purely scientific advances, critical race theorists should seek to propagate social justice.

SOURCE: Tony N. Brown. 2003. "Critical Race Theory Speaks to the Sociology of Mental Health." *Journal of Health and Social behavior* 44:292–301. This is taken verbatim from page 294 of Brown. Reprinted by permission of the American Sociological Association.

recognizing sexism, classism, homophobia, and so on (Valdes, Culp, and Harris, 2002). Central to CRT is the assumption/problem that race is completely embedded in U.S. laws and policies. Exhibit 2.2 lists the five fundamental tenets of CRT, listed by Tony Brown (2003). It is worth noting that student activism around increasing diversity in higher education in the 1960s through 1990s has been credited with the development of CRT (Cho and Westley, 2002), and CRT continues to develop (Valdes, Culp, and Harris, 2002). As Derrick Bell (1992, ix) claims, the struggle for racial justice must continue despite the fact that "racism is an integral, permanent, and indestructible component of this society."

Although there are limited applications of CRT to studies of crime, a recent one addresses the idea of schools representing relatively safe havens for youths until the 1990s. Watts and Erevelles (2004) point out that violence in urban schools in areas with social exploitation and high unemployment was ignored until violence hit the suburban and rural White schools in high-profile shootings (e.g., Columbine High School). Today, according to the authors, many public schools serve simply as institutions of social control, and school violence is not a result of a few "violent" students but rather institutions that base norms on whiteness and disability status. They conclude that whether the violent students are inner-city African Americans and Latino/as or middle- and upper-class White boys, "[t]heir failure to measure up (to the rigid social norms including those of masculinity) ensured their isolation and provoked them to commit horrifying acts" (ibid., 293). Thus, the answer to school violence is not to get rid of the "rotten kids" but to provide institutions that are not oppressing the students.

In summary, consistent with less liberal approaches, the Marxist or "new criminologists" of the early 1970s were just as guilty as the traditional theorists of omitting women and girls from their theories and analyses, despite the powerful potential of gender and sexual stratification in society to explain criminal behavior and processing. CLS emerged in an attempt to explain how the laws were inherently oppressive to the poor, racial minorities, and women. However, CLS was dominated by White male elites and criticized by women and people of color in leftist academia who became frustrated with its well-meaning but limited views. Subsequently, CRT emerged. The end of this chapter addresses the following emergence of *critical race feminist theory*.

WOMEN'S LIBERATION/EMANCIPATION HYPOTHESIS (WLEH)

As we have seen, traditionally, criminological theory showed only a passing interest in explaining the offending and the system's crime processing of females. All this changed in 1975, however, with the publication of Freda Adler's *Sisters in Crime* and Rita Simon's *Women and Crime*. These books, particularly Adler's, received a great deal of attention regarding their hypothesis that the women's "liberation" movement is linked to the female crime rate.

Also called the "emancipation hypothesis," this approach suggests that the feminist movement, although working toward equality for women, increased the female crime rate. Although similar overall, Adler and Simon differed concerning the types of crime the women's movement was expected to affect. Adler proposed that the violent crime rate would increase because of women's "liberation." In contrast, Simon proposed that only the property crime rate would increase with women's "liberation." Simon suggested further that women's violent crime would decrease because women's frustrations with life would diminish as they gained access to new work and educational opportunities.

Naffine (1987) summarizes some of the troubling assumptions of the women's liberation/emancipation hypothesis (WLEH): (1) Feminism brings out women's competitiveness; (2) the women's movement has opened up structural opportunities to increase places where women can offend; (3) women have fought and won the battle of equality; (4) feminism makes women want to behave like men; and (5) crime itself is inherently masculine. There are obvious problems with these assumptions. Even the most plausible assumption—that feminism has opened up women's structural opportunities—loses credibility when faced with statistics showing that women have not achieved equality in high-paying and managerial professions (see Chapters 9–11). These assumptions, and WLEH in general, have been soundly criticized for being wrong and also for misusing and manipulating statistics and their interpretations in efforts to prove that gender equality breeds female crime (see Crites, 1976; Feinman, 1986; Leonard, 1982; Morris, 1987; Naffine, 1987; Smart, 1976, 1982). A study published in 1983 on incarcerated violent females reported these women to be generally "traditional," "feminine" (not "feminist"), and "conformist" in terms of sex roles, hardly the hard-core feminists Adler's (1975) theory predicted (Bunch, Foley, and Urbina, 1983).

Another problem with WLEH is that it predicts the opposite of previous strain and class theories: that crime will increase with an improvement of opportunities. This implies an underlying fundamental difference between male and female criminality. The theories discussed thus far, when they accounted for class—as they often did—hypothesized that crime would increase with blocked or worsened economic opportunities (see Steffensmeier and Streifel, 1992).

Most important, however, the hypothesis that women's violent crime rates are catching up with men's is questionable. (This topic, a gender comparison of offending, is addressed more fully in the following chapter.) Analyses of changes in women's and girls' offending in the 1970s and 1980s reported that females' violent crime rate remained relatively stable (see Feinman, 1986; Steffensmeier, 1980), whereas research on property crimes, particularly larceny and petty property crimes, indicated women's rates increased during this time period (for example, Box and Hale, 1983, 1984; Chilton and Datesman, 1987; Smith and Visher, 1980; Steffensmeier and Streifel, 1992). But the increase in women's property crime rates has been attributed more to the declining economic situation for women than to their increased equality. Thus, the "feminization of poverty," the increased number of women (with and without dependents) living in poverty, is a better predictor of women's criminality—and then, of property crimes—than is the strength or weakness of the feminist movement. In fact, the types of crime for which women were increasingly arrested after the women's movement of the 1970s, prostitution and offenses against the family (such as desertion, neglect, and nonsupport), are crimes not "altogether compatible with the view of the emancipated female" (Steffensmeier and Allan, 1988).

In addition to the feminization of poverty, sentencing changes in the 1970s and 1980s to "get tough on crime" have done more than the feminist movement to increase females' (and males') official crime rate reported by the police (Box and Hale, 1984). Furthermore, if the women's movement has had any negative effect on women's criminality, it is that women appear to have become more likely to have their behaviors defined as criminal or delinquent by judges and police officers (Curran, 1984; Morris, 1987). Notably, researchers specifically examining the effect of young women's adherence to feminist ideals in the 1980s (for example, regarding women and work and gender roles in the family) found that pro-feminist women and girls were no more likely than their more traditional sisters to report aggression and criminal or delinquent behavior (Figueira-McDonough, 1984; Tremblay, McCord, and Otten, 1983). Kruttschnitt's careful overview of tests of Adler's and Simon's hypothesis concludes that economic marginalization, drug use, and changes in formal social control provide better predictors of female offending than WLEH or opportunity theories, but "they have yet to be formally integrated into an explanatory model of female offending or of gender differences in offending" (1996, 137).

BIOSOCIAL AND EVOLUTIONARY PSYCHOLOGICAL THEORIES

Some of the more recent efforts to explain violence against women, particularly rape, as completely or partially biologically driven are somewhat reminiscent of the early positivistic theories. Specifically, since the 1990s, biosocial and evolutionary psychological theories have gained increasing recognition for their claims that we cannot ignore biology in the commission of crimes. Notably, the resurgence of evolutionary theories has been used most to explain rape, intimate partner abuse, child abuse (including child sexual abuse), and infidelity ("cheating" on one's romantic/sexual partner). Even in her groundbreaking book *Against Our Will: Men, Women and Rape* (discussed more fully in Chapters 6 and 7), feminist Susan Brownmiller (1975) viewed rape as possible because men have penetrating penises and women have penetrable vaginas. The evolutionary psychological and biosocial explanations of men's violence against women emphasize that "sexually aggressive behavior is a biopsychosocial phenomenon that is primarily engaged in by males" (Hall et al., 1993, 1). But both males and females have genitalia that can be "fondled" (a troubling word for sexual abuse), and Cahill (2001) effectively argues that males also have penetrable anuses that could be sexually abused (by males or females). If we consider that it is the ability to overpower (force) or coerce sexual contact, then clearly sexual abusers and victims alike can be either male or female. Given that most babysitting, child-care work, childhood teaching, and parenting is performed by women (or girls) who typically have considerable physical power over the children they oversee, if we buy into the physical domination ability as the main determinant of sexually abusing, we would expect child sexual abuse to be predominantly committed by females. This is clearly not the case.

Many proponents of these new theories claim to integrate the biosocial approach with social theory, and some, even with feminist theory. But the end result of most of the recent publications touting biosocial or evolutionary theories is that biology, with perhaps a smattering of sociological forces, predicts why females are victims and males are offenders. In this context, rape and domestic violence are typically explained (or my fear is that they are excused) by such biological forces as sex drives and hormones. Key to the evolutionary theory approach is the concept of adaptation, which thus "investigates the adaptive value of a given behavior; how this behavior would increase the reproduction or survival of descendants and, therefore, that person's genetic material" (Burch and Gallop, 2004, 244).

Ellis (1993, 23) uses natural selection to explain that our gender roles are a result of our biological dispositions, whereby men gain by being "pushy" about sex and women gain by showing such feminine traits as "coyness" and "hesitancy." Ultimately he claims that males compete with each other for access to female sex partners whereas females compete with each other to find the best male who can provide for their offspring. Ellis (ibid., 24) believes that males do not rape because they want to *dominate* females but that they use these dominating and aggressive rape behaviors simply in their efforts to "copulate" (have sexual intercourse). Sociobiologists believe that men "naturally" pursue more sexual partners (to better plant their seeds), while women are more "naturally" monogamous (to be choosier in picking the father of their future children). One book, *Sperm Wars*, details (without *any* references to other research and no subsequent validation) ways in which sperm are "egg-getters" (try to fertilize ova) and "egg-killers" (try to kill other men's sperm inside of women), and how confusing, unpredictable, and moody women are relative to men (Baker, 1996). Ellis and Walsh (1997) claim that women resist sex/rape until they are confident the male will provide for their offspring. Of course, this simplistic reasoning does not explain why men and boys, premenstrual girls, postmenopausal women, women and girls on effective birth control, and so on would resist rape. Not surprisingly, Ellis and Walsh's (1997) perspective is not only sexist but it is also racist and classist. For example, they suggest African Americans are more criminal than Whites and Asian Americans due to "an evolutionary foundation for racial/ethnic differences" (ibid., 252).

In 2000, Randy Thornhill and Craig T. Palmer published the controversial book *A Natural History of Rape: Biological Bases of Sexual Coercion*, claiming that an evolutionary approach is better suited to understanding the causes of rape than are social science and social learning. Similarly to Ellis (1993), they view rape as an *adaptation* used by men who are unsuccessful in their efforts to have consensual sex with women. The book has been soundly criticized on numerous fronts, including ignoring scientific evidence, misrepresenting facts, and being simplistic and misleading (e.g., Coyne and Berry, 2000; Ward and Siegert, 2000). With an amusing example, Coyne and Berry (2000, 122) point out that evolutionary psychology and the focus on adaptation, specifically that natural selection is the basis for all human actions, are problematic: "The most imaginative and committed sociobiologist would be hard-pressed to show that masturbation, sadomasochism, bestiality, and pornography's enthusiasm for high heels are all direct adaptations."

Biosocial and evolutionary psychological perspectives are not only insulting to girls and women, viewing them as pathetic, needy competitors for male attention, but are also insulting to boys and men, viewing them as incapable of controlling their biological urges or in a constant need of fertilizing eggs (Belknap, 1997). Although some others support this new trend of using biology as a "cause" of crime and violence against women (e.g., Booth and Osgood, 1993; Crawford and Johnston, 1999; Wrangham and Peterson, 1996), other authors offer more progressive and insightful efforts to question the use of biology to explain male aggression against females (e.g., Cahill, 2001; Fausto-Sterling, 2000; Small, 1996; Taylor, 1996). *Evolution, Gender, and Rape*, edited by Cheryl Brown Travis (2003), is an interdisciplinary book comprised solely of responses to Thornhill and Palmer and is unanimously critical of the "bad science" employed in *A Natural History of Rape*. Perhaps Ann J. Cahill (2001, 24) sums it up best when she poignantly argues in her book, *Rethinking Rape*: "It is at least theoretically possible to understand the penis as other than a penetrating, violent tool, and indeed to rid it of such meaning entirely; and it is this theoretical possibility that affords room for hope."

A book edited by Kaj Bjorkqvist and Pirkko Niemela (1992b), entitled *Of Mice and Women: Aspects of Female Aggression*, reports studies by leading scholars regarding sex differences and similarities in aggressive behavior. One study concludes: "The majority of evidence indicates that in the general population differences in aggressiveness reflect the level of testosterone only to a limited extent, if at all. There is no reason to suggest that testosterone causes the behavior of males and females to differ markedly" (Benton, 1992, 46). Other studies reported in this book are convincing in their overview of scientific research, maintaining that "too much" is being made of biological differences between males and females in attempts to "explain away" cultural differences. Indeed, a chapter on "biology and male aggression" concludes: "Finally, we can look forward to the day when the myth that male animals are more aggressive than females can no longer be used by those who would argue that war is the product of biology rather than culture" (Adams, 1992, 24). Indeed, in the introductory chapter, the editors state: "There is no reason to believe that women overall should be less motivated to be aggressive than men" (Bjorkqvist and Niemela, 1992b, 14). Rather, they claim that males' and females' style differences in aggressive behavior depend on culture, age, and situations. One study (not in this edited volume) examining the aggressive nature of males and females from ages 8 to 30, conducted blood tests on sixty of the males and found no relationship between their aggression and testosterone levels (Huesmann et al., 1984).

Scientist Anne Fausto-Sterling (2000) points out how current-day evolutionary psychologists attribute as "fact" that girls and women have "evolved" (adapted?) to be more sexually reserved than boys and men, partly because they must protect their few eggs in contrast to males' vast numbers of sperm, and that women are "naturally" less ambitious than men, inferring that affirmative action will result in inferior hires. "And, as if that weren't enough, some evolutionary psychologists believe that women did not even evolve their own orgasms; it seems we just got lucky because it was so important for men to see constant sexual gratification" (ibid., 211). Fausto-Sterling also points out that while the evolutionary psychologists lean on research that draws on the animal kingdom, typically primates, to show males' "natural" aggression with each other and over females, more recent and sound research by women scientists disputes the findings that female primates are simply sexual receivers (as opposed to initiators) of sex, copulating solely to bear offspring. Similarly, Taylor (1996) criticizes sociobiologists for ignoring research supporting that rapists experience both *power* and *sexual pleasure* by raping, and like other critics of sociobiological explanations, he believes it is highly unlikely that many men rape in order to pass on their genes.

A landmark study of the role of sexual frustration as a cause of rape compared White, college undergraduate, unmarried heterosexual male students, 71 who identified as date rapists and 227 who did not (Kanin, 1985). All of the rapists reported raping girlfriends with whom they had previously experienced consensual sex. Contrary to what the biosocial and other theories would suggest, these men appeared to rape not because they did not have access to consensual sex (that is, were sexually frustrated) but rather because it was part of their socialization (see Exhibit 2.3). This study found that the rapists were sexual predators, using many tactics to try to gain sex: "Sexual exploitation of the female largely permeates their entire male-female approach" (ibid., 224). Moreover, those young men with the most success at obtaining heterosexual outlets consensually were also the young men most likely to date rape. The self-identified date rapists were far more likely to report their obtaining-sex–obsessed behaviors as beginning with their peer groups in high school. The findings confirm the importance of the role of active hyper-erotic peer cultures as influencing young men to rape their dates. Indeed, the rapists viewed their "prestige as being enhanced for sexually exploiting select women" (ibid., 228). It is clear from the findings that these men do not experience

**E X H I B I T   2.3   Eugene Kanin's (1985) Study Comparing Date Rapists
to a Control Group**

Goal
To test whether rape could be attributed to a lack of legitimate sexual outlets.

Method
Surveyed a sample of heterosexual, white, unmarried, undergraduate college men to
compare 71 *self-identified* date rapists to 227 self-identified non-date-rapists.

Findings
1.   All rapes occurred with women with whom the rapists had intensive consensual sexual
      encounters prior to the rape (usually oral sex).
2.   Only 6 of the 71 rapists were reported to the police, and all charges were dropped for
      all 6.
3.   None of the rapists used weapons or their fists to rape.

Differences between the Rapists and Non-Rapists

	Rapists	Non-Rapists
Experienced consensual coitus (intercourse) exclusive of rape events	100%	59%
Reported that "most of the time" they try to seduce a new date	62	19
Used alcohol and/or marijuana to attempt to seduce a date	76	23
Falsely professed love as a way to seduce a date	86	25
Falsely promised "pinning" (Greek system), engagement, or marriage to seduce a date	46	6
Threatened to end a relationship if date will not have sex	31	7
Threatened to leave a date stranded somewhere if she will not have sex	9	0
Reported high school peer culture of high pressure for heterosexual expression	85	26
Involved in a "gang-bang" or sequential sexual sharing of a female with a male friend	41	7
Reported first female-genital contact was due to being "fixed-up" by a friend	21	6
Reported that rape in the abstract can be justified under certain conditions	86	19

SOURCE: Kanin, Eugene J. 1985. Date Rapists: Differential Sexual Socialization and Relative Deprivation. Archives of
Sexual behavior 14(3):219–231.

deprivation of access to consensual sex compared to their nonrapist counterparts; in
fact, quite the opposite is true. However, the rapists appear to feel entitled to
frequent sexual encounters and seem to believe that they are deprived when they
cannot achieve those high expectations. Kanin concluded that date rapists have a
different sexual socialization that results in "an inordinately high value on sexual
accomplishment" and an "exaggerated sexual impulse" (ibid., 229). He speculated

that women who deny sexual attempts made by the date rapists with whom they previously had consensual sex are at risk of rape because these men fail to recognize these women's needs to establish intimacy outside of sex. One might also conclude that once these women say "yes" to sex, they are seen as the sexual property of these men.

Regarding sex/gender differences in general physically aggressive (not sexually aggressive) behavior, Harris's (1996) extensive overview concludes that aggressive behavior is more consistent with social learning, including cultural norms and specific experiences, than it is with biological factors. She states that biological factors can affect aggressive behavior, but research indicates that "cultural norms and gender role stereotypes, previous experiences with aggression, attitudes toward the aggression of others, and judgments of the justifiability of retaliation are even more important influences on aggression" (ibid., 141). However, behavioral genetic research in recent years reports the search for genetic characteristics associated with different forms of aggression (for a review, see Lesch and Merschdorf, 2000) but typically fails to compare women and men, and it is somewhat alarming that present-day studies are searching for what could cryptically be called "angry genes."

Not surprisingly, biosocial and evolutionary perspectives as explanations of *domestic violence* are also being promulgated (e.g., Janssen et al., 2005). Some of these studies focus on CDMs, short for "competitively disadvantaged males," hypothesizing that men who rate as low quality for mates due to their low socio-economic status and physical unattractiveness are more likely to use coerciveness and violence to gain sex (because it may be their only access to it) *and* to use violent sex against their wives *and children* in order to terrorize their wives (dominating their wives through abusing their children) into not leaving them (e.g., Figueredo and McCloskey, 1993; Figueredo et al., 2001). Once again, this approach is inherently offensive on numerous levels (e.g., class and societal ideas of attractiveness). Ironically, Figueredo and his colleagues' (2001, 315) test of this found the opposite of what was hypothesized: CDMs were actually *more* likely to abuse CDFs (competitively disadvantaged females) than the "higher mate quality [women] partners" they would seemingly need to abuse to "keep."

One study reported that men who are verbally and physically abusive to their wives had elevated levels of testosterone, but the study was limited by the small size ($N = 54$) and composition (recruited solely from social service sites) (Soler, Vinayak, and Quadagno, 2000). Another study used a meta-analysis, drawing on data from over thirty studies in eight countries, to test the modular theory of jealousy hypothesis that "natural selection shaped sexual jealousy as a mechanism to prevent cuckoldry, and emotional jealousy as a mechanism to prevent resource loss. Therefore, men should be primarily jealous over a mate's sexual infidelity [cheating] and women over a mate's emotional infidelity" (Harris, 2003, 102). In contrast to evolutionary theories, this study reported a significant lack of support for sex (biological) differences in men's and women's jealousy over infidelity. A large study in Barbados and Antigua proposing to test individual, social circumstances, and social relationship models to explain domestic violence concluded that it is a cultural myth that domestic violence can be explained by stress and strains (Handwerker, 1998). Rather, domestic violence was best explained by gender power differentials: Increasing gender equality decreased the likelihood that even "rotten" men abused their wives, and when gender inequality increased, the power "corrupted," resulting in some of these men becoming more violent. Handwerker (ibid., 206) suggests that we should shift our focus from violent people to the violent cultures that produce them.

FEMINIST AND PRO-FEMINIST THEORIES

Critical Race Feminism

Many people associate "feminism" with White women. Indeed, much of the early work written by White feminists (as discussed in the last chapter), assumed a monolithic experience of "womanhood" without recognizing the diversity of women's experiences based on their race/ethnicity, class, sexual identification, nationality, religion, immigrant status, and so on (see hooks, 2000). Similar to the centuries of documentation of White women's struggles and activism to fight sexism (as well as other forms of oppression), there is a massive amount of documentation of women of color advocating against sexism (as well as other forms of oppression). Records of African American women's resistance to slavery authenticate the many ways African American women resisted slavery and other forms of racism, sexism, and numerous types of abuse and oppression from the 1600s and since (see Crafts, 2002; Davis, 1981; Guy-Sheftall, 1995; King, 1988; Shaw, 1997)

The last chapter addressed the difference between sex and gender, with the former a biological distinction between males and females and the latter more socially constructed differences between the sexes. Gender, then, concerns the social, economic, political, and cultural opportunities associated with being female and male (The Development Assistance Committee, 1999). Similarly, in recent years many legal scholars, sociologists, and anthropologists have advocated for the necessity to view *race* as socially constructed (Lopez, 1996; Wing, 2003; Zuberi, 2001). Lopez (1996, 2003) carefully records manners in which race is a social construct whose social construction is reinforced through the legal system. (In particular, he traces how the dominant racial identity changed from Mexican American and, in some cases, White, to Chicano among this group's community and leadership through the "legal violence" during two trials against Chicano political activists [2003].)

Traditionally, race was viewed as identifiable through such characteristics as skin and hair color, hair texture, and bodily features and proportions. In his powerful book *Thicker than Blood: How Racial Statistics Lie*, Tokofu Zuberi (2001, 5) elaborates on how race historically became identified as a *concept*, and the continuing damaging implications of this:

> The concept of race is rooted in the 15th-century expansion of European nations. The advent of racial slavery and colonialism marked a turning point in how physical differences were viewed. . . . the white

supremacy that accompanied the racialization of slavery in the Americas has not existed since the dawn of human history and it continues to exert a peculiar influence today. The same can be said of colonialism. The racialization of colonization and slavery was historically unique, and its consequences have been lasting.

The "one drop of blood" theory maintained that anyone with any African ancestry is Black. But how does one measure "one drop of blood"? What about biracial and multiracial individuals? How can one scientifically decide someone's race? Given that it is impossible to identify distinguishable biological racial categories, it is important to view race, like gender, as a social construct. This is not to detract from the very real racism that individuals experience because they "look" and are of color (e.g., Asian, Asian American, African American, Native American, Latino/a). Rather, it is to understand that there are no scientific tests to identify exclusive racial categories. Indeed, Zuberi (2001, xviii) states: "Race is a socially constructed process that produces subordinate and superordinate groups." Viewing race this way provides clearer interpretations of race and racism, and how racism "works" to dominate and oppress.

Feminist jurisprudence was developed by White feminist legal scholars in the 1970s to address ways that lawmaking and enforcement work to the detriment of women and girls. As stated in the section on Marxist and radical theories, critical race theory emerged as a response to the view by some left-wing academic women and scholars of color that critical legal studies was limited by its framing by largely elite, White, male left-wing academics. In turn, the emergence of *critical race feminism* (CRF) is a response largely by women of color law professors in the United States in the early 1990s, concerned that feminist jurisprudence was dominated by White women law professors and CRT was dominated by African American men. Similar to the ways the designers of CRT accused the CLS theorists of limitations using the lens through which they see the world, CRF scholars suggest that CRT and feminist jurisprudence are not appropriately equipped to address women of color's double and multiple marginality when racism and sexism are combined with each other and/or additional forms of oppression (e.g., classism, homophobia, etc.). Hillary Potter's (2004) application of critical race feminism to understanding of the intimate partner abuse of African American women confirmed the utility of CRF to understanding these victims and the important ways that racism and sexism intersect with each other, as well as with classism and sexuality within the context of intimate partner abuse.

Messerschmidt's Masculinities and Crime Theories

Jeanne Flavin (2001) points out that ignoring the role of gender in criminological theories denies how gender not only shapes girls' and women's experiences and behaviors but how *gender also impacts boys' and men's experiences and behavior.* James Messerschmidt's (1993) rethinking of feminist theory focuses on structured action and gendered crime. Messerschmidt addresses the impact of gender not only on women's criminality but also on men's. He defines *social structures* as "regular patterned forms of interaction over time that constrain and channel behavior in specific ways" (1993, 63). Messerschmidt identifies three social structures as important to understanding our gendered society: the gender division of labor, gender relations of power, and sexuality. Moreover, class, race, and gender relations are interconnected to a number of social structures and thus are related to social actions.

To Messerschmidt, masculinity is key to explaining criminality. This is consistent with Naffine's (1996) contention that feminism, particularly using masculinity to assess why males behave more criminally than females, is useful for studying male as well as female offending. Messerschmidt carefully examines how race, class, and gender interact within various social structures that encourage the preponderance of criminality perpetrated largely by young males. Accounting for differences among males, Messerschmidt describes how middle-class White males can use power structures, such as a good education and respectable careers, to establish masculinity and provide for themselves and their families. Lower-class males and males of color have fewer legitimate options, however, and thus are more likely to use crime and delinquency to prove masculinity. Accounting for gender differences, it is far more important for males than for females to show power or to need to prove masculinity. Regarding sexuality, more respect is accrued to heterosexuals than to lesbians and gay men, and, as discussed in Chapter 4 of this book, consensual (hetero) sexuality is more permissible in society and the crime-processing system when it is exhibited by males than when it is by females. Messerschmidt effectively uses these variables of class, race, and sexuality to explain rape causality, the differential treatment of males and females who are sexually active, and participation in various crimes and offenses ranging from sexual harassment to robbery and homicide.

This relatively new approach to studying crime causation is appealing in that it accounts for both males and females, as well as the impact of gender, race, and class. Furthermore, it explains crime and criminal processing within the important social structures that shape society and the individuals in it. Bottcher (2001, 896) criticizes Messerschmidt, however, for failing to understand what gender tells us about crime by focusing on how gender "is expressed or enacted in crime": He does not "fully reveal the process by which crime becomes a resource for doing masculinity." Similarly, Laidler and Hunt (2001) question how we are to understand women's and girls' involvement in offending if crime is a mode for "doing" masculinity. Their extensive study found that "to be entirely feminine and respectable in their highly marginalized communities is unrealistic and dangerous" (ibid., 665). Another recent study of the role of gender and masculinity in violent retaliations in urban street life found that male-on-male retaliations were the most common violent retaliations and frequently involved "doing masculinity" to regain respect but that the second most common violent retaliation was female-on-female, typically in a dispute over a man (Mullins, Wright, and Jacobs, 2004). (Female-on-male was the least common type of street retaliation violence.) Interestingly, she compared the scrutiny of violent women street retaliators to the scrutiny of women in the "masculinized" business world (ibid, 934).

Cycle of Violence Theory

A major contributor to the understanding the causes of crime and delinquency is Cathy Spatz Widom, who developed the cycle of violence theory in 1989 to assess the relationship between childhood traumas and subsequent offending. Widom (1989) first compared the juvenile and adult offense records of more than 1,500 persons who had and had not been abused as children, and found that abused and neglected girls were significantly more likely than their nonabused/neglected counterparts to have both formal adult and formal juvenile criminal records. The abused/neglected girls, however, were no more likely than the nonabused/neglected girls to have a record of violent crimes. In another publication, Rivera and Widom (1990) reported that girls who were abused or neglected were at an increased risk for arrest for a violent crime while still a juvenile, although abused and neglected boys were not more likely than nonabused/nonneglected boys to face arrests for violent crimes.

In yet another study, Widom (1995) attempted to determine whether sexual abuse places youths at a greater risk for delinquent and adult criminal behavior than nonsexual child abuse and neglect. She compared 908 individuals who at the age of 11 years or younger had court-documented child abuse (physical or sexual) or neglect between 1967 and 1971 with a control group of of nonabused and non-neglected youths with similar characteristics (e.g., race, age, etc.). As expected, Widom (ibid.) found that individuals who experienced childhood abuse (physical or sexual) or neglect were more likely than their nonabused and nonneglected counterparts to be arrested later in life. Indeed, slightly over one-quarter (26 percent) of the youths who experienced abuse and/or neglect were arrested as juveniles, and about the same percent (29 percent) were arrested as adults. Although childhood sexual abuse victimization placed an individual at increased risk of future arrests, these childhood abuse survivors were no more likely to be arrested later in life than the individuals who experienced no (officially reported) sexual abuse but experienced (officially reported) physical abuse and/or neglect. However, individuals officially designated as "sexual abuse plus" victims, those who experienced sexual abuse plus physical abuse and/or neglect as a child, were at the greatest risk of being arrested for running away. A significant finding of this study was that childhood sexual abuse victims were far more likely to be arrested for prostitution than their nonsexually abused counterparts. (However, arrests for running away did not significantly predispose youths to prostitution arrests.) Additionally, careful analysis was conducted to determine the individual effects of three types of abuse: any sexual abuse, any physical abuse, and any neglect. Notably, "any sexual abuse" had the greatest impact on the likelihood of being arrested for prostitution, and "any non-sexual physical abuse" had the greatest impact on the likelihood of being arrested for rape or sodomy. Stated alternatively, regarding the link between the type of child-hood abuse victimization (sexual, physical, and neglect) and subsequent "sex crimes" offending, childhood sexual abuse has the greatest impact on subsequent prostitution offending, and (nonsexual) physical childhood abuse has the greatest impact on the likelihood of committing rape or sodomy. Unfortunately, these statistics lump females and males together, so we do not know how these dynamics may vary by gender. Widom's contributions are huge, but it is important to remember that she relies on court-documented cases of child abuse victimizations and neglect; thus, her studies do not include the many cases that do not reach the courts and likely disproportionately reflect the most extreme child abuse cases (Widom, 1995). Additionally, Fagan (2001) discusses the need for studies that better analyze the role of gender in the cycle of violence.

Life Course Theory (LCT)

A recent theoretical approach that is consistent in many respects with a pro-feminist method is the "Life Course Development Model." Sampson and Laub's (1993) construction of *life course theory* (LCT) drew significantly both from Hirschi's (1969) social control theory *and* Gottfredson and Hirschi's (1990) self-control theory (Taylor, 2001). LCT theorizes that various life events, particularly those during childhood and adolescence, affect one's risk of offending behavior. Thus, various developmental stages are "age specific," making offending behavior age associated (see Loeber, 1996). Indeed, adolescence is identified as a particularly "at-risk" time given the angst of puberty, the stress of changing schools, and peer pressure. In this sense, crime is viewed as a network of various causal factors. One aspect of LCT is that independent variables become dependent variables over time. For example, delinquency decreases one's chance of doing well in school, which in turn becomes a predictor for (re)turning to crime. Some of the key variables assessed in much of the life course research include antisocial behavior, intelligence, and income levels, as well as general criminal, delinquent, and deviant behaviors. Thus, a focus of some life course research is to assess whether antisocial behavior is continuous over an individual's life ("life course persistent") or whether there are periods of antisocial behaviors, usually limited to adolescence ("adolescence-limited") (Moffitt, 1993). The life course approach, then, examines "pathways through the age-differentiated life span," acknowledging different life stages, turning points, and transitions in individuals' lives (Elder, 1985). Therefore, this research tends to be longitudinal in nature (collecting data about individuals' lives over time).

The life course perspective, then, is a developmental perspective, focusing on individuals' behavioral changes from birth until death, the "social development over the full life course; specifically developmental processes from childhood and adolescence through adulthood" (Laub and Lauritsen, 1993, 236). Over the course of most individuals' lives, the formal and informal social controls vary, particularly the informal controls such as the family, school, and work, and these changes are largely age specific (Laub and Lauritsen, 1993). That is, most children do not have jobs, so we cannot examine that control for them, but their schools and parents typically have less control over them as they age, at the same time that they are usually increasingly influenced by their peers. In their work with the life course model, Sampson and Laub (1990) identify two hypotheses: first, that childhood antisocial behaviors predict problems in adult development; and second, that social bonds to work and family in adulthood explain changes in crime and development over the life span. They also identify two central concepts to the life perspective:

trajectories and transitions. Trajectories have to do with life's "pathways" or development lines over the life span, including a person's work life, marriage, parenthood, self-esteem, and criminal behavior. Transitions, on the other hand, are "specific life events that are embedded in trajectories and evolve over shorter time spans (e.g., first job or first marriage)" (ibid., 610). Sampson and Laub (ibid.) view one's social bonds in adulthood as potentially modifying events on the trajectory to criminal behavior. That is, stable and supportive social bonds (through attachment to a spouse, job stability, and commitment to occupational goals) in adulthood may ameliorate childhood experiences, setting one on the path to crime.

As stated previously, in many ways the life course perspective is seemingly pro-feminist in nature: It purports to address significant childhood and adult experiences and to view how these, particularly social bonds, are related to delinquent, criminal, and deviant behavior. Indeed, the research conducted from the life course perspective on boys and men has generally found considerable support for it. In practice to date, this research has less information to offer on girls and women. First, this research so far has focused almost exclusively on males (Laub, Nagin, and Sampson, 1998; Laub and Sampson, 1993; Li, 1999; Loeber, 1996; Moffitt, 1990, 1993; Nagin, Farrington, and Moffitt, 1995; Piquero, MacDonald, and Parker, 2002; Piquero et al., 2003; Sampson and Laub, 1990; Shover and Thompson, 1992; Stattin and Magnusson, 1991; Tremblay et al., 1992). In some sense, this is "excusable" given that the researchers are dealing with existing longitudinal data sets that began data collection in times when there was significantly less interest in females and gender. On the other hand, it is somewhat remarkable how little effort is made in the existing studies to mention how this research might apply to girls and women or the seeming lack of interest in it given that it is rarely or never mentioned as a limitation of the research.

One exception is Farrington's (1992) discussion of three large-scale longitudinal British data sets. At least one of the three data sets he discusses includes both males and females. Unfortunately, Farrington barely addresses any findings about the women and gender differences. Another article on the life course provides no empirical data but stresses the need for comparative studies across countries or even allowing for various structural locations within a country (including the United States) as important "next steps" for the life course perspective (Laub and Lauritsen, 1993). Unfortunately, the authors appear to be interested in race and class only as "structural location" variables and do not mention gender. Another seeming attempt to include gender is a lengthy article promising information on gender differences, entitled "Key Issues in the Development of Aggression and Violence from Child-hood to Early Adulthood" (Loeber and Hay, 1997). Remarkably, this long article scarcely touches on social learning or the many ways that boys' aggression is tolerated or even encouraged while girls' aggression is punished. Nor does the article begin to address the ways that childhood traumas are gendered and how this influences development. Instead, we learn that "some degree of aggression is age-normative, at least in boys" (ibid., 373), and "[i]t seems probably that girls during the preschool period outgrow aggression more speedily than boys" (ibid., 388). There is no indication why this is probable, and other studies suggest that girls do not "outgrow" aggression so much as their aggression is punished. Finally, Loeber and

Hay (1997) are comfortable identifying "gender differences" and "prediction" as the only key words for the article when the tables and figures are composed solely from data on boys. Therefore, similarly to most of the theories addressed thus far in this chapter, although LCT might be meaningfully applied to girls and women, this does not appear to occur. Or, as Kruttschnitt (1996, 141) states: "Failing to address how family and peer influences on delinquency change for males and females over the course of adolescence limits our ability to predict and explain the gender-crime relationship."

An exception to this is a study by Sommers and Baskin (1994). They briefly refer to LCT but claim their study "considers factors identified by previous works in integrated theory in order to understand pathways into violent offending for a specific sample of serious women offenders" (ibid., 469). They collected "life event histories" through interviews with eighty-five women arrested or incarcerated for violent crime in New York City, distinguishing between "early" and "normal/later" onset into offending and using self-report data. Notably, 60 percent reported an early onset of violent behavior, with 10 years as the average age of becoming involved in street fighting. There were no significant differences between the early and normal onset groups in terms of family background, largely because both sets "grew up in multiproblem households" with high rates of both experiencing and witnessing violence in the home. The neighborhood the woman grew up in, however, was significant. Girls raised in neighborhoods with high concentrations of poverty were more likely both to have an early onset into violent behavior and to report sexual and physical abuse by a stranger. Schooling was also significant, with the early onset offenders dropping out of school at a younger age than normal/late onset offenders. Another significant distinction between the early and normal/late onset violent offending females was initiation into and addiction to drugs. The early onset women were more likely than the normal/late onset women to have started using alcohol and marijuana at a younger age (typically before they turned 9 years old) and to be younger when they became addicted to more powerful drugs (ibid., 478).

One longitudinal study examined the short- and long-term effects of self-reported physical (nonsexual) violence perpetrated by family *and* nonfamily on youths' subsequent offending (Fagan, 2003). Both family-perpetrated and particularly nonfamily-perpetrated nonsexual violent victimizations increased the likelihood of these youths' immediate and lasting offending behaviors, and those youths reporting *both* family- and nonfamily-perpetrated violent victimization were the most frequent offenders. The only gender difference was that boys reported more of both family and nonfamily (nonsexual) violent victimizations (ibid.).

A study published prior to the development of LCT but consistent with it collected data over 22 years on more than 600 youths starting when they were 8 years old, about half of whom were girls (Huesmann et al., 1984). For both girls and boys, those that were identified by their school peers as most aggressive at age 8 were by age 30 the most aggressive and committed the most serious offenses. Furthermore, this aggressive/antisocial behavior was transmitted across generations (meaning that aggressive people are typically raised by aggressive parents and raise aggressive children). Thus, for both girls and boys, early aggressive behavior displayed in schools is a powerful predictor of serious antisocial and criminal behavior as adults, including child abuse. Notably, spouse abuse and driving violations were more common among males than females who had been identified as childhood aggressors (Huesmann et al., 1984). One of the rare LCT studies including girls (and boys), rarely mentioned or reported on gender, and though it collected detailed information on sexual activity, failed to account for whether it was consensual (Olds et al., 1998). A recent edited book, *Life-Course Criminology: Contemporary and Classic Readings* (Piquero and Mazerolle, 2000), includes many of the studies reviewed in this section. Unfortunately, throughout the entire book, gender, abuse, and trauma—seemingly important distinctions in early development, life experiences, and subsequent offending— are rarely mentioned.

Another point worth mentioning about LCT applications thus far is that in addition to being sexist, they are often heterosexist. Social ties as adults appear to be exclusively measured in terms of marriage and divorce. Also, although many of the life course studies claim to address variables loosely labeled "family diversity" or "poor family functioning," there is no mention of parental abuse or other types of abuse of these children and how this may influence their social bonds and subsequent delinquent and criminal behavior. To this end, Spohn (2000) used Widom's (1995) cycle of violence data to test LCT as informed by feminist research: that important life course events should include abuse and neglect. In addition to finding that males were five times as likely as females to have adult arrest records (even after controlling for the independent variables), Spohn found that childhood maltreatment had a "much greater influence on criminal involvement" (2000, 221) and "through a greater number of significant paths" (ibid., 223) among the females (as compared to the males). Spohn distinguishes LCT and "psycho-genic" perspectives, defining the latter to mean that the effects of childhood maltreatment extend "over and beyond the effects of a cumulative continuity and the labeling processes that promote a criminal career" (ibid., 219). While he finds some support for LCT for both males and females, it is more fitting for the males, while the "psychogenic" perspective is only fitting of the females. That is, for females, childhood maltreatment influences adult criminality and not simply through being stigmatized and labeled as a youthful offender, whereas for males the juvenile delinquent "label" mediated the effect of childhood maltreatment on adult offending. Finally, Spohn reported that the findings of the males are more con-sistent with LCT and the findings of the females are more consistent with the "psychogenic perspective."

Feminist Pathways Research

Research, at least since 1977, has increasingly used women's and girls' voices to determine "life course" events that place girls (and women) at risk of offending. Unlike the longitudinal data collected over time on individuals by the life course researchers (or using such existing prospective data sets), this research typically collects data at one point in time, usually interviewing incarcerated women (and sometimes girls) retrospectively about their lives, often pointedly asking or at least attempting to determine, "How did you end up being an offender/delinquent?" However, not all of these studies use incarcerated populations; the earliest ones used self-identified prostitutes "on the street" (as well as some incarcerated prostitutes). Thus, the feminist pathways research to date typically attempts to gain data that are quasilongitudinal by asking girls and women to discuss their lives and attempt to sequence major events (e.g., abuse by parents, school experiences, delinquent and criminal behavior, and so on).

Although the term *pathways* is used in this book and some of the more recent writings describing this phenomenon, this label did not exist in the earlier and even some of the later studies reported in this section. Also, grouping the studies in this "feminist pathways" section is a bit tenuous. For example, the pathways approach is consistent with the life course and cycle of violence theories, neither of which claim to be feminist. Furthermore, I am not sure that all of the scholars whose research is presented in this section personally identify as feminists or view their research as feminist. At any rate, it is hoped that the reader will see the common theme in what is included as "feminist pathways research" in this book: research that attempts to examine girls' and women's (and rarely, men's and boys') histories, allowing them, when possible, "voice" in order to understand the link between childhood and adult events and traumas and the likelihood of subsequent offending.

The first feminist pathways study I have found was a combination of data collected from two studies on prostitutes, both involving self-report data from questionnaires, interviews, and ethnographic field observations of prostitutes contacted on the street and in jail (James and Meyerding, 1977). The first data set, Study 1, was collected between 1970 and 1972 and included 72 adult and 20 adolescent prostitutes. The second data set, Study 2, was collected between 1974 and 1975 and included 136 prostitutes. The researchers, Jennifer James and Jane Meyerding, compared their data on prostitutes to existing "normal" population rates reported in publications, in an attempt to determine whether the prostitutes' rates of early/childhood sexual experiences differed from the "normal" (non-prostitute) population. As the researchers expected, the prostitutes reported more troubling sexual experiences than reported by the "normal" population: "The prostitutes had in common many negative experiences not found or found less often in other populations of young women. These include incestuous and/or coerced sex, lack of parental guidance, intercourse at a young age, and few or no meaningful relationships with males" (ibid., 1977, 1381). These scholars go on to speculate how these childhood experiences could lead to prostitution, and they postulate three factors that "may have influenced [the women] toward accepting prostitution as a lifestyle" (ibid., 1384). First, they see the lack of parental monitoring and guidance leading to the increased likelihood of early and casual sexual intercourse. Second, the young woman or girl learns that sex both adds to and detracts from her social status: She has a new-found "power" with males, but her nonvirgin status "makes her unacceptable to the majority of the culture" (ibid.). Third, rape and incest experiences are emotionally destructive. Although James and Meyerding's final analysis omits what many scholars say about some of these street prostitutes now, that they have little or no choice but to prostitute, their perspective into the double standard of males' and females' acceptable sexual agency is insightful and particularly profound, given when it was written:

> Because the range of acceptable sexual behaviors is much narrower for women than for men, and because women more than men are judged (by themselves and others) on the basis of their sexual desirability and behavior, sexual experiences may be a more important factor in a woman's development of self-identity. A woman who views herself as sexually debased or whose sexuality is more than normally objectified may see prostitution as a "natural"—or as the only—alternative. (ibid.)

The second feminist pathways study was likely one by Mimi H. Silbert and Ayala M. Pines (1981), who used word of mouth and public service announcements to recruit their sample. They interviewed 200 current and former prostitutes in the San Francisco Bay area. The sample ranged in age from 10 to 46 years, with an average age of 22 years. This impressive sample was also racially diverse: 69 percent White, 18 percent African American, 11 percent Hispanic, 2 percent Native American, and 1 percent Asian American. Although two-thirds of the sample came from middle- or higher-income families, almost 90 percent reported their financial situation at the time of the interview as "just making it" or "very poor" (ibid., 408). Silbert and Pines's profound findings include:

- Three in five participants (60 percent) reported being sexually abused before the age of 16 (although most were first abused at much younger ages) by an average of two sexual abusers each.

- Two-thirds of the sexual abuse victims were abused by fathers or father figures (stepfathers, foster fathers, and mothers' common-law husbands).

- "Only" 10 percent of the victims were sexually abused by strangers.

- The sexual abuse frequently led to running away from home, which led to prostitution and other street work.

- When asked why they started prostituting, nine-tenths said it was because they were hungry, needed money, and had no other options available to them. (ibid., 410)

(A more recent study interviewing street sex workers reported that 57 percent reported child sexual abuse and 49 percent reported being hit or beaten by a parent or caregiver until they had bruises or were otherwise physically injured. Regarding abuse suffered since becoming a sex worker, the following abuse rates were reported: 82 percent reported physical assaults, 83 percent reported being physically threatened with a weapon, 8 percent reported physical attacks by pimps or customers that resulted in serious injuries, 68 percent reported rapes, 49 percent reported pornography made of them while in doing sex work, and 32 percent reported being upset by having a customer request a sexual act viewed in prostitution [Farley and Barkan, 1998].)

The third feminist study examining women's and girls' pathways to offending, published in 1983 by Meda Chesney-Lind and Noelie Rodriguez, used intensive interviews with sixteen incarcerated women. Among their findings was the prevalence of severe nonsexual child abuse experienced by ten of the women, where violence included extreme brutality in homes devoid of affection and security. Similar to Silbert and Pines (1981), nine-tenths of the women reported involvement in prostitution, and for most this was an outgrowth of running away from home that started in their teens. Also similar to Silbert and Pines (1981, 55), their reasons for becoming prostitutes were "largely financial." Half of the women reported having been raped as children, and three-fifths reported some form of child sexual abuse victimization. Chesney-Lind and Rodriguez (1983) also reported how subsequent drug dependency was related to further entanglement with the law.

Regina A. Arnold (1990) conducted intensive interviews, participant observation, and questionnaires with sixty African American women prisoners. Similarly to the previous "pathways" studies, Arnold (ibid., 154) explains how these women were labeled and processed as deviants and delinquents as young girls "for refusing to accept or participate in their own victimization." This refusal led to their structural dislocation from three primary socialization institutions: the family, the educational system, and occupational systems. This dislocation, in turn, led to their entry into "criminal life." Arnold effectively discusses how patriarchal families and family violence, economic marginality, racist teachers, and a poor educational system individually and collectively produce environments leading to the criminalization of girls, where they are alienated in their own homes, schools, and communities. Furthermore, Arnold (ibid.) reports that these women and girls often "self-medicate" with drugs in attempts to numb the pain from their violent experiences and pasts.

In 1990, Lana Fox and Fran Sugar published a report on findings from interviews they conducted with thirty-nine Aboriginal women in Canada's federal prison for women. Fox and Sugar, themselves former prisoners and Aboriginal, reported not only that most of the women were in for violent offenses but that most had extensive experiences of violent victimization based on their gender, race/ethnicity, and often, age (they were very young and even more powerless for many of the victimizations). Over half reported rapes, many by fathers or male relatives, but also many of the women reported sexual and physical abuse suffered by "tricks" when they were sex workers on the street, often when they were still children (Fox and Sugar, 1990). Many reported victimizations in foster homes and juvenile delinquent and adult prison facilities. The authors state that the relationship between these Aboriginal women's victimization histories and subsequent violent offending is not accidental.

Margaret Shaw's (1991) study surveying women in Canadian prisons, convicted of both violent and nonviolent offenses, found that 68 percent reported having been physically abused at some time in their lives, and 53 percent reported sexual abuse experiences at some point. These rates were higher for the Aboriginal women: 90 percent reported physical victimization at some point, and 61 percent reported sexual victimization. "Some said that they had 'got over' what occurred, others that they felt they needed a great deal of help" (Shaw, 1995, 125). Shaw discusses how their physical and sexual victimization histories were not the only life experiences they reported that might be related to their criminal acts and behaviors:

> [S]eventy-five percent had an involvement with substance abuse, 66 percent had no work skills or regular legitimate employment, [and] almost half had severe disruption in their early lives. The Aboriginal women in particular have a history as victims of racism, violence in the home and on the street, dependence on drugs and alcohol from a very young age, being sent to institutions or [W]hite foster homes with sometimes as many as forty-seven different placements before the age of fifteen or sixteen. For some women, although not all, their contact with society has been one of violence and punishment almost all their lives. (ibid., 126)

Mary E. Gilfus (1992) conducted intensive interviews with twenty incarcerated women to understand their entries into street crime. These women also reported patterns of victimization to offending. Many of these women's survival skills to avoid victimization were criminal: running away from home, using drugs, and prostitution. The women were from economically disadvantaged backgrounds, particularly the African American women. In addition to abuse and poverty, prevalent in the women's childhoods, were educational neglect and extremely troubling school experiences. The African American women reported significant racial violence in their childhoods, including a girl who had witnessed her uncle murdered by two White men. The victimization, then, led to offending, which led to revictimization in their lives on the street, including rape, assault, and attempted murder. Many of the women in Gilfus's (ibid.) sample also reported experiencing battering by their intimate male partners in adulthood, as well. Similarly, Elizabeth Comack (1996) interviewed twenty-four incarcerated women and, while not trying to excuse their offenses, highlighted the manner in which these women's extreme adult and child physical and sexual abuses and subsequent offending cannot be removed from political, social, and economic analysis.

One of the most profound studies addressing "pathways" to crime is Beth E. Richie's (1996) research in *Compelled to Crime*, focusing on African American battered women in prison (although she also collected data from White battered and African American nonbattered women in prison). In this work, Richie used "life-history interviews" to elicit women's voices. Ultimately, she develops her theory of *gender entrapment* in an attempt to understand the "contradictions and complications of the lives of the African American battered women who commit crimes" (ibid., 4). More specifically, gender entrapment involves understanding the connections between (1) violence against women in their intimate relationships, (2) culturally constructed gender-identity development, and (3) women's participation in illegal activities. Two of the many important contributions of Richie's (ibid.) research are her dispelling of myths about battered women regarding "why they stay" and her investigation into the impacts of race and racism. For example, a major finding is that the African American battered women appeared to have had a more privileged childhood family environment (e.g., felt loved and important) than the White battered women and the African American nonbattered women. Richie (ibid.) suggests this "heightened status" in their families of origin is what makes

EXHIBIT 2.4 **Beth Richie's (1996) Battered Women's Pathways to Crime**

Pathways Associated with African American Battered Women
1. **Women Held Hostage:** This pathway involved women whose intimate partner batterers used extreme violence against them to keep them hostage and isolated, and these women were frequently charged in the deaths of their children that were caused by their batterers.
2. **Projection and Association:** This pathway involved battered women who committed violent crimes against men other than their batterers, where the new men served as "proxies" for their batterers, as projected or symbolic retaliation for past abuse.
3. **Poverty:** These were women arrested for property or other economically motivated crimes (e.g., burglary, forgery, robbery, and possession of stolen property).

Pathways Associated with both African American and White Battered Women
4. **Sexual Exploitation:** Although many of the women reported prostitution or sex-for-drugs experiences, this pathway involved women who ended up in prison due to illegal sex work. Notably, their batterers often forced/coerced them into the prostitution that landed them in prison, and the women in this category had higher rates of child and adulthood sexual abuse histories.
5. **Fighting Back:** This pathway involved battered women who committed offenses (arson, other property offenses, or assaults on their batterers) in the context of an assault against them by their batterers. The women did not deny their actions but viewed them more as "self-defense" than as crimes.

Pathway Associated with African American and White Battered Women and African American Non-Battered Women
6. **Addiction:** This pathway involved women whose primary offense landing them in prison was a drug offense. For the African American battered women, the drug use usually followed a battering incident, and drugs were used as a way to "reconnect" with the batterer (e.g., to create emotional intimacy). Indeed, some African American women indicated that their drug use/addiction started with being forced to take drugs by their batterers. The non-battered African American women reported more voluntary initiation into drug use. A White battered woman reported her arrest for selling drugs was due to her attempt to be able to afford to leave her batterer.

SOURCE: Beth E. Richie, 1996. *Compelled to Crime: The Gender Entrapment of Battered Black Women.* New York: Routledge.

these women vulnerable to entrapment when they become involved with batterers: They have become disappointed with their experiences in the public sphere where they encountered racism instead of a heightened status; thus, they refocus their goal on obtaining the perfect nuclear family. When the battering starts, they are optimistic about being able to "fix" things. In addition to reporting how battered women are "trapped by the violence" in their abusive intimate-partner relationships as adults, she also reports "six paths to crime," reported in Exhibit 2.4.

The goal of Joan W. Moore's (1999) study of Latino/a gang members and their families in East Los Angeles was to understand gang membership in terms of major themes relating to the family, including immigration and ethnicity, parental economic status, and the climate of the homes in which the gang members were raised. Ethnic identity was reported as confusing for many of these youths, as they were virtually all born in the United States yet were raised by their parents and treated by racist Whites as if they were Mexican. (For the parents, the Mexican identity was positive; for racist Whites, it was negative.) For both girls and boys, the racist experiences with Whites could lead to fights. For both sexes, the households in which they were raised were more reflective of "poverty" than of traditional extended Mexican families, and their parents typically had little formal education. Fathers were far more likely than mothers to work outside the home, and most of the parents "did not hold very good jobs" (ibid., 163). Notably, girls (44 percent) were far more likely than boys (19 percent) to report that their mothers worked outside the home. Despite these patterns of poverty, Moore reports that the emotional climate of the family during childhood was a far better predictor of youths in this area joining a gang than were the strains of poverty and immigrant life.

Moore (ibid., 165) reports that many of the gang members' families were not particularly happy, and some were "acutely unhappy." Moreover, one-third of the male members and two-fifths of the female members reported seeing their fathers beat their mothers. When asked about their reaction to their fathers' abuse of their mothers, about half of the females and two-thirds of the males reported "with-dr[awing] in fear" (ibid., 167). Notably, the females were more likely than the males to try to intervene and stop their fathers' abuse of their mothers or to fight their fathers themselves. About half of the males and two-thirds of the females were clearly afraid of their fathers, often "with good reason" (ibid., 168). Girls were also more likely to be afraid of their mothers than were boys, and consistent with other research, girls tended to be far more restricted than their brothers by their parents. Females were more likely than males to describe their parents as strict and to say their parents enforced rules with them. Although a few male members of the sample reported inappropriate sexual advances made to them as children, 29 percent of the females reported incest, usually perpetrated by a father but also by uncles, brothers, and grandfathers. Although Moore (ibid., 174) found that both male and female gang members report common experiences with "troubled" families, "clearly more women than men came from troubled families. They were more likely to have been living with a chronically sick relative, one who died, one who was a heroin addict, or one who was arrested. In fact, a large majority of the [gang] women had a relative die or be arrested [when the women were children]" (ibid.).

Candace Kruttschnitt's (1996) overview of research on gender and crime includes "exposure to parental deviance" in the rubric of social learning theory. However, in many senses, what she discusses is relevant for life course or pathways research as well. Specifically, she examines two aspects of parental deviance: exposure to parental violence, including harsh discipline; and the effects of parental deviance on their children's offending:

> In both cases there is evidence that gender modifies the outcomes. In the case of parental violence, girls who have been abused or neglected in their families or those who have witnessed family violence are less likely to engage in violent or aggressive behaviors . . . or to have an arrest record for substance use than comparable boys. . . . Interestingly, however, there is

some evidence of higher rates of depression among maltreated girls than boys. (ibid., 140)

Barbara Owen's (1998) study of face-to-face interviews with almost 300 with women in the largest women's prison in the world, the Central California Women's Facility (CCWF), provides a compelling argument that understanding these life histories is essential for understanding women prisoners. She addresses not only how childhood abuses and domestic violence are linked with offending but how they also impact the way these survivors experience prison. Specifically, Owen (ibid.) identifies five significant phenomena in the "pathways to imprisonment": (1) the multiplicity of abuse, (2) early family life, (3) children, (4) street life, and (5) spiraling marginality. The multiplicity of abuse is consistent with the other research reported in this section, in that the women in Owen's study reports numerous types of physical, sexual, and emotional abuse. For example, about 70 percent of the women experienced ongoing physical abuse under the age of 18 (usually perpetrated by a father, stepfather, or mother), and 62 percent experienced ongoing physical abuse at age 18 and older (usually perpetrated by a spouse or boyfriend). About 40 percent reported ongoing sexual abuse under the age of 18 (usually perpetrated by a father, stepfather, or other male relative), and 40 percent reported ongoing sexual abuse over the age of 17 (usually perpetrated by a spouse, partner, or boyfriend). Owen emphasizes that although most of the women did not experience gang activity or youthful incarcerations, for some of the women their "disordered" lives included early histories of juvenile crimes and gang membership. Owen (ibid.) found that once a girl/woman was involved with street life, she moved farther from attachments to conventional ties. Owen's (ibid., 61) final category of women's pathways to crime, spiraling marginality, is related to the intersection of substance abuse and street life: "The most often cited reason for not working was substance abuse problems.... The second most often cited reason for not working was 'made more money from crime and hustling,' with child care responsibilities a close third" (ibid., 61).

One of the most recent studies on girls' pathways to delinquency reported that *family issues* were key contributors, most commonly in the form of parental conflicts, absence, unavailability, and drug use (Bloom et al., 2003). Second, emotional, physical, and sexual *abuse* were instrumental as risk factors for delinquency, creating problems with secrecy, running away, and unhealthy sexual practices. School problems and difficulties and attitudes resisting help-seeking through adult authority figures were also identified as "risky" pathways for girls' subsequent delinquency. Some of the delinquent behaviors identified as "risky" for additional delinquent behaviors in this study included substance abuse and gang involvement.

In this discussion of feminist research on the pathways to crime, focusing largely on the victimization-to-offending trajectory, it is important to note Lisa Maher's (1997) feminist critique of both the traditional (non- or antifeminist) and feminist research. Maher claims that the approaches to women's involvement in crime dichotomize their *agency*, or self-determination. One approach (the more traditional approach) tends to ignore the gendered, classed, and raced world in which most female offenders exist, viewing them as "active subjects" seeking criminal opportunities with "over-endowed" agency (ibid., 1). The other approach, consistent with feminist pathways modeling, is in many ways the extreme opposite. Maher criticizes this approach for denying women any agency:

> . . . where women are portrayed as the passive victims of oppressive social structures, relations and substances, or some combination thereof. Women are cast as submissive objects, serving as mere automata for the reproduction of determining structures. Constituted by and through their status as victims, they are devoid of choice, responsibility, or accountability; fragments of social debris floundering in a theoretical tide of victimage. (ibid.)

Sterk (1999, 173) captures another dichotomy of agency in her study of crack-addicted women: "On the one hand, they saw themselves as victims, but on the other they recognized themselves as important, independent actors."

Numerous studies now document the pathways approach and the disproportionately high rates of trauma, particularly sexual and physical abuse, experienced by incarcerated women and girls, rates far higher than those reported in the general population (e.g., Browne, Miller, and Maguin, 1999; Coker et al., 1998; Cook et al., 2005; Daly, 1992; Gaarder and Belknap, 2002; Girshick, 1999; Johnson, 2003; Klein and Chao, 1995; Lake, 1993; Sharp and Marcus-Mendoza, 2001; Singer et al., 1995). Notably, a study of incarcerated mothers found the White women were more likely to report "bad homes" and "poor parenting" as their pathways to prison than African American or Latina women. African American women reported their mothers and other caretakers "as doing the best they could" in parenting them, but "the temptations of the street were too much for them to resist"; and Latinas were more likely to attribute their pathways to "the lure of quick money through drug sales" (Enos, 2001, 57). One recent study on women's and men's pathways to crack use in a non-inner-city sample (Evans, Forwyth, and Gautheir, 2002) reported that neglect (usually tied to intensive alcohol and/or drug use by parents) was a pathway for both men and women but that sexual abuse (mostly father-perpetrated incest) was a unique pathway to crack for women. Undeniably, trauma is a key pathway to offending.

A recent application of labeling theory identifies the way that labeling theory should be expanded to include *victims* of major traumas (Kenney 2002). This discussion is salient to the pathways research because it identifies the many ways that familial, social, and systemic responses to victims of significant trauma silence these victims and even label *them* as deviant (Kenney, 2002; Wortman and Lehman, 1983; Young, 1991).

With the exception of Widom's (1989) work, the pathways studies reported thus far are *retrospective* in nature, that is, asking individuals about their past experiences. A recent study was *prospective*; it sampled all of the cases of girl victims of child sexual abuse who went to an emergency room in the 1970s in a major northeastern city and sampled/matched them with girls with no such histories and then examined their offense histories (Siegel and Williams, 2003). Consistent with the pathways model, those sexually abused as girls were more likely to be arrested for running away (oddly, though, this was more often for cases where the girl was sexually abused by a stranger than by a family member), drug offenses, property offenses, and prostitution (ibid.).

SUMMARY

Theories attempting to explain the etiology of criminal behaviors (and reactions by the crime-processing system) have proposed biological, psychological, social, political, and economic causes. The earliest theories focused on biology and the individual, whereas more recent theories have focused on the societal, economic, and political sources of crime. Most of these theories were developed to explain male criminality. Until the mid-1970s, most theorists made little attempt to account for female criminality. When they did, their hypotheses were fraught with sexist stereotypes, often defining female crime in terms of sexuality. The findings of this research are inconsistent; it is still unclear how males' and females' socialization and responses by the criminal-processing system differ and how these may affect women's and girls' crime and delinquency rates.

In 1975, for the first time, a theory was developed to explain women's criminal behavior: women's "liberation" theory (Adler, 1975; Simon, 1975). Unfortunately, this theory was based on erroneous assumptions about the feminist movement, and statistics and their interpretations were often misleading. It is vital that future theory building and theory testing examine "pathways" to crime, sexuality, family factors, social and economic status, same-sex friendships, and mixed-sex friendships as equally relevant (or in the case of sexuality, perhaps irrelevant) for studies of both males and females (Campbell, 1990). Future theory building cannot assume, moreover, that women or girls as a group behave similarly to each other. Richie's (1996) work is a prime example.

Although there is a renewed interest in the troubling approach to use biology to determine gender differences in crime and to explain men's violence against women, at the same time, some of the new feminist and pro-feminist theories are offering exciting ways to assess how both girls' and boys' life experiences (e. g., experiences with abuse, schools, peers, and so on) are likely related to their subsequent offending. Unfortunately, the life course research, to date, rarely includes women in the sample, and even the research on men, though promising, does not appear to adequately assess childhood abuse variables. However, it offers the potential to enhance understanding of girls' trajectories into crime if girls and women are included in the samples and childhood victimizations and experiences can be validly measured. To date, the most useful data regarding understanding girls' and women's, and perhaps boys' and men's, entries into delinquency and crime, are the pathways models. Although they are considered somewhat "new," studies confirming a pathways model date back to the 1970s and have consistently suggested the need to understand the role of childhood and adulthood traumas as precursors to offending.

One study that uses qualitative data (interviews) with high-risk (for delinquency) youths perhaps provides the best testing of many of the traditional and more current theories. Jean Bottcher's (2001) study draws on detailed interviews with siblings of incarcerated boys and exemplifies the complexity of how gender and delinquency interact (see Exhibit 2.5). She stresses the role of *social practices* in how they simultaneously and routinely constrain girls' and encourage boys' delinquency. Specifically, she identifies how daily activities, sexual interests, surviving

E X H I B I T 2.5 Jean Bottcher's (2001) Social Practices of Gender That Restrain Girls' and Enable or Reward Boys' Delinquency

Making Friends and Having Fun

- **Friendship Groups**: Sex-segregated for both boys and girls; fewer in girls' groups
- **Boundary Maintenance**: Separation of boys and girls was enforced by the boys; delinquent boys more likely than nondelinquent boys to exclude girls
- **Types of Diversion**: More peer pressure for boys to be delinquent; girls spend more time with mothers and boys more time with fathers
- **Ideology of Gender**: Girls and boys viewed boys as more naturally bold, stubborn, and macho and girls as more naturally weak and cautious
- **Daily Paths**: Boys had more freedom in where they could go, what they could do, who they could be with, and how late they could be out

Relating Sexually and Becoming Parents

- **Heterosexual Relations**: Boys more sexually active, more partners, and less consumed by intimate relationships
- **Male Dominance**: Boys had more power in nature and pace of intimate relations
- **Meanings**: Girls more committed to intimate relationships and children than boys; boys exaggerate while girls understate sexual experiences
- **Female Restrictions**: Girls more restricted by parents from spending time with opposite sex and restricted from dating longer due to fear of pregnancy
- **Life Paths**: Girls assume more child-care responsibilities; girls establish independence from their parents sooner than boys

Surviving Hardship and Finding Purpose

- **Responsibility**: Girls do more work around the house
- **Discipline**: Boys more freedom outside the home and less accountable to parents
- **Focus**: Girls more focused on their intimate relationships and boys more focused on their friendships with other boys
- **Abuse**: Girls more likely to report sexual abuse, abuse from family members, and intimate partner abuse
- **Timing**: The older males increasingly focused on intimate partners and families and the older girls increasingly focused on work and school

SOURCE: Jean Bottcher. 2001. "Social Practices of Gender: How Gender Relates to Delinquency in the Everyday Lives of High Risk Youths." *Criminology* 39:893–931.

hardship and finding purpose, and having fun and spending time with peers are all manifestations of male dominance. For example, becoming a parent proved to be a deterrent to delinquency for girls but not for boys. "This study suggests that high-risk families usher boys out of their homes and into crime. Conversely, the most troubled of these families almost force girls out" (ibid., 922).

This chapter reported on numerous theories, many of which hold some promise for explaining offending and for examining gender and offending. One recent poignant overview of criminological theories emphasizes the need to examine not only families and childhood but also the interplay with institutions in U.S. society. Specifically, Fox and Benson (2000, 18) note that larger numbers of women than ever spend time incarcerated in institutions for offenders and that these institutions substitute family roles and destroy the families that were once "the surest pathways away from crime." Future research needs to include broader definitions of life experiences and understand how social processes are gendered, and thus how lawbreaking is also gendered.

REFERENCES

Abelson, Elaine S. 1989. The Invention of Kleptomania. *Signs* 15:123–143.

Adams, David. 1992. Biology Does Not Make Men More Aggressive than Women. Pp. 17–26 in *Of Mice and Women: Aspects of Female Aggression*, edited by K. Bjorkqvistand and P. Niemela. San Diego: Academic Press.

Adler, Freda. 1975. *Sisters in Crime: The Rise of the New Female Criminal*. New York: McGraw Hill.

Agnew, Robert. 1985. A Revised Theory of Delinquency. *Social Forces* 64:151–167.

———. 1992. Foundation for a General Theory of Crime. *Criminology* 30:47–87.

———. 2001. Building on the Foundation of General Strain Theory. *Journal of Research in Crime & Delinquency* 38:319–361.

———. 2002. Experienced, Vicarious, and Anticipated Strain. *Justice Quarterly* 19:603–632.

Alarid, Leanne Fiftal, Velmer S. Burton, and Francis T. Cullen. 2000. Gender and Crime among Felony Offenders. *Journal of Research in Crime and Delinquency* 37:171–199.

Arnold, Regina A. 1990. Women of Color: Processes of Victimization and Criminalization of Black Women. *Social Justice* 17:153–166.

Baker, Robin. 1996. *Sperm Wars: The Science of Sex*. New York: Basic Books.

Baron, Stephen W. 2004. General Strain, Street Youth and Crime: A Test of Agnew's Revised Theory. *Criminology* 42:457–483.

Bartusch, Dawn J., and Ross L. Matsueda. 1996. Gender, Reflected Appraisals and Labeling. *Social Forces* 75:145–177.

Becker, Howard S. 1963. *Outsiders: Studies in the Sociology of Deviance*. New York: Free Press.

Belknap, Joanne. 1997. Variations in Perspectives and Quality in Three Books on Rape. *Criminal Justice Review* 22:77–84.

———. 2001. *The Invisible Woman: Gender, Crime, and Justice*, 2nd ed. Belmont, CA: Wadsworth/Thomson Learning.

Bell, Derrick A. 1973. *Race, Racism and American Law*. Boston: Little, Brown, and Company.

———. 1992. *Faces at the Bottom of the Well: The Permanence of Racism*. New York: Basic Books.

Benton, David. 1992. Hormones and Human Aggression. Pp. 37–48 in *Of Mice and Women: Aspects of Female Aggression*, edited by K. Bjorkqvistand and P. Niemela. San Diego: Academic Press.

Bernburg, Jon Gunnar, and Marvin D. Krohn. 2003. Labeling, Life Chances and Adult Crime. *Criminology* 41:1287–1318.

Bjorkqvist, Kaj, and Pirkko Niemela. 1992a. New Trends in the Study of Female Aggression. Pp. 3–16 in *Of Mice and Women: Aspects of Female Aggression*, edited by K. Bjorkqvist and P. Niemela. San Diego: Academic Press.

Bjorkqvist, Kaj, and Pirkko Niemela (Eds.). 1992b. *Of Mice and Women: Aspects of Female Aggression.* San Diego: Academic Press.

Blackwell, Brenda Sims. 2000. Perceived Sanction Threats, Gender, and Crime: A Test and Elaboration of Power-Control Theory. *Criminology* 38:439–489.

———. 2003. Power-Control and Social Bonds: Exploring the Effect of Patriarchy. *Criminal Justice Studies* 16: 131–152.

Blackwell, Brenda Sims, Christine S. Sellers, and Sheila M. Schlaupitz. 2002. Victimization, Offending, and Deviant Role Exits: A Replication and Extension of Power-Control Theory. *Canadian Review of Sociology and Anthropology* 3:1–19.

Bloom, Barbara, Barbara Owen, Jill Rosenbaum, and Elizabeth Piper Deschenes. 2003. Focusing on Girls and Young Women: A Gendered Perspective on Female Delinquency. *Women & Criminal Justice* 14:117–136.

Bonger, Willem. 1969. *Criminality and Economic Conditions.* Bloomington: Indiana University Press.

Booth, Alan, and D. Wayne Osgood. 1993. The Influence of Testosterone on Deviance in Adulthood. *Criminology* 31:93–118.

Bottcher, Jean. 1995. Gender as Social Control. *Justice Quarterly* 12:33–58.

———. 2001. Social Practices of Gender: How Gender Relates to Delinquency in the Everyday Lives of High-Risk Youth. *Criminology* 39: 893–931.

Box, Steven, and Chris Hale. 1983. Liberation and Female Criminality in England and Wales. *British Journal of Criminology* 23:35.

———. 1984. Liberation/Emancipation, Economic Marginalization, or Less Chivalry: The Relevance of Three Arguments to Female Crime Patterns in England and Wales, 1951–1980. *Criminology* 22:473–498.

Britton, Dana M. 2000. Feminism in Criminology: Engendering the Law. *Annals of the American Academy of Political and Social Science* 571:57–76.

Broidy, Lisa M. 1995. Direct Supervision and Delinquency. *Journal of Criminal Justice* 23:541–554.

———. 2001. A Test of General Strain Theory. *Criminology* 39:9–36.

Broidy, Lisa, and Robert Agnew. 1997. Gender and Crime: A General Strain Theory Perspective. *Journal of Research in Crime and Delinquency* 34: 275–306.

Brown, Tony. 2003. Critical Race Theory Speaks to the Sociology of Mental Health. *Journal of Health and Social Behavior* 44:292–301.

Browne, Angela, Brenda Miller, and Eugene Maguin. 1999. Prevalence and Severity of Lifetime Physical and Sexual Victimization among Incarcerated Women. *International Journal of Law and Psychiatry* 22:301–322.

Brownmiller, Susan. 1975. *Against Our Will: Men, Women and Rape.* New York: Simon and Schuster.

Bunch, Barbara J., Linda A. Foley, and Susana P. Urbina. 1983. The Psychology of Violent Female Offenders: A Sex-Role Perspective. *The Prison Journal* 63:66–79.

Burch, Rebecca L., and Gordon G. Gallup, Jr. 2004. Pregnancy as a Stimulus for Domestic Violence. *Journal of Family Violence* 19, 243–247.

Cahill, Ann J. 2001. *Rethinking Rape.* Ithaca, NY: Cornell University Press.

Campbell, Anne. 1987. Self Definition by Rejection: The Case of Gang Girls. *Social Problems* 34:451–466.

————. 1990. On the Invisibility of the Female Delinquent Peer Group. *Women & Criminal Justice* 2:41–62.

Cernkovich, Stephen, and Peggy Giordano. 1979. A Comparative Analysis of Male and Female Delinquency. *The Sociological Quarterly* 20:131–145.

Chesney-Lind, Meda, and Noelie Rodriguez. 1983. Women under Lock and Key. *Prison Journal* 63:47–65.

Chilton, Ronald, and Susan K. Datesman. 1987. Gender, Race, and Crime: An Analysis of Urban Trends, 1960–1980. *Gender and Society* 1:152–171.

Clark, S. M. 1964. Similarities in Components of Female and Male Delinquency: Implications for Sex-Role Theory. P. 217 in *Interdisciplinary Problems in Criminology*, edited by W. C. Reckless and C. L. Newman. Columbus: Ohio State University.

Cloward, R. A., and L. E. Ohlin. 1960. *Delinquency and Opportunity: A Theory of Delinquent Gangs*. New York: Free Press.

Cohen, Albert K. 1955. *Delinquent Boys: The Culture of the Gang*. New York: Free Press.

Coker, Ann L., Nilam J. Patel, Shanthi Krishnaswami, Wendy Schmidt, and Donna I. Richter. 1998. Childhood Forced Sex and Cervical Dysplasia among Women Prison Inmates. *Violence Against Women* 4:595–608.

Comack, Elizabeth. 1996. *Women in Trouble: Connecting Women's Law Violations to their Histories of Abuse*. Halifax, NS Fernwood Publishing.

Cook, Sarah L., Sharon G. Smith, Chatal P. Tusher, and Jerris Raiford. 2005. Self-Reports of Traumatic Events in a Random Sample of Incarcerated Women. *Women & Criminal Justice* 16:107–126.

Cowie, John, Valerie Cowie, and Eliot Slater. 1968. *Delinquency in Girls*. London: Heinemann.

Coyne, Jerry A., and Andrew Berry. 2000. Rape as an Adaptation: Is this Contentious Hypothesis Advocacy, Not Science? *Nature* 404:121–122.

Crafts, Hannah. 2002. *The Bondwoman's Narrative*. New York: Warner Books.

Crawford, Charles C., and Marc A. Johnston. 1999. An Evolutionary Model of Courtship and Mating as Social Exchange. *Jurimetrics* 39:181–200.

Crenshaw, Kimberle W. 2002. The First Decade: Critical Reflections, or "A Foot in the Closing Door." Pp. 9–31 in *Crossroads, Directions, and a New Critical Race Theory*, edited by F. Valdes, J. M. Culp, and A. P. Harris. Philadelphia: Temple University Press.

Cressey, Donald. 1964. *Delinquency, Crime, and Differential Association*. The Hague: Martinus Nijhoff.

Crites, Laura. 1976. *The Female Offender*. Lexington, MA: D.C. Heath.

Cullen, Francis T., Kathryn M. Golden, and John B. Cullen. 1979. Sex and Delinquency. *Criminology* 17:301–310.

Curran, Daniel J. 1984. The Myth of the "New" Female Delinquent. *Crime and Delinquency* 30:386–399.

Daly, Kathleen. 1992. Women's Pathways to Felony Court: Feminist Theories of Lawbreaking and Problems of Representation. *Review of Law and Women's Studies* 2:11–52.

Datesman, Susan, Frank Scarpitti, and Richard Stephenson. 1975. Female Delinquency: An Application of Self and Opportunity Theories. *Journal of Research in Crime and Delinquency* 12:107–123.

Davies, Scott, and Julian Tanner. 2003. The Long Arm of the Law: Effects of Labeling on Employment. *Social Forces* 44:385–404.

Davis, Angela Y. 1981. *Women, Race, and Class*. New York: Vintage Press.

De Coster, Stacy, and Karen Heimer. 2001. The Relationship between Law Violation and Depression. *Criminology* 39:799–836.

DeKeseredy, Walter S. 1996. The Left-Realist Perspective on Race, Class, and Gender. Pp. 46–72 in *Race, Gender, and Class in Criminology*, edited by M. D. Schwartz and D. Milovanovic. New York: Garland.

Dembo, Richard, Gary Grandon, Lawrence La Voie, and William Burgos. 1986. Parents and Drugs Revisited: Some Further Evidence in Support of Social Learning Theory. *Criminology* 24:85–103.

Development Assistance Committee. 1999. DAC Guidelines for Gender Equality and Women's Empowerment in Development Co-Operation. OECD Publications, 2, rue Andre-Pascal, 7577 Paris Cedex 16- No. 80478 1999, 46pp. http://www.oecd.org/dataoecd/56/46/28313843.pdf

Dornfeld, Maude, and Candace Kruttschnitt. 1992. Do the Stereotypes Fit? Mapping Gender-Specific Outcomes and Risk Factors. *Criminology* 30:397–420.

Elder, Glen H. 1985. Perspectives in the Life Course. Pp. 23–49 in *Life Course Dynamics*, edited by G. H. Elder. Ithaca, NY: Cornell University Press.

Ellis, Lee. 1993. Rape as a Biosocial Phenomenon. Pp. 17–41 in *Sexual Aggression: Issues in Etiology, Assessment, and Treatment*, edited by G. N. Hall, R. Hisrchman, J. Graham, and M. Zragoza. Washington, DC: Taylor and Francis.

Ellis, Lee, and Anthony Walsh. 1997. Gene-Based Evolutionary Theories in Criminology. *Criminology* 35:229–276.

Enos, Sandra. 2001. *Mothering from the Inside*. Albany: State University of New York Press.

Erikson, Kai T. 1962. Notes on the Sociology of Deviance. *Social Problems* 9:309–314.

Esbensen, Finn-Aage, and David Huizinga. 1993. Gangs, Drugs, and Delinquency in a Survey of Urban Youth. *Criminology* 31:565–590.

Evans, Rhonda D., Craig J. Forwyth, and DeAnn K. Gautheir. 2002. Gendered Pathways into and Experiences within Crack Cultures Outside of the Inner City. *Deviant Behavior* 23:483–510.

Fagan, Abigail A. 2001. The Gender Cycle of Violence. *Violence and Victims* 168:457–474.

———. 2003. The Short- and Long-Term Effects of Adolescent Violent Victimization Experienced within the Family and Community. *Violence and Victims* 18:445–459.

Faith, Karlene. 1993. *Unruly Women: The Politics of Confinement and Resistance*. Vancouver: Press Gang Publishers.

Farley, Melissa, and Howard Barkan. 1998. Prostitution, Violence, and Posttraumatic Stress Disorder. *Women & Health* 27:37–49.

Farrington, David P. 1992. Criminal Career Research in the United Kingdom. *British Journal of Criminology* 32:521–536.

Fausto-Sterling, Anne. 1985. *Myths of Gender: Biological Theory about Women and Men*. New York: Basic Books.

———. 2000. Beyond Difference: Feminism and Evolutionary Psychology. Pp. 209–227 in *Alas, Poor Darwin*, edited by H. Rose and S. Rose. New York: Harmony Books.

Feinman, Clarice. 1986. *Women in the Criminal Justice System*, 2nd ed. New York: Praeger.

Figueira-McDonough, Josephine. 1984. Feminism and Delinquency: In Search of an Elusive Link. *British Journal of Criminology* 24:325–342.

Figueira-McDonough, Josephine, William H. Barton, and Rosemary C. Sarri. 1981. Normal Deviance: Gender Similarities in Adolescent Subcultures. Pp. 17–45 in *Comparing Female and Male Offenders*, edited by M. Q. Warren. Beverly Hills, CA: Sage.

Figueira-McDonough, Josephine, and E. Selo. 1980. A Reformulation of the 'Equal Opportunity' Explanation of Female Delinquency. *Crime and Delinquency* (July): 333–343.

Figueredo, Aurelio Jose, and Laura Ann McCloskey. 1993. Sex, Money, and Paternity: The Evolutionary Psychology of Domestic Violence. *Etiology & Sociobiology* 14:353–379.

Figueredo, Aurelio Jose, Victor Corral-Verdugo, Martha Frias-Armenta, Karen J. Bachar, Janine White, Prentiss L. McNeill, Beth R. Kirsner, and Irasema del Pilar Castell-Ruiz. 2001. Blood, Solidarity, Status, and Honor: 2001. The Sexual Balance of Power and Spousal Abuse in Sonora, Mexico. *Evolutiona and Human Behavior* 22:295–328.

Flavin, Jeanne. 2001. Feminism for the Mainstream Criminologist. *Journal of Criminal Justice* 29:271–285.

Fox, Greer Litton, and Michael L. Benson. 2000. Families, Crime and Criminal Justice: Charting the Linkages. *Families, Crime, and Criminal Justice* 2:1–21.

Fox, Lana, and Fran Sugar. 1990. *Survey of Federally Sentenced Aboriginal Women in the Community*. Canada: Correctional Service of Canada, 16pp. (or available at http://www.csc-scc.gc.ca/text/prgrm/fsw/nativesurvey/toce_e.shtml).

Freud, Sigmund. 1933. *New Introductory Lectures on Psychoanalysis*. New York: W. W. Norton.

Frigon, Sylvie. 1995. A Genealogy of Women's Madness. Pp. 20–48 in *Gender and Crime*, edited by R. E. Dobash, R. P. Dobash, and

L. Noaks. Cardiff: University of Wales Press.

Gaarder, Emily, and Joanne Belknap. (2002). Tenuous Borders: Girls Transferred to Adult Court. *Criminology* 40:481–517.

Gilfus, Mary E. 1992. From Victims to Survivors to Offenders: Women's Routes of Entry and Immersion into Street Crime. *Women & Criminal Justice* 4:63–90.

Giordano, Peggy C. 1978. Girls, Guys, and Gangs: The Changing Social Context of Female Delinquency. *Journal of Criminal Law and Criminology* 69:126–132.

Girshick, Lori B. 1999. *No Safe Haven: Stories of Women in Prison*. Boston: Northeastern University Press.

Gordon, David. 1973. Capitalism, Class, and Crime in America. *Crime and Delinquency* 19:163–186.

Gottfredson, Michael R., and Travis Hirschi. 1990. *A General Theory of Crime*. Stanford, CA: Stanford University Press.

Guy-Sheftall, B. (Ed.). 1995. *Words of Fire: An Anthology of African-American Feminist Thought*. New York: The New Press.

Hagan, John. 1988. *Structural Criminology*. Cambridge, UK: Polity.

Hagan, John, A. R. Gillis, and John H. Simpson. 1985. The Class Structure of Gender and Delinquency. *American Journal of Sociology* 90:1151–1178.

Hagan, John, John H. Simpson, and A. R. Gillis. 1979. The Sexual Stratification of Social Control: A Gender-Based Perspective on Crime and Delinquency. *British Journal of Sociology* 30:25.

———. 1987. Class in the Household: A Power-Control Theory of Gender and Delinquency. *American Journal of Sociology* 92:788–816.

Hall, Gordon N., Richard Hirschman, John Graham, and Maira Zragoza (Eds.). 1993. *Sexual Aggression.* Washington, DC: Taylor and Francis.

Handwerker, W. Penn. 1998. Why Violence? A Test of Hypotheses Representing Three Discourses on the Roots of Domestic Violence. *Human Organization* 57:200–208.

Harris, Anthony. 1977. Sex and Theories of Deviance: Toward a Functional Theory of Deviant Type-Scripts. *American Sociological Review* 42:3–16.

Harris, Christine. R. 2003. A Review of Sex Differences in Sexual Jealousy, Including Self-Report Data, Psychophysiological Responses, Interpersonal Violence, and Morbid Jealousy. *Personality and Social Psychology Review* 7:102–128.

Harris, Mary B. 1996. Aggression, Gender, and Ethnicity. *Aggression and Violent Behavior* 1:123–146.

Hayes, Terrell. A. 2000. Stigmatizing Indebtedness: Implications for Labeling Theory. *Symbolic Interaction* 23:29–46.

Heidensohn, Frances M. 1985. *Women and Crime: The Life of the Female Offender.* New York: New York University Press.

Heimer, Karen, and Stacy De Coster. 1999. The Gendering of Violent Delinquency. *Criminology* 37:277–318.

Hill, Gary D., and Maxine P. Atkinson. 1988. Gender, Familial Control, and Delinquency. *Criminology* 26:127–149.

Hill, Gary D., and Elizabeth M. Crawford. 1990. Women, Race, and Crime. *Criminology* 28:601–626.

Hindelang, M. 1971. Age, Sex and Versatility of Delinquent Involvement. *Social Problems* 21:471.

———. 1973. Cases of Delinquency: A Partial Replication and Extension. *Social Problems* 21:471.

Hirschi, Travis. 1969. *Cases of Delinquency.* Berkeley: University of California Press.

Hoffman, John P., and Felicia Gray Cerbone. 1999. Stressful Life Events and Delinquency Escalation in Early Adolescence. *Criminology* 37:343–373.

Hoffman, John P, and S. Susan Su. 1997. The Conditional Effects of Stress on Delinquency and Drug Use: A Strain Theory Assessment of Sex Differences. *Journal of Research in Crime & Delinquency* 34:46–78.

Hoffman-Bustamante, Dale. 1973. The Nature of Female Criminality. *Issues in Criminology* 8:117–136.

hooks, bell. (2000). *Feminist Theory: From Margin to Center,* 2nd ed. Cambridge, MA: South End.

Horwitz, Allan V. 1977. The Pathways into Psychiatric Treatment: Some Differences between Men and Women. *Journal of Health and Social Behavior* 18:169–178.

Howe, Adrian. 1994. *Punish and Critique: Towards a Feminist Analysis of Penality.* London: Routledge.

Huang, Bu, Rick Kosterman, Richard F. Catalano, J. David Hawkins, and Robert D. Abbott. 2001. Modeling Mediation in the Etiology of Violent Behavior in Adolescence. *Criminology* 39:75–107.

Huesmann, L. Rowell, Leonard D. Eron, Monroe M. Lefkowitz, and Leopold O. Walder. 1984. Stability of Aggression over Time and Generations. *Developmental Psychology* 20:1120–1134.

Hughes, Lorine A. 2005. The Representation of Females in Criminological Research. *Women & Criminal Justice* 16:1–27.

James, Jennifer, and Jane Meyerding. 1977. Early Sexual Experiences and Prostitution. *American Journal of Psychiatry* 134(12):1381–1385.

Jang, Sung Joon, and Marvin D. Krohn. 1995. Developmental Patterns of Sex Differences in Delinquency among African American Adolescents: A Test of the Sex-Invariance Hypothesis. *Journal of Quantitative Criminology* 11:195–222.

Janssen, Patricia A., Tonia L. Nicholls, Ravinesh A. Kuma, Harry Stefanka-kis, Alicia L. Spidel, and Elizabeth M. Simpson. 2005. Of Mice and Men: Will the Intersection of Social Science and Genetics Create New Approaches for Intimate Partner Violence? *Journal of Interpersonal Violence* 20:61–71.

Jensen, Gary F., and K. Thompson. 1990. What's Class Got to Do with It? A Further Examination of Power-Control Theory. *American Journal of Sociology* 95:1009–1023.

Jensen, Gary J., and Raymond Eve. 1976. Sex Differences in Delinquency. *Criminology* 13:427–448.

Joe, Karen A., and Meda Chesney-Lind. 1995. "Just Every Mother's Angel": An Analysis of Gender and Ethnic Variations in Youth Gang Membership. *Gender and Society* 9:408–431.

Johnson, Paula C. 2003. *Inner Lives: Voices of African American Women in Prison.* New York: New York University.

Johnson, Richard E. 1986. Family Structure and Delinquency: General Patterns and Gender Differences. *Criminology* 24:65–84.

Kanin, Eugene J. 1985. Date Rapists: Differential Sexual Socialization and Relative Deprivation. *Archives of Sexual Behavior* 14:219–231.

Kaplin, Hoard B., and Cheng-Hsien Lin. 2000. Deviant Identity as a Moderator of the Relation between Negative Self-Feelings and Deviant Behavior. *Journal of Early Adolescence* 20:150–177.

Kenney, J. Scott. 2002. Victims of Crime and Labeling Theory. *Deviant Behavior* 23:235–265.

King, D. K. (1988). Multiple Jeopardy, Multiple Consciousness: The Context of Black Feminist Ideology. *Signs: Journal of Women in Culture and Society* 14:42–72.

Kitsuse, John I. 1962. Societal Reaction to Deviant Behavior: Problems of Theory and Method. *Social Problems* 9:247–256.

Klein, Dorie. 1980. The Etiology of Female Crime: A Review of the Literature. Pp. 70–105 in *Women, Crime, and Justice*, edited by S. K. Datesman and F. R. Scarpitti. New York: Oxford University Press.

Klein, Dorie, and June Kress. 1976. Any Woman's Blues: A Critical Overview of Women, Crime, and the Criminal Justice System. *Crime and Social Justice* 5:34–49.

Klein, Hugh, and Betty S. Chao. 1995. Sexual Abuse during Childhood and Adolescence as Predictors of HIV-Related Sexual Risk during Adult-hood among Female Sexual Partners of Drug Users. *Violence Against Women* 1:55–76.

Konopka, Gisela. 1966. *The Adolescent Girl in Conflict.* Englewood Cliffs, NJ: Prentice Hall.

Kruttschnitt, Candace. 1996. Contributions of Quantitative Methods to the Study of Gender and Crime, or Bootstrapping Our Way into the Theoretical Thicket. *Journal of Quantitative Criminology* 12:135–161.

LaGrange, Teresa C., and Rovert A. Silverman. 1999. Low Social-Control and Opportunity: Testing the General Theory of Crime as an Explanation for Gender Differences in Delinquency. *Criminology* 37:41–72.

Laidler, Karen Joe, and Geoffrey Hunt. 2001. Accomplishing Femininity among the Girls in the Gang. *British Journal of Criminology* 41:656–678.

Lake, E. S. 1993. An Exploration of the Violent Victim Experiences of

Female Offenders. *Violence and Victims* 8:41–51.

Laub, John H., Daniel S. Nagin, and Robert J. Sampson. 1998. Trajectories of Change in Criminal Offending. *American Sociological Review* 63:225–238.

Laub, John H., and Janet L. Lauritsen. 1993. Violent Criminal Behavior over the Life Course: A Review of the Longitudinal and Comparative Research. *Violence and Victims* 8:235–252.

Laub, John H., and Robert J. Sampson. 1993. Turning Points in the Life Course: Why Change Matters to the Study of Crime. *Criminology* 31:301–325.

Lauritsen, Janet L. 1993. Sibling Resemblance in Juvenile Delinquency. *Criminology* 31:387–410.

Lemert, Edwin M. 1951. *Social Pathology: A Systematic Approach to the Theory of Sociopathic Behavior*. New York: McGraw Hill.

Leonard, Eileen B. 1982. *Women, Crime, and Society: A Critique of Criminology Theory*. New York: Longman.

Lerman, Paul. 1966. Individual Values, Peer Values and Subcultural Delinquency. *American Sociological Review* 33:219–235.

Lesch, Klaus P., and Ursula Merschdorf. 2000. Impulsivity, Aggression, and Seotonin: A Molecular Psychobiolgical Perspective. *Behavioral Sciences and the Law* 18:581–604.

Li, Spencer De. 1999. Social Control, Delinquency, and Youth Status Achievement: A Developmental Approach. *Sociological Perspectives* 42:305–324.

———. 2004. The Impacts of Self-control and Social Bonds on Juvenile Delinquency in a National Sample of Midadolescents. *Deviant Behavior* 25:351–373.

Loeber, Rolf. 1996. Developmental Continuity, Change, and Pathways in Male Juvenile Problem Behavior. Pp. 1–28 in *Delinquency and Crime*, edited by J. David Hawkins. New York: Cambridge University Press.

Loeber, Rolf, and David P. Farrington. 2000. Young Children Who Commit Crime. *Development and Psychopathology* 12:737–762.

Loeber, Rolf, and Dale Hay. 1997. Key Issues in the Development of Aggression and Violence from Childhood to Early Adulthood. *Annual Review of Psychology* 48:371–410.

Lombroso, Cesare, and William Ferrero. 1895. *The Female Offender*. London: Fisher Unwin.

———. 2004. *Criminal Woman, the Prostitute, and the Normal Woman* (trans. Nicole Hahn Rafter and Mary Gibson). Durham, NC: Duke University Press.

Lopez, Ian F. Haney. 1996. *White by Law: The Legal Construction of Race*. New York: New York University Press.

———. 2003. *Racism on Trial: The Chicano Fight for Justice*. Cambridge, MA: The Belknap Press of Harvard University Press.

Lorber, Judith. 1994. *Paradoxes in Gender*. New Haven, CT: Yale University Press.

Luthar, Suniya S., and Karen D'Avanzo. 1999. Contextual Actors in Substance Use. *Development and Psychopathology* 11:845–867.

Lynch, Michael J., and W. Byron Groves. 1989. *A Primer in Radical Criminology*, 2nd ed. New York: Harrow and Heston.

Maher, Lisa. 1997. *Sexed Work: Gender, Race and Resistance in a Brooklyn Drug Market*. Oxford, England: Clarendon Press.

Mann, Coramae Richey. 1984. *Female Crime and Delinquency*. Montgomery: University of Alabama Press.

Mazerolle, Paul. 1998. Gender, General Strain, and Delinquency: An Empirical Examination. *Justice Quarterly* 15:65–91.

McCarthy, Bill, John Hagan, and Todd S. Woodward. 1999. In the Company of Women: Structure and Agency in a Revised Power-Control Theory of Gender and Delinquency. *Criminology* 37:761–788.

McCarthy, Bill, Diane Felmlee, and John Hagan. 2004. Girlfriends are Better. *Criminology* 42:805–835.

Mears, Daniel P., Matthew Ploeger, and Mark Warr. 1998. Explaining the Gender Gap in Delinquency. *Journal of Research in Crime and Delinquency* 35:351–466.

Merton, Robert K. 1938. Social Structure and Anomie. *American Sociological Review* 3:672–682.

———. 1949. *Social Theory and Social Structure*. Glencoe, IL: Free Press.

Messerschmidt, James W. 1988. From Marx to Bonger: Socialist Writings on Women, Gender, and Crime. *Sociological Inquiry* 58:378–392.

———. 1993. Masculinities and Crime. Lanham, MD: Rowman & Littlefield.

Messner, Michael. A. 2000. Barbie Girls versus Sea Monsters: Children Constructing Gender. *Gender & Society* 14:765–784.

Miller, Susan L., and Cynthia Burack. 1993. A Critique of Gottfredson and Hirschi's General Theory of Crime: Selective (In)Attention to Gender and Power Positions. *Women & Criminal Justice* 4:115–134.

Moffitt, Terrie E. 1990. Juvenile Delinquency and Attention Deficit Disorder: Boys' Development Trajectories from Age 3 to Age 15. *Child Development* 61:893–910.

———. 1993. Adolescence-Limited and Life-Course-Persistent Antisocial Behavior: A Developmental Taxonomy. *Psychological Review* 100:674–701.

Moore, Joan W. 1999. Gang Members' Families. Pp. 159–176 in *Female Gangs in America: Essays on Girls, Gangs and Gender*, edited by M. Chesney-Lind and J. M. Hagedorn. Chicago: Lakeview Press.

Morash, Merry. 1983. Gangs, Groups, and Delinquency. *British Journal of Criminology* 23:309–335.

———. 1986. Gender, Peer Group Experiences, and Seriousness of Delinquency. *Journal of Research in Crime and Delinquency* 23:43–67.

Morash, Merry, and Meda Chesney-Lind. 1991. A Re-Formulation and Patriarchal Test of the Power Control Theory of Delinquency. *Justice Quarterly* 8:347–378.

Morris, Allison. 1987. *Women, Crime and Criminal Justice*. Oxford, England: Basil Blackwell.

Morris, Ruth R. 1964. Female Delinquency and Relational Problems. *Social Forces* 43:82–88.

———. 1965. Attitudes toward Delinquency by Delinquents, Non-Delinquents and Their Friends. *British Journal of Criminology* 5:249–265.

Naffine, Ngaire. 1987. *Female Crime: The Construction of Women in Criminology*. Sydney, Australia: Allen and Unwin.

———. 1996. *Feminism and Criminology*. Philadelphia: Temple University Press.

Nagasawa, Richard, Zhenchao Qian, and Paul Wong. 2000. Social Control Theory as a Theory of Conformity: The Case of Asian/Pacific Drug and Alcohol Nonuse. *Sociological Perspectives* 43:581–603.

Nagin, Daniel S., David P. Farrington, and Terrie E. Moffitt. 1995. Life-Course Trajectories of Different

Types of Offenders. *Criminology* 33:111–138.

Nakhaie, M. Reza, Robert A. Silverman, and Teresa C. LaGrange. 2000. Self-Control and Social Control: An Examination of Gender, Ethnicity, Class, and Delinquency. *Canadian Journal of Sociology* 25:35–59.

Norland, Stephen, Randall C. Wessel, and Neal Shover. 1981. Masculinity and Delinquency. *Criminology* 19:421–433.

Olds, David, Charles R. Henderson, Jr., R. Cole, J. Eckenrode, H. Kitzman, D. Luckey, L. Pettitt, K. Sidora, P. Morris, and J. Powers. 1998. Long-Term Effects of Nurse Home Visitation on Children's Criminal and Antisocial Behavior: 15-Year Follow-Up of a Randomized Trial. The *Journal of the American Medical Association* 280:1238–1244.

Olson, David E., Arthur J. Lurigio, and Magnus Seng. 2000. A Comparison of Female and Male Probationers. *Women & Criminal Justice* 11:65–79.

Owen, Barbara. 1998. *In the Mix: Struggle and Survival in a Women's Prison.* Albany: State University of New York Press.

Piquero, Alex R., John M. MacDonald, and Karen F. Parker. 2002. Race, Local Life Circumstances, and Criminal Activity. *Social Science Quarterly* 83:654–670.

Piquero, Alex R., Robert Brame, Paul Mazerolle, and Rudy Haapanen. 2003. Crime in Emerging Adulthood. *Criminology* 40:137–169.

Piquero, Alex and Paul Mazerolle, (Eds.). 2000. *Life-Course Criminology: Contemporary and Classic Readings.* Belmont, CA: Wadsworth.

Platt, Anthony. 1975. Prospects for a Radical Criminology in the U.S. Pp. 95–112 in *Critical Criminology,* edited by I. Taylor, P. Walton, and J. Young. London: Routledge and Kegan Paul.

Pollak, Otto. 1950. *The Criminality of Women.* Philadelphia: University of Pennsylvania Press.

———. 1961. *The Criminality of Women.* New York: A. S. Barnes.

Potter, Hillary. 2004. Intimate Partner Violence against African American Women: The Effects of Social Structure and Black Culture on Patterns of Abuse. A dissertation.

Quinney, Richard. 1972. The Ideology of Law: Notes for a Radical Alternative to Repression. *Issues in Criminology* 7:1–35.

———. 1975. *Criminology: Analysis and Critique of Crime in America.* Boston: Little, Brown.

Rafter, Nicole H., and E. M. Natalizia. 1981. Marxist Feminism: Implications for Criminal Justice. *Crime and Delinquency* 27:81–98.

Rafter, Nicole Hahn and Mary Gibson. 2004. Editors' Introduction Pp. 3–33 in *Criminal Woman, the Prostitute, and the Normal Woman* (translated by Nicole Hahn Rafter and Mary Gibson). Durham, NC: Duke University Press.

Rahav, Michael. 1984. Norm Set and Deviant Behavior: The Case of Age-Sex Norms. *Deviant Behavior* 5:151–179.

Rankin, Bruce, H., and James M. Quane. 2000. Social Contexts and Urban Adolescent Outcomes. *Social Problems* 49:79–100.

Rasche, Christine. 1975. The Female Offender as an Object of Criminological Research. Pp. 9–28 in *The Female Offender,* edited by A. M. Brodsky. Beverly Hills: Sage.

Rhode, Deborah L. 1990. Feminist Critical Theories. *Stanford Law Review* 42:617–638.

Rice, Marcia. 1990. Challenging Orthodoxies in Feminist Theory: A Black Feminist Critique. Pp. 57–69 in

Feminist Perspectives in Criminology, edited by L. Gelsthorpe and A. Morris. Buckingham, England: Open University Press.

Richie, Beth E. 1996. *Compelled to Crime: The Gender Entrapment of Battered Black Women.* New York: Routledge.

Ridgeway, Cecilia L., and Shelley J. Correll. 2004. Unpacking the Gender System: A Theoretical Perspective on Gender Beliefs and Social Relations. *Gender & Society* 18:510–31.

Risman, Barbara J. 2004. Gender as a Social Structure: Theory Wrestling with Activism. *Gender & Society* 18:429–450.

Rittenhouse, C. Amanda. 1991. The Emergence of Premenstrual Syndrome as a Social Problem. *Social Problems* 38:412–425.

Rivera, B., and Cathy S. Widom. 1990. Childhood Victimization and Violent Offending. *Violence and Victims* 5:19–35.

Rosenbaum, Jill L. 1989. Family Dysfunction and Female Delinquency. *Crime and Delinquency* 35:31–44.

Rosenbaum, Marsha. 1981. *Women on Heroin.* New Brunswick, NJ: Rutgers University Press.

Sampson, Robert J., and John H. Laub. 1990. Crime and Deviance over the Life Course: The Salience of Adult Social Bonds. *American Sociological Review* 55:609–627.

———. 1993. *Crime in the Making: Pathways and Turning Points through Life.* Cambridge, MA: Harvard University Press.

Sandhu, Harjit S., and Donald E. Allen. 1969. Female Delinquency: Goal Obstruction and Anomie. *Canadian Review of Sociology and Anthropology* 5:107–110.

Schur, Edwin M. 1984. *Labeling Women Deviant: Gender, Stigma, and Social Control.* New York: McGraw Hill.

Schwendinger, Herman, and Julia Schwendinger. 1970. Defenders of Order or Guardians of Human Rights? *Issues in Criminology* 5:123–157.

Segrave, Jeffrey O., and Douglas N. Hastad. 1983. Evaluating Structural and Control Models of Delinquency Causation. *Youth and Society* 14:437–456.

Seiler, Naomi. 2003. Identifying Racial Privilege: Lessons from Critical Race Theory and the Law. *American Journal of Bioethics* 3:24–25.

Sellers, Christine S. 1999. Self-Control and Intimate Violence. *Criminology* 37:375–405.

Sharp, Susan F. and Susan T. Marcus-Mendoza. 2001. It's a Family Affair: Incarcerated Women and Their Families. *Women & Criminal Justice* 12:21–49.

Shaw, Margaret. 1991. Survey of Federally Sentenced Women: Report to the Task Force on Federally Sentenced Women on the Prison Survey (User Report 1991–4: Ottawa, Ministry of the Solicitor General).

———. 1995 Conceptualizing Violence by Women. Pp. 115–131 in *Gender and Crime,* edited by R. E. Dobash, R. P. Dobash, and L. Noaks. Cardiff: University of Wales Press.

Shaw, Stephani J. 1997. Black Club Women and the Creation of the National Association of Colored Women. Pp. 499–503 in *Feminist Frontiers IV,* edited by L. Richardson, V. Taylor, and N. Whittier. New York: McGraw Hill.

Shover, Neal, and Carol Y. Thompson. 1992. Age, Differential Expectations, and Crime Desistance. *Criminology* 30:89–104.

Siegel, Jane A., and Linda M. Williams. 2003. The Relationship between Child Sexual Abuse and Female Delinquency and Crime. *Journal of*

Research in Crime and Delinquency 40:71–94.

Silbert, Mimi H., and Ayala M. Pines. 1981. Sexual Abuse as an Antecedent to Prostitution. *Child Abuse and Neglect* 5:407–411.

Simon, Rita. 1975. *Women and Crime.* Lexington, MA: D. C. Heath.

Singer, Mark I., Janet Bussey, Li-Yu Song, and Lisa Lunghofer. 1995. The Psychosocial Issues of Women Serving Time in Jail. *Social Work* 40:103–113.

Singer, Susan J., and Murray Levine. 1988. A Power-Control Theory, Gender, and Delinquency. *Criminology* 26:527–547.

Small, M. 1996. *Female Choices: Sexual Behavior of Female Primates.* Ithaca, NY: Cornell University Press.

Smart, Carol. 1976. *Women, Crime and Criminology: A Feminist Critique.* London: Routledge and Kegan Paul.

———. 1982. The New Female Offender: Reality or Myth? Pp. 105–116 in *The Criminal Justice System and Women,* edited by B. R. Price and N. J. Sokoloff. New York: Clark Boardman.

Smith, Douglas A. 1979. Sex and Deviance: An Assessment of Major Sociological Variables. *Sociological Quarterly* 20:183.

Smith, Douglas A., and Christy A. Visher. 1980. Sex and Involvement in Deviance/Crime: A Quantitative Review of the Empirical Literature. *American Sociological Review* 45:691–701.

Soler, Hosanna, Preeti Vinayak, and David Quadagno. 2000. Biosocial Aspects of Domestic Violence. *Psychoneuroendocrinology* 25:721–739.

Sommers, Ira, and Deborah R. Baskin. 1994. Factors Related to Female Adolescent Initiation into Violent Street Crime. *Youth and Society* 25:468–489.

Spender, Dale. 1981. *Men's Studies Modified.* Oxford, England: Pergamon Press.

Spohn, Ryan E. (2000). Gender Differences in the Effect of Child Maltreatment on Criminal Activity over the Life Course. *Families, Crime and Criminal Justice* 2:207–231.

Stattin, Hakan, and David Magnusson. 1991. Stability and Change in Criminal Behaviour Up to Age 30. *The British Journal of Criminology* 31:327–346.

Steffensmeier, Darrell J. 1980. Sex Differences in Patterns of Adult Crime, 1965–1977: A Review and Assessment. *Social Forces* 58:1080–1108.

Steffensmeier, Darrell J., and Emilie A. Allan. 1988. Sex Disparities in Arrests by Residence, Race, and Age: An Assessment of the Gender Convergence/Crime Hypothesis. *Justice Quarterly* 5:53–80.

Steffensmeier, Darrell J., and Cathy Streifel. 1992. Time-Series Analysis of the Female Percentage of Arrests for Property Crimes, 1960–1985: A Test of Alternative Explanations. *Justice Quarterly* 9:77–104.

Sterk, Claire E. 1999. *Fast Lives.* Philadelphia: Temple University Press.

Sutherland, Edwin. 1939. *Principles of Criminology,* 3rd ed. Philadelphia: J. B. Lippincott.

Sutherland, Edwin, and Donald Cressey. 1966. *Principles of Criminology.* Philadelphia: J. B. Lippincott.

Taylor, Claire. 2001. The Relationshp between Social and Self-Control. *Theoretical Criminology* 5:369–388.

Taylor, Ian, Paul Walton, and Jock Young (Eds.). 1973. *The New Criminology: For a Social Theory of Deviance.* New York: Harper and Row.

———. (Eds.) 1975. *Critical Criminology*. London: Routledge and Kegan Paul.

Taylor, Timothy. 1996. *The Prehistory of Sex*. New York: Bantam Books.

Thomas, W. I. 1907. *Sex and Society*. Boston: Little, Brown.

———. 1923. *The Unadjusted Girl*. Boston: Little, Brown.

———. 1967. *The Unadjusted Girl*. New York: Harper and Row.

Thornhill, Randy, and Craig T. Palmer. 2000. *A Natural History of Rape: Biological Bases of Sexual Coercion*. MIT Press.

Thornton, W. E., and J. James. 1979. Masculinity and Delinquency Revisited. *British Journal of Criminology* 19:225.

Torstensson, Marie. 1990. Female Delinquents in a Birth Cohort: Some Aspects of Control Theory. *Journal of Quantitative Criminology* 6:101–115.

Travis, Cheryl Brown (Ed.). 2003. *Evolution, Gender, and Rape*. Cambridge, MA: The MIT Press.

Tremblay, Richard, Joan McCord, and L. Otten. 1983. A Consideration of Sex Roles and Motivations for Crime. *Criminal Justice and Behavior* 10:3–12.

Tremblay, Richard E., Frank Vitaro, Lucie Bertrand, Marc Leblanc, Helene Beauchesne, Helene Boileau, and Lucille David. 1992. Parent and Child Training to Prevent Early Onset of Delinquency: The Montreal Longitudinal Experimental Study. Pp. 117–138 in *Preventing Antisocial Behavior: Interventions from Birth through Adolescence*, edited by J. McCord and R. Tremblay. New York: Guilford Press.

Uggen, Christopher. 2000. Class, Gender, and Arrest. *Criminology* 38: 835–860.

Valdes, Francisco, Jerome McCristal Culp, and Angla P. Harris, Eds. 2002. *Crossroads, Directions, and a New Critical Race Theory*. Philadelphia: Temple University Press.

Vander Ven, Thomas. 2003. *Working Mothers and Juvenile Delinquency*. New York: LFB Scholarly Publishing.

Vedder, Clyde, and Dora Somerville. 1970. *The Delinquent Girl*. Springfield, IL: Charles C. Thomas.

Ward, Tony, and Richard Siegert. 2002. Rape and Evolutionary Psychology: A Critique of Thornhill and Palmer's Theory. *Aggression and Violent Behavior* 7:145–168.

Watts, Ivan Eugene, and Mirmala Erevelles. 2004. These Deadly Times: Reconceptualizing School Violence by Using Critical Race Theory and Disability Studies. *American Educational Journal* 41:271–299.

Widom, Cathy S. 1989. The Cycle of Violence. *Science* 244:160–166.

———. 1995. *Victims of Childhood Sexual Abuse—Later Criminal Consequences. Research in Brief*, National Institute of Justice, U.S. Department of Justice.

Wing, Adrienne K. (Ed.) 1997. *Critical Race Feminism: A Reader*. New York: New York University Press.

———. 2003. *Critical Race Feminism: A Reader*, 2nd ed. New York: New York University Press.

Wortman, Camille B., and Darrin R. Lehman. 1983. Reactions to Victims of Life Crises. Pp. 463–489 in *Social Support*, edited by I. G. Sarason and B. R. Sarason. Boston: Martinus Nijhoff.

Wrangham, R., and D. Peterson. 1996. *Demonic Males: Apes and the Origins of Human Violence*. New York: Houghton Mifflin.

Young, Alison, and Peter Rush. 1994. The Law of Victimization in Urban Realism, Pp. 49–72 in *The Futures of Criminology*, edited by David Nelken. Thousand Oaks, CA: Sage.

Young, Marlene A. 1991. Survivors of Crime. Pp. 27–42 in *To Be a Victim: Encounters with Crime and Injustice*, edited by D. Sank and D. I. Caplan. New York: Plenum.

Zuberi, Tokofu. 2001. *Thicker than Blood: How Racial Statistics Lie*. Minneapolis: University of Minnesota Press.

3

The Frequency and Nature
of Female Offending

[D]ata indicate that men and women are actually quite similar in terms of
the offenses for which they are most often arrested and that the majority
are crimes that most would view as petty, for example, larceny-theft. . . .
The most striking difference is the absolute level
of men's and women's offending.

BRITTON, 2000, 60

Studies consistently show not only that females generally commit fewer crimes
than males but also that their offenses tend to be less serious and violent in
nature. Of U.S. arrests in 2003, females accounted for fewer than one in five of
the violent index offense arrests, fewer than one in three index property crime
arrests, and fewer than one in four of all arrests. That women are not as violent as
men is emphasized in a recent study where even among the most long-term
group of offenders, the "habitual" or "career" criminals, men were arrested for
four times as many violent crimes as women (and more property crimes, as well)
(DeLisi, 2002).

This chapter draws on prior and current research and data in order to assess girls'
and women's offending. However, for a complete understanding of the studies
and data, female offending must be examined and understood in a number of
contexts:

1. The extent of female offending: the types of crimes women and girls
   commit

2. The nature of female offending: the frequency with which women and girls
   commit crimes

3. Stereotypes and assumptions about female offending: How these influence
   legal codes and enforcement of laws

4. Gender comparisons in offending: how the nature and frequency of female and male offending compare

5. Historical aspects in offending: changes over time in the extent, nature, and gender differences in offending

The *extent* of offending, for the purposes of this book, is the frequency with which various offenses are committed. The *nature* of offending, on the other hand, addresses the type and seriousness of the offense. The term *offending* rather than *crime* is used, given that many of the studies are of youths and *status offenses*, behaviors that are not considered crimes when adults commit them (for example, truancy, drinking alcohol, and running away). Concerning the extent of female offending, regardless of whether crime rates are measured by arrest, victimization, or self-report rates, males offend at rates about five to ten times higher than females (Steffensmeier and Haynie, 2000). Regarding the nature of women's offending, the crimes for which females are most strongly represented are sex work (prostitution), running away, larceny-theft, fraud, and forgery, and embezzlement (see Table 3.1); this has been quite consistent historically.

Gender comparisons in offending are commonly evaluated by determining which offenses are gender related and which are gender neutral (Smart, 1976). Whereas *gender-related* crimes are more likely to be committed by one sex than by the other, *gender-neutral* crimes are equally likely to be committed by either sex. Given males' higher propensity to offend, *the majority of crimes are male-gender-related*, but rape and other violent crimes are especially so. The most common example of a female-gender-related crime is sex work.

Historically, legal codes for some offenses were written so that only one sex/gender could be a victim or offender. For example, until the 1970s many rape laws specified that only males could be offenders and only females could be victims. Similarly, many prostitution laws specified female offenders (and no "victims," but male clients, also offenders). But even if the legal code is gender neutral in identifying offenders and or victims (i.e., not specifying "penis," "female," and so on), the applications may still be gender specific (Morris, 1987). For example, even when the prostitution laws are changed to include male prostitutes or to go after clients as well as prostitutes, the police and judges may continue to disregard these male offenders because they do not fit their stereotypes of offenders (see Farley and Kelly, 2000). A recent study of sex workers reported that three-quarters were women, 13 percent were men, and 12 percent were transgendered (Farley and Barkan, 1998). Police may be less likely to detect male sex workers because they do not picture them in these roles.

The patterns of crime rates over time (especially of females) received increased attention with the advent of Adler's (1975) and Simon's (1975) "liberation" hypothesis. This hypothesis suggests that rather than stable differences between the sexes (Option A) or gender-divergence (increasing differences) between the sexes (Option B), gender-convergence (Option C) is likely to occur over time (see Figure 3.1) as gender equality increases. *Gender-stability* is any pattern over time where the differences between female and male

---

Comparative Perspectives: The Global Report on Crime and Justice: The Fifth United Nations Survey of Crime (UNSC) Trends

- The UNSC survey was returned by 91 countries.
- Countries were more likely to report rape rates to the UNSC than the rates of any other crimes.
- The ratio between adult male suspects and suspects of other age-gender groups varies among countries, but *males constitute the largest group of suspects in all countries*. For example, the male-to-female ratio for adult suspects was 91:1 in Western Samoa and 2:1 in Bolivia. Regarding the male-to-female ratio for juvenile arrests, in the country of Georgia the ratio was 79:1, while in Jamaica the ratio was 2:1.
- Globally, two in three victims of burglaries report their victimization to the police. Less than one in three female victims of violence do so.
- Far fewer women and girls were suspected of committing crimes in countries with low incomes than in countries with high incomes.

SOURCE: Graeme Newman (Ed.). 1999. *The Global Report on Crime and Justice.* Published for the United Nations Office for Drug Control and Crime Prevention, Centre for International Crime Prevention. New York: Oxford University Press. http://www.uncjin.org/Special/GlobalReport.html.

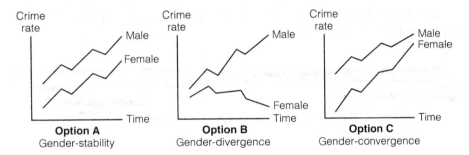

FIGURE 3.1 Examples of Comparing Gender-Offending Patterns over Time

rates are relatively stable. They co-vary: Female and male rates rise and fall together. For example, we might expect that in an era of "get-tough-on-crime" policies or in times of economic depression, men's and women's crime rates would be equally affected (unless the policy of economic hardship was likely to affect one sex more than the other). One in-depth study found that higher levels of many variables measuring *structural disadvantage* (e.g., poverty, income inequality, joblessness, etc.) increased both males' and females' offending (although they appeared to impact males' more significantly) (Steffensmeier and Haynie, 2000). With *gender-divergence* the disparity in crime rates between the sexes increases over time, with gender differences growing. *Gender-convergence*, consistent with the "liberation" hypothesis, occurs any time that the distance or gap between males' and females' rates is decreasing and their crime rates are becoming similar.

MEASURING CRIME AND MAKING GENDER COMPARISONS

Crime rates are measured a number of ways. Typically, the rate is the number of offenses per 100,000 people in the population. Other measures of crime rates include giving a group, for example, high school or college students, self-report surveys asking them how often (if ever) they participate in various offenses, or conducting interviews with sample participants. Alternatively, survey or interview data can measure crime rates by asking about victimization rates. Whatever the structure for collecting crime rates, these rates are used to examine the extent and nature of offending at one point in time or over a period of time (if conducted repeatedly). The most popular data sets used to assess crime rates in the United States are the Uniform Crime Reports (UCR). These reports summarize the yearly arrests for police departments in the entire country. Thus, the UCR data are a measure of arrests and therefore do not include crimes unknown and unreported to the police, nor do they include reported offenses for which the police choose not to arrest or are unable to arrest (e.g., there is insufficient evidence, or they cannot find or identify a suspect). Tables 3.1 and 3.2 in the chapter summarize some of the most recent available U.S. data on women and girls (and men and boys) available at the time of writing this edition (UCR data for 2003). (The most recent statistics are accessible through the Bureau of Justice Statistics website: http://www.ojp.usdoj.gov/bjs/).

As previously stated, regardless of whether crime rates are measured by arrest, victimization, or self-report rates, males offend at rates about five to ten times higher than females (Steffensmeier and Haynie, 2000). Almost one-quarter (23.2 percent) of all arrests in the United States in 2003 were of females (Table 3.1). Although not reported in the tables in this book, from the 2003 UCR data it can be calculated that women constituted 22.1 percent of all adult arrests, and girls constituted 29.0 percent of all juvenile arrests (Crime in the United States, 2003, 2004, Tables 39 and 40). Thus, females are a higher percentage of juvenile than adult arrests. Now turning back to Table 3.1 in this chapter, about 18 percent of all violent index crime arrests were of females (women and girls), and this was highest for aggravated assaults (21 percent). Females' arrests constituted slightly over one-tenth of the arrests for both murder/nonnegligent manslaughter and robbery arrests and about 1 percent of rape arrests. Almost one-third (30.8 percent) of property index crime arrests were of females, with the largest percent, 37.1 percent, for larceny-theft. Female arrests made up between 13 and 17 percent of the arrests for burglary, motor vehicle theft, and arson (see Table 3.1).

The data in Table 3.1 can also be used to identify which crimes are gender neutral and which are gender related. Of the twenty-eight individual offenses (as well as the composite index property and violent crime rates), *the vast majority*

TABLE 3.1 Arrest Rates in the United States: 2003 and Ten-Year Trends (Percent Change from 1994–2003)

Offense	Total N 2003	Percent Women 2003	Percent Men 2003	Percent Ten-Year Change 1994–2003 for Women		Percent Ten-Year Change 1994–2003 for Men	
				Total Women	Women <18	Total Men	Men <18
TOTAL	9,581,423	23.2	76.8	+12.3	−3.0	−6.7	−22.4
Murder/ manslaughter	9,119	10.3	89.7	−30.1	−48.7	−36.9	−68.9
Rape	18,446	1.3	98.7	−1.4	−30.0	−22.5	−24.6
Robbery	75,667	10.4	89.6	−12.4	−37.8	−26.2	−43.6
Aggravated assault	315,732	20.7	79.3	+14.0	−1.9	−17.3	−31.0
Burglary	204,761	13.7	86.3	−2.9	−26.9	−26.1	−41.2
Larceny-theft	817,048	37.1	62.9	−13.6	−18.6	−27.5	−42.8
Auto theft	106,221	16.6	83.4	−5.2	−44.1	−29.6	−53.6
Arson	14,330	15.6	84.4	−23.7	−38.0	−29.3	−36.0
Index violent arrest rate[1]	418,964	17.8	82.2	+9.6	−9.9	−20.0	−36.1
Index property arrest rate[2]	1,139,360	30.8	69.2	−12.5	−21.1	−27.4	−43.7
Other assaults[3]	877,105	24.2	75.8	+32.1	+35.9	−3.8	+1.2
Forgery/ counterfeiting	79,188	40.3	59.7	+10.5	−47.1	−3.8	−46.4
Fraud	208,469	44.6	55.4	−11.6	−27.5	−20.6	−29.2
Embezzlement	11,986	49.8	50.2	+42.0	+28.1	+2.1	+8.0
Stolen property	89,560	18.2	81.8	+6.3	−29.3	−25.2	−48.3
Vandalism	193,083	16.4	83.6	+5.2	−10.9	−21.2	−35.7
Weapons	117,844	8.2	91.8	−34.1	−21.6	−36.3	−42.4
Prostitution/ commercialized vice	51,686	64.2	35.8	−15.0	+86.5	−21.7	−23.9
Sex offense[4]	63,759	8.5	91.5	−3.4	+26.1	−10.3	−0.3
Drug violation	1,172,222	18.3	81.7	+34.8	+56.3	+19.9	+13.0
Gambling	7,414	10.9	89.1	−36.9	−70.2	−51.4	−58.1
Offense against family/children	94,488	23.0	77.0	+41.2	+31.2	+4.0	+12.2
Driving under the influence	1,005,777	18.2	81.8	+21.1	+83.5	−10.4	+24.9
Liquor law violation	431,912	25.8	74.2	+45.5	+25.6	+8.3	−5.2

(Continued)

[handwritten margin note beside Fraud/Embezzlement/Stolen property: "Gender Neutral crime"]

T A B L E 3.1   Arrest Rates in the United States: 2003 and Ten-Year Trends (Percent Change from 1994–2003)

Offense	Total N 2003	Percent Women 2003	Percent Men 2003	Percent Ten-Year Change 1994–2003 for Women		Percent Ten-Year Change 1994–2003 for Men	
				Total Women	Women <18	Total Men	Men <18
Drunkenness	389,626	14.5	85.5	–8.9	+24.4	–28.1	–18.3
Disorderly conduct	453,645	25.1	74.9	+4.2	+46.2	–15.6	+2.0
Vagrancy	20,052	21.5	78.5	+10.5	–36.6	+17.5	–52.9
Curfew/ loitering	95,052	30.3	69.7	+5.3	+5.3	–3.1	–3.1
Running away[5]	87,396	58.7	41.3	–40.2	–40.2	–44.3	–44.3

[1]Index violent crimes are murder, forcible rape, robbery, and aggravated assault.
[2]Index property crimes are burglary, larceny-theft, motor vehicle theft, and arson.
[3]"Other assaults" include assaults that are not the "aggravated assaults classified under the violent crime index."
[4]Except forcible rape and prostitution.
[5]This is a status offense, thus only a crime for minors.
SOURCE: U.S. Department of Justice. 2004. *Crime in the United States 2003: Uniform Crime Reports*. Federal Bureau of Investigation, U.S. Government Printing Office. Data for this table came from Tables 33 and 42.

of offenses are male-gender-related. Two offenses, prostitution (64 percent of arrests for females) and the status offense, running away (59 percent arrests of girls), are the only female-gender-related offenses. Additionally, only two of the twenty-eight offenses are gender neutral: embezzlement (50 percent female and 50 percent male arrests) and fraud (45 percent female and 55 percent male arrests). Thus, one in twelve offenses is female-gender related, one in twelve is gender neutral, and six out of seven offenses are male-gender-related.

Table 3.2 presents the top ten offense arrests for females and males. There are some interesting patterns in this table. First, nine of the top ten offenses are decisively male-gender-related. Stated alternatively, even for the ten offenses for which females are most frequently arrested, nine-tenths are offenses that far more frequently result in arrests for males. The only one not male-gender-related in Table 3.2 is gender neutral (fraud). A second important pattern in Table 3.2 is that, for the most part, eight of the ten most common arrests for females are also eight of the most common arrests for males. The exceptions are burglary and vandalism, which appear on the males' top ten, and fraud and "offenses against family," which appear on the females' top ten. Concerning the "offenses against family," I speculate that mandatory domestic violence arrest laws likely play a significant role in this. Research documents that whereas mandatory arrest policies have been implemented since the 1980s in efforts to deter male batterers, a major "side effect" has been a huge increase in *women's* arrests for domestic violence (see Dasgupta, 2001; Malloy et al., 2003; Martin, 1997; McMahon and Pence, 2003; Melton and Belknap, 2003; Miller, 2001). Most of these studies note grave concerns that women victims who resist their abusers in any way are

T A B L E 3.2 Top Ten Arrest Offenses for Females and Males in the United States in 2003

	Females		Males	
	Offense Type	Percent of arrests that are female	Offense Type	Percent of arrests that are male
1	Larceny-theft	37.1	Drug abuse violations	81.7
2	Drug abuse violations	18.3	Driving under the influence	81.8
3	Other assaults*	24.2	Other assaults*	75.8
4	Offenses against family	18.2	Larceny-theft	62.9
5	Driving under the influence	18.2	Disorderly conduct	74.9
6	Disorderly conduct	25.1	Drunkenness	85.5
7	Liquor law violation	25.8	Liquor law violation	74.2
8	Fraud	44.6	Aggravated assaults	79.3
9	Aggravated assaults	20.7	Burglary	86.3
10	Drunkenness	14.5	Vandalism	83.6

*Assaults other than aggravated assaults.

SOURCE: U.S. Department of Justice. 2004. *Crime in the United States 2003: Uniform Crime Reports.* Federal Bureau of Investigation, U.S. Government Printing Office. Data for this table came from Table 42.

often arrested as offenders. A third important pattern in Table 3.2 is the significant role that alcohol and drug offenses play in both females' and males' arrests (where males still constitute the bulk of arrests).

Analysis of Uniform Crime Reports (UCR) data—that is, arrest data—indicates that during the 1960s and early 1970s, although there was a temporary increase in larceny offenses and the number of girls arrested increased dramatically (by 250 percent), this was largely due to the "baby boomers" hitting the high-risk age group (Chesney-Lind and Shelden, 1992). Notably, national statistics on women in U.S. prisons from 1980 to 2000 indicate that their incarcerations for violent offenses were highest in 1980, decreasing significantly since then, while drug-related offense incarcerations were *lowest* in 1980 but climbed through 1999 (Johnson, 2003).

Despite the "liberation" hypothesis, most research published in the past twenty-five years that addresses gender and crime patterns over time reports a strong tendency toward gender-stability; it typically agrees that women's crime rates have basically stayed the same except in the areas of less serious property crimes and drugs (Bilchik, 1999; Boritch and Hagan, 1990; Canter, 1982; Chilton and Datesman, 1987; Giordano, Kerbel, and Dudley, 1981; Leonard, 1982; Naffine, 1987; Steffensmeier, 1981, 1993; Steffensmeier and Cobb, 1981;

Steffensmeier and Steffensmeier, 1980; Steffensmeier and Streifel, 1992). Thus, scholars often identify changes in crime rates (usually measured as arrest rates) as typically affecting females and males similarly; that is, females' and males' crime rates tend to co-vary (vary together: when one gender rate goes up, so does the other; when one goes down, so does the other). Moreover, the fluctuations are often tied to two cyclical patterns: economic well-being and crime policies. As expected, increases in "get-tough-on-crime" policies and depressed economic conditions often result in increases in arrests and imprisonment rates. Regarding the more stringent criminalizing of behaviors (e.g., tougher drug laws), although there may be no corresponding increase in actual offending behavior, arrest rates are likely to go up. This section reports some of the ways that net-widening policies may be affecting girls more than boys. However, overall, there is little evidence for a strong pattern of gender-convergence in crime rates.

A study of U.S. arrest trends from 1965 to 2000 reported gender-stability, probably because net-widening (policies that criminalize more behaviors) equally affected men and women (Steffensmeier and Schwartz, 2004). The largest increases for both sexes were for larceny, fraud, forgery, DUI, drug violations, and assault, with decreases for both sexes in arrests for public drunkenness, vagrancy, suspicion, and gambling (ibid.). When focusing on juvenile arrest rates from 1965 to 2000, this study again reported gender-stability (ibid.), consistent with earlier studies on the topic (Ageton, 1983). Thus, where gender-convergence appears to exist, it can be largely explained by (1) changes in law-enforcement practices, (2) the worsening economic position of women (the feminization of poverty), (3) changes in data collection methods, and (4) inflation in the small base of women's crimes (Boritch and Hagan, 1990; Canter, 1982; Chilton and Datesman, 1987; Giordano, Kerbel, and Dudley, 1981; Steffensmeier, 1993; Steffensmeier and Cobb, 1981; Steffensmeier and Schwartz, 2004; Steffensmeier and Steffensmeier, 1980). As one recent longitudinal study concludes, "crime—especially in its more serious and lucrative forms—largely remains a man's world" (Steffensmeier and Schwartz, 2004, 106). If the gender gap in offending is closing, it appears to be for less serious property crimes, and possibly for drug use.

Table 3.1 includes changes in arrest trends by sex in the United States between 1994 and 2003. Total females' and males' percentage changes over this time period are reported, as well as juvenile males' and females' arrests for this time period. "Eyeballing" these data suggests that gender-convergence is the most common pattern, but it is important to keep in mind that within this same table when we examine males' percentage of arrests for 2003, males still make up by far the bulk of arrests for all but four of the twenty-eight offenses listed.

Women and girls used to constitute about 15 percent of people arrested by the police (Mann, 1984), but as noted earlier, the 2003 UCR data indicate that today that rate is almost one-quarter of the arrests. But the UCR data may not be measuring changes in offending as much as changes in policies and practices disproportionately directed at girls and women. In recent years, there has been renewed interest in the "bad girl," exemplified by media, government, and research reports on girls' rising crime rates, particularly for violent crimes. These reports claim that the violent offending gap between girls and boys is narrowing.

While many of the media stories focus on anecdotal data, usually a particularly heinous crime by an individual girl or girls, the government and research reports typically cull their data from the UCR, that is, crimes officially reported to the police. Perhaps most unsettling is a government report that in the United States between 1989 and 1998, there was a 56 percent increase in girls' and a 20 percent increase in boys' juvenile detentions, which was largely a result of girls' 138 percent increase in crimes against persons (relative to the 49 percent increase in boys' crimes against persons) (Harms, 2002).

The most recent studies on gender trends, however, specify the need to examine how the data are collected: Official arrest data show gender-convergence, but youths' self-reported data support gender-stability and even gender-divergence. For example, while the UCR data indicate huge increases in girls' relative to boys' arrests between 1991 and 2000, self-report data suggest that both boys' and girls self-reported violence decreased during this time period, and the decrease was greater for girls than boys (Brener et al., 1999; Chesney-Lind and Belknap, 2004). Thus, Chesney-Lind and Belknap (2004) claim that assertions that the gender gap is closing for violence by youth are wrong. "Rather, it appears that changes in arrest data over time are likely the product of changes in the behavior of parents, school officials, and law enforcement" (ibid., 216). Similarly, another recent study using longitudinal self-report victimization and offending data to examine the gendered nature of youth violence patterns from 1980 to 2003 reported patterns of gender-stability and even gender-divergence (Steffensmeier et al., 2005).

Why, then, do the official data indicate gender-convergence when the self-report data indicate gender-stability, or even gender-divergence patterns? Researchers attribute the mismatch to changes in policies and practices that involve net-widening for girls and mostly agree that self-report data are a far more accurate reflection of the actual crime rate. Regarding net-widening, what "counts" as violence has expanded, a practice also known as "up-criming" (Acoca, 1999; Chesney-Lind and Belknap, 2004; Steffensmeier et al., 2005). For example, these studies report on parents who call the police on their daughters for such minor actions as throwing Barbie dolls or chocolate chip cookies at their mothers; the daughters are then charged with assault. "Up-criming" can also be seen in school "no-tolerance" policies where instances of youth-on-youth fighting, formerly handled by parents and teachers, now results in assault arrests. Sometimes parents will report their own daughters to the police, using detention as a "time out" for the parents, and this often occurs in cases where girls have run away because of the mother's boyfriend's inappropriate or illegal behavior (Lederman and Brown, 2000). As stated earlier, mandatory domestic violence arrest policies increased the arrests of women (most of whom are the victims). But this policy has also increased the likelihood of girls' arrests (see Steffensmeier et al., 2005). Concerning how the data are collected, the type of data used—official reports, victimization surveys, or self-reported offending—likely influences the representation of crime rates. This is partially because most offending goes undetected by the juvenile and adult crime-processing systems but also because official reports are apt to reflect bias, particularly in the forms of racism, classism, and sexism.

An example of how girls' increased victimization risks can cause police to arrest them more (addressed in more detail in the following chapter) is a study finding that when sexual abuse offenses went up, the arrest rate of girls for status offenses increased, while the corresponding arrest rates for boys stayed the same. "During times of increased sex crimes, police may be particularly harsh in their treatment of females whose behavior puts them at risk for victimization" (McCluskey, McCluskey, and Huebner 2003, 49). Ironically, what looks like an increase in girls' status offending is more likely an increase in police both "protecting" and punishing girls due to their perceived increased risk of sexual victimization (ibid.).

In sum, this section is likely confusing for the reader given the official/police statistics that indicate that the gender gap is closing and the self-report data suggesting that the gender gap is stable or even diverging. Clearly both economic and political/crime policy cycles impact offending: the former due to greater obstacles to live well or even survive, and the latter due to net-widening of what "counts" as a crime. Overall, the findings in this section indicate a closing of the gender gap concerning arrests, but a feminization of poverty and net-widening strategies, aimed particularly at delinquent girls and at women's drug use, that result in increases of labeling women and girls as offenders may be causing the rates to appear to converge when, in fact, they are not.

THE IMPORTANCE OF HOW CRIME RATES ARE MEASURED AND THE ROLES OF GENDER, AGE, RACE, CLASS, AND SEXUALITY

Chapter 2 pointed out how criminological theories have tended to be sex blind, either completely ignoring females or viewing them through a stereotypical lens that usually distorts women's and girls' real-life experiences. Any analysis of gender must avoid a similarly restricted view by accounting for differences among females based on their age, race, and social class (see Simpson, 1991). As noted already, the main source for measuring U.S. crime rates, the UCR, is limited for a variety of reasons, such as they only report on offenses that were reported to the police and where arrests were made. Additionally, they report *no* information on class or socioeconomic status, and the information they report on sex, race, and age is done so in a manner that too often makes it impossible to determine the intersection of these variables, such as race × sex, or race × sex × age. At any rate, it is important to keep in mind that officially collected crime data (e.g., the UCR) are likely a better indicator of those individuals detained by the police and formally processed by the system than of actual offending given that the majority of crimes are not reported to the police, and of those reported, the police do not always "solve" them. This section analyzes some of the important variables/ characteristics often related to actual offending and/or how offending is perceived.

Age and Juvenile Delinquency

Age is important because it has been well documented that there are relatively few "career criminals." Most people who break the law do so roughly between the ages of 15 and 24. Kruttschnitt's (1996, 139) careful review of existing studies reports that "the age-crime relationship may not be gender invariant," meaning that there exist gender differences depending on age. For example, the ratio of male-to-female offending varies significantly depending on the age group examined, and factors such as age at initiation into offending, age at which one escalates to more serious offending, and age at which offenders stop offending all vary by gender (ibid.). In 2003, 20 percent of all female arrests and 15 percent of all male arrests were for individuals under 18 years old (Crime in the United States, 2003, 2004, Tables 39 and 40). Thus, addressing youthful offenders is particularly relevant when examining gender. Overall, uniformity in female and male juvenile offending is most apparent in (1) less serious offenses, (2) self-report studies, and (3) more recent studies.

A study of court complaints filed against youths in Denver from 1916 to 1921 showed that girls were far more likely than boys to be charged with the following crimes: being out late at night, immoral conduct or indecent liberties, being beyond the control of parents/guardians, and being disobedient, and frequenting immoral places/persons. Boys were more likely than girls to be charged with taking things, truancy, breaking things, malicious mischief, taking automobiles, and assault (Colomy and Kretzmann, 1997). This is consistent with the long-standing pattern of policing girls' sexuality, addressed in more depth under the sexuality section later in this chapter.

In 1981, it was noted that the formerly male-dominated adolescent subculture of minor delinquency included girls (Figueira-McDonough, Barton, and Sarri, 1981). However, for the more serious offenses, gender differences appear to persist. In a comprehensive and more recent study of over 1,500 youths' self-reported offending (the National Youth Survey), for the twenty-two offenses listed under the categories of "status offenses," "vandalism," "theft," and "assault," boys were more likely to report every crime except running away and hitting a parent, for which boys and girls reported similar rates (about 5 percent of each ran away from home and about 4 percent of each hit a parent) (Triplett and Myers, 1995). Similar to other research, this study also found that the more serious the offense, the greater the gender gap in committing it. When this study examined the number of times (incidence) of the commission of the twenty-two offenses for those youths who had committed the offense at least once, there were few gender differences. Notably, for these few gender differences, girls reported higher frequencies than boys for all three offenses: running away, damaging school property, and carrying a hidden weapon.

Finally, this study attempted to determine gender differences in the context of juvenile offending (ibid.). Overall, for status, property, and theft offenses there were few gender differences in the context of committing the crimes. The exceptions for this regarded the destination when youths ran away, the form of assaults, the extent of injury in assaults, whether the youths were on drugs during the assaults, the purpose of force in assaults, and whether victims were hurt in the assaults (ibid.). More specifically, girls were more likely than boys to report (1) running to a friend's house when they ran away, (2) hurting their assault victims when the victims were students, and (3) using force for reasons other than to get money. Regarding the context of committing assaults, boys were more likely than girls to report (1) being on drugs during the assault, (2) hurting their victims if their victims were not students, (3) beating their victims or attacking them with a weapon, and (4) having their victims cut or hospitalized. Thus, there were few gender differences in the context of offending for status, vandalism (property), or theft offenses, and the context of offending resulted in gender gaps more often in the commission of violent offenses.

Race/Ethnicity

Race/ethnicity is vital to understanding crime rates because of limited legitimate opportunities available to many people of color, as well as their increased risk of being labeled "criminal" and "delinquent." Kruttschnitt (1996, 141) states that ignoring racial variations in gender comparisons of offending "presumes that Blacks and Whites are similarly situated in social life and so influenced by the same risk factors" and therefore is "short-sighted."

In 1981, Diane K. Lewis pointed out that it is almost impossible to make these important distinctions about racial/ethnic variations among women (and among men) due to the manner in which the UCR and prison data are typically reported. Unfortunately, the problem still exists. For example, if one accesses the Bureau of Justice Statistics website to examine crime rates for particular years or over time, the tables typically report looking at one, two, and possibly three variables at a time, but the format makes it impossible to understand how, for example, the rates break down when controlling for gender/sex, race/ethnicity, and age at the same time. Fortunately, government reports sometimes do this for the public, but these breakdowns are not always accessible. Additionally, until recently the racial/ethnic breakdowns were usually restricted to African American and White, which fails to account for variations among Latina/o, Asian American, American Indian, and other racial/ethnic individuals.

Significantly, official statistics such as the UCR, court convictions, and imprisonment rates rely on the crime-processing system actors' perceptions of whether or not a crime occurred. Theoretically, police arrest, and judges and juries convict only when they believe there is a strong likelihood that a person committed a crime. Thus, a major threat to the validity of using official statistics of crime rates is that discrimination may distort the statistics. For example, if Latinas are more likely than White women to be arrested for the same offense, the official statistics would exaggerate the Latinas' offending relative to White women. If African American women are more likely than Latinas to be arrested for the same offense, then official statistics will inflate African American women's crime rates. Thus, when differences are found based individually on gender, race/ethnicity, class, age, and so on, it is not clear whether there are distinct actual differences in the categories of these variables concerning crime rates or whether the differences among the categories represent differential (discriminatory) processing of offenders (e.g., sexist, racist, classist practices).

Lewis's (ibid, 93) review of research found that "correctional" statistics suggest that African American women "display somewhat greater involvement with violent and other personal crimes than [W]hite women." But Lewis (ibid, 93) also cautions that when examining arrest records or other data to compare various races' offending patterns, it is important to control for age because the higher ratio of African American to White females' violent crime rates might partially be explained by the fact that the African American population as a whole is younger (and thus in a higher-risk age group) than the White population. On the other hand, the age difference between African Americans and Whites cannot by itself, according to Lewis, explain the offending differences between White and African American women; these analyses must also consider economic deprivation, gender–status inequality, socialization, gender-role expectations, and racism.

> Black women, then, display gender role behavior, a social status and a crime pattern, all of which contradict acceptable feminine behavior, as defined by the dominant society. They tend to be assertive, function as unmarried heads of household and be convicted for violent person crimes. In short, they epitomize the type of deviant women the criminal justice system is committed to punish. (ibid., 102)

Diane K. Lewis's (1981) work, although reported in the early 1980s, is unfortunately still relevant today.

The importance of controlling for factors such as race and age, as well as the type of crime, can be seen in various studies. A study using national self-report data of women 18 to 23 years old found that although there were no significant differences between African American and White women in the composite crime rate, when the types of crime were broken down, White women reported significantly more drug use than African American women, and African American women reported more involvement in major property and assault crimes than White women. Furthermore, that African American women were more likely to report acquiring income from illegal activities suggested their increased economic vulnerability relative to White women (Hill and Crawford, 1990). Another study of female arrests found few racial differences overall, except that White women were more likely than African American women to be arrested for serious property crimes, and African American women were more likely than White women to be arrested for gambling, assault, family offenses, and violent crimes (Steffensmeier and Allan, 1988).

Class/Socioeconomic Status

It is also important to recognize that one's social class affects one's opportunities and can affect treatment by individuals in society in general (e.g., teachers, neighbors, store owners, etc.) and by the police, courts, and so on. Class also affects the likelihood that one will turn to crime for survival, and similarly limits one's abilities to pay bond and to pay for a good attorney. Unfortunately, data gatherers in both official statistics and many self-report studies are either unwilling or unable to account for class differences, so little is known about this seemingly powerful variable.

One exception is a self-report study on inner-city and suburban youth (arguably a class measure), which found suburban girls were the most likely to have tried alcohol and the most likely to have tried marijuana, while inner-city boys were the least likely to have tried alcohol and inner-city females were the least likely to have tried marijuana (Luthar and D'Avanzo, 1999). Contrary to popular class and race stereotypes, suburban males were most likely to have tried hard drugs, followed distantly by inner-city boys, inner-city girls, and suburban girls (respectively).

Those studies that simultaneously control for race, gender, class, and age often find these are important predictors of offending behavior, as well as treatment by the crime-processing system. Research has shown that making simple racial or gender comparisons is less useful than controlling for both race and sex to see how the experiences of women from different races compare and how men and women of the same race compare. It is important to emphasize the danger in relying solely on official crime-processing statistics (e.g., police and court records), in that they may be a better reflection of bias than offending. Researchers should also use self-report surveys and interviews to present a more valid measure of offending.

Sexuality

The next chapter includes discussions on the ways that sexuality is used to process girls' and women's charges of offending, but in the meantime, it is useful to be aware of the sexist ways in which, historically and currently, consensual sex is evaluated differently for females and males. There has been a concerted effort to control females' sexuality, both socially and legally, which has resulted in a double standard. For example, terms such as *promiscuous, loose,* and *nymphomaniac* are rarely applied to males. In fact, males are often expected to be sexually active, regardless of their marital status. Females, on the other hand, are often expected to be chaste or at least to limit themselves to one male partner. (Given the homophobia in our culture, it is unclear with whom the "healthy" boys are supposed to have sex.)

Although female sexuality has received increased latitude since the 1970s, women and girls still experience more social constraints on their sexuality than boys and men do. Current research documents the difficult time that many girls, delinquent and not, still have in "doing desire," particularly when compared to their male peers (Alder, 1998; Tolman, 1994). Schaffner (1998) stresses the need to examine girls' delinquency by contextualizing their experiences as a means of understanding the decisions girls make. Specifically, she describes how the social, political, and economic sexualizing of female adolescence can result in girls' harmful framings of their sexuality and role expectations, and she notes how some girls "solve" school, peer, and family problems through sex. Schaffner (ibid.) identifies four ways that the sexualization of girls' lives can be manifested in delinquency or perceptions of delinquency: (1) girls who are oppositional, resistant, or angry about the stereotypically prescribed gender roles; (2) girls whose empty family lives (abandonment or neglect by parents) result in them ending up with (much) older boyfriends; (3) girls who get "caught" in a homophobic system for exploring lesbian desire; and (4) girls with sexual injury in the form of abuse that results in anger, running away, drug use, and so on.

Legal codes until relatively recently often listed "promiscuity" and "adultery" as offenses, and these were applied almost exclusively to girls and women. Thus "promiscuity" and "adultery" appeared to be female-gender-related offenses when, in fact, boys and men are typically more promiscuous and "commit" adultery more often than girls and women. This is a useful example of how official statistics fail to reflect the actual behavioral representations in society. Many of the status offenses are directly or indirectly tied to both voluntary and abusive sexuality: for example, being sexually active (directly tied) or running away from home (indirectly tied). The status offenses of "running away" in the United States and "being in moral danger" in the United Kingdom are strongly related to sexual "promiscuity" (Smart, 1976).

Many girls (and boys) who run away from home are running away from sexual victimization or incest. In fact, 20 percent of girls and 7 percent of boys seeking help from runaway and homeless centers reported sexual abuse as a reason for their predicament; 9 percent of girls and 2 percent of boys who are runaways reported sexual abuse by a parent (U.S. Department of Health and Human Services, 1991). Moreover, many runaways experience sexual victimization and/or are coerced or forced into sex work after leaving home. Another study of runaways found that 38 percent of boys and 73 percent of girls reported sexual abuse, although they did not distinguish between sexual abuse experienced before and after running away (McCormack, Janus, and Burgess, 1986). Notably, the sexually abused runaway girls were more likely than the non-sexually abused runaway girls to report delinquent/criminal activities and to be arrested, to be placed in jail, and to participate in a violent act (ibid.). However, sexually abused runaway boys were no more delinquent/criminal than non-sexually abused runaway boys. Thus, not only are females and males labeled differently for consensual sexual activity but also sexual abuse appears to have a more detrimental effect on the subsequent delinquency of runaway females than of runaway males.

The crime-processing system, which has historically failed to respond to incest victims and other child abuse victimizations in the home, has diligently responded to girls who have run away from home or committed other offenses (see Gaarder and Belknap, 2002). Girls have been labeled and severely punished for running away, regardless of the circumstances motivating their flight. The system's processing of these "offenders" is covered in more detail in Chapter 4.

Clearly, a discussion of the role of sexuality must include mention of sex work. An overview of the global, political, gendered, and classed notions of sex work can be seen in international studies of sexual trafficking. The political economy of sex trafficking includes a "supply side" of Third World, poor women and girls; "exotic Asian women;" and a "demand side" of "men from industrialized and developing countries" (Bertone, 2000, 5). Suh (2000, 147) powerfully describes how "the social construction of Asian women as prostitutes can be traced both to the process of U.S. economic globalization that brought labor from Asia and to the gendered exclusion of Asian permanent residents." More specifically, she describes how in the late 1800s prostitution was listed as an occupation in the official census, and criminalizing it was a way to exclude Chinese from the United States. In the late 1800s, mining and railroad companies in the United States recruited Chinese men, who were not allowed to bring wives or children. Recruiters lured and kidnapped Chinese women to the United States, institutionalizing them as prostitutes. Thus, the social construction of Asian women as prostitutes can be traced both to the process of U.S. economic globalization that brought exploited labor from Asia and to the gendered exclusion of Asian permanent residents (ibid., 147). Suh (ibid., 156) points out the ramifications of this history today with regard to Asian women who marry U.S. military men who subsequently abuse them. If these women leave their abusive husbands before they are considered citizens, in a time when benefits for immigrants are decreasing, and they are forced into work in the sex (or drug) industry for survival, this clearly limits their ability to apply for citizenship and the benefits they should have received through citizenship or marriage.

THE FREQUENCY AND CONTEXT OF WOMEN'S AND GIRLS' OFFENDING FOR SPECIFIC CRIMES

Girl and Women Gangs

Although being in a gang is not a crime, gang membership is typically associated with delinquent and criminal activities. Until recently, the studies on girls and women in gangs have been few and fraught with methodological weaknesses. When the more dated studies included girls/women, it was as afterthoughts in studies on boys/men, and the studies viewed them through sexist, racist, and sexualized lenses (Chesney-Lind and Hagedorn, 1999). Not surprisingly, then, female participation in gangs has typically been viewed as an extension of male gang membership, with the female gang members viewed as sidekicks and sex objects for the male gang members (see Campbell, 1990; Chesney-Lind and Hagedorn, 1999).

Chesney-Lind and Hagedorn (1999) document a disturbing pattern where girls' roles in gangs have been invisible or sexualized, simplified, and misrepresented. For example, the historical writings on girls in gangs have minimized the sexual victimizations (including gang rapes) the girls reported at the same time that they presented their consensual sexual experiences, pregnancies, and motherhood as *indicators* of their delinquency and deviance (ibid.). More recent research suggests that "girls in gangs" are more dynamic, independent, and interesting than the criminologists from the 1950s and 1960s and earlier would have us believe (see Campbell, 1990; Chesney-Lind and Hagedorn, 1999; Laidler and Hunt, 2001; Wing and Willis, 1997).

Studies vary widely in what they report as girls' representation rate in gangs (see Bjerregaard, 2002. One study found them to make up 9 percent of gang members (Felkenes and Becker, 1995), another found that girls constituted 38 percent of gang members (Esbensen and Winfree, 1998), and yet another reported that females and males are equally likely to belong to a gang (Bjerregaard and Smith, 1993). Regarding the gendered nature of offending among gangs, the research is fairly consistent in reporting delinquency and criminal behavior as more prevalent in male than female gangs (Bjerregaard and Smith, 1993; Joe and Chesney-Lind, 1999; Esbensen and Winfree, 1998; Morash, 1983). One study found 90 percent of boys and 75 percent of girls had been arrested (Joe and Chesney-Lind, 1999). The only exceptions in the male-gender-related gang offending concern reports of drug use being gender neutral (no gender differences) (Esbensen and Winfree, 1998) and status offenses, particularly running away, as female-gender-related gang offenses (Joe and Chesney-Lind, 1999).

For both girls and boys, *peer influence/pressure* is the motivation for committing offenses (ibid.). As expected, the more time girls spend with delinquent girls, particularly girl gang members, the more likely they are to commit delinquent acts (Giordano, 1999). Whereas boys' peer influence plays a role in girls' delinquency, the approval of other girls is likely their most "important reference group, or at least the group to which they compare themselves" (ibid., 98–99).

Paramount in this discussion of gangs is the gendered use of violence. Research indicates that girls are more likely to fight when their personal, often sexual, reputation has been challenged, whereas boys are more likely to fight when the reputation of the gang has been challenged (which is never sexual) (Campbell, 1984). Fishman's (1999) analysis of the Vice Queens in Chicago in the 1960s reported that although the members would accompany the Vice Kings to their fights and subsequently fight the Vice Kings' enemy's auxiliary female gang members, the Vice Queens were far more likely to participate in their own fights with other female gangs, independently of what was going on with the Vice Kings. Most of the fights the Vice Queens engaged in had to do with issues of loyalty and integrity, with integrity involving a "threat to or attack on their public reputation" (ibid., 75). Notably, "fighting a male, and especially winning, carried a particular status among the girls" (ibid.). Campbell's (1999b, 115) study of Puerto Rican girl gang members in New York City from 1979 to 1981 found that the gang girls "took pride in their ability to fight" and "stress[ed] their aggressiveness and work[ed] hard at developing a reputation as a fighter." Campbell (ibid., 116) concluded: "More than winning a fight, it was important to be ready to enter one." A study of Los Angeles gangs reported that twice as many male (24 percent) as female (13 percent) gang members reported they would kill someone if asked to do so by the gang (Felkenes and Becker, 1995, 8).

Hagedorn and Devitt's (1999) extensive study of primarily Latina female gangs in Milwaukee in 1995 included eight gangs. One-quarter of their sample were African American female gang members. They reported that their sample was fairly evenly divided between the female gang members who "liked to fight" and those who fought to maintain solidarity with their gang members. The small number of women who reported that they were "not fighters" were frowned upon by their gang peers for violating the gang norms. Notably, the women who "liked to fight" had less of a male-centered outlook on life (e.g., were less likely to agree that all women "need" a man to order their lives), whereas the women who fought for gang solidarity were more likely to be in a current intimate relationship with a man. Latina gangs were most likely to fight because of turf battles or a rival gang "representing," whereas fights with other gangs constituted less than half of African American women gang members' fights. African American women gang members' fights were more likely over "respect" and "jealousy" issues than were the Latina women's gang fights.

Messerschmidt's (1999, 127) attempt to understand how female and male gang members "do gender" in the context of violence reports that participating in group violence is likely "the most positively sanctioned site for displaying one's 'badness.'" Messerschmidt is convinced that girl gang members' use of violence is conducted in a manner of "doing femininity" or accommodating their "proper" gender roles and masculine dominance. "For girls in the gang, doing femininity means occasionally, and in appropriate circumstances, doing violence" (ibid., 129). The girl gang members "doing violence," then, is not an attempt to "pass as males" but rather to construct "a specific type of femininity, race, and class" where "femininity is assessed both in terms of willingness to defend the 'hood' and on doing difference" (ibid., 130).

Girl gang members are well aware of the male gang members' sexualizing and conventional notions of them, and the girl gang members monitor other girls both in and out of their gang in terms of appearances and conduct that can be sexualized (Laidler and Hunt, 2001). Campbell's (1999b) analysis of Puerto Rican female gang members in New York City described their frustration with the public perception of them as "whores," or "ho's." Thus, the gang girls "exerted a good deal of social control over one another's sexual behavior," where "serial monogamy was the norm and sexual promiscuity was frowned upon" (ibid., 113). At the same time, they were quite aware of and frustrated with the double standard where males' infidelity in intimate relationships was accepted and even expected (ibid.). One study reported that because gang girls are often angered by their own mothers' use of drugs and violence and inability to realize their mothering roles, and in order to gain their own sense of respectability, they both adopt and reject some of the conventional gender roles. Thus, the girls work to maintain not only their femininity but also their autonomy from others, particularly males. Contrary to the early theorists on girls in gangs, "the girls develop their own notions of men and masculinity . . . In their eyes, a man has to have respect for her as a woman and as an individual" (Laidler and Hunt, 2001, 674).

Wing and Willis's (1997) research on gangs, race, and gender notes the racism and sexism of "gangs" being perceived as synonymous with African American male criminality. Additionally, they are troubled by the invisibility of African American women's roles in gang life. Wing and Willis (ibid., 244) identify six "frequently overlapping" roles of African American women's gang

---

EXHIBIT 3.1 Why Girls Join Gangs

- Gangs provide friendship and acceptance, a place of belonging, a "family."[1]
- Gangs provide an escape from isolation and harsh environments.[2]
- Gangs provide protection/safety, especially from undesirable men.[3]
- Gangs provide status.[4]

---

[1]Campbell, 1999a; Deschenes and Esbensen, 1999; Fishman, 1999; Joe and Chesney-Lind, 1999; Lauderback, Hansen, and Waldorf, 1992; Messerschmidt, 1999; Moore, 1999.
[2]Fishman, 1999; Joe and Chesney-Lind, 1999; Moore, 1999.
[3]Campbell, 1999a; Fishman, 1999; Messerschmidt, 1999.
[4]Fishman, 1999; Lauderback, Hansen, and Waldorf, 1992.

involvement: (1) full-fledged members of their own, female-only gangs; (2) auxiliaries to male gangs; (3) gangsters in coed gangs; (4) girlfriends and wives of male gang members; (5) mothers of male gang members' children; and (6) mothers, sisters, and daughters of male gang members. Thus, they conclude that African American women "have the capacity to affect gang members on profoundly intimate levels" and thus must play a pivotal role in providing solutions to the gang problem (ibid., 243). A study of largely Latino/a youth gangs in Los Angeles found that while over 90 percent of the youths reported pride in their Latino/a culture, about two-fifths of both the girls and boys reported that they believed they were discriminated against for being members of a Latino/a gang, and the authors indicated this race-based discrimination was related to the gang members' high school drop-out rate (about two-fifths of both sexes dropped out of high school) (Felkenes and Becker, 1995).

A frequently asked question regarding girls in gangs is, "Why would a girl want to join a gang?" Four main reasons that are somewhat overlapping have been identified in research, depicted in Exhibit 3.1 The primary reason is that gangs provide a *sense of belonging.* This overlaps with the second reason, that gangs provide *respite from the harsh environments* in the neighborhoods, families, and/or schools of many members. Third, gangs offer *safety and protection.* Finally, gangs can provide *status.* For example, Joe and Chesney-Lind's (1999, 229) study of Hawaiian gang members found that for both girls and boys, the gang provides a "social outlet and tonic" for growing up in communities "racked by poverty, racism, and rapid population growth" and lives fraught with boredom due to limited recreational outlets. In addition, for both sexes, gang membership provides a sense of family for those youths whose parents are forced (due to the economy) to work numerous hours, or worse, for those youths whose home lives are abusive (ibid.). Similarly, Moore's (1999) study of female and male gang members and their families in East Los Angeles reported that, while gang membership serves as a "family" for both sexes, given that female gang members are more likely than their male counterparts to report incest histories, more troubled families, living with a chronically sick relative, living with a relative who died, living with a relative who was a heroin addict, and living with a relative who was arrested, gang membership may represent a different peer group outlet and be more of a refuge from family for female than for male gang members. Another Los Angeles Latino/a gang study also noted that girls' reported lower satisfaction/happiness levels regarding their families (Felkenes and Becker, 1995).

In sum, the earliest research on girls in gangs, when the gang researchers bothered to include females, presented them in highly sexist manners. They were most frequently viewed as extensions, sidekicks, and sexual outlets for the important gang members: male gang members. More current analyses not only report far more dynamic and independent girls in gangs but also document that these earlier depictions, in addition to being racist and sexist, were inaccurate. Thus, girls in gangs, despite their often-difficult childhoods of sexism, racism, and poverty, show a significant amount of agency, and gang membership, as it does for boys, allows them an important sense of belonging and "family." At the same time, the research in recent years on females in gangs notes the heterogeneity of female gang membership. That is, there is considerable difference in the amount of violence used and what female gang membership means depending on the time/era, the location in the city, and the race/ethnicity of the gang. In short, female gang membership is far more complex and dynamic than the early studies implied.

Theft

Studies published in the 1980s identified larceny and thefts, such as forgery, counterfeiting, fraud, and embezzlement, as constituting considerable amounts of females' arrests and convictions but still identified these offenses as male-gender-related (Eaton, 1986; Leonard, 1982). Property offenses of a minor nature have often been attributed as female-gender-related. Stereotypes link women with shopping and portray them as being tempted by clothes, jewelry, and makeup; thus, shoplifting has frequently been assumed to be female-gender-related. A closer examination suggests that shoplifting may be gender neutral or male-gender-related. Most of the studies on shoplifting rates were published in the 1960s, 70s, and 80s. Two of these studies found no significant differences between males' and females' shoplifting rates (Hudson, 1989; Smart, 1976), whereas other studies reported that males are more likely than females to shoplift (Buckle and Farrington, 1984; Mawby, 1980) and are more likely to steal more items and items of greater value than the food and clothing typically shoplifted by females (Buckle and Farrington, 1984; Gibbens and Prince, 1962; Hoffman-Bustamante, 1973). A more recent study on shoplifting by drug addicts reported no gender differences in their rates (Byqvist, 1999).

Studies examining conviction rates from 1979 to 1986 (Kline, 1993) and arrest rates from 1960 to 1980 (Chilton and Datesman, 1987) reported that the crimes that suggested growing rates for women were larcenies and thefts (although these offenses were still male-gender-related). The study on arrests found women's arrest rate growth was particularly evident among African American women (ibid.). A more recent study found that among habitual or career criminals, women were significantly more likely than men to be arrested for forgery and fraud (DeLisi, 2002). Similarly, the 2003 arrest rates reported in Table 3.1 suggest that embezzlement is now a gender-neutral offense (50 percent of arrests for both females and males), while fraud (45 percent female arrests) and counterfeiting (40 percent female) are going in the direction of gender neutrality. Thus, it has been concluded that while men still dominate most property crimes, the women's rate is growing and as stated earlier has been linked with the "feminization of poverty" (women's growing poverty rates).

Robbery and Burglary

As seen in Table 3.1, about nine-tenths of both robberies and burglary arrests were of men/boys. Additionally, a recent study of career or habitual criminals found that men were significantly more likely than women to be arrested for both robbery and burglary (DeLisi, 2002). However, few studies examine gender and these crimes.

Although little effort has been made to study gender differences in burglary, in one notable exception, numerous gender differences were found: (1) Males were more likely than females to admit to crimes in addition to the burglary; (2) females were more likely than males to work with others in committing the burglary; (3) females were more likely than males to report being drug addicts; (4) males started their burglary "careers" at an earlier age than the females; (5) males reported committing more burglaries than the females; (6) females reported less contact with the crime-processing system than the males; and (8) females and males were equally likely to use drugs (Decker et al., 1993).

Sommers and Baskin's (1993) study of sixty-five violent females charged with robberies and aggravated assaults claimed the women varied significantly in the number of robberies they had committed (ranging from one to sixteen), although one-quarter had committed more than ten robberies. Two-thirds of the women reported the robbery occurring in the course of and subsequent to other crimes, such as prostitution, drug dealing, nonviolent theft, and fraud. Most of the robberies were not planned but were more spontaneous, or "spur-of-the-moment." Regarding motivations to rob, 89 percent reported committing the robbery to obtain money, with four-fifths of those committing it for money stating that it was money for drugs, with the remaining one-fifth wanting the money for clothes, jewelry, and electronic equipment. About 10 percent reported their motivation was loyalty to friends, vengeance, or the excitement. Notably, however, for many of these women, their early robberies were not motivated by financial desires, but their subsequent robberies were financial, usually to buy drugs. Now turning to the victims of these women's robberies, almost three-quarters were strangers, equally likely to be other women as men. However, when the women robbed without a weapon, their victims were more likely to be other women. They reported choosing stranger victims who looked weak and vulnerable. About two-thirds of the robberies were committed with accomplices, and of these, 60 percent were committed with other women.

From early on in their criminal careers, women in the robbery sample reported that they acted out of self-determination and not in concert with or for boyfriends. Although the women sometimes were involved in criminal activities that involved men or activities that at times were controlled by men, they did so most often as equal partners. (Sommers and Baskin, 1993, 149)

Miller's (1998) ethnographic study of fourteen women and twenty-three men robbers found overall gender similarities in motivation for robbing: Robbers of both sexes rob to get money, primarily for status or material goods (e.g., jewelry) and to a lesser degree to support a drug addiction. Less frequently, both males and females are motivated to rob by the "psychological thrill" it entails or for revenge. The only gender difference in motivation to rob was that young men were more likely to report the pressure to have their own money and to own status goods. The gender differences in Miller's (ibid.) study of robbers, then, had less to do with motivations to rob and more to do with how the robberies are carried out. The men used primarily one method to rob: "using physical violence and/or a gun placed on or at close proximity to the victim in a confrontational manner" (ibid., 47). Women, on the other hand, are more eclectic in their enactments of robbery, reporting three strategies. The most frequently reported strategy is targeting female victims, reported by 71 percent of the women robbers. Half of the women robbers reported two other strategies: (1) promising men sexual favors for money, where the women then don't "deliver" the sexual favors; and (2) working with men (friends, relatives, or boyfriends) to rob men. Maher's (1997) research on sex workers identified a type of robbery, "viccing," as specific to this group, where sex workers rob their clients. Maher and Curtis (1992) view "viccing" as motivated by sex workers' frustration with the devaluation of their work and their bodies and their extreme vulnerability to victimization.

White-Collar Crime

The "liberation" hypothesis implies that as women become more equal to men, their offending rates will converge with men's. Given that the slow movement toward gender equality has benefited middle-class women the most, we might expect to see a similarity in men's and women's offenses most clearly in the white-collar realm. There is limited research on the gendered nature of white-collar crime. A study of white-collar convictions in U.S. federal courts found major differences between convicted men and women: (1) Women were usually employed as clerical workers, and men were usually employed as managers and administrators; (2) 60 percent of convicted female embezzlers were bank tellers, whereas only 14 percent of male embezzlers were tellers; (3) men's financial gains were much larger than women's; (4) women tended to work alone in committing the crime, whereas men were more likely to work with others; (5) women were more likely than men to report "family need" as motivating their offense; (6) women's crimes were more petty than men's; (7) women's share of corporate crime was low; and (8) men were more likely than women to be influenced by other white-collar workers to commit the crime (Daly, 1989). In fact, the gender differences in these white-collar offenders were so extreme and the nature of the differences such to make one wonder whether the crimes of most of these women should really be classified under white-collar offenses.

A more recent study found that the gendered nature of white-collar crime depended on the type of white-collar crime committed: (1) *Asset misappropriation* (theft or misuse of an organization's assets) was reported as 48 percent women, (2) *corruption* (employees wrongfully using their influence in business transactions to obtain benefits for themselves that were contrary to duties to their employer) was reported as 45 percent women; and (3) *fraudulent statements* (falsification of the organization's records or documents) was reported as 31 percent by women (Holtfreter, 2005). This differs from Daly's (1989) finding that men were more likely to commit white-collar crime in groups (e.g., corruption). It is important, however, to acknowledge the similarities to Daly's (ibid.) findings: The less serious white-collar offenses (in terms of dollar loss), *asset misappropriation* and *corruption*, were equally likely to be committed by females and males. However, *fraudulent statements* (the more serious offenses) were distinctly linked to being male, being educated, and holding a higher-level position in the organization. This supports Daly's finding that gender differences in white-collar crimes are tied (at least in part) to positions within the organizational hierarchy.

Drug Use and Selling

Before reviewing the research on women and girls as drug users and drug sellers, it is useful to examine the political nature of women and drugs. Most research has been on men, and the research on both men and women has focused on the most economically and socially disenfranchised. Ironically, at the same time, "without any fanfare, the 'war on drugs' has become a war on women and has contributed to the explosion in women's prison populations," including the implementation of urinalysis and other technologies that are used on paroled women to send them back to prison at unprecedented rates for drug use (Chesney-Lind, 1997, 147). Moreover, women and girls who use drugs also face harsher societal disapproval than drug-using men and boys (Luthar and D'Avanzo, 1999; Sterk, 1999).

An analysis of gender and alcohol is insightful: In the general population, among both adolescents (Hussong, 2000) and adults (Green, Freeborn, and Polen, 2001), males tend to drink more heavily than females (Luthar and D'Avanzo, 1999). Notably, research on adolescents found girls are more likely than boys to report their first experience with alcohol and their first experience with drugs as coinciding with the first time they had sex, while boys are more likely than girls to report they had sex before the first time they used alcohol or drugs (Li et al., 2000). Contrary to stereotypes, studies on youths report suburban girls were the most likely to have used alcohol while inner-city boys were the least likely (Luthar and D'Avanzo, 1999), and African American females (and African American males) were significantly less likely to smoke cigarettes or drink alcohol than their Latina(o) and White counterparts (Bilchick, 1999).

Another youth study found that across gender, Whites reported the most poly-drug use, followed by African Americans and Latino/as (with similar rates), and Asian Americans with the lowest rates. There were few gender differences within race/ethnicity, but where differences existed, males used more than females, and the gender gap was most pronounced among Asian Americans (Epstein et al., 1999). Finally, a study of adult probationers reported no gender differences in illegal drug use histories but concluded that men were significantly more likely than women to have alcohol abuse histories (Olson, Lurigio, and Seng, 2000).

Regarding *reasons for using drugs*, research reports some interesting gender differences. First, women and girls are more likely to be introduced to drugs by husbands and boyfriends, while men and boys are more likely to be introduced by male friends (Evans, Forsyth, and Gauthier, 2002; Inciardi, Lockwood, and Pottieger, 1993; Lichtenstein, 1997), although research also suggests that many women and girls are introduced to drugs by girlfriends and parents (Sterk, 1999). Regarding crack use, however, Maher (1995) presents more varied initiation, claiming that few of the women were initiated by boyfriends or husbands; "rather, women's experiences of initiation were mediated by many factors including the influence of same-sex peers, previous drug use experience, availability and cost of the drug, patterns of consumption and the reciprocal relationship with popular cultural images" (ibid., 133). In fact, some women felt pressured by other women to try crack.

A second significant gender difference is that women are far more likely to be in a position to have to exchange sex and companionship for drugs from a dealer or other user (Inciardi, Lockwood, and Pottieger, 1993; Inciardi et al., 1991; Lichtenstein, 1997; Maher et al., 1996; Ratner, 1993; Sterk 1999). Third, while both females and males often begin using drugs out of curiosity and a desire to experiment, there are gender differences in the motivations for continued drug use. Women and girls are less likely than men and boys to use illegal drugs for pleasure or thrill seeking (Li et al., 2000) and from peer pressure. Fourth, a gender difference identified in drug use, at least as applied to crack, is that for men it is a means of "doing masculinity" (Evans, Forsyth, and Gautheir, 2002). However, some research on drug-using girls and women report them as motivated by a way to "act out" against their gender roles to society in general, their parents, and/or their teachers (Sterk, 1999; Friedman and Alicea, 1995).

Fifth, and finally, perhaps the major gender difference in drug use is women's and girls' "self-medication" to "treat" depression (Evans, Forsyth, and Gautheir, 2002; Inciardi, Lockwood, and Pottieger, 1993). A study of women crack users found that half started using in response to a traumatic experience or series of traumatic experiences (e.g., death in the family, losing a child, rape); the other half were in a progression of already serious drug use (Erickson et al., 2000). Women are more likely than men to continue drug use in response to crises and psychological stresses (and may be more likely to have crises and psychological stresses) and are more likely than men to have been depressed before developing a drug problem (Evans, Forsyth, and Gautheir, 2002; Inciardi, Lockwood, and Pottieger, 1993). A study of adolescents receiving drug abuse treatment found that the girls (and their parents) were more likely than the boys (and their parents) to report family dysfunction (Dakof, 2000). Notably, one study found that African American females' initiation into drugs is more likely a rite of passage, while White females' initiation is more likely a result of traumatic life events (Lichtenstein, 1997).

The limited research examining gender differences in *selling drugs* indicates that it is much tougher for women than men to break into the drug market. For lower-level drugs, particularly marijuana, women have more access to selling drugs. Women's drug selling may be a better indication of the feminization of poverty than of women's increased drug use (Diaz-Cotto, 1996). More specifically, not all women drug sellers are drug users, but rather, drug selling is one of the few options many poor women have to make money (ibid.). Some research contends that women who successfully gain access to drug selling do so through their husbands or boyfriends (Koester and Schwartz, 1993; Maher and Curtis, 1992). A study of six women and thirty-four men found that crack dealers "hang together" in groups for protection (the police are less likely to confront a group of suspects than individuals) and that this works to women crack dealers' advantage because they are viewed as just hanging out with the male dealers, not dealing themselves (Jacobs, 1996). One gender analysis of crack users' means to maintain their habits found (1) drug selling was limited to African American men and excluded all women and White men; (2) most of the women were in the position of having to exchange sex for drugs unless they had wealthy husbands, while male crack users generated income through exploiting women's and girls' sexual labor (prostituting them); (3) both males and females stole items, but only males robbed; and (4) while the men faced dangerous situations in robbing to make money to support their habits, the women faced extremely violent and sexually degrading encounters routinely in crack houses (Evans, Forsyth, and Gautheir, 2002). The men in this study reported committing extremely degrading sexual abuses of women and girls in the crack houses. This was a study of small–town, mainly White (and some African American) crack users, indicating that the sexual violence is not part of inner-city culture but simply part of crack culture.

An ethnographic study of the marijuana industry in rural Kentucky reported gender-distinguished roles, dependent on social class membership (Hafley and Tewksbury, 1996). The three distinct roles for women in the rural marijuana industry community are "strumpets," "decent women," and "women-in-between." A "strumpet" is typically young, uneducated, and unmarried and often has one or more children out of wedlock. Her role is to emotionally, sexually, and domestically support male marijuana growers. She is expendable to these men and knows it; thus, despite strong loyalty to men of the marijuana industry, if he goes to prison, moves, or drops her, she seeks the next man to take his place. Needless to say, she is looked down upon within her community. The "decent woman," then, is far more respected and typically a female relative of an active male in the marijuana industry (e.g., mother, sister, wife, grandmother, daughter, etc.). Although she is aware of the illegal activities of "her man" in the marijuana industry, she rarely participates herself. "However, decent women's expressed disapproval does not lead the men to curtail their activities, for after all, they are 'just women'" (ibid., 88). Finally, the "in-between-woman" falls between the strumpets and decent women and is unique in that she plays an active role in growing and distributing the marijuana. She is less respected than "decent women" but more respected and holds more power than "strumpets." "Across the board, women's roles are predominantly passive, although within the last decade women-in-between have begun to play more active roles. For the male marijuana grower, women fulfill essential, but subservient roles" (ibid., 91).

An important focus of the research on drug use and abuse is attempting to determine how it is related to other types of criminal acts and behavior. One study found that drug-using women prisoners are more likely than their non-drug-using counterparts to engage in a wide variety of both property and violent crimes, emphasizing the criminalizing aspect of drug addictions for women (Mullings, Pollock, and Crouch, 2002). A Swedish study of addicts found that relative to men, women were more likely to be unemployed and homeless, reported more severe drug use and habits that advanced more quickly, exhibited more complex psychological problems, and experienced more severe backgrounds, but despite all of this, they had significantly lower criminality (other than drug use) (Byqvist, 1999).

Although researchers disagree on the dynamics of the connection between drugs and sex, they agree a connection exists. Maher's (1997) ethnographic fieldwork with women crack users in the early 1990s in three Brooklyn (New York City) neighborhoods reports that income generation within the street-level economy falls into three overlapping and interdependent options: drug-business hustles, nondrug hustles, and sex work. Maher (ibid., 130) reports that "sex work was the only income-generating activity consistently available to women drug users," and given the risks of "death, rape, and disfigurement" that the sex work entailed, "suggests that overall these women had few [income-generating] choices indeed" (ibid., 189).

One study on women and crack cocaine found extremely high regularity of women performing oral sex (in particular) on men in crack houses in exchange for occasional hits of crack during the sexual act, an obvious form of sex work, and because the rules in the crack house were understood by all involved, there was little negotiating available to the women (Inciardi, Lockwood, and Pottieger, 1993). In another study, a crack-addicted woman reported witnessing a girl no older than 15 entering a crack house, trying to leave, and being beaten worse than anything she had ever seen. This witness was afraid to intervene because she believed the same would happen to her. She feared the girl was killed. Numerous men in this house gave the man who abused (or likely killed) this girl a rock of crack to "have their way" and "do all kinds of kinky shit to her" (Evans, Forsyth, and Gautheir, 2002, 503). When they were done, he threw something over her still body lying in her own blood and carried her out the door.

Maher (1995), however, challenges the research presentation of female drug users as "innocent" and "hapless victims," often lured into both drug use and sex work. "Such accounts perpetuate stereotypical images of women as weak and submissive; as incapable of exercising agency and unable to make any kind of choice in relation to drug use" (ibid., 132). She reports the gendered use of crack as far more complex than previous gender analyses of drug use. First, she is resistant to the existing paradigm of female drug using that denies women agency: "[W]omen, like me, choose to use drugs. Not one of the women in this study was forced to stick a needle in her arm or coerced into taking a blast off a crack stem" (ibid., 160). (However, Maher describes one woman user whose boyfriend "exerted considerable pressure," including "blowing the smoke in her mouth" [ibid., 141]). Maher's overall description of "the street-level drug users in one of the poorest neighborhoods in New York City" follows:

> The majority used a combination of crack cocaine and heroin on a daily basis. Most were members of racial/ethnic minorities. Nearly all were homeless. Many were mothers and a significant proportion were HIV positive. These women were both the perpetrators and victims of violence and all engaged in law-breaking, principally street-level sex-work, as a means of supporting their drug consumption. (1997, 29)

Maher (ibid.) noted, however, that while the initiation into crack use is less gendered than women's drug use is typically viewed in research, once immersed in the consumption of crack, their experiences and options are gendered. For example, women disproportionately suffered the economic marginalization and social stigma associated with crack use (Maher and Curtis, 1992), and the structure of the drug economy did not provide "equal opportunity employment," working to women's disadvantage (Maher, 1995). In fact, the advantages came to the male sellers (Maher and Daly, 1996). Homelessness for crack users was gendered in that men were more able to shelter themselves from the worst aspects of street life, particularly in terms of the risk of harassment, violence, and victimization (Maher, 1997). "By virtue of their economic position, many elderly males were able to accommodate their own demands for sexual activity and drug use by providing shelter to homeless women drug users" (ibid., 54), while impoverished crack-using women—in addition to providing these men with sex and domestic services—were sexually exploited and degraded by other men as well (Maher et al., 1996). Moreover, the advent of crack flooded the streets with new sex workers and thus the going rate for street sex workers decreased drastically (Maher and Curtis, 1992; Maher and Daly, 1996). At the same time as noting the gendered nature of crack use and selling crack, Maher (1997, x) is perhaps most effective in presenting these drug users more powerfully and with more agency than existing research: "As it turns out, the women I studied were remarkable in many ways, but perhaps most of all for their resilience, their capacity for the hardest of labors, and the sheer tenacity of the struggles to survive."

Interestingly, a study of an African American girl gang reported that the inception of crack sales in the mid-1980s by their boyfriends resulted in the formation of this female gang (Lauderback, Hansen, and Waldorf, 1992). More specifically, after continued dissatisfaction with the division of labor and profits from crack-selling ventures with their boyfriends, these young women entered into the crack-selling business themselves.

Another study concluded that women crack addictions "magnified their extreme vulnerability arising from conditions of poverty, arrest histories, loss of family, exposure to violence, and histories of sexual abuse" (Erickson et al., 2000, p. 769). But the authors also reported that most of the women did not see stopping crack use as an option, and most did not identify their addiction as a problem. Rather, crack was what made their lives bearable or interesting, and sex was the means to smoking crack (ibid.).

Friedman and Alicea's (1995) research is a departure from the vast majority of drug research in that their sample is composed of thirty White, middle- and upper-class women heroin and methadone users. This study found that many of these class- and race-privileged women reported their initial heroin use was a means to reject the patriarchy and the restrictive gender roles they perceived and experienced. These women, then, reported using heroin precisely because it "did not fit the traditional image of good girls" and "it felt empowering and gave them a sense of control because it required some degree of autonomy and assertiveness" (ibid., 437). Moreover, in addition to the "in-your-face" aspect of societal rejection by becoming heroin users, heroin use provided these women with feelings of pleasure and happiness and offered them "strength, self-confidence, and feelings of invincibility" (ibid., 438). However, over time, the drug stopped working as a "liberating mechanism," and they frequently reached a point of crisis where they redefined heroin as "the villain" instead of "the hero" (ibid., 439). Thus, while these wealthy White women's motivations for using the drug are likely different from those typically studied (the most marginalized of the population), their addictions resulted in both the positive and negative aspects that drug addiction does for everyone else. Also, while they had started using heroin as a rebellion against patriarchy and although it initially helped their self-esteem, addiction resulted in quite the opposite:

> They could not reconcile a perspective of being "in control" when they witnessed the horrible things they saw themselves doing for their men and their drug. They began to see the heroin world as a mirror of the dominant culture, which both relegated women to low status and devalued them as individuals. Heroin was no longer a vehicle for rejecting patriarchy. (ibid., 442)

The women in this sample described prostituting themselves to get more drugs for themselves and often their male partners/lovers or offering physicians "blow jobs" to get drugs. This was hardly the picture they had of themselves as independent women flaunting the patriarchy. Thus, distrust of men became another theme in their "epiphany" of realizing that heroin was "the villain." Unfortunately, they found the methadone clinics they went to in order to get off heroin often sexist and difficult to work with. The authors report: "At the point that women choose to use methadone, they believe that they have no resources (social and economic) and no other alternatives for survival" (ibid., 443). However, they also reported the treatment as unbearably sexist as well.

Claire E. Sterk (1999) offers one of the most detailed and comprehensive studies of crack-using women in her ethnographic research on 149 active crack-using women. In particular, her book *Fast Lives* describes far more variation among these women than is reported in other studies. Sterk identified four categories of crack-using women. Her first category, *queens of the scene*, had the highest status and the most control over their lives (relative to other crack-cocaine-using women) due to their ability to cook powder cocaine to form crack. Such cooking skills (the irony of this gendered job was not lost on the women) allowed these women access to the upper- and mid-level dealers, who also protected them. In addition to the "queens," Sterk's (ibid.) three other categories of women crack cocaine users were the *hustlers*, who "work" as criminals but not sex workers to support their habits (e.g, stealing cars, pickpocketing, etc.); the *hookers*, who use sex work (prostitution) to support their habits; and the *older struggling rookies*, who had no histories of drug using or other illegal activities until their 30s (or later) and were typically unemployed, concerned with social approval, and introduced to crack cocaine by their children. Sterk (ibid.) also reports that the existing research and media representations portraying crack cocaine as an aphrodisiac are misleading in the sense that for both men and women over time, the crack addiction and work to support the addiction result in decreased sexual activity.

The media abounds with degrading and humiliating images and names for women exchanging crack for sex, for example, "crack whores" and "chicken heads" (Comerford et al., 1996; Erickson et al., 2000; Evans, Forsyth, and Gauther, 2002; Metsch et al., 1996; Sterk, 1999). In addition to the gendered nature of sex work associated with drug use and addiction, one of the most gendered aspects of illegal drug use is the threat, perpetrated largely by the media, of drug-using pregnant women and mothers, particularly "crack mothers" (Humphries, 1999). A scholar in this area, Drew Humphries (ibid., 15) asks: "How and with what consequences did an unusually powerless category of women emerge as a threatening symbol of disorder, the unenviable enemy in the domestic war on drugs?" Humphries' (ibid.) focus is to merge the existing scientific data on rates of crack and cocaine use over time and research on the health of babies from women on crack with her careful research on how these rates and babies' health were represented in the television media between 1983 and 1994. The image presented in the media, and likely adopted by the general public, is of poor women of color in inner cities who use crack and who do not care that they are pregnant and what effect their crack use will have on the developing fetus. Through her careful examination of both research on the topic of drug-using women and content analysis of television news portrayal of these women, Humphries (ibid.) provides a powerful presentation of the four stages of the social construction of crack mothers by the media (see Exhibit 3.2). She states:

> The networks distorted the record on crack babies, representing the worst possible outcomes as the norm. . . . The prevailing wisdom, then, held that the prenatal cocaine exposure risked the life or health of the newborn, that crack-addicted women who used drugs during pregnancy should be prevented from inflicting avoidable harm to the fetus and newborn, and that someone should take action. (ibid., 66)

E X H I B I T 3.2 Humphries's Stages in the Social Construction of Crack Mothers as Presented in Television News Stories

Stage 1: Recreational Cocaine Use (1983–1985)—Characterized by affluent, white, remorseful women formerly addicted to cocaine, interviewed about their addictions from their own homes or a treatment facility. They were treated sympathetically by the news media as "vulnerable" to the "myth of recreational drugs." Discovery of pregnancy was not sufficient to stop the use. They tended to have healthy babies, however, although physicians had concerns about these babies' long-term health. These women were not subjected to punishment.

Stage 2: The Discovery of Crack (1985–1987)—Characterized by inner-city street corner African Americans and Hispanics after crack, a highly addictive, cheaper form of cocaine hit the drug market in 1985. Crack news stories overshadowed cocaine ones, except emotionally charged stories of white cocaine-using pregnant women and their afflicted babies.

Stage 3: The Crusade against Crack Mothers (1988–1990)—Characterized by inner-city, largely African-American pregnant women, or such women with recently born "crack babies," filmed on the streets or in hospitals shortly after the births. The babies in the coverage had serious defects. The sensationalist news coverage led to highly publicized cases of these women charged with manslaughter, injecting a minor with drugs, and child endangerment.

Stage 4: Recovering Mothers and Resilient Children (1991–1994)—News stories and researchers began questioning the reality and severity of trauma experienced by "crack babies" and documented that the prenatal transference of crack-cocaine was not as harmful as originally portrayed. "Crack mothers" were portrayed as "survivors" and interviewed in treatment. However, crack mothers were still vilified by the legal system with approaches and policies that made crack-addicted pregnant women, especially those of color or poor, reluctant to pursue treatment for fear of landing in jail or prison.

SOURCE: Drew Humphries. 1999. *Crack Mothers: Pregnancy, Drugs, and the Media*. Columbus, OH: Ohio State University Press, based on content analysis of television media representation from 1983–1994, using mostly ABC, CBS, and NBC news presentations (*N* = 84).

Similar to Humpries (ibid.), Boyd's (1999, 14) extensive literature review of research on the effects of illicit drug use on mothering reports that although it "is viewed as inconsistent with good mothering, many researchers have demonstrated that women who use illicit drugs can be adequate parents." Boyd cites research that found that drug-addicted mothers are no more likely to be child abusers and indeed are less likely than nonaddicted mothers to use physical forms of violence (Colten, 1982), and generally hold the same parenting values as non-drug-abusing mothers (Rosenbaum et al., 1990). Sterk (1999) found that most of the women in her study of crack users tried to quit crack when discovering they were pregnant, but they typically replaced crack with alcohol and other drugs, and all resumed crack after the pregnancies. Additionally, these women avoided getting prenatal care or going to detoxification programs for fear of being reported and thus having their babies taken away at birth.

Boyd (1999) notes that the only specific effect of pregnant women's use of drugs is the chance that their babies will experience drug withdrawal and that not all such babies experience withdrawal, also known as neonatal abstinence syndrome (NAS). Further, Boyd (ibid., 36) identifies NAS as appearing to be a "cultural fabrication" consistent with Humphries' (1999) identification of the social fabrication in "creating" a mythical image of "crack mother." Indeed, it appears that alcohol (via fetal alcohol syndrome) likely has a greater impact than drugs, although few of the pregnant woman drug studies have included alcohol intake as a variable in addition to drug intake (Boyd, 1999). Thus, Boyd (ibid., 25) concludes her review of the literature with the need to question the legal, medical, and social service assumption that "illicit drug use equals poor parenting, which places children at risk." Also consistent with Humphries' (1999) speculation, Boyd (1999) found that the twenty-eight illicit-drug-using women in her study were afraid to contact medical professionals for help when they found they were pregnant for fear of being stigmatized and jailed in their attempts to get "clean" and/or receive prenatal care. Boyd (ibid.) goes on to report not only horror stories about the medical community's treatment of drug-using women when their babies were born but also the truly deplorable conditions that their babies labeled with NAS were subject to at birth (e.g., little or no human touch, light, inability to bond with any human including a parent, and so on, for days at a time).

It is vital in the assessment of the crackdown on drug-using women to acknowledge the racist and racialized nature of the phenomenon and response to it. Roberts' (1997, 127) overview on the phenomenon of charging women who give birth to babies testing positive for drugs notes that most of these women are poor, African American, and addicted to crack:

> The prosecution of drug-addicted mothers is part of an alarming trend toward greater state intervention into the lives of pregnant women under the rationale of protecting the fetus from harm. Such government intrusion is particularly harsh for poor women of color. They are the least likely to obtain adequate prenatal care, the most vulnerable to government monitoring, and the least able to conform to the [W]hite middle-class standard of motherhood. They are therefore the primary targets of government control.

Finally, a significant aspect of illegal drugs since the 1990s is methamphetamine (for an excellent overview of the drug and women's use and selling of it, see Strauss and Falkin, 2001). Similar to other studies of women's methamphetamine use, a recent study of women users committed to prison or a community drug treatment program reported that they were predominantly White and unmarried, started using in their late teens, and typically started using alcohol and marijuana about six years before their initiation into methamphetamine (Strauss and Falkin, 2001). The three most common reasons for using this drug were (1) because close friends or partners did (28 percent), (2) to "party" (27 percent), (3) and to "get high." Notably, though, 13 percent started using it to lose weight, 9 percent to get things done, and 6 percent to "feel better" (ibid.). Seventy percent of the women had been involved in selling, manufacturing, and/or distributing methamphetamine.

General Aggression

Although other sections in this chapter have addressed or will address gender differences in aggression in terms of juvenile delinquency, gangs, child abuse, and homicide, it is also useful to devote a section simply to aggression. Chapter 1 included a discussion on the role of biology versus social learning as an explanation for the consistent finding that males are more aggressive than females, concluding that this is primarily a gender, not a sex, difference. More specifically, males are generally more aggressive than females due to prescribed and gendered social roles. Mary B. Harris has conducted a significant amount of research, ongoing since the 1970s, addressing gender differences in aggression and accounting for race/ethnicity and context (see, for example, Harris 1973, 1974a, 1974b, 1976, 1992, 1996). She has used both experimental and survey research designs on large populations of college students; her conclusions are shown in Exhibit 3.3.

Harris's research indicates the importance of examining many factors in attempting to address gender differences in aggressive behavior, including not only gender differences in the use of aggression but also differences in how aggression is used depending on the sex of the victim, gender differences in what "provokes" one to use aggression, differences in people's perceptions about the adequacy of using aggression based on whether the aggressor is female or male, and racial/ethnic differences in perceptions and use of aggression. These studies indicate that both personal use and assessment of others' use of aggression are highly gendered. The use and assessment of others' use of aggression is less affected by race/ethnicity, yet some differences indicated that "the use of verbal and physical aggression may be different for members of different ethnic groups" (Harris, 1996, 128).

A study examining the context of assaults committed by sixty-five violent women offenders reported that the motivations were often aggressive responses to aggression from those designated as their victims (Sommers and Baskin, 1993). "These women are not roaming willy-nilly through the streets engaging in 'unprovoked' violence. They are frequently thrust in violence-prone situations in which the victim enters into it as an active participant, shares the actor's role, and becomes functionally responsible for it" (ibid., 154). However, the respondents' aggression was typically more aggressive than that of their victims. The authors describe these women as primarily associated with others involved in crime, who become increasingly socially and psychologically alienated from conventional life (ibid., 156). These women's assaults were described as "often impulsive and unorganized," frequently involving weapons and occurring when they were intoxicated (ibid., 152). One-fifth of the assaults were planned, and these usually involved vengeance, "either related to money or false accusations" (ibid.). Fourteen percent of the assaults were related to drug dealing.

Another study documents how the official juvenile system "routinely criminalizes girls who are victims of extreme abuse" (Simkins and Katz, 2002, 1474). Girls who are traumatized, abused, and neglected are often ignored in terms of interventions but harshly punished when they act out aggressively (ibid.; Gaarder and Belknap, 2002).

E X H I B I T 3.3 **Gender and Race/Ethnicity Differences in College Students' Use of Aggression**

- Men generally report more aggressive behavior than women, particularly at the more serious levels of aggression.
- When women are the aggressors, men are more likely to be slapped or called unethical or cruel.
- Men generally report being the target/victim of aggressive behavior, with the exception of rape, more than women.
- When the target/victim is a female, males are more likely than females to report teasing her or making obscene gestures toward her.
- Men and women are more likely to report receiving aggressive behavior from men than women, with the exception of being slapped.
- Men and women are more likely to report directing their aggressive behavior at men than at women.
- Men are more likely than women to report inciting others to act aggressively.
- Men are more likely than women to report yelling at, committing property damage toward, and harming the target/victim when they are aggressive.
- Women are more likely than men to report feeling guilty, telling others, and crying about their aggressive behaviors.
- Both women and men are more likely to cry about the aggression they perpetrated if it was against the opposite sex.
- Both men and women are more likely to report threatening men than women.
- Men are more likely than women to report physical injuries and legal problems resulting from the aggression they initiated, whereas women are more likely than men to report interpersonal difficulties resulting from the aggression.
- Almost all men and women identified at least some positive effect of their own use of aggression.
- Men are more likely than women to report being angered by a man hurting another person or a woman using physical aggression.
- Women were more likely than men to report as highly anger provoking (1) condescending or insensitive behavior from either sex, (2) verbal aggression from a woman, or (3) physical aggression from a man.
- Being called "promiscuous" was reported as more insulting for women than men.
- Being called a "coward" or "wimp" by either sex or being called an obscene term (including implying someone was sexually inadequate) by a woman was reported as more insulting for men than women.
- African Americans, especially African American women, were more likely than Whites to report physical aggression from men as highly anger provoking.
- African American women were more likely than White women to report physical aggression from a woman as the most anger provoking.

SOURCE: Mary B. Harris. 1996. Aggression, Gender, and Ethnicity. *Aggression and Violent Behavior.* 1:123–146.

Nonlethal and Lethal Child Abuse

The nonsexual abuse of children and infants, such as neglect, cruelty, and abandonment, has long been considered a female-related offense (Smart, 1976). Whether these crimes are actually committed more by women than men is debatable, especially if the amount of contact a parent has with her or his child is taken into consideration. If women are indeed more likely than men to be reported for cruelty to children, it is likely due to the fact that they shoulder most of the responsibility for child care (ibid.). Analyses of mothers who abuse their children usually ignore the influence of patriarchy within the family and how females' own past and present experiences of victimization, especially of male violence, may be related to the abuse they perpetrate (Dougherty, 1993).

Nowhere is the violation of culturally bound gender roles more sensationalized and symbolic than in women who murder their own children. Although national studies indicate that men and women are equally likely to kill their children and stepchildren (Fox and Zawitz, 2004; Greenfeld and Snell, 1999), there is some indication that mothers are more likely to kill very young children (including abandonments that result in infant death) and fathers are more likely to kill children over age 8 (Greenfeld and Snell, 1999; Rodriguez and Smithey, 1999). However, one study found infanticides committed by the mother's boyfriend (16.4 percent) *plus* those committed by the baby's father (24.7 percent) actually exceeded the infanticides committed by the baby's mother (32.4 percent) (Smithey, 1998). Again, women and girls' primary responsibilities for newborns must be considered; men and boys are in less of a position to be frustrated by the responsibility of a baby. Regarding women who commit infanticide, they are typically young and trying to conceal a pregnancy, which "if it were to become known, could result in rejection and ostracization by significant others, such as parents, husbands, or boyfriends" (Smithey, 1998, 287).

Notably, while the response to infanticide in the United States is often the death penalty, "England's infanticide law provides probation and mandates psychiatric treatment for mothers with mental illness who commit infanticide" with the idea "that a woman with postpartum psychosis who commits infanticide needs treatment rather than punishment and that appropriate treatment will deter her from killing again" (Spinelli, 2004). The psychiatric literature on infanticide typically explains it through a biological emphasis, most notably postpartum psychosis (Smithey, 1997). But Smithey (ibid.) insists that understanding infanticide requires consideration of social structure on families and patterned social interactions. Her qualitative study of fifteen mothers who killed their infants found the mothers to be typically (1) young, (2) with high expectations for themselves as mothers and for their infants (which when unfulfilled resulted in stress and low self-esteem); (3) children of abusive and disapproving parents themselves; (4) daughters of alcoholic or chemically dependent fathers; (4) in relationships with abusive, antagonistic, or unsupportive husbands/boyfriends; (4) economically deprived, with stressful day-to-day lives; and (5) dealing with the absence of the infants' fathers (ibid.). Thus, the babies' fathers typically devoted little emotional or financial support *and* were often critical of the babies and the mothers. The precipitating factors leading to the infant killings were often undue emotional stress responses of and substance abuse by these mothers.

Alder and Baker's (1997) study of maternal filicide (a mother who kills her own child) found that 55 percent of all filicide (a parent who kills her/his own child) cases were committed by women ($N = 32$), and in all cases they were the biological mothers. The study identified three categories. *Filicide/suicides* comprised over a third of the cases and involved a murder-suicide (sometimes a murder–attempted suicide), typically when the mothers believed they were altruistic in killing their children given their life circumstances. For example, the father/husband was abusive or had abandoned the mother and child. In one case, the child was severely brain injured in a car accident and the father abandoned them and moved in with another woman. Also, over a third of the cases were the *neonaticides*. These were cases where an infant was killed in the first twenty-four hours after birth, and typically the mother was a teenage, unmarried woman in denial about her pregnancy. These births often occur in the toilet at home, where the young mothers make a limited effort to conceal the offense. Usually they immediately strangle or suffocate the infant, then place the body in a bag in a nearby location, such as a garbage bin, or simply abandon the live baby in a similar location. One-quarter of the maternal filicides were classified as *fatal assaults*. These typically involved cases where the mothers had previously been physically abusive to the children, which was often known to authorities. Alder and Baker (1997) believed that in the majority of these cases, the intent was not to kill but to punish the child, and the lethal violence was the end of an escalating pattern of violence over time. These mothers were typically around 25 years old and married at the time of the murder, and the children were usually babies under 9 months old. Typically, the mothers had financial problems, isolation, frustration, exhaustion, dislike of the child, and/or lack of support, and the murder event occurred with the mother lashing out at a child's specific behavior, usually crying. These women frequently reported their husbands' failure to help with the children and that they (the women) hit the children repeatedly to "make" them stop crying.

Smithey's (2001) findings regarding mothers who fatally injured their infants are consistent with Alder and Baker's (1997) *fatal assaults* but provide more detail. Smithy (2001, 65) identified three types of "transaction" events (characterized by the infant's behavior) that initiated the fatal injury and frustrated the mother because she was unable to comfort or control her infant: (1) incessant crying, (2) prolonged or frequent illness, and (3) difficulty with training (i.e., getting a child to use the toilet, sleep, or eat). Smithey (ibid.) views part of the responsibility as resting with society, which increasingly demands mothers to be able to comfort and control their infants, a virtually impossible task 100 percent of the time.

When abortion and birth control are illegal or simply difficult or impossible to obtain, a likely consequence both historically and currently is the occurrence of maternal infant killings. Whether this was acted out in the past by housemaids or factory workers raped by their male employers, unable to afford raising children, and resistant to the label of "bastard" for their children (and worse for themselves) or more recently by such high-profile cases as the girl who delivered her baby in the bathroom at her senior prom and left him there to die, it is clear that women's and girls' infanticide acts are not simply a historical phenomenon. What is clear is that both historically and presently, girls and women have often been faced with inadequate or no birth control and inadequate or no access to abortion when female sexuality outside of marriage and "unmarried mother-hood" are still stigmatized.

At the same time that we live in a highly sexualized culture (e.g., music videos, television commercials, films, and billboards) and a culture where sexual victimization, especially of young women and girls, occurs at epidemic levels (see Chapters 6 and 7), girls and young women are told not to have sex, and most schools are resistant to providing birth control or even lecturing on the need for it if one chooses to be sexually active. When women commit infan-ticide, they are usually considered "mad" (insane) or "bad" (evil and criminal) (Frigon, 1995), with little focus on the males who impregnated them (including when the pregnancy is a result of rape) and often aid in the actual killing of the infant.

A study conducted on twenty men and twenty-eight women in Wales and England who killed their own children examined the gender differences and similarities (Wilczynski, 1995). It is important to note that, similarly to findings from other such studies of parents killing their own children, most of these killings "were not instrumental or premeditated—they were usually sudden and impulsive" (ibid., 168). Wilczynski (ibid.) divided the motivations for killing the children into ten categories, ranging from retaliating to altruistic killings (there is also an eleventh category called "motive unknown"). Although Wilczynski's (ibid.) is far from "the final answer" on the issue of gender and parent killings, particularly given the small sample size, it is certainly an important first step in examining the relationship between parents' gender and their motivations for killing their own children.

Exhibit 3.4 summarizes the seven motivations Wilczynski (ibid.) estimates as likely to be gender related. In summary, fathers are more likely than mothers to commit retaliating, jealousy/rejection, and discipline killings of their children, while mothers are more likely than fathers to commit altruistic, psychotic, and Munchausen Syndrome by Proxy killings, and to kill their children (usually infants) because they were unplanned and not wanted. Again it is important to remember that Wilczynski's (ibid.) sample is small and future research is necessary on this topic. There were three other types of child killings by parents Wilczynski (ibid.) found in the literature that she did not locate in her sample. First is the secondary to sexual or ritual (or organized) abuse, where a child is killed (usually inadvertently) during sexual or ritual abuse or the child is killed purposely because the parent is afraid the child will inform others of the abuse. Another motivation not noted in this sample for child killings by parents is self-defense killing, where a parent kills a child in self-defense (because the child is assaulting the parent). The final category of child-killing parent motivation (also not found in Wilczynski's sample) is the "no intent to kill or injure the child" killing. This category includes parents who batter their children but do not intend the physical abuse to result in the children's death or parents whose neglect of their children results in their children's deaths. Given that Wilczynski (ibid.) did not find these final three categories in her sample, she was unable to estimate whether gender was related.

E X H I B I T 3.4 Wilczynski's Gender Analysis of Child-Killings by Parents

Male-Dominated Child-Killings by Parents

- *Retaliating killings*—Anger toward another person, usually the person's spouse, is displaced onto the child.

- *Jealousy of, or rejection by, the victim*—e.g., cases where the parent believes the child is not biologically his, resents the other parent's attention given to the child, feels rejected by the child (often because he has abused the child in the past)

- *Discipline killings*—children killed during the course of being disciplined or punished

Female-Dominated Child-Killings by Parents

- *Unwanted child killings*—children unwanted or unplanned; usually involved killings of children less than 24 hours old

- *Altruistic killings*—The parent believes it is in the child's best interest to be killed because the child is suffering from an illness ("mercy killing") or because the parent believes her or his own depression or situation results in an unacceptable situation for the child.

- *Psychotic killings*—parents diagnosed as psychotic at the time of the killing, often killing under some delusion

- *Munchausen Syndrome by Proxy*—A parent induces an illness in a child or fakes one, often presenting the child repeatedly to medical authorities.

SOURCE: Ania Wilczynski. 1995. "Child-Killing by Parents." Pp. 167–180 in *Gender and Crime,* edited by R. E. Dobash, R. P. Dobash, and L. Noaks. Cardiff: University of Wales Press. Reprinted by permission.

When women kill their children, they receive typically far more media attention than when men do, especially in cases where the mothers are White. In 1994, the world was shocked when a South Carolina mother, Susan Smith, admitted to strapping her young children into their car seats and setting the car in motion into a lake, resulting in their drowning. At first Smith told the police and TV cameras that an African American man had carjacked her automobile with the children inside. As the case unfolded, the gendered, as well as raced, nature of it was difficult to ignore. First, how would this crime have been viewed if it had been the children's father instead of their mother? Second, Ms. Smith's stepfather, high up in the "Christian Right," had molested her as a child. Should this be considered relevant? Although Susan Smith was convicted of killing her children, to many people's surprise she was not given the death penalty. The jury opted for life in prison. Perhaps this was because unlike consumers of the media, the jurors were able to actually hear the context and consequences of Smith's life. This is not to excuse Susan Smith but rather to understand what places someone at risk for infanticide or child murder.

Another high-profile mother murderer case was that of Andrea Yates, a Texas mother who in 2001 drowned her five children in the bathtub after she suffered years of severe mental instability and recent severe postpartum depression. In addition to the seriously troubling act of murdering her children, the act was even harder to believe given that this highly religious mother was a registered nurse, former high school athlete, National Honor Society member, and valedictorian. Her husband and the medical community missed numerous signs and diagnoses regarding the nature of her mental illness, closely related to postpartum depression, and the threat she posed to her children. Similarly to the Susan Smith case, the jury for Yates's case declined the death penalty in favor of life in prison.

Homicide

Researchers estimate that 10 to 20 percent of all homicides in the United States are committed by women, but evidence suggests that women's "share" of homicides has been decreasing in recent years. The percentage of female homicide arrests decreased from 17 percent in 1960 (Steffensmeier, 1993) to 10 percent in 1990 (Gauthier and Bankston, 1997; Steffensmeier, 1993), and we can see from the 2003 data in Table 3.3 that the rate has remained relatively stable. Moreover, a recent government report on homicides in the United States from 1976 to 2002 reports female-perpetrated homicides have decreased since the early 1980s, whereas males' homicide offending rates peaked in the early 1990s and have fallen markedly since (Fox and Zawitz, 2004). In 1876, 17,056 males and 3,296 females committed homicides. In 2002, about 500 fewer homicides were by men (16,536), while women's almost halved (1,711) (ibid.).

Thus, men commit the vast majority of homicides. Although in the United States men commit far more homicides than women overall, when women kill, their victims are typically their male partners (boyfriends, husbands, ex-husbands, etc.) (e.g., Browne and Williams, 1989; Gauthier and Bankston, 1997; Greenfeld and Snell, 1999). Moreover, a study of murders in the United States between 1976 and 2002 reported that although men kill their current and former wives and girlfriends more often than women kill their current or former husbands or boyfriends, a much higher percentage of female than male-perpetrated homicides involve intimate partners (see Table 3.3).

Gauthier and Bankston's (1997) study of homicides in 1990 in U.S. cities with populations of 100,000 or greater reported the importance of examining the type of homicide (intimate partner or not) and the role of gendered economic equality (see Exhibit 3.5). Consistent with findings from similar studies, Gauthier and Bankston (ibid.) found that while women make up a tiny minority of arrests for nonintimate homicides, the gender gap narrows for intimate partner homicides. Moreover, this gender gap is mediated by the gender equality in the economic structure for the city in which the homicide arrest occurs. Contrary to what the "liberation" or "emancipation" hypothesis suggests (Adler, 1975), women constitute a lower proportion of intimate partner homicide arrests in cities where they are doing better economically, and this is particularly true in southern states of the United States (Gauthier and Bankston, 1997). These authors conclude: "Again, we find a consistent explanation in suggesting males are increasingly exercising violence to maintain control over women in a context in which male status dominance is most threatened" (ibid., 594). Similarly Jensen's (2001) study of women-perpetrated homicides in the United States found that women's increased economic and social status decreases their

T A B L E 3.3 A Gender Comparison of Homicides in the United States, 1976–2002[1]

Variable	Percent
All Homicides	
Victim Sex	
Female	23.6%
Male	76.4
Offender Sex	
Female	11.4
Male	88.6
Sex of Offender/Sex of Victim	
Male/male	65.1
Male/female	22.6
Female/male	9.9
Female/female	2.4

Variable	Percent Male Offenders	Percent Female Offenders
Victim–Offender Relationships		
Intimate partner	64.8%	35.2%
Family	70.3	29.7
Infanticide	61.6	38.4
Eldercide	85.4	14.6
Circumstances		
Felony murder	93.3	6.7
Sex-related	93.6	6.4
Drug-related	95.7	4.3
Gang-related	98.4	1.6
Argument	85.3	14.7
Workplace	91.4	8.6
Weapon		
Gun homicide	91.0	9.0
Arson	79.5	20.5
Poison	62.9	37.1
Multiple Victims or Offenders		
Multiple victims	93.5	6.5
Multiple offenders	91.8	8.2

[1]These data come from an estimated 544,909 murders in the United States for this time period, for which there were varying amounts of information, for example, identifying who committed the murder.

SOURCE: James Alan Fox and Marianne W. Zawitz. 2004. *Homicide Trends in the United States*. http://www.ojp.usdoj.gov/bjs/homicide/homtrnd.htm.

**E X H I B I T 3.5 Gauthier and Bankston's Gender Analysis
of 1990 U.S. Homicides**

Overall Homicides
Men were arrested for 10 percent of all homicides.

Nonintimate Homicides
For every 100 nonintimates killed by men, women kill 6 nonintimates.

Intimate-Partner Homicides
—Intimate-partner homicide arrests constitute 6 percent of all homicide arrests
(and 10 percent of all homicide arrests where the victim and offender know
each other).

—On average, 62 women kill their intimate male partners for every 100 men that kill their
intimate female partners.

—Men's proportion of intimate-partner homicides is greater in cities where women's
economic advantage is relatively high, and this is particularly true in cities in the
southern United States (where, arguably, the gender roles are more restricted).

SOURCE: DeAnn K. Gauthier, and William B. Bankston. 1997. "Gender Equality and the Sex Ratio of Intimate
Killing." *Criminology* 35(4):577–600.

likelihood of offending, suggesting the importance of gender equality in decreasing women's homicide offending (the opposite of what the Liberation Theory
hypothesizes). An analysis of intimate partner homicides in the United States
from 1976 to 2002 reported that the number of men murdered by intimate
partners decreased by 71 percent over this time period, whereas the number of
women killed by intimate partners remained steady for two decades and then
declined after 1993, reaching the lowest recorded level and staying there in 2001
(Fox and Zawitz, 2004).

SUMMARY

In the studies of female offending, particularly those examining gender differences and patterns over time, the findings are inconsistent; however, some
patterns have emerged. First, if there is any support for gender-convergence in
offending, it appears to be for less serious property offenses and, to a lesser extent,
drug use. Regarding the property offense increases for women, the cyclical
fluctuations suggest that these are at least partially due to the feminization of
poverty (decreased economic well-being). Second, gender-convergence for more
serious crimes, especially violent offenses, is represented in some of the official
data but not much or at all in the self-report data. This indicates that the official
data may be measuring changes in policies and law enforcement practices more
than actual levels of offending. It appears that regarding most offenses, especially
serious and violent crimes, it is still a "man's world."

REFERENCES

Acoca, Leslie. 1999. Investing in Girls. *Juvenile Justice* 6:3–13.

Adler, Freda. 1975. *Sisters in Crime: The Rise of the New Female Criminal.* New York: McGraw Hill.

Ageton, Suzanne S. 1983. The Dynamics of Female Delinquency, 1976–1980. *Criminology* 21:555–584.

Alder, Christine M. 1998. "Passionate and Willful" Girls: Confronting Practices. *Women & Criminal Justice* 9:81–101.

Alder, Christine M., and June Baker. 1997. Maternal Filicide. *Women & Criminal Justice* 9:15–41.

Bertone, Andrea Marie. 2000. Sexual Trafficking in Women. *Gender Issues* 18:4–22.

Bilchik, Shay. 1999. Minorities in the Juvenile Justice System. U.S. Department of Justice. Office of Juvenile Justice and Delinquency Prevention, http://www.ncjrs.org/pdffiles1/ojjdp/179007.pdf

Bjerregaard, Beth. 2002. Operationalizing Gang Membership: The Impact of Measurement on Gender Differences in Gang Self-Identification and Delinquent Involvement. *Women & Criminal Justice* 13:79–100.

Bjerregaard, Beth, and Carolyn Smith. 1993. Gender Differences in Gang Participation, Delinquency, and Substance Use. *Journal of Quantitative Criminology* 9:329–355.

Boritch, Helen, and John Hagan. 1990. A Century of Crime in Toronto: Gender, Class, and Patterns of Social Control, 1859 to 1955. *Criminology* 28:567–599.

Boyd, Susan C. 1999. *Mothers and Illicit Drugs: Transcending the Myths.* Toronto: University of Toronto Press.

Brener, Nancy D., Thomas R. Simon, Etienne G. Krug, and Richard Lowry. 1999. Recent Trends in Violence-Related Behaviors among High School Students in the U.S. *Journal of the American Medical Association* 282:330–446.

Browne, Angela, and Kirk R. Williams. 1989. Exploring the Effect of Resource Availability and the Likelihood of Female-Perpetrated Homicides. *Law and Society Review* 23:75–94.

Buckle, Abigail, and David P. Farrington. 1984. An Observational Study of Shoplifting. *British Journal of Criminology* 24:63–73.

Byqvist, Siv. 1999. Criminality among Female Drug Abusers. *Journal of Psychoactive Drugs* 31:353–362.

Campbell, Anne. 1984. GIRLS' TALK: The Social Representation of Aggression by Female Gang Members. *Criminal Justice and Behavior* 11:139–156.

————.1990. Female Participation in Gangs. Pp. 163–182 in *Gangs in America,* edited by G. R. Huff. Newbury Park, CA: Sage.

————.1999a. Female Gang Members' Social Construction of Female Gangs. Pp. 248–255 in *Female Gangs in America: Essays on Girls, Gangs and Gender,* edited by M. Chesney-Lind and J. M. Hagedorn. Chicago: Lakeview Press.

————.1999b. Self-Definition by Rejection: The Case of Gang Girls. Pp. 100–117 in *Female Gangs in America: Essays on Girls, Gangs and Gender,* edited by M. Chesney-Lind and J. M. Hagedorn. Chicago: Lakeview Press.

Campbell, Gayle. 1990. Women and Crime. *Juristat* 10:1–8.

Canter, Rachelle J. 1982. Sex Differences in Self-Report Delinquency. *Criminology* 20:373–393.

Chesney-Lind, Meda. 1997. *The Female Offender: Girls, Women, and Crime*. Thousand Oaks, CA: Sage.

Chesney-Lind, Meda and Joanne Belknap. 2004. Trends in Delinquent Girls' Aggression. Pp. 203–220 in *Aggression, Antisocial Behavior, and Violence among Girls*, edited by M. Putallaz and K. L. Bierman. New York: The Guilford Press.

Chesney-Lind, Meda, and John M. Hagedorn, eds. 1999. *Female Gangs in America: Essays on Girls, Gangs and Gender*. Chicago: Lakeview Press.

Chesney-Lind, Meda, and Randall G. Shelden. 1992. *Girls, Delinquency, and Juvenile Justice*. Pacific Grove, CA: Brooks/Cole.

Chilton, Ronald, and Susan K. Datesman. 1987. Gender, Race, and Crime: An Analysis of Urban Trends, 1960–1980. *Gender and Society* 1:152–171.

Colomy, Paul, and Martin Kretzmann. 1997. The Gendering of Social Control: Sex Delinquency and Progressive Juvenile Justice in Denver, 1901-1927. Pp. 48–81 in *Governing Childhood*, edited by Anne McGillivray. Aldershot, England: Dartmouth Publishing.

Colten, M. 1982. Attitudes Experiences, and Self-Perceptions of Heroin-Addicted Mothers. *Journal of Social Issues* 38:77–92.

Comerford, Mary, Dale D. Chitwood, James Inciardi, and David K. Griffin. 1996. inner-City Crack Houses. Pp. 15–23 in *The American Pipe Dream: Crack Cocaine and the Inner City*, edited by D. D. Chitwood, J. E. Rivers, J.A. Inciardi, and The South Florida AIDS Research Consortuim. Orlandlo, FL: Harcourt Brace College Publishers.

Dakof, Gayle A. 2000. Understanding Gender Differences in Adolescent Drug Abuse. *Journal of Psychoative Drugs* 32:25–32.

Daly, Kathleen. 1989. Gender and Varieties of White-Collar Crime. *Criminology* 27:769–794.

Dasgupta, S. 2001. Towards an Understanding of Women's Use of Non-Lethal Violence In Intimate Heterosexual Relationships. http://www. vawnet.org/Domestic Violence/Research/VAWnetDocs/AR_ womviol.php.

Decker, Scott, Richard Wright, Allison Redfern, and Dietrich Smith. 1993. A Woman's Place Is in the Home: Females and Residential Burglary. *Justice Quarterly* 10:143–162.

DeLisi, Matt. 2002. Not Just a Boy's Club: An Empirical Assessment of Female Career Criminals. *Women & Criminal Justice* 13:27–45.

Diaz-Cotto, Juanita. 1996. *Gender, Ethnicity, and the State: Latina and Latino Prison Politics*. Albany: State University of New York.

Dougherty, Joyce. 1993. Women's Violence against Their Children: A Feminist Perspective. *Women & Criminal Justice* 4:91–114.

Eaton, Mary. 1986. *Justice for Women? Family, Court and Social Control*. Philadelphia: Open University Press.

Epstein, Jennifer A., Gilbert J. Botvin, Kenneth W. Griffin, and Tracy Diaz. 1999. Role of Ethnicity and Gender in Polydrug Use among a Longitudinal Sample of Inner-City Adolescents. *Journal of Alcohol and Drug Education* 45:1–12.

Erickson, Patricia G., Jennifer Butters, Patti McGillicuddy, and Ase Hallgren. 2000. Crack and Prostitution. *Journal of Drug Issues* 30:767–788.

Esbensen, Finn-Aage, and L. Thomas Winfree. 1998. Race and Gender Differences between Gang and Nongang Youths: Results from a Multisite Survey. *Justice Quarterly* 15:505–526.

Evans, Rhonda D., Craig J. Forsyth, and DeAnn K. Gautheir. 2002. Gendered Pathways into and Experiences within Crack Cultures Outside of the Inner City. *Deviant Behavior* 23:483–510.

Farley, Melissa, and Howard Barkan. 1998. Prostitution, Violence and Posttraumatic Stress Disorder. *Women & Health* 27:37–49.

Farley, Melissa, and Vanessa Kelly. 2000. Prostitution: A Critical Review of the Medical and Social Sciences Literature. *Women & Criminal Justice* 11:29–64.

Felkenes, George T., and Harold K. Becker. 1995. Female Gang Members: A Growing Issue for Policy Makers. *Journal of Gang Research* 2:1–10.

Figueira-McDonough, Josephine, William H. Barton, and Rosemary C. Sarri. 1981. Normal Deviance: Gender Similarities in Adolescent Subcultures. Pp. 17–45 in *Comparing Female and Male Offenders*, edited by M. Q. Warren. Beverly Hills, CA: Sage.

Fishman, Laura T. 1999. Black Female Gang Behavior: A Historical and Ethnographic Perspective. Pp. 64–84 in *Female Gangs in America: Essays on Girls, Gangs and Gender*, edited by M. Chesney-Lind and J. M. Hagedorn. Chicago: Lakeview Press.

Fox, James Alan, and Marianne W. Zawitz. 2004. Homicide Trends in the United States. http://www.ojp.usdoj.gov/bjs/homicide/homtrnd.htm.

Friedman, Jennifer, and Marisa Alicea. 1995. Women and Heroin: The Path of Resistance and Its Consequences. *Gender and Society* 9:432–449.

Frigon, Sylvie. 1995. A Genealogy of Women's Madness. Pp. 20–48 in *Gender and Crime*, edited by R. E. Dobash, R. P. Dobash, and L. Noaks. Cardiff: University of Wales Press.

Gaarder, Emily, and Joanne Belknap. 2002. Tenuous Borders: Girls Transferred to Adult Court. *Criminology* 40:481–517.

Gauthier, DeAnn K., and William B. Bankston. 1997. Gender Equality and the Sex Ratio of Intimate Killing. *Criminology* 35:577–600.

Gibbens, T. C. N., and J. Prince. 1962. *Shoplifting*. London: ISTD.

Giordano, Peggy C. 1999. The Changing Social Context of Female Delinquency. Pp. 90–99 in *Female Gangs in America: Essays on Girls, Gangs and Gender*, edited by M. Chesney-Lind and J. M. Hagedorn. Chicago: Lakeview Press.

Giordano, Peggy C., Sandra Kerbel, and Sandra Dudley. 1981. The Economics of Female Criminality: An Analysis of Police Blotters, 1890–1976. Pp. 65–82 in *Women and Crime in America*, edited by L. H. Bowker. New York: Macmillan.

Green, Carla A., Donald K. Freeborn, and Michael R. Polen. 2001. Gender and Alcohol Use. *Journal of Behavioral Medicine* 24:383–399.

Greenfeld, Lawrence A., and Tracy L. Snell. 1999. Women Offenders. Bureau of Justice Statistics: Special Report. U.S. Department of Justice, December, 14pp.

Hafley, Sandra R., and Richard Tewksbury. 1996. Reefer Madness in Bluegrass County: Community Structure and Roles in the Rural Kentucky Marijuana Industry. *Journal of Criminal Justice* 29:75–94.

Hagedorn, John M., and Mary L. Devitt. 1999. Fighting Female: The Social Construction of Female Gangs. Pp. 256–276 in *Female Gangs in America: Essays on Girls, Gangs and Gender*, edited by M. Chesney-Lind and J. M. Hagedorn. Chicago: Lakeview Press.

Harms, Paul. 2002. *Detention in Delinquency Cases, 1989–1998. OJJDP Fact*

Sheet, No. 1. Washington, DC: U.S. Department of Justice.

Harris, Mary B. 1973. Field Studies of Modeled Aggression in a Field Experiment. *Psychological Reports* 69:1–2.

———. 1974a. Aggressive Reactions to a Frustrating Phone Call. *Journal of Social Psychology* 92:193–198.

———. 1974b. Mediators between Frustration and Aggression in a Field Experiment. *Journal of Experimental Social Psychology* 10:561–571.

———. 1976. Instigators and Inhibitors of Aggression in a Field Experiment. *Journal of Social Psychology* 98:27–38.

———. 1992. Sex, Race, and Experiences of Aggression. *Aggressive Behavior* 18:201–217.

———. 1996. Aggression, Gender, and Ethnicity. *Aggression and Violent Behavior* 1:123–146.

Hill, Gary D., and Elizabeth M. Crawford. 1990. Women, Race, and Crime. *Criminology* 28:601–626.

Hoffman-Bustamante, Dale. 1973. The Nature of Female Criminality. *Issues in Criminology* 8:117–136.

Holtfreter, Kristy. 2005. Is Occupational Fraud "Typical" White-Collar Crime? A Comparison of Individual and Organizational Characteristics. *Journal of Criminal Justice* 33:353–365.

Hudson, Barbara. 1989. Justice or Welfare? English and French Systems. Pp. 96–113 in *Growing Up Good*, edited by M. Cain. London: Sage.

Humphries, Drew. 1999. *Crack Mothers: Pregnancy, Drugs, and the Media.* Columbus, OH: Ohio State University Press.

Hussong, Andrea M. 2000. The Settings of Adolescent Alcohol and Drug Use. *Journal of Youth and Adolescence* 29:107–119.

Inciardi, James, Anne E. Pottieger, Mary Ann Forney, Dale Chitwood, and Duane C. McBride. 1991. Prostitution, IV Drug Use, and Sex-for-Crack Exchanges among Serious Delinquents: Risks for HIV Infection. *Criminology* 29:221–235.

Inciardi, James, Dorothy Lockwood, and Anne E. Pottieger. 1993. *Women and Crack-Cocaine.* New York: Macmillan.

Jacobs, Bruce A. 1996. Crack Dealers' Apprehension Avoidance Techniques. *Justice Quarterly* 13:359–382.

Jensen, Vickie. 2001. *Why Women Kill.* Boulder, CO: Lynne Rienner Publishers, Inc.

Joe, Karen, and Meda Chesney-Lind. 1999. Just Every Mother's Angel: An Analysis of Gender and Ethnic Variations in Youth Gang Membership. Pp. 210–222 in *Female Gangs in America: Essays on Girls, Gangs and Gender,* edited by M. Chesney-Lind and J. M. Hagedorn. Chicago: Lakeview Press.

Johnson, Paula C. 2003. *Inner Lives: Voices of African American Women in Prison.* New York: New York University.

Kline, Sue. 1993. A Profile of Female Offenders in State and Federal Prisons. Pp. 1–6 in *Female Offenders: Meeting the Needs of a Neglected Population.* Laurel, MD: American Correctional Association.

Koester, Stephen, and Judith Schwartz. 1993. Crack, Gangs, Sex and Powerlessness. Pp. 187–203 in *Crack Pipe as Pimp,* edited by M. S. Ratner. New York: Lexington.

Kruttschnitt, Candace. 1996. Contributions of Quantitative Methods to the Study of Gender and Crime, or Bootstrapping Our Way into the Theoretical Thicket. *Journal of Quantitative Criminology* 12:135–161.

Laidler, Karen Joe, and Geoffrey Hunt. 2001. Accomplishing Femininity among the Girls in the Gang. *British Journal of Criminology* 41:656–678.

Lauderback, David, Joy Hansen, and Dan Waldorf. 1992. Sisters Are Doin' It for Themselves: A Black Female Gang in San Francisco. *Gang Journal* 1:57–72.

Lederman, Cindy S., and Eileen N. Brown. 2000. Entangled in the Shadows: Girls in the Juvenile Justice System. *Buffalo Law Review* 48:909–925.

Leonard, Eileen B. 1982. *Women, Crime, and Society: A Critique of Criminology Theory.* New York: Longman.

Lewis, Diane K. 1981. Black Women Offenders and Criminal Justice: Some Theoretical Considerations. Pp. 89–105 in *Comparing Female and Male Offenders,* edited by M. Q. Warren. Beverly Hills, CA: Sage.

Li, Xiaming, Bonita Stanton, Lesley Cottress, James Burms, Robert Pack, and Linda Kaljee. 2000. Patterns of Initation of Sex and Drug-Related Activities among Urban Low-Income African American Adolescents. *Journal of Adolescent Health* 28:46–54.

Lichtenstein, Bronwen. 1997. Women and Crack-Cocaine Use. *Addition Research* 5:279–96.

Luthar, Suniya S. and Karen D'Avanzo. 1999. Contextual Actors in Substance Use. *Development and Psychopathology* 11:845–867.

Maher, Lisa. 1995. Women and the Initiation to Illicit Drugs. Pp. 132–166 in *Gender and Crime,* edited by R. E. Dobash, R. P. Dobash, and L. Noaks. Cardiff: University of Wales Press.

———. 1997. *Sexed Work: Gender, Race and Resistance in a Brooklyn Drug Market.* Oxford: Clarendon Press, p. x.

Maher, Lisa, and R. Curtis. 1992. Women on the Edge of Crime: Crack Cocaine and the Changing Contexts of Street-Level Sex Work in New York City. *Crime, Law and Social Change* 18:221–258.

Maher, Lisa, and Kathleen Daly. 1996. Women in the Street-Level Drug Economy. *Criminology* 34:465–491.

Maher, Lisa, Eloise Dunlap, Bruce D. Johnson, and Ansley Hamid. 1996. Gender, Power, and Alternative Living Arrangements in the Inner-City Crack Culture. *Journal of Research in Crime and Delinquency* 33:181–205.

Malloy, K. A., K. A. McCloskey, N. Grigsby, and D. Gardner. 2003. Women's Use of Violence within Intimate Relationships. *Journal of Aggression, Maltreatment, and Trauma* 6:37–59.

Mann, Coramae Richey. 1984. *Female Crime and Delinquency.* Montgomery: University of Alabama Press.

———. 1987. Black Women Who Kill. Pp. 157–186 in *Violence in the Black Family,* edited by R. L. Hampton. Lexington, MA: Lexington Books.

Martin, Margaret E. 1997. Double Your Trouble: Dual Arrest in Family Violence. *Journal of Family Violence* 12:139–157.

Mawby, Rob. 1980. Sex and Crime: The Results of a Self-Report Study. *British Journal of Sociology* 31:525–541.

McCluskey, John D., Cynthia Perez McCluskey, and Beth Huebner. 2003. Juvenile Female Arrests. *Women & Criminal Justice* 14:35–51.

McCormack, Arlene, Mark-David Janus, and Ann W. Burgess. 1986. Runaway Youths and Sexual Victimization: Gender Differences in an Adolescent Runaway Population. *Child Abuse and Neglect* 10:387–395.

McMahon, M., and Ellen Pence. 2003. Making Social Change: Reflections on Individual and Institutional Advocacy with Women Arrested for Domestic Violence. *Violence Against Women* 9:47–74.

Melton, Heather C., and Joanne Belknap. 2003. He Hits, She Hits: Assessing

Gender Differences and Similarities in Officially Reported Intimate Partner Violence. *Criminal Justice and Behavior* 30:328–348.

Messerschmidt, James. 1999. Feminist Theory, Criminology, and the Challenge of Diversity. Pp. 118–132 in *Female Gangs in America: Essays on Girls, Gangs and Gender*, edited by M. Chesney-Lind and J. M. Hagedorn. Chicago: Lakeview Press.

Metsch, Lisa R., H. Virginia McCoy, and Norman L. Weatherby. 1996. Women and Crack. Pp. 49–66 in *The American Pipe Dream: Crack Cocaine and the Inner City*, edited by D. D. Chitwood, J. E. Rivers, J. A. Inciardi, and The South Florida AIDS Research Consortium. Orlando, FL: Harcourt Brace College Publishers.

Miller, Jody. 1998. Up It Up: Gender and the Accomplishment of Street Robbery. *Criminology* 36:37–66.

Miller, S. L. (2001). The Paradox of Women Arrested for Domestic Violence: Criminal Justice Professionals and Service Providers Respond. *Violence Against Women* 7(12):1139–1376.

Moore, Joan W. 1999. Gang Members' Families. Pp. 159–176 in *Female Gangs in America: Essays on Girls, Gangs and Gender*, edited by M. Chesney-Lind and J. M. Hagedorn. Chicago: Lakeview Press.

Morash, Merry. 1983. Gangs, Groups, and Delinquency. *British Journal of Criminology* 23:309–335.

Morris, Allison. 1987. *Women, Crime and Criminal Justice*. Oxford: Basil Blackwell.

Mullings, Janet L., Joycelyn Pollock, and Ben M. Crouch. 2002. Drugs and Criminality: Results from the Texas Women Inmates Study. *Women & Criminal Justice* 13:69–96.

Naffine, Ngaire. 1987. *Female Crime: The Construction of Women in Criminology*. Sydney, Australia: Allen and Unwin.

Olson, David E., Arthur J. Lurigio, and Magnus Seng. 2000. A Comparison of Female and Male Probationers. *Women & Criminal Justice* 11:65–79.

Ratner, Mitchell S. 1993. Sex, Drugs, and Public Policy. Pp. 1–36 in *Crack Pipe as Pimp*, edited by M. S. Ratner. New York: Lexington Books.

Roberts, Dorothy E. 1997. Punishing Drug Addicts Who Have Babies: Women of Color, Equality, and the Rights of Privacy. Pp. 127–135 in *Critical Race Feminism*, edited by Adrien K. Wing. New York: New York University Press.

Rodriguez, S. Fernando, and Martha Smithey. 1999. Infant and Adult Homicide. *Homicide Studies* 3:170–184.

Rosenbaum, M., S. Murphy, J. Irwin, and L. Watson. 1990. Women and Crack: What's the Real Story? *The Drug Policy Letter* 11:2–6.

Schaffner, Laurie. 1998. Female Juvenile Delinquency: Sexual Solutions, Gender Bias, and Juvenile Justice. *Hastings Women's Law Journal* 9:1–25.

Simkins, Sandra, and Sarah Katz. 2002. Criminalizing Abused Girls. *Violence Against Women* 8:1474–1499.

Simon, Rita. 1975. *Women and Crime*. Lexington, MA: D. C. Heath.

Simpson, Sally S. 1991. Caste, Class, and Violent Crime: Explaining Difference in Female Offending. *Criminology* 29:115–135

Smart, Carol. 1976. *Women, Crime and Criminology: A Feminist Critique*. London: Routledge and Kegan Paul.

———. 1982. The New Female Offender: Reality or Myth? Pp. 105–116 in *The Criminal Justice System and Women*, edited by B. R. Price and N. J. Sokoloff. New York: Clark Boardman.

Smithey, Martha. 1997. Infant Homicide at the Hands of Mothers. *Deviant Behavior* 18:255–272.

———. 1998. Infant Homicide. *Journal of Family Violence* 13:285–297.

———. 2001. Maternal Infanticide and Modern Motherhood. *Women & Criminal Justice* 13:65–83.

Sommers, Ira, and Deborah R. Baskin. 1993. The Situational Context of Violent Female Offending. *Journal of Research in Crime and Delinquency* 30:136–162.

Spinelli, M. G. 2004. Maternal Infanticide Associated with Mental Illness: Prevention and the Promise of Saved Lives. *American Journal of Psychiatry* 161:1548–1557.

Steffensmeier, Darrell J. 1981. Crime and the Contemporary Woman: An Analysis of Changing Levels of Female Property Crime, 1960–1975. Pp. 39–59 in *Women and Crime in America*, edited by L. H. Bowker. New York: Macmillan.

———. 1993. National Trends in Female Arrests, 1960–1990: Assessment and Recommendations for Research. *Journal of Quantitative Criminology* 9:411–441.

Steffensmeier, Darrell J., and Emilie A. Allan. 1988. Sex Disparities in Arrests by Residence, Race, and Age: An Assessment of the Gender Convergence/Crime Hypothesis. *Justice Quarterly* 5:53–80.

Steffensmeier, Darrell J., and Michael J. Cobb. 1981. Sex Differences in Urban Arrest Patterns, 1934–1979. *Social Problems* 29:37–50.

Steffensmeier, Darrell, and Dana Haynie. 2000. Gender, Structural Disadvantage, and Urban Crime. *Criminology* 38:403–438.

Steffensmeier, Darrell, and Jennifer Schwartz. 2004. Trends in Female Criminality. Pp. 95–112 in *The Criminal Justice System and Women*, 3rd edition, edited by Barbara Raffel Price and Natalie J. Sokoloff. Boston: McGraw Hill.

Steffensmeier, Darrell J., Jennifer Schwartz, Hua Zhong, and Jeff Ackerman. 2005. An Assessment of Recent Trends in Girls' Violence Using Diverse Longitudinal Sources. *Criminology* 43:355–404.

Steffensmeier, Darrell J., and R. H. Steffensmeier. 1980. Trends in Female Delinquency. *Criminology* 18:62–85.

Steffensmeier, Darrell J., and Cathy Streifel. 1992. Time-Series Analysis of the Female Percentage of Arrests for Property Crimes, 1960–1985: A Test of Alternative Explanation. *Justice Quarterly* 9:77–104.

Sterk, Claire E. 1999. *Fast Lives: Women Who Use Crack Cocaine*. Philadelphia: Temple University Press.

Strauss, Shiela M., and Gregory P. Falkin. 2001. Women Offenders Who Use and Deal Methamphetamine. *Women & Criminal Justice* 12:77–97.

Suh, Alexandra. 2000. Military Prostitution in Asia and the United States. Pp. 144–158 in *States of Confinement: Policing, Detention, And Prisons*, edited by Joy James. New York: St. Martin's Press.

Tolman, Deborah L. 1994. Doing Desire: Adolescent Girls' Struggles for/with Sexuality. *Gender and Society* 8:324–342.

Triplett, Ruth, and Laura B. Myers. 1995. Evaluating Contextual Patterns of Delinquency: Gender-Based Differences. *Justice Quarterly* 12:59–84.

U.S. Department of Health and Human Services. 1991. Annual Report to the Congress on the Runaway and Homeless Youth Program, Fiscal Year 1990. Washington, DC: Office of Human Development Services.

U.S. Department of Justice. 2005. *Crime in the United States 2004*. Uniform Crime Reports. Federal Bureau of Investigation. U.S. Government Printing Office. http://www.fbi.gov/ucr/cius_04/documents/CIUS2004.pdf

Wilczynski, Ania. 1995. Child-Killing by Parents. Pp. 167–180 in *Gender and Crime*, edited by R. E. Dobash, R. P. Dobash, and L. Noaks. Cardiff: University of Wales Press.

Wing, Adrien K., and Christine A. Willis. 1997. Sisters in the Hood: Beyond Bloods and Crips. Pp. 243–254 in *Critical Race Feminism*, edited by Adrien K. Wing. New York: New York University Press.

4

❖

Processing Women and Girls in the System

But men have indeed molded our legal system, which echoes the
contradictions felt toward women: at times regarding them as evil and
deceptive, at times treating them as childlike and defenseless.

LEONARD, 1982, 44

Until the 1970s, it was unusual for anyone to question whether males and
females were differently treated and processed by the police, prosecutors,
judges, jurors, probation officers, prison guards, and parole boards. Although
mainstream criminologists have agreed for some time that a defendant's race is
inappropriate as a classification for processing in the system, the question of
whether a person's sex is an equally inappropriate consideration has been unresolved. This is likely because "unlike claims of racism in the application of laws and
sanctions, there is no general presumption that women have historically been
subjected to a consistent pattern of discrimination" in crime processing (Nagel and
Hagan, 1983, 92).

Regardless of the historical lack of documentation of sexism in the official
decision making of alleged offenders, it has long been the case that the official
agents at every level of the system are "overwhelmingly male" (Schur, 1984,
224). Unfortunately, increased interest in female offenders since the 1970s has
focused more on questioning whether the feminist movement increased female
offending than on stimulating awareness of the paucity of scholarly attention and
programmatic change directed at female offenders (Chesney-Lind, 1987).

Crime processing refers to responses by the juvenile and crime-processing
decision makers, from the police to parole boards, regarding the handling of alleged
offenders. (For simplicity, the term *crime processing* will include the processing of
status offenses, although technically these are not crimes.) Research on crime
processing has been conducted at many different stages of decision making in the

system (such as arrest, pretrial, conviction versus acquittal, and sentencing) and in many jurisdictions. Since the 1970s, increased attention has been given to exploring whether sex discrimination in crime processing exists. Unfortunately, this endeavor is hampered by the fact that there are no routinely collected statistics for court decision making (for example, sentencing length and conviction rates) in various states and jurisdictions, comparable to the statistics the Uniform Crime Reports provide for police decision making (for example, arrest rates) (Schur, 1984).

This chapter discusses how sex discrimination has surfaced in both criminal and sentencing laws and describes current gender differences in crime processing in various jurisdictions and stages of the system. In addition, the processing of juveniles is discussed, as well as the ways age, race, and class have affected how females are handled by the crime-processing system. Finally, the adherence of females to gender stereotypes is examined to see how this influences the like-lihood of leniency or increased harshness toward female offenders.

CRIMINAL LAWS AND SEX DISCRIMINATION

The drafters of criminal law have been accused of attempting to perpetuate women's dependency (Scutt, 1981), and the criminal laws themselves have been described as a measure of the gender inequality in society (Leonard, 1982). This section discusses how criminal laws and their applications are often gendered. *Gender-neutral laws* are written so that no differentiation is made regarding applicability to females and males. *Gender-specific laws*, on the other hand, specify in writing that they apply to only one sex or apply differently to the sexes. (Gender-neutral and gender-specific may also be used to describe noncriminal laws, which are evaluated more closely in Chapter 9.) There are three general forms of sex discrimination in criminal laws: (1) implementing and applying gender-specific laws, (2) applying gender-neutral laws differently to female and male defendants, and (3) applying gender-neutral laws in a manner that values males' victimizations more seriously than females' victimizations.

Historically, most laws have been gender-neutral, and with the exception of affirmative action laws, gender-specific laws have increasingly become gender-neutral over time. For example, until recently, most rape laws defined the offender as male, and most prostitution laws defined the offender as female. In addition, the infanticide law, even as recently as the 1970s in England and Australia, and 1980s in Canada, applied only to women. (Scutt, 1981; Shaver, 1993; Smart, 1976)

An important aspect of U.S. history in terms of gender-specific laws sur-rounds the efforts in the latter part of the 1800s and the early part of the 1900s to raise the age of statutory rape (Odem, 1995). Odem (ibid.) documents how during this period White middle- and upper-class women engaged in formal efforts to raise the age at which a girl could legally consent to sex in 1885 from as young as age 7 (and usually age 10). This movement was successful in terms of raising the age; by 1920, most states had raised the age of consent to 16 or 18 years old. Clearly, this was a sex-specific law because it did not address at what age a male was able to consent to sex. The reformers who brought about the law change, however, were far more concerned with White girls' well-being than that of girls of color, particularly African American girls (ibid.). That is, the White women reformers were motivated by efforts to save poor White girls from lecherous older men. However, African American women reformers were concerned about African American girls' vulnerability to lecherous older men as well and thus were motivated to have the statutory rape age raised as well. The history of this movement is useful not only in terms of examining racism within this "feminist" movement to raise the statutory rape law but also in examining ways the law backfired for these women advocating for (White) girls. Specifically, while successful in raising the age in statutory rape law, in practice the law most directly affected girls in general and young African American men. White men processed in adult courts for violating the statutory rape laws were rarely punished, whereas African American men charged with having sex, no matter how consensual, with "underage" girl were far more likely to be punished (ibid.). Moreover, girls who had sex with men, either by consent or via force (rape), were processed harshly in the juvenile courts and punished for being sexually active (ibid.). Thus, the history of the statutory rape law not only symbolizes the important intersection between racism and sexism but it also exemplifies how a law designed to protect girls can backfire and result in more harm.

Over time, particularly during the 1970s and 1980s, many gender-specific laws were revised to make them gender neutral, consistent with the majority of the laws. Writing laws as gender neutral, however, does not ensure that their application will be gender neutral. That is, some laws that were intended to be gender neutral have treated males and females differently in their applications. An example is the Contagious Diseases Acts passed during the 1860s in England and designed to guarantee sailors and soldiers a "clean" supply of prostitutes by incarcerating prostitutes with venereal diseases. The police had free reign to arrest any "suspicious" women (Windschuttle, 1981). Numerous authors cite prostitution/sex work as an example of institutionalized sex discrimination in criminal laws and crime processing for focusing primarily on female sex workers as the offenders and ignoring the "clients," who are primarily male, as offenders, (Bernat, 1984; Edwards, 1984; Farley and Kelly, 2000; Leonard, 1982; Schur, 1984; Smart, 1976). In 1978, the implementation of a gender-neutral New York state statute to make prostitution and patronization of prostitute crimes of equal severity did not result in gender-neutral application. The police continued their nonenforcement toward patrons and continued their discrimination against the women (Bernat, 1985). Moreover, sex workers often face significant harassment by police, and when they are victims of crimes including rape and murder, their victimizations are rarely scrutinized by the police or courts (Frohmann, 1991; Morris, 1987).

The huge gender discrepancy between the sanctioning of female sex workers and male customers is further compounded when one accounts for race and class: The customers are typically White, employed, middle-class, middle-aged men living in the suburbs, while those penalized for this crime are usually poor women of color (Bernat, 1984; Leonard, 1982). Commercial sex businesses are most typically zoned in urban neighborhoods of people of color, creating a hostile environment where women and girls are harassed and recruited by pimps and johns driving through (Farley and Kelly, 2000).

The third manner in which criminal laws may result in sex discrimination is not concerned with how male and female defendants are differently treated but rather how the laws' enactments may judge the harshness of the crime based on whether the victim was male or female. Chapters 6 through 8 discuss this in more detail regarding female victims of rape and battering. Another example of this, however, is in the enactment of the gender-neutral death penalty laws, where women's and children's lives are generally less valued than men's. An in-depth analysis found that killing strangers for gain is much more likely to result in receiving the death penalty than killing a spouse (usually a woman) or child in anger (Rapaport, 1991). One study found that the crimes most likely to receive the death penalty are committed by men against men or by men who killed women and children in another man's family (ibid., 1991). Moreover, the death penalty is given in such a manner that male and parental dominance is supported because crimes in the home, of which women and children are disproportion-ately victims, are seen as less deserving of the death penalty than violence against (usually male) strangers, such as the "luckless clerk on night duty at a convenience store" (ibid., 379). However, a more recent study reported that murders of White female victims were the cases most likely to receive the death penalty (Holcomb, Williams, and Demuth, 2004).

Rapaport (ibid.) does not aim to weigh the moral grounds of the death penalty or to minimize the murder of night clerks. Rather, she shows how the murder of women and children by men they know is ranked far less seriously than the murder of men by strangers (usually for financial gain) when examining who receives the death penalty. Another study found that decisions to try a case (rather than plea bargain) are based on the strength of evidence and the credibility and blamelessness of the victim. This study also found that cases where the victims were male were more likely to go to trial than be plea-bargained, suggesting gender differences in credibility and blamelessness of victims (Myers and Hagan, 1979).

But gender of the victim is not the only factor influencing the decision making regarding female offenders' sentences. Dodge (2002) refers to victim devaluation theory (VDT) to explain differences between White women's slightly longer sentences for murder than those received by African American women in the first half of the twentieth century in Illinois. According to VDT, "legal authorities value the lives of white victims more highly than those of black victims and thus punish their killers more harshly" (ibid., 105). Given that White women's murder victims were far more likely than African American women's murder victims to be White, White women received harsher sentences (in a system that otherwise treated African American women far worse than White women).

In conclusion, with the exception of rape and prostitution laws, most laws are gender neutral, written to apply equally to both sexes. In the 1970s and 1980s, most of the few gender-specific laws were rewritten as gender-neutral laws. Unfortunately, the practice of enforcing laws does not always follow the gender neutrality written in most law codes. The next section of this chapter discusses how gender-specific legislation on sentencing has worked to the disadvantage of female offenders. The final section of this chapter discusses empirical research findings on gender differences in crime processing at various stages of the system.

SENTENCING LAWS AND SEX DISCRIMINATION

Many of the efforts to improve the lot of women in the crime-processing system have backfired, resulting in worse treatment or stricter guidelines for females. Examples of this include the first sex-segregated penal institutions and sex-specific sentencing laws. This section shows how the history of sex-segregated prisons is related to discriminatory sex-specific sentencing laws. Chapter 5 discusses in more depth how sex-segregated prisons often increase incarcerated women's oppression.

The first women-only prisons in England and the United States were designed to help women. They were labeled "reformatories" and "industrial homes" in an effort to distinguish them from the harsher "penitentiaries" housing male offenders. Women's prisons were designed to rehabilitate, whereas men's penitentiaries had punishment as the primary goal (Temin, 1980). The assumption was that women were more malleable and amenable to rehabilitation than men.

The result of this supposed better rehabilitative treatment of female offenders was that judges' sentences for women became indeterminate (uncertain) and longer than males' determinate (fixed) sentences for the same crimes. The justification was that women should stay in prison until they were rehabilitated. Although most states had a limit on the maximum sentence for each crime, women were actually serving more time than men were for the same crimes.

This patronizing "helping" of women offenders is analogous to the effects the juvenile and family courts created for children in the late 1800s. The supposed increased care of minors through *parens patriae* (where the court is assigned to act in a protective parental role toward children) did more to restrict than to liberate children (see Chesney-Lind, 1982; Naffine, 1989). This is consistent with the contention that "the deprivation of rights of women as a group has been historically justified by their definition as inferior human beings" (Figueira-McDonough and Sarri, 1987, 13–14), including treating them as children. The fact that both women and children have been subjected to this denial of rights in the name of "help" should not be lost. (The "infantalization" of women offenders is discussed further in Chapter 5.)

Indeterminate sentencing laws for women in Illinois in the 1930s and 40s resulted in women having one parole hearing at the end of the first year of their prison sentence, and if they were not released then, they did not receive another hearing, thus "maxing out" women's sentences (Dodge, 2002). The 1913 Muncy Act of Pennsylvania is the most famous example of sex discrimination in sentencing. The act required judges to sentence women age 17 and older who were convicted of an offense punishable by more than one year to an indeterminate sentence in the Muncy State Industrial Home for Women. The act gave judges much less discretion for sentencing female than male offenders, particularly with regard to shortening women's sentences. The effect of this act was that women were not eligible for parole as early as men convicted of the same offenses. As recently as the 1970s, Arkansas, Connecticut, Iowa, Kansas, Maine, Maryland, Massachusetts, New Jersey, and Ohio had laws similar to the Muncy Act, which permitted longer sentences for females than males convicted of the same offense (Temin, 1980).

The first attack on the Muncy Act occurred in 1966. Jane Daniel, a convicted robber, was originally sentenced to one to four years. One month later, her sentence was extended to three and a half to ten years, as stipulated by the Muncy Act. Had Jane Daniel been a male, the judge would have been allowed to give "him" the one- to four-year sentence. The Superior Court of Pennsylvania denied that this was an infringement of her rights, stating that men's and women's inherent physical and psychological differences justified differential treatment. Therefore, it was deemed reasonable for women to receive longer sentences, especially because they supposedly received more effective rehabilitation while incarcerated.

The one judge who dissented in this opinion was sufficiently convincing for the Supreme Court of Pennsylvania to hear the appeal. Daniel's appeal was joined by the case of Daisy Douglas, a woman convicted of aggravated robbery with a male codefendant. Douglas's record consisted only of prostitution arrests, whereas her paramour and codefendant had six prior convictions for burglary. Following the Muncy Act, Douglas received the maximum allowable sentence—twenty years—while her codefendant received a three- to ten-year sentence. The appeal centered on denial of the Fourteenth Amendment's equal protection clause. The Douglas case was crucial in overturning Muncy because it could actually show that a woman and a man were treated differently in the same case. The court could find no reason why women should receive longer sentences and ruled in favor of Douglas and Daniel. Connecticut followed suit shortly afterward, striking down their equivalent of the Muncy Act.

Unfortunately, two weeks after the Daniel decision, the Pennsylvania legislature passed the Muncy Act Amendment, which ordered the court not to fix a minimum sentence for a woman convicted of a crime; only a maximum sentence not to exceed the maximum term specified in the law could be given. Thus, women were still denied equal treatment, making the Daniel decision practically moot. Sex discrimination was further institutionalized because a man was entitled to have a minimum sentence set by a judge in an open hearing with mandated counsel, whereas women's sentences were decided in closed sessions by parole boards. "Arguably, this constitutes as much a denial of equal protection as the imposition of mandatory maximum sentences" (Temin, 1980, 267). Feinman (1992) traced a similar sentencing practice in New Jersey (*State v. Costello*, 1971). A 1973 State Supreme Court ruling struck down indeterminate sentencing of women when men received minimum–maximum term sentences, on the grounds that such decision making violated the equal protection clause of the Fourteenth Amendment (*State v. Chambers*, 1973). However, this practice ended only when a state code was implemented in 1979 (Feinman, 1992).

More recent laws also have significant gendered impacts. For example, the "three-strikes" laws requiring incarceration after three offenses impact poor, single mothers disproportionately because they are typically the hardest hit when the economy worsens and are in the most dire straights to support themselves and dependents on a limited budget (or no budget), particularly when social services are limited as well (Danner, 1998). Sokoloff (2005, 128) similarly accounts for the manner in which three-strikes laws, as well as "mandatory minimum" and "truth-in-sentencing" laws driven by the current conservative punishment era, have "intensified the burden" for women. The prisons and punishments designed for the violent male offender have resulted in more incarcerations for longer periods of time with fewer opportunities for parole or rehabilitation (ibid.).

In summary, during the 1960s and 1970s, there was a concerted effort to challenge many of the gender-specific laws requiring different sentencing practices for women and men. Observers of the implementation of these laws recognized that they resulted in de jure discrimination against women, who were receiving significantly longer sentences than men convicted of the same crimes. Challenges to these laws were resisted, but eventually most sexist laws were overturned in favor of gender-neutral sentencing laws. More recent laws, such as "three strikes, you're out," have also overly burdened women's sentencing.

THREE HYPOTHESES OF SEX DISCRIMINATION
IN CRIME PROCESSING

Three hypotheses can be tested to establish whether there is sex discrimination in crime processing and if so, whether it is against females or males: (1) the equal treatment hypothesis, (2) the chivalry (or paternalism) hypothesis, and (3) the "evil" woman hypothesis. The *equal treatment* (or the null) *hypothesis* states there is no sex discrimination in crime processing: Males and females are treated identically. An example of equal treatment would be minor males and females receiving similar sentences if caught drinking beer by a police officer. The *chivalry or paternalism thesis* hypothesizes that there is sex discrimination against male offenders; that is, females are treated or processed more leniently than males. This belief was first suggested by Thomas (1907) and then by Pollak (1950), who were discussed in Chapter 2. For example, a girl caught drinking beer would be told to pour her beer out and go home, whereas a boy caught drinking beer would be arrested and brought before juvenile court. The third category, the *evil woman hypothesis,* purports that sex discrimination against females exists in crime processing: Females are treated more harshly than males for similar offenses. The reasoning behind this belief is that offending females have violated gender roles as well as laws; thus, "female defendants will be sanctioned not only for their offenses but also for their inappropriate sex role behavior" (Nagel and Hagan, 1983, 116). The evil woman hypothesis is often viewed as the counter thesis to the chivalry or paternalism thesis. In this case, the beer-drinking boy would be sent home with no record, while the beer-drinking girl would be sanctioned and sent to juvenile court.

Farnsworth and Teske (1995) identified three corollaries to the chivalry hypothesis: (1) the typicality hypotheses, (2) the selectivity hypothesis, and (3) the differential discretion hypothesis. The *typicality hypothesis* "proposes that women are treated with chivalry in criminal processing, but only when their charges are consistent with stereotypes of female offenders" (1995, 23). The *selectivity hypothesis,* on the other hand, states that decision makers extend chivalrous treatment disproportionately to White females. Finally, the *differential discretion hypothesis* suggests that the stage in the system matters, specifically that chivalrous decision making is more likely in informal decision making, such as charge reduction decisions (Farnworth and Teske, 1995).

CHIVALRY AND PATERNALISM

It has been noted that criminologists and lay people frequently assume that chivalry is the most common practice of the three hypotheses (Curran, 1983; Leonard, 1982; Morris, 1987; Visher, 1983). Therefore, much of the research on sex discrimination in crime processing has focused on the idea of chivalrous treatment as an example of "reverse discrimination." Where it exists, however, chivalrous treatment is far more complex than the simple preferential treatment of females. Rather, chivalrous treatment is usually a bartering system in which women in general are viewed as being less equal. This bartering system is extended to only certain kinds of females, according to their race, class, age, sexual orientation, demeanor, and adherence to "proper" gender roles. Chivalrous treatment may be viewed as an exchange or bargain, where the interaction between the usually male official and the female violator "is transformed into an exchange between a man and a woman" (Visher, 1983, 6). The chivalrous treatment is likely extended, then, only to females who conform to traditional gender stereotypes (ibid.).

To understand the current costs and complexities of chivalrous treatment, it is necessary to be aware of the historical underpinnings of chivalry and paternalism.

> The term *chivalry* emerged in Europe during the Middle Ages. It described an institution of service rendered by the crusading order to the feudal lords, to the divine sovereign, and to woman kind. "Ladies" were special beneficiaries of the practice of chivalry—knights were sworn to protect their female weakness against dragons and devils. After the disappearance of chivalry as a formal institution, however, a number of chivalrous practices regarding women continued to exist in the world of social convention. (Moulds, 1980, 279)

Some believe that it is important to distinguish between chivalry and paternalism (Moulds, 1980; Nagel and Hagan, 1983). Chivalry is associated with placing an individual on a pedestal and behaving gallantly toward that person, whereas paternalism involves taking care of the powerless and dependent. Both chivalry and paternalism, however, imply weakness and a need to protect another person or group, which can have dangerous repercussions when "protect" becomes "control." It is often difficult to tell whether preferential treatment of female defendants, when it occurs, is due to chivalry or paternalism, some combination of the two, or other factors.

A cursory look at the chivalrous treatment of women and girls may indicate that females inevitably benefit, often at the expense of males. This form of human interaction, however, is more in tune with "political paternalism," for which there may be a cost. "If the gentle treatment women are said to enjoy is based on this political inferiority, we should be aware of the high price paid for the so-called benefits of chivalry" (Moulds, 1980, 278). On the other hand, some question whether equal treatment is necessarily the right objective because it ignores the fact that men and women have different access to power in society and often experience different roles and responsibilities (such as in child rearing) (Daly, 1989a; Morris, 1987). These issues resurface later in this chapter and again in Chapter 9, when we examine laws that have been used to "protect" women from "men's" employment, often restricting women to the unpaid and devalued work in the home. In short, there is often a high price to pay for chivalrous/paternalistic treatment: Women are viewed as children in "need" of additional attention and control.

EMPIRICAL FINDINGS ON GENDER DIFFERENCES IN CRIME PROCESSING

It is difficult to evaluate the validity of the equal treatment, chivalry, or evil woman hypotheses without accounting for the type of offense, the stage in the crime-processing system, the demographic characteristics of the alleged offender, and the degree to which defendants fit gender stereotypes. In their review of research that tests the chivalry and evil woman hypotheses, Nagel and Hagan (1983, 135–136) suggest that the evil woman hypothesis is not the opposite of the chivalry hypothesis but rather its corollary. Women may receive chivalrous treatment as long as they commit less serious crimes, exhibit the "appropriate" passive demeanor, and have little evidence against them.

> Thus it may be that women are preferentially treated, compared with men, until such time as the basis for that preferential treatment—chivalry or paternalism—is rendered inappropriate. Then, by virtue of the seriousness of the offense charged, the lessening of the presumption of innocence, and the evidence of deviation from traditional female patterns of behavior, the woman is moved into the evil woman category, and preferential treatment ceases. (Nagel and Hagan, 1983, 135–136)

The earliest research on gender differences in crime processing found strong support for the chivalry hypothesis rather than the equal treatment or evil woman hypotheses. For the most part, however, these findings supporting the preferential treatment of females could be explained by the studies' failure to account or control for two important legal variables: the defendant's prior record and the type of offense the defendant was accused of committing. If the crime-processing system is indeed just, then we expect the decision making to be related to legal variables about the case and not extralegal variables, such as the defendant's sex, race, and class.

Since the 1980s, studies evaluating gender bias in crime processing have been more likely to include the type of offense and prior record. Consequently, there is less support for the chivalry hypothesis and more for the equal treatment hypothesis. To understand how this works, consider a study that simply compares the raw percentages of males' and females' arrest, conviction, and sentencing severity and finds that males are far more likely than females to be arrested, convicted, and given lengthy sentences. These percentages imply chivalry, or the lenient treatment of females. Suppose, however, that after the analysis controls for the seriousness of the offense and the defendant's prior record, it finds that males and females with similarly serious offenses and similar prior records receive the same rates of arrest, conviction, and sentence length. Such findings (which are common) point to a more fundamental gender difference (already discussed in the last chapter) than how alleged offenders are processed: Males generally receive harsher sanctions than females in crime processing because they generally commit more serious crimes and have lengthier and more serious records.

Despite the increasing evidence that chivalrous treatment is less common than once thought, the picture of gender differences in crime processing is more complex than simple support for the equal treatment hypothesis. First, there is some evidence that chivalrous treatment still exists in some situations, even when controlling for the legal variables. Second, some studies have found support for the evil woman hypothesis when controlling for the legal variables. Most important, even when analyses find evidence for chivalrous treatment or equal treatment in crime-processing decisions, there is often additional evidence that different factors were used to determine males' and females' culpability and punishment. For example, one study found that what appeared on the surface to be chivalrous treatment was actually the result of extraordinarily harsh sanctioning of African American males relative to everyone else (all females and White males), implying that the intersection of race and sex alone can have a huge impact (Spohn, Welch, and Gruhl, 1985). Thus, regardless of which of the three hypotheses is supported by the overall findings, many studies find that different factors are used to make decisions about females' versus males' culpability.

The remainder of this chapter describes findings from empirical studies that tested the three hypotheses on gender discrimination in crime processing: the equal treatment, chivalry, and evil woman hypotheses. The factors that need to be considered to determine whether gender bias occurs in crime processing include (1) the race, class, and age of the alleged offender; (2) the importance of reforms in the processing of juveniles; (3) the stage in the crime-processing system; (4) the type of offense; and (5) how gender-role stereotypes affect gender bias in crime processing.

Access to Chivalry: Discrimination among Women

Any evaluation of crime processing must first recognize that there are different life experiences among females, depending on such factors as their race, ethnicity, class, age, nation of origin, and sexuality. The idea behind chivalry is that women are placed on a pedestal and need to be protected, but crime-processing decisions are often based on stereotypes that White women are more feminine, fragile, and deserving of protection than women of color (see Young, 1986). Similarly, with regard to social class, poorer women may be less likely to be treated as "ladies" than their wealthier sisters and thus be less likely to experience chivalrous crime-processing treatment. Regarding the age variable, there is evidence that the evil woman approach is more predominant for girls than for women (Nagel and Hagan, 1983, 115).

A considerable amount of research confirms that chivalrous treatment may be reserved for "certain kinds" of females, based on their personal characteristics, a practice referred to as *selective chivalry* (Dodge, 2002). Regarding race and gender, historical analyses of the United States report White female offenders viewed as amenable to rehabilitation, whereas stereotypes of African American female offenders as "aggressive" and "virile" were used to justify their harsher punishments (Seitz, 2005); immigrant women (particularly immigrant women of color) also face harsher sentencing (Butler, 1997; Dodge, 2002). A number of more recent crime-processing studies report that African American women/girls and other women/girls of color tend to receive more severe responses by the system than White women/girls (Agozino, 1997; Bortner and Reed, 1985; Butler, 1997; Chigwada-Bailey, 1997; Dodge, 2002; Krohn, Curry, and Nelson-Kilger, 1983; Kruttschnitt, 1981; Lieber and Mack, 2003; Seitz, 2005; Spohn, Gruhl, and Welch, 1987; Steffensmeier, Ulmer, and Kramer, 1998; Visher, 1983), poorer women receive more severe responses than wealthier women (Butler, 1997; Dodge, 2002; Kruttschnitt, 1981; Worrall, 1990), and younger women/girls are discriminated against compared to older women (Chesney-Lind and Shelden, 1992; Farrington and Morris, 1983; Hiller and Hancock, 1981; Krohn, Curry, and Nelson-Kilger, 1983; Steffensmeier, Ulmer, and Kramer, 1998; Visher, 1983).

"Little is known about the numbers and experiences of lesbian, bisexual, queer, and questioning young women in the juvenile corrections system" (Schaffner, 2004, 120). Three recent studies report the overrepresentation of lesbians among both juvenile and adult offenders, suggesting disproportionately harsh actions ("evil" woman) for these offenders (Belknap and Holsinger, 2006; Farr, 2004; Schaffner, 2004). Schaffner (2004) documents a variety of ways that lesbian delinquent girls experience harassment and abuse about their sexual orientation in the schools, their homes, and the "justice" system. "The effects of homophobia, both on the girls who are victims of violence and on the girls who perpetrate violence because of it, must be taken into account by those seeking to understand the environment of violence for female juveniles" (ibid., 120).

Some studies provide notable variations among characteristics. For example, one study found that whether a woman defendant was older or younger than 35 had no impact on the sentencing outcome (Brennan, 2002). Another study reported that welfare status had a more detrimental impact on sentencing severity than either race or income (Kruttschnitt, 1981). A study of the sentencing of women in Illinois from the 1920s to 1940s found discrimination against White women intimately involved with men of color (Dodge, 2002). A large study on the sentencing of women in New York City found that legal variables (e.g., charge severity and prior record) were the best (and most direct) predictors of sentencing outcomes but that extralegal socioeconomic variables (e.g., race/ethnicity, class, age, martial status, and educational attainment) had more complicated (indirect) impacts on the sentences. Thus, the author concluded that studies that fail to account for different sentences for different groups of women/girls may be omitting important indirect effects (or ways the socioeconomic variables interact with each other or the legal variables in predicting criminal-processing decision outcomes) (Brennan, 2002). Albonetti's (1997) study of the effect of drug-offense sentencing guidelines found that being a woman among Whites provided a more chivalrous impact in the likelihood of an incarceration sentence than being a woman among African Americans. Conversely, among African Americans, women received shorter prison terms than White women did among Whites. Thus, chivalry was greater for White women than for African American women among their own race in the decision to incarcerate, but chivalry was greater for African American than White women regarding the prison sentence length (ibid.).

Few studies address how educational attainment affects women's sentencing, but one such study found that, as expected, women with less (formal) education were more likely than more educated women to receive jail time (Brennan, 2002).

Regarding sexuality, while there is almost no research on how a girl's or women's lesbian or "queer" status may affect sentencing, there is a long history of every stage of the criminal legal system reserving extra harsh treatment for any women or girls where adultery is insinuated in any manner (Dodge, 2002). A study of female offenders in Illinois in the 1920s through 1940s found that women admitted to prison routinely tested for sexually transmitted infections, and unlike their male counterparts, if they tested positive their sentence included staying in prison at least until the STI was cleared (Dodge, 2002).

These findings confirm that not all females are treated similarly in the crime-processing system. As a rule, women of color, poor women, younger women, women immigrants, and lesbians are afforded less leniency or are processed more prejudicially than other females.

Reforms in the Processing of Juveniles

The juvenile court has been accused of punishing the noncriminal (status) offenses of girls the same as or more harshly than the criminal offenses of boys (or girls) (Chesney-Lind, 1973, 1981, 1987; Conway and Bogdan, 1977; Datesman and Scarpitti, 1977; Schlossman and Wallach, 1982). Also, girls charged with promiscuity have historically been treated more harshly than girls committing other nonsexual offenses (Terry, 1967). Girls not only have been formally and informally punished for consensual sexual activities that boys are more likely to "commit", but girls additionally have had their sexual victimizations merged with their sexual "offenses":

> One of the most problematic aspects of the juvenile justice system is its failure to distinguish offenders from victims. Nowhere is this more true than in the case of sexual abuse and sexual behavior. Females are often identically handled for abuse and promiscuous behavior or prostitution. (Sarri, 1983, 382)

Perhaps the most disturbing aspect of the processing of females has been the historically pervasive forced submissions of juveniles to gynecological exams. The excuses given for these exams were to determine whether they had STIs and whether they were virgins. (The courts were apparently unconcerned with STIs or virginity in boys.) The first study to document this practice was conducted on Honolulu juvenile court cases between 1929 and 1964 (Chesney-Lind, 1973). Only one-quarter of boys' but three-quarters of girls' arrests were for status offenses, and 70 to 80 percent of the girls were forced to have "physical exams," even for nonsexual charges such as larceny. The girls were more likely than the boys to be sent to pretrial detention, and they spent three times as long there as their male counterparts.

> Besides the jail-like atmosphere that confronts young people held in detention facilities, young women in the past underwent an extra and significant violation of their civil rights: pelvic examinations and, more recently, vaginal searches. . . . The accounts suggest that blanket administration of pelvic examinations occurred well into the 1970s in various parts of the United States. (Chesney-Lind and Shelden, 1992, 149–150)

Shelden's (1981) study of Memphis, Tennessee, court records between 1900 and 1917 found that nonconsensual sexual experiences (rape victimizations) as well as consensual sexual activity of girls resulted in harsh sanctions against them. Such sanctions were nonexistent for boys. Gynecological exams to determine whether girls were virgins (in order to assess their criminality) were commonplace. Even when controlling for race, class, and offense, girls were treated more harshly than boys.

In the context of the research reporting a focused policing of girls' sexuality, it is remarkable to examine research on the juvenile courts in Denver, Colorado, from 1901 to 1927. Progressive reformers, with Judge Ben B. Lindsey at the helm, developed a juvenile court system dedicated to "normalizing" girls' sexuality, attempting to educate the citizenry on the frequency across groups (regardless of race, class, and immigrant status) that young people were sexual (Colomy and Kretzmann, 1997). Lindsey and his court staff were so trusted by girls that the girls came to them to ask questions and broach concerns they were unwilling to ask their own parents.

> In a limited way, Lindsey gave voice to girls frequently juxtaposing their intelligence, honesty, and integrity to their parents' obtuseness and hypocrisy. By doing so, Lindsey intended to rest the court's authority and the validity of its judgments, in part, on an appreciation and first-hand knowledge of the actual life conditions, burgeoning "modern" sex code, and changing gender roles that regulated the life of young women. . . . Far from subjecting girls to the status degradation ceremonies practiced in other courts, the Denver court was organized so as to protect their dignity, self-respect, and privacy. (ibid., 58)

A more recent British study found that girls' sexual activity is monitored more closely and punished more severely than boys', and the harsh treatment of girl runaways is linked to their sexual "promiscuity" (Gelsthorpe, 1989). A study of U.S. family court records found that boys received harsher dispositions than girls for criminal offenses (felonies and misdemeanors), but girls received harsher dispositions than boys for status offenses. Half of the girls but only one-fifth of the boys had been referred to family court for status offenses (Datesman and Scarpitti, 1980). U.S. studies also report that the family courts are most likely to warrant official intervention of status offenders when they are White girls and least likely

when they are African American boys; this is consistent with race–gender stereotypes (Datesman and Aickin, 1984; Datesman and Scarpitti, 1980). An Australian
court study on juveniles found that girls are more likely to be given such "rehabilitative" sentences as probation, supervision, and institutionalization, while boys are
"treated" with more legalistic measures such as bonds, fines, and adjournment (Hiller
and Hancock, 1981).

A study of France, England, and Wales found that girls were only one-sixth of
the youths with criminal charges, yet they made up half of the juveniles removed
from the home and placed in institutions (Hudson, 1989). Moreover, girls received
special scrutiny and discrimination. They were judged by their "femininity" and
were sanctioned for typical adolescent behavior, including immaturity in judgment
and acting "silly." Boys who exhibited these same behaviors were less likely to be
sanctioned for them. A study of youths recommended for supervision (a court
punishment that requires checking in with a supervisor for two to three years) in
England and Wales reported discrimination against girls in that they were far more
likely than boys to be recommended for supervision for trivial offenses (Webb,
1984). Similarly, a comparative analysis of ten European criminal courts found that
girls are still more severely punished than boys for status offenses, especially for sexual
activity, and are more likely to be incarcerated and for longer periods than boys
(Cain, 1989, 232).

The role of parents in the offense processing of youths is particularly important, especially when the goal is to examine gender differences. There is ample
evidence that parents play a crucial role in many juveniles' first formal contact with
the crime-processing system and that girls are at much greater risk than boys of
having their parents turn them into the police or juvenile courts (Chesney-Lind
and Shelden, 1992; Colomy and Kretzmann, 1997; Hiller and Hancock, 1981;
Sarri, 1983; Teilmann and Landry, 1981). Parents are often less tolerant of their
daughters' than their sons' identical behaviors, whether they are status offenses (for
example, running away, breaking curfews, drinking alcohol, and being sexually
active) or more traditional offenses (for example, larceny and assaults). Moreover,
parents are more likely to report problems with daughters than with sons, and they
are more likely to physically and sexually abuse their daughters (Chesney-Lind and
Shelden, 1992). (This victimization often causes juveniles to run away, to drink
alcohol, and to engage in other "acting out" behaviors, as discussed in Chapter 3.)
Finally, one study reported that almost one-third of families refused to take their
children back after their release from court custody as "persons in need of supervision" (PINS) (Conway and Bogdan, 1977).

The establishment of the juvenile court in 1899 was the culmination of the
"child-savers'" efforts to control youths' lives. This was particularly apparent for
girls who were the "losers in the reform movement," which resulted in girls' high
referral rates to juvenile courts and subsequently high institutionalization rates for
"immorality" and "waywardness" (Chesney-Lind and Shelden, 1992, 120). The
police and the juvenile courts have historically condoned more punitive reactions
to female than male status offenders, reaffirming a double standard for male and
female sexuality. Although this was more common in the early years of the

juvenile court, "there is evidence that the pattern continues" (Chesney-Lind and Shelden, 1992, 115).

The Juvenile Justice and Delinquency Prevention Act (JJDPA) of 1974 was designed to divert and deinstitutionalize status offenders from secure facilities. For states to receive federal funding for delinquency prevention programs, they had to discontinue institutionalizing status offenders in "training schools," detention centers, and adult jails and to develop plans to treat status offenders in places other than juvenile detention or correctional facilities. Because girls have been disproportionately sanctioned as status offenders, it was predicted that this would have a huge impact on the processing of girls. As expected, there was a decline in the admission of girls to detention facilities and "training schools" following the 1974 JJDPA (Alder, 1998; Chesney-Lind, 1986, 1988; Sarri, 1983). Between 1975 and 1979, males' detention rates decreased by 20 percent, and females' rates decreased by 44 percent. These gender differences were largely due to the overrepresentation of girls in status offenses and to the policy's goal to divert status offenders from detention (Krisberg and Schwartz, 1983). Another study assessing the impact of the JJDPA on deinstitutionalization of delinquent youth found that girls are "transinstitutionalized" into mental health facilities for "inappropriate" behaviors, while African American youth are "warehoused in the public system of juvenile institutions," and thus, White males are the most likely to have benefited from deinstitutionalization (Federle and Chesney-Lind, 1992).

The initial optimism that accompanied the deinstitutionalization of status offenders is tempered by the findings from (1) monitoring deinstitutionalization rates over time and (2) examining the private juvenile "correctional" system that replaced the traditional secure facilities. Regarding the first point, there is some concern that the decline of institutionalized status offenders leveled off between 1979 and 1982 and that "the gains made against judicial sexism are very much in jeopardy" (Chesney-Lind, 1986, 90). In fact, between 1982 and 1986, arrests for both male and female runaways increased (Chesney-Lind, 1988). Moreover, while female admissions to "training schools" decreased 37 percent in the five years after the JJDP Act, male admissions increased by 9 percent (Krisberg and Schwartz, 1983).

Turning to the second point, it is not clear that the diversionary programs have resulted in any less stigmatizing of juvenile offenders than the detention facilities before the JJDPA (Datesman and Aickin, 1984). More importantly, however, a study in Minnesota discovered that many of the status offenders who previously would have been institutionalized in the traditional secure facilities (such as "training schools") were institutionalized in increasing numbers in the "hidden" or private juvenile "correctional" system following the 1974 JJDPA. This system includes mental health and chemical dependency programs (Schwartz, Beeck, and Anderson, 1984). Although this study did not examine gender per se, case studies portray many of these youth as females whose parents disapproved of their (often sexual) behavior: "More often than not, these youth are referred by their parents . . . [and] many of the admissions are not as 'voluntary' as one might think" (ibid., 382). The authors describe the case of a 16-year-old girl with no history of serious delinquency or chronic status offending, whose parents had her repeatedly institutionalized in private mental hospitals for periods as long as nine months simply because her father, a prominent university administrator, was embarrassed by her "punk" attire and "punk" friends. The authors question what rights parents should have to institutionalize their children against their will in psychiatric or chemical-dependency programs. It is also important to examine how this is "hidden." Similarly, a study of girls institutionalized in delinquent "homes" in England found that many girls were in these homes not for delinquent offenses but because of emotional and family problems, such as their parents' fighting (Gelsthorpe, 1989). In comparison, South Australia implemented a policy in 1979 to abolish status offenses. This act has been far more successful than the JJDPA in the United States and other countries' attempts to curb the criminalization of juveniles. South Australia's abolishment of status offenses appears to have resulted in equal treatment for boys and girls and a decreasing concern with girls' sexuality (Naffine, 1989). However, more recent research in Australia reported girls are still held in public and private juvenile justice and medical facilities for minor and status offenses (Alder, 1998). In particular, the girls face contradictions over how to balance independence with the feminine expectation of subservience, and the girls' sexuality is tied into this, with the double standard of boys' sexual behavior identified as "sowing wild oats" while sexually active girls are labeled as "sluts" (Alder, 1998).

The Presence of Gender Bias in Different Stages of Processing

Many studies examine gender bias at various crime-processing decision points in the system: arrest, detention versus pretrial release, prosecution, dismissal of charges, negotiations and the guilty plea, conviction versus acquittal, incarceration, sentence severity, parole, and reconviction. It is often difficult to compare these studies because they are conducted in numerous and varied jurisdictions, at various stages or decision points in the system, and in different time periods. It is necessary, however, to attempt to determine the overall findings from these studies.

As stated in Chapter 3, women are generally far less serious offenders than men and have less extensive prior records. Thus, they are less likely to have their cases reach the final stages of the crime-processing system. Therefore, analyses that focus only on the latter stages may not adequately represent the processing of female offenders.

The first evaluation of studies on gender bias in crime processing stated that chivalry was most likely in the beginning stages and least likely in the later stages (Nagel and Hagen, 1983). A more recent review, however, found the opposite: Chivalry is least likely in the beginning stages of crime processing and most prominent in the latter stages (Chesney-Lind, 1987). These opposing findings are likely because the more recent evaluation was able to include more studies on the original contact with the system (the police) and because the more recent studies have been more likely to control for legal variables. The overall findings regarding studies evaluated for this section of the chapter are consistent with the more recent (ibid.) review.

The most support for the evil woman hypothesis is at the earliest stages of decision making (the police); support for the equal treatment hypothesis is most evident in the middle decision-making stages (the decisions to prosecute, dismiss charges, and convict); and support for the chivalry hypothesis is most evident in the final decision-making stages (the decision to incarcerate, the severity of the sentence, and the likelihood of reconviction). Most studies did not find sex to be a strong predictor, as the legal variables usually are. Many researchers found that evidence for chivalry in the original analyses of their data disappeared (or gender differences became negligible) when they controlled for other, usually legal, variables (Farrington and Morris, 1983; Fisher and Mawby, 1982; Landau, 1981; Landau and Nathan, 1983; Spohn, Welch, and Gruhl, 1985).

Police Decision Making   Decision making by police is the stage that has the most support for the evil woman hypothesis. Even here, however, this support is not consistent and can be explained by the unusually harsh police treatment of female status offenders. Two studies found that women were discriminated against in police decision making (Ghali and Chesney-Lind, 1986; Wilbanks, 1986), three found lenient or chivalrous treatment by the police (DeFleur, 1975; Krohn, Curry, and Nelson-Kilger, 1983; Mastrofski, Worden, and Snipes, 1995), and one found equal treatment (Visher, 1983). Notably, the strongest and most consistent support for the evil woman hypothesis in police decision making was found in research on police responses to status offenders (Chesney-Lind and Shelden, 1992; Hiller and Hancock, 1981; Sarri, 1983; Teilmann and Landry, 1981).

In the past it was common for the police, when looking into nonsexual offenses of juveniles, to question girls—but not boys—about their sexual experiences and then to add the sexual offense charges to the original offense (Chesney-Lind, 1974). Most young women, then, enter the crime-processing system as status offenders for running away from home, incorrigibility, waywardness, curfew violations, and so on. Although females constitute a small proportion of the system, when they are in the system, it is most often for status offenses (Chesney-Lind, 1981). Most empirical research, then, dispels the notion that females are treated chivalrously at the beginning stages of the crime-processing system. Indeed, this is where most practices consistent with the "evil woman" occur. An area of processing women that has received little research attention, and yet impacts many women, is the intersection of racism and anti-immigrant sentiment with sexism where noncitizen African American women are disproportionally detained by airport authorities because of the mythical assumption that "Black immigrant equals [drug] courier, unless otherwise proven" (Agozino, 1997, 142).

An area of the police "processing" of women and girls that has received little research could also be included in the victimization section of this book. More specifically, Kraska and Kappeler (1995) researched the sexual exploitation and abuse of females perpetrated by police officers. They label this phenomenon police sexual violence (PSV) and report how it occurs on a continuum ranging from invasions of privacy to using force to rape (see Exhibit 4.1). The various unethical, unprofessional, violating, and exploitative behaviors are perpetrated against a variety of women and girls, including female victims and female defendants. An example of police PSV against female victims was a woman whose business partner, without her consent and knowledge, had videotaped them having sex and was

E X H I B I T 4.1 **Kraska and Kappeler's Continuum of Police Sexual Violence (PSV)**

Unobtrusive Behavior	Obtrusive Behavior	Criminal Behavior
Viewing victims, photographs, and sexually explicit videos Invasions of privacy, secondary victimization	Custodial strip searches, body cavity searches, warrant-based searches, illegal detentions, deceptions to gain sexual favors Provision of services for sexual favors, sexual harassment	Sexual harassment, sexual contact, sexual assault, rape

SOURCE: From Kraska and Kappeler (1995, 94). Adapted by permission.

using this illegally taped sex to extort insurance money from her by threatening to show the tape to her family. The police convinced the woman that they needed the tape to process the case, assuring her that it would be handled discreetly and confidentially (Kraska and Kappeler, 1995). Instead it was widely viewed by members of the police department, including the chief of police. An example of the sexual exploitation of female defendants/offenders was what Kraska and Kappeler (ibid.) reported as a seemingly common practice among some officers to wait outside bars for women exiting alone and follow them, stop them for drinking under the influence, and either coerce them to have sex in order to get out of tickets or outright rape them with force. (Notably, not all of these women were drunk.) Finally, Kraska and Kappeler (ibid.) suggest that the most marginalized women in society may be those most at risk of PSV, particularly poorer women, young women, and women of color. They also offer considerable support for how PSV is a part of the policing tradition, both in the institution of police department and in the media and films that portray women as flirting with police officers and as eager participants with police they have never met (ibid.). Although more research needs to be done on this extreme violation by the police, the secret nature of these events and the code of covering up for fellow officers make such research difficult.

Pretrial Court Decisions   Most of the research on sexism in courtroom decision making focuses on judge, jury, and trial decisions, although fewer than one in ten cases go to a full trial (Figueira–McDonough, 1985). Not only are pretrial decisions more common but much of the pretrial decision making is not subject to the due process requirements of formal trials, leaving more room for discrimination.

An important stage in crime processing is the detention versus pretrial release decision, which "refers to the terms under which a defendant may be allowed to remain free in the interim between arrest and case disposition" (Kruttschnitt and McCarthy, 1985). This decision not only is important regarding a defendant's immediate freedom but can also have implications on the subsequent processing of the case: A defendant who has been detained may be more likely to be viewed as a confirmed offender or "inmate" (see Frazier and Cochran, 1986). One study found females received leniency in the pretrial release decision, although they were just as likely as males to fail to appear for court (Steury and Frank, 1990). A study on juveniles reported chivalry regarding the probability of receiving a recommendation for further court processing, but this was only available to girls in two-parent homes (Leiber and Mack, 2003). Other research on gender bias at the detention/pretrial release decision suggests that chivalrous treatment may be reserved for adult women who are not prostitutes; or stated alternatively, the treatment of juveniles and prostitutes at the detention/release stage was more consistent with the evil woman hypothesis (Bernat, 1985; Frazier and Cochran, 1986; Kruttschnitt, 1984; Kruttschnitt and Green, 1984; Teilmann and Landry, 1981).

Research examining gender bias in the decision to prosecute or dismiss charges largely supports the equal treatment hypothesis (Curran, 1983; Ghali and Chesney-Lind, 1986; McCarthy, 1987; Nagel, Cardascia, and Ross, 1982; Steffensmeier, Kramer, and Streifel, 1993; Teilmann and Landry, 1981), although there is also some support for chivalry (Albonetti, 1986; Gruhl, Welch, and Spohn, 1984; Spohn, Gruhl, and Welch, 1987; Wilbanks, 1986). A study of California felony theft and assault cases found an important interaction between court defendants' race and sex in the decision to reduce charges. Specifically, controlling for prior record and the type and severity of the offense, 72 to 76 percent of females of all races and White males received reduced charges, while African American males (66 percent) were the least likely group to receive reduced charges (Farnworth and Teske, 1995). Moreover, this study found that the charge reduction decision significantly affected the final sentence in a gendered manner: Females with no charge reduction were less likely (22 percent) than males with no charge reduction (37 percent) to be sent to prison.

A study examining the likelihood of referring juveniles to juvenile court found chivalry in court referrals for youth charged with delinquent acts but support for the evil woman hypothesis for youth charged with status offenses (Datesman and Aickin, 1984). One study on juveniles, however, found that the sex of the offender had a significant interaction with her or his race regarding charge dismissal: White boys had the best chance for dismissal, White girls for diversion, African American girls for probation, and African American boys for formal processing (Sarri, 1983). Another study of a juvenile district court in Iowa from 1980 to 1989 reported no gender differences in the processing of the youthful offenders at the various stages of court processing (from intake through disposition); however, African Americans and Native Americans fared worse than Whites at every decision-making point (Leiber, 1994).

Regarding the likelihood of pleading guilty or negotiating a plea, two studies found equal treatment of the sexes (Curran, 1983; Gruhl, Welch, and Spohn, 1984), while two found support for the evil woman hypothesis (Ghali and Chesney-Lind, 1986; Figueira-McDonough, 1985). Figueira-McDonough's (1985) is perhaps the most important of these studies because it was the most carefully conducted. She found that although women and men were equally likely to plead innocent, men were nearly twice as likely to plead guilty to a lesser charge. Furthermore, the use or possession of a gun added seriousness to women's but not men's offenses, and the presence of a witness was more likely to influence women than men to plead guilty. Women were less able to bargain and more willing to plead guilty, which may have been due to their limited access to attorneys, education, and experience (or power in general). Men were also more likely to receive both charge reductions and sentence reductions. Finally, only men were rewarded for their guilty pleas.

Trial and Posttrial Decision Making   Research on the conviction stage of decision making is most consistent with the equal treatment hypothesis (Curran, 1983; Ghali and Chesney-Lind, 1986; Gruhl, Welch, and Spohn, 1984; Koons-Witt, 2002; Steffensmeier, Kramer, and Streifel, 1993), except for one study that supported the chivalry hypothesis (Wilbanks, 1986). The research on gender bias at the incarceration decision generally supports the chivalry hypothesis (Albonetti, 1997; Farnworth and Teske, 1995; Gruhl, Welch, and Spohn, 1984; Nagel, Cardascia, and Ross, 1982; Nobiling, Spohn, and DeLone, 1998; Spohn, 1990; Steffensmeier, Kramer, and Streifel, 1993; Steffensmeier, Ulmer, and Kramer, 1998) more often than the equal treatment hypothesis (Ghali and Chesney-Lind, 1986; Kruttschnitt and Green, 1984). One study that reported support for the chivalry hypothesis found it was important to understand the interactions between sex and race/ethnicity. Specifically, Farnworth and Teske's (1995) analysis of California felons found, as stated earlier, that African American males were least likely to have charges reduced and that charge reduction significantly affected later decisions. For example, for those without charge reductions, males were more likely than females to be sentenced to prison (the females were more likely than the males to be sentenced to jail and receive probation). For those with reduced charges, males were more likely to be sent to jail, and females were more likely to receive probation. White women were about twice as likely to have assault charges reduced to nonassault charges, while White men were about one-and-a-half times as likely as African American men to receive such a charge reduction. Finally, "females with no prior record were more likely than similar males to receive charge reductions, and this enhanced females' chances for probation" (Farnworth and Teske, 1995, 23).

Again, the Urban Reform Era study in Ontario supported the evil woman hypothesis regarding sentence severity (Boritch, 1992), but more recent research findings fairly consistently support the chivalry hypothesis in the sentencing-severity stage of decision making (Albonetti, 1997; Curran, 1983; Farrington and Morris, 1983; Kruttschnitt, 1984; Nagel, Cardascia, and Ross, 1982; Spohn, 1990; Steffensmeier, Kramer, and Streifel, 1993; Steffensmeier, Ulmer, and Kramer, 1998; Wilbanks, 1986). Exceptions are two studies reporting "equal treatment" of the sexes at the sentencing phase (Nobiling, Spohn, and DeLone, 1998; Zatz, 1984). One study conducted using fifty data sets on gender and court sentencing from the 1970s through the 1990s reported varied actions dependent on the severity of the offense, whether it was in an urban area, and whether the stage was sentencing or incarceration: (1) half of these cases were cases were consistent with the chivalry hypothesis, and one-quarter showed mixed or no effects; (2) chivalrous sentencing in the courts was most likely in felony offenses, cases prosecuted in felony courts, and in courts in urban areas; and (3) chivalry was more likely in the decision to incarcerate (women were less likely to be sentenced to prison) and less likely in the length of the sentence (which evidenced more "equal treatment" processing than the decision to incarcerate) (Daly and Bordt, 1995). Other studies emphasize the need for looking at how race, gender, and class intersect. A Canadian study found not only that Aboriginal/First Nation members were imprisoned disproportionately compared to Whites but also that this was particularly true for women (LaPrairie, 1989). A study of Pennsylvania court decision-making found that in addition to overall chivalry for both the decision to incarcerate and the length of sentence, young African American males (18–29 years old) were treated the most harshly by far (Steffensmeier, Ulmer, and Kramer, 1998). They conclude that research cannot examine the impact of race, gender, or class alone without including how they interact with each other: "To list some examples, Black females aged 18–29 and 30–49 are more likely to be incarcerated than both Black and White males aged 50 and over, and White females aged 18–29 are more likely to be imprisoned than White males 50 and over" (ibid., 783).

Similarly, studies on gender bias in reconviction (Farrington and Morris, 1983) and probation (Ghali and Chesney-Lind, 1986; Nagel, Cardascia, and Ross, 1982) decision making consistently supported the chivalry hypothesis, except for one study that found equal treatment of the sexes in probation decisions (Kruttschnitt, 1984). A more recent study comparing adult probationers in Illinois (similar to federal data on prisoners), however, found that the women tended to be less likely to have a prior violent offense conviction before the current case *and* "women were more likely to be on probation for property or drug offenses, whereas men were more likely to be on probation for violent crimes or driving under the influence" (Olson, Lurigio, and Seng, 2000). Despite this, women's charges were more likely to be classified as felonies than men's, which the researchers attributed to women's increased likelihood of drug law violations, whereas the men were more likely to have DUI violations, which were classified as misdemeanors (ibid.). (This is particularly interesting given that it could be argued the DUIs are probably more dangerous to the general population than illegal drug use.) Overall, there were no gender differences in the length of the probation sentence when controlling for the severity of the offense, except a slight chivalrous advantage for women regarding property crimes. Turning to the conditions of probation, there were no significant differences in terms of court orders to require drug testing or perform community service, but women were more likely than men to be ordered to drug treatment, and men were more likely than women to be assessed court costs, supervision fees, or fines (possibly because they were more likely to be employed and report higher incomes) (ibid.). Although women were far more likely to have UAs (required urinalysis drug tests), there were no differences in "hot" UAs (positive drug tests). Finally, there were no gender differences for revocations of probation, but men were more likely to be rearrested during probation and to have a technical violation (the latter only when controlling for many variables including prior record and offense type).

A final area of gender differences in court processing, one that has received little attention, is death penalty sentencing. Since 1900, forty-nine women have been executed in the United States, and the race and social statuses of both the victims and offenders indicate a significant pattern, as does geographical location (Seitz, 2005). More specifically, African American women were executed for convictions of murdering White domestic employers, and these cases occurred almost exclusively in the South (ibid.). Between 1976 and 1987, 14 percent of those charged with murder or nonnegligent manslaughter were women; however, only 2 percent of the prisoners on death row are female (Rapaport, 1991). This appears to be chivalrous treatment of female offenders, but a closer examination by Rapaport (ibid.) suggests otherwise. First, felony murders are rarely committed by women (4 to 6 percent), and women are more likely to kill intimates in anger or defense than to kill strangers for a predatory purpose (such as economic or sexual gain) (ibid.). Second, male murder defendants are four times more likely than female murder defendants to have a prior conviction for a violent felony. Third, females are far less likely than males to be accused of murdering multiple victims (ibid.). Given these gender differences in murders and murderers, it is "logical" that women constitute only 2 percent of death row prisoners. Finally, a recent study depicts the extraordinarily high rate of lesbians among women on death row in the United States and documents ways their lesbianism likely resulted in additionally harsh processing of their offenses (Farr, 2004).

Gender Differences in Crime Processing Based on the Type of Offense

In addition to determining the validity of the equal treatment, chivalry, and evil woman hypotheses based on personal characteristics of the offender and the stage in the crime-processing system, it is important to control for the type of offense. It is likely that the direction of sex discrimination (whether it is against males or females) may be closely linked with the nature of the offense. In fact, Naffine (1987, 2) states: "The agents of the law are clearly inconsistent, even in their paternalism." Her review of gender and crime-processing studies concluded that chivalry is more likely when women commit less serious crimes but that women are treated more harshly than men when they commit more serious crimes. The less serious and more serious offenses, however, are closely linked with gender-role stereotypes. It has been stated that women whose offenses more closely fit traditional gender stereotypes (for example, shoplifting) will fare better than their less traditional counterparts who commit robberies, assaults, and so on (Nagel and Hagan, 1983, 116). Therefore, women who commit traditionally "masculine crimes" are expected to be treated more harshly than men (Chesney-Lind, 1987). Some studies, however, have found that women are treated more chivalrously for felony or violent crimes and less chivalrously for minor and property offenses (Hepburn, 1978; Steffensmeier, Kramer, and Streifel, 1993; Visher, 1983). A study of juveniles found that girls were treated chivalrously for property crimes but as "evil women" for status offenses (Hiller and Hancock, 1981).

Sarri (1987) states that examining the interaction between the offense type and the gender likelihood of committing the offense is necessary to determine gender disparities in crime processing. For some crimes, females and males are equally likely

Comparative Perspective: Gender Differences in Criminal Legal Processing: An International Comparison

Surprisingly, research comparing gender differences in criminal legal processing, or even comparing women and/or girls, across countries is almost nonexistent. An exception is a study by Professor Linda Harvey and her colleagues (1992). They analyzed the second and third United Nations Crime Surveys to examine gender in terms of suspects, apprehension, prosecution, conviction, and imprisonment throughout the world. They found the following global patterns:

- The types of crimes for which females and males were convicted remained fairly constant over the time period.

- In 1980 and 1985 (and to some extent in 1975), women were more likely than men to be filtered out of the criminal legal system as they progressed through the various stages (from suspect, to arrest, prosecution, etc.).

- Women were more likely to be suspected, prosecuted, and convicted in 1985 than they were in 1980. (Stated another way, more women were suspected, prosecuted, and convicted of crimes in 1985 than in 1980.)

SOURCE: Linda Harvey, R. W. Burnham, Kathy Kendall, and Ken Pease. 1992. Gender Differences in Criminal Justice: An International Comparison. *British Journal of Criminology* 32:208–217.

to be involved, yet females are sanctioned more harshly (for example, running away and prostitution); for other crimes, males and females are equally likely to be involved and are treated equally (for example, larceny); and for yet others, females are much less likely to commit the crimes but are more severely sanctioned when they do (for example, sexually abusing children) (Sarri, 1983). Similarly, a study on the abduction and fondling of children found that women are treated more harshly than men throughout the crime-processing system, while for charges of fraud, men are treated more harshly than women (Wilbanks, 1986). Another study found chivalry for women in the sentencing of four felonies (second-degree murder, manslaughter, larceny, and forgery) but equal treatment for all of the misdemeanors except child abandonment, a gender-inappropriate crime, for which women had longer sentences than men (Zingraff and Thomson, 1984). A California study on males' and females' felony theft and felony assault cases found no indication of gender discrimination based on the type of offense at the court level (Farnworth and Teske, 1995), and a Milwaukee study found equal treatment regarding pretrial decisions for crimes more typically committed by women (Steury and Hochstedler, 1990). However, a large study of women in New York City showed important distinctions among the women's sentences: (1) for prostitution cases, White women received more lenient sentences than African American or Latina women; (2) for drug charges, Latinas were more likely to receive jail sentences, followed by White, then African American women (Brennan, 2002). In summary, there are no consistent findings regarding the relationship between the type of offense and the presence of chivalry. This investigation merits further inquiry.

Gender Stereotypes and Crime Processing

Early studies on sex discrimination in crime processing recognized that chivalrous treatment was often reserved for females who displayed "appropriate" feminine behavior. In the 1980s, an important addition to the understanding of gender bias in crime processing was the recognition that chivalrous treatment in the processing of adult offenders may not be the direct result of sexist behavior on the decision makers' parts alone but could also be the indirect effects of sexism and the very real gender differences in the responsibilities of women's and men's lives. That is, the specified gender roles in society likely influence differences in the processing of female and male defendants. Moreover, "women are more likely than men to be processed according to an assessment of their personal circumstances, rather than their offense" (Worrall, 1981, 90).

For example, rightly or wrongly, persons in charge of dependent children and with little access to legitimate means may be given special consideration by crime-processing decision makers. In most cultures, such persons are usually women. Thus, evidence of chivalrous treatment in crime processing might in fact be a manifestation of institutionalized gender roles in society at large. If women are fulfilling their "natural" roles as mothers and, to some extent, wives, they may be given more lenient sanctions. Thus, some of the "chivalry" directed at women may not be chivalry directly but rather making sentences at least partially in the best interests of defendants' children, and since women are more likely to be taking care of children, particularly as single parents, then women receive more lenient sentences.

A study of the Urban Reform Era (1871 to 1920) in Ontario, Canada, concluded that "judges appeared to view women's criminality as prima facie evidence of their inadequacy as mothers and showed little hesitancy in removing them from their child-care roles" (Boritch, 1992, 319). With one exception, the more recent research on dependent children suggests that chivalrous sanctioning may be a result of women's increased likelihood (over men) to have dependent children (see Daly, 1989a, 1989b; Eaton, 1986; Steffensmeier, Kramer, and Streifel, 1993; Worrall, 1990). A study of female defendants in New York City found that women who reported living with dependent children were less likely than women not living with their children to be sentenced to incarceration (Brennan, 2002). Another study found that pregnant women, as well as women with children, received more lenient sentencing from judges, but this was partly due to some judges' belief that the bad conditions in women's prisons resulted in extra-harsh punishment for women (Steffensmeier, Kramer, and Streifel, 1993). One study, however, found that among women incarcerated for drug offenses, those with dependent children in the home were more likely to have longer sentences than those without dependent children (prior to incarceration) (Sharp and Marcus-Mendoza, 2001).

Eaton's (1986) analysis of court cases in a London suburb found that while men and women were treated similarly when they were in similar circumstances, women and men were rarely *in* similar circumstances. It was difficult to tell from the design of this study whether the more lenient sentences for women were due to chivalry or to women's generally less extensive offending: The court did not overtly discriminate based on sex; it endorsed separate and unequal roles for men and women, particularly with respect to traditional families. Men were expected to provide financially for families, while women's roles included emotional support and child care. Thus, when a probation officer conducted a home visit, a description of the home was more common with a female defendant than with a male defendant (ibid., 67). Thus, chivalrous processing may be due more to an inherently unequal society than to an inherently biased crime-processing system.

Therefore, women's chivalrous treatment may in fact be a result of a response to their increased likelihood to be "familied." A study of British magistrates (judges) found that they favored giving women probation because it least disrupted their domestic duties (Worrall, 1990). Conversely, another study found that men, but not women, who provided significant emotional support for dependents were less likely to receive prison sentences, and men who provided significant economic support for their children were not granted a break in sentencing (Bickle and Peterson, 1991). This led the authors to conclude that taking care of familial dependents is rewarded "only when it is not a part of traditional gender-based role expectations" (ibid., 385). A more recent study found charged women with dependent children more likely than those without to get community alternative placements, while women without dependent children were more likely to get prison sentences (Koons-Witt, 2002).

The most recent study is also the most comprehensive, able to tease out some of the questions left by previous studies. Flavin (2001) examined how African American drug defendants' ties to their children and other family members affected their likelihood of being sentenced to incarceration. Although prior convictions and drug use were predictive of the sentence, so was whether the offender lived with a child or family member and, when it was a mother, whether someone was able to step in and take over the parenting duties. Notably, legal characteristics, such as the seriousness of the offense, had more impact for male than female defendants. This study found: (1) women were two-and-a-half times as likely as men to live with a child and eight times more likely to be a child's only care provider; (2) women had less extensive prior records; (3) women were more likely to be unemployed; (4) overall, both men and women who lived with a child were less likely to be incarcerated, and this relationship was especially strong for women; (5) family status variables did not impact men's sentencing, but women who were sole providers for their children were less likely to be incarcerated if they had no other person to take over child care, while women who were child–care providers but lived with another family member able to take over child care were *more* likely to be incarcerated; and (6) legal characteristics of the case had a bigger impact on men's than women's sentencing (ibid.). These findings suggest that African American women defendants with child-care responsibilities benefit from having these duties taken into account in ways that African American men defendants do not. Flavin (2001, 630) concluded from this study that the criminal legal decision making in these cases helped reproduce patriarchy, and compared the high incarceration rate of African Americans to slavery, consistent with Mullings (1997). The findings reinforce patriarchy with the suggestion that "women's place—but not men's—is in the home. Among women, the likelihood of incarceration is greatest for those women whose lack of ties to children and/or family most threaten conventional gender role expectations because they fail to care for dependents or to be dependent on someone else" while men's sentences do not take their child-care responsibilities into account (ibid.).

The marital status of a defendant appears in crime processing, similar to society at large, to be a more relevant factor for women than for men. Some studies found that being married helped women but not men in crime-processing outcomes (Erez, 1992; Nagel, Cardascia, and Ross, 1982). (Stated alternatively, being unmarried hurt women but not men in crime-processing outcomes.) Similarly, being divorced or separated hurt women more than men in sentencing (Dodge, 2002; Farrington and Morris, 1983). Although another study found that being married decreased the chances of both sexes being held in detention, this was afforded to men only when they had dependents as well as being married (Daly, 1989b). Unexpectedly, another study found that marital status was unrelated to the sentencing of women, whereas men were treated more harshly if they were married than if they were not (Bickle and Peterson, 1991). A study in New York City found that, overall, married women were less likely than unmarried women to be sentenced to incarceration, but when the analysis included only the African American women, married women were *more* likely than unmarried women to be incarcerated (Brennan, 2002). The overall findings on the gendered nature of the effect of marital status on crime processing are particularly interesting given recent research on felons reporting that being married or attached to a female partner had no impact on males' offending; however, with the exception of violent crimes, being married or attached to a male partner increased the likelihood of women's offending (Alarid, Burton, and Cullen, 2000). Stated alternatively, becoming intimately involved with men is a risk factor for women's offending. Taken a step further, if marital status is defined as a legal (instead of an extralegal variable), it "should" operate to reward unmarried women.

Some research has focused on the influence of employment status and economic dependence on the crime processing of women (and men). Generally, women have been sanctioned more harshly for working outside of the home than for being homemakers (Boritch, 1992; Kruttschnitt, 1981, 1982). One study found that being employed decreased men's sentences, while being unemployed decreased women's sentences (Crew, 1991). Another study found that unemployed women generally received harsher sentences than employed women, but unemployed students and full-time homemakers received more lenient sentences than women employed outside of the home (Kruttschnitt, 1981). One study, however, found employment status related equally to women's and men's sentencing (Kruttschnitt, 1984), and another found that among women defendants, their employment status had no impact on their likelihood of being sentenced to jail (Brennan, 2002). Probation and parole officers in other studies were more concerned with men's than women's employment problems, although women reported equal or more severe employment problems (Erez, 1989, 1992). Similarly, employment status affected men's more than women's pretrial release likelihood (Kruttschnitt and McCarthy, 1985).

In addition to the variables typically associated with gender differences (such as marital and employment status, child dependents, and demeanor), studies have found other variables that differently affect male and female sanctioning. Some studies found that legal variables (for example, prior record and offense seriousness) tend to influence men's sanctions more than women's (Boritch, 1992; Kruttschnitt and McCarthy, 1985; Nagel, Cardascia, and Ross, 1982; Steffensmeier, Kramer, and Streifel, 1993). One of these studies of court outcomes in Ontario, Canada, from 1871 to 1920 concluded that "judges appeared to adopt the attitude that the form a woman's criminality took was secondary to the fact a woman appeared before the court on any charge" (Boritch, 1992, 317). On the other hand, another study found that both being from a "broken home" and acting with another offender influenced women's sanctioning more than men's (Farrington and Morris, 1983). There is some evidence, although this needs to be further explored, that characteristics about the victim may influence females' and males' sanctions differently (See Jamieson and Blowers, 1993; Kruttschnitt, 1992; Visher, 1983). For example, in one study, the victim–offender relationship did not influence police decisions to arrest female suspects, but police were less likely to arrest male subjects who knew their victims (as friends or relatives) than those males who were unacquainted with their victims (Visher, 1983). A more recent study found acute gender bias in the processing of product liability cases during discovery and trial: Women, but not men, who sue corporations for physical, emotional, and/or financial injuries in product liability cases have their histories "paraded" in legal settings in ways that portray them as immoral and thus undeserving of redress in civil courts (Szockyj, 1999).

In conclusion, despite which of the three sanctioning hypotheses is supported (equal treatment, chivalry, or evil woman), studies that have provided in-depth analysis find other variables often interact with gender in a manner that provides a different pattern for crime processing of male and female offenders. Most studies confirm that being married, caring for dependent children, and being a homemaker increase a woman's chance of chivalrous sanctioning. For men, having stable employment and providing for families appear to effect leniency in their sanctioning. Overall, because women are more likely than men to be "familied" and because "familied" women generally fare better than "familied" men, much of the chivalry in crime processing, at least at the sentencing stage, may be explained by these gender differences in responsibilities. Consistent with gender stereotypes, such factors as employment and legal variables appear to influence men's sentences more than women's. It should be noted that, with regard to the preceding factors, there is a built-in discrimination against lesbians and gays, people who are not married, and people who are childless.

SUMMARY

This chapter covered the numerous factors likely to affect the crime processing of male and female offenders. Criminal laws and sentencing laws have historically included legal codes that specified different treatment of the sexes. Even when these laws are gender neutral, however, this does not guarantee that male and female defendants will be treated equally. To determine support for the three sanctioning hypotheses on gender differences (equal treatment, chivalry, and evil woman), it is first necessary to acknowledge that the treatment of females may vary based on such characteristics as their race, class, and age and that the treatment of female offenders may vary based on the types of offenses they commit. Moreover, the stage in the crime-processing system appears to influence gender patterns in crime processing: The evil woman hypothesis is supported most at the beginning stages, equal treatment at the middle stages, and chivalry during the latter stages. Finally, this chapter discussed the extraordinarily harsh treatment of female status offenders as well as the impact of gender stereotyping in crime processing concerning the marital, dependent-child, and employment status of women.

REFERENCES

Agozino, Biko. 1997. *Black Women and the Criminal Justice System*. Aldershot, England: Ashgate Publishing Company.

Alarid, Leanne Fiftal, Velmer Burton, and Francis Cullen. 2000. Gender and Crime among Felony Offenders. *Journal of Research in Crime and Delinquency* 37:171–199.

Albonetti, Celesta A. 1997. Sentencing under the Federal Sentencing Guidelines: Effects of Defendant Characteristics, Guilty Please, and Departures on Sentence Outcomes for Drug Offenses, 1991–1991. *Law and Society Review* 31:789–822.

Alder, Christine M. 1998. 'Passionate and Willful' Girls: Confronting Practices. *Women & Criminal Justice* 9(4):81–101.

Belknap, Joanne, and Kristi Holsinger. 2006. The Gendered Nature of Risk Factors for Delinquency. *Feminist Criminology*.1:48–71.

Bernat, Frances P. 1984. Gender Disparity in the Setting of Bail: Prostitution Offenses in Buffalo, NY, 1977–1979. Pp. 21–48 in *Gender Issues, Sex Offenses, and Criminal Justice: Current Trends*, edited by S. Chaneles. New York: Haworth Press.

———. 1985. New York State's Prostitution Statute: Case Study of the Discriminatory Application of a Gender Neutral Law. Pp. 103–120 in *Criminal Justice Politics and Women*, edited by C. Schweber and C. Feinman. New York: Haworth Press.

Bickle, Gayle S., and Ruth D. Peterson. 1991. The Impact of Gender-Based Family Roles in Criminal Sentencing. *Social Problems* 38:372–394.

Boritch, Helen. 1992. Gender and Criminal Court Outcomes: A Historical Analysis. *Criminology* 30:293–326.

Bortner, M., and W. Reed. 1985. Race and the Impact of Juvenile Deinstutionalization. *Crime & Delinquency* 31:35–46.

Brennan, Pauline K. 2002. *Women Sentenced to Jail in New York City*. New York: LFB Scholarly Publishing.

Butler, Anne M. 1997. *Gendered Justice in the American West*. Urbana: University of Illinois Press.

Cain, Maureen (Ed.). 1989. *Growing Up Good: Policing the Behavior of Girls in Europe*. London: Sage.

Chesney-Lind, Meda. 1973. Judicial Enforcement of the Female Sex Role. *Issues in Criminology* 8:51–70.

————. 1974. Juvenile Delinquency: The Sexualization of Female Crime. *Psychology Today* (July):43–46.

————. 1981. Judicial Paternalism and the Female Status Offender: Training Women to Know Their Place. Pp. 354–366 in *Women and Crime in America*, edited by L. H. Bowker. New York: Macmillan.

————. 1982. Guilty by Reason of Sex: Young Women and the Juvenile Justice System. Pp. 77–104 in *The Criminal Justice System and Women*, edited by B. R. Price and N. J. Sokoloff. New York: Clark Boardman.

————. 1986. Women and Crime: The Female Offender. *Signs* 12:78–96.

————. 1987. Female Offenders: Paternalism Reexamined. Pp. 114–140 in *Women, the Courts, and Equality*, edited by L. L. Crites and W. L. Hepperle. Newbury Park, CA: Sage.

————. 1988. Girls and Status Offenses: Is Juvenile Justice Still Sexist? *Criminal Justice Abstracts* 20:145–165.

Chesney-Lind, Meda, and Randall G. Shelden. 1992. *Girls, Delinquency, and Juvenile Justice*. Pacific Grove, CA: Brooks/Cole.

Chigwada-Bailey, Ruth, 1997. *Black Women's Experiences of Criminal Justice*. Winchester, England: Waterside Press.

Colomy, Paul, and Martin Kretzmann. 1997. The Gendering of Social Control: Sex Delinquency and Progressive Juvenile Justice in Denver, 1901–1927. Pp. 48–81 in *Governing Childhood*, edited by Anne McGillivray. Aldershot, England: Dartmouth Publishing.

Conway, Allan, and Carol Bogdan. 1977. Sexual Delinquency: The Persistence of a Double Standard. *Crime and Delinquency* 23:131–135.

Crew, Keith B. 1991. Sex Differences in Criminal Sentencing: Chivalry or Patriarchy? *Justice Quarterly* 8:59–84.

Curran, Deborah. 1983. Judicial Discretion and Defendant's Sex. *Criminology* 21:41–58.

Daly, Kathleen. 1987. Structure and Practice of Familial-Based Justice in a Criminal Court. *Law and Society Review* 21:267–290.

————. 1989a. Rethinking Judicial Paternalism: Gender, Work-Family Relations, and Sentencing. *Gender & Society* 3:9–36.

————. 1989b. Neither Conflict Nor Labeling Nor Paternalism Will Suffice: Intersections of Race, Ethnicity, Gender, and Family in Criminal Court Decisions. *Crime and Delinquency* 35:136–168.

Daly, Kathleen, and Rebecca L. Bordt. 1995. Sex Effects and Sentencing: An Analysis of the Statistical Literature. *Justice Quarterly* 12:141–176.

Danner, Mona J. E. 1998. Three Strikes and It's Women Who Are Out. Pp. 1–11 in *Crime Control and Women*, edited by Susan Miller. Thousand Oaks, CA: Sage.

Datesman, Susan K., and Mikel Aickin. 1984. Offense Specialization and Escalation among Status Offenders. *Journal of Criminal Law and Criminology* 75:1246–1275.

Datesman, Susan K., and Frank R. Scarpitti. 1977. Unequal Protection for Males and Females in the Juvenile Court. In *Juvenile Delinquency*, edited by T. N. Ferdinand. Newbury Park, CA: Sage.

DeFleur, Lois B. 1975. Biasing Influences on Drug Arrest Records: Implications for Deviance Research. *American Sociological Review* 40:88–103.

Dodge, L. Mara. 2002. *Whores and Thieves of the Worst Kind: A Study of Women, Crime, and Prisons, 1835–2000*. DeKalb: Northern Illinois University Press.

Eaton, Mary. 1986. *Justice for Women? Family, Court and Social Control*. Philadelphia: Open University Press.

Edwards, Susan. 1984. *Women on Trial: A Study of the Female Suspect, Defendant and Offender in the Criminal Law and Criminal Justice System.* Manchester, England: Manchester University Press.

Erez, Edna. 1989. Gender, Rehabilitation, and Probation Decisions. *Criminology* 27:307–327.

———. 1992. Dangerous Men, Evil Women: Gender and Parole Decision-Making. *Justice Quarterly* 9:105–126.

Farley, Melissa, and Vanessa Kelly. 2000. Prostitution: A Critical Review of the Medical and Social Sciences Literature. *Women & Criminal Justice* 11:29–64.

Farnworth, Margaret, and Raymond H. C. Teske. 1995. Gender Differences in Felony Court Processing. *Women & Criminal Justice* 6:23–44.

Farr, Kathryn Ann. 2004. Defeminizing and Dehumanizing Female Murderers: Depictions of Lesbians on Death Row. Pp. 249–260 in *The Criminal Justice System and Women*, 3rd edition, edited by Barbara Raffel Price and Natalie J. Sokoloff. Boston: McGraw Hill.

Farrington, David P., and Allison M. Morris. 1983. Sex, Sentencing and Reconviction. *British Journal of Criminology* 23:229–248.

Federle, K. H., and Meda Chesney-Lind. 1992. Special Issues in Juvenile Justice: Gender, Race, and Ethnicity. Pp. 165–195 in *Juvenile Justice and Public Policy: Toward a National Agenda*, edited by I. M. Schwartz. New York: Macmillan.

Feinman, Clarice. 1992. Criminal Codes, Criminal Justice and Female Offenders: New Jersey as a Case Study. Pp. 57–68 in *The Changing Roles of Women in the Criminal Justice System*, 2nd edition, edited by I. L. Moyer. Prospect Heights, IL: Waveland Press.

Figueira-McDonough, Josefina. 1985. Gender Differences in Informal Processing: A Look at Charge Bargaining and Sentence Reduction in Washington, D.C. *Journal of Research in Crime and Delinquency* 22:101–133.

Figueira-McDonough, Josefina, and Rosemary C. Sarri. 1987. Catch-22 Strategies of Control and the Deprivation of Women's Rights. Pp. 11–33 in *The Trapped Woman: Catch-22 in Deviance and Control*, edited by J. Figueira-McDonough and R. Sarri. Newbury Park, CA: Sage.

Fisher, C. J., and R. I. Mawby. 1982. Juvenile Delinquency and Police Discretion in an Inner City Area. *British Journal of Criminology* 22:63–75.

Flavin, Jeanne. 2001. Of Punishment and Parenthood. *Gender & Society* 15:611–633.

Frazier, Charles E., and John C. Cochran. 1986. Detention of Juveniles: Its Effects on Subsequent Juvenile Court Processing Decisions. *Youth and Society* 17:286–305.

Frohmann, Lisa. 1991. Discrediting Victims' Allegations of Sexual Assault: Prosecutorial Accounts of Case Rejection. *Social Problems* 38:213–226.

Gelsthorpe, Loraine. 1989. *Sexism and the Female Offender.* Aldershot, England: Gower.

Ghali, Moheb, and Meda Chesney-Lind. 1986. Gender Bias and the Criminal Justice System: An Empirical Investigation. *Sociology and Social Research* 70:164–171.

Gruhl, John, Susan Welch, and Cassia Spohn. 1984. Women as Criminal Defendants: A Test for Paternalism. *Western Political Quarterly* 37:456–467.

Hepburn, John R. 1978. Race and the Decision to Arrest: An Analysis of Warrants Issued. *Journal of Research in Crime and Delinquency* 15:54–73.

Hiller, Anne Edwards, and Linda Hancock. 1981. The Processing of

Juveniles in Victoria. Pp. 92–126 in *Women and Crime*, edited by S. K. Mukherjee and J. A. Scutt. North Sydney, Australia: Allen and Unwin.

Holcomb, J. E., M. R. Williams, and S. Demuth. 2004. White Female Victims and Death Penalty Disparity Research. *Justice Quarterly* 21: 877–902.

Hudson, Barbara. 1989. Justice or Welfare? A Comparison of Recent Developments in the English and French Juvenile Justice System. Pp. 96–113 in *Growing Up Good: Policing the Behavior of Girls in Europe*, edited by M. Cain. London: Sage.

Jamieson, Katherine M., and Anita Blowers. 1993. A Structural Examination of Court Disposition Patterns. *Criminology* 31:243–262.

Koons-Witt, Barbara. 2002. Gender and Justice: The Effect of Gender and Gender-Related Factors on the Decision to Incarcerate before and after Sentencing Guidelines. *Criminology* 40:297–328.

Kraska, Peter B., and Victor E. Kappeler. 1995. To Serve and Pursue: Exploring Police Sexual Violence against Women. *Justice Quarterly* 12:85–112.

Krisberg, Barry, and Ira Schwartz. 1983. Rethinking Juvenile Justice. *Crime and Delinquency* 29:333–365.

Krohn, Marvin, James P. Curry, and Shirley Nelson-Kilger. 1983. Is Chivalry Dead? An Analysis of Changes in Police Dispositions of Males and Females. *Criminology* 21:417–437.

Kruttschnitt, Candace. 1981. Social Status and Sentences of Female Offenders. *Law and Society Review* 15:247–265.

———. 1982. Women, Crime, and Dependency. *Criminology* 19:495–513.

———. 1984. Sex and Criminal Court Dispositions: The Unresolved Controversy. *Journal of Research in Crime & Delinquency* 21:213–232.

———. 1992. 'Female Crimes' or Legal Labels? Are Statistics about Women Offenders Representative of Their Crimes? Pp. 81–98 in *The Changing Roles of Women in the Criminal Justice System*, edited by I. L. Moyer. Prospect Heights, IL: Waveland Press.

Kruttschnitt, Candace, and Donald E. Green. 1984. The Sex-Sanctioning Issue: Is It History? *American Sociological Review* 49:541–551.

Kruttschnitt, Candace, and Daniel McCarthy. 1985. Familial Social Control and Pretrial Sanctions: Does Sex Really Matter? *Journal of Criminal Law and Criminology* 76:151–175.

Landau, Simha. 1981. Juveniles and the Police. *British Journal of Criminology* 21:27–46.

Landau, Simha, and Gad Nathan. 1983. Selecting Delinquents for Cautioning in the London Metropolitan Area. *British Journal of Criminology* 23:128–149.

LaPrairie, Carol P. 1989. Some Issues in Aboriginal Justice Research: The Case of Aboriginal Women in Canada. *Women & Criminal Justice* 1:81–92.

Leiber, Michael J. 1994. A Comparison of Juvenile Court Outcomes for Native Americans, African Americans, and Whites. *Justice Quarterly* 11:257–279.

Leiber, Michael J., and Kristin Y. Mack. 2003. The Individual and Joint Effects of Race, Gender, and Family Status on Juvenile Justice Decision-Making. *Journal of Research in Crime & Delinquency* 40:34–70.

Leonard, Eileen B. 1982. *Women, Crime and Society*. New York: Longman.

Mann, Coramae R. 1990. Female Homicide and Substance Use: Is There a Connection? *Women & Criminal Justice* 1:87–110.

Mastrofski, Stephen D., Robert E. Worden, and Jeffrey B. Snipes. 1995. Law Enforcement in a Time of

Community Policing. *Criminology* 33(4):539–563.

Morris, Allison. 1987. *Women, Crime and Criminal Justice.* Oxford: Basil Blackwell.

Moulds, Elizabeth F. 1980. Chivalry and Paternalism: Disparities of Treatment in the Criminal Justice System. Pp. 277–299 in *Women, Crime, and Justice,* edited by S. K. Datesman and F. R. Scarpitti. New York: Oxford University Press.

Myers, Martha A., and John Hagan. 1979. Private and Public Trouble: Prosecutors and the Allocation of Court Resources. *Social Problems* 26:439–451.

Naffine, Ngaire. 1987. *Female Crime.* Sydney, Australia: Allen and Unwin.

———. 1989. Towards Justice for Girls: Rhetoric and Practice in the Treatment of Status Offenders. *Women & Criminal Justice* 1:3–20.

Nagel, Ilene H., John Cardascia, and Catherine E. Ross. 1982. Sex Differences in the Processing of Criminal Defendants. Pp. 259–282 in *Women and the Law,* Vol. I, edited by D. K. Weisberg. Cambridge, MA: Schenkman.

Nagel, Ilene H., and John Hagan. 1983. Gender and Crime: Offense Patterns and Criminal Court Sanctions. Pp.91–144 in *Crime and Justice,* Vol. 4, edited by M. Tonry and N. Morris. Chicago: University of Chicago Press.

Nobiling, Tracy, Cassia Spohn, and Miriam DeLone. 1998. A Tale of Two Counties: Unemployment and Sentencing Severity. *Justice Quarterly* 15:459–486.

Odem, Mary E. 1995. *Delinquent Daughters: Protecting and Policing Adolescent Female Sexuality in the United States, 1885–1920.* Chapel Hill: The University of North Carolina Press.

Olson, Davd E., Arthur J. Lurigio, and Magnus Seng. 2000. A Comparison of Female and Male Probationers. *Women & Criminal Justice* 11:65–80.

Pollak, Otto. 1950. *The Criminality of Women.* Westport, CT: Greenwood Press.

Rapaport, Elizabeth. 1991. The Death Penalty and Gender Discrimination. *Law and Society Review* 25:368–383.

Sarri, Rosemary C. 1983. Gender Issues in Juvenile Justice. *Crime and Delinquency* 29:381–398.

———. 1987. Unequal Protection under the Law: Women and the Criminal Justice System. Pp. 394–427 in *The Trapped Woman: Catch-22 in Deviance and Control,* edited by J. Figueira-McDonough and R. Sarri. Newbury Park, CA: Sage.

Schaffner, Laurie. 2004. Capturing Girls' Experiences of Community Violence in the United States. Pp. 105–130 in *Girls' Violence: Myths and Realities,* edited by Christine Alder and Anne Worrall. Albany: State University of New York Press.

Schlossman, Steven, and Stephanie Wallach. 1982. The Crime of Precocious Sexuality: Female Juvenile Delinquency in the Progressive Era. Pp. 45–84 in *Women and the Law,* Vol. I, edited by D. K. Weisberg. Cambridge, MA: Schenkman.

Schur, Edwin M. 1984. *Labeling Women Deviant.* New York: McGraw Hill.

Schwartz, Ira, Marilyn Jackson-Beeck, and Roger Anderson. 1984. The Hidden System of Juvenile Control. *Crime and Delinquency* 30:371–385.

Scutt, Jocelynne A. 1981. Sexism in Criminal Law. Pp. 1–21 in *Women and Crime,* S. K. Mukherjee and J. A. Scutt. Sydney, Australia: Allen and Unwin.

Seitz, Trina N. 2005. The Wounds of Savagery: Negro Primitivism, Gender Parity, and the Execution of Rosanna Lightner Phillips. *Women & Criminal Justice* 16:29–64.

Sharp, Susan F., and Susan T. Marcus-Mendoza. 2001. It's a Family Affair: Incarcerated Women and Their

Families. *Women & Criminal Justice* 12:21–49.

Shaver, Frances M. 1993. Prostitution: A Female Crime?. Pp. 153–173 in *In Conflict with the Law: Women and the Canadian Justice System*, edited by E. Adelberg and C. Currie. Vancouver: Press Gang Publishers.

Shelden, Randall G. 1981. Sex Discrimination in the Juvenile Justice System: Memphis, Tennessee, 1900–1917. Pp. 55–72 in *Comparing Female and Male Offenders*, M. Q. Warren. Beverly Hills, CA: Sage.

Smart, Carol. 1976. Women, Crime and Criminology. London: Routledge and Kegan Paul.

Sokoloff, Natalie J. 2005. Women Prisoners at the Dawn of the 21st Century. *Women & Criminal Justice* 16:127–137.

Spohn, Cassia. 1990. The Sentencing Decisions of Black and White Judges. *Law & Society Review* 24:1197–1215.

Spohn, Cassia, John Gruhl, and Susan Welch. 1987. The Impact of the Ethnicity and Gender of Defendants on the Decision to Reject or Dismiss Felony Charges. *Criminology* 25:175–191.

Spohn, Cassia, Susan Welch, and John Gruhl. 1985. Women Defendants in Court: The Interaction between Sex and Race in Convicting and Sentencing. *Social Science Quarterly* 66:178–185.

Steffensmeier, Darrell, John Kramer, and Cathy Streifel. 1993. Gender and Imprisonment Decisions. *Criminology* 31:411–446.

Steffensmeier, Darrell, Jeffery Ulmer, and John Kramer. 1998. The Interaction of Race, Gender, and Age in Criminal Sentencing. *Criminology* 36:763–797.

Steury, Ellen Hochstedler, and Nancy Frank. 1990. Gender Bias and Pretrial Release. *Journal of Criminal Justice* 18:417–432.

Szockyj, Elizabeth. 1999. Playing the Sex Card in Female Product Liability Litigation. *Women & Criminal Justice* 10:91–111.

Teilmann, Katherine S., and Pierre H. Landry. 1981. Gender Bias in Juvenile Justice. *Journal of Research in Crime and Delinquency* 18:47–80.

Temin, Carolyn E. 1980. Discriminatory Sentencing of Women Offenders: The Argument for ERA in a Nutshell. Pp. 255–276 in *Women, Crime, and Justice*, edited by S. K. Datesman and F. R. Scarpitti. New York: Oxford University Press.

Terry, Robert M. 1967. Discrimination in the Handling of Juvenile Offenders by Social Control Agencies. *Journal of Research in Crime and Delinquency* 4:218–230.

Thomas, W. I. 1907. *Sex and Society*. Boston: Little, Brown.

Visher, Christy A. 1983. Gender, Police Arrest Decisions, and Notions of Chivalry. *Criminology* 21:5–28.

Webb, David. 1984. More on Gender and Justice: Girl Offenders on Supervision. *Sociology* 18:367–381.

Wilbanks, William. 1986. Are Females Treated More Leniently by the Criminal Justice System? *Justice Quarterly* 3:517–529.

Windschuttle, Elizabeth. 1981. Women, Crime, and Punishment. Pp. 31–50 in *Women and Crime*, edited by S. K. Mukherjee and J. A. Scutt. North Sydney: Allen and Unwin.

Worrall, Anne. 1981. Out of Place: Female Offenders in Court. *Probation Journal* 28:90–93.

———. 1990. *Offending Women: Female Lawbreakers and the Criminal Justice System*. London: Routledge and Kegan Paul.

Young, Vernetta D. 1986. Gender Expectations and Their Impact on

Black Female Offenders and Victims. *Justice Quarterly* 3:305–328.

Zatz, Marjorie. 1984. Race, Ethnicity, and Determinate Sentencing. *Criminology* 22:147–171.

Zingraff, Matthew, and Randall Thomson. 1984. Differential Sentencing of Women and Men in the U.S.A. *International Journal of Sociology and the Law* 12:401–410.

5

❖

Incarcerating, Punishing, and "Treating" Offending Women and Girls

What I had *not* anticipated when I began going to Rikers Island [Correctional Facility] was the extent to which physical assaults, emotional degradation, marginalized/tenuous status and overt racism formed a seemingly impermeable web of despair around the African American battered women in the jail. Nor did I expect to find such stories of resistance, resolve and respectability. For despite the seemingly overwhelming circumstances, the lives of the African American battered women I met at Rikers Island Correctional Facility reflected a complex dualism; they are at once victims and survivors, inspiring and over-whelmed, courageous and terrified, sometimes engaged social actors and other times passive witnesses to the oppressive chaos around them.

RICHIE, 1996, 3–4

Our nation's response to the crises in drugs, unemployment, undereducation, mental illness, and the like is not to deal with those social ills but to find a way to control and capture those female prisoners who have no voice in where they live, sleep, or eat.

COLLINS, 1997, 12

This chapter presents the many issues surrounding incarcerated females. Like males, females are incarcerated in juvenile institutions, such as "training" schools; in the short-term facilities known as jails; or in prisons, which are usually reserved for adults with sentences of a year or more. Cooper's (1993) treatise on the history of Canadian women prisoners identifies response themes of *neglect* and *paternalism*. These themes are certainly prevalent in

177

Comparative Perspectives: Sudbury's (2005) *Celling Black Bodies: Black Women in the Global Prison Industrial Complex*

- The *prison industrial complex* is a result of "an intricate web of relations between state penal institutions, politicians and profit-driven prison corporations."
- The *war on drugs* "is symbiotically related and mutually constituted by the transnational trade in criminalized drugs."
- In the past two decades, women's incarceration has exploded in Europe, North America, and Australia.
- This explosion in women's incarceration has co-occurred with a boom in prison construction.
- Three new regimes "of accumulation and discipline...build on older systems of racist and patriarchal exploitation to ensure the super-exploitation of black women within the global prison industrial complex":
    - The fundamental shift in the role of the state due to neoliberal globalization
    - The emergence and global expansion of the "prison industrial complex"
    - The emergence of the U.S.-led global war on drugs

Conclusion: "[T]he profitable synergies between drug enforcement, the prison industry, international financial institutions, media and politicians...are sending women to prison in ever increasing numbers."

SOURCE: Julia Sudbury. 2005. Celling Black Bodies: Black Women in the Global Prison Industrial Complex. *Feminist Review* 80:162–179.

U.S. and United Kingdom treatises, too: Women and girl offenders are typically invisible (neglected) or, when responded to specifically as females, are treated in a paternalistic manner.

The first major studies on women prisoners were not conducted until the 1960s (Heidensohn, 1985), and female offenders were not even mentioned in the huge 1967 report, a national study of crime by the President's Commission on Law Enforcement and the Administration of Justice. In contrast to the vast and extensive research on men's prisons since the 1940s, little was known about the isolated and inaccessible women's prisons until the 1970s (Pollock 2002b; Sarri, 1987). Furthermore, the earliest books on women's prisons have been noted more for their focus on the female prison subculture, especially homosexuality, than for their examination of the deplorable conditions of women's incarceration (see Giallombardo, 1966; Ward and Kassebaum 1965). Like homeless and mentally ill women, women prisoners are among the most neglected, oppressed, and misrepresented groups in society. A study on the media (particularly film and television) portrayals of incarcerated women reports how they exploit these women based on their gender, race/ethnicity, class, and sexuality (specifically, lesbianism), fostering false and damning representations of them similar to Lombroso's portrayal of criminal women as monsters (Faith, 1993a).

Three reasons have been offered for the invisibility of incarcerated women (relative to incarcerated men): (1) Women have constituted a small proportion (typically 5 to 7 percent) of the total prison and jail population, (2) generally women are incarcerated for less dangerous and serious crimes than men, and (3) incarcerated women are less likely than incarcerated men to "riot, destroy property and make reform demands" (Mann, 1984, 190). Historically, women prisoners, who have suffered the dual stigmas of "woman" and "prisoner," have been neglected even within the women's rights and prisoners' rights movements (Haft, 1980). In fact, the first decade of U.S. federal court prisoners' rights cases, the 1960s, failed to benefit women prisoners (Leonard, 1983). Moreover, in the 1970s, when male prisoners in North America were filing case after case to address inhumane institutional conditions, the few cases women prisoners brought were to obtain parity with the inhumane and unfair conditions and opportunities in men's prisons (Faith, 1993b). Even today, despite significantly worse prison conditions and opportunities, females are far less apt than males to file lawsuits against prisons and jails (Aylward and Thomas, 1984; Barry, 1991; Rafter, 1989; Pollock, 2002b; Schupak, 1986; Van Ochten, 1993; Wheeler et al., 1989).

Significantly, since the 1980s and the fanfare of the women's "liberation" hypothesis, women's incarceration has grown at an astounding rate, with particular discrimination and increase focused on women of color (for an excellent review, see Sokoloff, 2005). Sokoloff (2005) notes that there were 5,600 women in U.S. prisons in 1970, about 12,500 in 1980, and 94,336 in 2001 (ibid.), and in 2004, the number rose to 97,491 (Harrison and Beck, 2005). During the 1980s, the number of women in U.S. prisons tripled (Church, 1990; Fletcher and Moon, 1993a; Immarigeon and Chesney-Lind, 1992; Kline, 1993) while the corresponding increase in males' incarceration rates "only" doubled (Kline, 1993). Then, between 1980 and 1994, U.S. women's incarceration rates almost quadrupled (increased 386 percent) while men's rates "only" doubled (increased 214 percent) (Acoca and Austin, 1996). Moreover, in 1996 alone, there was a 9.1 percent increase in women's incarceration in the United States while the corresponding increase in men's imprisonment was 4.7 percent (Mumola and Beck, 1997, 5). Between 1995 and 2004, the average annual growth rate for incarcerated women was 5.0 percent while men's was 3.3 percent, and women increased from 6.1 percent of the prison population in the United States in 1995 to 6.9 percent in 2004 (Harrison and Beck, 2005). Notably, women typically constitute a higher percentage of jail detainees than prisoners; in 2004, 11.4 percent of jail detainees were female, and from 1995 to 2004, the women's jail incarceration grew 7.0 percent annually while the rate for men in jail was 4.2 percent annually (ibid.).

These massive increases in women's incarceration are despite falling rates for women's incarceration for violent offenses. Women were most likely incarcerated for nonviolent larceny-theft, forgery, fraud, and prostitution offenses, until the 1980s and the explosion in women's incarceration for drug sales and possession (Sokoloff, 2001). Some see this significant increase since the 1970s as the result of and the second wave of the women's movement with women's quest for equality; what Chesney-Lind has called "equality with a vengeance" (Chesney-Lind and Pollock-Byrne, 1995).

> Thus, despite the fact that prisons and punishments were designed for the violent male offender, women have gotten the same harsh sentences applied to them in a conservative punishment era that intensified under the burden of "mandatory minimum," "three-strikes" laws, and "truth-in-sentencing" laws. All such laws had the effect of incarcerating more people, for longer periods of time, with less options for diversion from prison or opportunities for parole or rehabilitation. (Sokoloff, 2005, 128)

In fact, women's rates of incarceration for drug offenses have grown (e.g., Chesney-Lind, 2003; Immarigeon and Chesney-Lind, 1992; Kelley, 2003; Moon, Thompson, and Bennett, 1993; Morris, 1987; Pollock, 1998; 2002b; Sokoloff, 2005). "Roughly twice as likely as men to be imprisoned for drug-related offenses, women inmates are more likely to have entrenched alcohol and other drug dependencies" (Acoca, 1998a, 51–52). Additionally, many women incarcerated for nondrug offenses report drug and alcohol addiction problems (Belknap, 2000; Chesney-Lind and Rodriguez, 1983). Notably, a governmental report states that for every measure of drug use in the month prior to incarceration and used during the commission of the offense that "landed" them in prison, women in state prisons reported higher usages than similarly situated men reported (Greenfeld and Snell, 1999).

THE HISTORY OF INSTITUTIONALIZING
FEMALE OFFENDERS

Punishment

Women and men were subject to the same penalties in preindustrial societies; most of the penalties were noncustodial and included burnings at the stake, whippings, hangings, and public ridicule (Cooper, 1993; Dobash, Dobash, and Gutteridge, 1986; Heidensohn, 1985; Morris, 1987). Although confinement in castles, monasteries, and nunneries existed during the Middle Ages, confining women and men for prolonged periods was unusual until the late sixteenth century and was not accepted as the most appropriate response to criminals and deviants until the nineteenth century (Dobash, Dobash, and Gutteridge, 1986).

Historians have noted that although the overall punishments of women and men were similar, the exceptions were largely to women's disadvantage and involved punishing them for crimes against their husbands, violating the standards for sexuality, or both. For example, during the Middle Ages, it was not uncommon for women to be burned to death for committing adultery or murdering a spouse, while male adulterers and wife killers were rarely considered offenders (ibid.). Similarly, during colonial times in the United States (1620 to the 1760s), women were punished far more harshly than men for adultery, and they could be punished by the church as well as the state (Feinman, 1983). Public humiliation was also more common in the punishing of women than men, such as forcing female convicts to give confessions before they were hanged (Cooper, 1993; Dobash, Dobash, and Gutteridge, 1986; Feinman, 1983). The strength of these antiwoman and antisex (for women) values carried over into the twentieth century. In 1923, half of the women in U.S. prisons were convicted of sex offenses (prostitution, fornication, and adultery) (Lekkerkerker, 1931), and until 1950, women in Massachusetts convicted of having sex outside of marriage were charged with fornication and sentenced to prison (Janusz, 1991).

In the early 1700s in England, a new alternative for a commuted death sentence was to transport convicts to the American colonies and Australia with various work sentences. One in eight of those sent to Australia were women. They were usually young (in their teens or twenties) and typically were transported for a first offense, such as a petty theft (Dobash, Dobash, and Gutteridge, 1986). The conditions for the transported women were far worse than those for the transported men, and the women's "sentences" usually included being forced into prostitution in Australia (ibid.).

With the exception of a few private and often religious experiments, men and women prisoners were housed in the same institutions until the 1850s in England, the 1870s in the United States (and 1915 in the Western United States), and 1913 in Canada. Usually these prisons provided separate rooms for women and men, but both sexes were under the supervision of exclusively male wardens and guards. A similar regime was used for both male and female prisoners because the system was designed to respond to the majority of prisoners—the male prisoners (Butler, 1997; Cooper, 1993; Dodge, 2002; Heidensohn, 1985; Morris, 1987). Although most historical accounts of imprisoning women and men together emphasize their similar treatment, the differences that existed were significant. First, women prisoners played gender-stereotyped roles in keeping the prison running; second, and more importantly, the women prisoners faced a high risk of rape. In Canada, women were first incarcerated in 1835 in the Kingston Penitentiary for Men. Given their small numbers, their incarceration experience was predicated on what best served the administration and the male prisoner population; thus, their primary task was making and mending the male prisoners' bedding and clothing (Cooper, 1993). Even so, these women were deemed "more difficult to manage than the men" by the first (male) wardens and thus were subjected to extreme corporal punishment (ibid., 37).

Moreover, incarcerated women were often blamed for the "sexual disturbances"—their rapes (Rafter, 1985, 12). There existed a policy of calculated neglect of women in the "men's" prisons, where the sexual abuse often resulted in pregnancy and the floggings sometimes caused death (Feinman, 1981, 1983). Similarly, Butler's (1997, 136) account of the Huntsville, Texas prison in 1874 describes the fourteen women convicts, twelve of whom were African American, roaming the prison yard carrying babies "conceived and born in the penitentiary." One older African American prisoner gave birth to a biracial baby whose conception was caused by the White prison doctor, who bragged about how he had coercive sex with the prisoner. The guards punished the *woman* by taking the baby, publicly shaving the prisoner's head, and putting her in the dungeon (Butler, 1997). In the Arizona Territorial Prison in 1890, a 21-year-old prisoner (who had an 8-year-old child) was moved by the male superintendent of the prison to an open shack in the prison yard, where guards and male prisoners had sexual access to her (ibid.). Butler's description of African American women prisoners serving as sexual rewards to male prisoners and guards is reminiscent of the Korean "comfort women" in Japan who were forced into prostitution for soldiers in World War II (see Yoshimi, 2000). Thus, prison-sanctioned rape was a common theme in these prisons designed for incarcerated men but holding convicted women. In addition to the women's high risk of rape, services for incarcerated women were substantially limited relative to those for incarcerated men, and the authorities were unwilling to hire female guards to supervise them because of their small numbers.

> These prisoners were thus often left entirely on their own, vulnerable to attacks by one another and male guards. Secluded from the main population, women had less access than men to the physician and chaplain. Unlike men, they were not marched to workshops, mess halls, or exercise yards. Food and needlework were brought to their quarters, where the women remained day in and day out, for the years of their sentences. (Rafter, 1985, xx)

Butler's (1997, 192) description of women in Western U.S. prisons from 1865 to 1915 is similar: "Women either stayed in their cells in forced inactivity, provided sexual diversion for male officials and inmates, cleaned and cooked for officers, plowed and planted, or worked merciless hours in the prison industry."

The first official inquiry to examine the treatment of women prisoners in Canada occurred in 1921 (by a male judge). Notably, the report was instructive and forceful regarding some of the coarse conditions the women faced both within the prison and upon their release, but it also defined the women prisoners as sexual deviants whose sexual desires were out of control and placed the *male staff* at risk (Cooper, 1993). Thus, while women and men imprisoned in the same institutions were treated similarly overall, the few differences were largely to the gross disadvantage of women.

Reform

The movement for reform in women's prisons has occurred in fits and starts, without consistent progress. The most active reform in the imprisonment of women began in the nineteenth century and was conducted by wealthy White women who often held conflicted views of women's roles in society. On the one hand, they recognized that women offenders were often not deviant per se but rather victims in male economic and criminal legal systems. On the other hand, these same women reformers generally strove to "purify" and control the "fallen women," whom they viewed as a threat to society (Feinman, 1983). In both the United States and England, the women's prison reformers were particularly concerned with the sexual abuse of incarcerated women by male officials in institutions housing both sexes.

The reformers' solution was to help these women rather than to punish them. The first penal reformer to focus exclusively on women was Elizabeth Fry, who established the Ladies Society for Promoting the Reformation of Female Prisoners in England. A Quaker, Fry developed reforms based on the Society of Friends when she began her work in 1816. Her approach was to convince the authorities that women and men had different needs, women's specific needs being "useful" labor, which included needlework and personal hygiene, and religious instruction, requiring the hiring of "decidedly religious" female guards (Dobash, Dobash, and Gutteridge, 1986, 52). Elizabeth Fry promoted the idea that female offenders were not dangerous criminals but rather "fallen women" who needed a helping hand. Fry and her committee of "ladies" experimented on the women at London's Newgate Gaol in 1818 with their program of resocializing the prisoners. The experiment was claimed a success by most (Windschuttle, 1981).

Despite Fry's experimental success, only three of her requests in 1818 were passed by Parliament. However, they were significant: (1) segregating prisons by sex, (2) hiring women to supervise women prisoners, and (3) decreasing the hard labor required of women prisoners (Morris, 1987). With the exception of the sex of the employees and the requirement for hard labor, however, men's and women's institutions were still similar in their harsh regimens. Some reformers continued to believe after Fry's death that there should be more differences between men's and women's prisons, given that men were usually incarcerated for serious crimes while women were typically imprisoned for drunkenness, prostitution, and petty thefts. Suffragists imprisoned between 1905 and 1914 in England provided the public with graphic descriptions of the deplorable conditions for these mostly petty offenses (ibid.).

The reform movement for incarcerated women in the United States began somewhat later than in England and was also led by middle- and upper-class White women. Similar to Fry's experiment, a group of these women established the Magdalen Home in 1830 to reform prostitutes through religious instruction and motivational instruction. The reform goal was to remold by encouraging "proper" gender roles rather than to punish women (Feinman, 1981; Rafter 1985). The deaths of hundreds of thousands of soldier "breadwinners" in the Civil War resulted in a new class of poor women who filled the jails as prostitutes, vagrants, and thieves during the 1860s (Freedman, 1974). After the Civil War, U.S. society was obsessed with controlling social disorder and credited restoring "women's inherent purity" as one means of doing so. Therefore, female offenders were considered deserving of harsher punishment than male criminals and thus experienced worse aspects of the prisons (ibid.).

In the 1860s, women activists in the United States heightened public awareness of the significant increase in the rate of women's imprisonment, the horrendous conditions for incarcerated women, and the sexual abuse of women prisoners by male guards. The reformers of this time started questioning the "fallen woman" label and pointed out that "fallen men" were aiding and abetting women and girls into prostitution. Moreover, once confined in prison, it was not unusual for incarcerated women to be lashed until they would have sex with male prison officials. This is similar to the situation of the female offenders transported from England to Australia, who were forced into prostitution as part of their sentence. As in England, the U.S. reform movement called for single-sex prisons where women prisoners would be administered by women (Freedman, 1982). "Freed" slaves, both men and women, after the Civil War encountered the prison system as a new means of enslavement: Laws were passed, and unethical enforcement practices were used to imprison African Americans so that they were forced into a new slave state (Collins, 1997). African American women prisoners "were put to work on the large, decaying plantation cotton fields or assigned to mill work sewing in a large central building" (ibid., 7).

The reformers of the 1870s and 1880s in the United States were from the northern states, and they were Quakers, charity workers, and feminists. They viewed women prisoners as victims of male judges, wardens, and prison guards (Freedman, 1982, 142). Rafter (1985, 1989) distinguishes between custodial institutions and reformatories. Custodial institutions were the traditional prisons that were usually designed for men but also housed women, where the goal was not rehabilitation but rather to "confine inmates at the lowest cost (a profit, if possible) until their sentences expired" (Rafter, 1989, 91). Initially, most custodial women's institutions were smaller structures attached to men's prisons (ibid.). Women felons were routinely housed in these men's prisons in the late eighteenth and early nineteenth centuries. At the same time that they were isolated and neglected, they had limited control over privacy from both male guards and male prisoners (ibid.). The mortality rate of infants born to incarcerated women was very high (ibid., 92).

> The custodial model, although eventually supplemented by women's institutions of the reformatory type, did not disappear. Most of the states that established a separate reformatory for women continued to operate a custodial unit, in or nearby their central prison, for female offenders convicted of the most serious crimes and those transferred out of reformatories for misbehavior. Other states—particularly those in the South and West—never created a women's reformatory. (ibid.)

Reformatories, as noted in Chapter 4, were designed specifically to house women offenders, White women offenders for the most part, while African American and other women of color were confined in the harsher penitentiaries (Collins, 1997). The reformatory structure reflects gender stereotypes, often entailing a cottage-style architectural design. To this day, many women's prisons (and some delinquent facilities) are called reformatories. Rafter (1989) states that the reformatory model began to evolve in the United States in the Northeast and Midwest after the Civil War, organized by women's groups, run by women, and based on the view of women as innately different from men and on a rehabilitation approach (ibid.). The first women's reformatory in England was constructed in London in 1853, and the first women's reformatory in the United States was opened in 1874 in Indiana. Shortly afterward, women's reformatories were built in Massachusetts and New York (Freedman, 1974). Most women's reformatories were not established in the United States until 1910, with half established in the 1920s, largely in response to women activists in the World War I era battling prostitution, sexually transmitted infections, and promiscuity (Dodge, 2002). The adoption of women's reformatories in Illinois in 1927 represented a significant net-widening for women offenders: Women who committed adultery and prostitution were typically fined before the reformatories, but with the reformatories they were sentenced to confinement. Additionally, indeterminate sentencing emerged with the reformatories, so not only were women confined for a broader range of offenses but their sentences were far longer with the limitation of one parole hearing after the first year (ibid.).

Despite resistance and hostility from the male authorities who supervised the first sex-segregated and woman-managed reformatories, they were claimed a success. Thus, they were allowed to transition from housing a small number of young, White, and nonimmigrant female offenders to a larger and more diverse group of convicted women. The female staff in the first U.S. reformatories practiced Elizabeth Fry's correctional theories (Freedman, 1974). Similar to some of the disparate laws based on gender, these institutions were in theory designed to protect women and were based on a view of women as more like children than like men: "[T]hey discouraged inmates from acting as independent adults— from competing with men in the industrial job market and participating in the activities (meeting men in dance halls, smoking cigarettes, traveling alone) of other working-class women" (Rafter, 1989, 93). Men's reformatories, though rare, were established in the late nineteenth and early twentieth centuries and were limited to felons, while the misdemeanants were housed in jails and state institutions (ibid.). Many of the women sent to reformatories were women convicted of minor sex offenses such as prostitution, lewdness, and pregnancy out of wedlock—offenses for which men were not prosecuted, much less convicted (ibid.). The loose sentencing available to judges with the perceived view of reformatories as light sentences encouraged a double standard in sentencing and punishing, given that the differential sentencing and institutions resulted in harsher punishment for female than male prisoners (ibid.).

The founders of the U.S. reformatories saw their goals as reform and refuge; their aim was to train the prisoners in the "important" female role of domesticity (Feinman, 1981, 1983; Freedman, 1982). Thus, an important part of the reform movement in women's prisons was to encourage and ingrain "appropriate" gender roles, such as vocational training in cooking, sewing, and cleaning. To accommodate these goals, the reformatory cottages were usually designed with kitchens, living rooms, and even some nurseries for prisoners with infants. Despite their relatively gentle appearances, these institutions were run with "firmness, authority, and strict discipline" (Freedman, 1982, 145). Moreover, parole frequently involved being released to a "good" Christian home as a domestic servant (Feinman, 1983; Rafter, 1985). This indentured servant format was new in the United States but not in Europe and was supported by the middle class who could afford/exploit these inexpensive yet hardworking laborers (Janusz, 1991).

The Progressive era, the first two decades of the 1900s, brought in a new generation of reformers. The two characteristics distinguishing this era's reformatories were the increased professionalism of the female prison administrators and the incorporation of a medical model (Rafter, 1985). For the first time, the reformatories were managed by educated and experienced women professionals, who put more distance between themselves and the prisoners than their predecessors had. The Progressive era was also distinguished by the establishment of physicians,' psychiatrists,' and psychologists' roles in classifying offenders and by an obsession with identifying and responding to incarcerated women's venereal diseases.

Their approach was more feminist than that of the first wave of reformers. Although they continued to support a sex-segregated prison system, they questioned the treatment of women that encouraged them to stay in traditional roles, as these reformers had rejected such roles in their own lives (Freedman, 1982). The second wave of reformers were less likely than their foremothers to base their beliefs on religious and biological underpinnings. They were less concerned with the "moral uplifting" valued by the first wave of reformers, and they targeted what they viewed as the cause of women's crime: low wages and limited opportunities for women in work and education (ibid.). The reformers during the twentieth century were also invested in the suffrage movement, partly because they believed that the conditions for incarcerated women would improve with women's right to vote. But the success of the women's prisons soon resulted in their overcrowding, and legislators were unwilling to fund the needed expansion of vocational, recreational, and educational programs (ibid.). Moreover, overcrowding resulted in disciplinary problems (Rafter, 1985). Ironically, in 1915, just as the reformers started realizing that sex segregation meant reduced opportunities for incarcerated women (relative to incarcerated men), state officials were finally supporting the legitimacy of the sex-segregated facilities (Freedman, 1982).

After 1915, the population of incarcerated women began to change, with a huge influx of incarcerated prostitutes and drug users and an increase in African American women prisoners due to the northern migration of southern African Americans (ibid.). African American women and drug users were perceived as dangerous and in need of being controlled, and racially segregated housing was used in the cottages (ibid.). In the 1920s, the training of the women prisoners in "homemaking" became popular again. The women prisoners' "rights," therefore, were changed to include less rigid clothing rules and more freedom to decorate their walls. The vocational training, however, continued to support gender stereotypes (ibid.).

Sex-Segregated Custodial Prisons

The custodial and reformatory models of women's incarceration merged about 1930, "pooling their respective disadvantages to create the women's prison system as we know it today" (Rafter, 1989, 93). Although sex segregation and the gender stratification of male and female institutional regimes became standard throughout the United States (Freedman, 1982), after the Great Depression, many custodial institutions were closed, and most women were imprisoned in the reformatories, which lost many of the reformatory ideals and took on more of the custodial regimes (Chesney-Lind, 2003; Rafter, 1985). "The majority of prisons built between 1930 and 1966 were built with the reformatory model as the goal for young white women, while blacks were confined to arduous physical farm camps" (Collins, 1997). The 1940s and 1950s have been characterized as a time in which the reformatories switched the goal from turning women prisoners into good housemaids to making them good housewives (Carlen, 1983; Morris, 1987; Windschuttle, 1981). Regardless, valuing women as domestic servants, in their own or others' homes, was commonplace in the women's penal reform movement, and racist views of women of color further impacted their difficulty in serving time. After this period, the reform movement for incarcerated women temporarily died down, and there was little change in women's imprisonment in the middle of the twentieth century (Collins, 1997; Heidensohn, 1985).

Racist Segregation and Treatment in Girls' and Women's Institutions

It is also useful to examine the significant role of racism, similar to the founding of women's prisons, in the establishment of juvenile institutions. Vernetta D. Young (1994) offers a comprehensive historical accounting of this, beginning with the refuge movement for juveniles out of adult facilities in the Southern United States. This began prior to the Civil War, and although it was a serious demand, it did not occur for another three decades, at the end of the 1890s. Young (ibid.) argues that the development of institutions for youth was predicated on the need to control different segments of the population in the South, tracing how the development of incarceration varied among youth depending on their sex and race. More specifically, White male youths were separated from White male adults in adult prisons, while African American male youths prior to the Civil War were controlled by slavery and the adult penal system. After abolition, African American male youths remained in the adult prison system and were processed through the convict lease system (ibid.). Juvenile institutions for African American male youths were introduced only to maintain social control, once the mechanisms of the convict lease system failed, and the "new" method of maintaining social control was by using these youths as needed laborers. The institutions designed for White female delinquents were motivated by the desire to save these girls from sexual immorality by providing them with instruction in "women's" work. Special institutions for African American female youths were not implemented until it became practically or fiscally prohibitive to remand them to adult institutions or "ship" them out of state (ibid.).

But the impact of racism during slavery and reconstruction (the post–Civil War era) was obviously not limited to juveniles. For example, Johnson (2003,

p. 23) discusses the "Black Codes" that replaced the "Slave Codes" during Reconstruction: "Although the Reconstruction era reforms promised independence and self-determination for freed slaves, southern states responded by enacting laws that reinscribed the perceived racial inferiority and inherently criminal status of people of African descent." Given that African Americans were highly criminalized under Black Codes, they were also those most impacted by the convict lease system (ibid.) There was a racialized pattern where White women were more likely to be "channeled out of prisons" because their offending was more likely to be seen as the result of being "victims of circumstance," while African American women offenders were seen as inherently immoral with "uncontrolled lust" and thus were more likely to be sentenced to jail, prison, and hard labor (ibid., 32). Anne M. Butler's (1997) research on women in men's prisons in the Western United States from 1865 to 1915 and L. Mara Dodge's (2002) historical research on women in Illinois prisons from 1835 to 2000 describe the significant impact of race *and* immigrant status among the imprisoned women. For example, in addition to racial segregation in the housing of the women, African American women were more likely to be required to do heavy labor (Butler, 1997).

Women's Prisons in the 1960s, 1970s, and 1980s

Three occurrences in the 1960s and 1970s renewed interest in women's penal reform: (1) the rise of modern feminism and reappraisal of women's roles in society as deviants and as victims; (2) concern that women's crime rates were growing faster than men's; and (3) in England, a 1968 policy that claimed women offenders should be treated uniquely given their special physical and psychological problems (Heidensohn, 1985). With the reemergence of feminism in the 1970s, U.S. reformers began to question the value of sex-segregated prisons. Although these segregated facilities had significantly decreased the abuse (especially sexual) of women prisoners, they had also served to promote damaging gender stereotypes and restricted incarcerated women's opportunities (Freedman, 1982). Structures built specifically to be used as women's reformatories in the United States usually have a cottage-style design and are often compared to college campuses. In addition to their "tamer" architectural appearance, these women's prisons are less likely to have gun towers, armed guards, high concrete walls, and other intimidating, prison-like features. However, in the United States since the 1990s, there has been a growing tendency to place high fences with rolls of barbed wire around these "campuses," and the recent prison building is more consistent with custodial than cottage-style women's prisons.

The lack of adequate women's prisons concerned feminists in the 1970s because women prisoners were often sent out of state if there were no institutions to house them in their own state (Chesney-Lind, 1991, 2003; Rafter, 1989). Unprepared for the explosion in women sentenced to incarceration in the 1980s in both the United States and England, in addition to more women's prisons being built, convicted women were held in "holding tanks," including former men's and juveniles' facilities, hospitals, and even motels (Chesney-Lind, 1991,

2003). In fact, two out of three facilities used as women's prisons in 1990 were not designed to house females (American Correctional Association, 1990). Whether built or created to hold convicted women, women's prisons have appeared at exponential rates. Only two or three women's prisons were built or created per decade between 1930 and 1950, but there were an additional seven built in the 1960s, seventeen in the 1970s, and thirty-four in the 1980s (Chesney-Lind, 1991). Similarly, women's prison programs are designed along the same lines as those for men, with no consideration of the special needs of women, many of whom have survived rape and battering (Hannah-Moffat, 1994). Thus, feminists have increasingly questioned why women's prisons should be expanded when they appear to harm more than help the women they so severely punish (Chesney-Lind, 1991, 2003; Hannah-Moffat, 1994; Rafter, 1989).

THE WOMEN'S PRISON REGIME

U.S. women's prisons changed relatively little from the beginning of the twentieth century into the 1980s (Feinman, 1981; Sarri, 1987). Women's prisons have always been (and still are) smaller, fewer in number, and different than men's prisons, but since the early 1990s women's prisons have grown larger and been built at unprecedented rates, and in some manners, there appears to be increased uniformity in administering women's and men's prisons (Pollock, 2002). In both the United States and England, women' smaller proportion of prisoners (about 5 to 9 percent) has resulted in institutionalized sexism:

1. Women's prisons are generally a farther distance from prisoners' friends and families because of their sporadic and isolated locations, making visits from children, other family, and friends more difficult, particularly for the poor.

2. The relatively small number of women in prison and jail is used to "justify" the lack of diverse educational, vocational, and other programs available to incarcerated women.

3. The relatively small number of women in prison and jail is used to "justify" low levels of specialization in treatment and failure to segregate the more serious and mentally ill offenders from the less serious offenders (as is done in male prisons and jails).

Feminists who have worked toward establishing gender equality in the treatment of prisoners are mounting growing concerns about the response of prison administrators and policy makers (Chesney-Lind, 1991; Hannah-Moffat, 1994; Wheeler et al., 1989). With the boom in women's incarceration, governmental establishments can no longer consider them "correctional afterthoughts" (Chesney-Lind, 2003, 5). "Gender equality" has resulted in (1) a building "binge" to imprison more women (Chesney-Lind, 1991, 2003) and (2) an assumption that female prisoners can simply "fit into" male prisoners' building structures and programs (Chesney-Lind, 1991, 2003; Hannah-Moffat, 1994).

The regime of women's prisons has been described as intending to "discipline, infantalize, feminize, medicalize, and domesticize" (Carlen and Tchaikovsky, 1985). Discipline for incarcerated women is overly harsh, especially relative to that for incarcerated men. A study of women in a North Carolina prison found that the control of the prisoners was strict *and* arbitrary (Girshick, 1999). A study of Texan prisoners found that women were far more likely than men to be cited for rule infractions, particularly minor ones, and far more severely punished for them (McClellan, 1994). The women received citations for drying their underwear, talking while waiting in lines, displaying too many family photographs, and failing to eat all of the food on their plates. "Contraband" included having an extra bra or pillowcase, a borrowed comb or hat, and candy. Sharing shampoo in the shower and lighting another prisoner's cigarette were classified as "trafficking." Such minor everyday occurrences never resulted in citations or punishment in men's prisons (ibid.). Thus, in addition to reinforcing gender stereotypes such as domesticity and femininity, women's prison policies and supervision treat women like children (Carlen, 1983; Fox, 1975; Leonard, 1983; Moyer, 1984).

The medicalization of incarcerated women is also evident (Carlen and Tchaikovsky, 1985; Dobash, Dobash, and Gutteridge, 1986). For example, even women returning from such permitted leaves as court appearances, furloughs, and giving birth in hospitals are often subjected to vaginal searches for contraband (and the searches are typically by security, not medical, staff). These searches are not only humiliating but also often painful and dangerous, resulting in bleeding and infection (Holt, 1982; Mann, 1984; McHugh, 1980). "What is ironic about this procedure is that these vaginal examinations are frequent, yet the preventive pap test for cervical cancer is not often given" (Mann, 1984, 213). Furthermore, despite a change of policy in England and Scotland in the 1960s and 1970s that assumed an inherent mental instability and illness of women prisoners, treatment is difficult to obtain and when obtained is rarely helpful (Dobash, Dobash, and Gutteridge, 1986).

Women defendants, as noted in Chapter 4, face a number of restrictions in the legal system en route to prison. One study found that 50 percent of incarcerated women saw their public defenders for fifteen minutes or less, most did not even know the names of their public defenders, and the women who saw public defenders for more than fifteen minutes were those charged with a capital crime and even then met with their defenders for only about an hour (Pendergrass, 1975). Incarcerated women's legal battles begin well before incarceration and extend well into their incarceration. Legal cases in the 1980s challenged why women prisoners had to have their lights out earlier than male prisoners did and why they received vocational training only in sewing prison clothes while male prisoners in the same state received training in a variety of vocational skills (such as electronics or carpentry) (Leonard, 1983). Limitations for incarcerated women also include disadvantages (relative to incarcerated men) in access to law libraries, jailhouse lawyers, and, consequently, the courts (Alpert, 1982; Carlen, 1983; Haft, 1980; Wheeler et al., 1989). In fact, only about half of U.S. women's prisons have law libraries available for prisoner use (American Correctional Association, 1990). One study found a lack of legitimate channels for incarcerated women to report abuses or seek effective help for their problems, reinforcing their belief that they are not taken seriously (Carlen and Tchaikovsky, 1985).

While both male and female prisoners are expected to be submissive, this is likely a more rigorous expectation in women's prisons. Additionally, this population with massively high sexual abuse histories is given little control over their bodies in prison, starting with the "degradation ceremonies" they face upon prison entry (Maeve, 1999a). Similarly, one of the worst legal problems incarcerated women and girls have faced historically involves reproductive freedom. Not only have many imprisoned and institutionalized women and girls had abortions against their will (Holt, 1982; Leonard, 1983; McHugh, 1980), but those who want abortions, particularly indigents, are not necessarily guaranteed access to them (Haft, 1980; Holt, 1982; Knight, 1992; McHugh, 1980; Resnick and Shaw, 1980; Vitale, 1980; Vukson, 1988). Additionally, girls in juvenile institutions and women prisoners are encouraged and sometimes forced to give up their babies for adoption (Baunach, 1992; Haft, 1980; Haley, 1980; Mann, 1984; Ross and Fabiano, 1986), even if they became pregnant while incarcerated (Mann, 1984). A more recent assessment of imprisoned women's access to reproductive health care reports: "There are no consistently applied policies regarding contraception, abortion, and general reproductive education and counseling for incarcerated women. When these services are available, they are rarely provided in a comprehensive or consistent manner" (Acoca, 1998a, 56). Morever, access to the most basic of needs, toilet paper and sanitary pads, is often highly restricted in women's prisons: They are allotted a certain amount of toilet paper and pads per time period, regardless of the frequency of their cycles or rate of bleeding (Maeve, 1999a). Thus, incarcerated women are at the mercy of the staff for everyday needs (Compton-Wallace, 2003; Kruttschnitt, Gartner, and Miller, 2000; Pollock, 2002).

RATES OF IMPRISONMENT AND A PORTRAYAL OF INCARCERATED GIRLS AND WOMEN

The media, academics, and prison reformers have noted the surge in incarceration rates in recent years. Although women's recent incarceration rates are growing at a faster pace than men's, the discussions on the rates frequently fail to account for women or simply lump them in with the men. Increases in women's incarceration rates have exceeded men's every year since 1981 (Kline, 1993; Pollock, 2002), although some jurisdictions have been slowing their incarceration rates with the new century (Pollock, 2002). The number of women in U.S. prisons tripled during the 1980s (Church, 1990; Fletcher and Moon, 1993a; Immarigeon and Chesney-Lind, 1992; Kline, 1993), while the number of incarcerated men about doubled (Kline, 1993). Similar incarceration-rate explosions for women have occurred in England (Morris, 1987). Between 1980 and 1994, men's rates of incarceration in the United States skyrocketed by doubling (increasing 214 percent), but women's corresponding rates were almost twice the rate of the men's, almost quadrupling (increasing 386 percent) (Acoca and Austin, 1996).

There are a number of interesting points regarding women's disproportionately high increases in incarceration rates. First, there does not appear to be a corresponding increase in women's criminality overall (Immarigeon, 1987a; Morris, 1987; Pollock, 2002). Second, the overall proportion of women imprisoned for violent crimes has actually decreased (Immarigeon and Chesney-Lind, 1992; Sokoloff, 2001). In fact, most of the increase in women's imprisonment can be accounted for by minor property crimes (mostly larceny-theft) and drug and public order offenses (Chesney-Lind, 1991; Immarigeon 1987a; Immarigeon and Chesney-Lind, 1992; Kline, 1993; Mann, 1984; Sarri, 1987; Sokoloff, 2005). Exhibit 5.1 presents the most recent statistics regarding incarceration in the United States (Harrison and Beck, 2005). The findings mirror earlier patterns: (1) The increase in women's incarceration (4.0 percent) was double the rate of men's (1.8 percent) in 2004; (2) half of men's incarcerations (52 percent) were for violent offenses, which accounted for a third of women's incarcerations (33 percent); (3) a higher percentage of women (29 percent) than men (20 percent) were incarcerated for property offenses; and (4) a higher percentage of women (32 percent) than men (21 percent) were incarcerated for drug offenses (ibid.).

A third important point is that the growth in the building of women's prisons and the addition of female units in existing prisons are unprecedented (Immarigeon, 1987a; Immarigeon and Chesney-Lind, 1992; Pollock, 2002; Sarri, 1987), although most incarcerated women are not dangerous, but rather tend to be property offenders, drug abusers, and/or victims of domestic violence (Immarigeon, 1987a; Sokoloff, 2005). Some reports say sentence lengths have not increased (Immarigeon, 1987a), while others say that women's sentence lengths have increased along with their increased likelihood of incarceration (Sarri, 1987). Overall, there appears to be an increasing willingness to incarcerate women (Harrison and Beck, 2005; Immarigeon and Chesney-Lind, 1992; Sokoloff, 2005).

Fourth, women's increased incarceration rates can be traced to implicit policy changes. Chesney-Lind (1991, 2003) believes the "war on drugs" has been translated into a "war on women," given the extreme growth of women's incarcerations for drug crimes. She attributes the increase in women's imprisonment to this war on drugs/women and to changes in decision making in the crime-processing system (such as the implementation of new sentencing guidelines). Significantly, despite the huge increase in women's incarceration, women constituted only about 6 percent of incarcerated persons in the United States in 1990 (U.S. Department of Justice, 1992).

Finally, offending women's and girls' help-seeking behaviors can themselves be criminalized. For example, Sterk's (1999) study of women using crack reported that the women were deterred from pursuing treatment in clinics when they were pregnant for fear of being put in jail and/or having their babies taken away. Moreover, many of the women reported encountering long waiting lists and/or a six-month approval for public-funding to get into drug treatment when they were desperate to stop using (ibid.).

E X H I B I T 5.1 Recent Facts on Women's Incarceration in the United States

■ In 2004 women's incarceration in state and federal prisons increased 4.0 percent, while the corresponding increase for males was 1.8 percent.

■ In 2004, there were 104,848 women and 1,391,781 men in prison. Thus, women constituted 7.0 percent of all prisoners in 2004 (and were 5.7 percent in 1990 and 6.1 percent in 1995).

■ Since 1995, the number of male prisoners has increased by 32 percent while the number of female prisoners has increased by 53 percent.

■ Oklahoma, Mississippi, and Louisiana, respectively, have the highest female incarceration rates.

■ Across age, African American females were more than twice as likely as Latinas and 4 times as likely as White females to be incarcerated in 2004.

■ In 2004, the racial/gender breakdown of U.S. State and Federal Prisoners is as follows:

	Female Prisoners	Male Prisoners
● Percent White	44.2	33.6
● Percent African American	41.2	33.4
● Percent Latina/o	19.5	15.6

■ Percent of U.S. prisoners that are female under state jurisdiction in the United States in 2002 by offense:

Offense	Female	Male
Total	100.0%	100.0%
Total Violent Offenses	33.0	51.7
Murder	10.2	12.1
Manslaughter	2.0	1.3
Rape	0.6	5.2
Other sexual assault	1.3	6.9
Robbery	8.0	14.2
Assault	8.3	9.5
Other violent offense	2.6	2.4
Total Property Offenses	28.7	19.9
Burglary	6.0	10.9
Larceny	9.0	3.5
Motor Vehicle Theft	1.0	1.5
Fraud	10.5	1.9
Other Property Offense	2.3	2.0
Drug Offenses	31.5	20.7
Public-Order Offenses	6.1	7.1
Other/unspecified Offenses	0.8	0.6

SOURCE: Paige M. Harrison and Allen J. Beck. 2005. *Prisoners in 2004*. Bureau of Justice Statistics Bulletin. U.S. Department of Justice, October, NCJ 210677. http://www.ojp.usdoj.gov/bjs/pub/pdf/p04.pdf.

The most obvious characteristic distinguishing women and girls who have been incarcerated from those who have not is race (e.g., Binkley-Jackson, Carter, and Rolison, 1993; Brewster, 2003; Rafter, 1985; Ross, 1998; Sarri, 1987; Sharp, 2003). The women's prisons, like the men's, have a long history of reflecting the criminal legal system's racism. Even prior to 1865, African American women were disproportionately incarcerated, and after the Civil War the rate of impris-oned African American women swelled even more (Butler, 1997; Collins, 1997; Rafter, 1985). It has been pointed out that the recent media and academic recognition of the highly disproportionate incarceration of African Americans has focused almost exclusively on males, although some researchers report there have often been higher rates of African Americans in women's than in men's prisons (Binkley-Jackson, Carter, and Rolison, 1993; Goetting and Howsen, 1983; Rafter, 1985), and Aboriginal women are even more disproportionately overrepresented than Aboriginal men in Canadian prisons (Johnson and Rodgers, 1993). The most recent statistics from the United States, however, suggest that the overrepresentation of people of color in men's prisons is more severe than it is in women's. More specifically, in 2004, African American men were 6.9 times more likely than White men to be incarcerated, whereas African American women were 4.4 times more likely than White women to be incarcerated. Latino men were 2.4 times as likely as White men to be incarcerated, whereas Latina women were 1.7 times as likely as White women to be incarcerated (Harrison and Beck, 2005). African American men in their 20s and 30s have the highest incarceration rates of all the gender-race-age groups; it is estimated that 13 percent of African American men in their late 20s were in prison or jail in 2004 (ibid.).

A little-addressed problem in prisons is the representation of American Indians. Luana Ross (1998) points out that although American Indians constituted 6 percent of Montana's population in 1995, 17 percent of the men's prison population and 25 percent of the women's prison population in Montana were classified as American Indian. It is painfully apparent that poor women of all races are vastly overrepresented in women's prisons (Brewster, 2003; Morris, 1987) and that poor men and men of color are vastly overrepresented in men's prisons. A British study reported that in 1994, 25 percent of the female prison population were ethnic minorities, with the vast majority African American (21 percent) (Chigwada-Bailey, 1997, 13). Notably, 16 percent of the British male prisoners were ethnic minority members (ibid.). Perhaps the most telling of the studies on racial identity in women's prison is a recent study reporting that the women's racial identities were seriously different from the official prison race data, partic-ularly for women who identified as American Indian (Abril, 2003). The Ohio Reformatory for Women (ORW) reported that of the 1,700 prisoners, 56 percent were African American and 44 percent were White. They reported only 1 Asian American and 2 Native Americans (out of 1,700). However, when the author was able to survey 601 of the 1,700 women, 255 reported American Indian heritage, which translates into 42 percent of those answering the survey and at least 14 percent of the entire prisoner population (assuming that of those who did not or could not take the survey, none would report American Indian heritage) (ibid.). Many of the women wrote of being bi- or multiracial and of being perceived by the rest of the population as a race other than how they defined themselves. This study suggests huge flaws in classifying offenders' race and ethnicity and how formal documents likely misrepresent prisoners' race/ethnicity, particularly concerning American Indian heritage.

Although collecting data on class is more difficult than gathering data on race, a recent government report indicated that incarcerated women are significantly more economically disadvantaged than incarcerated men (a largely poor group) (Greenfeld and Snell, 1999). For example, in this study comparing incarcerated men's and women's financial status prior to the arrest for the offense that led them to a U.S. state prison, (1) 40 percent of women and 60 percent of men were employed full-time, (2) 37 percent of women and 28 percent of men had incomes of less than $600 per month, and (3) almost 30 percent of women and less than 8 percent of men were receiving welfare.

In addition to race and class, a distinguishing characteristic of incarcerated females is their significantly increased likelihood of having survived sexual and/or physical violence, particularly by a male relative or intimate partner (American Correctional Association, 1990; Acoca, 1998b; Arnold, 1990; Bunch, Foley, and Urbina, 1983; Carlen, 1983; Chesney-Lind and Rodriguez, 1983; Coker et al., 1998; Fletcher, Rolison, and Moon, 1993; Fox and Sugar, 1990; Gilfus, 1992; Gray, Mays, and Stohr, 1995; Greenfeld and Snell, 1999; Immarigeon, 1987a, 1987b; Lake, 1993; Mullings, Marquart, and Brewer, 2000; Sable et al., 1999; Sargent, Marcus-Mendoza, and Yu, 1993; Simkins and Katz, 2002; Singer et al., 1995). Research also shows that women in prison have experienced unusually high rates of extremely abusive "discipline" from parents, involvement in drugs, and prostitution, whether they were imprisoned for these crimes or not (Bunch, Foley, and Urbina, 1983; Chesney-Lind and Rodriguez, 1983), and of witnessing domestic violence (Fox and Sugar, 1990). Many of the incarcerated women and girls report that they believe their offending/incarceration, sexual victimization, drug abuse, and prostitution are all interrelated (Chesney-Lind and Rodriguez, 1983; Fox and Sugar, 1990; Gilfus, 1992; Sargent, Marcus-Mendoza, and Yu, 1993; Sterk, 1999).

One study was conducted to try to determine how chronic female offenders in prison differed from nonchronic incarcerated females (Danner et al., 1995). The greatest differences between the chronic and nonchronic females, reported in order of most to least predictive, were age of first arrest, substance abuse, offense seriousness, and racial/ethnic group status. Specifically, the chronic group was about four years younger than the nonchronic group at age of first arrest; the chronic group reported more drug-use problems than the nonchronic group; the chronic group tended to be serving time for a less serious offense; and chronic offenders were more likely to be African American. The authors explain the surprising finding that the nonchronic group were in for more serious offenses, by the possibility that the findings are skewed by battered women who kill their batterers but have no offense history (ibid.). It is also likely that the finding of African American females as overrepresented is related to the racist processing of females (and males) and that African American girls/women are more harshly processed and labeled by the system than White girls/women.

E X H I B I T 5.2   **A Profile of Incarcerated Girls in the United States**

- On average, 14 to 15 years old (although may have started acting out a few years earlier)
- Poor and grew up in a neighborhood with a high crime rate
- Belong to an ethnic minority (50 percent of female juveniles in detention are African American, 34 percent are White, and 13 percent are Latina)
- Have a history of poor academic performance and may be high school drop-outs
- Victims of physical, sexual, and/or emotional abuse or exploitation
- Used and abused drugs and/or alcohol
- Gone without medical and mental health needs addressed
- Feel that life is oppressive and lack hope for the future

SOURCE: Greene, Peters, and Associates. 1998. *Guiding Principles for Promising Female Programming*. Office of Juvenile Justice and Delinquency Prevention, October, p. 2. http://ojjdp.ncjrs.org/pubs/principles/contents.html.

A study of women incarcerated in Oklahoma reported that 30 percent are married, almost 30 percent never married, almost 20 percent divorced, and the rest separated, divorced, or something else (Holley and Brewster, 1996). Over 40 percent of the prison population was African American, 7 percent American Indian, and 43 percent White. Five percent were White–Latina and 8 percent were African American–Latina (biracial). Three-quarters reported having at least one child, with 60 percent giving birth to their first child when they were 18 or younger. Over 70 percent had used drugs at age 19 or younger, over 25 percent at age 14 or younger. Over one-third experienced sexual abuse as a child or adult, and almost half had experienced physical abuse, usually by current or former boyfriends or husbands (ibid.). Over half had another family member incarcerated, usually a brother. Over one-third had run away from home at some time, and over one-third had experienced drug treatment prior to their incarceration. Sixty percent reported needing more education. Most were serving time for an economic or drug crime, and most were in prison for the first time (ibid.). (See Exhibit 5.2 for a summary of characteristics of incarcerated girls.)

GIRLS' "CORRECTIONAL" INSTITUTIONS

Although separate penal institutions were developed for adult women in the mid-1800s, separate facilities for girls date from the early 1900s (Sarri, 1987). Often, women and girls in jails are usually placed in what are essentially male facilities. For the arrested girls, this usually amounts to solitary confinement in jail, which places them at high risk for suicide, particularly given girls' high rates of prior sexual and physical victimizations (Chesney-Lind and Shelden, 1992). Not only are girls more likely than boys to be placed in jail for trivial (status) offenses but the conditions for girls in jail are worse than those for boys. In addition to experiencing high rates of solitary confinement, they appear to be at risk of being sexually assaulted by the male staff and other jail inmates (Chesney-Lind and Rodriguez, 1983).

One study of adolescent offenders found that girls (65 percent) were more than twice as likely as boys (26 percent) to report that they had thought about suicide, and girls (56 percent) were more than twice as likely as boys (26 percent) to attempt suicide (Miller, 1994). Although for both boys and girls the most frequently given reason for thinking about suicide (80 percent) was due to feelings of "hopelessness," girls who attempted suicide were far more likely (92 percent) than boys who attempted suicide (60 percent) to report "hopelessness" as a reason they attempted suicide (ibid.). Notably, boys (20 percent) were more likely than girls (0 percent) to report a family member dying as a rationale for attempting suicide. A study on juvenile delinquents' emotional disorders did not separate the boys' from the girls' responses but found that for a large population of delinquent youth in Ohio, the delinquent youths' psychometric profiles were more similar than dissimilar to a clinical, mentally ill population (Davis et al., 1991). About one-fifth of the youths had made suicide threats, and 13 percent had attempted suicide. Although the authors only briefly discussed gender differences in the sample, they found "striking" findings regarding a comparison between the department of youth services (delinquent) girls and the profiles of girls in psychiatric facilities. Specifically, the delinquent girls had "both greater behavioral and emotional difficulties," reporting greater emotional distress and social immaturity than the psychiatric sample (ibid., 8). The authors conclude this study highlights the need to respond to youths exhibiting mental illness problems so that they do not become delinquents or are not processed and labeled as delinquents when the correct diagnosis and treatment would be for mental health needs (ibid.).

Like women's prisons, juvenile girls' institutions often reinforce gender stereotypes and roles (Gelsthorpe, 1989; Kersten, 1989; Smart, 1976). Girls are subject to greater rule rigidity and control and are offered fewer vocational and other programs than boys (Kersten, 1989; Mann, 1984). A British study comparing incarcerated boys and girls found that despite no set gender differences in policies, the gender differences practiced in treatment and activities were quite severe (Gelsthorpe, 1989). The girls were rewarded for feminine behavior such as acting maternal, being affectionate, showing sensitivity, and crying. Moreover, even the activities were sex-prescribed: Boys swam, jogged, and played ping-pong, darts, soccer, and volleyball, while girls watched from the sidelines. If girls attempted to join in the "boys'" activities, they were negatively labeled "tomboys" or "unladylike." Conversely, the girls' activities included exercises to keep slim, sewing, and cooking because the staff viewed the girls as "destined for marriage and family life" (ibid., 114).

At worst, like the jails, delinquent girls' institutions have proven to be dangerous for female juvenile offenders. "Studies of the conditions in the nation's detention centers and training schools indicate that rather than protecting girls, many neglect their needs and, in some instances, further victimize the girls" (Chesney-Lind and Shelden, 1992, 164). This is particularly disturbing given that in 1989, 22 percent of girls and 3 percent of boys held in public juvenile facilities were there for nondelinquent reasons (for example, status offenses, abuse and neglect, and voluntary commitment) (U.S. Department of Justice, 1991a). An important area of penal reform, then, is changing the institutionalization and treatment of female youth offenders. Given the vastly growing number of women prisoners, this could be an important preventive effort.

PSYCHOLOGICAL ASPECTS OF WOMEN'S IMPRISONMENT

The penal system that castigates women prisoners for being more manipulative and demanding of medical needs (relative to incarcerated men) ignores the tendency to pathologize these women far more than the male prisoners (Maeve, 1999a). Stated alternatively, the prison system treats these women as "sick" but complains about being inundated with their subsequent requests for help with depression as well as physical ailments.

A disturbing aspect of women's and girls' confinement is the relatively high rate of self-destructive behaviors. Some speculate that incarcerated women's disproportionately high suicide attempts (e.g., Maeve, 1999a; Miller, 1994), cell destruction, and self-mutilation ("cutting") are a result of women's tendency to internalize anger, while incarcerated men are more likely to externalize anger by assaulting other prisoners or prison staff (see Dobash, Dobash, and Gutteridge, 1986; Fox, 1975). One reason offered for the self-mutilation is that it is a way for incarcerated females to feel *something*, particularly for those who, in their efforts to survive traumatic pasts, have effectively trained themselves to cut off all emotions (see Morris, 1987). Indeed, Faith (1993b, 230) views incarcerated women's and girls' self-mutilation related to two phenomena: First, women and girls are often "unable to direct their anger at more appropriate targets" (than themselves). Second, women and girls who injure themselves are disproportionately survivors of childhood sexual abuse (ibid.). Addressing the high rates of tattoos (which some view as self-mutilation), Faith (ibid., 239) states: "Traditionally, they have been a key means by which Western 'deviants' in general, and prisoners in particular, could lay claim to their own bodies, as well as signify their identification with the outcast culture."

Despite the now well-documented trauma histories that the majority of women prisoners report, access to adequate mental health workers has been an ongoing problem in women's prisons. As recently as the 1970s, Dwight Prison in Illinois had a visiting **psychiatrist** who worked at the prison one day a month and no **psychologist**, while unqualified persons, such as wives of the guards and the prison switchboard operator, were hired as therapists (Dodge, 2002). Without reporting male prisoners' rates of receiving medication for emotional disorders, a recent governmental report stated that 17 percent of women in jails and 23 percent of women in state prisons in the United States receive psychotropic drug prescriptions (Greenfeld and Snell, 1999). There is, however, considerable evidence that such drugs are far more common in women's than in men's prisons (Auerhahn and Leonard, 2000; Heidensohn, 1985; Mann, 1984; Morris, 1987; Ross and Fabiano, 1986). Incarcerated women's and girls' increased levels of psychotropic and tranquilizer drug prescriptions may be due to (1) females experiencing imprisonment more severely than males (Morris, 1987), (2) women experiencing more pain due to separation from children (ibid.), and/or (3) an increased likelihood of prison staff to value or justify the nonmedical use of drugs to socially control females (relative to males) (Auerhahn and Leonard, 2000; Compton-Wallace, 2003; Fletcher and Moon, 1993b; Sarri, 1987). Unfortunately, there is also some indication that the medical staff frequently prescribe these drugs without checking to determine whether the woman is pregnant, although these drugs can be quite harmful to fetuses (McHugh, 1980). Equally troubling is a recent study finding that the women jailees who were given these drugs (often for nonmedical reasons) experienced "disproportionately harsh outcomes" in their trials, where they were falling asleep or too drugged to take part in their own defenses (Auerhahn and Leonard, 2000). Another important point has been made by Luana Ross concerning prison prescriptions of psychotropic drugs for Native American women:

> Many Native women at the WCC [Montana's Women's Correctional Center] responded to the harsh prison environment by being detached, by observing how things were conducted. Prison counseling staff misinterpreted their behavioral reaction as a suppression of anger, which led to the overprescribing of a variety of mind-altering drugs. The women believed that because the counseling staff did not know how to relate to them as Native Americans, they tried to control them with drugs, which they were forced to take. (2000, 134)

It is more than a little ironic that the war on drugs fueled the massive explosion in women's incarceration rates, yet women often have trouble accessing drug treatment programs both *before* their arrests and incarceration (Alemagno, 2001; Sterk, 1999) and *during* their incarceration (Alemagno, 2001; Belknap, 2000; Gray, Mays, and Stohr, 1995; Moon, Thompson, and Bennett, 1993; Pollock, 2002; Prendergast, Wellisch, and Falkin, 1995; Wellisch, Prendergast, and Anglin, 1996). Moreover, while many incarcerated women have difficulty accessing programs to become "clean and sober" while incarcerated, they are frequently provided with abundant amounts of psychotropic drugs for nonmedical reasons (Auerhahn and Leonard, 2000). Many incarcerated women also worry about how they will stay off drugs *after* completing their prison sentences. The lack of adequate drug treatment programs before, during, and after incarceration is problematic on many levels but mostly because drug-abusing convicts have a high rate of reoffending and returning to prison (Moon, Thompson, and Bennett, 1993; Singer et al., 1995). When implemented, drug/alcohol treatment programs for women should take two issues into account: First, the extensive physical and sexual abuse women prisoners have survived may require special consideration in chemical dependency treatment (Moon, Thompson, and Bennett, 1993; Singer et al., 1995). Second, too often the drug treatment programs employ shaming tactics that backfire for these women with already very low self-esteem (Sterk, 1999).

Another disturbing irony in the treatment and holding of incarcerated women is the manner in which the prison experience further shames, stigmatizes, victimizes, and neglects the needs of this already highly shamed, stigmatized, abused, and neglected group (see Dodge and Pogrebin, 2001; Pogrebin and Dodge, 2001). Somehow these women are supposed to leave prison with new skills to make up for the poverty, sexism, racism, and classism that most of them experienced prior to offending and incarceration. Their prison experiences often exacerbate their poor self-images, and they must find legal ways to provide for themselves and their dependents without skills, with incarceration records, and often with lagging self-esteems.

Another source of psychological stress that is addressed in more detail in the next section is guilt and worry about separation from their families, especially their children (Dodge and Pogrebin, 2001). As stated earlier, a form of institutionalized sexism in incarceration is that given the fewer number of women's prisons, women prisoners are generally incarcerated farther away from their family members, support systems, and their children than are men (Farrell, 1998). Women prisoners are more likely than men to feel guilty about their incarceration because of the lack of contact with their children. Women prisoners are more likely to worry that grandparents, foster parents, and others given temporary custody of their children may not adequately supervise the children (see Baunach, 1992). Women who believe that their convictions were unjust are likely to feel even more traumatized by the separation from their children. Thus, policies need to be developed that recognize not only the pain incarcerated women experience by being separated from their children but also the pain the children, particularly young, dependent children, experience by being separated from their mothers (see Bloom and Steinhart, 1993; Farrell, 1998; Sharp and Marcus-Mendoza, 2001).

Finally, the geographic isolation of women's prisons is not the only reason women prisoners get so few visits. The different values families place on the male members (husbands, fathers, sons, and brothers) as opposed to the female members (wives, mothers, daughters, and sisters) is evident in that incarcerated females receive fewer visits from family members than men receive. "Even while women are still at the county jail level (before being sent off to the remote prisons), they are not visited and stuck by with the same loyalty as men are by families, partners, and friends" (Swain, 1994). One recent study reported that almost half of the incarcerated women had lost touch with their families. In most cases, the woman had tried repeatedly to contact family members but after no response gave up because the rejection was so painful (Dodge and Pogrebin, 2001).

PARENTHOOD: A GENDER DIFFERENCE
AMONG PRISONERS

The average number of dependent children per incarcerated woman is between two and three (Abril, 2003; American Correctional Association, 1990; Baunach, 1985; Fletcher, Rolison, and Moon, 1993; Greenfeld and Snell, 1999; Johnston,

1995a; McGowan and Blumenthal, 1976, 1978; Sharp and Marcus-Mendoza, 2001), and a 1999 government document reported that 233,600 children in the United States had mothers in jail or state or federal prisons; additionally, over a million children had mothers on probation (Greenfeld and Snell, 1999). Approximately four out of five women and three out of five men entering prison are parents, and research indicates that almost all incarcerated women have custody of their children prior to imprisonment, while fewer than half of the men do (Church, 1990; Johnston, 1995b; Koban, 1983). However, a recent study found that 65 percent of incarcerated women with minor children and 47 percent of incarcerated men with minor children reported that their children lived with them prior to incarceration (Schafer and Dellinger, 1999).

One of the greatest differences in stresses for women and men serving time is that the separation from children is generally a much greater hardship for women than for men. Incarcerated fathers are far more likely than incarcerated mothers to have the other parent taking care of the child during their sentence (Bloom, 1993; Rafter 1985; Sharp et al., 1999). Indeed, about 90 percent of incarcerated fathers report that the other parent has primary custody of their children during their imprisonment (Johnston, 1995b; Schafer and Dellinger, 1999), whereas 20 to 30 percent of incarcerated women report their children's fathers as having primary custody when the women entered prison (Enos, 2001; Johnston, 1995b; Schafer and Dellinger, 1999; Sharp and Marcus-Mendoza, 2001). In fact, children of incarcerated women are about five times as likely to be placed in foster care as children of incarcerated fathers (Johnston, 1995b; Sharp et al., 1999). Testimony to incarcerated women's increased dedication to be reunited with their children relative to incarcerated men is evidenced in a recent study that found women prisoners are significantly more amenable to sentencing alternatives to prison (and are willing to endure them for longer periods) than are incarcerated men, particularly when they are primary caregivers (Wood and Grasmick, 1999). In her study of almost 300 women prisoners, Owen (1998, 101) describes most women's relationships with their children as "sacred," providing "a basis for attachment to the outside world not always found among male prisoners."

In addition to acknowledging the pain that incarcerated women suffer from being separated from their children, it is of utmost importance to acknowledge the suffering most children experience when their mothers are incarcerated (Bloom and Steinhart, 1993; Henriques, 1996; Kampfner, 1995; Owen, 1998; Pollock, 2002; Sharp et al., 1999). It is likely that children's separation from their mothers due to their mothers' imprisonment increases these youths' chances of going to prison (American Correctional Association, 1990; Bloom and Steinhart, 1993; Luke, 2002; Myers et al., 1999; Sharp et al., 1999). Given that most incarcerated mothers want to be reunited with their children upon their release and that most children of incarcerated mothers want to be reunited with their mothers, it is important and necessary to examine these occurrences and dynamics. "Positive reunion is often the result of opportunities for continued contact between mothers and their children during a mother's incarceration" (Henriques, 1996, 85). Thus, it is necessary not only that prisons have such visitation programs and possibilities in place but also that it is recognized that incarcerating women, particularly poor women (most of the women in prison), at great distances from their children not only exacerbates a woman's incarceration experience, but it likely has devastating and lasting effects on her children as well (ibid.).

Significantly, incarcerated women are far more likely than incarcerated men to be the emotional and financial providers for children. Indeed, incarcerated men are less likely than incarcerated women to even know where their dependent children are living (Sharp et al., 1999). Not only do women prisoners exhibit more concern than men about their children, but children are far more likely to be affected by an incarcerated mother than an incarcerated father. The general acceptance that children whose parents go to prison are likely to be far more affected by their mothers' than their fathers' incarceration is apparent from the titles of the first books on this topic: *Unfit Mothers* (Mahan, 1982), *When Mothers Go to Jail* (Stanton, 1980), and *Why Punish the Children?* (McGowan and Blumenthal, 1978). In fact, it is difficult to find studies on parenting issues with regard to incarcerated fathers. One study found that the primary source of family income for an incarcerated woman with dependent children before coming to prison was her job, and after her incarceration, "help from others" tripled and became the primary source (Sharp and Marcus-Mendoza, 2001). Moreover, the average family income for a woman with dependent children was halved from about $29,400 annual income to $10,700 with her incarceration, at the same time that 10 percent of the families prior to the mothers' incarceration, but only 2 percent of the families after their incarceration were receiving government child support. This may be because incarcerated women are afraid to apply for financial help for the relatives caring for their children while they are imprisoned because it may lead to institutionalizing the children rather than letting them live with their relatives (Carlen, 1983), although these families are likely financially strapped as well (Sharp and Marcus-Mendoza, 2001).

The most likely caregiver for a child whose mother has been incarcerated is a grandparent, and this is usually the maternal grandmother (Belknap, 2000; Bloom and Steinhart, 1993; Enos, 2001; Farrell, 1998; Owen, 1998; Schafer and Dellinger, 1999; Sharp and Marcus-Mendoza, 2001, Sharp et al., 1999). Most women prisoners want to take an active role in determining where their children will stay while they are incarcerated, and when given a choice, they most frequently request their own mothers (or the children's maternal grandmothers). This is largely because the maternal grandmothers often play a major role in the children's lives, and the incarcerated mothers will have fewer difficulties regaining custody after release (Baunach, 1992). Although some studies report that fathers were the next most likely caregiver to incarcerated women's dependent children (after maternal grandmothers) (Enos, 2001; Sharp and Marcus-Mendoza, 2001; Sharp et al., 1999), other research indicates that the next most common caretaker is another relative of the mother's (e.g., an aunt) (Owen, 1998). The children of incarcerated women run a high risk of having to change schools (as well as caretakers) and are less well off financially after their mothers' incarceration (Sharp and Marcus-Mendoza, 2001; Stanton, 1980). There is also no guarantee that the initial placement of a child, say with a family member, will last the duration of the mother's incarceration (Johnston, 1995b; McCarthy, 1980). As expected, incarcerated mothers with longer sentences and those mothers unhappy about the custody arrangements for their dependent children report higher levels of strain while imprisoned (Berry and Eigenberg, 2003). Not surprisingly, many caretakers, particularly if they are grandparents, find the child care financially, emotionally, and/or physically exhausting (see Enos, 2001).

Incarcerated mothers often worry about the competency and even dangerousness of their children's caretakers (Enos, 2001; Sharp and Marcus-Mendoza, 2001). One study found some fathers who had taken over custody while the women were in prison were using drugs in front of the children and/or were abusive to the children (Enos, 2001), although another study of women and men incarcerated for drug offenses found the women were more likely than the men to report using drugs in the home while a child was there (Sharp et al., 1999). (Of course, given that women are more likely to have custody of their children, this is not terribly surprising.) A key factor only recently examined is the intersection between incarcerated women's highly dysfunctional families of origin and the strong likelihood of the incarcerated women's children going to their parents' (the children's maternal grandparents') homes. Sharp and Marcus-Mendoza (2001) analyzed this and found significant rates of incarcerated women's children going to grandparents who had drug/alcohol problems during the women's childhood. Even more alarming was that incarcerated women who reported parents who were physically and/or sexually abusive to them when they were children were just as likely as incarcerated women reporting no such parental abuse to have their own children sent to these abusive "guardians" (ibid.).

One of the most controversial debates surrounding the imprisonment of women is whether they should be allowed to keep infants and small children with them in prison. On the one hand, some argue that innocent children should not be raised in prisons. On the other hand, others claim that it is unfair for innocent children to be separated from their mothers. A comprehensive book on children of prisoners states: "Often they are removed abruptly from their homes, schools, and communities, shuttled from one caretaker to another, deprived of seeing their parents or siblings, teased and avoided by their peers, and left to comprehend on their own what is happening" (McGowan and Blumenthal, 1978). It is not surprising that these children's school performance and behavioral problems begin or get worse after their mothers' incarceration (Sharp and Marcus-Mendoza, 2001; Stanton, 1980). Although a small number of women are imprisoned specifically for neglecting, abusing, or killing their children, a far greater number are in prison for stealing or prostituting in order to provide for themselves and their children. Notably, those few women in prison for harming or killing their children face more ostracism from the other prisoners than anyone else does (Kaplan, 1988; Mahan, 1984).

Not surprisingly, a study of incarcerated mothers in Oklahoma found their children reported high rates of depression, running away, bad school performances and dropping out of school, problems with guardians, and alcohol/drug problems (Sharp and Marcus-Mendoza, 2001). Fifteen percent of the women reported their children had been arrested during their own incarceration (ibid.).

Prisons and jails have varying policies regarding visitation with children and placement of babies born to incarcerated women. Many of the early women's reformatories allowed babies and young children to stay in the prisons with their mothers until they were 2 years old (Lekkerkerker, 1931). A reformatory in Massachusetts built a nursery in 1880 and encouraged all of the women to visit and care for the babies. "This 'communal' maternal care proved to be, in many ways, the most effective therapy" (Janusz, 1991, 11). More recently, social workers have decided whether babies born to pregnant prisoners would be cared for by relatives or put up for adoption (Baunach and Murton, 1973). Ironically, the women's prisons champion gender-stereotyped roles at the same time that they tend to ignore "mother–infant bonding or the fostering of female convicts' mothering skills as central to their rehabilitation" (Dodge, 2002, p. 245).

Some places in Denmark, England, Russia, Taiwan, Jamaica, Peru, India, and Canada allow women to keep children up to 5 or 6 years old (Henriques, 1994; Vachon, 1994; Weintraub, 1987). A comparative study of women's prisons reported that children forbidden from living with their incarcerated mothers frequently ended up on the streets (Weintraub 1987). Overall, flexibility to allow contact and maintain the mother–child relationship appears to be limited in the United States. Only two out of five prisons allow extended visits between mothers and children (American Correctional Association, 1990). A few U.S. women's prisons still allow infants to live in the prisons, sometimes up to the age of 2 (Baunach, 1982, 1992; Haft, 1980; Haley, 1980; Heidensohn, 1985; Holt, 1982; McCarthy, 1980; Schupak, 1986).

Most U.S. women's prisons with nurseries house the babies only temporarily, until placement with foster parents or other caregivers is determined (Boudouris, 1985; Pollock, 2002b). One recent study found that while several state prisons had accommodations for babies in the early part of the 1900s, "only four states—New York, California, Nebraska, and South Dakota—continue to allow women to spend any length of time with their newborns today" (Pollock, 2002a, 144). Fewer than half of the jails allow women contact visitation (where they can touch, hold, and move freely) with children, but all U.S. women's prisons allow mothers contact visitation with their children (American Correctional Association, 1990). Over half of incarcerated women in one study reported that their children had never visited them in prison, with the most-cited reason being the great distance between the children's home and the prison (Bloom, 1993). It can be disconcerting to children, especially young children, to have limited communications with their mothers, especially if they are feeling abandoned. Moreover, it is not uncommon for U.S. prisoners to be allowed only one fifteen-minute (collect) phone call per month.

Incarcerated women's children are cared for by relatives, state foster homes, or other institutions. "One of the most painful problems confronting mothers in prison is the possibility of gradual loss of their children. . . . There is also the feeling of helplessness arising from concern for the welfare of children" (Fox, 1975, 192). Many women justifiably worry that it will be difficult or impossible to regain custody from a foster parent or relative when they are released from prison. There are also cases of fathers who "disappear" with the children during the mothers' incarceration. Child welfare laws allow "termination of parental rights if the parent has failed to maintain an adequate relationship with a child who is in foster care," a scenario many incarcerated mothers, particularly single mothers, face (Bloom, 1993, 66). Indeed there is some history of prison sentences alone being used as reasons to negate parental rights for women (Haley, 1980; Knight, 1992), if not directly, than indirectly, even today (Pollock, 2002). Research documents that some incarcerated women report having to send their children to the parents or guardians who abused them as children (Maeve, 1998; Sharp and Marcus-Mendoza, 2001). Furthermore, the 1997 Adoption of Safe Families Act allows the termination of custody for incarcerated mothers whose children were placed in foster care for 15 or more months (Raeder, 2003). Other child welfare policies also work to the disadvantage of incarcerated mothers committed to maintaining custody of dependent children (Luke, 2002). Inherent in many of these policies, laws, and practices is institutionalized discrimination against single mothers who likely have fewer alternatives for caretakers (Raeder, 2003). Ironically, incarcerated women are more likely than incarcerated men to have their parental rights revoked (Fletcher and Moon, 1993b).

Not surprisingly, one of the first goals of many women released from prison is to reestablish custody of their children. They may first be required to prove that they have stable housing and employment, which is difficult for anyone leaving prison. Even getting back on welfare can be time consuming because of the enormous amount of "red tape." Often the woman is placed in a position of having to borrow from loan sharks or friends and family (Stanton, 1980). Moreover, a number of jailed mothers report desertion or divorce by their male partners or husbands while incarcerated (ibid.). In conclusion, it is ironic that prisons have unabashedly programmed female offenders into their "proper" gender roles as wives and mothers but simultaneously make few or no provisions for them to maintain contact with even their youngest children (Haft, 1980; Knight, 1992; Sarri, 1987).

EDUCATIONAL, VOCATIONAL, AND RECREATIONAL PROGRAMS

Women prisoners have typically been viewed as unworthy of or not smart enough for training or education, thus confirming their dependent status in and out of prison. "In general, treatment and training programs for female offenders are distinctively poorer in quantity, quality, and variety, and considerably different in nature from those for male offenders" (Ross and Fabiano, 1986). Moreover, frequently women have less access to or are simply excluded from educational and vocational opportunities, work release programs, halfway houses, furloughs, and other programs available to incarcerated men in the United States (Janusz, 1991; Pollock, 2002; Rafter, 1989). (This is not to imply that education and training programs in men's prisons are adequate or should be the model.) Indeed, most of the lawsuits brought by incarcerated women in the past few decades have to do with sex discrimination in access to equal treatment, for example, regarding disparity in recreational facilities, the size of their cells, and so on (Rafter, 1989): "All [sex discrimination lawsuits brought by incarcerated women] contrast the conditions of male and female prisoners; conclude that women's conditions are poorer; and argue that the differences constitute sex discrimination in violation of the Fourteenth Amendment's Equal Protection Clause" (ibid., 90).

Historically, the justifications offered for discrimination against women prisoners include that they are not major "breadwinners" or in need of remunerative employment (Smart, 1976). Although this situation has improved somewhat, there is still a theme in prison programming for women to reflect society's bias that the most acceptable roles for women are those of mother and wife (Carlen, 1983; Diaz–Cotto, 1996; Feinman, 1983; Natalizia, 1991). The focus on women as domestic servants or wives and mothers clearly belies the vast and growing number of single women who are heads of households. Furthermore, assumptions about who "deserves" jobs and programs are often sexist. Other excuses offered for the lack of women's prison programs argue that women constitute a small portion of prisoners and that they are in prison for relatively short time periods compared to men. Few work assignments are available to women incarcerated in the United States; those that exist "are not considered prison industries with marketable job skills" (American Correctional Association, 1990, 38). It should be noted that programs in jails are even more limited for incarcerated women than in the prisons (Glick and Neto, 1982; Gray, Mays, and Stohr, 1995) and that work-release programs are far more available to incarcerated men than to incarcerated women (Diaz–Cotto, 1996; Ross and Fabiano, 1986). Indeed, at least through the 1980s, few changes were made in the programs and opportunities offered to women prisoners since the beginning of the 1900s (Sarri, 1987).

Historically, women's prisons have had programs in cosmetology, office skills, typing, sewing, hairdressing, and homemaking, but few train women in skills to help them become financially independent on their release. This is particularly troubling when examining the gender differences in educational and vocational programs in prisons: "[W]hereas men may have access to programs in welding, electronics, construction, tailoring, computers, and plumbing, and to college programs, women may have cosmetology, and child-care, keypunch, and nurse's aide programs, and often high school is the only education available to women" (Pollock, 2002, 56). Diaz–Cotto's (1996, 284) study of New Bedford Prison in Massachusetts reported that vocational classes offered in the 1970s were data processing and cosmetology, but during the 1980s, the programming broadened to also include electronics, general business education, building maintenance, computer programming, commercial art, food service, and printing. She reports that in the 1980s, occasionally vocational training in nontraditional ("men's") jobs was implemented (e.g., auto mechanics), but it never lasted long due to factors such as the inability to place women in these jobs upon release, staff resistance, and competion with support for programs in men's prisons. Given that the traumatic childhoods of many imprisoned women "may threaten their ability to parent effectively when they are home with their children," parenting programs are needed in women's prisons (Myers et al., 1999) (and also in men's, for that matter).

Furthermore, women prisoners who have questioned policies and attempted to change their restricted educational and vocational opportunities are often punished—sometimes with long periods in solitary confinement (Sarri, 1987). While some legal cases have successfully challenged the sex discrimination in prison vocational programs and educational opportunities, the decisions of the federal courts "have had little impact because of prison overcrowding, the dominance and resistance of male administrators, the punitive attitudes of legislators and court officials, and the fact that many social action organizations have ignored the plight of these offenders" (ibid., 417).

Both the prisoners and the staff rank education as the most valuable resource for women during incarceration (Glick and Neto, 1982; Mawby, 1982). Women prisoners typically have less education prior to incarceration than men do (e.g., Sharp et al., 1999); less than one-third of all incarcerated females hold a high school degree at intake (American Correctional Association, 1990). Moreover, women with more education prior to incarceration are the most likely to participate in prison educational programs (Mawby, 1982). A study on coed prisons found that the women were more likely than the men to request academic programs, while women and men were equally likely to request vocational programs (Wilson, 1980). A recent study found that while incarcerated women who acquired GEDs were less likely to recidivate (than women without them, the hypothesized relationship), the women's completion of a vocational-technical program actually *decreased* their time for recidivism (the opposite of the hypothesized relationship). The author speculates that this might be because the vo-tech programs are either unmarketable or they unrealistically raise the hopes of the women who complete them (Brewster, 2003).

Research has also found sex discrimination in the availability of activities for incarcerated men and women. A study in Scotland found that male prisoners were allowed to play darts, cards, ping-pong, dominoes, and so on, whereas these activities were unavailable to imprisoned women (Carlen, 1983). Another study reported, as if this were perfectly normal and acceptable, that an activity called the "Hen House" provided an opportunity for the women in a coed prison to get together with the staff wives to make Christmas cookies and spend the evening sewing, knitting, and talking (Campbell, 1980). Men's prisons have vastly better recreational facilities and programs, based on the myth that men need more physical exertion than women (Goetting, 1987). Apparently there is a related assumption that men are more in need of heterosexual contact than women, given that some states allow male prisoners conjugal visits, while providing no such opportunity for female prisoners (Boudouris, 1985).

Little research addresses gender differences among prisoners and access to religious and spiritual opportunities. An exception to this is Luana Ross's (2000) description of how the American Indian Religious Freedom Act of 1978 affected incarcerated Native men more than Native women. This act states that "imprisoned Natives have the right to fully practice their Native traditions" (ibid., 141). In her study of Montana, Ross reports that White women and men have "full access" to their Judeo-Christian–based religions and Native men have access to the sweat lodge, but Native women do not have access to a sweat lodge, which Ross points out is a violation of the 1978 act.

Although little research exists examining women incarcerated in jails, two such studies indicate that the gender discrimination in jails is similar to that in prisons, although likely even worse (Gray, Mays, and Stohr, 1995; Prendergast, Wellisch, and Falkin, 1995). One of these studies reported that the major finding was that, with the exception of treatment programs provided by community groups, such as Alcoholics Anonymous and Narcotics Anonymous, "the programming in women's jails is woefully inadequate" (Gray, Mays, and Stohr, 1995). Only 12 percent of the women received any educational, vocational, or work training or programming, despite the sample of women reporting these as their top-priority program desires. The jail administrators claimed they were constrained by their budget to provide better programming for these jailed women. Despite high rates of the incarcerated women's reports of sexual victimization, only about 4 percent of the women had access to programs on this topic (ibid.).

Scholars have suggested that for both prisons and jails, one partial solution to provide better programming and treatment is to expand the utilization of community volunteer and private resources (Gray, Mays, and Stohr, 1995; Rafter, 1989). These could include violence-against-women organizations, drug programs, and so on.

HEALTH CARE SERVICES

"If one were to rank population subgroups by the seriousness of their health problems, female prisoners would be located near the top of the ladder" (Anderson, 2003, 50). Overall, incarcerated women have more serious health problems than women outside of prison because of their increased likelihood of living in poverty, limited access to preventive medical care, poor nutrition, chemical dependency, and limited education on health matters (see Anderson, 2003; Girshick, 1999; Maeve, 1999a; Ross and Fabiano, 1986; Pollock, 1998, 2002). The historical neglect of women prisoners combined with the massive increase in women's incarceration in recent years has resulted in a health crisis for these women (Anderson, 2003).

The health care in women's prisons is lacking in both quantity (availability) and quality (Compton-Wallace, 2003; Pollock, 1998, 2002; Zaitzow and West, 2003). One of the major problems in women's prisons is the lack of skilled and available medical care (Compton-Wallace, 2003; Fletcher and Moon, 1993a; Pollock, 2002; Resnick and Shaw, 1980). In fact, most lawsuits filed by or on behalf of incarcerated women are for problems in receiving medical services (American Correctional Association, 1990; Aylward and Thomas, 1984; Maeve, 1999a). Access to medical care is difficult for women prisoners, and the staff often patronize and minimize the prisoners' requests for medical care (Compton-Wallace, 2003; Dobash, Dobash, and Gutteridge, 1986).

Maeve's (1999a) in-depth work with incarcerated women traces the important ways that abusive, traumatic, neglect-filled, and poverty-ridden childhoods exacerbate incarcerated women's health perceptions and issues and construct their perceptions of health care. More specifically, she found that the incarcerated women sexually abused as children often adopted a complex self-view as "evil woman" (blaming themselves for the abuse) and internalized anger for experiencing the abuse and anger at the abuser. The people with the authority to help them were often the same people who abused them. This is not unlike many nonincarcerated women with child sexual abuse histories, but Maeve reports that poverty combined with "unrelenting abuse" often leads to "nihilism, despair, and ultimately self- and community-harming behaviors" for these women (ibid., 61). She contrasts nonprisoners, who view health care as an individual responsibility and a right, to incarcerated women, who view access to health care as both *punishment* (because they only had access to health care when they were in jail or prison) and *protection* (because health care in the United States is reserved for "good" and privileged people). Similarly, Moe and Ferraro's (2003, 62) work reports incarcerated women's conflicted evaluations of their health care as "dismal and inadequate, while simultaneously better than what could often be obtained on 'the outside.'" But because the women must access prison health care through a myriad of rules and red tape, they rarely "find any resolution to their health problems in prison, and if anything, become less healthy" (Maeve, 1999a, 66). Thus, what could be a unique opportunity to empower and educate women heretofore without access to health care and education does little good and too often further damages them. At the same time, some of the women in Girshick's (1999) study stated that while they struggled with the many limitations and lack of resources in the prison, prison was a way to escape some of the other stresses in their lives, such as staying off drugs, abusive husbands/boyfriends, and being able to get a GED or job training. Some women made references to suicide and stated that prison turned their lives around.

HIV/AIDS

Although the media and individuals often express the concern that sex workers are tempting and infecting their male customers, the medical evidence is that HIV is far more likely to be spread from men to women (Farley and Kelly, 2000). The epidemic of women with HIV/AIDS is a crisis in women's prisons largely because of the sex-work and drug-abuse backgrounds of many of these women (Anderson, 2003; Maeve, 1999a; Mullings, Marquart, and Brewer, 2000; Sterk, 1999; Zaitzow and West, 2003). Furthermore, child sexual abuse survivors, which are disproportionately high among women prisoners, have exceptionally high rates of HIV/AIDS (Farley and Kelly, 2000; Mullings, Marquart, and Brewer, 2000; Sterk, 1999). Thus, it is hardly surprising that female prisoners are more likely than male prisoners to test HIV-positive

(Greenfeld and Snell, 1999; Hankins et al., 1994; Lawson and Fawkes, 1993; Maeve, 1999a). In 1997, about 2,200, or 3.5 percent, of women in state prisons in the United States tested positive for HIV, while 2.2 percent of the male prison population was HIV-positive (Greenfeld and Snell, 1999). "The percentage of the female inmate population that was HIV-positive peaked in 1993 at 4.2 percent" (ibid.). A Canadian study reported that 6.9 percent of the incarcerated women tested HIV-positive and that 13 percent of those with drug injection histories and 13 percent of those reporting prostitution as their primary income source prior to incarceration tested HIV-positive (Hankins et al., 1994). Notably, a warden at one Northeastern women's prison reported that between 25 and 30 percent tested HIV-positive in the prison's routine testing for the virus, a much higher rate than other studies indicate (Acoca, 1998a). Research on crack-addicted women reports the difficulties these women encountered in requiring condoms from both their intimate partners (who are often drug users as well) and their clients if the women are sex workers (Sterk, 1999). In sum, HIV medication and caretaking is yet another area where the medical facilities are sorely lacking in responding to incarcerated women (see Acoca, 1998a; Clark and Boudin, 1990; Compton-Wallace, 2003; Hankins et al., 1994; Lawson and Fawkes, 1993).

Prenatal, Pregnancy, and Postpartum Health Care

Given that most of incarcerated women's increased needs for medical attention (relative to incarcerated men's needs) are related to gynecological issues, it is problematic that one in five U.S. women's prisons do not have gynecological/ obstetrical services available at least once a week (American Correctional Association, 1990). In addition to standard medical treatment, some of the concerns include "the detection and treatment of sexually transmitted infections; cancer examinations (breast and pelvic); general gynecological care; prenatal, childbirth, and postpartum care; abortion; menstrual problems; and problems associated with poor nutrition and the abuse of drugs" (Ross and Fabiano, 1986, 52).

Especially poignant are the medical needs of incarcerated pregnant women and girls. Although pregnancy tests do not appear to be routine in the intake of women prisoners, research suggest that between 5 and 6 percent of U.S. women offenders are pregnant at intake into jails or prisons (American Correctional Association, 1990; Greenfeld and Snell, 1999). Another study estimated that 9 percent of all incarcerated women are pregnant (Bloom and Steinhart, 1993). Still others estimate that one-quarter of women prisoners either were pregnant at intake or gave birth during the previous year (Church, 1990). Given the large and growing number of incarcerated females, this is not an insignificant number.

Women's prisons often fail to provide prenatal care or even appropriate nutrition, such as milk (Barry, 1991; Daane, 2003; Mann, 1984; McHugh, 1980; Resnick and Shaw, 1980), or care for chemically dependent pregnant women and their fetuses or babies (Acoca, 1998b; Daane, 2003). A survey of

U.S. women's prisons found that (1) less than half provided prenatal care, (2) only 15 percent provided special diets and nutritional programs for pregnant women, (3) only 15 percent provided counseling to help mothers find suitable placement for the infant after birth, and (4) only 11 percent provided postnatal counseling (Wooldredge and Masters, 1993). Additionally, the wardens listed the following as problems not addressed in the survey: (1) inadequate resources for false labors, premature births, and miscarriages; (2) a lack of maternity clothes; (3) a requirement for prisoners in labor to wear belly chains on the way to the hospital; and (4) the housing of minimum-security pregnant women in maximum-security prisons (ibid.). A more recent governmental report indicated that about half of those pregnant when jailed and four-fifths of those pregnant when admitted to state prisons receive prenatal care; however, there was no indication of the quality of this care (Greenfeld and Snell, 1999).

In addition to inadequate medical care, pregnant and postpartum prisoners often face considerable hostility and resentment for their "special" medical and physical needs and face discrimination by the staff (Compton-Wallace, 2003; Holt, 1982; McHugh, 1980). Relatively recent research details outright physical abuse of pregnant girls by police and juvenile hall staff (Acoca, 1998b), and there is some indication that women with gynecological complaints are given unnecessary hysterectomies (McHugh, 1980). Ironically, while the prison system seems to be intolerant of offending women procreating and has a history of forced abortions, sterilizations, and adoptions, there appears to be little effort to educate incarcerated women and girls on birth control and their gynecological health.

Many pregnant women in prisons and jails still face horrible conditions when they go into labor (Vaughn and Smith, 1999). Furthermore, after delivering their babies and being forced to give them up for adoption, many suffer from not being given medication to dry up their breast milk, which not only often results in breast infections but also increases their sense of loss and depression (Acoca and Austin, 1996). Research has established that the conditions for pregnant women housed in jails are equally deplorable or worse (Barry, 1991).

MENTAL HEALTH PROBLEMS AND CARE

Now turning to mental health, it has been pointed out that mental illness is often the cause of behaviors criminalized by the state resulting in incarceration, which further exacerbates the mental illness (Suh, 2000). Additionally, the abusive and traumatic backgrounds of most incarcerated women, not surprisingly, typically result in a serious amount of depression and even posttraumatic stress disorder (PTSD) (Farley and Kelly, 2000; Marcus-Mendoza and Wright, 2003; Pollock, 2002). The overlap between sexual abuse, chemical dependency, and mental health problems is significant for incarcerated women (Mullings, Pollock, and Crouch, 2002; Singer et al., 1995). Most drug-treatment programs in women's prisons are drug education classes, typically twelve-step programs designed for male addicts (Mullings, Pollock, and Crouch, 2002). At the same time, substance-using incarcerated women were far more likely than non-substance-using incarcerated women to report violent victimizations as children, violent victimizations as adults, and greater likelihood of seeking mental health help in the past; to be diagnosed with a mental health problem; and to have ideated or attempted suicide (ibid.). While one study found that incarcerated women positively evaluated self-help substance abuse programs, they were also worried that these programs failed to address "the long-standing, serious problems which contributed to their drug use, such as abuse and mental illness, nor the drug-using milieu which awaited them upon release" (Moe and Ferraro, 2003, 69).

The psychological strain of being a pregnant prisoner is also evident. Owen (1998) found that pregnant women's presence alone was hard on women separated from their dependent children outside of prison. She also reported "pains of pregnancy" for prisoners. "First, many women report that being pregnant in prison was an 'ugly feeling.' Second, not having a place to send one's child was very painful. . . . Third, many women said that returning to prison after giving birth was extremely difficult" (ibid., 101–102).

In one study on incarcerated women, more than one in five reported attempting suicide in the past (Holley and Brewster, 1996). Another study reported that 45 percent of incarcerated women in the United States need mental health treatment (Acoca and Austin, 1996). Perhaps not surprisingly, then, one study of women's prisons found that social workers were more accessible than medical personnel. (Of course, they are much less costly than physicians, too.) Unfortunately, the social workers' time was consumed with responding to the women's practical concerns (such as contact with children, legal and court problems, and securing employment and housing on release), limiting their abilities to provide counseling (Dobash, Dobash, and Gutteridge, 1986). The psychiatrists available to the prisoners were more concerned with the women's criminal and mental health histories than with the stresses of incarceration, and the women requesting psychiatric help were often labeled mentally unstable. Therapy, consistent with other programs in women's reformatories, was considered "successful" when gender stereotypes, such as dependence and compliance, were reestablished (Dobash, Dobash, and Gutteridge, 1986). Similar findings on mental health responses to incarcerated women were reported in a more recent study (Compton-Wallace, 2003). On a more encouraging note, a recent study found incarcerated women were very positive about "general counseling" that was a program addressing domestic violence and anger management through watching videos and discussing them. They found this approach supportive and something they would not be able to do outside of prison (Moe and Ferraro, 2003).

But worse than deficiency, some studies have found the medical "care" in women's prisons to be abusive, with the psychiatrists among the "worst offenders" (Faith, 1993b, 257). Faith (ibid.) recounts stories of imprisoned women coerced into being guinea pigs to test ineffective medications, psychiatrists who viewed and treated all incarcerated women's problems as "penis envy," and hysterectomies given indiscriminately to large numbers of women by unaccredited medical establishments and retired general practitioners with no gynecology experiences. In my own research, incarcerated women reported horrific practices by the dentist, including not changing gloves between patients, talking on the phone while removing teeth, and ignoring all dental needs (including cleaning and filling teeth) except pulling teeth (Belknap, 2000). Although the physicians appeared to be less abusive, the women reported waiting so long to see a doctor that by the time they saw one, sometimes weeks later, they no longer had the condition (ibid.). Other studies report the staff and administration ignoring serious health crises for imprisoned women, until it is too late to save the woman's life (e.g., Wallace-Compton, 2003).

INCARCERATED WOMEN AND GIRLS
WITH DISABILITIES

A study of delinquent youth in Ohio reported severe learning problems, including speech and language disorders, in almost one-fifth of the sample, far exceeding the general population (Davis et al., 1991). In addition to recognizing that medical needs for prisoners may be gendered, it is important to recognize varied needs among offending women and girls. Rarely addressed is the topic of incarcerated women and girls with physical and/or mental disabilities. In her historical account of women incarcerated in the West, Butler (1997) notes the high rate of deaf women, wondering if they had the opportunity to communicate in the processing of the crime charges that led them to prison. She reported that the guards and wardens had little concern for the blind and deaf women. "Disabled prisoners, confused by their surroundings, hampered by narrow societal perceptions, and removed from even the semblance of care, must have yielded to fear, anger, and depression," which "further alienated them from a disinterested administration" (ibid., 156–157).

Owen (1998) briefly discusses issues for incarcerated women in wheelchairs in her study of a California women's prison. She discusses how these women are more restricted in the prison, largely given their greater reliance on staff. She states: "Women in wheelchairs have specific problems in the prison world such as mobility, obtaining specialized care, developing a satisfactory program, and establishing satisfactory relationships with other prisoners" (ibid., 102). Acoca (1998a) begins an article on incarcerated women's health with a prisoner in a wheelchair who is badly sunburned after being left out in the yard. Maeve (1999a) provides anecdotal data on an incarcerated woman whose hearing was damaged by antibiotics as a child and who then lost most of the rest of her hearing after being pistol-whipped by her boyfriend shortly before her incarceration. She was 31, HIV-positive and in prison for the first time, and was placed in isolation where the health care providers had little access to her and could only yell through a door where they could not be heard (ibid.). The most comprehensive study of incarcerated women's disabilities was a large survey of Oklahoman women. Two-fifths of the women reported impaired vision, over 5 percent reported a hearing impairment, and one-fifth indicated a physical disability (Holley and Brewster, 1996).

In conclusion, the few studies that address women prisoners who are physically disabled suggest quite dire implications. More research is needed in this area. Additionally, a growing problem regarding the health needs of incarcerated women concerns older women, particularly given that traditional prison health care systems are "designed for young, healthy men" (Reviere and Young, 2004).

THE PRISON SUBCULTURE

The information reported to this point suggests that just about everything that is bad in men's prisons is worse in women's prisons (e.g., the increase in incarceration rates; HIV rates; proximity to friends and family; access to educational, vocational, medical, and recreational programs and professionals; and possibly the disproportionate number of prisoners of color). However, one significant gender distinction that is arguably in favor of women is the prison subculture, particularly how the prisoners treat each other. The prison subculture has to do with prisoners' norms and values and the adjustment and coping prisoners do to counterbalance the negative aspects of confinement (Hart, 1995, 71). Owen (1998, 63) states: "In the simplest sense, a study of prison is about doing time." She reports that in a practical sense, "the majority of women shape the day around a job, vocational training, or a school assignment" (ibid., 103). However, it is useful to remember the incarcerated women are individuals who "do time" differently, often dependent on their age, ethnicity, class, family relations, abuse histories, and sexual orientation (Bosworth, 1999), and just as women's experiences outside of prison are diverse, so are their prison experiences (Kruttschnitt, Gartner, and Miller, 2000). Girshick (1999, 82) found incarcerated women's adaptation to prison was based on "acceptance [realize you are in prison and make the best of it], isolation, state families, religious dedication and resignation." Similarly, Butler (1997) identified various strategies adopted by individual women, including compliance (submissive), resistance (rebellious), acting alone, and acting in concert with other prisoners. Some of the women "chose escape through death. Many endured a day-to-day stoicism until release" (ibid., 17).

There is speculation that males are more likely to adapt to incarceration by isolating themselves, while females, conversely, adjust by forming close relationships with other prisoners (Fox, 1975. Maeve, 1999b). The friendships and networks women prisoners form are based on a variety of characteristics. Diaz-Cotto (1996, 295) describes this best: "Women prisoners generally formed informal groups based on housing assignments, race and ethnicity, homegirl networks, social and recreational activities, prison family/kinship networks, and political underground reform-oriented activities.... Latinas further subdivided according to nationality and language spoken." Girshick (1999) states that most of the women find it difficult to trust anyone and are most likely to trust other prisoners from their own "home" towns. Kruttschnitt and her colleagues (2000) also found a significant lack of trust but that it varied across the prisons they studied. Most women reported friendship networks of one or two other prisoners, not groups of other women. She also found that while women interacted regularly across race/ethnicity, there was often an underlying level of racial prejudice. However, another study found that racial differences among the women were not a source of conflict and did not impact the prisoners' relationships (Kruttschnitt, 2000).

Research assessing how "doing time" varies across incarcerated women suggests there are no significant racial differences regarding how women relate and adapt to the institution and those around them, whether they were politically active, socially isolated, resistant, or religious (Kruttschnitt, Gartner, and Miller, 2000; Owen, 1998). However, social class impacted women's reactions to prison. Those few prisoners from middle-class backgrounds were far more likely to bring up their class and found the initial adaptation to prison far more difficult. Some of the poorer prisoners speculated it was because conditions in the prison were better than those many poor women experienced outside of prison (Kruttschnitt, Gartner, and Miller, 2000). Age was also somewhat of a predictor of how the women "did time." Women under 30 reported a broad range of prison experiences, from good to terrible, whereas women in their 30s seemed comfortable with the prison life and code. The older "lifers" (women with life sentences who had been in prison for a long time) largely reported coming into prison depressed or rebellious, but they learned to develop a resigned attitude (ibid.). The women in their 40s and older who were not life-term prisoners, like the women under 30, were varied in their responses of doing time. Some isolated themselves from others, and many had been in prison before and found the routine easier to come back to. Regardless of how long they had been in prison, the older prisoners viewed the younger prisoners as difficult to understand and get along with and viewed them with some disdain for seeing prison as a game (ibid.). Notably, some women who were survivors of abuse outside of the prison, particularly intimate-partner abuse, reported similarities in experiencing the abuse outside of prison with the prison experience (ibid.). Doing time was also impacted by the culture of the prison staff; not surprisingly, in institutions where the staff was less hostile and more respectful to the prisoners, the prisoners evaluated their experiences more positively.

Gender differences in the prison/jail subculture is evidenced by a study reporting the implementation of a state-of-the-art "new generation" jail that was experienced very differently by incarcerated men and women, with men reporting far higher satisfaction than women (Jackson and Stearns, 1995). This gender difference was largely explained by a changed "guarding" style of a direct supervision structure designed to "undermine negative peer relationships" through dismantling power hierarchies (ibid., 216). The overall male evaluation was strong support, and the overall female reaction was one of dissatisfaction. The authors report that the new style "may not necessarily be well-suited to handle more dependent, cooperative, family-like relationships that exist among female inmates" (ibid.). The study concluded that the "new generation" design assumed a male prisoner and thus focused on what would overcome the problems in men's jails, wrongly assuming that what worked for males would work for females, despite very different peer relations (Jackson and Stearns, 1995).

In contrast to the gendered nature of women prisoners' tighter relationships with each other relative to men prisoners, some research suggests that male prisoners "stick together" in adherence to the "convict code" more so than female prisoners do (Kruttschnitt, 1981; Owen, 1998). The women in Owen's (1998, 73) study report that this is because they are more afraid than the men prisoners of losing days (due to rule violations) because they are more stressed out about their families outside of prison. "[F]or many women, reuniting with their children becomes a primary goal and acts as a form of informal social control during the days in prison" (ibid., 120). Similarly, Diaz-Cotto's (1996, 271) analysis of women prisoners in the 1960s and 1970s points out that the women tended to prioritize "family matters over other concerns," such as engaging in work strikes, riots, or widespread litigation. A result of this was that they were seen as "apolitical" relative to incarcerated men who were active, and women's "apolitical" practices deemed them as unworthy by the media, Department of Corrections administrators, and others of the reform and support offered to some of the more political and active male prisoners at that time. Thus, women prisoners tend to focus more on how they are going to get out as quickly as they can to be reunited with family, while the male prisoners appear to feel more empowered to fight the oppressions in the prisons. Further, Owen (1998, 120) claims that the primacy of incarcerated women's relationships with their children "has an impact on the values shaping prison culture in several ways, such as making conversations about children sacred, acknowledging the intensity and grief attached to these relationships, sanctioning those with histories of hurting children, and other child-specific cultural beliefs or behaviors." However, Diaz-Cotto (1996, 298) reports that pseudofamilies (which she refers to as "prison family/kinship networks") "were created to address a wide range of prisoner concerns. While the politicizing capability of such groups has generally been denied or ignored by social scientists, their structure included the potential for contributing to prisoner politicization and reform-oriented organizing."

Despite the consistent findings that imprisoned women and girls are far kinder to each other than institutionalized males, the focus on gender differences in the prison subculture has been almost exclusively on how incarcerated women (and girls) are far more likely than incarcerated men (and boys) to form close emotional and sexual bonds with each other. Some rather dated (and often homophobic) research suggests that females' socialization to be caring and to value family relationships has resulted in the structuring of pseudofamilies in women's prisons and girls' juvenile institutions (see Carter, 1981; Ford, 1929; Giallombardo, 1966, 1974). Despite the homophobic context in which these early studies presented the pseudofamilies and lesbian relationships, more recent research also identifies the existence of the pseudofamilies but not through a homophobic lens (e.g., Bowker, 1981; Girshick, 1999; Owen, 1998). Rather, these studies suggest that pseudofamilies are a logical extension for incarcerated women, who, like most women, have "been socialized to concentrate their energies on family relationships [...] women presumably miss these relationships more than men do and therefore create pseudofamilies to replace lost familial relationships" (Bowker, 1981, 415). Mann (1984) reported that both heterosexual and lesbian girls and women are in these "family" systems, although not all incarcerated females are in a "family." A recent study of girls tried and convicted as adults and serving time in an adult women's prison found that whereas most of the girls reported some negative experiences with the adult prisoners, none "reported unwanted sexual behaviors outside of verbal remarks" (Gaarder and Belknap, 2004, 64–65). All girls (almost one-fifth) who reported sexual involvement with adult woman prisoners indicated the relationships were consensual, and some girls discussed adult prisoners they called "Mom" who "babied" and mothered them (ibid., 66).

Some research from the 1980s suggests that the pseudofamilies were either exaggerated in earlier studies or became less common in women's prisons (Bowker, 1981; Mahan, 1984; Mawby, 1982). What is clear is that incarcerated women's romantic or sexual interest with each other has been carefully monitored in most institutions, starting with reformatories (Dodge, 2002). Ironically, the reformatory climate intended to make women subservient instead cultivated defiance, providing a powerful inmate subculture (Dodge, 2002). However, given that women are raised to value others and friendship more than men are, it should not be surprising that incarcerated women form closer and more intimate bonds than incarcerated men. An example of this is a recent study assessing gender differences in prisoners' reported levels of social support (Hart, 1995). "Social support refers to interpersonal ties that are rewarding to and protective of an individual" (ibid., 68). Similar to studies on nonincarcerated populations, Hart (ibid.) found that women prisoners report higher levels of social support than men prisoners and that in women's prison there was a relationship between social support and psychological well-being, whereas no such relationship existed in men's prisons.

The partnerships in these prison families are not necessarily sexual. In fact, many of the lesbian relationships reported in prison are based more on affection with a sexual connotation than actual sexual activity (Pollock, 2002). Furthermore, while some women and girls arrive at prison or juvenile institutions already identifying themselves as lesbians, others assume a lesbian status only while incarcerated, and others "come out" as lesbians while institutionalized and maintain this status after their release (see, for example, Diaz-Cotto, 1996; Girshick, 1999). As in the world outside of prison, this confirms a high degree of both lesbianism and bisexuality. Owen's (1998, 138) study of almost 300 women in a California prison reported that some women come into prison "straight" and stay that way, while others come in lesbian and stay that way, and still others, while identifying as lesbian before coming to prison, "avoid any sexual or emotional entanglements while in prison." Faith's (1993b) thoughtful research on this topic provides insight. First, she states that not all incarcerated women who love another woman prisoner are "lesbian" (ibid., 214). Second, she notes that some incarcerated women who "learn to love" another woman in prison learn to love themselves in the process. Specifically, she addresses, often through incarcerated women's own words, how these first experiences of loving another woman were the first times they had someone who knew a lot about them still love them and how they came to feel better about themselves and their bodies through this love of another woman (ibid.). Girshick (1999) believes that most of these sexual relationships are driven by the desire for emotional closeness. Faith (1993b) does not view these woman-loving-woman relationships as simply a replacement because the women have no men available to love but rather observes that many of the women who have their first lesbian experience in prison "discover they are attracted to women in their own right." Moreover, Faith states:

> Prisons tend to intensify every emotion, and when women fall in love it can become a consuming passion even if the circumstances prevent sexual contact. As is the case with many lesbians in the "free" world, for women in prison sexual passion is often subordinate to the shared emotional comfort, social camaraderie, spiritual communion and political connectedness that can be achieved in balanced relationships. (ibid., 215)

Owen (1998, 146) reports that same-sex relationships are sometimes the source of fights in the prison; given their intensity, "jealousy seems to be at the base of many of the [prison] conflicts." Maeve (1999b) discusses the ways in which women prisoners have taken on all the guilt and "the bad girl" identification both from their child sexual abuse histories and their offending histories, and then if they identify as lesbians in prison, this is one more confirmation to them, supported by the homophobic policies of the prisons, that makes them feel bad about themselves and reinforces their "evil woman" self-images.

Research from the 1970s and 1980s indicates that approximately one-quarter of incarcerated women report involvement in a lesbian relationship (Mawby, 1982; Moyer, 1978). More recent research states that no reliable means are available to identify the number of women in prisons in intimate sexual relationships but that conservative estimates are that between 30 and 60 percent of incarcerated women are in lesbian relationships in prison (Owen, 1998, 138), and may be over 80 percent (Maeve, 1999b). According to one study, the lesbian prisoner relationships typically end when one of the partners is released from prison or the staff separates the women (Moyer, 1978). Notably, one study found that a strict policy against homosexuality in women's prisons is more likely to foster than discourage homosexuality (Mahan, 1984). Moreover, the staff's obsession with deterring homosexuality often results in women being penalized simply for forming friendship bonds with other prisoners. Subsequently, many women report a fear of developing emotional ties with other prisoners, which exacerbates their feelings of isolation and loneliness and their inability to cope with imprisonment (Maeve, 1999b; Moyer, 1980).

Due to the intensity of homophobia, there is a troubling tendency by prison experts/researchers, prison administrators and workers, and lay people alike to mistakenly lump consensual homosexuality and same-sex rape together. This alarming practice is most prevalent when discussing prisons. It is important to distinguish consensual homosexual sex from homosexual rape, just as it is important to distinguish consensual heterosexual sex from heterosexual rape. Given the gender roles and misogyny in the outside world, it is hardly surprising that the subculture in men's prisons views homosexual rape as acceptable, while consensual gay relationships are considered taboo (see Bowker, 1980; Wooden and Parker, 1982). The opposite is true in women's prisons; consensual lesbian relationships are more common and less taboo. The rape of women in prison by other prisoners is rare.

Regarding prisoner-on-prisoner violence, although some research reports that incarcerated females and males are equally violent toward each other, Faith (1993b, 232) explains how this biased presentation occurs: "If men in prison beat up and rape each other it receives little attention because it is so commonplace. Exaggerated perceptions of female violence are formed because when two women get into a serious physical fight it is a noteworthy event." At the same time, Maeve's (1999b) small study on sexual and romantic relationships between women in prison found that many of these pairings ultimately become violent, typically due to jealousy, and this is most common in the couples where there is an identified "male" and "female." Maeve (1999b) carefully describes the impact of severe child sexual abuse histories and the sexist society within and outside of prison that views women through sexual lenses, and how these combine to create (nonsexual) violence in the intimate pairings among women prisoners.

Finally, future research needs to compare and contrast the supportive bonds that both women and men prisoners form that help them survive prison. It is possible that researchers with stereotypical views of gender, emotions, and friendship have overlooked male prisoners' bonds. One woman who was incarcerated in a federal prison and now works with female and male prisoners states:

> I think there are some differences between the way women bond with each other in prison and the way men bond to each other in prison, but I know that it happens in both populations. And I believe it is what allows both men and women to survive prison with at least a little bit of our emotional beings intact. (Swain, 1994)

An important distinction between incarcerated women and incarcerated men reported in some research is the degree to which race is emphasized (Owen, 1998). That is, race is much less of a social organizing factor in women's than men's prisons. This does not mean that racism is never an issue and does not come up in women's prisons, but it seems most likely to be a factor in terms of some types of resources, particularly unfair access to prisoners' jobs (ibid., 154). Ross's (2000) research on incarcerated American Indian women reported strained relationships between them and White women in prison: "[R]acism spilled over into their interactions," and this was largely due to racism regarding Native women's culture, such as ridiculing religion. Diaz-Cotto (1996, 296) reports that although personal and sexual relationships among the women were often interracial and interethnic, "divisions based on race and ethnicity were entrenched enough to make the formation of coalitions among large numbers of prisoners difficult." She describes the unique problem for monolingual Spanish-speaking prisoners, who were forbidden to speak Spanish to anyone. Thus, they were not only penalized when they spoke Spanish but their inability to understand the prison rules, provided only in English, made them more prone to rule infractions they were unaware existed (Diaz-Cotto, 1996, 2000).

SEXUAL ABUSE OF WOMEN PRISONERS

Current research on the incarceration of women and girls rarely mentions sexual abuse by the male staff. Although sexual abuse likely has decreased from earlier times, there has been no systematic research to determine the extent to which it still exists. Research published as recently as the 1970s, however, documented the high risk of women in southern U.S. jails being sexually assaulted by male sheriffs and jail trustees (Sims, 1976). In addition to outright rape, it was not unusual for male staff to coerce or force women and girls into doing sexual "favors" in order to get their basic needs met (for example, food and family contact). Sexual assault of jailed females in the South was overlooked until 1974, when Joan Little, an African American in jail appealing a larceny conviction, struggled with a White male jailer who was trying to orally rape her. During the struggle, the jailer fell on the ice pick he was using to assault her and died. Little's case received national recognition when she claimed she could not get a fair trial in Beaufort County, North Carolina, and she was acquitted after a change of venue (Human Rights Watch Women Rights Project, 1996).

What is apparent from the little scholarly or journalistic research conducted on rape in women's prisons is that sexual abuse perpetrated by prison administrators and guards, much of it extremely violent and all of it inherently coercive, occurs far too commonly. Thus, while male prisoners are more likely to be raped by fellow prisoners than are female prisoners, female prisoners are more likely than their male counterparts to be raped by prison guards or administrators. A powerful documentation of this is a 1996 book by the Human Rights Watch Women's Rights Project entitled *All Too Familiar: Sexual Abuse of Women in U.S. State Prisons*. This book describes not only violent rapes of incarcerated women by male guards but also the vulnerability of many incarcerated women to sexual "relationships" with guards (and other prison staff), which appear consensual at first. For example, the book describes how the sheer loneliness of prison life places women at risk of "falling for" an unprofessional and unethical guard who pursues romantic and sexual relationships.

Accounts of these sexually exploitative guards is similar to the research on lecherous college professors who develop reputations for "hitting on" female students and forming romantic and sexual relationships with them (e.g., Glaser and Thorpe, 1986). In both instances, the incarcerated women as well as the women college students realize too late the seriousness of the power difference and that there is a cadre of women they have (ab)used similarly, often at the same time. To compound the trauma of these exploitative and abusive experiences, a study of sexual abuse of women in U.S. prisons found that the perpetrator himself, other guards, or the entire system frequently retaliated against the women who reported the abuses (Human Rights Watch Women Rights Project, 1996).

Moreover, women who became pregnant from sexual encounters with guards were sometimes forced to have abortions they did not want, one reporting being dragged through abortion protesters at an abortion clinic (ibid.). The "punishment" of the sexual abusers and exploiters in the prison system is similar to findings about sexual harassers: They were simply transferred to other (usually male) prisons (ibid.).

There have been other allegations of women prisoners being sexually assaulted and sexually harassed by male staff (Aylward and Thomas, 1984; Van Ochten, 1993). From May 22 to May 25, 2005, *The Detroit News* reported on an extensive investigation by journalists into the sexual abuse of women incarcerated in Michigan. The reporters, Melvin Claxton, Norman Sinclair, and Ronald J. Hansen (see Claxton, Hanson, and Sinclair, 2005a–d; Hanson, Sinclair, and Claxton, 2005a–c; Sinclair, Claxton, and Hanson, 2005a, b), read thousands of pages of prisoners' statements from the Department of Corrections Internal Affairs and interviewed current and former prisoners and guards and national experts on the topic of the sexual abuse of women prisoners. The resulting newspaper stories in *The Detroit News* documented women who (1) experienced serious sexual assaults at the hands of guards, some of which resulted in pregnancies (and children); (2) struggled to file charges against sexually abusing officers that were ignored by the prison authorities; and (3) killed themselves after the continued sexual abuse that went unchecked. Coercive sex was also rampant where the guards demanded sex for perks. Despite the fact that female prisoners are far more likely to be sexually abused by male guards than male prisoners are to be abused by female guards, there is more sex integration of workers in women's than men's prisons (Goetting, 1987). This is due to the unfounded belief that women workers pose a security risk in men's prisons.

Another point related to sexual abuse in prison is the different way that incarcerated men and women may experience cross-gender searches (Farkas and Rand, 1999). In a 1993 court case, *Jordan v. Gardner* (986 F2d. 1521 Ninth Circuit), the court "appropriately recognized that because of their histories of abuse, female prisoners are more likely to be psychologically harmed by cross-gender [body] searches in prison" (ibid., 33). That is, given the extraordinarily high incidence of abuse in incarcerated women's lives, particularly sexual abuse perpetrated by males, having strip searches performed by males can be extremely traumatic. Farkas and Rand (1999) point out that cross-gender searches for survivors of these abuses are likely counter to any treatment that may be provided by the prison regarding healing from these abuses.

CO-CORRECTIONS

It is important to remember that the first prisons were coed or "co-corrections" (housing women and men in the same institution), although the few women prisoners were typically housed in "special" sections of what were basically men's prisons (Faith, 1993b, 135). While the original and primary goal of women's prison reformers was sex-segregated institutions, in the early 1970s sex-segregated prisons were offered as the major reason for gender inequality in prisons. The first attempt in almost 100 years to reestablish coed prisons occurred in 1971 in Fort Worth, Texas. Although men and women are still housed in separate buildings or cottages, they share some or all prison programs and services in co-corrections (Dodge, 2002; Schweber, 1985). Five federal co-correctional institutions opened in the 1970s, and fifteen state co-correctional facilities were in operation in 1977.

An examination of the early literature on co-corrections suggests that prison administrators and feminists perceived very different potential advantages of co-corrections. Prison administrators who implemented co-corrections in the 1970s hoped that sex integration would normalize the prison experience, making reintegration of ex-prisoners into society easier. To these administrators, an added benefit of co-corrections would be a supposed decrease in homosexual activity. To feminists, the two potential advantages of co-corrections were (1) reducing sex discrimination in prison experiences and increasing women's access to educational, vocational, work, social, and medical programs and activities; and (2) decreasing the chances that women would be detained at a great geographic distance from their children, other family, and friends.

While there is little information to support or refute that co-corrections has increased incarcerated women's likelihood of being near friends and family members, the remaining perceived potential advantages of co-corrections have not been realized. It is difficult, however, to assess most of the research on co-corrections because the research itself is often based on sexist and homophobic assumptions. It is apparent, however, that co-corrections has done little to make things better for imprisoned women (and they may in fact be worse).

The traditional gender roles continue to be encouraged in co-corrections (see Campbell, 1980; Heffernan and Krippel, 1980). For example, women are likely to be given positions subservient to men, who dominate the high-status positions in the prison community (Schweber, 1985); co-corrections men are more likely than co-corrections women to rank the furlough and work/education programs as positive and fairly distributed (Almy et al., 1980); co-corrections men have more freedom to move around the facility than co-corrections women (Chesney-Lind and Rodriguez, 1983); co-corrections women are more likely than co-corrections men to be disciplined (Chesney-Lind and Rodriguez, 1983; Wilson 1980); co-corrections rarely decreases the traditional women's programs; and when men prisoners are "added" to women's prisons to make them co-correctional, the men get many of the best prisoner jobs (Ross and Heffernan, 1980). One study in a co-correctional facility found that women were routinely denied access "to virtually all programs at the facility" (Chesney-Lind and Rodriguez, 1983). Thus, women frequently are the "losers" when co-corrections is implemented (see Rafter, 1989).

> Critics have noted that co-corrections "normalizes" in another way—it places women in a minority situation in which their needs are subordinated in a male-dominated environment. There is nothing about a co-correctional institution which prohibits management from deciding in

allotting programs and services to focus on the needs of the majority—
the men. (Ross and Fabiano, 1986, 66–67)

Nowhere in co-corrections is sex discrimination more obvious than in sexual
control. Both homosexual and heterosexual activity are against institutional
regulations; however, both homosexual and heterosexual activity still occur. In
fact, there is evidence not only of pregnancies occurring during incarceration in
co-correctional facilities but also of prostitution, where women are coerced or
agree to do sexual favors in return for cigarettes or contraband (Chesney-Lind
and Rodriguez, 1983; Heffernan and Krippel, 1980; Ruback, 1980). Although
current information does not exist on the rules for romantic interactions, early
reports indicated that some variation in heterosexual romantic activity was
allowed, although no homosexual romantic behaviors were allowed. For example, some institutions did not allow any physical contact between heterosexuals,
others allowed hand-holding, and still others allowed hand-holding and putting
arms around each other as long as the couple was not lying down (Anderson,
1978). Notably, co-corrections does not appear to have decreased the rate of
homosexuality in the prisons for either women or men (Campbell, 1980; Ross
and Fabiano, 1986).

Women in the co-correctional facilities who are "caught" having heterosexual sex are more likely than men to receive punishment. The burden of
upholding the "no sexual contact" policy in co-correctional facilities falls more
heavily on the women, which has resulted in closer observation of the women
than the men in these facilities (and closer observation of the women in co-
corrections than in women-only prisons) (Schweber, 1985). One study reported
that while 29 men and 29 women were written up for being in a "compromising
sexual situation," 29 women and only 7 men were written up for having sexual
intercourse. This discrepancy was attributed to the fact that women who get
pregnant are automatically "caught" and that even when caught "in the act," men
are somehow better able to avoid identification (Anderson, 1978). In a similar
study, a staff member reported: "When a female gets pregnant by another inmate
in here, it's all hers. There are no attempts to make the father take responsibility
for the child after the initial disciplinary hearings are over" (Mahan, 1984, 235).
When Illinois' Dwight Correctional Center became co-correctional in the mid-
1970s, "several female prisoners became pregnant each year" (Dodge, 2002, 254).

Finally, the obsession with keeping the women and men prisoners separated
in the co-correctional facilities did not prevent the male staff from sexually
harassing and exerting pressure for sexual favors on the women prisoners
(Chesney-Lind and Rodriguez, 1983). One study confirmed reports of staff–
prisoner sexual relations in co-corrections but did not discuss its exploitative
nature (Mahan, 1989). Thus, co-corrections appears to be one of those "nice in
theory, not so great in practice" institutions. Perhaps co-corrections institutions
could provide the best possibility of gender equity in imprisonment regarding the
costs (e.g., distance the prison is from family) and opportunities (e.g., educational,
vocational, medical, and recreational access). Unfortunately, to date, that does
not appear to be the case. Notably, Faith (1993b) reviews a Canadian survey of

convicted women lawbreakers that reports that incarcerated women who have not been in a prison that also holds men tend to believe that they would prefer being held with men. However, those who have experienced co-corrections report being doubly exploited in terms of being treated and perceived as both sex objects and nurturers (Shaw et al., 1990).

By 1984, only six states had co-correctional facilities (Ryan, 1984). Long-term policies toward co-corrections in both state and federal prisons appear to have mostly disappeared by 1989 (Mahan, 1989), although two federal co-correctional institutions remained open as recently as 1994 (Smykla and Williams, 1996). A 1990 survey by the American Correctional Association reported that 45 percent of "correctional" facilities housed both males and females. Faith (1993b, 136) concludes her discussion of co-corrections with the observation that in both the United States and Canada, women continue to be held with men in places "where there are too few women to justify the cost of building separate prisons," despite the poor evaluations of co-corrections.

The availability of programs for women in co-corrections and the degree of interaction allowed between the male and female prisoners vary among institutions (Schweber, 1985). Only about one-third of these facilities allow interactions between females and males during such activities as recreation/leisure, prison programs, dining, and work crews, and 13 percent allow men and women to work together in prison industry (American Correctional Association, 1990, 95). These percentages suggest that the programs and opportunities probably remain separate and unequal. In a more recent comprehensive review of the impact of co-corrections, the general finding was that "co-corrections offers women prisoners few, if any, economic, educational, vocational, and social advantages. Co-corrections benefits male prisoners and system maintenance" (Smykla and Williams, 1996, 61).

In a recent overview of co-correctional prison facilities in the United States, Smykla and Williams (ibid., 74) conclude: "It is disconcerting to find that co-corrections is still beset with divergent policies, wide ranges in the level of policy implementation, inconsistent modes of action, and heated debates about the actual and ideal policies, programs, and objectives." These authors state that co-corrections have been implemented in a manner to "meet the system needs," and by failing to alter standard prison operations in the process when the prison begins to house both males and females, it inevitably fails. They suggest that a key component to making the implementation of co-corrections successful is through the assigned roles and training of the guards in these institutions, who should provide guidance as well as a security role (Smykla and Williams, 1996).

WOMEN AND THE DEATH PENALTY

The first person to receive the death penalty in Canada was a 16-year-old girl convicted of theft in 1640 (Cooper, 1993). Relatively little research has been conducted on women receiving execution for their offenses. A notable exception is a study by Baker (1999) on executions of females in the United States between 1632 and 1997. Baker (ibid.) establishes how the executions of these 357 women had a considerable amount to do with their race and the political climate. For example, most women who received the death penalty did so for murder convictions; African American women constitute all of the females "executed for robbery, arson, poisoning and unspecified felonies"; and White women constitute all of the females executed for "witchcraft, spying/espionage, adultery, and concealing the birth or death of an infant" (ibid., 82–83). Three-fifths (59 percent) of U.S. women receiving the death penalty were African American, two-fifths (39 percent) were White, 1.5 percent were American Indians, and 0.9 percent were Latinas (ibid.). Baker (ibid., 83) states that the "preponderance of African American female executions during slavery" was a result of these women "who spurned White male sexual exploitation." Thus, once again, the processing of alleged female offenders must not be examined without considering race.

SUMMARY

This chapter traced the beginnings of the punishment of women and the treatment of incarcerated women historically to current responses to convicted females. The development of women's reformatories during the nineteenth and early twentieth centuries has had long-term effects on the institutionalization of female offenders. While the reformatories were important in providing safety from sexual abuse, they were built on a foundation that stereotyped women and girls into roles of homemakers and maids. To this day, women's prisons are fraught with programs and activities that reaffirm women's "appropriate" role as homemakers. Gender differences in women's and men's prison experiences and access to services and activities generally show discrimination against incarcerated females. Although the implementation of co-corrections was perceived as a means to decrease gender discrimination in prison opportunities, this appears not to have happened. One result apparent from comparing the gender differences in incarceration in the United States, regarding most factors, is that the conditions of women's prisons are worse than the deplorable conditions of men's prisons. Whether we measure this as proximity to family and loved ones or access to health care, recreation, education; or disproportionate rates of people of color and HIV-positive status; or distribution of psychotropic drugs; or likelihood of being raped by a guard, women in prison appear to be far worse off than most men in prison. The only way that women appear to be better off—and it is a significant one—is that incarcerated women appear to be far less likely than their male counterparts to be raped by fellow prisoners. Finally, the issues of pregnancy and parenting for incarcerated women are some of the most difficult and heart-rending in the prison system today.

REFERENCES

Abril, Julie C. 2003. Native American Identities among Women Prisoners. *Prison Journal* 83:38–50.

Acoca, Leslie. 1998a. Defusing the Time Bomb: Understanding and Meeting the Growing Health Care Needs of Incarcerated Women in America. *Crime and Delinquency* 44:32–48.

———. 1998b. Outside/Inside: The Violation of American Girls at Home, on the Streets, and in the Juvenile Justice System. *Crime and Delinquency* 44:561–589.

Acoca, Leslie, and James Austin. 1996. *The Crisis Women in Prison*. San Francisco, CA: The National Council on Crime and Delinquency.

Alemagno, Sonia A. 2001. Women in Jail: Is Substance Abuse Treatment Enough? *American Journal of Public Health* 91:798–800.

Almy, Linda, Vikki Bravo, Leslie Burd, Patricia Chin, Linda Cohan, Frank Gallo, Anthony Giorgianni, Jeffrey Gold, Mark Jose, and John Noyes. 1980. A Study of a Co-Educational Correctional Facility. Pp. 120–149 in *Co-Ed Prison*, edited by J. O. Smykla. New York: Human Services Press.

Alpert, Geoffrey P. 1982. Women Prisoners and the Law: Which Way Will the Pendulum Swing? Pp. 171–182 in *The Criminal Justice System and Women*, edited by B. R. Price and N. J. Sokoloff. New York: Clark and Boardman.

American Correctional Association. 1990. *The Female Offender: What Does the Future Hold?* Arlington, VA: Kirby Lithographic Company.

Anderson, David C. 1978. Co-corrections. *Corrections Magazine* (Sept. 4):33–41.

Anderson, Tammy L. 2003. Issues in the Availability of Health Care for Women Prisoners.: Pp. 49-60 in *The Incarcerated Woman*, edited by S. F. Sharp. Upper Saddle River, NJ: Prentice Hall.

Arnold, Regina. 1990. Processes of Victimization and Criminalization of Black Women. *Social Justice* 17:153–166.

Auerhahn, Kathleen, and Elizabeth Dermody Leonard. 2000. Docile Bodies? Chemical Restraints and the Female Inmate. *Journal of Criminal Law and Criminology* 90:599–634.

Aylward, Anna, and Jim Thomas. 1984. Quiescence in Women's Prison Litigation. *Justice Quarterly* 1:253–276.

Baker, David V. 1999. A Descriptive Profile and Socio-Historical Analysis of Female Executions in the United States: 1632–1997. *Women & Criminal Justice* 10:57–94.

Barry, Ellen M. 1991. Jail Litigation Concerning Women Prisoners. *The Prison Journal* 71:44–50.

Baunach, Phyllis Jo. 1982. You Can't Be a Mother and Be in Prison . . . Can You? Impacts of the Mother–Child Separation. Pp. 155–170 in *The Criminal Justice System and Women*, edited by B. R. Price and N. J. Sokoloff. New York: Clark and Boardman.

———. 1985. *Mothers in Prison*. New Brunswick, NJ: Transaction Books.

———. 1992. Critical Problems of Women in Prison. Pp. 99–112 in *The Changing Roles of Women in the Criminal Justice System*, edited by I. L. Moyer. Prospect Heights, IL: Waveland Press.

Belknap, Joanne. 2000. Programming and Health Care Responsibility for Incarcerated Women. Pp. 109–123 in *States of Confinement: Policing, Detention, and Prisons*, edited by Joy James. New York: St. Martin's Press.

Berry, Phyllis E., and Helen M. Eigenberg. 2003. Role Strain and Incarcerated Mothers. *Women & Criminal Justice* 15:101–119.

Binkley-Jackson, Deborah, Vivian L. Carter, and Garry L. Rolison. 1993. African-American Women in Prison. Pp. 65–74 in *Women Prisoners: A Forgotten Population*, edited by Beverly R. Fletcher, Lynda D. Shaver, and Dreama G. Moon. Westport, CT: Praeger.

Bloom, Barbara, and D. Steinhart. 1993. *Why Punish the Children?* San Francisco: National Council on Crime and Delinquency.

Boudouris, James. 1985. *Prisons and Kids*. College Park, MD: American Correctional Association.

Bosworth, Mary. 1999. *Engendering Resistance: Agency and Power in Women's Prisons*. Dartmouth, MA: Ashgate.

Bowker, Lee. 1980. *Victimization in Prisons*. New York: Elsevier.

———. 1981. Gender Differences in Prisoner Subcultures. Pp. 409–419 in *Women and Crime in America*, edited by L. H. Bowker. New York: Macmillan.

Brewster, Dennis R. 2003. Does Rehabilitative Justice Decrease Recidivism for Women Prisoners in Oklahoma? Pp. 29–45 in *The Incarcerated Woman*, edited by S. F. Sharp. Upper Saddle River, NJ: Prentice Hall.

Bunch, Barbara J., Linda A. Foley, and Susana P. Urbina. 1983. The Psychology of Violent Female Offenders: A Sex-Role Perspective. *The Prison Journal* 63:66–79.

Butler, Anne M. 1997. *Gendered Justice in the American West*. Urbana: University of Illinois Press.

Campbell, Charles F. 1980. Co-Corrections—FCI Fort Worth after Three Years. Pp. 83–109 in *Co-ed Prison*, edited by J. O. Smykla. New York: Human Services Press.

Carlen, Pat. 1983. *Women's Imprisonment: A Study in Social Control*. London: Routledge and Kegan Paul.

Carlen, Pat, and Chris Tchaikovsky. 1985. Women in Prison. Pp. 182–186 in *Criminal Women*, edited by P. Carlen, J. Hicks, J. O'Dwyer, and D. Christina. Cambridge, MA: Polity Press.

Carter, Barbara. 1981. Reform School Families. Pp. 419–431 in *Women and Crime in America*, edited by L. H. Bowker. New York: Macmillan.

Chesney-Lind, Meda. 1991. Patriarchy, Prisons, and Jails: A Critical Look at Trends in Women's Incarceration. *The Prison Journal* 71:51–67.

———. 2003. Reinventing Women's Corrections. Pp. 3–13 in *The Incarcerated Woman*, edited by S. F. Sharp. Upper Saddle River, NJ: Prentice Hall.

Chesney-Lind, Meda, and Joycelyn Pollock-Byrne. 1995. Women's Prisons: Equality with a Vengence. Pp. 155–175 in *Women, Law and Social Control*, edited by Joycelyn Pollock-Byrne and Alida Merlo. Boston: Allyn & Bacon, 1995.

Chesney-Lind, Meda, and Noelie Rodriguez. 1983. Women under Lock and Key. *Prison Journal* 63:47–65.

Chesney-Lind, Meda, and Randall G. Shelden. 1992. *Girls, Delinquency, and Juvenile Justice*. Pacific Grove, CA: Brooks/Cole.

Chigwada-Bailey, Ruth. 1997 *Black Women's Experiences of Criminal Justice*, Winchester, England: Waterside Press.

Church, George. 1990. The View from behind Bars. *Time Magazine* (Fall) 135:20–22.

Clark, Judy, and Kathy Boudin. 1990. Community of Women Organize Themselves to Cope with the AIDS Crisis: A Case Study from Bedford Hills Correctional Facility. *Social Justice* 17:90–109.

Claxton, Melvin, Ronald J. Hanson, and Norman Sinclair. 2005a. Guards Assault Female Inmates. *The Detroit News*, May 22, 2005. http://detnews.com/2005/specialreport/0505/24/A01-189215.htm

———. 2005b. State Fumbles Sexual Misconduct Probe. *The Detroit News*, May 22, 2005. http://detnews.com/2005/specialreport/0505/24/A13-188917.htm

———. 2005c. Suicides Follow Unheeded Complaints. *The Detroit News*, May 22, 2005. http://detnews.com/2005/specialreport/0505/24/A13-188918.htm

———. 2005d. Inmates Struggle to File Charges against Officers. *The Detroit News*, May 22, 2005. http://detnews.com/2005/specialreport/0505/24/A13-188916.htm

Coker, Ann L., Nilam J. Patel, Shanthi Krishnaswami, Wendy Schmidt, and Donna L. Richter. 1998. Childhood Forced Sex and Cervical Dysplasia among Women Prison Inmates. *Violence Against Women* 4:595–608.

Collins, Catherine Fisher. 1997. *The Imprisonment of African American Women.* Jefferson, NC: MacFarland & Co.

Compton-Wallace, Veronica. 2003. *Eating the Ashes: Seeking Rehabilitation within the U.S. Penal System.* New York: Algora Publishing.

Cooper, Sheelagh. 1993. The Evolution of the Federal Women's Prison. Pp. 22–49 in *In Conflict with the Law: Women and the Canadian Justice System*, edited by E. Adelberg and C. Currie. Vancouver: Press Gang Publishers.

Daane, Diane M. 2003. Pregnant Prisoners. Pp. 61–72 in *The Incarcerated Woman*, edited by S. F. Sharp. Upper Saddle River, NJ: Prentice Hall.

Danner, Terry A., William R. Blount, Ira J. Silverman, and Manual Vega. 1995. The Female Chronic Offender: Exploring Life Contingency and Offense History Dimensions for Incarcerated Female Offenders. *Women & Criminal Justice* 6:45–66.

Davis, Daniel L., Gerald J. Bean, Joseph E. Schumacher, and Terry Lee Stringer. 1991. Prevalence of Emotional Disorders in a Juvenile Justice Institutional Population. *American Journal of Forensic Psychology* 9:5–17.

Diaz-Cotto, Juanita. 1996. *Gender, Ethnicity, and the State: Latina and Latino Prison Politics.* Albany: State University of New York.

———. 2000. Race, Ethnicity, and Gender in Studies of Incarceration. Pp. 123–131 in *States of Confinement: Policing, Detention, and Prisons*, edited by Joy James. New York: St. Martin's Press.

Dobash, Russell P., R. Emerson Dobash, and Sue Gutteridge. 1986. *The Imprisonment of Women.* Oxford, England: Basil Blackwell.

Dodge, L. Mara. 2002. *Whores and Thieves of the Worst Kind: A Study of Women, Crime, and Prisons, 1835–2000.* DeKalb: Northern Illinois University Press.

Dodge, Mary, and Mark Pogrebin. 2001. Collateral Costs of Imprisonment for Women. *Prison Journal* 81:42–54.

Enos, Sandra. 2001. *Mothering from the Inside: Parenting in a Women's Prison.* Albany: State University of New York Press.

Faith, Karlene, 1993a. Media, Myths and Masculinization: Images of Women in Prison. Pp. 174–211 in *In Conflict with the Law: Women and the Canadian Justice System*, edited by E. Adelberg and C. Currie. Vancouver: Press Gang Publishers.

———. 1993b. *Unruly Women: The Politics of Confinement and Resistance.* Vancouver: Press Gang Publishers.

Farkas, Mary Ann, and Kathryn R. L. Rand. 1999. Sex Matters: A Gender-Specific Standard for Cross-Gender

Searches of Inmates. *Women & Criminal Justice* 10:31–56.

Farley, Melissa, and Vanessa Kelly. 2000. Prostitution: A Critical Review of the Medical and Social Sciences Literature. *Women & Criminal Justice* 11:29–64.

Farrell, Ann. 1998. Mothers Offending against Their Role: An Australian Experience. *Women & Criminal Justice* 9:47–69.

Feinman, Clarice. 1981. Sex-Role Stereotypes and Justice for Women. Pp. 383–391 in *Women and Crime in America*, edited by L. H. Bowker. New York: Macmillan.

———. 1983. A Historical Overview of the Treatment of Incarcerated Women: Myths and Realities of Rehabilitation. *Prison Journal* 63: 12–26.

———. 1986. *Women in the Criminal Justice System*, 2nd ed. New York: Praeger.

Fletcher, Beverly R., and Dreama G. Moon. 1993a. Introduction. Pp. 5–14 in *Women Prisoners: A Forgotten Population*, edited by Beverly R. Fletcher, Lynda D. Shaver, and Dreama G. Moon. Westport, CT: Praeger.

———. 1993b. Conclusions. Pp. 5–14 in *Women Prisoners: A Forgotten Population*, edited by Beverly R. Fletcher, Lynda D. Shaver, and Dreama G. Moon. Westport, CT: Praeger.

Fletcher, Beverly R., Garry L. Rolison, and Dreama G. Moon. 1993. The Woman Prisoner. Pp. 15–26 in *Women Prisoners: A Forgotten Population*, edited by Beverly R. Fletcher, Lynda D. Shaver, and Dreama G. Moon. Westport, CT: Praeger.

Ford, C. 1929. Homosexual Practices of Institutionalized Females. *Journal of Abnormal and Social Psychology* 23:442–448.

Fox, James G. 1975. Women in Crisis. Pp. 181–205 in *Man in Crisis*, edited by H. Toch. Chicago: Aldine-Atherton.

Fox, Lana, and Fran Sugar. 1990. Survey of Federally Sentenced Aboriginal Women in the Community. Canada: Correctional Service of Canada, 16pp. (or available at http://www.csc-scc.gc.ca/text/prgrm/fsw/nativesurvey/toce_e.shtml).

Freedman, Estelle. 1974. Their Sisters' Keepers: A Historical Perspective on Female Correctional Institutions in the United States, 1870–1900. *Feminist Studies* 2:77–95.

———. 1982. Nineteenth-Century Women's Prison Reform and Its Legacy. Pp. 141–157 in *Women and the Law: A Social Historical Perspective*, Vol. I, edited by D. Kelly Weisberg. Cambridge, MA: Schenkman Publishing.

Gaarder, Emily, and Joanne Belknap. 2004. Little Women: Girls in Adult Prison. *Women & Criminal Justice* 15:51–80.

Gelsthorpe, Loraine. 1989. *Sexism and the Female Offender*. Aldershot, England: Gower.

Giallombardo, Rose. 1966. *Society of Women: A Study of a Women's Prison*. New York: John Wiley.

———. 1974. *The Social World of Imprisoned Girls*. New York: Wiley.

Gilfus, Mary E. 1992. From Victims to Survivors to Offenders: Women's Routes of Entry and Immersion into Street Crime. *Women & Criminal Justice* 4:63–90.

Girshick, Lori B. 1999. *No Safe Haven: Stories of Women in Prison*. Boston: Northeastern University Press

Glaser, R. D., and J. S. Thorpe. 1986. Unethical Intimacy: A Survey of Sexual Contact and Advances between Psychology Educators and Female Graduate Students. *American Psychologist* 41:43–51.

Glick, Ruth M., and Virginia V. Neto. 1982. National Study of Women's

Correctional Programs. Pp. 141–154 in *The Criminal Justice System and Women*, edited by B. R. Price and N. J. Sokoloff. New York: Clark and Boardman.

Goetting, Ann. 1987. Racism, Sexism, and Ageism in the Prison Community. *Federal Probation* 49:10–22.

Goetting, Ann, and Roy M. Howsen. 1983. Women in Prison: A Profile. *The Prison Journal* 63:27–46.

Gray, Tara, G. Larry Mays, and Mary K. Stohr. 1995. Inmate Needs and Programming in Exclusively Women's Jails. *The Prison Journal* 75:186–202.

Greene, Peters, and Associates. 1998. Guiding Principles for Promising Female Programming. The Office of Juvenile Justice and Delinquency Prevention, October, 94pp.

Greenfeld, Lawrence A., and Tracy L. Snell. 1999. Women Offenders. Bureau of Justice Statistics: Special Report. U.S. Department of Justice, December, 14pp.

Haft, Marilyn G. 1980. Women in Prison: Discriminatory Practices and Some Legal Solutions. Pp. 320–338 in *Women, Crime, and Justice*, edited by S. K. Datesman and F. R. Scarpitti. New York: Oxford Press.

Haley, Kathleen. 1980. Mothers behind Bars. Pp. 339–354 in *Women, Crime, and Justice*, edited by S. K. Datesman and F. R. Scarpitti. New York: Oxford Press.

Hankins, Catherine A., Sylvie Gendron, Margaret A. Handley, Christiane Richard, Marie Therese Lai Tung, and Michael O'Shaughnessy. 1994. HIV Infection among Women in Prison. *American Journal of Public Health* 84:1637–1640.

Hannah-Moffat, Kelly. 1994. Unintended Consequences of Feminism and Prison Reform. *Forum on Corrections Research* 6:7–10.

Hanson, Ronald J., Norman Sinclair, and Melvin Claxton. 2005a. Pregnant

Inmates Name Guards as Dads. *The Detroit News*, May 23, 2005. http://detnews.com/2005/specialreport/0505/24/A08-189818.htm

———. 2005b. Prison Affairs Hard to Control. *The Detroit News*, May 23, 2005. http://detnews.com/2005/specialreport/0505/24/A09-189816.htm

———. 2005c. State keeps guards with past crimes. *The Detroit News*, May 23, 2005. http://detnews.com/2005/specialreport/0505/24/A01-190120.htm

Harrison, Paige M., and Allen J. Beck. 2005. Prison and Jail Inmates at Mid-year 2004. U.S. Department of Justice Statistics Bulletin, NCJ 208801.

Hart, Cynthia B. 1995. Gender Differences in Social Support among Inmates. *Women & Criminal Justice* 6:67–88.

Heffernan, Esther, and Elizabeth Krippel. 1980. A Co-ed Prison. Pp. 110–119 in *Co-ed Prison*, edited by J. O. Smykla. New York: Human Services Press.

Heidensohn, Frances M. 1985. *Women and Crime: The Life of the Female Offender*. New York: New York University Press.

Henriques, Zelma W. 1994. Imprisoned Mothers and Their Children: A Cross-Cultural Perspective. Paper presented at Prisons 2000, an International Conference on the Present and Future State of Prisons. Leicester, England, April.

———. 1996. Imprisoned Mothers and Their Children: Separation–Reunion Syndrome Dual Impact. *Women & Criminal Justice* 8:77–96.

Holley, Philip D., and Dennis Brewster. 1996. The Women at Eddie Warrior Correctional Center: Descriptions from a Data Set. *Journal of the Oklahoma Criminal Justice Research Consortium* 3:107–114.

Holt, Karen E. 1982. Nine Months to Life: The Law and the Pregnant Inmate. *Journal of Family Law* 20:523–543.

Human Rights Watch Women Rights Project. 1996. *All Too Familiar: Sexual Abuse of Women in U.S. State Prisons.* New York: Human Rights Watch.

Immarigeon, Russ. 1987a. Women in Prison. *Journal of the National Prison Project* 11:1–5.

———. 1987b. Few Diversion Programs Are Offered Female Offenders. *Journal of the National Prison Project* 12:9–11.

Immarigeon, Russ, and Meda Chesney-Lind. 1992. *Women's Prisons: Overcrowded and Overused.* San Francisco: National Council on Crime and Delinquency.

Jackson, Patrick G., and Cindy A Stearns. 1995. Gender Issues in the New Generation Jail. *The Prison Journal* 75:203–221.

Janusz, Luke. 1991. Separate but Unequal: Women behind Bars in Massachusetts. *Odyssey* (Fall):6–17.

Johnson, Holly, and Karen Rodgers. 1993. A Statistical Overview of Women and Crime in Canada. Pp. 95–116 in *In Conflict with the Law: Women and the Canadian Justice System*, edited by E. Adelberg and C. Currie. Vancouver: Press Gang Publishers.

Johnson, Paula C. 2003. *Inner Lives: Voices of African American Women in Prison.* New York: New York University.

Johnston, Denise. 1995a. Jailed Mothers. Pp. 41–55 in *Children of Incarcerated Parents*, edited by K. Gabel and D. Johnston. New York: Lexington Books.

———. 1995b. The Care and Placement of Prisoners' Children. Pp. 103–123 in *Children of Incarcerated Parents*, edited by K. Gabel and D. Johnston. New York: Lexington Books.

Kampfner, Christina Jose. 1995. Post-Traumatic Stress Reactions in Children of Imprisoned Mothers. Pp. 89–102 in *Children of Incarcerated Parents*, edited by K. Gabel and D. Johnston. New York: Lexington Books.

Kaplan, Mildred F. 1988. A Peer Support Group for Women in Prison for the Death of a Child. *Journal of Offender Counseling, Services, and Rehabilitation* 13:5–13.

Kelley, Margaret S. 2003. The State-of-the-Art in Substance Abuse Programs for Women in Prison. Pp. 119–148 in *The Incarcerated Woman*, edited by S. F. Sharp. Upper Saddle River, NJ: Prentice Hall.

Kersten, Joachim. 1989. The Institutional Control of Girls and Boys. Pp. 129–144 in *Growing Up Good: Policing the Behavior of Girls in Europe*, edited by M. Cain. London: Sage.

Kline, Sue. 1993. A Profile of Female Offenders in State and Federal Prisons. Pp. 1–6 in *Female Offenders: Meeting the Needs of a Neglected Population*, edited by American Correctional Association. Laurel, MD: American Correctional Association.

Knight, Barbara. 1992. Women in Prison as Litigants: Prospects for Post Prison Futures. *Women & Criminal Justice* 4:91–116.

Koban, Linda A. 1983. Parent in Prison: A Comparative Analysis of the Effects of Incarceration on the Families of Men and Women. *Research in Law, Deviance and Social Control* 5:171–183.

Kruttschnitt, Candace. 1981. Prison codes, Inmate Solidarity and Women. Pp. 123–141 in *Comparing Male and Female Offenders*, edited by Marguerite Q. Warren. Beverly Hills, CA: Sage.

Kruttschnitt, Candace, Rosemary Gartner, and Amy Miller. 2000. Doing Her Own Time? Women's Responses to Prison in the Context of the Old and the New Penology. *Criminology* 38:681–717.

Lake, E. S. 1993. An Exploration of the Violent Victim Experiences of Female Offenders. *Violence and Victims* 8(1):41–51.

Lawson, W. Travis, and Lena Sue Fawkes. 1993. HIV, AIDS, and the Female Offender. Pp. 43–48 in *Female Offenders: Meeting the Needs of a Neglected Population.* Laurel, MD: American Correctional Association.

Lekkerkerker, Eugenia C. 1931. *Reformatories for Women in the United States.* J. B. Wolters' Groningen-The Hague: Batavia.

Leonard, Eileen B. 1983. Judicial Decisions and Prison Reform: The Impact of Litigation on Women Prisoners. *Social Problems* 31:45–58.

Luke, Katherine P. 2002. Mitigating the Ill Effects of Maternal Incarceration on Women in Prison and Their Children. *Child Welfare* 81:929–948.

Maeve, M. Katherine. 1998. Methodologic Issues in Qualitative Research with Incarcerated Women. *Family & Community Health* 21:1–15.

———. 1999a. Adjudicated Health: Incarcerated Women and the Social Construction of Health. *Crime, Law and Social Change* 31:49–71.

———. 1999b. The Social Construction of Love and Sexuality in a Women's Prison. *Advances in Nursing Science* 21:46–65.

Mahan, Sue. 1982. *Unfit Mothers.* Palo Alto, CA: R and E Associates.

———. 1984. Imposition of Despair: An Ethnography of Women in Prison. *Justice Quarterly* 1:357–384.

———. 1989. The Needs and Experiences of Women in Sexually Integrated Prisons. *American Journal of Criminal Justice* 13:228–239.

Mann, Coramae Richey. 1984. *Female Crime and Delinquency.* University, AL: University of Alabama Press.

Marcus-Mendoza, Susan T., and Erin Wright. 2003. Treating the Woman Prisoner. Pp. 107–117 in *The Incarcerated Woman,* edited by S. F. Sharp. Upper Saddle River, NJ: Prentice Hall.

Mawby, R. I. 1982. Women in Prison: A British Study. *Crime and Delinquency* 28:24–39.

McCarthy, Belinda R. 1980. Inmate Mothers: The Problems of Separation and Reintegration. *Journal of Offender Counseling, Services and Rehabilitation* 4:199–212.

McClellan, Dorothy S. 1994. Disparity in the Discipline of Male and Female Inmates in Texas Prisons. *Women & Criminal Justice* 5:71–97.

McGowan, Brenda, and Karen L. Blumenthal. 1976. Children of Women Prisoners: A Forgotten Minority. Pp. 121–136 in *The Female Offender,* edited by L. Crites. Lexington, MA: D. C. Heath.

———. 1978. *Why Punish the Children? A Study of Children of Women Prisoners.* Hackensack, NJ: National Council on Crime and Delinquency.

McHugh, Gerald A. 1980. Protection of the Rights of Pregnant Women in Prisons and Detention Facilities. *New England Journal on Prison Law* 6:231–263.

Miller, Darcy. 1994. Exploring Gender Differences in Suicidal Behavior among Adolescent Offenders. *Journal of Correctional Education* 45:134–138.

Moe, Angela, and Kathleen J. Ferraro. 2003. Malign Neglect of Benign Respect: Women's Health Care in a Carceral Setting. *Women & Criminal Justice* 14:53–80.

Moon, Dreama G., Ruby J. Thompson, and Regina Bennett. 1993. Patterns of Substance Use among Women in Prison. Pp. 45–54 in *Women Prisoners: A Forgotten Population,* edited by Beverly R. Fletcher, Lynda D. Shaver, and Dreama G. Moon. Westport, CT: Praeger.

Morris, Allison. 1987. *Women, Crime and Criminal Justice.* Oxford: Basil Blackwell.

Moyer, Imogene L. 1978. Differential Social Structures and Homosexuality among Women in Prison. *Virginia Social Science Journal* 13:13–19.

———. 1980. Leadership in a Women's Prison. *Journal of Criminal Justice* 8:233–241.

———. 1984. Deceptions and Realities of Life in Women's Prisons. *Prison Journal* 64:45–56.

Mullings, Janet L., James W. Marquart, and Victoria E. Brewer. 2000. Assessing the Relationship between Child Sexual Abuse and Marginal Living Conditions on HIV/AIDS Related Risk Behavior among Women Prisoners. *Child Abuse and Neglect* 24:677–688.

Mullings, Janet L., Joycelyn Pollock, and Ben M. Crouch. 2002. Drugs and Criminality: Results from the Texas Women Inmates Study. *Women & Criminal Justice* 13:69–96.

Mumola, Christopher J., and Allen J. Beck. 1997. Prisoners in 1996. Bureau of Justice Statistics. U.S. Department of Justice, June, 15pp.

Myers, Barbara J., Tina M. Smarsh, Kristine Amlund-Hagen, and Suzanne Kennon. 1999. Children of Incarcerated Mothers. *Journal of Child and Family Studies* 8:11–25.

Natalizia, Elana. 1991. Feminism and Criminal Justice Reform. *Odyssey* (Fall):19–20.

Owen, Barbara. 1998. *In the Mix: Struggle and Survival in a Women's Prison*. Albany: State University of New York Press.

Pendergrass, Virginia E. 1975. Innovative Programs for Women in Jail and Prisons. Pp. 67–81 in *The Female Offender*, edited by A. M. Brodsky. Beverly Hills, CA: Sage.

Pogrebin, Mark, and Mary Dodge. 2001. Women's Accounts of their Prison Experiences. *Journal of Criminal Justice* 29:531–541.

Pollock, Joycelyn M. 1998. *Counseling Women in Prison*. Thousand Oaks, CA: Sage.

———. 2002a. Parenting Programs in Women's Prisons. *Women & Criminal Justice* 14:131–154.

———. 2002b. *Women, Prison, and Crime*, 2nd Ed. Belmont, CA: Wadsworth/Thomson Learning.

Prendergast, Michael L., Jean Wellisch, and Gregory P. Falkin, 1995. Assessment of and Services for Substance-Abusing Women in Community and Correctional Settings. *Prison Journal* 75:240, 256.

Raeder, Myrna S. 2003. Gendered Implications of Sentencing and Correctional Practices. Pp. 173–208 in *Gendered Justice*, edited by Barbara E. Bloom. Durham, NC: Carolina Academic Press.

Rafter, Nicole Hahn. 1985. *Partial Justice: Women in State Prisons, 1800–1935*. Boston: Northeastern University Press.

———. 1989. Gender and Justice: The Equal Protection Issues. Pp. 89–109 in *The American Prison*, edited by Lynne Goodstein and Doris MacKenzie. New York: Plenum Press.

Resnick, Judith, and Nancy Shaw. 1980. Prisoners of Their Sex: Health Problems of Incarcerated Women. Pp. 319–413 in *Prisoners' Rights Sourcebook*, Vol. 2, edited by Ira P. Robbins. New York: Clark Boardman.

Reviere, Rebecca, and Vernetta D. Young. 2004. Aging behind Bars: Health Care for Older Female Inmates. *Journal of Women & Aging* 16:55–69.

Ross, James, and Esther Heffernan. 1980. Women in a Co-ed Joint. Pp. 248–261 in *Co-ed Prison*, edited by J. O. Smykla. New York: Human Services Press.

Ross, Luana. 1998. *Inventing the Savage: The Social Construction of Native American Criminality*. Austin: University of Texas Press.

————. 2000. Imprisoned Native Women and the Importance of Native Traditions. Pp. 132–144 in *States of Confinement: Policing, Detention, and Prisons*, edited by Joy James. New York: St. Martin's Press.

Ross, Robert R., and Elizabeth A. Fabiano. 1986. *Female Offenders: Correctional Afterthoughts*. Jefferson, NC: McFarland.

Ruback, Barry. 1980. The Sexuality Integrated Prison. Pp. 33–60 in *Co-ed Prison*, edited by J. O. Smykla. New York: Human Services Press.

Ryan, T. A. 1984. *Adult Female Offenders and Institutional Programs: A State of the Art Analysis*. Washington, DC: U.S. Department of Justice.

Sable, Marjorie R., John R. Fieberg, Sandra L. Martin, and Lawrence L. Kupper. 1999. Violence Victimization Experiences of Pregnant Prisoners. *American Journal of Orthopsychiatry* 69:392–397.

Sargent, Elizabeth, Susan Marcus-Mendoza, and Chong Ho Yu. 1993. Abuse and the Woman Prisoner. Pp. 55–64 in *Women Prisoners: A Forgotten Population*, edited by Beverly R. Fletcher, Lynda D. Shaver, and Dreama G. Moon. Westport, CT: Praeger.

Sarri, Rosemary. 1987. Unequal Protection under the Law: Women and the Criminal Justice System. Pp. 394–426 in *The Trapped Woman: Catch-22 in Deviance and Control*, edited by J. Figueira-McDonough and R. Sarri. Newbury Park, CA: Sage.

Schafer, N. E., and A. B. Dellinger. 1999. Jailed Parents: An Assessment. *Women & Criminal Justice* 10:73–91.

Schupak, Terri L. 1986. Comments: Women and Children First: An Examination of the Unique Needs of Women in Prison. *Golden Gate University Law Review* 16:455–474.

Schweber, Claudine. 1985. Beauty Marks and Blemishes: The Co-ed Prison. *Prison Journal* 64:3–15.

Sharp, Susan F. 2003. Mothers in Prison. Pp. 151–166 in *The Incarcerated Woman*, edited by S. F. Sharp. Upper Saddle River, NJ: Prentice Hall.

Sharp, Susan F., and Susan T. Marcus-Mendoza. 2001. It's a Family Affair: Incarcerated Women and Their Families. *Women & Criminal Justice* 12:21–49.

Sharp, Susan F., Susan T. Marcus-Mendoza, Robert G. Bentley, Debra B. Simpson, and Sharon R. Love. 1999. Gender Differences in the Impact of Incarceration on the Children and Families of Drug Offenders. Pp. 217–246 in *Interrogating Social Justice*, edited by Marilyn Corsianos and Kelly A. Train. Toronto: Canadian Scholar's Press.

Shaw, Margaret, with Karen Rodgers, Johanne Blanchette, Lee Seto Thomas, Tina Hattem, and Lada Tamarack. 1990. *Survey of Federally Sentenced Women*. Ottawa: Ministry of the Solicitor General, Corrections Branch.

Simkins, Sandra, and Sarah Katz. 2002. Criminalizing Abused Girls. *Violence Against Women* 8:1474–1499.

Sims, Patsy. 1976. Women in Southern Jails. Pp. 137–148 in *The Female Offender*, edited by L. Crites. Lexington, MA: D. C. Heath.

Sinclair, Norman, Melvin Claxton, and Ronald J. Hanson. 2005a. Michigan Faces Conflict of Interest. *The Detroit News*, May 24, 2005. http://detnews.com/2005/specialreport/0505/24/A08-190953.htm

————. 2005b. Prisoner Complaints Unheeded. *The Detroit News*, May 24, 2005. http://detnews.com/2005/specialreport/0505/24/A01-191652.htm

Singer, Mark I., Janet Bussey, Li-Yu Song, and Lisa Lunghofer. 1995. The Psychosocial Issues of Women Serving Time in Jail. *Social Work* 40:103–113.

Smart, Carol. 1976. *Women, Crime and Criminology: A Feminist Critique.* London: Routledge and Kegan Paul.

Smykla, John O., and Jimmy J. Williams. 1996. Co-Corrections in the United States of America, 1970–1990: Two Decades of Disadvantages for Women Prisoners. *Women & Criminal Justice* 8:61–76.

Sokoloff, Natalie J. 2001. Violent Female Offenders in New York City. Pp. 132–146 in *Crime and Justice in New York City*, Vol. 1, edited by Andrew Karmen. Cincinnati: Thomson Learning.

———. 2005. Women Prisoners at the Dawn of the 21st Century. *Women & Criminal Justice* 16:127–137.

Stanton, Ann M. 1980. *When Mothers Go to Jail.* Lexington, MA: Lexington Books.

Sterk, Claire E. 1999. *Fast Lives: Women Who Use Crack Cocaine.* Philadephia: Temple University Press.

Suh, Alexandra. 2000. Military Prostitution in Asia and the United States. Pp. 144–158 in *States of Confinement: Policing, Detention, and Prisons*, edited by Joy James. New York: St. Martin's Press.

Swain, Lorry. Personal correspondence, May 19, 1994.

U.S. Department of Justice. 1991a. Children in Custody, 1989. Office of Juvenile Justice and Delinquency Prevention. NCJ-127189. Washington, DC, January.

———. 1991b. Drugs and Jail Inmates, 1989. Special Report NCJ-130836. Bureau of Justice Statistics. Washington, DC, August.

———. 1992. Census of State and Federal Correctional Facilities, 1990. NCJ-137003. Bureau of Justice Statistics. Washington, DC: Government Printing Office.

Vachon, Marla M. 1994. It's about Time: The Legal Context of Policy Changes for Female Offenders. *Forum on Corrections Research* 6:3–6.

Van Ochten, Marjorie. 1993. Legal Issues and the Female Offender. Pp. 31–36 in *Female Offenders: Meeting the Needs of a Neglected Population*. Laurel, MD: American Correctional Association.

Vaughn, Michael S., and Linda G. Smith. 1999. Practical Penal Harm Medicine in the United States. *Justice Quarterly* 16:175–232.

Vitale, Anne T. 1980. Inmate Abortions: The Right to Government Funding behind the Prison Gates. *Fordham Law Review* 48:550–567.

Vukson, Todd M. 1988. Inmate Abortion Funding in California. *California Western Law Review* 24:107–126.

Ward, David A., and Gene G. Kassebaum. 1965. *Women's Prison: Sex and Social Structure.* Chicago: Aldine.

Weintraub, Judith F. 1987. Mothers and Children in Prison. *Corrections Compendium* 11:1, 5.

Wellisch, Jean, Michael L. Prendergast, and M. Douglas Anglin. 1996. Needs Assessment and Services for Drug-Abusing Women Offenders: Results from a National Survey of Community-Based Treatment Programs. *Women & Criminal Justice* 8:27–60.

Wheeler, Patricia A., Rebecca Trammell, Jim Thomas, and Jennifer Findlay. 1989. Persephone Chained: Parity of Equality in Women's Prisons. *The Prison Journal* 69:88–102.

Wilson, Nancy K. 1980. Styles of Doing Time in a Co-ed Prison: Masculine and Feminine Alternatives. Pp. 150–171 in *Co-ed Prison*, edited by J. O. Smykla. New York: Human Services Press.

Windschuttle, Elizabeth. 1981. Women, Crime, and Punishment. Pp. 31–50 in *Women and Crime*, edited by

S. K. Mukherjee and J. A. Scutt. North Sydney, Australia: Allen and Unwin.

Wood, Peter B., and Harold G. Grasmick. 1999. Toward the Development of Punishment Equivalencies: Male and Female Inmates Rate the Severity of Alternative Sanctions Compared to Prison. *Justice Quarterly* 16:19–50.

Wooden, Wayne S., and Jay Parker. 1982. *Men behind Bars: Sexual Exploitation in Prison.* New York: Plenum.

Wooldredge, John D., and Kimberly Masters. 1993. Confronting Problems Faced by Pregnant Inmates in State Prisons. *Crime and Delinquency* 39:195–203.

Yoshimi, Yoshiaki. 2000. *Comfort Women.* New York: Columbia University Press.

Young, Vernetta D. 1994. Race and Gender in the Establishment of Juvenile Institutions: The Case of the South. *Prison Journal* 73:244–265

Zaitzow, Barbara H., and Angela D. West. 2003. Doing Time in the Shadow of Death: Women Prisoners and HIV/AIDS. Pp. 73–90 in *The Incarcerated Woman,* edited by S. F. Sharp. Upper Saddle River, NJ: Prentice Hall.

6

The Image
of the Female Victim

Although constitutional law may be blind to disparities of power and
status between private citizens, most victims of sexual and domestic
violence are not. Victims often perceive quite accurately that their
abusers are acting with the tacit permission, if not active complicity, of
family, friends, church, or community. Moreover, any illusions a victim
might have entertained about her status relative to the offender are most
convincingly dispelled by the crime itself. By their nature, these crimes
are displays of raw power, intended to subordinate the victim and to
teach her to know her place. Unlike property crimes, they result in no
obvious material gain for the perpetrator; rather, their goal is to gain or
maintain dominance over the victim. The perpetrator seeks to establish
his dominance not only by terrorizing the victim but also,
often most effectively, by shaming her.
HERMAN, 2005, 572

The image of the female victim has changed considerably in recent years.
Until the 1970s, female victims were relatively invisible. Since then, not
only has awareness of the frequency of male violence against women and girls
grown significantly but new types of these victimizations have been identified
and studied. All the types of victimizations discussed in this section have always
occurred, yet they have been recognized as significant social and legal problems
only since the 1970s. For example, the term *battered woman* did not exist until
1974 (Schechter, 1982, 16), *sexual harassment* was not a labeled behavior until
1975 (Evans, 1978), and *date rape* was first identified as a problem in the early
1980s (Warshaw, 1988). *Stalking* has been defined as the crime of the 1990s
(Wallace, 1995). Chapman (1990) provides a more global list of violence-against-
women phenomena, including suttee, foot binding, infibulation, clitoridectomy,

dowry death, selective malnourishment, bride burning, female infanticide, daughter neglect, forced prostitution, international sexual trafficking and slavery, homicide, human sacrifice, and pornography. This chapter looks at how women victims of male violence have been viewed historically and how awareness of their victimization has changed over time.

Today we all have some idea of what these words (woman battering, date rape, sexual harassment, and stalking) mean, although we may not agree on the behaviors that constitute each. For example, some people still believe a woman or girl was not raped if she drank or used drugs, invited the man or boy on the date, wore certain types of clothes, had a bad reputation, or initiated intimacy. Some people still believe it is justifiable for a man to abuse his wife or girlfriend if she talks back, gets a job, flirts with someone else, or breaks up with him. Although many people continue to believe the stereotypes surrounding female victimization, the frequency and facts about the sexual, physical, and emotional/psychological victimization of women and girls have been increasingly documented across the globe: From a comparative standpoint, violence against women occurs across all geographical regions and among societies that range in complexity from hunter-gatherers to advanced industrial societies (Michalski, 2004, 652). The focus of the next few chapters is on the victimizations most frequently associated with women and girls: sexual victimization and battering, which were labeled in 1979 as the most underreported crimes against persons in the criminal justice system (Gelles, 1979, 121). Unfortunately, it is beyond the scope of this book to address some of the other victimizations associated with women, particularly those involving reproductive freedom. There is substantial evidence not only of botched legal and illegal abortions but also of coerced and forced sterilization of women, especially poor women and women of color (see Davis, 1981; Gordon, 1977).

Both the physical and sexual victimization of women and girls have been shrouded in beliefs that these occurrences are rare, the victim's fault, and shameful for the victim. The understanding of sexual victimization has been muddled because of puritanical views of rape as an unmentionable crime (Sanders, 1980). Historically, battered women have been thought of as deserving victims, nags, and inadequate wives. Although the stereotype of the real rape victim usually assumed the victim to be White and middle or upper class (Estrich, 1987), the stereotype of a battered woman was of a woman involved in a family "disturbance" in a working-class or poor neighborhood. Research has shown that these stereotypes are myths: All women and girls are at risk of male violence, regardless of race, class, age, or ethnicity.

Although male violence against women and girls has been a historical constant, recognition of the epidemic proportions of these crimes has been relatively recent. Russell (1984) traced the recognition of various phenomena as identified social problems. Social problems are phenomena that have often occurred for centuries but were not labeled as problematic or common until data were collected and a critical mass of society accepted them as problematic. Russell (ibid., 20) identifies, in order of their appearance from the 1960s to the early 1980s, the following social problems that came to the public's

---

Comparative Perspectives: Abuse during Pregnancy: A Global Issue

Jacquelyn Campbell, Claudia Garcia-Moreno, and Phyllis Sharps (2004) summarized the existing research on abuse of pregnant women. They found:

- There is increasing global documentation about the risk of violence for women and girls when they are pregnant.

- Abuse during pregnancy has a significant impact on both maternal and infant health, particularly in North America.

- The range of reported abuse of pregnant women and girls is much wider in developing (3.8–41.6 percent) than industrial (3.4–11.0 percent) countries.

- The range of intimate partner assaults during pregnancy in the United States is 0.9–20.1 percent (Gazmararian et al., 1996).

Conclusion: Although there are methodological differences and ranges in the amount of abuse during pregnancy reported across studies and regions, abuse during pregnancy is a significant social and health problem affecting pregnant women and girls and infant health.

SOURCE: Jacquelyn Campbell, Claudia Garcia-Moreno, and Phyllis Sharps. 2004. Abuse during Pregnancy in Industrialized and Developing Countries. *Violence Against Women* 10: 770–789; Julie A. Gazmararian, Suzanne Lazorick, A. M. Spitz, T. J. Ballard, Linda E. Saltzman, and J. S. Marks. 1996. Prevalence of Violence against Pregnant Women. *Journal of the American Medical Association* 4:79–84.

---

attention: (1) nonsexual child abuse, (2) the rape of women by strangers and other nonintimates, (3) nonsexual wife abuse, and (4) the sexual abuse of children (particularly incest). The identification of each of these social problems helped set the stage for the others to follow. Since the publication of Russell's (ibid.) book, the threats and reality of physical and sexual dating violence, marital rape, sexual harassment, stalking, and satanic cult victimization of women and girls have been increasingly documented. It appears that for all types of family or domestic violence, girls and women are the losers.

For example, studies on *elder abuse* committed by family members highlight this as yet another area where women are the most frequent targets (Anetzberger, 1997; Jonson and Akerstrom, 2004). Intimate partner abuse of older women is prevalent across racial/ethnic groups in the United States (Grossman and Lundy, 2003) and in many other countries, such as Ireland, the United Kingdom, Italy (Ockleford et al., 2003), and Australia (Mears, 2003). Recent research also documents older women's significant risks of sexual abuse at the hands of caretakers when they are in the home needing help, and typically these caretakers are family members (Roberto and Teaster, 2005). Additionally, older women in nursing homes and similar facilities are at risk of sexual abuse, mostly from fellow residents in these homes (ibid.). One study on intimate partner abuse of older women found that 10 percent were sexually abused by their current or former male partners, as well as three-quarters reporting physical abuse and over 95 percent reporting emotional abuse by these men (Grossman and Lundy, 2003).

For women of any age, sexual abuse is very personal and highly intrusive and requires extraordinary intervention efforts (Roberto and Teaster, 2005, 474).

Finally, sexual abuse, intimate partner abuse, and stalking are not always distinct victimizations. Homes where woman battering occurs are often homes where children are physically and sexually abused as well (Edleson, 1999). Additionally, physical and sexual violence in dating or courtship relationships often go hand in hand. Many men who batter their wives or girlfriends also sexually victimize these women (Bergen, 2004; Finkelhor and Yllo, 1985; Meyer, Vivian, and O'Leary, 1998; Russell, 1984, 1990; Schechter, 1982; Tjaden and Thoennes, 2000). More recent research has identified the significant role that stalking plays in woman battering, such as women and girls being followed and threatened by current or former male partners (Lowney and Best, 1995).

THE LINK BETWEEN ACTUAL VICTIMIZATIONS AND THE FEAR OF CRIME

A number of (male) researchers have claimed that males are far more likely to be victims of crime in general than are females (for example, Cohen and Felson, 1979; Gottfredson, 1986; Miethe, Stafford, and Long, 1987). Other research has consistently shown that females have higher fear of crime than males (Braungart, Braungart, and Hoyer, 1980; Clemente and Kleiman, 1976; LaGrange and Ferraro, 1989; Ortega and Myles, 1987). One study stated that women think they are more likely [than men] to be the victim of a personal crime (LaGrange and Ferraro, 1989). Certainly for the crimes we typically associate with female victims—rape and battering—most people and researchers agree these are gendered in that males are usually the perpetrators and females are usually the victims. However, even looking at overall violent crime rates (except murder) collected across the United States through the National Crime Victimization Survey (NCVS) in 2003, 2.0 percent of females and 2.6 percent of males reported violent victimizations (Catalano, 2004). As expected, males were more commonly victims of robbery, total assault, simple assault, and aggravated assault, while females were more commonly the victims of sexual assault/rape. Also, males (54 percent) were more likely than females (32 percent) to report violent victimizations by strangers (ibid.). An NCVS study of college students from 1995 to 2002 found 4.3 percent of females and 8.0 percent of males reported violent victimizations (Baum and Klaus, 2005). Notably, the gender gap of 18- to 24-year-olds who were *not* college students was much smaller: 7.1 percent of females and 7.9 percent of males reported violent victimizations (ibid.). Similar to the NCVS study of the general U.S. population, males were more likely than females to be victims of robbery, aggravated assault, and simple assault, but females were far more likely to report rape/sexual assault (ibid.). Another study using NCVS data to study workplace violence between 1992 and 1996 in the United States indicates that 83 percent of the perpetrators of violence in the workplace are men, and one-third of the victims are women (Warchol, 1998).

Given the lower rates of female victimization reported in most statistics, some criminologists have suggested that women's higher fear of crime is irrational, and indeed women's and the elderly's low victimization rates compounded with their high fear of crime has been labeled the paradox of fear (by Warr, 1984, as cited in Madriz, 1997). The major problems with this rationale—that women and girls are unduly afraid of crime—are that (1) awareness of the extent and frequency with which females are victimized is relatively recent and often ignored, (2) the nature of the victimization is different for crimes associated with female victims (rape and battering), and (3) U.S. culture *encourages* women and girls to be afraid of crime. Regarding the first point, the extent and frequency of females' victimizations are not clearly known because sexual victimization and battering are the least likely offenses to be reported to the police (Young, 1992). The earliest comprehensive, valid study of rape victimization not relying on police-reported rapes found that 44 percent of women reported being the victims of rape or attempted rape at least once, and only 8 percent of those victimized reported it to the police (Russell, 1984). Other researchers estimate that 40 to 50 percent of women in the United States experience battering at the hands of intimate male partners (Smith, 1994; Walker, 1979).

If crimes such as rape and battering were reported to the police (or even the NCVS) as consistently as the types of crimes males tend to experience, statistics would likely begin to define females as significantly more at risk of violence than males. Females' high levels of fear and low reported victimizations are likely due to researchers' unwillingness to accept fear levels as realistic assessments of risk (Young, 1992). Other research found that most women rarely tell anyone about physical and sexual intrusions because of fear, humiliation, and self-blame. Moreover, when they do tell someone, a decision is usually made to keep the incident private (Stanko, 1992). A number of reasons have been offered as to why women do not report physical and sexual abuse to researchers or to the police: too personal to discuss, embarrassment or shame, fear of reprisal by the abuser, or repression due to the trauma (Smith, 1994).

It is vital to address the nature of crimes regularly perpetrated against females (Riger, 1981). With the exception of murder, rape is the most fear-inducing crime (Brodyaga et al., 1975). The severity and threat of rape cannot be overemphasized. One study in New Orleans specifically challenged the assumption that crimes are not gendered and that the effects of gender on the fear of crime should operate similarly regardless of the crime type (Reid and Konrad, 2004). When controlling for the type of crime and perceived risk, the findings were that only for sexual assault does the impact of gender have an unambiguous effect on fear (as expected, women reported more fear), while there were no gender difference in the fear of burglary, and men reported greater fear than women of robbery victimization (ibid.).

The third problem (noted earlier) with perceiving women and girls as irrational in their fear of crime is that most women and girls are raised and conditioned to be afraid of male violence—particularly rape. Madriz (1997) provides convincing documentation of this conditioning, starting with child-hood fairy tales such as *Little Red Riding Hood* that teach us to constantly fear predatory males but to rely on good males to save us from the predatory ones. Women's and girls' conditioning to fear male violence comes from all around us: our parents, our siblings, and the numerous media depictions instilling fear. The media depictions range from television news magazines that often sensa-tionalize rapists, stalkers, and batterers to MTV videos and slasher films that eroticize male violence against women or at least use it as entertainment value. To compound this problem of raising girls to be afraid (addressed more thoroughly in the sections on the effects of culture on gender roles and victim blaming), when women and girls fail to follow the socially prescribed roles, such as going out alone, drinking alcohol, or wearing certain clothes, then they are often blamed by their families, the police, the courts, and others for their victimizations.

> The fear of crime, and specifically the fear of male violence, not only perpetuates the image that women are powerless, weak, and more vulner-able than men but also feeds into the notion that women and men are not entitled to the same rights: women should not and cannot go places where men can go; women cannot engage in activities which are open to men; women should wear proper attire so that they are not molested by men; and since women must protect themselves and their children from criminal victimization, they had better stay home and be good girls. Further, the fear of crime reinforces the subordinate role of women [and heterosexism]: if a woman wants to be safe and protected, she had better be accompanied by a man. (Madriz, 1997, 15–16)

Madriz (1997) also addresses this everyday management of the threat of male violence in girls' and women's lives, adding significant understanding to the problem. First, she notes that fear and concern are not the only responses women and girls have to this threat; many also report *anger.* Second, Madriz (ibid.) documents significant race/ethnicity and class differences in females' fears about and experiences with crime. More specifically, she found that White women report the highest fears of rape, which she attributes partly to the media that most often cast White women as rape victims. Madriz (ibid.) effectively docu-ments the important intersection between racism and sexism in the lives of women and girls of color, not only in their risks of victimization but also in how the police and courts respond to them. But Madriz (ibid.) also points out the unique and significantly additional types of violence that poorer women and girls experience, such as being mugged, robbed, or even murdered in their neighborhoods and higher levels of school violence. Others point out that while men are more afraid of robbery than women are, this is likely due to men participating in more risk-taking behaviors making them vulnerable to robbery, such as walking alone (Reid and Konrad, 2004). A study of fear of crime in the United States from 1973 to 1994 indicates the gender gap may be closing some as women's fear of crime stabilized while men's increased (Haynie, 1998).

Websdale (1996) points out how the social construction of whom women are most threatened by is consistent with patriarchal ideology. To make his case, he examines Washington State's 1990 law on "sexual predators" and the media coverage leading up to this law. He argues that the law and media focused on predators as sick strangers, ignoring the far greater sexual predator threat to children and women *by men in their own families*. Websdale (ibid.) does not believe the passage of the act was conspiratorial in terms of legislators trying to let the most threatening men, marital rapists, and incest-perpetrating males off the hook. Rather, he states that the legislators reasoned that it would be difficult, primarily for financial reasons, for women to turn their abusive mates in if this law covered husbands and other relatives. "Nevertheless, because of the definitional imperatives of the predator law and the media sensationalization of rare one-on-one stranger violence, everyday sexual violence against women and children remains marginalized" (ibid., 49).

Studies on gender and fear of crime in other countries are consistent with findings in the United States. A study on the fear of crime in Ghana found that not only were women more fearful but allowing for contextual accounts helped explain women's increased fear. For example, women's fear of crime was highest in the community that had the highest murder rate of women (Adu-Mireku, 2002). A qualitative study on fear of crime in London, England, found it highly gendered, with women far more likely to report threatening experiences in their own neighborhoods. Fear of crime was most apparent among low-income mothers of dependent children (Whitley and Prince, 2005). A study of two major universities in Greece reported that women college students are significantly more afraid of rape than their male counterparts, they view it as a more serious crime, and they consider themselves far more likely to be raped (Softas-Nall, Bardos, and Fakinos, 1995), which is hardly surprising but confirms how not just actual rape victimization but also the fear of rape is an important gendered aspect of our lives.

EFFECT OF CULTURE ON GENDER ROLES

Sex-role stereotyping begins even before birth. Not only do the names parents choose for their children often differ depending on the child's sex but frequently parents' expectations of that child depend on the child's sex. The societal image of women as weaker, less intelligent, and less valued influences the likelihood of victimization.

In a sense, then, many women and girls have been socialized to be victims of male violence. Girls are rewarded for passivity and feminine behavior, whereas boys are rewarded for aggressiveness and masculine behavior. These stereotypes are often reaffirmed in the media, where strong, independent female characters are rare, but violent, controlling male characters are abundant. Moreover, these images affect both males' and females' perceptions of males' dominance and females' (in)ability to resist male dominance. A woman or girl resisting an attacker is in need of resistance techniques that she has often been conditioned or instructed not to use (Estrich, 1987).

Our culture often suggests that women need men for protection and financial security. For example, a social expectation is that women on dates usually assume their dates will take care of them. This expectation leaves women vulnerable to date rapists who often plan situations where the woman has little control (Ehrhart and Sandler, 1985; Kanin, 1985; Martin and Hummer, 1989; Medea and Thompson, 1974; Sanday, 1990; Schwartz and DeKeseredy, 1997). To compound this, men who perpetrate physical and sexual violence against women they know, or are even intimately involved with, often receive peer support from male friends who may encourage the abuse (DeKeseredy, 1988; Gwartney-Gibbs and Stockard, 1989; Martin and Hummer, 1989; Schwartz et al., 2001). One study concluded: "The data presented ... strongly suggest that sexually abusive male undergraduates' peers encourage them to assault their girlfriends or dating partners" (Schwartz et al., 2001, 641).

There is a tendency to view instances of male aggressiveness (violence) against women and girls as somehow "natural," just as females are supposedly inherently passive (as described in Chapter 2 under the biosocial and evolutionary theories). Explanations of women experiencing male violence often focus on whether male aggression was "natural" in relation to the woman's behavior (Stanko, 1985, 10). This implies that particular behavioral patterns and roles inherent biologically in both males and females encourage and justify the victimization of females by males. Furthermore, it implies that women are the precipitators of men's violence and that in some cases men are justified in their violent behavior. In 1993, a judge in Ohio released a man with a criminal record, who had severely beaten his estranged wife and her daughter (from another relationship) with a crow bar, to shock probation. The judge blamed the woman because she had allegedly been in bed with another man when her estranged husband barged into her home. Such an image of male and female roles and behavior clearly deters the correct assignment of blame and the inhibition of male violence.

Gender stereotyping perpetuates mythical perceptions of both sexual assault offenders and victims. There is a tendency to think that only certain types of women and girls are sexually victimized and battered and that certain types of men are batterers and rapists. Raped women are often stigmatized for being provocative and sexually uncontrolled and for not knowing where to draw the line (Stanko, 1985). This is particularly acute in acquaintance (as compared to stranger) rapes (Frese, Moya, and Megias, 2004). Gender stereotypes are frequently associated with racist and classist assumptions, such as that poor, African American women are more likely to be battered women, and young, White, middle-class women are more likely to be sexual assault victims. Similarly, rapists and batterers are frequently assumed to be poor, African American men, often mentally ill or drug addicted. Such perceptions are not based on reality and inhibit our ability to understand and protect ourselves from sexual victimizations. In the United States, most rapists are White, and 90 percent of rapes are intraracial (within race); yet African American men are disproportionately convicted of rape (Fonow, Richardson, and Wemmerus, 1992).

GENDER DISPARITIES IN POWER

Susan Brownmiller's book *Against Our Will: Men, Women and Rape* (1975) received a great deal of attention. As well as enlightening its many readers on the history and terror of rape, *Against Our Will* exposed the anger many women feel about living in a culture where rape is minimized, ignored, or joked about. *Against Our Will* was a path-breaking book and the first widely read feminist analysis of rape. Unfortunately, despite the power of this book in raising awareness about rape, it has also been criticized for reinforcing myths about African American rapists (Davis, 1981; Tong, 1984; Williams, 1981). However, Brownmiller addresses how lynchings of African Americans in the United States were racially motivated, targeting African American men for fabricated rapes of White women. Overall, *Against Our Will* has had a significant impact on the discourse of rape.

A controversial contention in *Against Our Will* is the statement that rape is nothing more or less than a conscious process of intimidation by which all men keep all women in a state of fear (Brownmiller, 1975, 5). Brownmiller, then, views rape as a conscious means by which men control women. Russell (1984, 153), on the other hand, views rape and other male violence against women as a consequence of the power disparity between the sexes that has existed as long as recorded history. Visano (2002, 52) also views rape as a sociopolitical consequence of inequality. Brownmiller sees rape as causing the disparity between women and men, whereas Russell and Visano view the power disparity between the sexes as causing rape. Consistent with Russell's (1984) belief, a cross-cultural study found that rape levels were related to the levels of society's adherence to patriarchal roles. Rape-prone societies were associated with lower levels of female power and authority, including women's lack of participation in public decision making (Sanday, 1981). Similarly, studies on Serbia (Mrsevic and Hughes, 1997) and the former Yugoslavia (Nikolic-Ristanovic, 1999) exemplify how wars often not only enhance the militarism, nationalism, and poverty within a country but also often increase adherence to tradition and patriarchy in manners that ultimately result in increased violence toward women both inside and outside the home. Notably, a study assessing the relationship between gender inequality and rape, relying on panel data for over 100 U.S. cities over three decades (1970, 1980, and 1990), found that the short-term effect of gender equality is rape (as a sort of backlash), while the long-term effect is a reduced rape rate and improved climate for women (Whaley, 2001). Conversely, the short-term effect of gender inequality is a decreased rape rate, while the long-term effect of gender-inequality is high rape rates (ibid.). Thus, levels of gender equality/inequality are associated with rape rates, with more equality, overall, associated with lower rape rates.

A more accurate depiction of the preceding debate is that female victimization and gender-power disparity reinforce each other (see Figure 6.1). More specifically, victimization and the threat of victimization of females decrease the power of women and girls. Simultaneously, inequalities in power between males and females make females more likely to be victims and

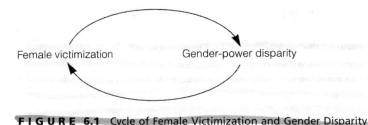

FIGURE 6.1 Cycle of Female Victimization and Gender Disparity

males more likely to be aggressors/offenders. Society, culture, and the crime-processing system contribute to this cycle of female victimization and gender-power disparity in many ways, such as advertisements linking sex and violence, images of women as passive, and police and court officials who blame victims. Thus, we need to simultaneously construct the empowerment of women and girls as equal to that of men and boys in the minds of both females and males.

This power disparity is not limited to physical power but pervades most facets of our lives—men also tend to have higher economic, political, and social status than women. (For example, the Whaley [2001] study just cited measured gender equality through gender inequality to income, education, and access to high-status occupations and legal status data.) A study of fifty U.S. cities found that as the economic, political, and legal status of women decreased, the rape rate increased (Baron and Straus, 1987). These more obvious power differences result in less obvious social and psychological power disparities between men and women. The aggregated gender status differences are equally obvious at the individual level. The verbal and psychological abuses of battered women exemplify this:

> Battered women consistently complain of degrading verbal abuse: You can't do anything right; How could I have ever married a pig like you! Verbal assaults, like physical ones, may go on for hours in a relentless attack on a woman's sense of dignity and self-worth and almost always include threats: I'll cut your throat from one end to another; If you try to leave me, you're dead. (Schechter, 1982, 17)

Thus, power may be asserted in many forms: physically (battering), sexually, economically, and verbally. Male power, perceived and real, limits the freedom and rights of women and girls.

Sexual victimization, like woman battering, is an act of power. Sexual offenders are motivated by a desire to dominate, not simply to achieve sexual gratification. The forced sexual submission is clearly a manner of controlling and humiliating a victim; it is a way for a victim to experience that she does not have control over her own body, whereas the rapist does.

THREATS OF VIOLENCE

Although both male and female children lead lives that are restricted because children are vulnerable and need protection, such limitations often follow females for the rest of their lives. Women are constantly reminded of their vulnerability by messages from friends, family, and the media. "Such fear can induce a continuing state of stress in women and can lead to the adoption of safety precautions that severely restrict women's freedom, such as not going out alone at night or staying out of certain parts of town" (Riger and Gordon, 1981, 73). Similarly, the threat of rape may deny women employment, keep them off the streets at night, and influence them to be "passive and modest for fear that they will be thought provocative" (Griffen, 1971, 35). This myth is not confirmed by recent research reports that unemployed women are more at risk of rape than employed women (Avakame, 1999). However, the message of the vulnerability of women and girls is deeply and culturally embedded: Females should restrict their behavior, actions, and clothing, or something dreadful will happen. Women are reminded of their vulnerability and male violence every time they read or hear of another woman being raped. Moreover, women are rarely able to predict when a threatening or intimidating form of male behavior will escalate to violence. As a result, many women are frequently on guard to the possibility of men's violence, particularly if they have already been victimized (Stanko, 1985, 1990).

The abuse of women by their husbands or boyfriends, similar to their sexual victimization, keeps women under the control of men. The belief that a man is the "king of his castle" is still accepted by some people in society. Abuse, whether physical or threatened, reduces the control the battered woman has over her life while increasing the batterer's control. Just as sexual assault is more likely in a culture with large power disparities between the sexes, the same can be expected of the battering of women. The more authority men are perceived to hold over women, the more likely that battering will occur. The implications of woman battering are significant:

> Violence signifies crossing a boundary in which violation and degradation, previously unacceptable in a loving relationship, are now used as tools of power and coercion. Battering is far more than a single event, even for the woman who is hit once, because it teaches a profound lesson about who controls a relationship and how that control will be exercised.... Self-consciously exercised, violence temporarily brings a man what he wants—his wife acquiesces, placates him, or stops her demands. As a form of terrifying intimidation, violence signifies that the man's way will prevail even when the woman struggles against this imposition. Leaving her in a constantly vigilant state, violence forces a woman to worry about the time, place, or reason for the next attack. (Schechter, 1982, 17)

The threatened and actual victimization of women and girls (whether it is sexual, physical, psychological, or verbal) serves to define the "place" of females in the culture. It restricts the freedom and quality of life of women and girls. Brownmiller's (1975) assertion that all men benefit from rape is more understandable when one recognizes that it is not necessary for all men to victimize all women in order for all women to be afraid of male violence. The fact that some men victimize some women serves to control most females' lives through at least some degree of fear.

This fear affects many aspects of women's lives, such as enrolling in day classes, deciding to walk on the opposite side of the street when they see an unknown male walking toward them, or deciding not to wear certain clothes for fear of being perceived as "fair game" to all men. "Women worry more than men do in the same situations: going to laundromats, using public transportation, or being downtown alone after dark" (Gordon and Riger, 1989, 14). Many women report that the fear of rape crosses their mind regularly (Gordon and Riger, 1989). Compounding the fear of victimization by strangers is the growing awareness that women and girls are more likely to be victimized by males they know.

VICTIM BLAMING

Women and girls who do not follow society's unwritten rules are often blamed if they are raped. Persons who believe that women and girls should lead restrictive lives also tend to believe that a woman or girl who violates these rules is at least partially responsible if she is victimized. Thus, many people believe that girls or women who drink alcohol, especially to the point of getting drunk, are at least partly at fault for their victimization (e.g., Bromley and Territo, 1990). Notably, while research supports the contention that alcohol (and drug) use increases the risk of sexual victimization (e.g., Schwartz and Pitts, 1995; Ward et al., 1991; Warshaw, 1988), research also indicates that women and girls are most at risk of rape committed by current or former boyfriends and husbands (e.g., Russell, 1984). It is not a coincidence that cultural norms dictate that women should not drink but they *should* date and marry men. One study of college women found that in addition to greater alcohol consumption being related to a greater likelihood of being raped, women who are friends with men who get women drunk in order to have sex with them are at a greater risk of sexual victimization (Schwartz and Pitts, 1995). Notably, although a study of college students evaluating rape scenarios found little relative victim-blaming overall, alcohol-consuming victims were viewed by *female* raters as more careless and more culpable for their victimizations (Scronce and Corcoran, 1995).

Victims of rape and battering are more likely to be blamed than victims of any other crimes. Both battered women and sexual assault victims are frequently accused of having provoked the abusive behavior. In fact, "battered wives and rape victims are often accused of 'asking for,' 'deserving,' or 'enjoying' their victimization" (Gelles, 1979, 121). If a batterer tells the police he hit his wife because she was not home when he got home from work, the police officer may ask the battered woman, "Why weren't you home when your husband got home from work?" Similarly, the police officer investigating a sexual assault may ask the victim why she left her door unlocked.

Rape victims are blamed for wearing certain clothing, failing to lock doors or windows, drinking alcohol, waiting for buses late at night, or hitchhiking. It is important for potential victims to know what situations increase their risk of victimization, but it is also important to remember that women do not always have access to their own transportation and that offenders, not victims, are responsible for violence. Again, although reliable statistics inform us that women are most at risk of being raped by husbands and boyfriends (see Russell, 1984), few people are prepared to tell women and girls not to date and marry.

It is not only the "person on the street" who often has preconceived ideas of what "kinds" of people get victimized. Persons responsible for the treatment of victims and punishment of offenders also are frequently misinformed. One study on the perception of sexual assault victims' reputations in court found that divorced women, women of color, and women out alone at night are stereotyped as more readily consenting to more men in more situations (Burt and Albin, 1981). "Having assumed a generalized propensity to consent and attached it to whole classes of women, this line of reasoning then particularizes the argument to this woman (victim) in this situation (alleged rape) and infers consent to this man (alleged assailant). Therefore, following this reasoning, this situation is not a rape" (ibid., 214). A review and meta-analysis of existing studies on attributions of rape victims' responsibility in their own victimizations indicated that the revealing nature of the victim's clothing and character (e.g., sexual reputation) are most likely to result in blaming the victim, whereas the victim–offender relationship and her physical attractiveness were less important (Whatley, 1996). The implication is that certain women are fair game to be sexually victimized, and therefore they cannot be assessed as legitimate rape victims. Such women have supposedly lost their rights to determine with whom they are sexual. Moreover, women and girls are expected to be "sexy but modest, and attractive but not provocative" (Gordon and Riger, 1989, 53). Obviously, these are absurd notions.

Similar to females who are sexually victimized, battered women are frequently blamed for the abuse they receive. "When activists speak about battered women, even sympathetic audiences continually scrutinize the victim's behavior, moral 'failings,' or 'stupid' reactions, returning repeatedly to the question, 'Why do these women stay?'" (Schechter, 1982, 16). One myth is that violence is a way of life for some people; therefore, women who are members of these violence-prone groups will not be as traumatized by rape or battering as other women are. This assertion carries inherently classist and racist overtones. Victimization hurts regardless of whom it happens to, and violence is appropriate only when used in self-defense. The following is an excerpt from a 1984 journal article in *Victimology* depicting the abused wife's responsibility in her own victimization:

The husband, perhaps burdened with a childhood in which violence was a fact of life, strikes the wife; she insults him, perhaps assaulting his masculinity or dredging up an incident from the past, or cringes, begging him to please stop, or runs away with him in hot pursuit, or laughs, or returns the blow. Any of these responses—it's a no-win game—leads to further blows, followed by further counters, etc. In a few weeks or months, the couple is locked into the twisted sequence of regenerative feedback, with no easy way out, rather like two super-powers maniacally escalating an arms race. (Erchak, 1984, 251)

This is not only an example of relieving the offender of responsibility (he was abused as a child) and blaming the victim (she insults him, insults his masculinity, and laughs at him) but is a clear example of ignoring gender-power disparity. It is unrealistic to refer to the husband and wife as two superpowers. This is not a situation of two equals battling it out. In analyses of why some men are violent, a common problem is the claim that they are violent because of the violence that has occurred to them. Why then aren't most females violent because they have experienced so much more victimization? Feminist legal scholar Wendy Murphy (1997, 14) describes court practices that perpetuate the very environment that offers redress to victims of gender-based violence. Regarding women's and girls' violent victimizations by men and boys, she describes how these victims are revictimized in the courts by the lack of accountability for poor treatment of the victims by judges, defense attorneys, and others (ibid.).

Why are some victims blamed for their victimization? One explanation is Lerner's (1965) just-world hypothesis, which states that most people want to believe that we get what we deserve (Karmen, 1984). Therefore, when we hear of bad things happening to people, we often question behaviors that put them more at risk. In this way, we comfort ourselves by thinking, "This won't happen to me because I didn't do...." For instance, often when we hear that someone has cancer, one of our first thoughts is, "Did she (or he) smoke?" This makes some sense because we know smoking may lead to cancer (but it is certainly not a very sensitive question!). In cases of rape, people often ask, "What was she wearing?" This denies that violence is random and rarely predictable.

The just-world approach not only results in the assumption that only certain types of people can be victimized but also serves as a way for people to deceive themselves that they are free from victimization because of who they are and how they behave. Unfortunately, this is not the case—anyone can be a victim. Studies of rape victims and battered women have a difficult time determining who is most at risk because the focus of research has often been on what is unusual about the victims rather than what it is about offenders that makes them likely to rape or batter. Recent research indicates that just-world believers are more likely to blame victims of rape (Murray, Spadafore, and McIntosh, 2005). Similarly, much of the research on woman battering has been sexist, where "aberrant behavior" is more likely to be attributed to the victim than to the offender (Wardell, Gillespie, and Leffler, 1983).

In line with having to accept that violence is random, it is also necessary to acknowledge that the battering and sexual victimizations of most women and girls are committed by persons known to them. Research suggests that about four in five rape victims know their assailants (National Victim Center, 1992; Russell, 1984). Estrich (1987, 10) explains how simple rape cases, where a woman is forced to have sex without consent by only one man whom she knows and who does not beat her or attack her with a gun, are far more common than aggravated rape cases, characterized by extrinsic violence, multiple assailants, or no prior relationship between the victim and the offender. The issue of victim blaming is exemplified by Wolfgang's (1958) coining of the term *victim precipitation*, which focuses on the role victims play in their own victimization. This approach implies that victims are at least partially responsible. In 1975, a psychiatrist published the following statement in the respected *British Journal of Criminology*: "Apparently, some pedophilia offenses never lead to prosecution and consequently are not recorded by courts. Obviously, this is the case in particular when the offense is a minor one and the victim's precipitation very strong" (Virkkunen, 1975, 178).

Victim blaming for the battered woman usually comes in the form of the question, "Why does she stay with him?" The implication is that if she does not want to be battered, she should leave her partner. This view ignores the fact that many women *do* leave; we just do not often hear about them. Blaming battered women for staying also ignores the economic dependence many women and their children have on the batterers and the fear many battered women have developed of being either financially destitute and/or further victimized—even killed by their abusers—if they leave. There are also the issues of family, friends, and the crime-processing system workers who often ignore the offense or encourage the victim to try to work things out. Again, victim blaming often includes asking the woman what she did to precipitate the violence. She is often blamed for starting the violence and for staying in the battering relationship. This diverts the focus from the real problem: the offender.

THE VICTIMIZATION OF WOMEN
AND GIRLS OF COLOR

The diversity of the U.S. population is such that cultural differences and the effects of racism and classism often provide vastly different life experiences. Williams (1981, 18–19) claims that Third World women in the United States (in which she includes African Americans) are disproportionately victims of rape, battering, and sterilization abuse. A study of homeless women found that women of color were more victimized overall—and raped in particular—than White women (Costin, 1992). Using NCVS data for the United States, one study reported that between 1993 and 1998, African American women experienced the highest rates of intimate partner violence, 35 percent higher than White women's rates and about 2.5 times the rate of women of all other races (Rennison and Welchans, 2000). This same study showed no significant differences in intimate partner abuse rates between Latinas and non-Latinas. A U.S. survey reported that American Indian/Alaskan Native women had the highest lifetime rates of being raped (34 percent), followed by mixed-race women (24 percent), African American women (19 percent), White women (18 percent), and Asian/ Pacific Islander women (7 percent) (Tjaden and Thoennes, 1998). Finally, an Australian study found that Black/Aboriginal women were at increased risk of male violence, yet they are silenced and their victimizations are too often invisible (Lucashenko, 1996).

Robert Hampton and his colleagues (2003) report that intimate partner abuse is more common and violent in African American than in White communities and attribute this to structural, cultural–community, and situational contexts, where institutional racism affects African Americans' intimate relationships. They cite other research indicating that African American men are displacing onto their wives and lovers the anger, hatred, and frustrations caused by institutional racism (Hampton, Oliver, and Magarian, 2003, 533). Moreover, institutional racism doubly victimizes African American women as they try to break out of the cycle of violence (ibid.).

African American women have been particularly vulnerable to sexual assault, historically in slavery and currently because of the negative images associated with them, such as being hot-natured and morally loose (Davis, 1997; Giddings, 1984, 31). DeFour (1990) and Cho (1997) effectively document the intersection between sexism and racism regarding the risk of sexual harassment for women-of-color students on college campuses. In a discussion of racist stereotypes of African American, Latina, Asian American, and Native American women, DeFour (ibid., 48) describes how "[t]hese images either portray the women as weak and thus unlikely to fight back if harassed, or they are perceived as very sexual and thus desiring sexual attention." Ontiveros (1997, 188) carefully portrays the gender and race dynamics in sexual harassment in the workplace:

> Since workplace harassment is a power dynamic, women of color serve as likely targets because they are the least powerful participants in the workplace. Unlike White women, they are not privileged by their race. Unlike men of color, they are not privileged by gender. Although a White man might harass any woman, a man of color is not likely to feel that he has the prerogative to harass a White woman. He may feel that he is not able to harass her because of his lack of racial status or because he knows he could be subject to disproportionate reaction stemming from society's deep-seated, historical fears of attacks on White women by non-White men. Harassers may also prefer those women of color, such as Latinas and Asian American women, whom they view as more passive and less likely to complain.

A study of 37 highly educated African American women ranging from 23 to 56 years old found *racialized sexual harassment* as a distinct construct from either racial harassment or sexual harassment (Buchanan and Ormerod, 2002, 114). One example of this is White coworkers asking sexually explicit questions of them, reflecting an underlying assumption that African American women's sexual boundaries, both the behaviors they will engage in and their comfort in discussing sex, are looser than those of White women (ibid.). Another example is White coworkers making comments about African American women's clothing, implying that they look like sex workers or that their clothes are exotic or offensive.

Compounding this is the fact that it is common for society or for crime-processing workers to treat women of color as if they are not really victims. Thus, women of color appear to have disproportionately high victimization rates, yet they are much less likely to have their victimizations acknowledged. This limited and racist legal response is even more profound for immigrant women of color, particularly when they are not legal immigrants (Ontiveros, 1997). Chapter 1 discussed the dichotomy of women into Madonnas or whores (Feinman, 1986). Women more consistent with the Madonna image (for example, virgins and White women) are more likely than women in the whore category to be viewed as legitimate victims. None of Young's (1986) categories of African American women portrays a woman who could be perceived as a legitimate victim: Amazons are viewed as capable of protecting themselves, sinister sapphires are viewed as vindictive or as precipitating the violence against them, and seductresses receive no validation as credible victims. Similarly, Tong (1984, 155) discusses how the view of African American women as less sexually puritanical than White women is objectionable and racist, and it furthermore implies that African American women do not want or need protection against male violence. Clearly, these mythical and racist views of women and girls of color affect how they are treated (or not treated) by the crime-processing system.

Racism and the rape laws are unquestionably inseparable (Schwendinger and Schwendinger, 1983, 110). Even the laws well into the twentieth century stated that women who worked outside the home or whose race had a history of sexual exploitation were outside the realm of "womanhood" and its prerogative (Giddings, 1984, 49). Thus, the law implied that women of color were not legally capable of being raped. In fact, rape laws were originally mandated to protect upper-class White men whose wives and daughters could be assaulted (Davis, 1981). Thus, in addition to the rape laws emerging because of a view of women as men's property, there were significant racist and classist components in the development of these laws.

The criminal legal system and society as a whole, then, tend to minimize female victims of male violence, and this is particularly true if the victims are of color and/or poor. The incongruity between high victimization rates and low validation rates for persons of color in this society serves to further victimize and oppress this group. The lack of response by the crime-processing system may lead victims to take matters into their own hands to protect themselves. However, any female victim of sexual assault or battering who uses self-defense runs the risk of being charged with a crime herself. This is most evident for women of color, as Williams (1981) exemplifies through a large number of cases of women of color who were incarcerated for protecting themselves against violent men. These women failed to be taken seriously as victims but were taken extremely seriously as so-called offenders in their efforts to protect themselves and their children.

There is a significant need for progressives to join forces in fighting *both* racism and violence against women (Matthews, 1993; Tong, 1984; Williams, 1981). Historically, there has been a cleavage between White and African American women fighting male violence because the African American women have also had to fight the stereotype of African American male offenders. In the late 1800s, African American activist Ida B. Wells publicly stated that there was a focus on accusing African American males of raping White females, whereas the rape of African American girls and women by White males was overlooked (Giddings, 1984). While slave masters and other White men raped African American women freely, death was the punishment for an African American man convicted of raping a White woman (Schwendinger and Schwendinger, 1983, 108). Indeed, because most slave codes did not recognize the rape of African American women, there was no punishment for enslaved, free, or White men who did so (Johnson, 2003).

African American males, the guilty and innocent alike, are still indiscriminately brought to justice for rape (Davis, 1981). More recent research confirms the disproportionately harsh treatment of African American males charged with rape compared to the treatment of White males (Walsh, 1987). Davis (1981) discusses how it has been difficult for African American women to be active in the antirape movement, given the treatment of African American men (particularly innocent African American men) charged with rape. The antirape movement in the United States began at the same time as African American feminism and at the same time that African American women began feeling distrustful of White feminists (Matthews, 1993). In more recent years, however, rape-crisis centers and battered-women's shelters have become more integrated and more dedicated to combating racism as well as sexism and male violence.

Recent research identifies the added burden among African American women to uphold a strong African American woman image (Donovan and Williams, 2002; Potter, 2004). Perhaps this is why recent scholarship found that White women are far more likely than women of color to engage in more advanced help-seeking behaviors, such as police reporting, asking for help from family and friends, and seeking help from psychiatrists and social service agencies (Kaukinen, 2004). However, another study found no racial differences among victims of intimate partner abuse in terms of distrust of the criminal legal system (Bui, 2001).

THE VICTIMIZATION OF IMMIGRANT WOMEN AND GIRLS

Until recently, the unique experience and challenges of immigrant women and girls who are victimized has been largely ignored, although one study states that intimate partner abuse of immigrant women is at epidemic proportions (Raj and Silverman, 2002, 367). To date, the bulk of the research on the victimization of immigrant women is on intimate partner abuse, with limited research on sexual victimizations (outside of those committed by intimate partners). The research includes immigrant women who are partners of immigrant men, as well as immigrant women married to men from the United States. In both cases, whether their male partners are immigrants or not, immigrant status poses unique and troubling experiences for women abused by their partners.

One of the earliest treatises on this topic is Margaret Abraham's (2000) book *Speaking the Unspeakable: Marital Violence among South Asian Immigrants in the United States*. This and subsequent studies on immigrant women who are victims of intimate partner abuse provide insight into the vulnerability of women in the United States whose national origin, and possibly language and citizenship barriers, place them as outsiders and isolated. Abraham's book explains (1) how immigrant status can serve as a risk factor in domestic violence; (2) how both informal and formal responses to domestic violence are related to immigrant status; (3) how immigrant status is related to resistance factors for battered women; (4) how immigrant status, gender, race, and class intersect; and (5) the development and struggles of advocacy groups for battered women within South Asian communities in the United States (Abraham, 2000). Similarly, Hoan Bui's (2004) book examines Vietnamese immigrant women to the United States and, like Abraham (2000), allows the reader to understand the significant intersection between gender, race, class, nationality, and domestic violence experiences, including how the criminal legal system responds to victims and abusers. A review of the research on the intimate partner abuse of immigrant women explains how immigrant women's cultures, contexts, and legal status can (1) increase vulnerability to abuse, (2) be used by batterers to control and abuse immigrant women, and (3) create barriers to women seeking and receiving help (Raj and Silverman, 2002).

A recent study of Latina immigrants to the United States concluded that although the women unanimously affirmed that intimate partner abuse was an extensive problem in the Latino/a community, they also reported that it was made invisible because victims are expected to see it as their lot in life (Adames and Campbell, 2005). Furthermore, the women reported that intimate-partner abuse in immigrant Latino/a communities is rooted in external factors, including cultural norms and stresses related to immigration changes (ibid., 1359). Another study examined the intimate partner abuse against immigrant wives and fiancées at the hands of U.S. military men (Erez and Bach, 2003). The study concluded: "The immigration circumstances and status interact with the military context to compound the abuse, further marginalize victims/survivors, and weaken the military social service and legal systems' response" (ibid., 1093).

As previously stated, most of the research on the victimization of immigrant women and girls focuses on intimate partner abuse (sometimes addressing marital rape in these cases). Two studies expand beyond intimate partners. A study of thirty-six Ethiopian immigrants to Israel who were admitted as psychiatric patients reported that even prior to Jewish Ethiopians fleeing their country, many were raped, robbed, or murdered by marauding militias (Grisaru, Irwin, and Kaplan, 2003, 242). Upon fleeing Ethiopia, typically through Sudan, the escapees faced serious violations by marauding bands and Ethiopian authorities, who not only stripped, imprisoned, and emotionally and physically tortured them but who also raped the women in front of their families (ibid., 242). A recent study of girls and young women in racialized immigrant communities in western Canada found that to truly understand these young women's lives, it is necessary to analyze how racism interlocks with other systems of domination to influence the life chances and reality of girls who are racialized (Jiwani, 2005, 853). Indeed, these young women identified racism as the dominant and most pervasive form of violence they encountered in their daily lives (ibid., 858). Racism permeated their lives and resulted in their "othering" through inferiorization, trivialization, exoticization, and erasure (ibid., 867). These girls/young women were described as having to walk the tightrope of trying to fit into a mainstream society that often conflicted with their families' ideals.

THE VICTIMIZATION OF WOMEN AND GIRLS WITH DISABILITIES

Many people assume that women and girls with physical or mental disabilities are less at risk for victimization of any kind. This erroneous assumption is based largely on two faulty beliefs. First is the belief that no one would want to harm someone who is already harmed or vulnerable. The second faulty belief, which is most pronounced for sexual victimizations, is that no one would find such women or girls sexually attractive. The reality is that disabled women and girls are at an increased risk of victimization, but the silence surrounding this violence makes their victimizations invisible and unknown (Chenoweth, 1996, 391; see also Roberto and Teaster, 2005). One study reported that children with disabilities in the United States are almost twice as likely as children without disabilities to be sexually victimized (Cross, Kaye, and Ratnofsky, 1995, as cited in Chenoweth, 1996). Mentally and/or physically disabled women and girls who are institutionalized are at particularly high risk of sexual victimization (Chenoweth, 1996). Chenoweth (ibid., 405) also states that disabled women and girls are in a paradox of being perceived as both asexual and sexually promiscuous and depraved. Once a woman's identity is constructed as asexual, the license to commit many abuses usually follows (ibid.).

Women with disabilities are more at risk than nondisabled women, given their weakened status to defend or care for themselves (Curry, Hassouneh-Phillips, and Johnston-Silverberg, 2001; Gilson, Cramer, and DePoy, 2001a, 2001b). Whether their dependence on caregivers is in their homes, hospitals, or other institutions, this dependency places them at risk of physical, emotional, and sexual abuse. Gilson and his colleagues (2001b), however, also point out that battered women are at risk of developing disabilities, or even an illness, as a result of the intimate partner abuse. Abuse of disabled women can include such actions and inactions as failing to provide medications, threats to institutionalize if they fail to comply with sexual requests or to report abuse, taking away access to telephones and/or wheelchairs, and so on (see Gilson, Cramer, and DePoy, 2001b). A qualitative study of intimate partner survivors who are disabled women found three subthemes characterizing the unique forms of intimate partner abuse directed at disabled women *and* these women's responses to them (ibid.) as reported in Exhibit 6.1. The types of abuse

E X H I B I T 6.1   **Forms of Intimate Partner Abuse Directed at Disabled Women and Their Responses to This Abuse**

Unique Forms of Intimate Partner Abuse Directed at Disabled Women

Physical and Emotional Assault
- Conveying judgmental attitudes based on her disability
- Threatening her with the loss of her children because of her disability
- Threatening to institutionalize her

Neglect
- Physical
- Withholding personal assistance
- Erecting or refusing to remove architectural barriers in the home
- Lifting a wheelchair out of the way with her in it
- Not contacting a physician when one is needed

Control/Restraint
- Withholding medications
- Controlling access to needed items on persons
- Controlling assistive services
- Using disability to demean, discredit, or dismiss
- Refusing access to social support
- Refusing to communicate using assistive devices

Types of Disabled Women's Responses to Intimate Partner Abuse

Bad Self
- Trying to be good
- Internalizing blame for the abuse
- Doubting herself

Stuck
- Feeling that she cannot leave the relationship
- Feeling dependent on her abuser
- Not knowing where to go or what to do

Movement
- Confronting the abuser
- Threatening to leave if the abuse continues
- Separating from or divorcing the abuser
- Finding role models
- Spending time with positive people
- Sharing stories with other abused women
- Developing a support system
- Connecting with service providers
- Volunteering to help other abused women

SOURCE: Stephen French Gilson, Elizabeth P. Cramer, and Elizabeth DePoy. 2001. Redefining Abuse of Women with Disabilities. *Affilia* 16:228.

are physical and emotional assault, neglect, and control/restraint, acted out in manners unique to disabled women's vulnerabilities. The women's responses include self-blame (bad self), feeling stuck, moving to confront and/or leave the abuser, and working with other abused women (ibid.).

Elman's (1997, 257) research on disability pornography, the pornography made of disabled girls and women, reports that these media both sexualize and ridicule women and girls whose health and relative immobility make them especially vulnerable to sexual abuse. Although some of these portrayals, such as in *Playboy*, claim to liberate women with disabilities from the stigma of sexual unattractiveness, Elman (ibid., 258) claims that pornography has never promoted sexual liberation for any women, and for disabled women and girls, their disabilities are used to sexualize their passivity and immobility, fetishizing their disabilities. Indeed, one adolescent humor magazine, *Slam*, told how to rape mentally retarded girls and advised that "[the boy readers] will probably get away with it" (ibid., 259). Elman compares the pornography of disabled women and girls to that of African American women, where the woman is portrayed as a sexual object who delights in her brutal subordination (ibid., 262). Finally, Elman (ibid., 265) describes how the sadomasochistic representations of disabled women and girls include tying women to wheelchairs and showing where orthopedic bandages replace the leather and rope in sadomasochistic pornography.

SUMMARY

The foremost image of the female victim has been invisibility. Battering and sexual victimization are the most underreported crimes against persons in the criminal legal system. Information on the victimization of females is becoming more widespread, including knowledge that it happens more frequently than once thought and that the nature of these victimizations is more threatening and violent than once acknowledged. Moreover, culture and society tend to support gender roles that encourage the likelihood of male violence against females. Women and girls are encouraged to be passive and ladylike, whereas men and boys are encouraged to be aggressive.

Determination of the causes of the victimization of females is grounded in the acceptance of gender disparities in power. This chapter discussed the victimization of females as both a result and a reinforcement of gender-power disparity. That is, the threat and existence of the victimization of females decreases the power of women and girls; simultaneously, this power disparity encourages victimization. Furthermore, the threat of violence against females restricts the freedom of women and girls. Fear of sexual victimization influences where, when, and how women will work, take classes, socialize, and live. Women learn they are not safe alone, at night, in certain areas of town, and with certain types of people. Compounding these restrictions is the more recent acknowledgment of the high degree of sexual victimization perpetrated by persons known, often well known, to the victim. Awareness of the prevalence and controlling nature of woman battering has also grown.

Stereotypical images in society imply that some women ask for rape through their clothing, behavior, and even race or class. Therefore, this view perpetuates the myth that the real rape victims are White, wealthy virgins who resisted the attack. Similarly, stereotypical images imply that women who nag, who commit adultery, or who engage in other demasculizing or obnoxious behavior precipitate their battering victimizations. Victim blaming not only holds victims responsible for the violence and exploitation against them but also mistakenly assures persons that violence is not random.

REFERENCES

Abraham, Margaret. 2000. *Speaking the Unspeakable: Marital Violence among South Asian Immigrants in the United States*. New Brunswick, NJ: Rutgers University Press.

Adames, Sandra Bibiana, and Rebecca Campbell. 2005. Immigrant Latinas' Conceptualizations of Intimate Partner Violence. *Violence Against Women* 11:1341–1364.

Adu-Mireku, Samuel. 2002. Fear of Crime among Residents of Three Communities in Accra, Ghana. *International Journal of Comparative Sociology* 43:153–168.

Anetzberger, Georgia J. 1997. Elderly Adult Survivors of Family Violence. *Violence Against Women* 3:499–514.

Avakame, Edem F. 1999. Females' Labor Force Participation. *Violence Against Women* 5:926–949.

Baron, Larry, and Murray A. Straus. 1987. Four Theories of Rape: A Macrosociological Analysis. *Social Problems* 34:467–489.

Baum, Katrina, and Patsy Klaus. 2005. Violent Victimization of College Students, 1995–2002. Bureau of Justice Statistics. U.S. Department of Justice. September, 12pp.

Bergen, Raquel Kennedy. 2004. Studying Wife Rape. *Violence Against Women* 10:1407–1416.

Braungart, Margaret M., Richard G. Braungart, and William J. Hoyer. 1980. Age, Sex, and Social Factors in Fear of Crime. *Sociological Forces* 13:55–66.

Brodyaga, A. L., M. Gates, S. Singer, M. Tucker, and R. White. 1975. *Rape and Its Victims: A Report for Citizens, Health Facilities and Criminal Justice Agencies*. Washington, DC: Government Printing Office.

Bromley, M. L., and L. Territo. 1990. *College Crime Prevention and Personal Safety Awareness*. Springfield, IL: Charles C. Thomas.

Brownmiller, Susan. 1975. *Against Our Will: Men, Women and Rape*. New York: Simon and Schuster.

Buchanan, NiCole T. and Alayne J. Ormerod. 2002. Racialized Sexual Harassment in the Lives of African American Women. Pp. 107–124 in *Violence in the Lives of Black Women*, edited by C. M. West. New York: Haworth Press.

Bui, Hoan H. 2001. Domestic Violence Victims' Behavior in Favor of Prosecution. *Women & Criminal Justice* 12:51–76.

——— 2004. *In the Adopted Land: Abused Immigrant Women and the Criminal Justice System*. Westport, CT: Greenwood.

Burt, Martha R., and Rochelle S. Albin. 1981. Rape Myths, Rape Definitions, and Probability of Conviction. *Journal of Applied Social Psychology* 11:212–230.

Catalano, Shannan. 2004. Criminal Victimization, 2003. Bureau of Justice Statistics. U.S. Department of Justice. September, 12pp.

Chapman, Jane Roberts. 1990. Violence against Women as a Violation of Human Rights. *Social Justice* 17: 54–70.

Chenoweth, Lesley. 1996. Violence and Women with Disabilities. *Violence Against Women* 2:391–411.

Cho, Sumi K. 1997. Converging Stereotypes in Racialized Sexual Harassment: Where the Model Minority Meets Suzie Wong. Pp. 203–220 in *Critical Race Feminism*, edited by A. K. Wing, New York: New York University Press.

Clemente, Frank, and Michael B. Kleiman. 1976. Fear of Crime among the Aged. *Gerontologist* 16:211–219.

Cohen, L. E., and M. Felson. 1979. Social Change and Crime Rate Trends: A Routine Activity Approach. *American Sociological Review* 44: 588–608.

Costin, Charisse T. M. 1992. The Influence of Race in Urban Homeless Females' Fear of Crime. *Justice Quarterly* 9:721–730.

Cross, S. B., E. Kaye, and A. C. A. Ratnofsky. 1995. *A Report on the Maltreatment of Children with Disabilities*. Washington, DC: National Center on Child Abuse and Neglect.

Curry, Mary Ann, Dena Hassouneh-Phillips, and Anne Johnston-Silverberg. 2001. Abuse of Women with Disabilities. *Violence Against Women* 7:60–79.

Davis, Angela Y. 1981. *Women, Race, and Class*. New York: Vintage Press.

Davis, Deidre E. 1997. The Harm That Has No Name: Street Harassment, Embodiment, and African American Women. Pp. 192–202 in *Critical Race Feminism*, edited by A. K. Wing, New York: New York University Press.

DeFour, Darlene C. 1990. The Interface of Racism and Sexism on College Campuses. Pp. 45–52 in *Ivory Power: Sexual Harassment on Campus*, edited by M. A. Paludi. Albany: State University of New York Press.

DeKeseredy, Walter S. 1988. *Woman Abuse in Dating Relationships: The Role of Male Peer Support*. Toronto: Canadian Scholars Press.

Donovan, Roxanne, and Michelle Williams. 2002. Living at the Intersection: The Effects of Racism and Sexism on Black Rape Survivors. Pp. 95–105 in *Violence in the Lives of Black Women*, edited by C. M. West. New York: Haworth Press.

Edleson, Jeffrey L. 1999. The Overlap between Child Maltreatment and Woman Battering. *Violence Against Women* 5:134–154.

Ehrhart, Julie K., and Bernice R. Sandler. 1985. *Campus Gang Rape: Party Games?* Washington DC: Project on the Status and Eduction of Women, Association of American Colleges.

Elman, R. Amy. 1997. Disability Pornography: The Fetishization of Women's Vulnerabilities. *Violence Against Women* 3:257–270.

Erchak, G. M. 1984. The Escalation and Maintenance of Spouse Abuse: A Cybernetic Model. *Victimology* 9:247–253.

Erez, Edna, and Shayna Bach. 2003. Immigration, Domestic Violence, and the Military. *Violence Against Women* 9:1093–1117.

Estrich, Susan. 1987. *Real Rape*. Cambridge, MA: Harvard University Press.

Evans, Laura J. 1978. Sexual Harassment: Women's Hidden Occupational Hazard. Pp. 202–223 in *The Victimization of Women*, edited by J. Roberts-Chapman and M. Gates. Beverly Hills, CA: Sage.

Feinman, Clarice. 1986. *Women in the Criminal Justice System*. New York: Praeger.

Finkelhor, David, and Kersti Yllo. 1985. *License to Rape: Sexual Abuse of Wives*. New York: Free Press.

Fonow, Mary Margaret, Laurel Richardson, and Virginia Wemmerus. 1992. Feminist Rape Education: Does It Work? *Gender and Society* 6:108–121.

Frese, Bettina, Miguel Moya, and Jesus L. Megias. 2004. Social Perception of Rape: How Rape Myth Acceptance Modulates the Influence of Situational Factors. *Journal of Interpersonal Violence* 19:143–161.

Gelles, Richard J. 1979. *Family Violence*. Beverly Hills, CA: Sage.

———. 1983. An Exchange/Social Control Theory. Pp. 151–165 in *The Dark Side of Families*, edited by D. Finkelhor, R. J. Gelles, G. T. Hotaling, and M. A. Straus. Beverly Hills, CA: Sage.

Giddings, Paula S. 1984. *When and Where I Enter: The Impact of Black Women on Race and Sex in America*. Toronto: Bantam Books.

Gilson, Stephen French, Elizabeth P. Cramer, and Elizabeth DePoy. 2001a. Linking the Assessment of Self-Reported Functional Capacity with Abuse Experiences of Women with Disabilities. *Affilia* 16:220–235.

———. 2001b. Redefining Abuse of Women with Disabilities. *Affilia* 16:220–235.

Gordon, Linda. 1977. *Women's Body, Women's Right: A Social History of Birth Control in America*. New York: Penguin Books.

Gordon, Margaret T. and Stephanic Riger. 1989. *The Female Fear*. New York: Free Press.

Gottfredson, Michael R. 1986. Substantive Contributions of Victimization Surveys. In *Crime and Justice: An Annual Review of Research*. Chicago: University of Chicago.

Griffen, Susan. 1971. Rape: The All-American Crime. *Ramparts* (September): 26–35.

———. 1981. *Pornography and Silence*. New York: Harper Colophon Books.

Grisaru, Nimrod, Martin Irwin, and Zeev Kaplan. 2003. Acute Psychotic Episodes as a Reaction to Severe Trauma in a Population of Ethiopian Immigrants to Israel. *Stress and Health* 19:241–247.

Grossman, Susan F., and Marta Lundy. 2003. Use of Domestic Violence Services across Race and Ethnicity by Women Aged 55 and Older. *Violence Against Women* 9:1442–1452.

Gwartney-Gibbs, Patricia, and Jean Stockard. 1989. Courtship Aggression and Mixed-Sex Peer Groups. Pp. 185–204 in *Violence in Dating Relationships*, edited by M. Pirog-Good and J. E. Stets. New York: Praeger.

Hampton, Robert, William Oliver, and Lucia Magarian. 2003. Domestic Violence in the African American Community. *Violence Against Women* 9:533–557.

Haynie, Dana L. 1998. The Gender Gap in Fear of Crime, 1973–1994. *Criminal Justice Review* 23:29–50.

Herman, Judith Lewis. 2005. Justice from the Victim's Perspective. *Violence Against Women* 11:571–602.

Jiwani, Yasmin. 2005. Walking a Tightrope: The Many Faces of Violence in the Lives of Racialized Immigrant Girls and Young Women. *Violence Against Women* 11:846–875.

Johnson, Paula C. 2003. *Inner Lives: Voices of African American Women in Prison*. New York: New York University Press.

Jonson, Hakan, and Malin Akerstrom. 2004. Neglect of Elderly Women in Feminist Studies of Violence: A Case of Ageism. *Journal of Elder Abuse & Neglect* 16:47–63.

Kanin, Eugene J. 1985. Date Rapists. *Archives of Sexual Behavior* 6:67–76.

Karmen, A. 1984. *Crime Victims: An Introduction to Victimology*. Monterey, CA: Brooks/Cole.

Kaukinen, Catherine. 2004. The Help-Seeking Strategies of Female Violent-Crime Victims: The Direct and Conditional Effects of Race and the Victim-Offender Relationship. *Journal of Interpersonal Violence* 19: 967–990.

LaGrange, Randy L., and Kenneth F. Ferraro. 1989. Assessing Age and Gender Differences in Perceived Risk and Fear of Crime. *Criminology* 27:697–718.

Lerner, M. 1965. Evaluation of Performance as a Function of Performer's Reward and Attractiveness. *Journal of Personality and Social Psychology* 1:355–360.

Lowney, Kathleen S., and Joel Best. 1995. Stalking Strangers and Lovers: Changing Media Typifications of New Crime Problem. Pp. 33–57 in *Images of Issues: Typifying Contemporary Social Problems*, 2nd edition, edited by Joel Best. New York: Aldine De Gruyter.

Lucashenko, Melissa. 1996. Violence against Indigenous Women. *Violence Against Women* 2:378–390.

Madriz, Esther. 1997. *Nothing Bad Happens to Good Girls: Fear of Crime in Women's Lives*. Berkeley: University of California Press.

Martin, Patricia Y., and Robert A. Hummer. 1989. Fraternities and Rape on Campus. *Gender and Society* 3:457–473.

Matthews, Nancy A. 1993. Surmounting a Legacy: The Expansion of Racial Diversity in a Local Anti-Rape Movement. Pp. 177–192 in *Violence against Women: The Bloody Footprints*, edited by P. B. Bart and E. G. Moran. Newbury Park, CA: Sage.

Mears, Jane. 2003. Survival Is Not Enough: Violence against Older Women in Australia. *Violence Against Women* 9:1478–1489.

Medea, Andra, and Kathleen Thompson. 1974. *Against Rape*. New York: Farrar, Straus and Giroux.

Meyer, Shannon-Lee, Dina Vivian, and K. Daneil O'Leary. 1998. Men's Sexual Aggression in Marriage. *Violence Against Women* 4:415–435.

Michalski, Joseph H. 2004. Making Sense out of Trends in Intimate Partner Violence. *Violence Against Women* 10:652–675.

Miethe, T. D., M. C. Stafford, and J. S. Long. 1987. Social Differentiation in Criminal Victimization: A Test of Routine Activities/Lifestyle Theories. *American Sociological Review* 52:184–194.

Mrsevic, Zorica, and Donna M. Hughes. 1997. Violence against Women in Belgrade, Serbia. *Violence Against Women* 3:101–128.

Murphy, Wendy. 1997. Gender Bias in the Criminal Justice System. *Harvard Women's Law Review* 20:14–26.

Murray, John D., Jo Ann Spadafore, and William D. McIntosh. 2005. Belief in a Just World and Social Perception. *Journal of Social Psychology* 145:35–47.

National Victim Center. 1992. *Rape in America*. Arlington, VA, 18pp.

Nikolic-Ristanovic, Vesna. 1999. Living without Democracy and Peace: Violence against Women in the Former Yugoslavia. *Violence Against Women* 5:63–80.

Ockleford, Elizabeth, Yvonne Barnes-Holmes, Roberta Morichelli, Orjaria Asesha, Francesca Scocchera, Freerick Furniss, Claudio Sdogati, and Dermot Barnes-Holms. 2003. Mistreatment of Older Women in Three European Countries. *Violence Against Women* 9:1453–1464.

Ontiveros, Maria L. 1997. Three Perspectives on Workplace Harassment of Women of Color. Pp. 188–192 in *Critical Race Feminism*, edited by A. K. Wing. New York: New York University Press.

Ortega, Suzanne T., and Jessie L. Myles. 1987. Race and Gender Effects on Fear of Crime: An Interactive Model with Age. *Criminology* 25:133–152.

Potter, Hillary. 2004. Intimate Partner Violence against African American Women: The Effects of Social Structure and Black Culture on Patterns of Abuse. Unpublished dissertation. Boulder: University of Colorado.

Raj, Anita, and Jay Silverman. 2002. Violence against Immigrant Women. *Violence Against Women* 8:367–398.

Reid, Lesley Williams, and Miriam Konrad. 2004. The Gender Gap in Fear. *Sociological Spectrum* 24:399–425.

Rennison, Callie Marie, and Sarah Welchans. 2000. Intimate Partner Violence. Bureau of Justice Statistics. Department of Justice. Special Report, May, 11pp.

Riger, Stephanie. 1981. On Women. Pp. 47–66 in *Reactions to Crime*, edited by D. A. Lewis. Beverly Hills, CA: Sage.

Riger, Stephanie, and Margaret T. Gordon. 1981. The Fear of Rape: A Study in Social Control. *Journal of Social Issues* 37:71–92.

Roberto, Karen A., and Pamela B. Teaster. 2005. Sexual Abuse of Vulnerable Young and Old Women. *Violence Against Women* 11:473–504.

Russell, Diana E. H. 1984. *Sexual Exploitation: Rape, Child Sexual Abuse, and Workplace Harassment*. Beverly Hills, CA: Sage.

———. 1990. *Rape in Marriage*. Bloomington: Indiana University Press.

Sanday, Peggy R. 1981. The Socio-Cultural Context of Rape: A Cross-Cultural Study. *Journal of Social Issues* 37:5–27.

———. 1990. *Fraternity Gang Rape*. New York: New York University Press.

Sanders, William B. 1980. *Rape and Woman's Identity*. Beverly Hills, CA: Sage.

Schechter, Susan. 1982. *Women and Male Violence*. Boston: South End Press.

Schwartz, Martin D., and Walter S. DeKeseredy. 1997. *Sexual Assault on the College Campus*. Thousand Oaks, CA: Sage.

Schwartz, Martin D., Walter S. DeKeseredy, David Tait, and Shahid Alvi. 2001. Male Peer Support and a Feminist Routing Activities Theory: Understanding Sexual Assault on the College Campus. *Justice Quarterly* 18:623–649.

Schwartz, Martin D., and Victoria L. Pitts. 1995. Exploring a Feminist Routine Activities Approach to Explaining Sexual Assault. *Justice Quarterly* 12:9–31.

Schwendinger, Julia R., and Herman Schwendinger. 1983. *Rape and Inequality*. Beverly Hills, CA: Sage.

Scronce, Christine A., and Kevin J. Corcoran. 1995. The Influence of the Victim's Consumption of Alcohol on Perceptions of Stranger and Acquaintance Rape. *Violence Against Women* 1:241–253.

Smith, Michael D. 1994. Enhancing the Quality of Survey Data on Violence against Women: A Feminist Approach. *Gender and Society* 8: 109–127.

Softas-Nall, Basilia, Achilles Bardos, and Michael Fakinos. 1995. Fear of Rape. *Violence Against Women* 1:174–186.

Spencer, Cassie C. 1987. Sexual Assault: The Second Victimization. Pp. 54–73 in *Women, Courts, and Equality*, edited by L. L. Crites and W. L. Hepperle. Newbury Park, CA: Sage.

Stanko, Elizabeth A. 1985. *Intimate Intrusions: Women's Experience of Male Violence*. London: Routledge and Kegan Paul.

———. 1990. *Everyday Violence: How Women and Men Experience Sexual and Physical Danger*. London: Pandora.

———. 1992. The Case of Fearful Women: Gender, Personal Safety and Fear. *Women & Criminal Justice* 4:117–135.

Tjaden, Patricia, and Nancy Thoennes. 1998. Prevalence, Incidence, and Consequences of Violence against Women. U.S. Department of Justice. Research in Brief. November, 16pp.

———. 2000. Prevalence and Consequences of Male-to-Female and Female-to-Male Intimate Partner Violence as Measured by the National Violence Against Women Survey. *Violence Against Women* 6:142–161.

Tong, Rosemarie. 1984. *Women, Sex, and the Law*. Totawa, NJ: Rowman and Allanheld.

Virkkunen, M. 1975. Victim-Precipitated Pedophilia Offenses. *British Journal of Criminology* 15:175–180.

Visano, Livy A. 2002. A Critical Critique of the Cultures of Control: A Case study of Cyber Rape. Pp. 51–72 in *Sexual Violence*, edited by J. F. Hodgson and D. S. Kelley. Westport, CT: Praeger.

Wallace, Harvey. 1995. A Prosecutor's Guide to Stalking. *Prosecutor.* February 29, Vol 26.

Walker, Lenore E. 1979. *The Battered Woman*. New York: Harper and Row.

Walsh, Anthony. 1987. The Sexual Stratification Hypothesis and Sexual Assault in Light of the Changing Conceptions of Race. *Criminology* 25:153–174.

Warchol, Greg. 1998. Workplace Violence, 1992–1996. Bureau of Justice Statistics. U.S. Department of Justice, July, 8pp.

Ward, S. K., K. Chapman, S. White, and K. Williams. 1991. Acquaintance Rape and the College Social Scene. *Family Relations* 40:65–71.

Wardell, Laurie, Dair L. Gillespie, and Ann Leffler. 1983. Science and Violence against Wives. Pp. 69–84 in *The Dark Side of Families*, edited by D. Finkelhor, R. J. Gelles, G. T. Hotaling, and M. A. Straus. Beverly Hills, CA: Sage.

Warr, Mark. 1984. Fear of Victimization: Why Are Women and the Elderly More Afraid? *Social Science Quarterly* 65:681–702.

Warshaw, Robin. 1988. *I Never Called It Rape*. New York: Harper and Row.

Websdale, Neil S. 1996. Predators: The Social Construction of "Stranger-Danger" in Washington State as a Form of Patriarchal Ideology. *Women & Criminal Justice* 7:43–68.

Whaley, Rachel Bridges. 2001. The Paradoxical Relationship between Gender Inequality and Rape. *Gender & Society* 15:531–555.

Whatley, Mark A. 1996. Victim Characteristics Influencing Attributions of Responsibility to Rape Victims: A Meta-Analysis. *Aggression and Violent Behavior* 1:81–96.

Whitley, Rob, and Martin Prince. 2005. Fear of Crime, Mobility and Mental Health in Inner-City London, UK. *Social Science and Medicine* 61:1678–1688.

Williams, Lynora. 1981. Violence against Women. *The Black Scholar* (January/ February):18–24.

Wolfgang, Marvin. 1958. *Patterns in Criminal Homicide*. Philadelphia: University of Pennsylvania Press.

Young, Vernetta D. 1986. Gender Expectations and Their Impact on Black Female Offenders and Victims. *Justice Quarterly* 3:305–328.

———. 1992. Fear of Victimization and Victimization Rates among Women: A Paradox? *Justice Quarterly* 9:419–442.

7

❖

Sexual Victimization

Survivors of rape face institutionally sanctioned forms of scrutiny,
incredulity, and distrust, which are directed at them in ways that are
virtually unknown, if not only exceptionally employed, in the
investigation and trial processes of any other criminal offense. The rules
of evidence and the judicial procedures that have long granted aggressive
cross-examinations of female complainants ... [are] particularly true for
women who are sexually active, women who have sought counseling or
therapy, and women from marginalized groups, such as women of color
and women who have been institutionalized.

DENIKE, 2002, 101

DEFINING SEXUAL VICTIMIZATION

Problems arise from the limitations implied when defining the word *rape*. From 1770
to 1845 in England, rape was defined as penetration of the vagina by the penis, where
ejaculation had taken place (Clark, 1987, 8–9). This was extremely difficult to prove in
court. The traditional, common-law definition of rape states: "A man commits rape
when he engages in intercourse ... with a woman not his wife; by force or threat of
force; against her will and without her consent" (Estrich, 1987, 8). Historically, then,
rape has most commonly been defined as forced penile–vaginal intercourse, committed by an adult male stranger against an adult female. In reality, rape can occur between
a variety of persons (female and male, young or old) and in many forms, for example,
oral and anal rape, and sexual assaults using foreign objects. Recent work documents
the dynamics of woman-to-woman sexual violence, and similar to heterosexual rape,
this is most common by current or former partners or dates (Girschick, 2002a, 2002b).
Since the 1970s, most states have worked to expand the legal definition of rape or
sexual conduct to include these other serious forms of sexual abuse.

In addition to legislation, researchers have also worked to change and broaden
the definitions of sexual abuse. Russell (1984, 21) believes that even the term

266

Comparative Perspectives: Rape and Death in Darfur

Genocide against Africans living in villages and on farms in the Darfur region of Sudan began in February 2003. Briefly, genocide refers to the killing and otherwise harming of a group of people based on their race, religion, color, or ethnic origin, with the intent of destroying that group of people. "The Arab-dominated Sudanese government seeks to use its military power to preserve and extend its control over the land and inhabitants of Darfur by empowering local Arab Janjaweed militias to destroy and drive the non-Arab African tribal groups from their farms and villages" (Hagan, Rymond-Richmond, and Parker, 2005, 531).

Since 2003, close to 400,000 Africans have been killed in state-supported and militarily unjustified racially motivated attacks. John Hagan and his colleagues (2005) carefully analyzed about 500 surveys from face-to-face interviews conducted with Darfurian survivors living in refugee camps in Chad. Their analysis concluded that "the racialized and gendered hierarchies of power and control" effected the following patterns:

- More men are killed than women so that the men cannot rebel or defend their villages or farms.

- Women are raped and killed in order to:
  - Terrorize them
  - Keep them from having their "own" children
  - Alter the race of the children "in this patrilineal culture where descent is understood as being transmitted along male lines" (ibid., 544)
  - Get rid of their "blackness"
  - Shame the women to make it more difficult to report the rapes
  - Dislocate the African Sudan people

Conclusion: "Both killing and rape are instruments of terror, and more than 2 million Africans from Darfur have been displaced from their homes and today are living and dying in refugee camps in Sudan and Chad" (ibid., 552).

SOURCE: John Hagan, Wenona Rymond-Richmond, and Patricia Parker. 2005. The Criminology of Genocide: The Death and Rape of Darfur. *Criminology* 43:525–562.

---

sexual assault is too restrictive because some forms of sexual conduct (in particular some instances of child sexual abuse and sexual harassment) are violating rather than violent. Russell (1984) prefers the term *sexual exploitation* to sexual assault because rape, child sexual assault, and sexual harassment all include abuse of power by the offender over the victim, whether that power is economic, physical, and/or status in nature. Similarly, Medea and Thompson (1974, 12) define rape as "any sexual intimacy forced on one person by another."

Restricting the definition of sexual victimization (or rape) decreases understanding of the problem and overlooks many cases of sexual victimization. It is important to recognize that sexual victimization consists of a variety of forms and occurs between a wide variety of persons. Because the term *rape* is associated with such a restrictive definition, the term *sexual victimization* will be used in this book in order to include the various forms of sexual violations discussed. Thus, sexual victimization will include penile–vaginal rape, anal and oral rape, molestation, sexual harassment, attempted rape, and sexual assault with foreign objects. For the purposes of this book, *sexual victimization is any forced or coerced sexual intimacy.*

HISTORICAL ISSUES IN DEFINING SEXUAL VICTIMIZATION

Few words in the English language have as powerful an impact as the word *rape.* Historically, children have not been educated about the meaning of rape. In spite of ignorance of its meaning, girls are raised to know that rape restricts them and is something to fear. The lifestyles of girls and women are affected by the specter of potential rape. They learn that their vulnerability restricts their options: where and how they live, and where and when they work and go out. They learn the conflicting messages that men are to be both feared and depended on for protection. The fine line between victimization and protection regarding women, men, and rape has been compared to the victimization and protection in the Mafia; the Mafia is often feared by the very people who depend on it for protection (Griffen, 1971). Similarly, women are frequently victimized by men and yet are socialized to view men as their protectors. It is assumed that known men will protect women from aberrant strange men's violence (Stanko, 1992), yet women are more likely to be victimized by known men.

Turning to ancient history, *lex talionis,* better known as an eye-for-an-eye system of crime processing, viewed women and girls as men's (fathers' or husbands') property. "A rape for a rape" meant that the father of a raped daughter was permitted to rape the rapist's wife (Brownmiller, 1975). Bride capture, where a male staked a claim to a woman by raping her, was the earliest form of permanent mating relationships (ibid.). Brownmiller (ibid.) points out that rape has been so ingrained and accepted as part of society that Hebrew law did not include "Thou shalt not rape" in the Ten Commandments (although, significantly, the Ten Commandments warn against committing adultery).

Throughout history, rape laws were aimed mostly at protecting virginal daughters in wealthy families (ibid.). In the late eighteenth century, rape was used to justify women's place in the home (Clark, 1987). The system went from trivializing rape, then, to using it as an excuse to restrict women from working or traveling outside the home. In eighteenth-century England, sexually victimized women were in a double bind if they wished to involve the court system to receive justice (ibid.). Being raped itself caused a woman to lose her credibility. Any woman charging rape had by admittance had sex (although forced) with a man not her husband. By raping a woman, a man not only victimized her but also stripped her of her credibility as a victim. Subsequently, conviction was extremely rare unless (1) the woman proved her chastity was preserved by being only the victim of an *attempted* rape (it was much more difficult to obtain convictions for completed rapes because they implied the victim's culpability), or (2) a husband or father of a raped woman went to court to challenge his loss of property value (ibid., 47). Unfortunately, some men still view women as their property. This is addressed more thoroughly in the next chapter.

In the 1970s, when sexual victimization was first becoming defined as a social problem, the focus was on adult–stranger rapes. These were the rapes focused on in the media and the ones disproportionately reported to the police. Since speak-outs on rape in the 1970s, it became clearer that acquaintance rapes far outnumbered stranger rapes.

Sexual victimization runs on a continuum from coercion to force. Force is a physical method to obtain power, such as holding down, hitting, or stabbing. Coercion is a psychological method to obtain power. Using coercion, a rapist may achieve sexual intimacy through various threats. For instance, a man may threaten a girl with telling her parents that she was smoking if she does not comply sexually. A boyfriend may tell his girlfriend he will break up with her if she will not have sex with him. A foster father may threaten a girl with removal of support if she does not submit to his sexual demands. A minister or priest may promise special favors for sexual compliance. These examples of coercion show how physical force is not always necessary in order to sexually victimize.

STATISTICS ON SEXUAL VICTIMIZATION

Determining the rates of sexual victimization has been problematic for a number of reasons. First, it has been difficult to gather sexual victimization statistics. Until 1973, the Uniform Crime Reports (UCR) provided most of the victimization data in the United States. The UCR data are limited for any crime because they include only crimes reported to the police. This is particularly problematic for sexual victimizations because these are the most underreported of the index crimes. The humiliation and intimate violation involved in sexual victimizations make them difficult to report to strangers, be they researchers or police officers. Because many victims/survivors do not report rapes to the police or even to interviewers, the statistics on sexual victimization are often invalid. In 1973, the National Crime Survey (NCS), a national victimization survey, was implemented to get around the problems inherent in the solely police-reported crimes in the UCR. A major criticism of the NCS was the failure to ask about rape (or any kind of sexual assault) unless a respondent answered "yes" to having been attacked (see Eigenberg, 1990). Thus, the NCS was revised with an expanded question sequence for forced or coerced sexual activity and implemented in 1992, and the name was changed to the National Crime Victimization Survey (NCVS).

A second limitation of sexual victimization statistics is that some victimization cases are disproportionately reported to the police depending on characteristics of the victim and the assailant. Sexual victimizations that the culture and the criminal legal system view as "real" rapes—those occurring between strangers, those where the victim is White, those where the offender is African American, those where the victim has a "good reputation," and so on—are disproportionately reported to the police. Acquaintance rapes are underreported to the police because they are often more difficult to prove and the victim is more likely to feel some responsibility. "Pressure not to involve the police, fear of causing an embarrassing situation for themselves in a relatively closed community, and fear that their names will not be kept confidential often prevent victims from reporting" acquaintance rape (Parrot, 1986, 2). Similarly, although many prostitutes experience sexual victimization, these assaults are rarely reported to the police because they usually are not taken seriously. Notably, one study found that rape victims who know their attackers are not just less likely to report to the police but they are more likely to delay telling *anyone* about the rape than do stranger-rape victims (Sudderth, 1998). Sexual victimization is particularly troublesome when the victims are children. Children and youths typically are less informed of their rights, and access to criminal legal authorities is more limited. Furthermore, they are usually in less powerful positions than adults to report, particularly if the rapist is related to them.

Another significant problem concerns acquaintance rapes in which the victim and the offender had a consensual sexual relationship prior to the rape. Victims of date and marital rape sometimes fail to define their experiences as rapes or sexual victimizations. Even if they do, they believe (often correctly) that the police and the courts will not define their experiences as rapes, so they do not report them. One study found that younger women and women who were raped by men they knew were the least likely to define the assaults as rapes (ibid.).

Just as characteristics of the victim and the offender influence reporting to the police, characteristics of the sexual victimization itself also influence the validity of rape statistics. For instance, anal and oral sexual assaults, as well as sexual victimizations with a foreign object, are less likely to be reported to the police because of the additional humiliation sometimes associated with these experiences. Also, many rape statistics do not "count" these as "real" rapes. Another reason that sexual victimization statistics are difficult to collect accurately is the tendency among some victims (especially victims of attempted rape) to believe their victimizations are not important enough to report to the police. Finally, many times rape victims fail to label their own victimizations as rapes (e.g., Russell, 1984; Schwartz and Leggett, 1999; Sudderth, 1998). They may not consider it rape because it is confusing and does not fit the stranger-in-the-bushes-or-alley image they have been told about, or they do not want to admit that a man they would go out with is a rapist, or they blame themselves. (For a review of measuring sexual victimization, see Belknap, Fisher, and Cullen, 1999.)

As mentioned in Chapter 6, Russell's (1984) San Francisco study found that 44 percent of the 930 randomly sampled women age 18 and older had been victims of completed or attempted rape (defined as completed or attempted forced penile–vaginal penetration) at some point in their lives, and 24 percent had experienced completed rapes. We refer to these rates over a person's lifetime as *prevalence rates*. In Russell's (1984) study, White (46 percent) and African American (44 percent) women reported similar levels of having experienced a completed or attempted rape, and though few American Indian women were in the sample (thus the finding must be interpreted cautiously), they reported the highest rate (55 percent). Thirty percent of the Latina women and 17 percent of the Asian American women reported completed or attempted rapes (ibid.). Similarly, 53 percent of women in a study in Charleston County, South Carolina, reported experiencing sexual assault at least once in their lives (Murphy et al., 1988). A study by Gail E. Wyatt and her colleagues (1993) involved in-depth interviews about both consensual and nonconsensual (sexual abuse) sex with 122 White women and 126 African American women in Los Angeles. (The interviewers restricted their definition of nonconsensual sex to vaginal and anal, excluding oral, rapes.) Wyatt and her colleagues (ibid.) found that 22 percent of the women experienced rape or attempted rape as adults, and the only racial/ethnic difference was that the African American women were more likely to delay disclosing their rape victimization to *anyone* until years later. (However, a more recent study on African American rape survivors did *not* find a delayed reporting of the rape to others [Neville and Pugh, 1997].)

A study, termed the National Women's Study, conducted a national probability sample of over 4,000 women in the United States (National Victim Center, 1992). Rape was defined as force or threat of force to penetrate the victim's vagina, mouth, or rectum. The researchers projected that over 12 million U.S. women (or one in eight) have been the victims of rape at some point in their lives. A more recent national telephone survey on violence against women conducted in 1995 and 1996, the National Violence against Women (NVAW) Survey, sampled 8,000 women and 8,000 men. The NVAW survey results indicated that 18 percent of women and 3 percent of men experienced a completed or attempted rape at some point in their life, with rape defined as forced oral, anal, or vaginal intercourse (Tjaden and Thoennes, 1998). This translates into one in six women and one in thirty-three men in the United States reporting an attempted or completed rape as a child and/or as an adult. Similar to Russell (1984), in this study Asian/Pacific Islander women reported the lowest lifetime rape rates (7 percent), while American Indian/Alaska Native women reported the highest rates (34 percent). Eighteen percent of White women, 19 percent of African American women, and 24 percent of mixed race women reported having experienced rape (Tjaden and Thoennes, 1998).

Incidence rates, on the other hand, are measured as rates within some period, usually a year, prior to the interview or survey. The NCS/NCVS and UCR statistics are incidence rates. Russell (1984) compared her 1974 incidence rates with the 1974 UCR and NCS incidence rates because all of these methods measured rape and attempted rape in the traditional method (penile–vaginal). Russell (ibid.) found that the incidence rate in her study (3 percent in the prior year) was thirteen times greater than the UCR incidence rate and over seven times greater than the NCS incidence rate.[1] Although NCS techniques, unlike those of the UCR, capture some rapes not reported to the police, even the NCS questionnaire design is fraught with problems, bringing into question the validity of this rape measure (see Eigenberg, 1990). The NCS interviewers never directly ask respondents whether they have been raped or sexually victimized. This information is assumed to be volunteered when the respondents are asked if they have been assaulted. Nonetheless, it has been suggested that NCS data are a likely approximation of trends in rape frequencies, while the UCR statistics better reflect police organizations' management of rape cases (Jensen and Karpos, 1993). As stated, the NCS in its revised form, the National Crime Victimization Survey (NCVS), addressed some of the problems in the original form with measuring rape (Bachman and Taylor, 1994). However, even this new improved measure is still fraught with problems in defining rape (see Belknap, Fisher, and Cullen, 1999; Koss, 1996). Antonia Abbey and her colleagues (2001) conducted an intensive review of research on sexual assault and concluded that conservative estimates suggest that at least 25 percent of American women have been sexually assaulted in adolescence or adulthood and that 18 percent have been raped. Furthermore, at least 20 percent of American men report having perpetrated sexual assault and 5 percent report having committed rape (ibid., 1).

A detailed study of 1,162 female-victim sexual assaults presented to a sexual assault center at the Women's Hospital in Toronto, Canada, provides some useful data to describe this community sample of rapes (Stermac, Du Mont, and Dunn, 1998). The survivors ranged in age from 14 to 87 years old, with an average age of 27. Regarding victim–offender relationship (VOR), 31 percent were by strangers (S), 15 percent were by husbands or boyfriends (H/B), 14 percent were by acquaintances the victim knew less than 24 hours (AK<24), and 40 percent by acquaintances known more than 24 hours (AK>24) (ibid.). The number of assailants (per incident) ranged from one to six, with stranger-rape victims reporting the most assailants. The VOR was related to where the sexual assaults occurred: The stranger assaults were more likely to be committed outside or in a vehicle, husband/boyfriend rapes were more likely to be committed in the victim's home, and both types of acquaintance rapes were more likely to be committed in the assailant's home (ibid.). Among these sexual assault survivors, 82 percent reported penile-vaginal penetration, 17 percent reported fellatio, 11 percent reported anal rape, 6 percent reported cunnilingus, and 2 percent reported rape by a foreign object. Again, the VOR was related to the type of assault: Stranger rapists were more likely than acquaintance or husband/boyfriend rapists to force fellatio and penile-vaginal penetration. (There was no difference among the various VORs for cunnilingus, anal, and foreign object sexual assaults.) Although stranger rapists were the most likely to use a weapon (23 percent), 17 percent of husband/boyfriend rapists used weapons (as did 10 percent of acquaintances of less than 24 hours and 15 percent of acquaintances of more than 24 hours) (ibid.).

The various studies indicate quite varied estimates of the prevalence and incidence of rape. This is likely due to the varied measures (Do they include anal and oral rapes?), the sampling plans (Are they phone interviews, written surveys, or in-person interviews?), and the wording. Although Russell's (1984) research design is often held up as the ideal, even it is limited because of her restricted definition of rape as penile–vaginal and because her sample excluded such high-risk women as those confined in prison and mental institutions. What is clear from the studies is that rape is a serious social and legal problem and that it is highly gendered in both its perpetration and victimization.

WHO ARE THE VICTIMS?

Traditionally, real rape has tended to be viewed as something that happens in alleys to young, White women who are alone late at night. The offenders are often viewed as insane perverts, usually African American. Chapter 6 addressed many of these stereotypes. These misleading portrayals have been largely perpetuated by the media. Research, on the other hand, portrays all women at risk, regardless of age, race, or class. Anyone can be a victim.

Females are much more likely than males to be victims of sexual assault. Statistics from the NCS covering a ten-year period between 1973 and 1982 reported that 762 females were victims of rape or attempted rape. (Information on other sexual victimizations was not collected.) For this same time period, only 36 males reported rape or attempted rape. Because of gender power inequalities (see Chapter 6) and the societal view of women and girls, it is not surprising that females are more likely than males to be sexually victimized.

Research has also pointed out some commonalities regarding who is most at risk of rape. It is important to remember, however, that official statistics on sexual victimization overrepresent stranger assaults (because they are disproportionately reported); most sexual victimizations occur between nonstrangers. The statistics imply that rape tends to occur to women between the ages of 16 and 24 (Amir, 1971; Belknap, 1987; Russell, 1984; Skogan, 1976). African American females appear to be more at risk of rape than White females (Amir, 1971; Costin, 1992; Schram, 1978; Skogan, 1976). Russell (1984) found that African American females were more at risk of stranger rapes, while White females were more at risk of acquaintance rapes. Women and girls have a high risk of being raped in their own homes—even by strangers (Belknap, 1987; Sanders, 1980; Schram, 1978). Research focusing on stranger rapes also finds that rapes are more likely to occur at night and in the summer months (Amir, 1971; Belknap, 1987; Sanders, 1980).

WHO ARE THE OFFENDERS?

Groth's (1979) research on convicted sex offenders warns against describing rapists as simply oversexed. In fact, one-third of the rapists in his study were sexually active with their wives at the time of the rapes. Similarly, many mothers of incest victims are shocked on discovering that their husbands sexually abused their daughter(s), given that their own sex lives with the perpetrator were very active (Russell, 1986). Sexual victimization is fundamentally a power issue—a need to dominate. Groth (1979, 13) describes rape as "sexual behavior in the primary service of nonsexual needs." Thus, domination is the goal, and sex is the means by which domination is achieved.

Groth's (1979) attempts to categorize types of rapists have been somewhat limited because of his focus on convicted rapists. Because only a small percentage of rapists are convicted, it is highly unlikely that convicted rapists are representative of rapists at large. Nonetheless, his three categories are useful to examine. *Anger rapes* are characterized by physical brutality, where sex is used to express rage and anger. Excessive force is used to dominate the victim. The second pattern, *power rapes*, are characterized not by the rapist wishing to harm his victim but rather by the rapist wanting to possess the victim sexually (ibid., 25). The goal is sexual conquest, and only the amount of force necessary to achieve this is used. The final pattern, the *sadistic rape*, fuses sexuality and aggression so that aggression itself becomes eroticized (ibid., 44). This type of rapist finds the victim's suffering sexually gratifying. Groth's (ibid., 58) study found that 55 percent of the cases were power rapes, 40 percent were anger rapes, and about 5 percent were sadistic rapes. He contends that if his sample were not restricted to convicted rapists, he would have seen more power rapists and fewer anger and sadistic rapists, given that anger rapes are more likely than power rapes to include corroborating evidence, and sadistic rapes are more likely to provide evidence of force—both of which increase conviction rates.

Another study of convicted rapists' perceptions of themselves and their victims found that most of the men experienced no guilt or shame regarding their behavior (Scully, 1988). Furthermore, their inability to empathize influenced their self-control, or lack thereof. Scully (ibid., 211) identified two groups of rapists: Some of the men viewed women as opponents to be reduced to abject powerlessness. Others, adopting the cultural view of women as sexual commodities, reduced their victims to meaningless objects.

Although the crime statistics tend to show African American males overrepresented as sexual offenders, Tong (1984, 166) suggests this is because African American offenders are more likely to be reported to and taken seriously by the criminal legal system. Despite the fact that the vast majority of rapes are intraracial (White on White, African American on African American, and so on), the U.S. legal system has followed a legacy from slavery to the present day that treats the rape of White women by African American men more harshly than any other kind of rape (Wriggins, 1983, 116). Wriggins (ibid.) argues this is a result of patriarchal values (controlling both White women and African American men). Moreover, she points out the numerous consequences of focusing on African American-on-White rapes: (1) It denies all sexual victimizations of African American women, (2) it denies the majority of sexual victimizations of White women (those perpetrated by White men), and (3) it falsely depicts rape as largely African American on White and stranger oriented (given the highly segregated U.S. society). This focus on African American-on-White rapes discriminates against African American men and leaves out victims who are other women of color, in addition to African American women. As Wriggins (ibid., 117) states, "[R]ape is painful and degrading ... regardless of the attacker's race."

Just as with sexual-assault victims, rapists come from every racial, ethnic, and economic group. They include doctors, lawyers, ministers, priests, professors, politicians, and many others. Thus, just as anyone can be a rape victim, so too, can anyone be a rapist. Why, then, do we have the common image of rapists as abnormal, African American, and oversexed? First, the media often portrays them as such. Second, women are socialized to be wary of strangers, especially strange men, with strong racist implications regarding which men are strange and threatening. Third, akin to the previously discussed just-world hypothesis, it is probably another attempt to feel control over one's environment. We feel safer if we think we can determine whether someone is a rapist by his appearance. Unfortunately, this is not the case. Furthermore, when we hold racist and other misinformed stereotypes, we not only promote a rape ignorant culture but we also promote a racist culture.

THE VICTIM–OFFENDER RELATIONSHIP

Research reports vary in the stranger-versus-acquaintance rates of sexual victimizations. This is largely a result of how the studies were conducted. For example, in a classic study from the book *Forcible Rape,* using police UCR data, 42 percent of the rapes in a study of police reports were committed by strangers (Amir, 1971), whereas in an NCS study 50 percent of the single-offender and 58 percent of the multiple-offender (gang) attempted and completed rapes were committed by strangers (Belknap, 1987). Russell's (1984, 59) random study of women found that only 16 percent of completed and attempted rapes were committed by strangers.

Russell's (ibid.) study no doubt has the highest rates of nonstranger rapes because of her data-collection method (a process that did not rely on cases reported to the police, as did UCR statistics) and because she used a random sample where the respondents were directly asked whether they were raped (unlike NCS statistics). In any sexual victimization situation, it is difficult for the victim to report it to the police or even to an interviewer. This is particularly the case if the offender is known to the victim. First, the victim is likely to feel ashamed to admit that a friend or loved one sexually victimized her. Second, she may fear retaliation if the offender finds out that she reported him (particularly to the police but also to an interviewer or a friend). Finally, the victim of acquaintance rape may not define the situation as rape or sexual victimization. "Many acquaintance rape victims feel that they were forced to have intercourse but deny that they were raped. This discrepancy in terms stems from our socialization and cultural standards, which leads to the common notion that rape only happens when a stranger jumps out of the bushes" (Parrot, 1986, 4).

A more recent study examined the victim–offender relationship, comparing the NCS with the NCVS. That is, it compared the rates when the national survey always asked whether someone had been raped, instead of only asking if someone had been raped if there was a yes answer to whether someone had been attacked. Table 7.1 shows the significant differences in the victim–offender relationship when the rape question was specified: More nonstranger rapes and more of the less violent rapes (as measured by levels of injury, force, and weapons) were reported to the interviewers when the rape question was asked of everyone (Baumer, Felson, and Messner, 2003). Notably, with the change in questioning, stranger rapes reported to this national survey as a percentage of total rapes reported to the study decreased by two-thirds, from 47 percent in the NCS to 15 percent in the NCVS. The proportion of intimate partner and well-known acquaintance rapes more than doubled with the new questioning. It is clear from these results that the probing questions in the redesigned

T A B L E 7.1   Change in the Victim–Offender Relationship in Rape Reports When the Questioning Changed: NCS vs. NCVS Findings

Victim–Offender Relationship	NCS (National Crime Survey)[1] 1973–1991	NCVS (National Crime Victimization Survey)[2] 1992–2000
Stranger	46.8	14.8
Nonstranger[3]	53.2	85.2
Intimate partner	4.6	10.7
Other family member	2.9	3.6
Well-known acquaintance	18.6	40.2
Casual acquaintance	17.8	24.0
Sight-only acquaintance	9.3	6.7

[1]NCS questions did not directly ask about sexual coercion or force unless person reported attack.

[2]NCVS questions always asked if person experienced sexual coercion or force.

[3]Nonstrangers were further divided into five categories: intimate partner, other family member, well-known acquaintance, casual acquaintance, and sight-only acquaintance.

SOURCE: Eric P. Baumer, Richard B. Felson, and Steven F. Messner. 2003. Changes in Police Notification for Rape, 1873–2000. *Criminology* 41:841–872.

survey produce a sample of incidents quite different from the NCS in terms of relationship, as illustrated in Table 7.1 (ibid., 854).

One form of acquaintance rape is by co-workers. Sadly, women soldiers serving in the U.S. military have reported "fellow American soldiers" for sexually assaulting them:

> At least 37 female service members have sought sexual-trauma counseling and other assistance from civilian rape crisis organizations after returning from war duty in Iraq, Kuwait and other overseas stations, *The Denver Post* has learned. The women, ranging from enlisted soldiers to officers, have reported poor medical treatment, lack of counseling and incomplete criminal investigations by military officials. Some say they were threatened with punishment after reporting assaults. (Moffeit and Herdy, 2005)

WHAT CAUSES SEXUAL ABUSE?

Rape Myths

Too often, perceptions about the primary causes of rape center around four myths. First is the *victim-is-not-a-real-victim myth*, implying that most rape victims caused their rapes and other sexual victimizations. Significant numbers of people believe women precipitate or cause their rape victimizations (e.g., Lee et al., 2005). Victim-blaming not only affects how outsiders view rape victims and their assailants but it also affects how assailants view themselves and excuse or justify their sexually abusive or exploitative behaviors. Moreover, victim-blaming cultures also limit sexual victimization survivors' ability to label their victimizations as rape or another sexual victimization. Some victims are so preoccupied with blaming themselves for wanting to be with their date that they view the entire episode as their fault. If any romantic exchanges, such as innocent hugging or kissing, took place prior to the attack, the victim often feels she went too far before she said "no" and therefore caused the rape to occur by pushing the man to the edge of sexual frustration (Glavin, 1986, 3). One recent intensive study of undergraduate women's labeling of unwanted sexual experiences with dating partners found they were more likely to label their experiences as sexual abuse or sexual assault when they had clearly and repeatedly indicated their lack of consent and when the assailant threatened or actually used force (Harned, 2005). Notably, women who were coerced into sex through excessive pressure and/or manipulation were divided as to whether this was sexual abuse. In this study, not only did alcohol and drugs play a role in *incapacitating* the women (by being blacked out, unconscious, or extremely drunk) but many of these rape victims did not view the intoxication as diminishing their ability to consent (which is the legal stand) but rather as making them *responsible* for their victimizations (e.g., self-blame) (ibid.).

This leads us to the second myth: *Alcohol and drugs cause sexual assault and rape.* There is no doubt that alcohol and drugs are often present and consumed in sexual abuse incidents. An extensive overview of the research on alcohol consumption and rape stipulates that in approximately half (with a range from 34 percent to 74 percent) of sexual assault cases, the assailants were drinking alcohol; and likewise, in approximately half (with a range from 30 percent to 70 percent) of these cases, the victims were drinking alcohol (Abbey et al., 2001). In most cases, the drinking by the victim and abuser co-occur (ibid.). While it is necessary to examine the role that alcohol/drugs play in placing potential victims (all of us) at risk of sexual victimization, it does not follow to conclude that alcohol/drugs *cause* rape. In a study of Greek students, both women and men reported that the opposite sex's consumption of alcohol makes them sexier (Alva, 1998). Another study of college students found that the mere *presence* of alcohol, not so much its consumption, triggered the initiation of sex (Corcoran and Thomas, 1991). In sum, in society the consumption, and even presence, of drugs and alcohol wrongly indicates a free-for-all, no-one-needs-to-establish-consent license for sex (rape) to many individuals, even though this is not consistent with the law.

Alcohol/drugs enhance gendered roles, making women and girls who use them more vulnerable to victimization due to decreased resistance abilities (and victim-blaming by the public, and often police, jurors, judges, and other officials); at the same time, alcohol/drugs may disinhibit men and boys to allow them to rape. One study using NCVS data, however, found that a man's drinking of alcohol decreases the chances that the attempt at rape will be completed but increases the likelihood of victim injury (Martin and Bachman, 1998). Notably, there is an assumption that when intoxicated women have been raped without force, but through taking advantage of their intoxicated state, this is not traumatic, and calling it rape is simply a way to get over the guilt for having sex with a bad date (Roiphe, 1993). However, research testing this assumption found it to be false: Women raped through an inability to give consent due to intoxication were just as likely as women raped through physical force to report emotional trauma resulting from the rape (Schwartz and Leggett, 1999).

Drinking and/or drug use do not excuse sexual abuse. Most of us would not kick our pets, hit our friends and family members, yell racial epithets, and so on when we are drunk or on drugs, just as we do not do these things when we are sober. Drinking and drugs do not *cause* rape; rather, they are used by some rapists to plan disempowerment of potential victims and/or to excuse the rapists' own sexually abusive behavior toward the victims. Referring back to Harned's (2005) study in the discussion of the victim-blaming myth, it is noteworthy that when rapists use alcohol/drugs to incapacitate their victims (or search out victims who are incapacitated by drugs/alcohol), they are less likely to have to use force or threats of force to have sex (rape), *and* the victim is more likely to view the rape as her fault.

The third myth is reserved for those (rare) cases where the victims are viewed as truly innocent and undeserving of their sexual victimizations, and this is the myth that *rapists are sick*. The typical rapist has frequently been portrayed as crazy, sexually starved, or psychotic. However, empirical research is unable to confirm these beliefs, and rapists are no more likely than nonrapists to be mentally ill (see Bart and O'Brien, 1985; Russell, 1984; Scully, 1990). Interviews with men who confessed to raping, as well as with men who had not raped demonstrated how many men who are not rapists often (1) blame women for turning them on, (2) link sex and violence, and (3) report wanting to be violent toward women they perceive as trying to tease them (Beneke, 1982).

The final myth, *rape is simply a miscommunication between the assailant and the victim*, is buoyed by the belief that the assailant did not realize she did not want to have sex. This may explain a minutia of cases but does not explain the vast majority. Examples of this are where the woman perceives her own flirtatious behavior as simply meaning "I *may* be interested in you" or even "I *am* interested in you"; she likely does not mean it to be interpreted as "I will have sex with you under any conditions." The assailant may believe, on the other hand, that he has the license to force sex with her because he read signals from her indicating she was attracted to him. After a date rape, even though the victim knows she said "no" and did not want sex with the rapist and he physically forced her, she may still not define the behavior as rape. Fear, shock, confusion, guilt, disbelief, degradation, and loss of control are some of the common reactions of acquaintance rape victims. Many women, overcome with guilt, often do not realize they have been raped when it was committed by a date or boyfriend.

Although it is important to address the role of miscommunication in the occurrence of date rapes, as well as the accompanying gender differences associated with this miscommunication, it is also important not to use miscommunication as the explanation of date, marital, and other acquaintance rapes. Clearly, many date rapists proceed to rape despite significant communication from victims that they are not consenting or when the victims are asleep or passed out and unable to consent. Nonetheless, perceptions about consent are the crux of almost every rape trial, and nowhere is this more complex and significant than in date rapes—especially if the victim invited the rapist out, she "let" him pay for dinner, she invited him to her apartment, she let him kiss her, and so on. Research from the 1980s suggests that a gender gap in sexual communication exists (Weiner, 1983, 147) and that males are more likely than females to interpret various behaviors and verbal communications as sexual (Abbey, 1987; Miller and Marshall, 1987; Muehlenhard, 1989). However, a more recent study reports no significant gender differences in what men and women report as indicators of sexual interest/consent, sexual refusal/nonconsent, and sexual coercion (McCaw and Senn, 1998):

> There was a striking similarity in the cues that men and women used, across all categories that were examined.... [M]ale participants did not over-estimate women's interest in sex.... Men did not dismiss women's refusals as token, nor did they simply not perceive them.... Finally the results of the present study suggest that most men may be well aware of those behaviors that women experience as sexually coercive, so that relatively few men may engage in sexual coercion without realizing, or being able to realize, that is what they are doing. (ibid., 621–622)

Similarly, another study of college men comparing sexually aggressive with sexually nonaggressive men found that more in-depth qualitative data (unlike closed-ended quantitative survey data) indicate profound differences between these two groups of college men (Yescavage, 1999). More specifically, the sexually aggressive men were more accusatory of the victims' responsibility in getting herself raped, and the sexually aggressive men's comments implied that forced sex is a woman's consequence for allowing some sexual activity to occur (ibid., 809). Moreover, the sexually aggressive men's comments suggest these men know that force is being used to inflict harm. Thus, this study concludes that college men rape out of a sense of male entitlement more than a sense that the victim only offered token resistance. Similarly, a study of 114 men aged 17 to 43 years old found men's general sense of *men's entitlement* and their specific sense of men's *sexual* entitlement of women were strong predictors of "an array of rape-related attitudes and behaviors" (Hill and Fischer, 2001, 45).

The Role of Rape Myths and Other Causes
of Sexual Victimization

So now we have established the rape myths. What then, are the causes of rape? To some extent, the rape myths cause rape. When they are accepted by individuals as excuses for them to rape or to blame victims, a rape culture is in place. Moreover, earlier I stated that miscommunication legitimately explained a very small percentage of rapes. However, it is necessary to examine the role of a rape climate in those cases where individual assailants truly believe they are not sexual abusing/assaulting. For example, if a fraternity member or athlete is convinced by his brothers or team members that the drunk women at a party truly want to have sex with him, then we must not only hold individuals accountable but also the institutions (be they workplaces, universities and colleges, teams, fraternities, dormitories, friendship groups, etc.). More specifically, we need to ask ourselves if the team or university has some accountability when, for instance, 17-year-old young men are being recruited from high school to play on a university or college team and during their recruit visit are taken to a party where other players are having sex with drunk/drugged women and are informed, "This is how we do things here." In this example, the young player may get the idea that not only is sex with drunken women not rape, but it is expected. We could make the same analogy for a young man joining a fraternity: in his first week at college attending a party where his future Greek brothers are having sex with women too drunk to consent and expecting him to do likewise. In a perfect world, everyone knows that sex with someone unable to freely consent is not only unethical but also illegal. However, given that often people are unaware of the law/morals, it is important that institutions be held accountable for promoting rape climates, just as they should be held accountable for promoting climates that are racist, anti-Semitic, anti-immigrant, homophobic, and so on.

Thus, antiwoman climates, pro–violence-against-women climates, and so on feed a rape culture. Thus, rape is institutionalized when we see strong adherence to rape myths and institutions' general lack of willingness to punish abusers. What are some of the ways the male-stream culture feeds rape myths? A study of the fifty top-grossing films of 1996 found that the movies present patriarchal views of sex and rape and foster the myth that rapists are predominantly sadistic, disturbed, lower-class individuals who prey on children and the vulnerable (Bufkin and Eschholz, 2000, 1317). In this study, 17 percent of the sex scenes involved rapes, and the only two sex scenes showing same-sex sexuality both depicted rapes where adult men raped teenage boys (ibid.). Thus, these top films not only encourage stereotypes that rapists are sick and poor but stereotypes of homosexual sex as deviant (ibid.). An extensive study of cyber rapes (cultural articulations of rape found using web search engines) found no rapes of men, all depicted explicit violence and domination, and gang rapes made up one-third of the rape depictions (Visano, 2002). The graphic rape images often included labels, such as "skank," "slut," "bitch," and "whore," indicating the victim's need to be punished. The rape images were clearly designed to link rape with erotic power and to depict the degradation and objectification of women and girls for sexual pleasure (ibid.). In addition to misogyny, the images were replete with racism. African American followed by Asian American women and girls were the biggest targets of violence, and the racist portrayals were reinforced with racist captions packed with racial epithets and harmful stereotypes. These cyber rapes are particularly disturbing when we understand how easily accessible they are (ibid.).

Another important source of male-stream antiwoman/girl media is television music videos. They not only enhance negative self-images about women's and girls bodies (Tiggenmann and Slater, 2004), but they also portray aggressive sex in about one-third of the implicit or explicit sex scenes. Although the males did not appear as sexual masochists, the females were typically viewed as the recipients (not initiators) of sex and as enjoying aggressive sex more than the males did (Sommers-Flanagan, Sommers-Flanagan, and Davis, 1993). An article in *The New York Magazine* referred to MTV as the date rape channel (Christgau, 2003). Finally, video games are played by millions of people, mostly boys, and these games also promote violence. The worst is likely *Grand Theft Auto*, which encourages the players to commit virtual murder and rape of sex workers.

CHILD SEXUAL VICTIMIZATION (CSA)

One of the most disturbing aspects of sexual victimization is the high degree to which children are victims, and this appears to be most hidden when the victimization is incest. Child sexual victimization was once thought to be a rare occurrence, particularly cases of incest. Child sexual abuse (CSA) was reported to social service agencies during the 1800s, but it was not labeled as a social problem until the early 1980s (Gordon and O'Keefe, 1984). A 1987 article in *Psychology Today* claimed that 40 million Americans (about one in six) may have been sexually victimized as children (Kohn, 1987, 54). "There is scarcely a study, report or investigation into aspects of human sexuality that does not indicate that child–adult sex is an active, prevalent pastime" (Rush, 1980, 5).

While boys face epidemic risks of CSA, this abuse is still very gendered. One overview of studies reported that girls constitute about 70 percent of the cases (Finkelhor and Baron, 1986), a more recent overview suggested that girls are 2.5 to 3 times more likely than boys to be victims (Putnam, 2003), and another study found girls were 85 percent of CSA victims (Heger et al., 2002). Ninety-five percent of the perpetrators of sexual abuse against girls and approximately 80 percent of the perpetrators of sexual abuse against boys are male (Finkelhor and Baron, 1986; Russell, 1984). In sum, the victims of CSA tend to be girls, and the abusers tend to be men.

The National Women's Study found the majority of rape cases occur during childhood and adolescence. Twenty-nine percent of all forcible rapes occurred when the victim was less than 11 years old, while another 32 percent occurred between the ages of 11 and 17 (National Victim Center, 1992, 3). Similarly, the National Violence against Women Survey revealed that of women who were raped, 22 percent reported their first rape was when they were under 12 years old, 32 percent reported they were 12 to 17 years old, 29 percent reported they were 18 to 24 years old, and 17 percent reported they were 25 years old or older at the time of their first rape (Tjaden and Thoennes, 1998). Gail Wyatt and her colleagues' (1993) in-depth interviews with 248 adult women in Los Angeles about their childhood sexual abuse reported that when noncontact sexual victimization (e.g., exposure, masturbating in front of a child, or asking the child to engage in sex) was combined with contact CSA (e.g., molesting or attempted or completed rape), almost two-thirds (62 percent) of the women reported such experiences. When Wyatt and colleagues (ibid.) restricted the abuse to only contact CSA, almost half (45 percent) of the women reported such childhood experiences. In one-third of these cases, the child told no one, and 70 percent of the undisclosed cases were contact sexual abuse cases (ibid.). Regarding incest, Russell (1984) found that 12 percent of the women reported familial CSA occurring when they were under the age of 14, and 16 percent reported it occurred when they were under the age of 18. The offenders were most likely to be fathers or uncles. These are extremely high rates for a crime that we know has such devastating psychological, and often physical, effects. A review of empirical research on the prevalence of CSA states:

> [T]here is considerable variation in the prevalence rates for child sexual abuse derived from the various North American studies. Reported rates range from 6 percent to 62 percent for females and from 3 percent to 31 percent for males. Although even the lowest rates indicate that child sexual abuse is far from an uncommon experience, the higher reported rates would point to a problem of epidemic proportions. (Peters, Wyatt, and Finkelhor, 1986, 19)

As mentioned previously, child sexual victimization was not acknowledged as a social problem until the 1980s. Prior to this, it was viewed as a taboo that rarely occurred. Just as it has been extremely difficult for adult women to speak out about sexual victimization, this has also been the case for children. The power of children is even further minimized by their increased psychological, emotional, and financial dependencies, in addition to their small physical statures. Given these conditions, it is not surprising that the crime of child sexual victimization has remained so invisible, despite its wide occurrence. Most CSA victims do not report their victimizations until they are adult survivors. Even then, many choose to keep it a secret or even repress the memory. There are a number of reasons Rush (1983) identified for why children may keep sexual abuse victimization a secret: they feel shamed, they have no protection, they are afraid they made it up, they want to forget, or they may even be blamed for their victimization. Another reason is that they do not remember it; they have repressed it. For example, a study that interviewed 136 women 17 years after they had received medical care for documented CSA (ranging from ages 10 months to 12 years old for the index abuse) found that over a third did *not* report the CSA event for which they had been hospitalized, suggesting that a significant proportion of CSA survivors do not remember the abuse (have repressed it) (Williams, Siegel, and Pomeroy, 2000). This study found a large number of additional CSA incidents in addition to the index one for which the women (as girls) had received hospital treatment (ibid.). Thus, when asking adults retrospectively about their childhood sexual abuse experiences, we can expect a huge amount of underreporting given not only the shame and fear but that individuals have quite literally buried the memories.

Psychiatrist and pioneer of psychoanalysis Sigmund Freud is partly to blame for the cover-up of CSA. He was amazed at the large numbers of women who reported having experienced sexual victimization as children, most often naming their fathers as the offenders. Although he initially believed his clients, other psychologists doubted him. He then restructured his theories and proposed the Oedipus complex, which is the theory of innate erotic attraction of children to parents (Rush, 1980, 84).

Although it is unusual for a child to wish to be seduced, as children do not understand sexuality and sexual feelings, it is apparent that sometimes children's behavior is sexual. Often this is a natural curiosity, customarily acted out by exploring their own and often their peers' bodies (for example, playing doctor).

People who work with children who have been sexually abused note that these children have heightened and often troubling sexual behavior. This is hardly surprising given that they have learned that this is appropriate. This sexual behavior might also make these children more at risk for revictimization. It is the adult's responsibility to make sure that he or she does not cross sexual boundaries with the child. Unfortunately, the child victim often feels guilty about the crime that was committed against her or him.

Similar to the other victimizations discussed previously, the sexual abuse of children occurs in all races/ethnicities, neighborhoods, and income levels, and it happens with alarming frequency. It is difficult to determine patterns and realistic statistics because CSA is a covered-up crime. However, researchers have uncovered some tendencies: Abusers are usually male and usually well known to the child, the abuse is often not limited to a single episode, and the abuser rarely uses force (Gomes-Schwartz, Horowitz, and Cardearelli, 1990; Kohn, 1987). A recent comprehensive examination of the existing research on CSA concludes (1) girls are 2.5 to 3 times more likely than boys to be victims; (2) the risk of CSA increases with a child's age; (3) physical disabilities (e.g., blindness, deafness, mental retardation) that increase a child's dependency, institutional care, and communication problems increase her/his risk of CSA, as well; (4) the absence of one or both parents, with girls at a particularly high risk of CSA by stepfathers (Putnam, 2003). However, this overview did not find class or race/ethnicity to be risk factors for CSA (ibid.).

Why do some people sexually abuse children? Just like motivations for battering and the sexual victimization of adult women, the sexual victimization of children is strongly related to power and inequality. Children are particularly at risk: With their naiveté and their natural capacity for affection, children are far more capable of idolatry than any of the adults the abuser knows (Crewdson, 1988, 63). Groth (1979, 154) discusses how perpetrators of CSA use sex as a weapon to discharge power and/or anger in order to control their victims. Such offenders capitalize on the relative helplessness of a child to coerce her or him into the sexual activity (ibid.). Children abused by parents, on whom they are economically and emotionally dependent, are in extremely powerless and vulnerable positions.

> Father–daughter incest is not only the type of incest most frequently reported but also represents a paradigm of female sexual victimization. The relationship between father and daughter, adult male and female child, is one of the most unequal relationships imaginable. It is no accident that incest occurs most often precisely in the relationship where the female is most powerless. The actual sexual encounter may be brutal or tender, painful or pleasurable; but it is always, inevitably, destructive to the child. The father, in effect, forces the daughter to pay with her body for affection and care which should be freely given. (Herman, 1981, 4)

Society has been blamed for encouraging CSA through advertisements, media, and pornography, which frequently blur distinctions between adult women and girl children—women are photographed to look childish, and girls are photographed to look sensuous (Bass, 1983). It is not unusual for pedophiles to photograph their victims and exchange the photographs with other pedophiles. *Playboy* published a cartoon of a lecherous worker in a doll factory assembly line who changed one doll's voice from saying "Momma" to "Wanna have a party, big boy?" (Crewdson, 1988, 249). Such forms of entertainment perpetuate the myth that children are willing participants and are not being assaulted, abused, exploited, and raped when they have sex with adults. In reality, children are not in a position to make decisions about sex with adults.

Similar to men who rape adult women, the child sexual abuser is indistinguishable in the population (ibid., 55). In fact, as evidence to contradict the myth that child sexual abusers are dirty old men, one study found that 71 percent of child sexual abusers were under the age of 35 (Groth, 1979). One trait that seems to be prevalent among (although not exclusive to) child sexual abusers is a high propensity toward narcissism (Crewdson, 1988). The abusers may feel unworthy and powerless, but they attempt to portray an image of importance and superiority. They often have inflated views of their appearance, abilities, and intelligence (ibid., 61). Additionally, the narcissist is better able to overcome the taboos associated with CSA because he secretly believes that rules and laws are meant for others and thus is less concerned with the consequences of being apprehended (ibid., 64). In this view, the child sexual abuser is primarily focused on his own well-being and gratification and sees himself as above the law.

A further disturbing aspect of child sexual abusers is the movement among some to publicly encourage adult–child sex as healthy and natural. A number of groups such as the Rene Guyon society, which was founded in 1962 and boasts thousands of members, advocate legalizing sex with children (ibid., 97). Their slogan is "sex by year 8, or else it's too late." CSA quadrupled between the early 1900s and the early 1970s (Russell, 1986, 82). Five explanations for this epidemic increase include (1) an increase in child pornography and the sexualization of children; (2) the sexual revolution with its all-sex-is-okay philosophy; (3) the backlash against sexual equality (men who cannot cope with women as equals turn to girls); (4) the recycling of untreated CSA, in which victims grow up to become victimizers; and (5) the increase in stepfamilies, where girls are especially at risk of incest (Russell, 1986).

A study of adult survivors of CSA found that the main reasons for children's delayed disclosures of their victimizations were due primarily to the high level of trauma associated with the abuse but also were due to "a belief in the importance of obedience to grownups, mistrust of people, fear of social rejection, and fear of the criminal justice system" (Somer and Szwarcberg, 2001, 332). Research has shown that initial reactions to CSA include anxiety, depression, fear, anger and hostility, and inappropriate sexual behavior (Browne and Finkelhor, 1986). While some victims of CSA become quite withdrawn, many victims react by becoming very sexual; they have learned that their most important asset is to service others sexually. Other research on the immediate impact of CSA found differing ranges of the effects, ranging from very serious damage to apparently unaffected children (Conte and Schuerman, 1987). In the long term, most adults and children psychologically survive CSA, but its effects can be extremely painful.

In addition to the trauma and danger that victims of CSA experience during and immediately after abuse, they frequently also experience long-term effects. Adult survivors of CSA report depression, self-destruction, anxiety, isolation, stigma, negative feelings about men, fear, and mistrust (Browne and Finkelhor, 1986; Murphy et al., 1988; Russell, 1984). Long-term behaviors associated with adult survivors of CSA include drug and alcohol abuse and sexual dysfunction (Browne and Finkelhor, 1986). Research also shows that sexually abused children have an extremely high rate of rape revictimization (Browne and Finkelhor, 1986; Kimerling et al., 2002; Murphy, 1991; Murphy et al., 1988; Russell, 1986; Tjaden and Thoennes, 1998), and one study found this more prevalent for those sexually abused as adolescents than for those sexually victimized before the age of 13 (Siegel and Williams, 2003). Revictimization may be associated with low rates of self-esteem and high rates of chemical dependency. Low self-esteem and chemical dependency are associated with surviving sexual victimization as well as being sexually victimized. That is, rapists often pick victims who look vulnerable, and vulnerability is often an effect of sexual victimization.

In summary, child sexual abuse can occur to anyone, and its effects are often devastating.

> The sexual abuse of children spans all races, economic classes, and ethnic groups. Even babies are its victims—hospitals treat three-month-old infants for venereal disease of the throat. Sexually abused children are not more precocious, pretty, or sexually curious than other children. They do not ask for it. They do not want it. Like rape of women, the rape and molestation of children are most basically acts of violation, power, and domination. (Bass, 1983, 24)

The frequency and prevalence of CSA occurances are outrageous. Again, power plays a tremendous role, as it does in other forms of sexual assault and sexual harassment.

DATE RAPE

Date rape is forced or coerced sexual intimacy by someone with whom one has had a romantic or dating relationship but does not include such sexual victimization by someone with whom one has been living as a spouse. Some studies show that women tend to be more at risk of date rape the longer they have been dating someone (Henton et al., 1983; Muehlenhard and Linton, 1987). However, date rape can also occur early on in the dating relationship, even on the first date. For college campuses, rape is particularly important to address given that it is the most prevalent serious crime on these campuses (Adams and Abarbanel, 1988).

Date rape is not a recent phenomenon, although it has only recently been made public. Clark (1987) traces sexual assault in England between 1770 and 1845 and found that rape in courtship was not particularly unusual. She examined why some men raped the women they dated and found it was not because the women had refused them sexually but rather because the men refused to acknowledge women's right to desire or refuse them and believed they had a right to women's bodies (ibid., 85). Some of the women raped during courtship felt pressured into marrying the rapist because views were such that a woman should be sexual only with her husband. Unfortunately, more recent research has also found that some women who are raped by their boyfriends or fiancés feel an obligation to marry them because they have already been sexual with them, however forced it was (Russell, 1982, 1984).

In 1957, Kanin published an article in a well-known sociology journal claiming that 62 percent of first-year college women reported experiencing some level of offensive erotic intimacy in the twelve months prior to starting college. Nonetheless, date rape remained unrecognized publicly until Mary P. Koss's study in conjunction with *MS.* magazine, published early in the 1980s, for which she developed the Sexual Experiences Survey to measure acquaintance/date rape (Barrett, 1982). In studies of college women, 70 to 80 percent reported having a man misinterpret the degree of sexual intimacy they desired or having a man use sexual aggression (Koss and Oros, 1982; Muehlenhard and Linton, 1987). Furthermore, 15 percent of the women and 7 percent of the men reported being involved in sexual intercourse against the woman's will, or rape, as it is commonly defined. In a more recent and larger-scale study of over 6,000 students at thirty-two U.S. colleges and universities, 12 percent of the women had experienced attempted rape, and another 15 percent had experienced completed rape. A total of 6.5 percent of the women reported experiencing completed rape in the twelve months prior to the study. Approximately 3 percent of men reported committing attempted rapes, and 4 percent admitted committing completed rapes (Koss, Gidycz, and Wisniewski, 1987). A recent review of this research finds that most of the studies of college women's acquaintance rape victimizations place these as occurring to between 15 and 25 percent of college women (Rubenzahl and Corcoran, 1998). Schwartz and DeKeseredy (1997) report similar levels of sexual victimization using a slightly modified version of Koss's Sexual Experiences Survey on almost 2,000 women and over 1,000 men in community colleges and universities in Canada. More specifically, regarding incidence levels, about 28 percent of the women reported sexual assaults in the previous year, and 11 percent of the men reported sexually assaulting a female dating partner in the previous year. Regarding prevalence levels, 45 percent of the women reported a sexual assault victimization since leaving high school, and 20 percent of the men reported committing at least one incident of sexual assault since leaving high school (ibid., 15).

It is apparent that roughly three-fourths of college women have experienced sexual victimization (excluding sexual harassment). Approximately one in four has experienced completed or attempted rape since the age of 14. Eighty-four percent of these rapes were acquaintance rapes, and "[f]ifty-seven percent of the rapes happened on dates" (see Warshaw, 1988, 11). College students may be particularly vulnerable "[s]ince the majority of acquaintance rape victims are between the ages of 15 and 24, with the average age of 18" (Glavin, 1986). In fact, college women are less likely to be victims of acquaintance rape the longer they are in college: Freshmen women are most at risk, and senior women are least at risk (Parrot, 1986). Culture and society have been blamed for the high rates of date and acquaintance rapes.

Our culture's dating scheme often sets up conditions where the woman is at risk. For instance, if she is expected to have her date pick her up and bring her home, she is somewhat dependent on him. There are additional unwritten assumptions adopted by some men (and women): If he pays for dinner, movies, and so on, then she owes him sex; if she drinks or uses drugs with him, she is giving up her right to say no to sex; if she consensually goes to one level of sexual intimacy, she must continue; or if she once had a sexual relationship with someone, she has no right to say no to such a relationship in the future.

In addition to dating practices negatively affecting gender differences in power, there are also more fundamental beliefs regarding masculinity and femininity. Women are supposed to be passive, weak, dependent, and yet in control of sexual encounters with men. They are in the double bind of having to appear attractive to men but not being sexual. Men, on the other hand, are expected to be aggressive, strong, and independent and to take control with women (and other men). Despite recent awareness surrounding date rape, many people still believe women do not mean it when they say "no" to sex with men.

Women who have been using drugs or alcohol, who wear revealing clothing, who have a reputation for being sexually free, or who have been intimate with the rapist prior to the rape, are even less likely to be viewed as legitimate rape victims— that is, as women who had a legitimate right to say "no." Men's and women's different socialization may result in different interpretations of the same behaviors. Men interpret as an invitation to sex some behaviors that women interpret as friendly or showing some interest in a man; such behaviors include a woman visiting a man's apartment or accepting a ride home from a party (Spencer, 1987).

Research also indicates that to truly understand and deter sexual assaults on campuses (and likely elsewhere), it is necessary to understand the role of male peer support. In particular, Schwartz and DeKeseredy (1997) effectively document in their study of Canadian college students how male peer support, particularly in terms of belonging to male friendship/peer groups where masculinity is narrowly and traditionally defined, where there is a high degree of group secrecy and loyalty, and where women are sexually objectified, is a strong precursor to date rape. They convincingly demonstrate how the socialization of males in North America in a male-dominated/patriarchal society, replete with rape myths and pornography, prepares boys/men to rape. Certainly, anecdotal cases indicate that men who belong to high-profile sports teams and fraternities have a greater sense of entitlement to rape and abuse women and girls. For example, Benedict (1998, 93) reports that demonstrated masculinity is an occupational necessity for male athletes, and when this is combined with an abundance of groupies who willingly provide sex to the male athlete, the athlete views women and girls as a purely sexual function that, in turn, shortens the distance between socially irresponsible behavior and criminal sexual assault. Descriptions of rapes in fraternities provide a similar sense of the members viewing their sexual access to women and girls as a given (see Sanday, 1990, 1996).

Studies comparing the Greek and non-Greek students on college campuses indicate that (1) Greek men drink significantly more than anyone else (i.e., non-Greek men and women and Greek women); (2) Greek women drink more than non-Greek women, and (3) non-Greek men and Greek women consume similar levels of alcohol (Alva, 1998; Wechsler, Kuh, and Davenport, 1996). Boeringer's (1996) study of almost 500 U.S. male college students found fraternity members significantly more likely than nonfraternity members to report using intoxicants and verbal coercion to obtain sex, but they were no more likely to use physical force than nonfraternity members. Male athletes reported the highest proclivity toward rape but no greater coercive or aggressive sexual behaviors than nonathlete males. In another study, Boeringer (ibid.) found that male athletes, followed by male fraternity members and finally a control group of male students (who were neither fraternity nor athletic team members), reported the strongest adherence to rape myths.

Another study of the judicial affairs offices in Division I universities found overrepresentation of male student athletes in reports of the sexual victimization and intimate partner battering of women on college campuses (Crosset et al., 1996). Schwartz and Nogrady's (1996, 148) study of a large Midwestern university found that while "there was strong evidence uncovered that male peer support for victimization of women exists and that it is related to extensive alcohol use, ... there is no evidence that fraternity men are different on these factors from other men." In summarizing some of the diverse findings from these studies regarding differently situated male college students (e.g., athletes v. non-athletes and fraternity members v. independents), Koss and Cleveland (1996) suggest we interpret these studies with caution given some of the methodological and conceptual problems, and support the need for more research addressing how the environment and culture affect fraternity members' and athletes' proclivity toward and attitudes about the victimization of women.

A study comparing African American and White fraternities found institutional racism related to aggression and alcohol and drug (ab)use: The African American fraternities did not have their own houses, so they had to rent dance/party halls that they had to hire security guards for, which resulted in far more monitoring of African American than of White fraternities (Black, Belknap, and Ginsburg, 2005). This lack of monitoring likely impacted the finding that rapes (and drugs and alcohol) were far less common in African American than in White fraternities, yet African American fraternities were far more likely to face sanctions from the police and their universities (ibid.). Unlike the African American fraternities, some White fraternities had contests marginalizing women and placing marginalized women at risk of rape. For example, one fraternity had a "hogging" activity to see who could sleep with the fattest girl. One of the African American women in this study reported being raped at a White fraternity because of a contest checklist that included having sex with an African American woman (ibid.).

Date rapes on college and university campuses, then, particularly in the form of gang rapes, are related to the environment of fraternities and other campus parties (Boswell and Spade, 1996; Ehrhart and Sandler, 1985; Martin and Hummer, 1989; Sanday, 1990, 1996). These studies indicate that women are most at risk of rape in settings where there is general misogyny and devaluing of women. Although most male students do not gang rape, it is important to respond to those who do. Campus gang rapes can take many forms; however, there is usually a pattern. They tend to take place during parties where there is a free flow of alcohol (and often drugs), the music is loud, and women can be easily controlled and isolated. Gang rapes are particularly humiliating in that these rapes are often watched by others, are photographed, and otherwise occur with a multitude of witnesses who either decide to participate or refuse to take action (Warshaw, 1988, 102). Most victims of such gang rapes transfer to another college or drop out.

Gang rapes exhibit a bonding between the rapists, where the participants feel a need to perform in front of their peers. Instigators of gang rape place pressure on onlookers to participate (Groth, 1979). This pressure is probably particularly apparent between fraternity brothers. Also, male athletes' disproportionately high rates of sexual assaults have been attributed to the intense bonding of living and playing with other male athletes (Eskenazi, 1990). A combination of high–status privilege (often attributed to male athletes) and a pack mentality likely influences male athletes' rape-prone behavior. It is also disturbing that these onlookers (whether they are fraternity brothers, friends, or so on) usually choose to join in or at least watch but rarely feel an obligation to stop the victimization.

Frequently, the date rapists purposely work to create an environment that minimizes the victim's control. Two factors often associated with acquaintance rapes are (1) the consumption of alcohol/drugs prior to the victimization, and (2) the playing of loud music (Parrot, 1986, 10). One study of campus rape found that almost all campus gang rapes involved alcohol or drugs, and every one of the fraternity gang rapes they identified involved alcohol or drugs, which helped decrease men's inhibitions and weakened women's ability to determine threatening situations and resist sexual victimizations (Ehrhart and Sandler, 1985).

The playing of loud music is probably used in acquaintance rapes to cover the victim's sounds of noncompliance and increase the victim's feeling of helplessness (Parrot, 1986, 10). Alcohol and drug use and the playing of loud music serve to further debilitate the woman's ability to resist sexual victimization. Many date rapists actually plan the situation in advance in order to maximize their advantages and limit their victims' resistance (Warshaw, 1988, 87). It is not unusual for these men to invite their dates to their own or a friend's apartment on the pretext of seeing the friend or picking something up. The victim later realizes her victimization was planned, often in collusion with the friend who vacated the apartment. Even more disturbing, 84 percent of the men in one study who committed rape said that what they did was definitely not rape (ibid., 90).

A significant form of rape in recent years is what has been labeled *drug-facilitated sexual assault* (DFSA) (McGregor et al., 2003). The typical scenario consists of the assailant adding a drug that induces disinhibition and amnesia to an unsuspecting woman's drink:

> [The assailant then waits] for her to succumb to the effects of the drug before sexually assaulting her. Upon regaining consciousness, victims may recall sensations of drunkenness that are incongruent with the amounts of alcohol consumed, have fragmentary memories of events, and a sense that someone has had sex with them, all of which leads them to suspect they have been sexually assaulted. (ibid., 72)

The most common date rape drugs are rohypnol (roofies) and gamma hydroxyl-butryrate (GHB). A Canadian study that followed sexual assault cases reported to an emergency room between 1993 and 1999 found: (1) the rate of suspected DFSA cases more than double that of the prior six years (from 10 percent to 23 percent); (2) DFSAs were delayed in getting to the emergency room (ER); (3) DFSA cases were less likely to be reported to the police; and (4) DFSA cases had lower levels of injury (ibid.). The delayed reporting to the ER was likely due to the survivor's debilitated state. The problem is that many date rape drugs vanish from the system within 12 hours; thus, delays to the ER make it difficult for women to know whether they were drugged or to establish it for a legal case. The reduced likelihood of reporting to the police is perhaps due to survivors' fears that they have no case. Returning to the previous discussion on MTV, in 2003 a 22-year-old woman reported being raped after consuming a drink and blacking out at the house where MTV's *Real World* was being filmed; another woman witnessed the man who gave her the drink slipping a drug into it and was told by him, "I just hit that" (referring to the survivor who was passed out) (NBC San Diego, 2003).

To better understand date rape, it is important to study men as well as women. One study of college men found that over half thought it was somewhat justifiable to force kissing with tongue contact, and over one-fifth thought it was somewhat justifiable to touch the woman's genitals against her wishes (Muehlenhard, Friedman, and Thomas, 1985). Thirty-five percent of college males in a study in the United States and Canada reported they would commit rape if they knew they could get away with it (Malamuth, 1981). Still another study of male college students found that 15 percent reported forcing intercourse at least once, 28 percent reported using directly coercive methods at least once, and only 39 percent denied coercive sexual involvement. Consistent with the earlier contention that some men do not listen when a woman says "no" or "stop," over one-third of college men reported ignoring a woman's protests (Rapaport and Burkhart, 1984). The most recent study on this topic involved over 100 college men, with an average age of 23.5 years old, using Koss's Sexual Experiences Survey (Rubenzahl and Corcoran, 1998). This study found that using a more encompassing definition of sexual victimization, including engaging in sexual intercourse with a woman who did not want it by overwhelming her with continual arguments and pressure, indicated that 24 percent of these college men responded affirmatively to at least one type of acquaintance rape. When the definition was restricted to a more traditional definition of acquaintance rape, such as threatening or actually using force to obtain sex from a woman who did not want to give it, 10 percent of these college men reported such rape behavior (ibid.).

Data in recent years have shown the extent to which date rape affects young women's lives. To date, most of this research has taken place on college campuses. While a few date rape studies have been conducted in high schools, none have been conducted on older women or younger women not in college. Future research must address this class and institutionalized bias. Additionally, research on fraternity rapes and rapes committed by male athletic stars suggests that some fraternity members and sports stars perceive that their fraternity or star association allows them to have sex with whomever they desire, whether it is voluntarily, coercively, or forcefully. Future research must address these perceived privileges and how they are fostered.

MARITAL RAPE

I've heard from many different people that marital rape cannot possibly be as bad as being raped by a stranger. To me, it is worse. It was devastating to know that the one person I trusted and shared a part of my life with could violate and traumatize me in such a way.
BURTON, 1999, 1084

Many people still view marital rape as a contradiction in terms, believing that husbands should have complete say on when, how, and how often they have sex with their wives. Persons who adhere to these beliefs, however, are often unaware of the extreme brutality in many marital rapes, as well as the effects of routinely having sex against one's will with someone who is supposed to be loving. Unfortunately, media images of marital rape as simply a conflict over sex or an unpleasant but not particularly serious marital squabble have resulted in a sanitary stereotype of marital rape (Finkelhor and Yllo, 1985, 13). Marital rape is either minimized as a petty conflict (Finkelhor and Yllo, 1985) or romanticized as highly erotic for the husband and the wife (for example, in movies such as *Gone with the Wind* and *The Thorn Birds*). Bergen (1996, 13) sums it up best by presenting "marital rape" as ranging "from assaults that were relatively quick in duration and involved little physical force to sadistic, torturous episodes that lasted for hours." Bergen (1996) identifies three causes of marital rape: (1) the husband feels entitled to sex with his wife under any (even violent) conditions; (2) the husband uses rape to punish his wife for something she or someone else did (e.g., he is mad at their child); and (3) the husband rapes to assert power over and control the wife.

Although there is still a lot to learn, research in the 1980s first addressed the issues surrounding marital rape. Most research conducted on marital rape defines it as rape in a marital relationship, including common-law marriages and sometimes persons living together as spouses although not legally married. Rape by former spouses is also typically included under the label *marital rape*. Rape occurs in marriage with alarming frequency (Finkelhor and Yllo, 1983, 1985; Russell, 1982, 1984;

Shields and Hanneke, 1983). Russell's (1984, 62) random sample found that 12 percent of the married women had experienced sexual assault by a husband. Another study examining marital sexual aggression in the previous year compared married couples seeking marital counseling with a community sample of married couples not seeking such counseling (Meyer, Vivian, and O'Leary, 1998). This study found that 5 percent of the women in the counseling group reported experiencing threatened forced or actual forced sex in the previous year, whereas about one-half of one percent (0.5 percent) of the noncounseled community group reported such aggressive sexuality in their relationships in the previous year. However, turning to husbands' use of sexual coercion (the pressuring of wives for sex), over one-third (36 percent) of the women in the couples' counseling group reported sexual coercion, and almost one-quarter (23 percent) of women in the community (non-counseling group) reported sexual coercion in the previous year. Research is consistent in reporting a significant overlap between couples where the man is nonsexually physically aggressive and relationships where the man is sexually aggressive. That is, men who severely abuse their wives in nonsexual ways are also likely to sexually victimize their wives (e.g., Campbell and Soeken, 1999; Finkelhor and Yllo, 1983, 1985; Meyer, Vivian, and O'Leary, 1998; Russell, 1982, 1984). Moreover, women who reported that their husbands used psychological aggression/abuse against them were also more likely to report that their husbands were sexually coercive, pressuring for sex (Meyer, Vivian, and O'Leary, 1998).

Researchers have identified two typologies of marital rape. The first, by Finkelhor and Yllo (1985), categorizes marital rapes as *battering rapes, nonbattering rapes*, and *obsessive rapes*. In battering rapes, sexual violence occurs in addition to verbal and physical violence, or rather, as part of the battering. Nonbattering rapes are marital rapes in relationships where there is little nonsexual physical violence but rape occurs (usually as a result of sexual conflicts). Obsessive rapes are marital rapes that involve "bizarre sexual obsessions," largely perpetrated by men who view (consume) considerable amounts of pornography (Finkelhor and Yllo, 1983, 123–125).

The second typology of marital rapes, by Russell (1982), is a result of her belief that Finkelhor and Yllo's typology is too limiting and not exhaustive. Russell is concerned that the Finkelhor and Yllo typology neglects the less extreme forms of wife rape. In fact, Russell (ibid., 145) believes that although many men who physically abuse their wives also sexually abuse them, probably many more wives are raped by their husbands but not (physically) battered in extreme and repeated forms. Therefore, Russell (ibid., 133–143) proposes the following typology of husbands in relation to wife rape:

1. Husbands who prefer raping their wives to having consensual sex with them
2. Husbands who are able to enjoy both rape and consensual sex with their wives or who are indifferent to which it is
3. Husbands who prefer consensual sex with their wives but are willing to rape when their sexual advances are refused
4. Husbands who would like to rape their wives but don't act on these desires
5. Husbands who have no desire to rape their wives

E X H I B I T   7.1   **Basile's Five Types of Unwanted Marital Sex/Rape by Acquiescence**

1. **Unwanted turns to wanted:** The woman did not initially want to have sex but was able to enjoy it ultimately.

2. **It's my duty:** The woman has sex because she believes it is her marital obligation, not because she wants to have sex.

3. **Easier not to argue:** The woman has sex because she can't tolerate any more verbal or nonverbal behavior from her partner, and sex is the easiest way out of the situation.

4. **Don't know what might happen if I don't:** The woman has sex because she is afraid of a negative consequence if she doesn't.

5. **Know what will happen if I don't:** The woman knew from experience that, if she didn't comply, she would be raped and/or experience other serious forms of violence.

Rape by intimates is difficult to uncover. The victims themselves often redefine what they experience, believing it cannot be rape if the offender is a husband, a boyfriend, or a relative. Marital rape victims often attempt to minimize or forget that they were sexually abused by their husbands (Basile, 1999; Bergen, 1995, 1996; Kelly, 1988). In fact, many times it is not until years later, looking back at a situation, that a woman recognizes that the forced sex she experienced with her husband was indeed rape (Basile, 1999; Kelly, 1988; Sheiner, 1987). It is important in any discussion on marital rape to understand that some of the most violent rapes are rapes occurring in marriage and that some of the marital rapes, while highly coercive in nature, are not violent per se. Regarding the former point, one study found women sexually assaulted by their husbands to be most at risk of being killed by their partners (Campbell and Soeken, 1999). Research on marital rape using the NCVS data reports that marital rapes involve not only more frequent sexual assaults than other acquaintance rapes and stranger rapes but also that marital rape survivors are less likely than the survivors of acquaintance and stranger rapes to seek medical, police, or agency help (Bergen, 1996; Mahoney, 1999). Regarding the latter point, that many marital rapes are more coercive than forceful, one study found five ways in which women give in to unwanted sex with their husbands, presented in Exhibit 7.1 (Basile, 1999). These five types of acquiescence ranged from less serious (I don't feel like it, but maybe I can) to more serious (If I don't do this "voluntarily," he's going to make/rape me). Thus, in this and other studies many women reported that when they tried to resist marital rape, they received worse injuries. thus, nonresistance was a learned mechanism to minimize the level of injuries accompanying the rape (Basile, 1999; Bergen, 1995, 1996). These studies emphasize that even the less violent/more coercive marital rapes are often symbolic of the potential for rape, gender inequality, and the perceived and real consequences when women do not respond to their husbands' sexual demands. It is likely that these same behaviors are experienced by men and women in dating relationships.

Notably, marital rape was made illegal in many other countries before it was made illegal in the United States (X, 1999). In the mid 1970s in Michigan, a courageous judge, Judge Victor Baum, took the liberty of breaking with legal precedent by insisting to the jury that Judy Hartwell had a right to defend herself from her husband who was trying to rape her, even though marital rape was not illegal anywhere in the United States at that time (ibid.). Hartwell had been charged with murdering her husband. Despite considerable resistance, the United States has gone from marital rape being a crime in only five states in 1978 to marital rape being a crime in all fifty states in the 1990s (ibid.).

SEXUAL HARASSMENT

- A woman is walking by a construction site, and one of the workers whistles at her.
- A student goes to her professor to discuss a paper she is writing for his class, and he asks her on a date.
- A woman's supervisor tells her she has nice legs.
- A woman's pastor tells her he knows he shouldn't, but he has sexual fantasies about her.

These are all examples of sexual harassment. Sexual harassment is typically viewed as something that happens only in the workplace or on the street. However, sexual harassment can occur anywhere, including in a college classroom, in a doctor's office, and at social gatherings. Sexual harassment can gradually erode the victim's sense of self-respect and privacy, whether it is a junior executive looking down one's blouse, an obnoxious drunk at the next table making lewd comments, or a construction worker whistling and catcalling (Medea and Thompson, 1974, 50). Similar to discussions on other victimizations of women and girls, power plays a huge role in sexual harassment. The unwanted, intrusive, and insulting behaviors included in sexual harassment have the effect of controlling, angering, and humiliating women and girls.

Most research on sexual harassment has focused on sexual harassment in the workplace. In fact, Stanko (1985, 60) defines sexual harassment as "many forms of unwanted sexual attention that occur in working situations: visual (leering) or verbal (sexual teasing, jokes, comments, or questions) behavior; unwanted pressure for sexual favors or dates; unwanted touching or pinching; and unwanted pressure for sexual favors with implied threats of retaliation for noncooperation." The most comprehensive study on sexual harassment in the workplace was conducted by the Merit Systems Protection Board and initiated by the Subcommittee on Investigations of the House Committee on Post Office and Civil Service. This 1981 report involved questionnaires completed by 20,000 randomly selected federal employees. They found that 15 percent of all male employees and 42 percent of all female employees reported sexual harassment on the job. A study conducted on almost 1,000 workers in Taiwan found that 36 percent of the women and 13 percent of the men reported sexual harassment at work (Luo 1996). The harassment typically took the form of unwanted sexual jokes and comments, followed by deliberate body touching and requests and pressure for dates. Most of the harassment was by coworkers of the opposite sex and the victims attributed the harassment to the harassers' insensitivity (ibid.).

Sexual harassment has been viewed as existing on a continuum of five levels: (1) *Gender harassment* involves sexist remarks putting down women but not necessarily sexual in nature; (2) *seductive behavior* includes behaviors such as sexual advances or requests to discuss the victim's personal and sexual life; (3) *sexual bribery* is where sex is solicited with a promise of a reward; (4) sexual coercion involves threatening someone with punishment for failing to comply with a sexual demand; and (5) *sexual assaults*, gross sexual imposition, and indecent exposures constitute the last and most severe level (Till, 1980). For clarification, an example of sexual bribery is where a student is asked out on a date by her professor, indicating that it will help her grade, whereas sexual coercion would be a professor telling a student if she did not go out with him, she would flunk the course. Thus, these five levels, as listed, imply the least to the most serious types of sexual harassment. It is evident that sexual harassment is often confusing for the victims, who feel they "should" be flattered by the attention but are not or are even afraid.

Legally, sexual harassment has been identified as potentially occurring in two manners. The first, *quid pro quo* harassment involves trading educational or work sustenance or advancement for sexual favors. That is, the victim is promised a grade, a job, a promotion, or some other educational or work favor for complying with a sexual request. The second way sexual harassment has been legally defined as operating is called *hostile environment* sexual harassment. This type of sexual harassment involves behaviors, "decorations," and so on that make a person's work or educational environment intimidating or offensive.

A study of over 1,000 men and over 300 women serving in combat positions in the U.S. military exemplified the causes of sexual harassment (Rosen and Martin, 1998). This study found that the male officers' *tolerance of sexual harassment* was related to their reported levels of *hostility toward women*, negative masculinity (measured as characteristics believed to be socially undesirable for both sexes but more prevalent in males, such as greed, arrogance, selfishness, cynicism, and boastfulness), *acceptance of women as equals*, and *race*. As expected, men reporting higher levels of tolerance for sexual harassment reported higher levels of hostility toward women and hypermasculinity and lower levels of acceptance of women as equals (ibid.). Notably, African American male soldiers were significantly less tolerant of sexual harassment than were White soldiers, and African American female soldiers were less tolerant of sexual harassment than were White female soldiers.

The coercion involved in sexual harassment cannot be overstated. Just as a woman may decide to take a less convenient route to her destination to avoid sexual harassment on the street, women students or women workers may reasonably fear they will do poorly in a class or be fired or denied promotions at work if they refuse to put up with the sexual harassment. It has been suggested that such women keep their jobs at the expense of their self-respect (Farley, 1978). Women are increasingly deciding to confront their harassers, either informally or through university or job policies or laws. The 1991 U.S. Senate confirmation hearings regarding the appointment of Clarence Thomas helped advance awareness on sexual harassment more than anything to date. Thomas was confronted with accusations of sexually harassing Anita Hill, a former employee, at the Equal Employment Opportunity Center office. Although Thomas was confirmed, much of the country was moved by Hill's integrity, and many victims and survivors of sexual harassment came forward to tell their stories as well.

Many people view sexual harassment as harmless or even flattering. Besides having an effect that is often demeaning (making victims feel "cheap" or like a "piece of meat" or a "sexual object"), sexual harassment is yet one more manner in which women are controlled. One article on sexual harassment on the street states that "the message is not that you are attractive enough to make a man lose his self-control but that the public realm belongs to him and you are there by his permission as long as you follow his rules and as long as you remember your place" (Benard and Schlaffer, 1997, 396). The threat behind sexual harassment cannot be minimized. The victim is often unsure as to what degree the harasser will go to in the attempt to demean or control her. If she confronts the harasser for whistling, might she end up being physically sexually assaulted? The severity of sexual harassment is witnessed in a study where more than one in five women reported being sexually assaulted (that is, raped) by someone they knew from work (Schneider, 1991). One study involved the researchers asking street sexual harassers why they do it (Benard and Schlaffer, 1997). Most of these men minimized their behaviors and claimed it was a result of boredom or the camaraderie they felt with other men when they did it. Most had not given it any thought, but about 15 percent claimed that they purposely set out to humiliate and anger their victims (ibid.).

Fear of losing jobs or promotions or failing courses and so on if they stand up to sexual harassment at work and school keeps women and girls from pursuing their goals and careers. The threat of sexual harassment also serves to keep women from pursuing or maintaining jobs traditionally held by males, which are also the jobs that pay the most. The 2005 film *North Country* tracks the true story of sexual harassment of women miners in Minnesota in 1980 and their court resistance. But women in traditionally female jobs are also sexually harassed, often as an expected part of their job (MacKinnon, 1979). Mink (2000) describes high-profile sexual harassment cases, particularly Paula Jones, who charged President Bill Clinton with sexual harassment. Mink also describes her own sexual harassment in graduate school. More than any other researcher, she describes how even some feminists distanced themselves from Jones and other victims, and how the media and many Democratic supporters were insistent on describing Jones as "trailer trash" and other classist and sexist "gold-digging" portrayals.

Clearly, sexual harassment is not harmless when it has such devastating effects. Yet, a study of prime-time television shows reported that sexual harassment on television is both highly visible *and* highly invisible. That is, 84 percent of the shows had at least one incident of sexual harassment, but these situations were presented as humorous, harmless, and easy for the victims to end (Grauerholz and King, 1997). Some research has been conducted at universities in order to determine levels of sexual harassment. A review of research on sexual harassment on college campuses reported that the most common perpetrators of sexual harassment on college campuses are professors and that approximately one-third of undergraduate and graduate women report sexual harassment victimizations by a faculty member over the course of their education (Belknap and Erez, 1997). A study comparing 1989 and 1993 rates of undergraduate women who were seniors at a northeastern public university in the United States found that the incidents of sexual harassment decreased during this four-year period from 25 percent to 20 percent (McCormack, 1995). Although the rate decreased, still one in five of these women had experienced sexual harassment over the course of her undergraduate experience. Also, even though faculty members and to some extent university staff were identified as offenders, the most common perpetrators were fellow students (ibid.).

One recent study was a broad-based, careful analysis of workplace sexual harassment (WSH) as a gendered expression of power (Uggen and Blackstone, 2004). This study is unique in that it included males in the sample and it distinguished between sexual harassment at jobs *during* and *since* high school. Adult women were most subjected to sexual harassment, but high rates of adolescent WSH and clear WSH syndromes occurred across age and gender. The findings indicate that workplace sexual harassment derives from power and masculinity for both males and females and across age groups and that sexual harassment is a general social phenomenon (ibid., 88). Financially vulnerable females and males were the most subjected to WSH (ibid.). Although the quantitative part of the study did not code for the sex of the WSH perpetrators, the qualitative data indicated that almost all of the WSH of both women and men, regardless of age, was by men (personal correspondence with Christopher Uggen, October 14, 2005). A study of high school students who worked part-time found that about two-thirds of the girls and one-third of the boys reported sexual harassment at their jobs (Fineran, 2002). About one-fifth of the harassment was committed by supervisors, another fifth by others at their workplace (e.g., customers), and three-fifths by their coworkers. Consistent with other research comparing gender on victimization, the girls reported higher levels of threats and fear than the boys who reported workplace sexual harassment (ibid.).

Sexual harassment is a problem that occurs on the job, on the street, in the classroom, in the library, and in many other places. Sexual harassment even occurs in religious settings (Majka, 1991; Whitson, 1997), another a place not covered by the work or education legal definition of where sexual harassment can occur. Notably, a focus group study of African American Methodist women found that, although they reported significant levels of sexual harassment in the male-dominated church setting, they were reluctant and unlikely to report it to their church community or leaders because they were afraid they would be blamed for it (Whitson, 1997).

In sum, sexual harassment can be as "mild" as leering or as extreme as a physical sexual assault. Sexual harassment demeans women; it poses a threat, thus serving as a control over women. It can limit women economically from pursuing certain careers or cause them to lose jobs, wages, or promotions. Sexual harassment can dictate when and where women and girls feel safe to walk and in which social communities they can even informally report it. In short, sexual harassment occurs to many women in many environments.

SEXUAL VICTIMIZATION AND THE CRIMINAL LEGAL SYSTEM

Reform efforts to overcome rape survivors' perception that the criminal justice process is out of their control, painful, or degrading have developed along several lines. Since the 1970s, feminists have pursued statute reform to dismantle legal requirements for resistance, corroboration, and spousal exclusions from prosecution and to restrict the manner in which rape survivors are questioned in the courtroom. These changes in law are intended to protect rape survivors from the most traumatic aspects of testifying and ultimately alter societal perceptions that involvement in prosecution is not worthwhile. Research reveals, however, that statute changes are limited in their effect because legal personnel exercise discretion in the implementation of the new laws.

KONRADI AND BURGER, 2000, 351–352

Unfortunately, there is still significant victim-blaming of sexual abuse victims, particularly when they know their offenders and have been intimately involved with the offenders, and they and/or the offenders have consumed alcohol and/or drugs. Thus, it is not surprising that some victims blame themselves and want to keep the sexual abuse a secret. Given that most sexual assaults have no witnesses save the victim, it is usually "easy" for victims to keep the victimization a secret. Unfortunately, this lack of witnesses further hurts victims' chances of being viewed as real victims if they decide to report the incident. Victims may decide not to tell anyone, to tell only a close friend or relative, to tell the police, and/or to tell a rape-crisis center. Rape-crisis centers have proven helpful in providing the victim with a variety of services. In addition to emotional support, they usually provide volunteers to accompany victims to the hospital, to the police department, and to court if they opt to use any of these services.

Victims who formally report the assault will likely have to deal with responses from a variety of persons, including physicians, counselors, family, and friends, as well as the various actors of the criminal legal system. Making their victimizations public, then, often requires survivors to deal with various persons' views and beliefs, as well as myths associated with rape. Regardless of responses by the police and courts, the community response is important. If there are no community services for rape victims, or if the community values sexist and rape-supportive myths, "then the victims' needs will undoubtedly go unaddressed" (Koss and Harvey, 1991, 95).

The sexual abuse victim has frequently been referred to as being twice victimized: once by her (or his) assailant and once by the criminal legal system. But not just police, judges, and juries have been reported to be ignorant about sexual victimization and hostile to the victims. Often even family members and friends respond with hostility toward rape victims; this is particularly true when women and girls are raped by men they know (Sudderth, 1998). There are also accounts of doctors, nurses, therapists, and administrators who behave insensitively to victims, often failing to take victimizations seriously. An analysis of 100 years (from 1880 to 1980) of medical indexes found a recurring theme, particularly in indexes prior to 1960, of advice to view rape victims as liars and "to be extremely meticulous in your examination and history, as many women and girls falsely accuse men of sexual assault; if you make erroneous hasty conclusions, you may be responsible for sending an innocent man to his death" (Mills, 1982, 53). Fortunately, Mills (1982) reports improvements by physicians and hospitals since then. With the second wave of the women's movement, the 1960s and 70s was a crucial era in enacting legislation directed at rape reform, particularly aimed at taking the focus from victim-blaming and improving the climate of the criminal legal system so victims would feel safer and more comfortable reporting rapes to the police (Clay-Warner and Burt, 2005). Unfortunately, though "[d]espite the seriousness of the offense, relatively little is known about the legal processing of sexual assault cases" (Du Mont and Myhr, 2000, 1110).

The Police

Sexual victimization is particularly difficult for the victims to make public because of the shame involved, the fear of retaliation by the assailant, and the need to convince others (sometimes even themselves) that they did not ask for or deserve the assault. The first contact most victims have with the criminal justice system is the police. The police serve an important function, not only in that they are the first contact but also in that victims are dependent on the police to make the case for them. Rape victims, unlike other victims, must often prove nonconsent, with the assumption that most women lie when charging rape (Spencer, 1987, 56). An exhaustive review of the criminal legal research on processing rape in the United States, Canada, and the United Kingdom concluded that few sex offenders are arrested and charged, and still fewer are prosecuted and convicted of sexual offenses. At the police level of processing, studies have found that approximately one-half to three-quarters of all reported sexual assaults are filtered out of the legal system (Du Mont and Myhr, 2000, 1111).

Most of the research on police responses to rape victims occurred in the 1980s. A focus of some of this research is on the practice of *unfounding*, which is when a case is dismissed because the police or prosecutors decide the woman was mistaken or trying to cover up consensual sex. One study revealed that the police unfounded rape cases because of complaints about the victim's moral character or conduct (71 percent), lack of victim cooperation (20 percent), and technical reasons (such as the rape occurring outside of the departmental jurisdiction) (9 percent) (LaFree, Reskin, and Visher, 1985). Notably, nonconforming victims—women who hitchhiked, had sex outside of marriage, went to bars without male escorts, and willingly went to the defendant's apartment—were less likely to have their cases result in arrests (ibid.). A study of over 2,000 police officers found that although police officers are not insensitive to rape victims overall, they are suspicious of victims who meet certain criteria, such as previous and willing sex with the assailant, or who "provoke" rape through their appearance or behavior (LeDoux and Hazelwood, 1985, 219). Furthermore, some of these officers strongly agreed with statements such as "Nice women do not get raped" and "Most charges of rape are unfounded." Rapes that police determine to be unfounded never appear in official statistics of victimization (such as the UCR), thus increasing the invisibility of sexual victimization. A more recent Canadian study reported that 8 percent of rapes were unfounded by the police and almost half resulted in arrest and rape charges. (Of the remaining cases, 27 percent were unsolved, 6 percent were women declining to press charges, and 5 percent were cleared in some other way) (Du Mont and Myhr, 2000).

As stated, one of the goals of legal reform in sexual assault cases was to increase victims' reports to the police (and follow-through with the courts). Examining the rates of rapes reported to the police emphasizes the significance of the type of abuse and the era. Russell (1984) found that only 8 percent of attempted or completed rapes were reported to the police, and the National Victim Center (1992) data indicated that 16 percent of forcible rapes were reported to the police. As expected, stranger rapes are far more likely than acquaintance rapes to be reported (ibid.). Other studies found that on the average, only 5 percent of child sexual assault cases (Russell, 1984) and 5 percent of date rape cases were reported to the police (Warshaw, 1988). Notably, 86 percent of U.S. women reported they would be less likely to report a rape to the police if the media disclosed victims' names (National Victim Center, 1992).

An analysis of UCR and NCVS data from 1973 to 1990 indicated a slight increase in rape victims' reports to the police following statute reforms (Bachman and Paternoster, 1994). But Clay-Warner and Burt (2005) point out that legal reform is unlikely to quickly change rape victims' likelihood to report to the police, but rather it is indicative of societal change; thus, legal rape reform is better studied over a vast number of years with a consistent data set. The researchers then drew on the NVAW data referred to earlier in this chapter to examine changes in rape reporting using information on 824 completed and attempted rapes reported to the National Victim Center (1992) to examine early reform (1975–1989) and modern reform (1990–present). This study found that a rape occurring in the modern reform period (1990–1996) was 88 percent more likely to be reported to the police than a rape occurring before 1978, but women with aggravated rapes (those involving a stranger and/or a weapon and/or a physical injury) were still significantly more likely to report rapes to the police than women with simple rapes, and the difference remained quite stable over eras (Clay-Warner and Burt, 2005). This study also found that victims who consumed drugs/alcohol were significantly less likely to report to the police (ibid.).

The study referred to earlier in this chapter that examined NCS and NCVS rape data also conducted analyses to determine if and how rape reporting to the police has changed over time and found (1) police notification of rapes has increased since the early 1970s, largely due to increases in third-party reporting and victims' increased likelihood to report nonstranger rapes; (2) the increase was particularly large for women raped by current or former husbands; (3) rape victims increasingly notified the police in the 1990s; (4) rapes by nonstrangers were significantly less likely to be reported to the police in the 1970s and 1980s; and (5) victim–offender relationship did *not* effect the likelihood of reporting rapes to the police in the 1990s (Baumer, Felson, and Messner, 2003). Stated another way, the researchers concluded that women raped by acquaintances (i.e., those known well, casually, or by sight only) are no longer *significantly* less likely to notify the police than are women raped by strangers (ibid., p. 858).

The reader likely notices the differences between the Clay-Warner and Burt (2005) study and the study by Baumer and his colleagues (2003). This is likely due to the difference in the data sources. Baumer, Felson, and Messner (ibid.) use the NCVS data which uses legal definitions of rape, while Clay-Warner and Burt's (2005) analysis is based on NVAW data, which defines a broader range of rapes and, in particular, likely includes more nonstranger rapes.

Finally, a Canadian study of 186 women whose rape cases were processed at a hospital found the women's age, race, marital status, employment status, mental health status, and whether they had used alcohol unrelated to whether they reported their rapes to the police (Du Mont, Miller, and Myhr, 2003). Higher levels of physical force and higher levels of injuries resulted in a greater likelihood of the rapes being reported to the police (ibid.). This study concluded that "women who did not resemble the mythologized 'real victim' were as likely as women who did to report the assault to the police. . . . It may be that women who have traditionally been viewed as hesitant to seek police protection, and most likely to bear the brunt of police bias, feel increasingly entitled to turn to law enforcement authorities for redress" (ibid., 477). Thus, while the authors posed their study to test whether traditional notions of chastity and respectability have been seen as effectively disqualifying the "experienced" and the "misbehaved" from claiming or achieving real victim status, including lesbians, sex trade workers, psychiatrized women, low-income women, hitchhikers, and those who frequent nightclubs and/or who have been drinking, and concluded that all types of women/girls feel more empowered to report to the police than ever before, it is unclear how these women fare with the police; the next section will discuss how they fare in court cases.

Using the same data, another study explored the relationship between client/victim and evidentiary factors on the impact of police decision making

(Du Mont and Myhr, 2000). Regarding client/victim variables, both older women and women who could not or did not physically resist were less likely to have their cases forwarded for prosecution. Surprisingly, however, the victim–offender relationship was not related to pressing charges: Police were just as likely to forward cases where a woman was sexually assaulted by a current or former partner *and* other cases where the victim and offender knew each other for more than 24 hours to the police as they were to forward sexual assaults by strangers. Turning to evidence, surprisingly, "[n]either penetration nor the collection of forensic evidence [i.e., a rape kit in the hospital] related to a case resulting in a charge" (ibid., 1123). However, the corroboration of the victim's statement by a witness increased by six times the likelihood of pressing charges. A recent study of nine law enforcement counties in North Carolina found that while there was some significant interaction between rape crisis and law enforcement agencies, all nine counties continued to focus on consent and the *victim's* behavior, and many only allowed cases with physical evidence (Lord and Rassel, 2002). In addition, many departments polygraphed *victims* (and some polygraphed the victims before the offenders), something we rarely see for other offenses (ibid.).

Given the perceptions held by a significant portion of the population of the police being (1) insensitive to rape victims, and (2) racist in processing cases, it is hardly surprising that women and girls of color may feel some community pressure not to report rapes (or batterings), particularly when their abusers are also of color. One of the few studies to address this involved interviews and surveys of African American women rape survivors (Neville and Pugh, 1997). The women in this study reported moderate support for the hypothesis that African American women experience police officers' reputation for hostility and unfairness to African Americans as a barrier to reporting their rape victimizations to the police. Notably, however, a more significant barrier reported by the women in this study was the nonracial reputation police as a group have for their treatment of rape victims (ibid.). Similarly, a study of African American sexual assault survivors reported that they unanimously perceived the criminal legal system as actively hostile to them, as individuals and as members of a broader racial community. Although some indicated they probably would report future sexual victimization to the police, they were clear that they would report only to get something on record, not because they felt they would be helped (Washington, 2001, 1279). The women did not believe crisis intervention services were actively hostile or consciously racist (like the police), but the "[l]ack of staff diversity was rightly or wrongly translated into lack of sensitivity to cultural differences" (ibid.).

In sum, the findings on reporting rapes to the police summarized in this section suggest that rape reform and cultural changes have influenced some significant changes in women's and girls' likelihood of formally reporting their sexual abuse victimizations to the police. Furthermore, although there still appears to be a greater likelihood for victims of the stereotypical rapes that "count," those by strangers where the victim was not drinking and so on are more likely to be reported to the police even though they make up a small percentage of all rapes. Recent research in New Zealand suggests rape survivors favorably report on their experiences with the police when they perceive the police as caring, supportive, and believing them (Jordan, 2001). A third of the women rated their police experiences negatively, citing perceptions of the officers' lack of empathy, judging them, and not believing them, and/or that the police did not think their rape victimization was important. Some women reported such dire experiences with their initial police reports that they quit pursuing the case (ibid.). Finally, this study found that rape survivors' were additionally upset with the police when they believed the lack of professional commitment to their cases in the earliest interviews resulted in lack of conviction for their rapists. In short, these women wanted to be believed, validated, and have the police actively pursuing their rapists (ibid.).

The Court Process, or Whose Trial Is It Anyway?

Assuming that the accuser's sexual abuse case is processed by the police and a suspect has been identified and charged, it is now the prosecutor's turn to determine whether the accuser is "really a victim" and whether the case is worth the prosecutor's time (often not taking the victim's wants or needs into account). Like many police, many prosecutors have relied on gender stereotypes in their efforts to assess "credible" female victims (Stanko, 1982). Thus, the prosecutor's reliance on irrelevant characteristics about the victim and the prosecutor's accept-ance of rape myths may result in the victim not being able to prosecute. In short, many prosecutors and judges have been accused of having the same limited attitudes about rape that many police hold (LaFree, 1989).

Less than 35 percent of arrests for rapes end in convictions (Estrich, 1987, 17); the rest are dismissed or acquitted. Of the 670 attempted and completed rapes reported in Russell's (1984) study, only 2 percent resulted in arrests, and 1 percent resulted in convictions. LaFree (1989) found that 37 percent of rape cases reported to the police ended in arrests, 12 percent resulted in guilty pleas or verdicts, 6 percent went to trial, and less than 5 percent resulted in a prison sentence. A more recent study of over 1,000 court rape cases in Detroit reported that, in 18 percent of the cases, all charges were dismissed, and in 34 percent of the cases, the court cases ended in a conviction, two-thirds of the defendants were incarcerated, and the average maximum sentence in months for the con-victed rapist was 167 (Spohn and Spears, 1996). Another study analyzed prose-cutors' unfounding (deciding the rape did not happen) of rape cases and found that of victims who report to the police, rape victims are just as likely to want to take their cases to court as aggravated assault, robbery, and burglary victims. However, rape victims are more likely to be perceived by prosecutors as lying than are aggravated assault, robbery, and burglary victims. "[R]ape victims are as willing to undergo the ordeal of the court process as are other victims, despite the fact that it may be more grueling for them. However, they are less frequently believed than other victims" (Williams, 1981, 32).

Similarly, a study of judges found that they often base their decisions on who they view as "genuine" or "real" rape victims, and women who are "risk takers"—women who hitchhike, walk alone late at night, go to a bar alone, or use alcohol or drugs—are less likely to have their court cases result in a conviction, particularly if the offender is African American and the victim is White (Spohn and Spears, 1996). A more recent Canadian study found that the conviction rate was 17 percent, while prosecutors or judges withdrew 16 percent of cases, dismissed 4 percent, and acquitted 5 percent of these cases (Du Mont and Myhr, 2000). Of the convictions, three-quarters were cases where the defendant pled guilty. Another Canadian study reported that a third of police-reported cases resulted in charges being filed, and 11 percent of police-reported rapes resulted in convictions (McGregor et al., 2002). Defendants were found guilty as charged in only 7 percent of the cases and found guilty of a lesser charge in the remaining 4 percent of police-reported rapes that resulted in a conviction. Only about 9 percent of the police-reported rapes resulted in any type of custodial (prison/jail) sentence (ibid.).

Prosecutors' ignorance of the dynamics surrounding sexual victimization negatively affects victims who attempt to secure prosecution of their rapists. A study of prosecutors' screening of sexual assault cases found a centrality of victim discredibility in the prosecutors' decisions to reject many rape cases (Frohmann, 1991). This was done by looking for discrepancies in the victim's account or between the victim's account and the police report and trying to determine whether the victim had ulterior motives for filing a false report (for example, not wanting to tell her boyfriend she got a STI from consensual sex with another man). These decisions were heavily based on the often incomplete and mistaken police reports and on the victim's criminal connections. "Rap" sheets chronicling a person's arrests and convictions were routinely run on rape *victims* who were homeless, who were involved in illegal activities, or who simply lived in African American and Latino neighborhoods, but they were not run on women from the wealthier, "White" part of the city (ibid.). Typifications of the victim's behavior and knowledge of the victim's personal life also influenced prosecutors' decisions to reject rape cases. What prosecutors may think is "typical" rape behavior is likely inaccurate, yet it often affects their perceptions of victims' credibility. "Unless we are able to challenge the assumptions on which these typifications are based, many rape cases will never get beyond the filing process because of unconvictability" (ibid., 224).

A more recent study, building on Frohmann (1991) by analyzing 1997 sexual battery cases in Miami, Florida, found that while prosecutors still used a variety of assumptions such as the victims' character, reputation, and time of incident to accept or reject rape cases, a substantial number of rape cases were dropped for acceptable reasons (e.g., the victim did not want to pursue it) (Spohn, Beichner, and Davis-Frenzel, 2001). Still, prosecutors' focal concerns on stereotypes about the victims' moral character and behavior highly influenced the prosecutors' evaluations of the victims' credibility, and over half of the sexually battery cases were not prosecuted. Thus, Estrich's (1987) "real rape" portrayals still influenced the prosecutors' decisions to purse rape charges in some cases (ibid.).

Once a prosecutor decides to advance a rape case to court, Estrich (ibid., 18–19) identified three factors that influence whether a rape charge results in a conviction: (1) the victim–offender relationship, (2) the amount of force used by the defendant and the level of resistance offered by the victim, and (3) the quality of the evidence (that is, the perceived plausibility of the victim's testimony and whether her account can be corroborated). First, studies on *the relationship between the victim and the offender* in sexual assault cases consistently find that convictions are less likely in cases where the victim knows the offender than in stranger rapes (Estrich, 1987; Russell, 1984; Williams, 1981). Although victims are much more likely to be able to identify the assailant in acquaintance rapes, stranger rapes are much more likely to be taken seriously by the criminal legal system (and most of the public) and to result in convictions. This is particularly troubling given that most sexual assaults are perpetrated by men known to the victim. Similarly, evidence about the victim's lifestyle, such as drinking, drug use, or extramarital sexual activity, also affects the verdict (LaFree, Reskin, and Visher, 1985).

In fact, rape trials often seem more concerned with the victims' than the offenders' accountability, responsibility, and personal characteristics. Ironically, one study found that while the defendant's criminal history did not affect the likelihood of his conviction, the victim's criminal history significantly affected whether the offender was convicted (Williams, 1981). Notably, the victim–offender relationship did not affect the likelihood of a guilty verdict in a more recent study (Du Mont and Myhr, 2000). An analysis of Canadian rape law and court cases emphasizes how survivors must show "great resistance" to prove they did not consent (Sheehy, 2001). In the courts, "women's actual resistance was frequently either minimized or ignored, such that judges continued to pronounce that the crime had not been proven as there was no 'great resistance'" (ibid., 99). This study concluded that the current Canadian law effectively immunized men from criminal responsibility when they raped women they had "doped" with alcohol or drugs, because, of course, these women were unable to use "great resistance" (ibid.).

Rape law reform in the 1970s in the United States centered on eliminating some of the worst aspects of the laws and the evidentiary standards (particularly, requiring the victim have corroboration when there were usually no witnesses to rapes) (Bernat, 2002). Additionally, rape reform laws were directed at addressing issues of consent, force, and intent. Unfortunately, a recent overview identifies extralegal factors such as the victims' characteristics as being used to determine police, judges', and jurors' decisions (ibid.). Moreover, the Violence Against Women Act of 1994 (VAWA), designed "to provide victims with redress when state legal systems are inadequate to respond," was invalidated by the U.S. Supreme Court in 2000 (Bernat, 2002, 97). This involved the heartbreaking case of a woman student at Virginia Polytechnic Institute who reported being raped by two male students in 1994. Charges were dropped against one student due to lack of evidence, while the other was found guilty of sexual assault and suspended for two semesters by the university's hearing committee until he appealed to the committee and his charges were lowered from sexual assault to "using abusive language." He was readmitted to the university without notice to the victim (ibid.). The woman filed a federal lawsuit under the new 1994 VAWA, but the court responded by invalidating VAWA, claiming that "Congress lacked constitutional authority to enact VAWA." This invalidation was reaffirmed in District Court and then the U.S. Supreme Court (Bernat, 2002, 95–96). Rape law reform in Canada is strikingly similar, where equality advocates and legislators attempt to consider women's dignity in the processing of these cases, but the Canadian Supreme Court's tactic is "to cast aspersion on rape complainants and to presume women's lack of credibility, their propensity to deceive, misrepresent facts, and malign men to protect their own reputations...and to render judgments that rely on and reinforce a view that the sexual and emotional proclivities of women pose a perpetual threat to the 'rights of man'" (Denike, 2002, 115).

Research has also addressed how levels of both *offender aggression and victim resistance* influence public perceptions that a rape actually occurred. Predictably, both influence impressions of rape culpability. The greater the level of force used by the offender, the more likely the behavior will be labeled rape (Burt and Albin, 1981; Goodchilds and Zellman, 1984). Similarly, the more actively a woman resists, the better chance she has of being viewed as a legitimate victim (Deitz, Littman, and Bentley, 1984; Gilmartin-Zena, 1988). In application to rape court cases, a recent Canadian study found that the level of physical force by the rapist but not the level of resistance by the victim affected the likelihood of a conviction (in the expected direction) (Du Mont and Myhr, 2000).

Regarding the *quality of the evidence* in rape cases, Williams (1981) found that witnesses and traces of physical evidence (such as torn clothing and the presence of sperm) positively affected the likelihood of conviction. Similarly, a review of empirical research found that medical corroboration and corroboration by a witness significantly improved the chances of conviction in sexual victimization cases (Estrich, 1987, 17). A Canadian study, consistent with other studies, found that only about half of the rape victims reporting to a hospital evidenced genital injury (McGregor et al., 2002). This study found, as expected, that higher levels of injury documented by a medical exam increased the likelihood of charges *and* of a conviction. In this study, a woman's willingness to have DNA/sperm collection attempts made by medical personnel (whether sperm or seminal fluid was actually found) increased the chances of the police pressing charges; however, this evidence was only sometimes crucial in terms of convictions (ibid.). At the same time, survivors' records at rape counseling and other therapy centers are increasingly required to be reported to the courts by judges in some cases, placing a chilling effect on women who had counseling *and* want to pursue justice (Denike, 2002).

Conditions for child sexual abuse victims also tend to lack adequate criminal legal system responses. One problem is that even when conclusive medical evidence exists, the child is frequently too young to testify. If the child does testify, she or he is not exempt from the typical abrasiveness and victim blaming of defense lawyers. Finally, given the alarming number of child sexual abusers, it is not unlikely that at least one will end up on a jury (Crewdson, 1988).

The process of making her victimization public is likely to be a painful process for the sexually assaulted victim. In addition to shame and depression, she is likely to experience frustration and anger toward persons who are supposed to be helping her bring the offender to justice. However, there are costs to not prosecuting. A victim may experience a sense of denial of her victimization if she does not prosecute, as well as inhibiting the possibility of punishing the rapist. The victim who does not report may also feel a sense of responsibility that the rapist is free to continue assaulting other victims. On the other hand, deciding to take the case through the criminal legal system may not necessarily result in a sense of vindication. As stated previously, many women who have experienced sexual victimization fear how the police, lawyers, judges, and juries will respond to them. Pretrial settlements in rape prosecutions can "undermine the effectiveness of rape law" and are "rarely subject to judicial review" (Hubbard, 1999, 1260).

Konradi's (1996) study of rape survivors' preparation for court describes how these women are aware of how they must battle victim-blaming and sexist stereotypes in their efforts to have their rapists found guilty. She found that these survivors engaged in six kinds of activities to prepare for the witness stand. First, they did *appearance work* through their clothing and make-up in order to demonstrate respect, conservatism, and nonsexual images. Second, they used the strategy of *rehearsal* by repeatedly telling the events of the rape to supporters before the trial due to their fears that they would become too emotional and cry and/or incorrectly remember the sequencing of events. Third, the survivors used *emotion work* in efforts to obtain the correct court demeanor: one who was polite, composed, deferent to the court's authority, and not angry or in pain. Fourth, the survivors worked on *team building*, or the recruiting of the appropriate support system to be available and present during the trial. (This might involve asking certain people, such as parents, not to attend.) Fifth, the survivors conducted *role research* in order to educate themselves about the rape law, the legal process, and potential court occurrences. Finally, the survivors used *case enhancement* by bringing documents supporting their case to the legal personnel or the court case itself (ibid.). Not surprisingly, in this study the survivors who were the most critical of the process heard irregularly from the legal personnel about their cases and felt that the prosecutors were not invested in their cases. In sum, it is evident that while many women in society are cognizant of the often sexist and victim-blaming court systems, many of the court practitioners are not.

Konradi and Burger (2000) identified four kinds of motivation for rape survivors taking part in the court sentencing of their rapists: (1) to influence the assailants' sentence; (2) to engage in the criminal legal process (including to own and tell their own experiences, which were often at odds with what the defense presented); (3) to reduce the imbalance of power with the assailant; and (4) to resolve emotional components of the rape (e.g., to purge self-doubt and/or anger, or to bring closure). Not surprisingly, when these survivors were encouraged by prosecutors, judges, or victim advocates to represent themselves through writing or speaking regarding the sentence, they were more likely to do so. Likewise, when discouraged to take part by these same court actors, they were less motivated and empowered to do so (ibid.).

A recent study of victims' wishes from the criminal legal system notes that the "wishes and needs of the victims are often diametrically opposed to the requirements of legal proceedings" (Herman, 2005, 574). Indeed, the victims and their loved ones are looking for *validation*, not just from the legal proceedings but also from their communities; for an *apology* from the abusers; and for the abusers' *accountability* (ibid.). Notably, of the four basic goals of the criminal legal system (retribution, deterrence, incapacitation, and rehabilitation), the goal most generally endorsed by the victims and their loved ones was incapacitation. However, most victims preferred ongoing community supervision or civil restraining orders over jail or prison for their abusers (ibid.)

Turning to sexual harassment, litigation of these cases did not occur until the mid-1970s. One review of the laws surrounding this victimization reported that sexual harassment in the workplace (via Title VII of the Civil Rights Act) and in educational settings (via Title IX of the Civil Rights Act) is illegal but that claiming sexual harassment outside of these environments is almost impossible legally (Belknap and Erez, 1997). "[S]exual harassment occurs in many other contexts in which unwelcome sexual remarks or advances may disadvantage their recipients, but there appears to be little legal recourse available to these victims" (ibid., 154).

SUMMARY

This chapter explained the limitations inherent in how the term *rape* has traditionally been defined. To fully understand and measure sexual victimization, it is necessary to acknowledge that people are sexually victimized in many ways in addition to forced penile–vaginal penetration between adult strangers. The rate of sexual victimization in this country is much higher than once thought, particularly between acquaintances. Increased awareness of the probability of stranger rapes of adult women occurred in the 1970s. Next, the uncovering of acquaintance rapes of adult women occurred. Finally, in the early 1980s, the sexual abuse of children, particularly incest, became defined as a social problem, if not a national epidemic. Awareness of date and marital rape followed shortly after the identification of child sexual abuse as a social problem.

Of the eight index crimes, rape is the least likely to be reported. In addition to the humiliation associated with sexual victimization, victims may fear the offenders' retaliation or lack of support by the criminal legal system, and/or they may blame themselves for the assault. In the case of child sexual abuse, the victim may not be in a situation to report the behavior or even to understand that she or he has been victimized. Thus, in spite of increased attention by the media and researchers, for many reasons sexual victimization remains a highly invisible crime.

Determination of rates of sexual victimization has been hampered by some of the following factors: (1) Rape is one of the crimes that victims are least likely to report to the police; (2) stereotypical characteristics of the victim and the offender (such as whether they are strangers, whether she has a bad reputation) often are mistakenly used to determine whether the rape was "real;" (3) the nature of the sexual victimization (that is, the increased humiliation of having been anally or orally raped or raped by a husband) may deter the victim from reporting; and (4) the victims of attempted rapes may perceive their victimizations as not important enough to report because they were not really raped.

Although the NCS data collection method provides a more accurate assessment than the UCR of the degree to which rapes occur in the United States, neither the NCS nor the UCR adequately assesses the frequency of sexual victimization because of their methods of questioning and, in the case of the UCR, data collection. (Specifically, the UCR relies on rapes reported to the police, which presents a skewed picture of the overall distribution of rapes.) Improved data-collection methods have uncovered the high likelihood of U.S. females being sexually victimized, particularly by their families, close friends, and dates.

It was not until the 1980s that child sexual abuse was labeled a social problem. In a relatively short period of time, we have become aware that it may occur to as many as 62 percent of female children and 31 percent of male children (Peters, Wyatt, and Finkelhor, 1986). Child sexual victimization has remained invisible for the same reasons that the sexual victimization of adult women has remained invisible. However, in most cases, children are even less empowered than adult women to physically resist sexual victimization and to be able to report their victimizations.

Young women who have recently left home (for college or work) are also a high-risk group for sexual victimization. Date rape has recently been identified as a sexual problem. Research has also highlighted gang rapes on college campuses, where the victim and rapists knew each other prior to the assault. This appears to be particularly prevalent during fraternity and dormitory parties and by male athletes. These rapes are frequently planned, using alcohol, drugs, and loud music to debilitate the victim (Parrot, 1986).

Sexual harassment is a form of sexual victimization. It is behavior that is sexual in nature and empowers the harasser by demeaning the victim. Occurrence of this behavior is most frequently associated with the workplace, but more recently, it has been recognized as occurring anywhere: in educational settings, at work, in social settings, and on the streets. Sexual harassment is one more method by which women are threatened and their lives are shaped.

Unfortunately, many persons experiencing sexual victimization are further victimized by their encounters with the criminal legal system. Police and courts have frequently been found to be suspicious of any women, and often children, who claim to have been sexually victimized. Disbelief and cynicism on the part of the criminal legal authorities is most prevalent in the cases that occur most frequently and in which the victim is most likely to be able to identify the offender: acquaintance rapes. It is necessary for police officers, judges, and lawyers to be educated about the realities of sexual victimization. This education is also necessary for the public, not only because they serve on juries but also in order that they may stop their own rape-prone behaviors and/or be supportive when someone they know experiences sexual victimization. Rape awareness education may reduce women's and girls' sexual victimization by making them aware of what places them most at risk, as well as educating males about what constitutes rape and why it is illegal and immoral.

NOTES

1.   Russell (1984) had to extrapolate her data to make the necessary comparisons with the UCR and NCS findings, based on differences in sampling and reporting techniques. For instance, Russell's data are for persons 18 years of age and older, the NCS is for persons 12 and older, and the UCR includes persons of all ages.

REFERENCES

Abbey, Antonia. 1987. Misperceptions of Friendly Behavior as Sexual Interest. *Psychology of Women Quarterly* 11:173–194.

Abbey, Antonia, Tina Zawacki, Philip O. Buck, A. Monique Clinton, and Pam McAuslan. 2001. Alcohol and Sexual Assault: National Institute on Alcohol Abuse and Alcoholism (NIAAA). *Alcohol Health and Research World* 25(1). http://www.athealth.com/Practitioner/ceduc/alc_assault.html

Adams, Antonia, and G. Abarbanel. 1988. *Sexual Assault on Campus: What Colleges Can Do*. Santa Monica, CA: Rape Treatment Center.

Alva, S. A. 1998. Self-Reported Alcohol Use of College Fraternity and Sorority Members. *Journal of College Student Development* 39:3–10.

Amir, Manachem. 1971. *Patterns in Forcible Rape*. Chicago: University of Chicago Press.

Bachman, Ronet, and Raymond Paternoster. 1994. A Contemporary Look at the Effects of Rape Law Reform: How Far Have We Really Come? *The Journal of Criminal Law and Criminology* 84:554–574.

Barrett, Karen. 1982. Date Rape: A Campus Epidemic? *Ms. Magazine* (September):49–51, 130.

Bart, Pauline B., and Patricia H. O'Brien. 1985. *Stopping Rape: Successful Survival Strategies*. New York: Pergamon Press.

Basile, Kathleen C. 1999. Rape by Acquiescence: The Ways in Which Women "Give in" to Unwanted Sex with Their Husbands. *Violence Against Women* 5(9):1017–1035.

Bass, Ellen. 1983. Introduction: In the Truth Itself, There Is Healing. Pp. 23–61 in *I Never Told Anyone*, edited by E. Bass and L. Thornton. New York: Harper and Row.

Baumer, Eric P., Richard B. Felson, and Steven F. Messner. 2003. Changes in Police Notification for Rape, 1973–2000. *Criminology* 41:841–872.

Belknap, Joanne. 1987. Routine Activity Theory and the Risk of Rape: Analyzing Ten Years of National Crime Survey Data. *Criminal Justice Policy Review* 2:337–356.

Belknap, Joanne, and Edna Erez. 1997. Redefining Sexual Harassment. *Justice Professional* 10:143–159.

Belknap, Joanne, Bonnie Fisher, and Francis Cullen. 1999. The Development of a Comprehensive Measure of the Sexual Victimization of College Women. *Violence Against Women* 5:185–214.

Benard, Cheryl, and Edith Schlaffer. 1997. "The Man in the Street": Why He Harasses. Pp. 395–398 in *Feminist Frontiers IV*, edited by L. Richardson and V. Taylor. New York: McGraw Hill.

Benedict, Jeffrey R. 1998. *Athletes and Acquaintance Rape*. Thousand Oaks, CA: Sage.

Beneke, Timothy. 1982. *Men on Rape: What They Have to Say about Sexual Violence*. New York: St. Martin's Press.

Bergen, Raquel Kennedy. 1995. Surviving Wife Rape. *Violence Against Women* 1:117–138.

———. 1996. *Wife Rape*. Thousand Oaks, CA: Sage.

Bernat, Frances P. 2002. Rape Law Reform. 85-99. Pp. 51–72 in *Sexual Violence*, edited by J. F. Hodgson and D. S. Kelley. Westport, CT: Praeger.

Black, Tyra, Joanne Belknap, and Jennifer Ginsburg. 2005. Racism, Sexism and Aggression: A Study of Black and White Fraternities. Pp. 363–392 in *African American Fraternities and Sororities: The Legacy and the Vision*, edited by Tamara L. Brown, Gregory S. Parks, and Clarenda M. Phillips. Lexington: The University Press of Kentucky.

Boeringer, Scot B. 1996. Influences of Fraternity Membership, Athletics, and Male Living Arrangements on Sexual Aggression. *Violence Against Women* 2:134–147.

Boswell, A. Ayres, and Joan Z. Spade. 1996. Fraternities and Collegiate Rape Culture. *Gender and Society* 10:133–147.

Browne, Angela, and David Finkelhor. 1986. Impact of Child Sexual Abuse: A Review of the Research. *Psychological Bulletin* 99:66–77.

Brownmiller, Susan. 1975. *Against Our Will: Men, Women and Rape*. New York: Simon and Schuster.

Bufkin, Jana, and Sarah Eschholz. 2000. Images of Sex and Rape: A Content Analysis of Popular Film. *Violence Against Women* 6:1317–1344.

Burt, Martha R., and R. S. Albin. 1981. Rape Myths, Rape Definitions, and Probability of Conviction. *Journal of Applied Social Psychology* 11:212–230.

Burton, Davie. 1999. My Struggle. *Violence Against Women* 5(9):1084–1085.

Campbell, Jacquelyn C., and Karen L. Soeken. 1999. Forced Sex and Intimate Partner Violence. *Violence Against Women* 5(9):1017–1035.

Christgau, Robert. 2003. Rock Out: Why MTV had to Destroy Rock and Roll in order to Save It. *New York Magazine* (April 7). http://newyorkmetro.com/nymetro/news/anniversary/35th/n_8586/

Clark, Anne. 1987. *Women's Silence, Men's Violence: Sexual Assault in England, 1770–1845*. London: Pandora Press.

Clay-Warner, Jody, and Callie Harbin Burt. 2005. Rape Reporting After Reforms: Have Times Really Changed? *Violence Against Women* 11:150–176.

Conte, John R., and John R. Schuerman. 1987. The Effects of Sexual Abuse of Children. *Journal of Interpersonal Violence* 2:380–390.

Corcoran, K. J., and L. R. Thomas. 1991. The Influence of Observed Alcohol Consumption of Perceptions of Initiation of Sexual Activity in a College Dating Situation. *Journal of Applied Social Psychology* 21:500–507.

Costin, Charisse T. M. 1992. The Influence of Race in Urban Homeless Females' Fear of Crime. *Justice Quarterly* 9:721–730.

Crewdson, John. 1988. *By Silence Betrayed: Sexual Abuse of Children in America*. Boston: Little, Brown.

Crosset, Todd W., James Ptacek, Mark A. McDonald, and Jeffrey R. Benedict. 1996. Male Student-Athletes and Violence against Women. *Violence Against Women* 2:163–179.

Deitz, Sheila R., Madeleine Littman, and Brenda J. Bentley. 1984. Attribution of Responsibility for Rape: The Influence of Observer Empathy, Victim Resistance, and Victim Attractiveness. *Sex Roles* 10:261–280.

Denike, Margaret A. 2002. Myths of Woman and the Rights of Man. Pp. 101–134 in *Sexual Violence*, edited by J. F. Hodgson and D. S. Kelley. Westport, CT: Praeger.

Du Mont, Janice, Karen-Lee Miller, and Terri L. Myhr. 2003. The Role of "Real Rape" and "Real Victim" Stereotypes in the Police Reporting Practices of Sexually Assaulted Women. *Violence Against Women* 9:466–486.

Du Mont, Janice, and Terri L. Myhr 2000. So Few Convictions: The Role of Client-Related Characteristics in the Legal Processing of Sexual Assaults. *Violence Against Women* 6:1109–1136.

Ehrhart, Julie K., and Bernice R. Sandler. 1985. *Campus Gang Rape: Party Games?* Washington, DC: Association of American Colleges.

Eigenberg, Helen M. 1990. The National Crime Survey and Rape: The Case of the Missing Question. *Justice Quarterly* 7:655–672.

Eskenazi, Gerald. 1990. The Male Athlete and Sexual Assault. *New York Times*, June 30, p. 27.

Estrich, Susan. 1987. *Real Rape*. Cambridge, MA: Harvard University Press.

Farley, L. 1978. *Sexual Shakedown: The Sexual Harassment of Women on the Job*. New York: Warner.

Fineran, Susan. 2002. Adolescents at Work: Gender Issues and Sexual Harassment. *Violence Against Women* 8:953–967.

Finkelhor, David, and Larry Baron. 1986. High Risk Children. Pp. 60–88 in *A Sourcebook on Child Sexual Abuse*, edited by D. Finkelhor. Beverly Hills, CA: Sage.

Finkelhor, David, and Kersti Yllo. 1983. Rape in Marriage: A Sociological View. Pp. 119–131 in *The Dark Side of Families: Current Family Violence Research*, edited by D. Finkelhor, R. J. Gelles, G. T. Hotaling, and M. A. Straus. Beverly Hills, CA: Sage.

———. 1985. License to Rape: *Sexual Abuse of Wives*. New York: Free Press.

Forward, Susan, and Craig Buck. 1978. *Betrayal of Innocence: Incest and Its Devastation*. Middlesex, England: Penguin Books.

Frohmann, Lisa. 1991. Discrediting Victims' Allegations of Sexual Assault: Prosecutorial Accounts of Case Rejection. *Social Problems* 38: 213–226.

Gilmartin-Zena, Pat. 1988. Gender Differences in Students' Attitudes toward Rape. *Sociological Focus* 21:279–292.

Girshick, Lori B. 2002a. No Sugar, No Spice: Reflections on Research on Woman-to-Woman Sexual Violence. *Violence Against Women* 8:1500–1520.

———. 2002b. *Woman-to-Woman Sexual Violence*. Boston: Northeastern University Press.

Glavin, A. P. 1986. *Acquaintance Rape: The Silent Epidemic*. Massachusetts Institute of Technology, Campus Police Department, March.

Gomes-Schwartz, Beverly, Jonathan M. Horowitz, and Albert P. Cardearelli. 1990. *Child Sexual Abuse: The Initial Effects*. Newbury Park, CA: Sage.

Goodchilds, Jacqueline D., and Gail L. Zellman. 1984. Sexual Signaling and Sexual Aggression in Adolescent Relationships. Pp. 233–243 in *Pornography and Sexual Aggression*, edited by N. M. Malamuth and E. Donnerstein. Orlando, FL: Academic Press.

Gordon, Linda, and Paul O'Keefe. 1984. Incest as a Form of Family Violence: Evidence from Historical Case Records. *Journal of Marriage and Family* 46:27–34.

Grauerholz, Elizabeth, and Amy King. 1997. Prime Time Sexual Harassment. *Violence Against Women* 3:129–148.

Griffen, Susan. 1971. Rape: The All-American Crime. *Ramparts* (September): 26–35.

Groth, A. Nicholas. 1979. *Men Who Rape: The Psychology of the Offender*. New York: Plenum Press.

Harned, Melanie S. 2005. Understanding Women's Labeling of Unwanted Sexual Experiences with Dating Partners: A Qualitative Analysis. *Violence Against Women* 11:374–413.

Heger, Astrid, Lynne Ticson, Oralia Velásquez, and Rápale Bernier. 2002. Children Referred for Possible Sexual Abuse. *Child Abuse and Neglect* 26:645–659.

Henton, J., R. Cate, J. Koval, S. Lloyd, and S. Christopher. 1983. Romance and Violence in Dating Relationships. *Journal of Family Issues* 4:467–482.

Herman, Judith L. 1981. *Father–Daughter Incest*. Cambridge, MA: Harvard University Press.

Herman, Judith Lewis. 2005. Justice from the Victim's Perspective. *Violence Against Women* 11:571–602.

Hill, Melanie S., and Ann R. Fischer. 2001. Does Entitlement Mediate the Link between Masculinity and Rape-Related Variables? *Journal of Counseling Psychology* 48:39–50.

Hubbard, William H. J. 1999. Civil Settlement during Rape Prosecutions. *The University of Chicago Law Review* 66:1231–1260.

Jensen, Gary F., and Mary Altani Karpos 1993. Managing Rape: Exploratory Research on the Behavior of Rape Statistics. *Criminology* 31:363–386.

Jordan, Jan. 2001. Worlds Apart? Women, Rape and the Police Reporting Process. *British Journal of Criminology* 41:679–706.

Kanin, Eugene J. 1957. Male Aggression in Dating–Courtship Relations. *American Journal of Sociology* 63: 197–204.

Kelly, Liz. 1988. How Women Define Their Experiences of Violence. Pp. 114–132 in *Feminist Perspectives on Wife Abuse*, edited by K. Yllo and M. Bograd. Newbury Park, CA: Sage.

Kimerling, Rachel, Alessandra Rellini, Vanessa Kelly, Patricia Judson, and Lee Learman. 2002. Gender Differences in Victim and Crime Characteristics of Sexual Assaults. *Journal of Interpersonal Violence* 17:526–532.

Kohn, Alfie. 1987. Shattered Innocence. *Psychology Today* (February):54–58.

Konradi, Amanda. 1996. Understanding Rape Survivors' Preparations for Court. *Violence Against Women* 2:25–62.

Konradi, Amanda, and Tina Burger. 2000. Having the Last Word: An Examination of Rape Survivors' Participation in Sentencing. *Violence Against Women* 6:351–395.

Koss, Mary P. 1996. The Measurement of Rape Victimization in Crime Surveys. *Criminal Justice and Behavior* 23:5–69.

Koss, Mary P., and Hobart H. Cleveland III. 1996. Athletic Participation, Fraternity Membership, and Date Rape. *Violence Against Women* 2:180–1990.

Koss, Mary P., C. A. Gidycz, and N. Wisniewski. 1987. The Scope of Rape: Incidence and Prevalence of Sexual Aggression and Victimization in a National Sample of Higher Education Students. *Journal of Consulting and Clinical Psychology* 55:162–170.

Koss, Mary P., and Mary R. Harvey. 1991. *The Rape Victim: Clinical and Community Interventions*, 2nd ed. Newbury Park, CA: Sage.

Koss, Mary P., and C. J. Oros 1982. Sexual Experiences Survey: A Research Instrument Investigating Sexual Aggression and Victimization. *Journal of Consulting and Clinical Psychology* 50:455–457.

LaFree, Gary D. 1989. *Rape and Criminal Justice: The Social Construction of Sexual Assault*. Belmont, CA: Wadsworth.

LaFree, Gary D., Barbara F. Reskin, and Christy A. Visher. 1985. Jurors' Responses to Victims' Behavior and Legal Issues in Sexual Assault Trials. *Social Problems* 32:389–407.

LeDoux, J. C., and R. R. Hazelwood. 1985. Police Attitudes and Beliefs toward Rape. *Journal of Police Science and Administration* 13:211–220.

Lee, Joohee, Elizabeth C. Pomeroy, Seo-Koo Yoo, and Kurt T. Rheinboldt. 2005. Attitudes toward Rape: A Comparison between Asian and Caucasian College Students. *Violence Against Women* 11:177–196.

Lord, Vivian B., and Gary Rassel. 2002. Law Enforcement Responses to Sexual Assault. Pp. 155–172 in *Sexual Violence*, edited by J. F. Hodgson and D. S. Kelley. Westport, CT: Praeger.

Luo, Tsun-Yin 1996. Sexual Harassment in the Chinese Workplace. *Violence Against Women* 2:284–301.

MacKinnon, Catherine A. 1979. *Sexual Harassment of Working Women*. New Haven, CT: Yale University Press.

Mahoney, Patricia. 1999. High Rape Chronicity and Low Rates of Help-Seeking among Wife Rape Survivors in a Nonclinical Sample. *Violence Against Women* 5(9): 993–1016.

Majka, L. 1991. Sexual Harassment in the Church. *Society* (May/June):14–21.

Malamuth, Neil M. 1981. Rape Proclivity among Males. *Journal of Social Issues* 37:138–157.

Martin, P. Y., and R. Hummer. 1989. Fraternities and Rape on Campus. *Gender and Society* 3:457–473.

Martin, Susan E., and Ronet Bachman. 1998. The Contribution of Alcohol to the Likelihood of Completion and Severity of Injury in Rape Incidents. *Violence Against Women* 4:694–712.

McCaw, Jodee M., and Charlene Y. Senn. 1998. Perception of Cues in Conflictual Dating Situations. *Violence Against Women* 4:609–624.

McCormack, Arlene Smith. 1995. Revisiting Sexual Harassment of Undergraduate Women. *Violence Against Women* 1:254–265.

McGregor, Margaret J., Madalena Lipowska, Seema Shah, Janice Du Mont, and Terri L. Myhr. 2002. Sexual Assault Forensic Medical Examination: Is Evidence Related to Successful Prosecution? *Annals of Emergency Medicine* 39:639–647.

McGregor, Margaret J., Madalena Lipowska, Seema Shah, Janice Du Mont, and Christine De Siato. 2003. An Exploratory Analysis of Suspected Drug-Facilitated Sexual Assault Seen in a Hospital Emergency Department. *Women & Health* 37:71–80.

Medea, Andra, and Kathleen Thompson. 1974. *Against Rape*. New York: Farrar, Straus and Giroux.

Meyer, Shannon-Lee, Dina Vivian, and K. Daneil O'Leary. 1998. Men's Sexual Aggression in Marriage. *Violence Against Women* 4:415–435.

Miller, Beverly, and Jon C. Marshall. 1987. Coercive Sex on the University Campus. *Journal of College Student Personnel* 28:38–47.

Mills, Elizabeth A. 1982. One Hundred Years of Fear: Rape and the Medical Profession. Pp. 29–62 in *Judge, Lawyer, Victim, Thief*, edited by N. H. Rafter and E. A. Stanko. Stoughton, MA: Northeastern University Press.

Mink, Gwendolyn. 2000. *Hostile Enviornment: The Political Betrayal of Sexually Harassed Women*. Ithaca, NY: Cornell University Press.

Moffeit, Miles, and Amy Herdy. 2005. Female GIs Report Rapes in Iraq War. *Denver Post*, January 25. http://www.commondreams.org/headlines04/0125-08.htm.

Muehlenhard, Charlene L. 1989. Misinterpreted Dating Behaviors and Risk of Rape. Pp. 241–256 in *Violence and Dating Relationships*, edited by M. A. Pirog-Good and J. E. Stets. New York: Praeger.

Muehlenhard, Charlene L., D. E. Friedman, and C. M. Thomas. 1985. Is Date Rape Justifiable? The Effects of Dating Activity, Who Initiated, Who Paid, and Men's Attitudes toward Women. *Psychology of Women Quarterly* 9:297–310.

Muehlenhard, Charlene L., and M. A. Linton. 1987. Date Rape and Sexual Aggression in Dating Situations: Incidence and Risk Factors. *Journal of Counseling Psychology* 34:186–196.

Murphy, John E. 1991. An Investigation of Child Sexual Abuse and Consequent Victimization: Some Implications of Telephone Surveys. Pp. 79–88 in *Abused and Battered: Social and Legal Responses to Family Violence*, edited by D. D. Knudsen and J. L. Miller. New York: Aldine De Gruyter.

Murphy, Shane M., Dean G. Kilpatrick, Angelynne Amick-McMullan, Lois J. Veronen, Janet Paduhovich, Connie L. Best, Lorenz A. Veilleponteaux, and Benjamin E. Saunders. 1988. Current Psychological Functioning of Child Sexual Assault Survivors. *Journal of Interpersonal Violence* 3:55–79.

National Victim Center. 1992. *Rape in America*. Arlington, VA, 18pp.

NBC San Diego. 2003. Woman Says She Was Raped in "Real World" House: Victim Blacks Out After Being Given Drink. http://www.nbcsandiego.com/entertainment/2665151/detail.html.

Neville, Helen A., and Aalece O. Pugh. 1997. General and Culture-Specific Factors Influencing African American Women's Reporting Patterns and Perceived Social Support following Sexual Assault. *Violence Against Women* 3:361–381.

Parrot, Andrea. 1986. *Acquaintance Rape and Sexual Assault Prevention Training Manual*. Department of Human Services Studies. Ithaca, NY: Cornell University.

Peters, Stefanie D., Gail E. Wyatt, and David Finkelhor. 1986. Prevalence. Pp. 15–59 in *Sourcebook on Child Sexual Abuse*, edited by D. Finkelhor. Beverly Hills, CA: Sage.

Putnam, Frank W. 2003. Ten-Year Research Update Review: Child Sexual Abuse. *Journal of the American Academy of Child and Adolescent Psychiatry* 42:269–278.

Rapaport, K., and B. R. Burkhart. 1984. Personality and Attitudinal Characteristics of Sexually Coercive Males. *Journal of Abnormal Psychology* 93:216–221.

Roiphe, Katie. 1993. *The Morning After.* Boston: Little, Brown.

Rosen, Leora N., and Lee Martin. 1998. Predictors of Tolerance of Sexual Harassment among Male U.S. Army Soldiers. *Violence Against Women* 4:491–504.

Rubenzahl, Samuel A., and Kevin J. Corcoran. 1998. The Prevalence and Characteristics of Male Perpetrators of Acquaintance Rape. *Violence Against Women* 4:713–725.

Rush, Florence. 1980. *The Best Kept Secret: Sexual Child Abuse of Children.* New York: McGraw-Hill.

———. 1983. Foreword. Pp. 13–14 in I Never Told Anyone, edited by E. Bass and L. Thornton. New York: Harper and Row.

Russell, Diana E. H. 1982. *Rape in Marriage.* New York: Collier Books.

———. 1984. *Sexual Exploitation: Rape, Child Sexual Abuse, and Workplace Harassment.* Beverly Hills, CA: Sage.

———. 1986. *The Secret Trauma: Incest in the Lives of Girls and Women.* New York: Basic Books.

Sanday, Peggy Reeves. 1990. *Fraternity Gang Rape: Sex, Brotherhood, and Privilege on Campus.* New York: New York University Press.

———. 1996. *A Woman Scorned: Acquaintance Rape on Trial.* New York: Doubleday Press.

Sanders, William B. 1980. *Rape and Woman's Identity.* Beverly Hills, CA: Sage.

Schneider, Beth E. 1991. Put Up and Shut Up: Workplace Sexual Assault. *Gender and Society* 5:533–548.

Schram, Donna D. 1978. Rape. Pp. 53–80 in *The Victimization of Women,* edited by J. R. Chapman and M. Gates. Beverly Hills, CA: Sage.

Schwartz, Martin D., and Walter S. DeKeseredy. 1997. *Sexual Assault on the College Campus.* Thousand Oaks: Sage.

Schwartz, Martin D., and Molly S. Leggett. 1999. Bad Dates or Emotional Trauma? The Aftermath of Campus Sexual Assault. *Violence Against Women* 5:251–271.

Schwartz, Martin D., and Carol A. Nogrady. 1996. Fraternity Membership, Rape Myths, and Sexual Aggression on a College Campus. *Violence Against Women* 2:148–162.

Scully, Diana. 1988. Convicted Rapists' Perceptions of Self and Victim: Role Taking and Emotions. *Gender and Society* 2:200–213.

———. 1990. *Understanding Sexual Violence.* Boston: Unwin Hyman.

Sheehy, Elizabeth. 2001. From Women's Duty to Resist. *Canadian Woman Studies.* 20:98–104.

Sheiner, Marcy. 1987. Battered Women: Scenes from a Shelter. *Mother Jones* (November):15–19, 43–44.

Shields, Nancy M., and Christine R. Hanneke. 1983. Battered Wives' Reactions to Marital Rape. Pp. 132–148 in *The Dark Side of Families: Current Family Violence Research,* edited by D. Finkelhor, R. J. Gelles, G. T. Hotaling, and M. A. Straus. Beverly Hills, CA: Sage.

Siegel, Jane A., and Linda A. Williams. 2003. Risk Factors for Sexual Victimization of Women. *Violence Against Women* 9:902–930.

Skogan, Wesley G. 1976. The Victims of Crime: Some National Survey Findings. In *Criminal Behavior in Social Systems,* edited by A. L. Guenther. Chicago: Rand-McNally.

Somer, Eli, and Sharona Szwarcberg. 2001. Variables in Delayed Disclosure of Child Sexual Abuse. *American Journal of Orthopsychiatry* 71:332–341.

Sommers-Flanagan, Rita, John Sommers-Flanagan, and B. Davis. 1993. What's

Happening on Music Television? A Gender Role Content Analysis. *Sex Roles* 28:745–753.

Spencer, Cassie C. 1987. Sexual Assault: The Second Victimization. Pp. 54–73 in *Women, Courts, and Equality*, edited by L. L. Crites and W. L. Hepperle. Newbury Park, CA: Sage.

Spohn, Cassia, Dawn Beichner, and Erika Davis-Frenzel. 2001. Prosecutorial Justifications for Sexual Assault Case Rejection. *Social Problems* 48: 206–235.

Spohn, Cassia, and Jeffrey Spears. 1996. The Effect of Offender and Victim Characteristics on Sexual Assault Case Processing Decisions. *Justice Quarterly* 13:649–680.

Stanko, Elizabeth A. 1982. Would You Believe This Woman? Prosecutorial Screening for "Credible" Witnesses and a Problem of Justice. Pp. 63–82 in *Judge, Lawyer, Victim, Thief*, edited by N. H. Rafter and E. A. Stanko. Stoughton, MA: Northeastern University Press.

———. 1985. *Intimate Intrusions: Women's Experience of Male Violence*. London: Routledge and Kegan Paul.

———. 1992. The Case of Fearful Women: Gender, Personal Safety and Fear of Crime. *Women & Criminal Justice* 4:117–135.

Stermac, Lana, Janice Du Mont, and Sheila Dunn. 1998. Violence in Known-Assailant Sexual Assaults. *Journal of Interpersonal Violence* 13:398–412.

Sudderth, Lori K. 1998. "It'll Come Right Back at Me": The Interactional Context of Discussing Rape with Others. *Violence Against Women* 4:559–571.

Tiggenmann, M., and A. Slater. 2004. Thin Ideals in Music Television: A Source of Social Comparison and Body Dissatisfaction. *International Journal of Eating Disorders* 35:48–58.

Till, F. J. 1980. *Sexual Harassment: A Report on the Sexual Harassment of Students*. Report of the National Advisory Council on Women's Educational Programs. Washington, DC.

Tjaden, Patricia, and Nancy Thoennes. 1998. *Prevalence, Incidence, and Consequences of Violence against Women*. U.S. Department of Justice. Research in Brief. November, 16 pp.

Tong, Rosemarie. 1984. *Women, Sex, and the Law*. Totowa, NJ: Rowman and Allanheld.

Uggen, Christopher, and Amy Blackstone. 2004. Sexual Harassment as a Gendered Expression of Power. *American Sociological Review* 69:64–92.

Visano, Livy A. 2002. A Critical Critique of the Cultures of Control: A Case study of Cyber Rape. Pp. 51–72 in *Sexual Violence*, edited by J. F. Hodgson and D. S. Kelley. Westport, CT: Praeger.

Warshaw, Robin. 1988. *I Never Called It Rape*. New York: Harper and Row.

Washington, Patricia A. 2001. Disclosure Patterns of Black Female Sexual Assault Survivors. *Violence Against Women* 7:1254–1283.

Wechsler, H., G. Kuh, and A. E. Davenport. 1996. Fraternities, Sororities, and Binge Drinking. *NASPA Journal* 33:260–279.

Weiner, Robin D. 1983. Shifting the Communication Burden: A Meaningful Consent Standard in Rape. *Harvard Women's Law Journal* 6: 145–161.

Whitson, Marian. 1997. Sexism and Sexual Harassment: Concerns of African-American Women of the Christian Methodist Episcopal Church. *Violence Against Women* 3:382–400.

Williams, Kirk R. 1981. Few Convictions in Rape Cases. *Journal of Criminal Justice* 9:29–40.

Williams, Linda M., Jane A. Siegel, and Judith J. Pomeroy. 2000. Validity of

Women's Self-Reports of Documented Child Sexual Abuse. Pp. 211–226 in *The Science of Self-Report*, edited by Arthur A. Stone, Javlan S. Turkkan, Christine A. Bachrach, Jared B. Jobe, Howard S. Kurtzman, and Virginia S. Cain. Mahwah, NJ: Lawrence Erlbaum.

Wriggins, Jennifer. 1983. Rape, Racism, and the Law. *Harvard Women's Law Journal* 6:103–141.

Wyatt, Gail Elizabeth, Michael D. Newcomb, and Monika H. Riederle.

1993. *Sexual Abuse and Consensual Sex*. Newbury Park, CA: Sage.

X, Laura. 1999. Accomplishing the Impossible: An Advocate's Notes from the Successful Campaign to Make Marital and Date Rape a Crime in All 50 States and Other Countries. *Violence Against Women* 5(9):1064–1081.

Yescavage, Karen. 1999. Teaching Women a Lesson: Sexually Aggressive and Sexually Nonaggressive Men's Perceptions of Acquaintance and Date Rape. *Violence Against Women* 5:796–812.

8

❖

Intimate Partner Abuse
and Stalking

[W]ives are much more likely to be slain by their husbands when separated from them than when co-residing.... One implication is that threats which begin "If you ever leave me..." must be taken seriously. Women who stay with their abusive husbands because they are afraid to leave may correctly apprehend that departure would elevate or spread the risk of lethal assault. As one Chicago wife, a victim of numerous beatings by her husband, explained to a friend who asked why she didn't leave her husband, "I can't because he'll kill us all, and he's going to kill me." He did.

WILSON AND DALY, 1993, 9–10

DEFINING INTIMATE PARTNER ABUSE
AND STALKING

Intimate Partner Abuse (IPA)

Naming the phenomenon of males who abuse their current or former intimate female partners has been problematic. Defining it as *domestic violence* confuses the issue of separating child abuse, "elder" abuse,[1] and sibling abuse from woman battering. Defining the phenomenon as *spouse abuse* hides the fact that women are the victims and men are the perpetrators approximately 95 percent of the time (Berk et al., 1983; see Browne, 1987; Dobash et al., 1992). Defining this phenomenon as *wife abuse* or *wife battering* ignores the fact that many of the couples are dating or cohabiting and are not married (even if we include common-law marriages) and that ex-wives are often at increased risk of abuse by their former husbands. Increasingly in recent years, in order to include same-sex

Comparative Perspectives: Intimate Partner Abuse in India

In India, "domestic violence" was first officially recorded as a criminal act in 1983. Huma Ahmed-Ghosh (2004), however, outlines that while laws are necessary to counter intimate partner abuse, they are not sufficient, particularly when aspects of the law reinforce patriarchy. The following are some of the historical-political facts described by Ahmed-Ghosh (2004) about IPA in India:

- Since the 1980s, women from diverse backgrounds and professions and with varied awareness about IPA have come together to fight this woman abuse. "Lawyers, academics, nongovernment organizations (NGOs), government agencies, and various women's groups are banding together in their efforts to better understand domestic violence in attempts to grapple with the enormity of the crisis" (ibid., 95).

- Men in India are privileged in both the private (home) and public (societal) spheres, and this privileged position not only is a cause of IPA but also hampers women's organized attempts to change domestic violence laws.

- Indian government statements and the legal system discuss domestic violence in the context of patriarchy in the form of "family values" and "tradition."

- In New Delhi and Bombay in 1980, the "Lawyers Collective" was formed by women lawyers as an NGO to address legal education, free legal aid for poor women, legal reform, and training for police, lawyers, and magistrates.

- In 2000, the Lawyers Collective drafted the Domestic Violence against Women bill in order to expand abuses in the legal definition of domestic violence (e.g., to civil law) and to include, in addition to wife victims, aged parents, female children, and female domestic help who experienced violence in the home. This draft was consistent with the 1993 United Nations Declaration on the Elimination of Violence against Women.

- The Protection from Domestic Violence Act of 2002 in India "is a reflection of male privilege and control" (ibid., 95). It ignored the Lawyers Collectives' and United Nations' definitions of domestic violence and of those besides wives who should be protected. Counter to what is known about the dynamics of IPA, the Act requires counseling for both the offender *and the victim, and stipulates that they should be counseled together.*

- The Lawyer's Collective were so upset by the changes made to their draft "that the women's movement has been galvanized to reject this act in its entirety" (ibid., 94).

SOURCE: Huma Ahmed-Ghosh. 2004. Chattels of Society: Domestic Violence in India. *Violence Against Women* 10:94–118.

partner abuse and to recognize that much of the violence occurs in dating or broken up relationships, the term *intimate partner abuse* (IPA) is used to describe current or former intimate relationships where one or both partners are violent toward the other. Although this label is appealing on many levels, it does not recognize the gendered nature of this serious and prevalent form of victimization, but it is used in this chapter as the best term for this definition. As this chapter will explain, much of the abuse perpetrated by current or former partners is not *violent* per se; thus, the term *intimate partner abuse* is preferred over *intimate partner violence*.

One force that keeps IPA invisible is that the victims themselves are often reluctant to define themselves as victims or battered (Walker, 1979). They may believe that because it happens only once or twice a year, they are not really victims. As was stated in Chapter 6, once the woman has been abused, she knows that potential is always there, and the threat of violence frequently serves to guide her relationship from then on. Furthermore, research has found that abused women usually understate the degree of violence or injury they incur (Browne, 1987, 15).

The tendency of abused women to minimize their victimization is further exacerbated by abusers' tendencies to minimize the frequency and seriousness of their violence (Goodrum, Umberson, and Anderson, 2001; Heckert and Gondolf, 2000). Studies of abusers found that they use excuses and justifications when confronted with their culpability (Dutton, 1988; Ptacek, 1988). Abusers use *excuses* in order to deny responsibility (Ptacek, 1988). Excuses are related to situational characteristics of the assault (Dutton, 1988). Abusers' excuses may include being drunk, being frustrated, or losing control. Notably, intimate partner abusers do not typically lose control with their bosses when they are mad at them. *Justifications*, on the other hand, are used to deny wrongness (Ptacek, 1988) and tend to include characteristics about the victim (Dutton, 1988). Justifications for IPA include blaming the victim for "causing" the abuse because she is a bad cook, is not sufficiently sexually responsive, is not deferential to the abuser, is not faithful, and does not know when to "shut up" (Ptacek, 1988). Clearly, none of these excuses and justifications legitimizes abuse. Notably, abusers are more likely to use justifications than excuses. That is, abusers are more likely to blame their victims for "making" them violent than they are to offer situations to explain their violence (Dutton, 1988).

Tong (1984) identified four categories of IPA. It is not uncommon for more than one of these to occur within the same abusive relationship. The first category is *physical abuse*, which consists of slapping, hitting, burning, kicking, shooting, stabbing, or any other form of nonsexual physical violence. This is IPA as it has been traditionally viewed. The second category, *sexual abuse*, occurs when there is a sexual nature to the violence, such as beatings on the breasts or genitals, and oral, anal, or vaginal rape. Marital rape is discussed in more detail in Chapter 7.

The third category of IPA, *psychological abuse*, is often minimized but is potentially extremely harmful. Many abused women report psychological abuse as the most damaging type of abuse. This exists when the offender threatens, demeans, and otherwise discredits the victim. The final category is the *destruction of pets and property*. It is not unusual for abusers to destroy the woman's property (anything from minor clothing to automobiles or even her house) and abuse or kill animals belonging to the woman. One study found that almost half of abused women seeking shelter reported that their abusers had threatened to harm or actually harmed their animals (Flynn, 2000). Underlying the clear loss of a beloved animal or cherished property is the message that the victim and her/their children are also capable of being cruelly destroyed.[2]

There are three commonalities among the four categories of IPA: They all result in harm to the victim, all are manifestations of domination and control, and all occur in an intimate relationship (Tong, 1984, 126). Nonetheless, there is not complete agreement on what qualifies as IPA. Researchers have disagreed over such issues as whether psychological battering alone qualifies a woman as an IPA victim/survivor. There is also disagreement as to whether a woman who is hit "only" once is abused. Some researchers' definitions of IPA require a systematic occurrence where IPA is an ongoing aspect of the relationship. In most cases, it appears that the violence and threat of violence are ongoing and that the different categories of violence operate simultaneously within IPA relationships. That is, it is not uncommon for an IPA victim to be physically, sexually, and psychologically abused as well as to experience destruction of property or pets.

A large Finnish study by Piispa (2002) identified four patterns IPA can take in intimate relationships. First, *a short history of violence* involves cases where the violence had started in the past few years. (Most of these were relatively young (new) marriages, but in some the couple had been together for twenty years or more before the abuse started.) Second, *partnership terrorism* involved relationships where the violence continued and had been part of the relationship for many years. This was most common among the most marginalized and dependent women (unemployed, with small children, etc.). The third pattern, *mental torment*, was IPA where the man had been abusive in the past but not for at least seven years prior to the survey. This typically involved some very serious abuse (knives, sexual violence, injuries, etc.). The final category of IPA patterns, *episode in the past*, involved abuse seven or more years earlier that was overall not very violent, injurious, or psychologically damaging (Piipsa, 2002).

Stalking

Douglas and Dutton (2001, 519) define *stalking* as repeated following, communication, and contacting a person in a threatening manner that causes the person to fear, on a reasonable basis, for his or her safety. It is important to note that many of the measures of common stalking behaviors, such as phone calls, e-mails, letters, and gifts, are not abusive or threatening in all social contexts (Roberts, 2005). These behaviors become problematic (stalking) when they are unwanted and form a persistent long-term pattern and become more sinister, especially if the victim suffers fear and distress as a result (ibid., 90). Similarly, a stalker has been described as someone who persistently pursues another individual in a way that instills fear in the target (Mustaine and Tewksbury, 1999, 44) and as one who conducts obsessional following (Meloy, 1996).

A study in the United Kingdom of women college students who had been stalked by former dating partners was conducted to identify risk factors for those formerly dating stalking cases that resulted in violence (Roberts, 2005). First, these dating relationships that resulted in stalking after the break-up were fraught with abuse and jealousy when they were still together: Almost half of these boyfriends committed physical abuse of their partners, over one-fifth were sexually violent, over half were excessively jealous, over two-thirds monitored their behavior, and about a third abused drugs during the relationship (ibid). Second, violence was extremely predominant in postrelationship stalking: Over a third of the 220 stalking victims experienced violence as part of the stalking. Former dating partners who became *violent* stalkers were more likely than former dating partners who became nonviolent stalkers if they used threats, were jealous, and abused drugs when the couple was still dating (ibid.). There were no differences in the likelihood of violence regarding race. This study as well as others on stalking violence found that *threats by stalkers should not be taken lightly as they frequently result in violence* (Brewster, 2000; Meloy, 2002; Roberts, 2005). Given the recognition that the most common victim of stalking is an ex-intimate partner (Douglas and Dutton, 2001, 519), it makes sense to address these two victimizations in the same chapter.

THE HISTORICAL IDENTIFICATION OF IPA AND STALKING AS SOCIAL PROBLEMS

Chapter 6 stated that the nonsexual physical abuse of women was not identified as a social problem until the 1970s. However, attempts had been made prior to the 1970s to bring attention to the problem of IPA. Physical abuse by men toward their wives not only has been recorded for hundreds of years but often has been portrayed as acceptable, even expected, behavior (Martin, 1976). Although there were a few laws criminalizing wife beating in the United States in the 1600s and 1700s, formal complaints numbered only one or two per decade (Pleck, 1989). In 1776, Abigail Smith Adams wrote a letter to her husband, John Adams, requesting the freedom of women by restricting the power men held in marriages (Dobash and Dobash, 1979, 4). This plea apparently was ignored.

During the struggle for women's suffrage during the latter part of the nineteenth century, liberal feminists Elizabeth Cady Stanton and Susan B. Anthony spent considerable time attempting to bring the plight of battered women into the public eye (Pleck, 1983). However, their efforts were less effective than those of conservative feminists Lucy Stone and her husband, Henry Blackwell. Unlike Stanton and Anthony, Stone and Blackwell did not advocate divorce as a necessary solution; rather, they simply advocated suffrage and protective legislation. The second time wife beating was addressed was as a part of the platform by British and U.S. suffragists during the beginning of this century (Dobash and Dobash, 1979). Thus, wife beating was legally acceptable throughout most of history and was not made illegal in every state until 1920 (Robbins, 1999, 208).

The most recent and successful movement questioning violence against wives began in 1971 in a small English town (ibid.). A group of over 500 women and children and one cow marched to protest rising food costs and the reduction of free milk for children. Although the march was not deemed a success regarding the problems it set out to address, it was a success and a historical event in that it led to solidarity among the marching women. This solidarity resulted in a community-gathering place for local women, the Chiswick's Women's Aid. During discussions at Chiswick's Women's Aid, women began revealing and discussing the systematic violence they had experienced from their husbands. IPA and its frequency, then, were accidentally discovered, changing the focus of Chiswick's Women's Aid to woman battering (ibid.).

Feminists in the United States followed the lead set by British feminists. Public information on IPA increased with Chiswick's Women's Aid founder Erin Pizzey's publication (1974) in England of *Scream Quietly or the Neighbors Will Hear* and Del Martin's publication (1976) in the United States of *Battered Wives*. Since the mid-1970s, shelters for abused women have been established all over the United States, England, Canada, and many European and other countries. These early shelters were very basic, starting as grass-roots, community-based efforts by feminists. Often the shelters were individual women's homes, which they volunteered as sanctuaries for abused women. Such make-do shelters still operate in some rural communities. Thus, the first step in the current abused women's movement was the setting up of emergency shelters by women within each community. "Since 1975, the movement has made substantial headway in three areas besides emergency shelter: legislation, government policy and programs, and research and public information" (Tierney, 1983, 208). However, even today IPA remains invisible to a large degree, and shelters are regularly underfunded and overpopulated, turning women and children away in large numbers.

Since the 1980s, literature has emerged portraying the widespread existence of what can be labeled *dating violence*, the sexual, psychological, and/or physical violence and abuse that occurs in dating relationships. A study that compared IPA in premarital, marital, and ex-spousal relationships reported to the police found that unmarried couples resort to physical violence and use weapons somewhat more frequently than the other types of couples (Erez, 1986). While premarital relationships have a higher percentage of assaults than the other two categories, marital, and particularly postmarital (ex-spousal), relationships have the most serious assaults and injuries (Erez, 1986; Mahoney, 1991). Indeed, research in recent years identifies leaving a violent relationship as one of the most dangerous/ lethal times for abused women (Campbell, 1992; Ellis, 1987; Ellis and DeKeseredy, 1989; Hardesty, 2002; Mahoney, 1991; Pagelow, 1993; Sev'er, 1997; Wilson and Daly, 1993), including lesbian battered women (Glass et al., 2004). Studies on the rates of dating violence suggest that between one-fifth and one-third of college students report experiencing nonsexual, physical dating violence (Bogal-Allbritten and Allbritten, 1985; Cate et al., 1982; Knutson and Mehm, 1986; Lane and Gwartney-Gibbs, 1985; Makepeace, 1981, 1986; Matthews, 1984; Stets and Pirog-Good, 1987).

Davies, Lyon, and Monti-Catania (1998) and Kanuha (1996) describe the social and public construction of the battered woman that activists and researchers devised. They call this depiction the "pure victim," characterized by a battered woman who (1) is not herself violent unless in self-defense, (2) has "experienced extreme physical violence separated by periods of emotional abuse," (3) suffers abuse in a pattern in which it escalates in severity and frequency over time unless someone intervenes, and (4) is terrified by the abuse (Davies, Lyon, and Monti-Catania, 1998, 15). While this image was useful in garnering public support and in accurately portraying many battered women, it failed in terms of classifying all battered women in this same venue. The pro-arrest laws (discussed later in this chapter) were geared toward these "pure victims," who did not hit back, wanted the police to arrest the abuser, and experienced the same violence in the same ways. Thus, women who did not fit this "pure victim" image were treated with disdain by the police and some advocates (Davies, Lyon, and Monti-Catania, 1998; Kanuha, 1996).

Stalking as a social problem has experienced a much more recent academic and criminal legal history. Although, like most of the offenses and victimizations noted in this book, stalking has always occurred, it was not until the high-profile celebrity cases of the 1980s and 1990s, which included President Ronald Reagan and actress Jody Foster's stalker, comedian David Letterman's stalker, and actor Rebecca Schaeffer's (from the television show *My Sister Sam*) stalker and murderer, that stalking received unprecedented attention. Increasingly researchers and the general public are aware that not only are noncelebrities also at risk of being stalked but that the vast majority of stalking is perpetrated in the context of intimate partner relationships and often those that already exhibit other forms of victimization and abuse. Indeed, one study of IPA survivors found that over 90 percent experienced at least some level of stalking (Melton, 2004).

THE FREQUENCY OF IPA AND STALKING

The gendered nature of intimate partner abuse is hotly debated and quite clearly rests on how the studies sampled their participants and the questions they used to identify IPA. A considerable amount of research suggests that men tend to batter women in approximately 95 percent of the IPA situations (Berk et al., 1983; see Browne, 1987, 8; Dobash et al., 1992). A study using NCVS data from the United States reported that about 85 percent of IPA cases in 1998 were women victims (Rennison and Welchans, 2000). Dobash and Dobash (1988, 69) claim that 25 percent of all violent crimes are wife assaults, and according to the UCR, 20 percent of violence experienced by women and 2 percent of violence experienced by men is from IPA (as cited in Burch and Gallup, 2004). The National Violence against Women survey discussed in the last chapter, which interviewed 8,000 women and 8,000 men in the United States by telephone, found that 22 percent of women and 7 percent of men reported experiencing IPA as victims (Tjaden and Thoennes, 1998a, 2000). A recent national study in Canada stated that 29 percent of the women who had ever been married or lived as common-law spouses with a man reported at least one incident of IPA (Johnson, 1995). Notably, 15 percent of women reported that their current partner had abused them; when asked about previous married or cohabitating relationships with men, 45 percent of the women reported IPA (ibid.). Others believe that as many as half of all women will be victims of IPA by a husband or boyfriend (Mills and McNamar, 1981; Slote and Cuthbert, 1997; Walker, 1979; Yoshihama, 1999).

The degree and frequency of abuse differ among relationships where IPA occurs, but it often begins early on in marriages (Dobash and Dobash, 1979, 124) or even during the courtship or dating stage (Dobash and Dobash, 1979, 84; Erez, 1986; Flynn, 1990; Makepeace, 1981; Pirog-Good and Stets, 1989; Schwartz and DeKeseredy, 1997; Stets and Pirog-Good, 1987). Indeed, a recent governmental report using NCVS data reported that women/girls aged 16 to 24 years old experienced the highest per-capita rates of IPA in the United States (Rennison and Welchans, 2000). An extensive survey of about 4,000 Massachusetts high school students reported that one in five female students reported being physically and/or sexually abused by a dating partner and that this abuse increased their risk of substance use, unhealthy weight-control behaviors (e.g., vomiting or laxatives), sexually risky behaviors, pregnancy, and thoughts or attempts of suicide (Silverman et al., 2001).

Determining the prevalence of IPA (similar to rape rates) is difficult, as is evident from the range these statistics present. Problems inherent in determining the prevalence of IPA are exemplified by researchers' frustrations in trying to find a control group of nonabused women to compare with a group of abused women; they often find abused women in their control group (Browne, 1987, 5).

One of the questions most often asked about IPA is, "What about men who are battered by women?" Some research views men and women as mutually combative or inflicting fairly equal amounts of violence on each other in intimate relationships (Steinmetz, 1977/1978; Straus, 1990, 1991; Straus and Gelles, 1986; Straus, Gelles, and Steinmetz, 1980). However, it is important to emphasize that the wide range of study reports on women's versus men's proportion of offending and victimization in IPA depends on the sample and the measurement instruments used (see Belknap and Melton, 2005). Greater gender similarity is found typically at the more minor levels of violence, such as slapping, and the greatest gender disparities in victimization and offending are at the more serious IPA levels, such as punching.

Much of the criticism regarding the findings reporting that women and men are "mutually combative" has centered around the Conflict Tactic Scale (CTS), a measurement instrument criticized by many as an incomplete and inadequate test to measure IPA (Berk et al., 1983; DeKeseredy, 1995; Dobash and Dobash, 1988; Kurz, 1993; Schwartz, 1987; Stark and Flitcraft, 1983; Yllo, 1988). Specifically, the CTS oversimplifies the complexities of IPA, focusing solely on behaviors and ignoring consequences of the social contexts in which the behaviors occur and their meanings to the victim and the offender (Dasgupta, 2001; DeKeseredy and Schwartz, 1998; Ferraro and Johnson, 1983; Smith, 1994; Yoshihama, 1999). For example, the CTS fails to take into account the difference between a 250-pound man slamming a 100-pound woman into a wall and her shoving *him* back forcefully. Notably, in a public-opinion poll, respondents tended to blame women for IPA whether they were the ones who hit or the ones who got hit (Greenblat, 1983). Finally, DeKeseredy (1995, 162) criticizes the CTS for ignoring "many injurious acts, such as suffocating, squeezing, sexual assault, stalking, and scratching" and for not providing "additional opportunities to disclose abusive experiences."

Thus, researchers and nonresearchers alike have had a tendency to blame women victims as equally responsible, if not more so, for IPA. A study interviewing both men and women about the abuse in their relationships found that, compared to women, men underestimate (1) the types/number of violence forms they use against their intimate female partners, (2) how often they use these forms of violence, (3) the likelihood of the abuse resulting in injuries, and (4) the types/ numbers of injuries the woman/victim receives (Dobash et al., 1998). A study on marital rape and aggression found very low correlation between wives' and husbands' versions in the same-couple reports of the husband's use of sexual aggression and coercion against the wife, with wives reporting far higher rates of sexual aggression and marital rape than did husbands (Meyer, Vivian, and O'Leary, 1998). This indicates that we will find very different rates of marital rape based on whether we ask women or men about rape in their marriages and on the strong tendency for men to lie about or discount marital rapes they commit. A study using the CTS to measure IPA among ninety-four U.S. military couples suggests not only that there is likely more violence in these than in nonmilitary couples but also that men reported higher rates of their abuse against their wives than the wives reported these husbands as perpetrating against them (Bohannon, Dosser, and Lindley, 1995).

Another important point is that the violence husbands direct at wives is not comparable to the violence wives direct at husbands: IPA damages women's self-esteem, whereas men's self-esteem often appears unaffected by violence from their wives (Mills, 1984). Not surprisingly, then, a study of college students revealed that females are more likely than males to report seeking an end to the relationship, informal controls, or formal controls if assaulted by an intimate partner (Miller and Simpson, 1991). A study of dating IPA among high school students found that girls who experienced abuse at the hands of their boyfriends most commonly reported *fear* and then *emotional hurt* as the effect. Boys reporting violence by their girlfriends, however, most commonly reported first that they thought it was funny and then anger as their responses (O'Keefe and Treister, 1998). Other research confirms that heterosexual IPA directed at women causes far more fear than IPA directed at men (Hamberger and Guse, 2002; Johnson and Bunge, 2001; Melton and Belknap, 2003; Morse, 1995; O'Keefe and Treister, 1998).

A study of dating aggression among 171 low-income African American youths found the girls were more likely than the boys to report strangling, attempted forced intercourse, and hurt feelings victimizations, and more likely than the boys to report *perpetrating* throwing objects, making threats, and hitting their partners (West and Rose, 2000). Boys were more likely than the girls to report attempting forced intercourse, and making a partner feel inferior and degrading her (ibid.). Furthermore, women usually resort to violence out of *self-defense* or *retaliation* or to *escape situations* where the man initiated and escalated the violence (Barnett, Lee, and Thelen, 1997; Hamberger and Guse, 2002; Hamberger et al., 1997; Molidor and Tolman, 1998; Saunders, 1988; Schwartz, 1987). Men, on the other hand, typically resort to violence against their intimate female partners to control them (Barnett, Lee, and Thelen, 1997; Edleson et al., 1991; Hamberger et al., 1997). Significantly, women are more likely than men to incur serious injury in IPA incidents (Berk et al., 1983; Holtzworth-Munroe, Smutzler, and Bates, 1997; Loving, 1980; Molidor and Tolman, 1998; Oppenlander, 1982; Stets and Straus, 1990). Finally, men's greater economic resources decrease their need for shelters (Straus, 1991), as do their lower levels of serious violence and fear.

Although stalking research is relatively new, research indicates that this behavior is also highly gendered. Tjaden and Thoennes's (1998b) National Violence against Women (NVAW) survey study found that of the 8,000 men and 8,000 women in the United States interviewed by phone, 8 percent of women and 2 percent of men reported stalking that involved high levels of fear. When they employed a broader definition of stalking, where the stalking also included somewhat or a little fear reported by the study participants, 12 percent of women and 4 percent of men reported stalking victimizations. Thus, 6 percent of women and 1.5 percent of men in the United States reported experiencing stalking victimization. Similar to the studies on rape, Native Americans/Alaskan Natives reported the highest rates of stalking victimization (5 percent of men, 17 percent of women), followed by individuals of mixed races (4 percent of men, 11 percent of women), Whites (2 percent of men, 8 percent of women), African Americans (2 percent of men, 7 percent of women), and Asians/Pacific Islanders (2 percent of men, 5 percent of women) (ibid., 5).

The gender differences reported in stalking are even greater when one looks at perpetration rather than at victimization. More specifically, the NVAW survey findings were that 78 percent of stalking victims are women (thus, 22 percent are men), and 87 percent of the stalkers (according to the victims) are males (thus, 13 percent of the stalkers are females) (Tjaden and Thoennes, 1998b). When one breaks this down further by sex, 94 percent of the stalkers identified by female victims and 60 percent of the stalkers identified by male victims were male (ibid., 5). When restricting stalking to current or former intimate partners, they found women were about eight times as likely as men to report stalking victimization (Tjaden and Thoennes, 2000). Tjaden and Thoennes (1998, 6) found some evidence that gay men are more at risk than straight men of being stalked and speculate that this is due to three factors: the stalking of gay men by homophobic/ "hate crime" stalkers, men stalking men based on sexual attraction, and males stalked in the context of gang membership/rivalries. A review of ten studies on stalking published between 1978 and 1995 reported that about three-fourths of these obsessional followers were male, and these males were typically in their 30s with prior psychiatric backgrounds and a history of failed heterosexual relationships, and they tended to be more intelligent than other criminal offenders (Meloy, 1996). Although half of these stalkers threatened their victims with violence; the frequency of actual violence ranged from 3 to 36 percent, with less than 2 percent resulting in a homicide. Meloy (ibid., 147) states that their preoccupation with their victims is "fueled by a disturbance in their narcissistic fantasy linking them to their victims. Such disruption is usually caused by an acute or chronic rejection that stimulates rage as a defense against shame." On the other hand, some of the more recent research on stalkers suggests they stalk their current or former girlfriends and wives because they are jealous, because they feel they "own" them, and because they can—no one challenges their infringement on these women's autonomy and, often, safety.

WALKER'S CYCLE THEORY OF VIOLENCE

Psychologist Lenore E. Walker (1979) is credited with developing the "cycle theory of violence," which describes the pattern of IPA over time. She identified three phases in the continuous cycle of IPA. Phase one is the *tension-building* stage. This is a sort of calm before the storm. The victim feels that the pressure is mounting and that a violent explosion is inevitable. While minor IPA incidents may occur during this time (for example, shaking or slapping), a major abusive assault is what she most fears. She may try to calm her partner down with something that worked in the past, such as cooking his favorite meal or keeping the children quiet.

Phase two of Walker's (ibid.) IPA cycle is the *acute abuse incident*. Phase two is when the major abuse actually occurs and is usually the briefest of the three phases in the cycle. If the police are notified at all (only 10 percent of Walker's sample had done so), it is usually during this phase. However, by the time the police arrive, the cycle has usually moved on to phase three.

Phase three is characterized by kindness and contrite loving behavior from the abuser. "He begs her forgiveness and promises her that he will never do it again" (ibid., 65). Usually, both the man and the woman want to believe that this violence was some fluke and that it will not occur again. It is easier for them to believe this when the abuse first starts, as opposed to after years of abuse. The abuser often appears sincere in his apology and in his commitment to change. He may lavish the woman with gifts, quit drinking, or do other things to convince her that he really loves her and that the abuse will never happen again. "It is during this phase that the woman gets a glimpse of her original dream of how wonderful love is. . . . The traditional notion that two people who love each other surmount overwhelming odds against them prevails" (ibid., 67–68). This phase is usually longer than phase two but shorter than phase one. At the beginning of an IPA relationship, women are often confused, shocked, depressed, and in need of reassurance, making them vulnerable to the abusers' promises to stop the abuse (Browne, 1987, 62–63).

As phase three ends, phase one begins again, and the cycle continues. Other researchers have noted that over time the violence tends to increase in frequency, severity, and injuries, and thus more formal social agency assistance becomes necessary (Dobash and Dobash, 1979, 179). "Each successive violent episode leaves the woman with less hope, less self-esteem, and more fear" (ibid., 140). In more recent research, Walker (1983a, 44) has found that the length of the three phases in IPA relationships changes over time. As the IPA relationship progresses, tension building (phase one) is longer and more evident, and loving and contrition (phase three) decline. Abusers are less likely over time to apologize for their violence and more likely to blame the victims for "making" them violent (ibid., 117–123). This implies that once the abuser has established his power over the victim, he feels less of a need to apologize to keep her. Thus, hopefulness (the belief that he may change) may be replaced with fear (that he will kill or severely harm her and/or her/their children if she leaves) as the motivation for staying in the relationship.

Although Walker's cycle appears to fit some battered women's experiences, it is important to note that it has not been extensively studied, and it is clear that it does not fit all battered women's and abusers' actions, responses, and experiences. More research is necessary in this area.

WHY DO (SOME) MEN (AND WOMEN) ABUSE AND STALK?

Many men do not batter, abuse, or stalk women regardless of how angry they may feel toward them or how worried they are that the relationship could end when they do not want it to. So why do some men behave in these ways? Most researchers on IPA focus on the family structure. For instance, Goode (1971) stresses the importance of viewing the family as a power system, where power is unequally distributed. He points out that such characteristics as being male, being older, and having control over property, money, and gifts serve to enhance the power of the father/husband in the family system. Additionally, there are fewer restraints against aggression in the family than exist in other social settings because fights between family members are viewed as more socially acceptable (Sebastian, 1983). Furthermore, the dependency of some family members on others requires that they tolerate the abuse. This is particularly apparent regarding child abuse.

It is necessary to assess the IPA of women and the family structure within a sociohistorical context. Gender disparities in the culture, economy, and political environment have an inherent impact on the family (Bograd, 1988; Breines and Gordon, 1983; Dobash and Dobash, 1979; O'Neill, 1998; Stark and Flitcraft, 1983; Yllo, 1983, 1988). Focusing on family inequality independently from the political context leads to an image of battered women dominated by rotten husbands. This removes the focus from such issues as inadequate governmental policies (such as welfare and child care) that encourage female subordination and patriarchal dependency (Stark and Flitcraft, 1983, 336). Similarly, Bograd (1988, 14) claims: "The reality of domination at the social level is the most crucial factor contributing to and maintaining wife abuse at the personal level." The family cannot be analyzed independently from the social, political, and economic structure of a society. These outside forces serve to reinforce the power disparity and dependence of women in marriage.

Stereotypical gender differences discussed earlier in this book are related to the expectations by some that men should be aggressive and women passive; these expectations have an impact on IPA. While aggression may have many aims, "one of the aggressor's objectives is the injury of the target" (Berkowitz, 1983, 179). Men's violent and aggressive behavior is often viewed as typical and therefore goes unquestioned (Stanko, 1985). Similarly, there is a tendency to view both sexism and violence as an inevitable part of culture (Klein, 1981). Male violence, then, is more conforming than aberrant behavior (Bograd, 1988, 17). Men are socialized to dominate women, and male aggression is not only encouraged but also often glorified. This can be seen in male sports such as football, hockey, and boxing, as well as in the media, with movies such as *True Lies, Lethal Weapon, Rambo, Robocop, Terminator,* and basically most of Arnold Schwartzenneger's and Sylvester Stallone's movies and the James Bond movies. Stalking is glorified and minimized in the movie *Something about Mary.* Woman abuse, then, has not occurred as an event isolated from the community or against the general principles of acceptable behavior; rather, it is an institution in its own right (Dobash and Dobash, 1981, 565). Not only is male violence in general often tolerated by the media and culture but male violence directed against females, specifically, is frequently tolerated and even glorified. In addition to some men, there are women who believe that IPA is justified under certain situations (Haj-Yahia, 1998).

What benefits do abusers obtain? It is clear that violence or the threat of violence results in a strong sense of power and dominance for the abuser. Abusers may not always be conscious of their desire to control, but IPA is typically a result of male entitlement—abusers are angry and feel justified to abuse when they do not have the control they have been socialized to believe they deserve (see Schechter, 1982, 219). Abusers may have a sense that their behavior is justified—their victims "needed" to be punished or "taught a lesson." Abusers often view their victims as their property or as children who need discipline. These men usually feel threatened by any indication of their victims' autonomy—even the time these women spend with their families or other women friends. It is not unusual for abusers to inflict violence when the victims are pregnant or when they feel jealous of attention the victims have given to their children (e.g., Burch and Gallup, 2004). Indeed, a study of men in an intervention program for intimate partner abusers found that one in seven *self-reported* violently abusing their wives/girlfriends when they were pregnant, and the men who did so were more likely to report higher levels of sexual jealousy (ibid.). Moreover, both the *severity* of the violence and the *frequency* of the violence were twice as high when the women were pregnant (ibid.).

Goolkasian (1986) claims there are two reasons why IPA continues to exist. First, "violence is a highly effective means of control" (ibid., 2). Thus, men batter in order to gain and maintain control over women. Second, "men batter because they can; that is, because in most cases no one has told batterers that they must stop" (ibid.). Although the victim and her/their children may make attempts to communicate to the abuser that his behavior is unacceptable, the abuser often gets messages from many others that he is the "king of his castle" and can treat "his woman" in whatever manner he pleases. These messages often come from the media, friends, family, and even the criminal legal system.

WHO ARE THE ABUSERS AND STALKERS?

Who are the abusers? The stereotype of the unemployed, alcoholic, lower-class abuser is not necessarily accurate. IPA abusers and victims come from a range of backgrounds and experiences. Research in the 1970s attempted to refute the myth that abusers were all mentally ill or had a psychological disorder (Gelles, 1980, 876). Numerous researchers have pointed out that IPA occurs in all socioeconomic and educational levels (Brisson, 1981; Flynn, 1977; Goolkasian, 1986; Holtzworth-Monroe, Smutzler, and Bates, 1997). However, some research suggests that arrest works as a deterrent for employed abusers but increases the likelihood of subsequent violence for unemployed abusers (Pate and Hamilton, 1992; Sherman et al., 1992). The reasoning is that arrest has the intended impact on employed abusers because they have more to lose (e.g., their jobs).

The greatest risk factor for being an abuser is being male. A study of a phone hotline for women and children in Belgrade, Serbia, in the early 1990s found that 94 percent of the calls involved abuse by male family members (Mrsevic and Hughes, 1997). Of the 770 calls to the hotline over three years, 83 percent involved abusive husbands (65 percent), former husbands (13 percent), or boyfriends (5 percent). Two percent of the abuse perpetrators were fathers of the victims, and 8 percent were sons of the victims (ibid.). Research suggests that it is not so much being male but rather being socialized as masculine that places a person at risk of IPA. More specifically, at least for White men, men who score higher on femininity scales are less likely to be abusive to their girlfriends than are those men who score lower on femininity scales (Boye-Beaman, Leonard, and Senchak, 1993).

While an abuser may come from any background, the description of abusers by battered women suggests that abusers all share certain characteristics (Walker, 1983a). Although this study found no "victim-prone" women (or types of women who were likely to become IPA victims), "violence-prone" personalities for men were identified, including adherence to traditional views of women, possessiveness, and abuse of alcohol (ibid.). As stressed in Chapter 6, no nonabusive behavior of the victim's, perceived or real, justifies violent behavior from the abuser. However, it is still useful to examine how abusers perceive their own behavior. Existing research identifies exceptionally *jealous* individuals as those most likely to be intimate partner abusers (Barnett, Martinez, and Bluestein, 1995; Brisson, 1981; Browne, 1987; Dobash and Dobash, 1979; Molidor and Tolman, 1998; O'Keefe and Treister, 1998; Piipsa, 2002; Straus, Gelles, and Steinmetz, 1980; Walker, 1979, 1983a), including men who murder their intimate partners (Dobash et al., 2004). This relates to the abusers' belief that their wives or girlfriends "belong" to them, and this "justifies" their violent behavior. This is also true for stalkers of former intimate partners, who often showed excessive jealousy while in the relationship (Langhinrichsen-Rohling et al., 2000; Roberts, 2002, 2005; Silva et al., 2000).

Regarding alcohol abuse, most researchers agree that violence is not caused by substance abuse but that such use and abuse may disinhibit violent behaviors. Most men who beat their wives when they are drunk also beat them when they are sober. One study on IPA found that "alcohol use at the time of violence is far from a necessary or sufficient cause for wife abuse despite the stereotype that all drunks hit their wives or all wife-hitting involves drunks" (Kantor and Straus, 1987, 224). Analyses of two national violence against women survey studies, one in Canada and one in the United States, found that in both samples/countries, the women's risk of injury during abuse increased when the men were using alcohol (Thompson, Saltzman, and Johnson, 2003).

Control is a concept repeatedly raised in discussions of IPA. Ironically, while the public and criminal legal system too often view IPA as losing control, the opposite is typically the reality: Abusers are usually very controlling people, and a key aspect of IPA is the abusers' desire for and practices in *controlling* their victims. Abusers use threats to control their victims, and when the threats do not work, they often resort to violence (Fleury, Sullivan, and Bybee, 2000). Piipsa (2002) identifies the many ways that male abusers' control limits and deny their intimate female partners. For example, they may limit the women's living spaces, call them names, humiliate them, and/or socially control them (e.g., keep victims from seeing friends and relatives). Indeed, many of the control tactics used by the abuser fit under Tong's (1984) category of psychological abuse (discussed earlier).

The belief that IPA is simply a result of the loss of control on the part of the abuser is increasingly disputed. In fact, groups who have organized to try to help abusers end their violent behavior concentrate on teaching abusers that IPA is a choice, and they may choose not to batter. Others have pointed out that IPA is indeed controllable if we assess IPA via the targets of the abuse (where the offenders place their blows) and the locations in which IPA occurs (whether the assault takes place in public or at home). For instance, an abuser may attempt to excuse his abuse of his intimate partner because he was angry at something his boss did that day. It is important to note, however, that the target of his violence was not his boss but rather his wife or girlfriend. Thus, if it is a matter of simply losing control, how is it that he is able to control himself from hitting his boss, who provoked his anger? Also, abusers are often controlled enough to restrict their blows to places on the body that are least likely to be visible to other people, such as the stomach, breasts, and thighs. Marital rape is also viewed as an effective tool of control by the abuser because the damage is not visible, and the victim is likely to be too ashamed to report it even to friends or family and particularly to law-enforcement officials. The fact that most abusers refrain from abusive behavior in public places also indicates a degree of control on the abuser's part in determining his own violent behavior.

A number of researchers have focused on a hypothesized *intergenerational transmission of violence* in an attempt to explain why men batter (Dutton and Painter, 1981; Fagan, Stewart, and Hansen, 1983). This theory contends that children who witness violence learn that violence is an acceptable way to resolve conflict (Dutton and Painter, 1981, 142). The intergenerational transmission of violence theory, then, views IPA as a learned behavior that passes down from one generation to another within the family system. In applying this theory, it is important to acknowledge that experiential learning is likely to be different for males and females. While both males and females may learn that physical conflict is a legitimate response to family or interpersonal conflict, males may learn to be the oppressors, whereas females learn to be the victims. One study found that adult male survivors of child abuse by their parents or adult males who had watched their fathers abuse their mothers were more likely than adult males from nonabusive homes to view violence as an adequate response to family conflict and to abuse their own wives or girlfriends later in life (Fagan, Stewart, and Hansen, 1983).

However, the theory of intergenerational transmission of violence has received criticism, too. For instance, it is possible that living in a violent home may result in an adult survivor's strong commitment to disallow violence in her or his own home (see Levendosky, Lynch, and Graham-Bermann, 2000). Adult survivors of homes where IPA occurred may not all behave uniformly. Although witnessing parental violence increases the likelihood of a boy growing up to be an abuser, "the majority of wife assaulters have never witnessed parental violence" (Dutton, 1988, 47). The studies testing the intergenerational transmission of violence have been accused of committing clinical fallacy by examining only adult abusers and failing to include the effects of childhood violence on non-violent adults (Breines and Gordon, 1983). An exception to this is a study that found that persons (male and female) raised in homes with "spousal violence" were at risk of being victims, not offenders, of IPA as adults; it also found that "vulnerability to aggression was transmitted more than the learned role of perpetrator" (Cappell and Heiner, 1990, 135). In conclusion, while there are likely some implications for condoning violence if one grows up with it, the overall impact on later violent behavior is unclear.

We now turn to the question, "Who are stalkers?" Once again it is clear that this behavior is highly gendered. As stated earlier, the NVAW survey findings indicate that women comprise 78 percent of the stalking victims and men comprise 87 percent of the stalking perpetrators (Tjaden and Thoennes, 1998b). Similar to previous research, the NVAW survey findings confirm that most stalking victims know their stalkers: "Only 23 percent of female stalking victims and 36 percent of male stalking victims were stalked by strangers" (ibid., 5). *Another significant manner in which stalking is gendered is that women are far more likely than men to be stalked by current or former intimate partners:*

> Thirty-eight percent of female stalking victims were stalked by current or former husbands, 10 percent by current or former cohabiting partners, and 14 percent by current or former dates or boyfriends. Overall,

59 percent of female victims, compared with 30 percent of male victims, were stalked by some type of intimate partner (Tjaden and Thoennes, 1998b, 6).

There is widespread belief that stalking in the context of intimate partner abuse is a result of the woman leaving the relationship, thus, that stalking in the context of IPA starts when women leave abusive or potentially abusive male partners/boyfriends. The NVAW study found that although 43 percent of the stalking experienced by women stalked by current husbands or partners occurred as speculated, that is, after the relationship ended, 21 percent stated that the stalking occurred before the relationship ended, and 36 percent reported that the stalking occurred both before and after the relationship ended. Thus, contrary to popular opinion, women are often stalked by intimate partners while the relationship is still intact (ibid.).

It is important to remember that IPA and stalking can and do occur in same-sex relationships as well as in heterosexual ones (e.g., Robinson, 2002). There is more research on lesbian than gay male IPA, but the research suggests that the dynamics tend to be similar except for the added burden of the threat of being "outed" if the abuse comes to light, the worry of giving the lesbian/gay/bisexual/transgender community a bad name, and threats to child custody for those with dependent children (see Allen and Leventhal, 1999; Banks, 2003; Giorgio, 2002; Gorshick, 2002; Perilla et al., 2003; Potoczniak et al., 2003; Renzetti, 1992; Russo, 2003).

The motivations for and risk factors of becoming a stalker strongly overlap with IPA, which is not surprising given that stalking is most frequent among former intimate partners. One study identified the following characteristics as co-occurring among ex-intimate partner stalkers and some intimate partner abusers: emotional volatility, attachment dysfunction, primitive defenses, weak ego strength, jealousy, anger, substance abuse, early childhood trauma, and rage reactions to real or perceived rejection (Douglas and Dutton, 2001).

INHIBITORS TO LEAVING AN ABUSIVE RELATIONSHIP

Battered women stay because they rarely have escape routes related to educational or employment opportunities, relatives are critical of plans to leave the relationship, parenting responsibilities impede escape, and abusive situations contribute to low self-esteem and negative emotions—especially anxiety and depression

FORTE ET AL., 1996, 69

Much of the writing on IPA, and even responses by the public as well as by the criminal legal system, have focused on asking why a woman stays in an IPA relationship. This response tends to be victim blaming in that it implies she would leave if she really did not like to be abused. IPA is a complex phenomenon, and it is important to understand why some women stay in or return to IPA relationships.

First, we must ask why the focus is on why she stays rather than on why he batters. Focusing on why abused women stay has resulted in the labeling of such women as deviant (Loseke and Cahill, 1984). Perhaps it would be more fruitful to ask questions such as "Why are men violent?" "Why are women so easily victimized?" "Why are violent men allowed to stay?" and "Why should the victims rather than the assailants be expected to leave?" (Hoff, 1990).

Second, it is rarely acknowledged that many women do leave IPA relationships. There is a tendency to hear only about women who stay in IPA relationships. Many women have left IPA relationships, even after the first violent episode. However, shame and the tendency of others to discount their victimizations keep these survivors from identifying themselves as formerly battered women. In fact, 70 percent of 251 battered women who had contacted a counseling unit associated with the county attorney's office decided to leave their abusive partners (Strube and Barbour, 1984). Nonetheless, many women do stay for a period of time or indefinitely. Thus, it is important to understand the numerous obstacles these women face and to ask what happens when abused women leave. One study that attempted to answer this question followed for two years women who had left abusive partners and found that one-third of them were reabused by their abusers during this time (Fleury, Sullivan, and Bybee, 2000). Moreover, the intimate partner abusers most likely to keep abusing after the women left them were those who used more threats and more violence and who had more jealousy/sexual suspicion during the relationship (ibid.). Thus, it is important to remember that leaving an abusive relationship does not necessarily stop the abuse. Indeed, it might increase it, including to lethal levels.

Third, some women stay in IPA relationships because they face overwhelming restrictions in their attempts to leave. The previous section discussed the importance of looking at aggregate political and social realities that maintain men's power over women, particularly within the institutions of marriage and the family. Economic and psychological factors also help to explain why women stay. Forces restricting women's autonomy, then, function at aggregate levels in the political and social structure, as well as at individual economic and psychological levels.

A study of heterosexual African American women college students in psychologically abusive dating relationships found a four-stage process to their leaving the relationships (Few and Bell-Scott, 2002). First was assessing the relationship, followed by separating from the abusive partner, then re-establishing social networks, and finally gaining a sense of self-empowerment (ibid.). Another study examined twenty-one African American women's acts of resistance and disengagement from abusive intimate partners and reported three stages of disengagement (Taylor, 2002). First came *defining moments*, which were life-altering and pivotal moments that many women called "the straw that broke the camel's back." For some women it was hearing other battered women's stories and others witnessing their abusers' violence toward another person. Second was *moving away*, or strategies to emotionally and physically distance themselves from their abusive partners (ibid., 88). For some this meant moving to a different city, and for others it involved going to a shelter The final stage, *moving on*, had to do with sustaining the separation from the former partner and typically included building a support network of friends and family (ibid.).

Economic Restrictions

Frequently, it is simply not economically feasible for a woman to leave the man who batters her. This is particularly problematic for women who have children. It is not uncommon for abusers to control all of the money in the household and to place the woman on a minuscule allowance for which she must justify all spending. Furthermore, many women do not possess the skills or education necessary to support themselves and their children. Some research has shown that unemployed women are less likely than employed women to leave the IPA relationship (Gelles, 1976; Strube and Barbour, 1984), while other research reports no difference in the employment status of abused women and their likelihood to leave/stay (Herbert, Silver, and Allard, 1991). In a study of women in a low-income area of Chicago, "women who experienced [intimate partner] male violence were as likely to be currently employed as those who did not, [but] they were more likely to have been unemployed in the past, to suffer from health problems, and to have higher rates of welfare receipt" (Lloyd and Taluc, 1999). This study also pointed out the complexity of the role of battered women in the labor force: "Employed women may be less likely to enter, tolerate, or stay in abusive relationships, and others may be employed because they are compelled by their partners to work and to contribute income to the household" (ibid., 386). A study of Vietnamese immigrant women in the United States reported that women's economic participation was not related to the IPA they experienced; however, "economic hardship could prevent women from leaving an abusive relationship to avoid further violence" (Bui and Morash, 1999, 789). A study of women's calls to a hotline in Belgrade, Serbia (discussed earlier in this chapter), found that the victims "were often forced to live with perpetrators because of the lack of available housing, which worsened due to privatization, economic sanctions against Serbia, and the influx of refugees. . . . Most refugees were housed in private homes, resulting in increased violence against women refugees and women hosts" (Mrsevic and Hughes, 1997, 101). Moreover, the study classified 6 percent of the calls to the hotline as reports of *economic violence*, which included property damage, controlling women's wages and property, and restricting their "allowances" to a level that made it impossible to buy food for the family.

Although abused women come from "all walks of life," recent research indicates that poor women may be at significantly increased risk of IPA (Browne, Salomon, and Bassuk, 1999; Craven, 1996; Forte et al., 1996; Kaplan, 1997; Pearson, Thoennes, and Girswold, 1999) and that leaving an abuser decreases a woman's income (Herbert, Silver, and Ellard, 1991). A longitudinal study of women living in extreme poverty in Worcester, Massachusetts, reported that women who experienced physical aggression/violence by a male partner in the previous twelve months were less likely/able to maintain employment in the subsequent year (Browne, Salomon, and Bassuk, 1999). Their mental health was also related to their capacity to maintain work (in the predicted direction), but job training, job placement services, and previous employment history enhanced the likelihood (as expected) of their subsequent work history. The authors conclude that the significant impact that recent IPA has on subsequent employment is problematic in terms of the work-to-welfare policies now popular in the United States (ibid.). A relevant issue in addressing abused women's economic concerns is that of child support. Legislation in 1996 in the United States, known as the Personal Responsibility and Work Opportunity Reconciliation Act (PRWORA), includes a good-cause exemption allowing a different process in filing for child support for cases where abused women are fearful that applying for child support could enable, through garnishment of wages, a current or former intimate partner abuser to locate and renew violence against them and their children (Pearson, Thoennes, and Girswold, 1999). Notably, a study of this found that while few women request this exemption, those who do appear to be in significantly dangerous circumstances (as are their children), and two-thirds are denied this request (ibid.).

Many abusers are so jealous and possessive that they do not want their wives or girlfriends to work outside the home for fear that the women will start having affairs. However, even abusers who confine their victims to the home frequently accuse the victims of having extramarital affairs. Some experts believe that abused women not only need access to shelters and adequate police and court protection but they also need to be able to learn skills and obtain financial resources in order to be free of the abusers (Tong, 1984).

Sociological Restrictions

Women are confined to IPA relationships in a number of cultural ways. First, people seem to have a need to believe that IPA is not happening or, if it is happening, that the victims deserve it. (This parallels Lerner's just-world hypothesis discussed in Chapter 6.) Second, attitudes about marriage negatively affect a woman's ability to leave an IPA relationship. Battered women frequently claim that their relatives, neighbors, and friends deny the IPA and, if confronted with it, imply to the victim that she is somehow responsible and that she must work harder on her marriage. This is also true of many women who turn to religious guidance, such as priests, ministers, or rabbis. To some clergy, marriage is viewed as sacred, to be held together at all costs, however dangerous doing so may be to women and children. The children not only witness their mother's victimization (a form of emotional child abuse) but may also be physically abused themselves (Bowker, Arbitell, and McFerron, 1988; Jaffe et al., 1986; Jaffe, Wolfe, and Wilson, 1990; Walker, 1989). A study of Asian Indian immigrant battered women in the United States found that these women's childhood socialization into the "ideals of 'good' wife and mother that include sacrifice of personal freedom and autonomy" placed them at risk, even when they had economic independence (Dasgupta and Warrier, 1996, 238). Moreover, they feared dishonoring their family by divorce and felt responsible for their families' reputations in India. Similarly, a study of Palestinian women from the West Bank and Gaza Strip found that those women who adhered to a patriarchal ideology were more likely to support "understanding" of abusers and not blame them solely for their abusive behavior (Haj-Yahia, 1998).

Abused women frequently report a feeling of having no escape (see Browne, 1987; Forte et al., 1996; Jones, 1994). They may have exhausted every resource in order to leave an IPA relationship. Many IPA survivors have discussed attempts to gain help from their own relatives, the abuser's relatives, the police, and the courts (such as through divorces or restraining or protection orders). Abusers continue to threaten and violate many of these victims, and sometimes their children (see Pagelow, 1993). One study of abused women reported:

> Almost all [of the abused women] have sought help from a variety of sources. Most have, at some time, called the police for physical protection. Over two-thirds had received counseling from marriage counselors or clergy at some point. Few women, however, reported that their husbands were willing to cooperate with counseling. Over one-half had consulted with attorneys and almost half turned to divorce for resolution of the problem. However, divorce was not always found to be the successful resolution, as occasionally the assaulter continued to seek out his former wife to assault her or assaults occurred at the time of visitation with the children. (Flynn, 1977, 18)

In fact, some studies have shown that abusers' violence often escalates when the victims attempt to leave the abusive relationship (Campbell, 1992; Ellis, 1987; Ellis and DeKeseredy, 1989; Mahoney, 1991; Pagelow, 1993; Sev'er, 1997; Wilson and Daly, 1993). Instead of asking why (some) battered women stay, perhaps we should be asking, "What happened to you when you left? What support did you get?" (Mahoney, 1991).

A specific area of sociological research that has only recently addressed IPA is the social experience of *environmental disasters*. Specifically, this area of research examines the sociology of communities experiencing floods, earthquakes, and so on, as well as how prepared communities are for these natural disasters. The sparse research on IPA in the context of disasters suggests that intimate partner abuse increases in the wake of natural disasters and is particularly problematic in the area of housing for the abused women and their children (see Enarson, 1999; Fothergill, 1999). Living through fear and intimidation on a daily basis, battered women are already in emotional crisis before disaster. Attending to preparedness or evacuation warnings, stabilizing their lives in a disaster-stricken neighborhood, or accessing recovery resources may be impossible tasks (Enarson, 1999, 748). Women's safety and well-being are likely to be additionally stressed if they are living in a shelter requiring their second evacuation (the first being from their home with the abuser), and "[r]elief funds may be more available to the abuser at home than to women living in shelter" (ibid., 749). These problems are especially acute for battered women who are poor and/or disabled (Fothergill, 1999).

While historical research documents that IPA has occurred over centuries, cross-cultural and comparative studies indicate that IPA occurs cross-culturally and globally. A recent phenomenon in the research on intimate partner abuse focuses on issues of IPA for immigrant women in the United States, with the majority of these studies focusing on Asian immigrant women. Regarding the unique experiences of immigrant women, Bui and Morash state:

> On one hand, immigrant women have brought their traditional cultures and their experience with legal norms and social structure of their countries of origin to America. On the other hand, they have also internalized to some degree American culture as a result of resettlement and adaptation to a new life, and they and their families often experience stress related to relocation and a change in social status. (1999, 770)

A study of Vietnamese immigrant women in the United States reported that "class, culture, gender, and immigration status could simultaneously affect women's experience of violence by husbands" (ibid., 769). A study of South Asian immigrant women in the United States reported their susceptibility to marital rape, sexual control through manipulation of reproductive rights (e.g., not allowing birth control and causing continual pregnancies or denying the woman the right to have a child by abusing her when she is pregnant to the point of losing the pregnancy), sexual abuse by flaunting another relationship (e.g., "If you don't have sex when and how I want it, I'll take a lover"), and sexual abuse by others (e.g., rape by a brother-in-law) (Abraham, 1999).

Psychological Restrictions

Many psychologists have suggested various explanations for staying in an IPA relationship. The victims themselves sometimes describe the psychological effects of abuse and exploitation as "brainwashing" (Finkelhor, 1983, 20). Efforts to determine which women are victim prone—or likely to become battered women—not only are victim blaming but have proven fruitless. Researchers have been unable to establish which types of women are battered (Walker, 1983a). This informs us that *any woman could become a battered woman—*a frightening thought and counter to those who want to believe a just world exists.

Walker (1979) uses the social learning theory called *learned helplessness* to explain abused women's behavior. She bases this on (ethically questionable) studies of animals where all options of escape are closed off. The animals in these tests experience uncontrollable pain or harm on a random, unpredictable basis. Learned helplessness is characterized by persons (or animals) who have learned through repeated failure that they cannot control their destiny. Because they have no control over their environments, there is no point in trying. Therefore, even when faced with what outsiders may view as viable escapes, the person or animal with learned helplessness cannot identify these alternatives as escapes. In a later study, Walker (1983a) claimed that this learned helplessness may occur early or later in life. For instance, it may be a result of women growing up in a violent family and viewing IPA as a coping strategy for family conflict, or learned helplessness may occur later in life within the confines of an IPA relationship. "Thus, learned helplessness has equal potential to develop at either time in the battered woman's life" (ibid., 35).

Walker's (1979, 1983a) learned helplessness theory has been criticized by some feminists (Dobash and Dobash, 1988; Gondolf and Fisher, 1988; Wardell, Gillespie, and Leffler, 1983). These critics believe that the learned helplessness approach suggests too strongly that abused women have wrongly assumed they cannot leave an IPA relationship. The abused woman's recognition of a lack of alternatives is often rational, not simply due to a poor self-image, after she has sought help repeatedly from friends, family, the police, and the courts and is still in a threatening position (Wardell, Gillespie, and Leffler, 1983). Social learning theory focuses on abused women overlooking some of the alternatives available to them. Even if such alternatives exist, people under conditions of high anxiety or terror may not see them, and people often make decisions that appear illogical to others, such as keeping their houses even though their neighbors have been burglarized twice or getting a Ph.D. when universities are not hiring (ibid., 1983).

The theory of learned helplessness diverts attention from the abuse to the victim by labeling her response as "unreasonable" (ibid., 76). The focus is on what the victim is doing wrong rather than on the abuser's behavior and the woman's lack of alternatives. For these reasons, it has been suggested (tongue-in-cheek) that the police and judges who do nothing to help abused women may be the ones with learned helplessness (Gondolf and Fisher, 1988). Certainly, a vast amount of research documents ways that abused women have depended on, or even reached out to, the criminal legal system and been disappointed with a lack of response, or even with responses that support the abusers more than they do the victims (e.g., Browne, 1987; Cahn, 1992; Erez and Belknap, 1998; Jones, 1994; Rosewater, 1988).

Another psychological theory used to explain reluctance or inability of women to leave IPA relationships is that of *traumatic bonding*. Dutton and Painter (1981, 146–147) define this as the development and course of strong emotional ties between two persons where one person intermittently harasses, beats, threatens, abuses, or intimidates the other. This approach has been used to explain why hostage victims, children abused by their parents, or members of malevolent cults frequently bond with their aggressors. If viewed within this context, the relationship between battered women and their abusers may not be an isolated phenomenon but rather is an example of traumatic bonding (ibid., 146). The two common features of the various forms of traumatic bonding are power imbalance and intermittent abuse. It is not uncommon for the power imbalance to grow as a relationship becomes increasingly violent: The violent person feels more powerful and the victim less powerful as the violence progresses. The intermittent nature of the abuse may be exemplified in IPA if we examine Walker's cycle, where violence is intermittently dispersed among expressions of sorrow, love, and affection (ibid., 150).

In tracing the various theoretical and historical perspectives on what causes IPA, it is clear that confronting IPA must occur in many contexts. These include adequate divorce laws, services available to abused women and their children to help them leave and start over, adequate legislation, and appropriate responses by the criminal legal system. Additionally, similar to the contention in Chapter 7 that sexual victimization and gender inequality reinforce each other, IPA and gender inequality do so as well. As men and women become more equal, we should expect women to have more economic, psychological, and societal resources to leave IPA relationships.

THE CONSTANT THREAT OF DANGER

All of the inhibitors (economic, sociological, and psychological) addressed in the preceding section are influenced by a constant threat of danger and fear for many abused women once the violence has begun. If the abuser threatens to assault or actually does assault the victim, they both become aware of his potential to harm her. One study found that almost all battered women report a fear that their abusers may completely "lose control" and kill them during a beating (Star et al., 1979). Even if none of the other negative conditions, such as those suggested earlier (economic, sociological, and psychological), exists for the victim, the danger is still present. For instance, if a woman is beaten by her husband and decides to leave him, she may feel assured in doing this on many levels—she may hold a good job, his family and her family and friends may support her leaving him, and she may not have fallen victim to some of the psychological syndromes previously addressed. Even if her parents and friends do not support her breakup with him, she may have access to a battered women's shelter. However, he may still pose a powerful threat of danger. He may tell her he will kill her, her/their children, and/or her parents if she does not return to him. She has learned he is capable of violence, and she likely has reason to believe he may follow through on his threats. Even if she is not completely convinced he will carry out his threats, the risk of destruction to loved ones is logically perceived as too great a gamble.

     If she is staying in a shelter or hotel or hiding with friends or relatives, she may have to quit her job because he could locate her at work. It is not unusual for women who have left abusers to have the abusers show up at their places of employment or trace their new residences through friends, family, coworkers, or private detectives. When the victim is staying with her family to escape from the abuser, he will often use sufficient threats and pressure that one or more members of her own family might begin to advise her to work it out with him. Although a victim may have received a protection or restraining order from the court not allowing the husband on her property, he may still have rights to child visitation, so avoiding him is almost impossible (McCann, 1985; Walker, 1989). Many abused women survivors have had to move to a new city or state and change their names in order to be free of the violence. Clearly, such women often lose their family and friends, in addition to their possessions, which is often some abusers' goal.

     Evidence shows that abusers' promises to kill their victims are not merely idle threats—some abusers do eventually kill the women they have abused. In fact, much of the worst violence abused women experience occurs after they have separated from or divorced their husbands (Campbell, 1992; Ellis, 1987; Ellis and DeKeseredy, 1989; Erez, 1986; Mahoney, 1991; Pagelow, 1993; Sev'er, 1997; Wilson and Daly, 1993). This may be most dangerous for unmarried battered women, whose rates of being murdered by their abusers increased from 1976 to 1987 (Browne and Williams, 1993).

A study of divorced women with children from a variety of backgrounds found that intimate partner abuse (1) is what caused many of the women to file for a divorce and (2) played an important and threatening role in their efforts to negotiate for assets after they left (Kurz, 1996). This was most evident in negotiating for child support, a critical issue in setting divorced women above the poverty line. Across women from different classes and races/ethnicities, 30 percent of the women reported fears in negotiating child support, and the more serious and frequent the violence they experienced in the marriage, the more fearful they were about child-support negotiations (ibid.).

Finally, a recent study of murder in Britain compared men who murder other men to men who murder an intimate partner (Dobash et al., 2004). While overall the men who murder intimate partners tend to be more conventional and ordinary than men who murder other men, the men who murder intimate partners have abused women in a previous relationship as well as the woman they murdered.

IPA AND STALKING AND THE CRIMINAL LEGAL SYSTEM

A historical account of communitywide and criminal legal system responses to the IPA of women leads one to believe that men were more likely to be punished for not dominating their wives than for beating them. A portrayal of community regulations of domestic authority since the fifteenth century states:

> Men could be subjected to ritualized rebukes if they were thought to be doing women's work, were henpecked, cuckolded, or believed to have been beaten by their wives—that is, when there was a perceived inversion of patriarchal authority and domination. . . . In addition to being ridiculed by the community for failing to maintain authority, men thought to have domineering or wayward wives were supported in their attempts to regain or retain dominance by ridiculing and shaming the woman publicly and/or by punishing her physically. (Dobash and Dobash, 1981, 566)

To challenge the accepted public beliefs and laws regarding women abused by current or former intimate partners, we must challenge the contention that wives (women) belong to husbands (men). It was not until the latter half of the nineteenth century that such challenges began to appear in the legal code. Only in the past thirty years, however, has IPA been recognized as a distinct criminal offense (Olson and Stalans, 2001, 1164).

The public and systemic response to abused women, consistent with the focus on why the woman stays, often gets stuck in viewing abused women as "uncooperative" or "reluctant." This brings us back to the earlier discussion about learned helplessness: Do abused women have this, or does the system that has historically failed to protect abused women asking for arrests and convictions have it (Gondolf and Fischer, 1988)? Research suggests that abused women, rather than being uncooperative, are more likely extremely frustrated with a system that fails to address their victimizations (see Browne, 1987; Erez and Belknap, 1998; Jones, 1994). For example, despite the widely held belief that all battered women are upset when their abusers are arrested, even to the point of attacking the police themselves, a considerable body of research reports that police have historically been unwilling to make arrests even when the abused woman requests it (Bowker, 1982; Brown, 1984; Buzawa and Austin, 1993; Dolon, Hendricks, and Meagher, 1986; Ferraro, 1989b; Oppenlander, 1982; Pagelow, 1981; Websdale, 1995; Websdale and Johnson, 1997; Zoomer, 1989), even though battered women may be more likely than other assault victims to make such a request (Eigenberg, Scarborough, and Kappeler, 1996; Oppenlander, 1982). Some research found that victim injury has no bearing on a police officer's likelihood of arresting a violent intimate partner (Berk and Loseke, 1981; Eigenberg, Scarborough, and Kappeler, 1996; Hatty, 1989; Smith and Klein, 1984; Worden and Pollitz, 1984). Moreover, although police are more likely to arrest intimate partner abusers when a weapon is present or used, the levels of arrest even when a weapon is present have historically been quite low (Bachman and Coker, 1995; Buzawa and Austin, 1993; Eigenberg, Scarborough, and Kappeler, 1996).

Finally, recent research documents the need for advocates and police and court officials responding to IPA to ask about and seriously respond to stalking when it happens in the context of IPA. Two-thirds of twenty-one IPA survivors who also reported stalking by their abusers described frustrating experiences with the police and courts, including minimization of the stalking and saying there was nothing they (the police or courts) could do about the stalking (Melton, 2004). At the same time, other research reports the ignorance and even disdain that many court officials (prosecutors, judges, and public defenders) hold for IPA victim advocates (Hartman and Belknap, 2003).

The Police

Despite the fact that IPA is the most common violent crime reported to police (Ventura and Davis, 2005, 255), before the 1960s, police training in IPA was rare, and few departments had policies on how the police should respond to these calls. In the 1960s, *mediation* training and policies were implemented in many departments. Mediation policies and training encouraged police officers to treat IPA as merely a breach of the public peace and to calm the parties down. However, a mediation response communicates to everyone involved—the victim, the offender, the children, witnesses, and the police—that a serious crime has not occurred. The abuser's violence goes unpunished and in some respects is actually sanctioned by the police department because they know what has occurred and still fail to restrict or punish the offender.

Evidence that mediation does not deter IPA is apparent from the vast number of repeat calls police receive to return to relationships where they previously used mediation. Furthermore, research suggests that mediation is not even a temporary solution. One study found that "[e]ven when the patrol officer leaves the scene of conflict, nearly a fourth of the domestic assault victims remain in a state of distress" (ibid., 455). At the same time, National Crime Survey data analysis reports that 37 percent of the battered women who call the police do so to prevent an incident from happening (Langan and Innes, 1986). Also disturbing are research findings that the police tend to focus most concern on the offender rather than adapt to the victim's needs (Oppenlander, 1982). In short, police response to IPA, unlike other assaults, has traditionally included a formal or informal policy of arrest avoidance (Bell and Bell, 1991; Dobash and Dobash, 1979; Erez, 1986; Finesmith, 1983; Gondolf and Fisher, 1988; Hanmer, Radford, and Stanko, 1989; Oppenlander, 1982; Rowe, 1985; Schechter, 1982; Stanko, 1985; Tong, 1984; Zorza, 1992).

Four factors helped to change the traditional police response of nonintervention (including mediation) in woman-abuse calls. First, it was clear that mediation was as ineffective as nonintervention (Finesmith, 1983; Gee, 1983; Rowe, 1985; Stanko, 1985; Tong, 1984). Second, the feminist movement was gaining momentum and organizing around male violence against women, including the implementation of the first battered women's shelters and rape-crisis centers. This was related to the third factor—court cases aimed at police departments. Third, battered women, often in class-action lawsuits, began taking police departments to court for failing to arrest their abusers and leaving them in dangerous and life-threatening situations (see Eppler, 1986). These women were successful in the court outcomes, using the Fourteenth Amendment to contend that they were not treated equally by the police as persons assaulted by strangers. Probably the most famous of these is the 1984 *Thurman v. City of Torrington* case, where Tracey Thurman's repeated calls to the police and the restraining order she obtained were ineffective in acquiring police protection. During Thurman's final battering, the police not only delayed in responding to the call but watched for some time as her abuser severely assaulted her. Thurman suffered severe and permanent physical damage. However, Thurman not only won her lawsuit against the police department but the aftermath of this lawsuit also resulted in Connecticut's governor forming a state task force to examine responses to IPA (Davies, Lyon, and Monti-Catania, 1998).

The fourth and final factor influencing police policy changes in response to IPA was research finding that arresting abusers works. Sherman and Berk (1984) conducted the first of these studies in Minneapolis, Minnesota, where offenders were randomly assigned to three options: (1) arrest, (2) mediation, or (3) an order that the offender leave the premises. This research found that arrested abusers were the least likely to recidivate and stated that an arrest should be made unless there are good, clear reasons why an arrest would be counterproductive (ibid., 270).

Sherman and Berk's (ibid.) "Minneapolis experiment" was replicated, and their findings were confirmed throughout the 1980s (Berk and Newton, 1985; Jaffe et al., 1986). These four factors (mediation's ineffectiveness, feminists organizing against male violence, abused women's successful lawsuits against police departments, and research findings that arrest deters abusers) resulted in the adoption of pro-arrest (presumptive or mandatory arrest) policies in most large U.S. cities. However, since the 1990s, a number of replications of the Minneapolis experiment (including ones conducted by the original researchers, Sherman and Berk) reported no differences in repeat violence by abusers who were and were not arrested (see Dunford, 1992; Dunford, Huizinga, and Elliott, 1990; Hirschel and Hutchison, 1992; Hirschel, Hutchison, and Dean, 1991, 1992; Pate and Hamilton, 1992; Sherman et al., 1992).

Notably, a study comparing police likelihood to arrest intimate partner assaulters versus other assaulters *before pro-arrest policies* found the police significantly more likely to arrest nonintimate partner assaulters more often (17 percent) (Eigenberg, Scarborough, and Kappeler, 1996), then a more recent *post–pro-arrest policy implementation* study found that nonwife assaulters are still more likely to be arrested than wife assaulters (Avakame and Fyfe, 2001). This study also found that police were more likely to arrest when the victim was a White, wealthy, older, suburban female (ibid.). A study in a city before a pro-arrest policy found that regardless of IPA offenders' personal characteristics (e.g., race, prior violence, etc.), they were less likely to recidivate if they felt the police acted in a procedurally fair manner (even when they arrested the suspects) (Paternoster and Bachman, 1997).

This effort by some to repeal pro-arrest policies is troubling to feminists for many reasons. First, just because arresting abusers may not stop their abuse does not in and of itself justify not arresting them. When many robbers keep robbing after being arrested, we do not throw our hands in the air and say, "Oh, we might as well not bother arresting them!" (robbery analogy made by Zorza [1992]). Second, arresting abusers gives abused women and their children an opportunity to escape if the abusers spend at least a few hours being processed and in jail. Given this assumption, it is not surprising that an Oregon study found that the implementation of a state pro-arrest policy resulted in a significant decrease in the number of domestic homicides (women or men killing their spouses) (Jolin, 1983). This study points out two important issues: (1) There is more than one way to measure the effectiveness of arrest, and (2) not only might pro-arrest policies save abused women's lives but these policies are also likely to reduce the number of women forced into a situation where they kill their abusers in self-defense. (Interestingly, Jolin's research has received no attention by the same policing scholars who evaluated the pro-arrest policies.) A recent study using national U.S. data reported that there were about 3,000 intimate partner murders in 1976, and this has decreased over time to 1998, when there were about 1,830 such murders (Rennison and Welchans, 2000). Thus, these data indicate that the development of shelters and the implementation of pro-arrest policies have saved the lives of women and men. A fourth area of concern is that research evaluating pro-arrest policies has found that police often fail to comply with the policy;

officers still tend not to arrest abusers even in jurisdictions with pro-arrest policies (Balos and Trotzky, 1988; Ferraro, 1989b; Lawrenz, Lembo, and Schade, 1988).

This does not mean that all feminists support pro-arrest policies. First, there is concern that these policies are implemented discriminately—that abusers of color and from less wealthy neighborhoods are more likely than their wealthier White counterparts to be arrested (Edwards, 1989; Hoff, 1990; Miller, 1989, 2005; Stanko, 1989; Stark, 2004). However, one study found that despite a pro-arrest policy, there was low compliance, and police were less likely to arrest intimate partner abusers when the victim was African American (26 percent) than when they were not African American (36 percent) (Robinson and Chandek, 2000). Second, considerable evidence exists that the police arrest some *victims* who resist or fight back against their abusers (Dasgupta, 2001, 2002, 2003; Hirschel and Buzawa, 2002; Jones and Belknap, 1999; Martin, 1997; Melton and Belknap, 2003; Miller, 2001, 2005; Perilla et al., 2003; Stanko, 1989; Stark, 2004). Thus, pro-arrest policies resulted in the previously almost unheard of, and certainly unintended practice of, arresting women for domestic violence, either instead of or along with their male intimate partners; these are called dual arrests. Needless to say, it is traumatizing for the victims to be arrested as offenders (Miller, 2005). One study found that dual arrests were most likely in departments where the officers perceived these arrests as the desire of their departments and in cases where both members of the couple were injured (Finn et al., 2004). Not surprisingly, when a victim is arrested as part of a dual arrest, she is less interested in pursuing prosecution of her abuser (Bui, 2001). Some departments, in order to get away from dual arrests, have opted for primary aggressor rules, directing that only one person in a couple should be arrested in most IPA calls. Unfortunately, women who use weapons, often a kitchen knife, to level the playing ground when they are being seriously threatened or assaulted are often arrested as the primary aggressor and the abusive man goes free.

Third, there has been some concern that arresting abusers may *increase* subsequent violence toward the victim. However, a reanalysis of the data from many of the studies evaluating pro-arrest policies concluded that arresting intimate partner abusers resulted in *lowered* aggression levels, if anything, in the future (Maxwell, Garner, and Fagan, 2001). A final but important feminist concern with the pro-arrest policies is that they take decision making completely away from the victims, who likely already feel powerless (Hoff, 1990; Mills, 1999, 2003; Rowe, 1985; Stanko, 1989). More specifically, if the victims do not want their abusers arrested, should their desires be honored?

Hirschel and Hutchison (2003) addressed these two concerns—Does arrest increase subsequent abuse, and should victims' wishes influence whether police should arrest their abusers?—and examined their overlap. In their study of 419 female IPA survivors, 30 percent wanted their abusers arrested. The remainder wanted the police to simply take him away (41 percent), warn him (12 percent), make him leave her alone (6 percent), enable her to leave by herself (4 percent), or some other nonarrest response (7 percent) (ibid.). Notably, victims who were African American (as opposed to White), poorer, had been hit more frequently in the preceding six months, had been hit more severely in the current incident, and whose offenders had prior arrest records were more likely to want their abusers arrested. Moreover, and importantly, victims who wanted their abusers arrested were more likely to be revictimized by their abusers following the arrest than victims who did not want their abusers arrested. Finally, victims whose abusers were arrested were no more likely to be revictimized than victims whose abusers were not arrested (ibid.).

These feminist criticisms of pro-arrest policies do not necessarily mandate a withdrawal of the policies. Rather, they suggest that the policies need to be implemented fairly and that officers who fail to do so should be punished or held accountable in some way. We also must question the logic of withdrawal of pro-arrest policies based on the possibility that arrest *may* make some abusers more violent. Instead, police departments and the remainder of the criminal legal system must become more responsible for protecting abused women and their children from these abusers who are likely the most dangerous and lethal to their victims.

Restraining orders, also known as orders of protection or stay-away orders, are a legal intervention in which one person who is deemed to be a threat to another is ordered to have no contact with the person and usually to stay a specified distance away from the individual (Sorenson and Shen, 2005, 912). They were developed in order to reduce IPA and to provide a remedy in addition to prosecution (Grau, Fagan, and Wexler, 1985, 15), and the vast majority of these orders are for IPA, typically to protect a female against a male (Sorenson and Shen, 2005). These orders potentially offer additional protections for IPA and stalking victims, but they are not without problems. First, acquiring restraining orders typically places the burden on the victim. This is unrealistic in many IPA situations in which an abuser leaves his victim with no access to transportation, and the fear of getting caught trying to acquire the order overrides the desire to obtain it. Also, although police officers often encourage abused and stalked women to obtain restraining orders, there is considerable evidence that police are often resistant to enforcing them, making them useless and frustrating for the battered and stalked women who went to the efforts to get them (Erez and Belknap, 1998; Logan, Shannon, and Walker, 2005; Pagelow, 1993; Rigakos, 1997; Tong, 1984).

One study found that 40 percent of women who initially pursue restraining/protection orders do not progress beyond the first step in the process (Fernandez, Iwamoto, and Muscat, 1997). The process was described as lengthy and some-what complicated; thus, not surprisingly, only about three in ten women who initially pursed protection orders continued to pursue and were granted them (ibid.). This study found that the more economically dependent women were on their abusers, the less likely they were to complete the application process of obtaining the orders. Additionally, the more severely abused the woman, the less likely she was to obtain the order, suggesting the abuse kept her in fear of completing the application (ibid.). Research indicates that women pursue restraining orders when they have decided they have had enough (Fischer and Rose, 1995), suggesting that this may be the time that some women feel ready to leave the relationship. Research on protection/restraining orders provides additional insight. Notably, one study found that over a fifth of the women obtaining protection orders also reported to researchers that they had been sexually assaulted by their intimate partners (Logan, Shannon, and Walker, 2005).

Although these orders may increase police responsiveness and empower some women with more emotional and financial independence to leave abusive relationships, some women are at increased risk of violence by the abuser for retaliation for acquiring the order (Chaudhuri and Daly, 1992). These orders have been found to be more useful to fiscally independent women in less severe IPA relationships but have not proven useful in more violent relationships with long histories of abuse (Chaudhuri and Daly, 1992; Grau, Fagan, and Wexler, 1985). Other research documents the additional problems that rural, as compared to urban, women face in obtaining protection orders (Logan, Shannon, and Walker, 2005). The problems faced by women who have protection orders but whose abusers are granted shared custody or visitation of their children are examples of how some abusers can continue to stalk, harass, and even abuse these women with protection orders (e.g., Kernic et al., 2005; Rosen and O'Sullivan, 2005).

Although some criminal legal system officials and victim advocates report frustration with battered women who obtain restraining orders and then drop them, Ford (1991) found that restraining orders are an important negotiating tool that abused women use to gain more power in their relationships with their abusers and to stop the abuse. Thus, regardless of whether some victims decide to drop restraining orders, police who routinely fail to enforce restraining orders when battered women report their violations are not only not doing their jobs but are likely reinforcing abusers' belief that it is their right to violate these women, and in doing so, these women are at risk of greater, even lethal, violence.

This section highlights a host of problems surrounding the policing of IPA. The police historically were resistant to arrest these abusers because they were not expected to do so. After the implementation of the pro-arrest policies, many resented that they had their discretion in this one offense taken away. But there is some indication that police officers are disproportionately likely, compared to the general population, to themselves be involved in IPA (see Neidig, Russell, and Seng, 1992). Moreover, and not surprisingly, officers who themselves are abusive to their wives are more likely to take antivictim stances in responding to IPA calls (Stith, 1990). Thus, some of the problems in policing IPA may have to do with the officers' own IPA offending. With the implementation of pro-arrest policies and increasing awareness about the damage resulting from IPA, there is some hope that more police are understanding of the dynamics behind IPA and thus respond more powerfully.

Thus, it is important to note studies with positive findings about police responses. One study of over 300 pregnant Latina women who were abused by an intimate male partner found that of the 23 percent who had used the police, almost three-fourths rated the police as somewhat or very effective, and women who used the police reported less serious abuse than those who had not used the police (Wiist and McFarlane, 1998). Another recent study found that 80 percent of women victims of IPA who encountered the police rated the experience with the officers favorably (Apsler, Cummins, and Carl, 2003). The women were most satisfied with the police efforts to arrest their abusers and help with obtaining restraining orders (when these were actions they desired) but were dissatisfied with the inability of the police to help them obtain counseling. The women with the lowest police satisfaction ratings were those who wanted their abusers arrested but they were not. Notably, even most of the women who did not want their abusers arrested but whose abusers were arrested reported that they would call the police again in the future (ibid.). Another study found that IPA women victims typically rated their police experience as between neutral and somewhat satisfied (Fleury, 2002). Notably, when the victims felt the police were supportive, they were more satisfied with the police response, and they reported higher satisfaction when one of the officers was female (ibid.).

What we do know is that pro-arrest policies need further examination to address the level of compliance with the policies and whether they are implemented in discriminating manners (e.g., based on race, class, sexuality, etc.). Furthermore, arresting victims who resist instead of arresting offenders further victimizes and alienates these already-abused women and empowers the offenders in additional ways. Finally, it would seem from the research that perhaps a good start in reconducting the pro-arrest policies would be implementing them in cases where the victims want the abuser arrested, given that they seem to understand their likelihood of revictimization better than anyone else.

The Courts

Historically, court officials (prosecutors, district attorneys, and judges), similar to the police, often failed to respond to the plight of abused women. Early British Common Law established the "rule of thumb," a ruling that allowed husbands to beat their wives with rods no larger than the thickness of their thumbs. A study of the abuse of women in San Diego County in the late 1800s found that the White male prosecutors, judges, juries, and police tended to respond with bipolar extremes: harshness or leniency (Parker, 1997, 294). More specifically, in those few cases where there was overwhelming evidence (particularly if the wife was murdered), serious action was taken against the male abuser. However, the more typical response was leniency, not wanting to compromise the husband's financial and social reputation. Similar to current-day processing, men of color were most likely to have the harshest responses, as were poor men, and women with bad reputations were rarely seen as worthy of the court's time. In 1824, the Mississippi Supreme Court upheld this ruling. "Progress" was made in 1864 with North Carolina's "curtain rule:" The law could interfere with a husband's chastisement of his wife (go beyond the curtain of the home) but only where the husband's violence resulted in permanent injury to the wife (Tong, 1984, 128). Thus, courts have historically defined some forms of wife abuse as legal. More recent research suggests that court officials (prosecutors, public defenders, and judges) rubber stamp police officers' resistance to pro-arrest policies and police ambivalence about IPA cases (Hartman and Belknap, 2003).

A particularly vulnerable time for women who have decided to press charges and follow through (assuming the prosecutor is willing to go through with the case) is the *pretrial period*. During this time, it is not unusual for the abuser to attempt to woo his estranged victim back by promising they can start over and that he will not be violent anymore. If this does not work, he is likely to try to intimidate her with threats of what he will do to her or to her loved ones if she goes to court. Indeed, one study found that many women who went in to drop IPA charges were escorted by their abusers, and fear was the major reason abused women gave for dropping charges against abusers (Quarm and Schwartz, 1985). To better aid IPA survivors in pursuing their cases, it is important to understand their concerns and experiences. One study interviewing women pressing charges against their abusers found four obstacles presented by the court system: (1) a confusing process; (2) a frustrating process; (3) fear of the abuser and fear the court is unwilling and/or unable to protect them from the abuser; and (4) conflict they feel over the prospect of their abusers' incarceration (Bennett, Goodman, and Dutton, 1999). But abused women may quit pursuing (drop) a case against their batterers if they are upset the case was minimized by being charged as a misdemeanor instead of a felony (Ptacek, 1999). Ptacek's (1999) interviews with judges found their attitudes frighteningly similar to the abusers' in the manners they minimized and denied the abuse the victims in their courtroom experienced. He also noted that the judges frequently incorrectly applied the law and used biased attitudes toward the victims in their processing and decisions (ibid.).

It is important to note that police officers also complain of the courts' failure to act. Understandably, police often wonder why they should bother trying to help the victim and make an arrest if prosecutors or judges are simply going to dismiss the case. Similarly, while abused women vary in what they want from prosecution, they have in common the experience of facing significant barriers to safe and effective participation as victim-witnesses in the criminal justice process (Hart, 1993, 625). Abused women frequently feel frustrated when they have made it to court, but the prosecutor decides to dismiss the case; or if the prosecutor pursues the case and it gets to court, the judge decides to take no action, to dismiss the case, or to acquit the abuser. One study in a pro-arrest jurisdiction (that had *not* implemented a no-drop policy as defined later in this section) found that two-thirds of the cases were dismissed, mostly by the prosecutor and a few by the judge for lengthy pending periods (Hirschel and Hutchison, 2001). The two factors, both legal characteristics, most likely to be associated with dismissed cases were the victims' wishes to dismiss and the lack of identifiable injuries (ibid.). One complaint many members of the criminal legal system pose is the cost of obtaining good evidence. A study assessing the effect of photographs (before digital photos), taped 911 calls, medical records, and police testimony on court outcomes found the 911 tapes never affected the outcome, the availability of photographs resulted in more days incarcerated, the availability of medical records resulted in more days of incarceration, and the testimony of police resulted in fewer days on probation (Belknap et al., 1999). The last effect was speculated to be the impact of police officers being completely unprepared by reviewing their own notes or by the prosecutor for their testimonies (ibid.). The only study on digital photos of the IPA victims' injuries found that this low-cost, high-quality evidence collection technology increased the likelihood of intimate partner abusers in a no-drop jurisdiction to plead guilty, be convicted, and receive more severe sentences (Garcia, 2003, 579).

A 1987 study in Minnesota and Illinois reported that arrested abusers are convicted of felonies less than 10 percent of the time, and "[j]udges don't usually do anything the first time a man violates an order of protection" (Blodgett, 1987). With the implementation of pro-arrest policies, there has been a huge increase in the number of IPA cases that reach the court system. A study on a post–pro-arrest jurisdiction reported that half (51 percent) of the cases were dismissed by the judge, one-twentieth (5 percent) were found not guilty, and 44 percent resulted in guilty verdicts (Belknap et al., 1999). The best predictor of the case outcome (verdict and severity of sentence) was how many times the prosecutor met with the victim, indicating that prosecutors' time spent with victims is crucial for convictions. Although whether a victim was subpoenaed had no affect on the case outcome, victim testimony increased the likelihood of a guilty verdict and resulted in a more severe sentence (ibid.). Surprisingly, neither the levels of abuse nor injury were related to the case outcomes, except that when strangling was included, the offenders received more days on probation. Another study in a post–pro-arrest implementation study in Toledo found that about a quarter of IPA cases resulted in convictions, and the cases were just as likely to result in conviction whether the defendant was male or female (Ventura and Davis, 2005). One-third of all of the cases that reached court (regardless of disposition) resulted in revictimization in the twelve months following the verdict (or dismissal). It is troubling that this study found that the defendants in the dismissed cases were significantly more likely than defendants in convicted cases to have histories of violent felonies. The authors speculate that the most violent intimate partner abusers are those whose victims are the most fearful to appear in court, and thus, the cases are dismissed (ibid.). Notably, when batterers were convicted, they were less likely to recidivate in the following twelve months. However, better predictors of the defendants' likelihood of recidivating (than the case disposition) were the IPA history, the age, and the gender of the defendants: Defendants who were younger, had longer IPA histories, and who were male, were more likely to recidivate (ibid.). Of the convicted defendants, those with the lightest sentences (fines or suspended sentences) were the most likely to recidivate, suggesting light sentences could be interpreted by an abuser as receiving a free pass to do as he pleases (ibid., 273).

A comparison of IPA probationers with other violent probationers found the groups were similar except that the IPA probationers were more likely to admit to substance abuse problems and were more educated, older, and more likely than the other violent probationers to be White (Olson and Stalans, 2001). Regarding court-imposed sanctions, the IPA probationers were more likely to be required to undergo intervention/treatment and to pay fines, more likely to be charged with a misdemeanor (instead of felony), and more likely to receive shorter sentences than the other violent probationers were. There were no differences between the groups' likelihood of violating probation sentences and likelihood of arrest while on probation. The tenacity of the IPA offenders to continue victimizing is apparent in the finding that the IPA probationers were three times more likely than the other violent probationers to revictimize their original victim (ibid., 1182). A finding of great concern was that IPA probationers court-ordered to intervention/treatment were five times more likely to revictimize their same victims than those IPA probationers not ordered to intervention/treatment. The authors speculate that this could be a result of the most serious offenders being the ones ordered to intervention, but it could also be that by exposing intimate partner abusers to other intimate partner abusers, group counseling teaches these abusers new techniques of both abusing and justifying their abuse (ibid., 1181).

Another spin on probation as a sentence for IPA offenders notes that while far below some victims' expectations of appropriate state sanctioning, probation can still serve to aid some IPA survivors (Ames and Dunham, 2002). For example, while a probation sentence is unlikely to reform abusers and stop the abuse, it does play the significant role of some degree of monitoring of these abusers we know are at a relatively high risk of reoffending.

Similar to the implementation of pro-arrest policies in policing, some domestic violence courts began implementing no-drop policies in the 1980s and 1990s. These mandated prosecutors to pursue domestic violence charges, even when the victims wanted the charges dropped and/or refused to testify. Again, similar to the pro-arrest policies, the no-drop policies have the potential to frustrate women who do not want their abusers convicted. At the same time, what message does it give to have known sexist violence in the home recognized but dismissed (see Robbins, 1999)? Despite feminist advocacy to require more consistent arrests, prosecutions, and harsher convictions of IPA defendants, the reality is that sanctions, even in the no-drop era, are typically quite light (Ames and Dunham, 2002). However, the no-drop policy has also been described as the single most effective method for getting domestic violence charges to stick (Robbins, 1999, 217). And in San Diego, intimate partner homicides decreased from thirty in 1985 to seven in 1994 following the implementation of a no-drop policy (ibid.).

At any rate, a growing body of documents label the pro-arrest and no-drop policies as coercive, as backfiring on victims, and as causing some women's disempowerment and feelings of entrapment, and that responses to IPA have resulted in overreliance on the state (e.g., Dasgupta, 2003; Ford, 2003; McDermott and Garofalo, 2004; Mills, 1999, 2003). For example, Ford (2003) describes a woman who had two different IPA abusers and had a keen sense that one would be stopped by prosecution but that the subsequent one would kill her. At the same time, other feminists are concerned that some of the criticisms of the pro-arrest and no-drop policies are cast too hastily without acknowledging or documenting the positive impacts they have had on abused women's lives (e.g., Flanakin and Walsh, 2005; Stark, 2003, 2004). Stark notes that while pro-arrest and no-drop policies are not flawless:

... there is some evidence that mandatory arrest has reduced bias in law enforcement; improved evidence gathering and innovative prosecutorial strategies, overcome the distaste traditionally shown for victims whose history, race, or social class might identify them as aggressive; and empowered new voices within the criminal justice system who value victim empowerment alongside the pragmatics of winning or closing cases. (2004, 1327)

Perhaps what makes the most sense is allowing some discretion in the arrest and no-drop policies without getting rid of the policies (Robbins, 1999). That is, the policies need to allow for some individualized justice (Corsilles, 1994). The problem is that police historically, and sometimes still, failed to arrest when the victims wanted and asked them to do so. Similarly, some prosecutors lack the commitment to pursue IPA cases in the courts (see Corsilles, 1994; Erez and Belknap, 1998).

WHEN WOMEN KILL ABUSIVE PARTNERS
IN SELF-DEFENSE

Men are more likely to kill battered women than women are to kill their abusers, even in self-defense (see, for example, Browne and Williams, 1993; Gauthier and Bankston, 1997; Glass et al., 2004; Greenfeld and Snell, 1999, and Chapter 3 in this book). Indeed, 40 to 50 percent of femicides (killings of females) in the United States are from intimate partner homicide (Glass et al., 2004). Historical accounts of women in prison abound with examples of women who injure or kill their abusive husbands in the context of self-defense (e.g., Butler, 1997), with scenarios strikingly similar to battered women who kill in self-defense today. Ironically, it has been noted that until quite recently the same court system and judges who have refused to take the victims of battering seriously appear to exercise little leniency toward women who kill their husbands in self-defense or after years of abuse (Crites, 1987, 45), and the few women who escaped charges of killing their abusers did so by pleading insanity. Such a plea negates the fact that women frequently have no other alternative but to kill their abusers.

Many women survivors who have killed their abusers in self-defense have received life imprisonment in spite of an otherwise clean record. In fact, it is common for battered women who kill not only to admit that they killed but also to notify the police. Although usually in a state of shock, they often assume that it will be apparent to the police and courts that they acted in self-defense. This, unfortunately, is not often the case, as was discussed in Chapter 4. The heartbreak of these cases is further confounded by women who have killed in order to save their own and their children's lives, only to be in prison and have their children placed in foster homes or possibly with relatives of the abuser. Most court cases of abused women who kill have resulted in convictions with no appeals (Gillespie, 1989).

What we do know is that despite the far greater risk women have of being murdered by current or former male intimate partners than men have of being killed by current or former female intimate partners, and that the former is far more likely to be in the context of self-defense after a long history of abuse victimization, the criminal legal system has historically treated men who murder their wives far less harshly than women who murder husbands. There are no existing statistics on how many women in the United States have served life sentences or are currently serving life sentences in prison for killing their abusive male partners in self-defense. But there is documentation of women who were not allowed to speak at their own trials and whose attorneys failed to enter any of their victimization histories. In this case and many others where abused women have killed their abusers, they had little or no say in the trial. Their lawyers were often unlikely to let them take the stand to tell their own stories in spite of the fact that they wished to do so (Marcus, 1981, 1728). This silencing of women resulted in extraordinarily harsh sentences. In a unique case, a law professor and a law student, after working pro bono with incredible dedication, were able in 1998 to free an African American woman, Juanita Thomas, who had been incarcerated for eighteen years at the time of her release, for killing her batterer in self-defense (Lyon, Hughes, and Thomas, 2001). Thomas had been convicted in a case fraught with injustices, including an all-White jury, prosecutors who hid and destroyed key evidence, and an incompetent public defender (ibid.).

What factors influence the likelihood of a woman killing her abuser? As noted previously in this chapter, *the most dangerous/lethal time for IPA victims is when they leave their abusers*. Research comparing women who killed (or almost killed) and women who have not (yet) killed their abusers identifies some distinctions between the two. First, battered women who kill are more likely to be involved with an abuser who physically and, often, sexually abuses her/their children (Browne, 1987; Ewing, 1987; Walker, 1989). Second, battered women who kill have perceived a more immediate sense of danger, usually involving violence that has increased in frequency, severity, and injury (Browne, 1987; Ewing, 1987; O'Keefe, 1997; Walker, 1989). Finally, battered women who kill are more likely to have received death threats and been terrorized with weapons (often firearms) (Browne, 1987; Ewing, 1987). It is useful to note that these findings suggest that the factors that trigger a battered woman to kill have more to do with actions of the abuser than with actions of the victim. For example, a woman in Browne's (1987) study was told by her husband that he was going to kill her if she did not find out what had happened to his current lover, whom he had also abused and who had left him. This woman had no idea where her husband's other victim had fled, but she believed his threat. In this instance, she had prepared to defend herself by locating one of his guns. She did not shoot him even when he was shooting at her (with another one of his guns). She did not shoot him until he attempted to kill their child. Notably, a study comparing incarcerated battered women who killed their abusers with those in for other offenses found not only that the ones who killed experienced more sexual assaults, more frequent battering, more severe battering, more injuries, higher levels of danger, and a longer duration of violence in the relationship, but surprisingly, they also reported *less* violence against their partners (prior to the lethal incident), and they were *less likely* to have a prior criminal record or to have served time in jail/prison (O'Keefe, 1997).

It is difficult to question a woman's rationality in the vast majority of the cases where women have killed their abusers in self-defense: They usually do so only after having exhausted alternatives, including leaving him and contacting the criminal legal system. Starting in the late 1970s, battered women's syndrome (BWS) started to be used as a defense in U.S. courts. This diagnosis is typically brought in as a defense for women who killed their abusers and usually requires an expert witness to verify that the woman suffers from BWS. Before defining BWS, it is important to address the dynamics behind women killing their abusers. As identified by Lenore Walker (1979), BWS has three components: Walker's cycle of violence, learned helplessness, and posttraumatic stress disorder (PTSD). The former two components were discussed earlier in this chapter. PTSD, developed to explain responses of U.S. Vietnam War veterans, claims that certain psychological symptoms result from experiencing severe and unexpected trauma or being unexpectedly and repeatedly exposed to abuse. Research suggests, as expected, that the likelihood of a battered woman being diagnosed with PTSD is related to the severity of the abuse and the types of abuse, as well as other life events and the availability of social support systems, in the predicted directions (see Astin, Lawrence, and Foy, 1993; Kemp et al., 1995). However, there is some concern with using PTSD and defining abused women as psychotic or mentally ill. Also, we must approach BWS with caution, in that it may define others as experts, disallowing the woman's experience and reports of her own unique IPA situation (Davies, Lyon, and Monti-Catania, 1998).

Expert witnesses have been employed since the 1980s to educate judges and juries about the dynamics behind IPA (Attorney General's Task Force on Family Violence, 1984, 41). Testimony regarding BWS is usually used to provide evidence that the woman was indeed battered, as suggested by psychological indicators. Although feminists in part have supported the use of expert witnesses in cases where women have killed their abusers, the result is that abused women, particularly until more recently, have not had the chance to tell their own stories.

Some scholars believe the BWS defense is necessary because the current interpretation of the self-defense law is largely patriarchal and fails to understand the threat of great bodily harm and death that victims experience (see Gillespie, 1989). However, a number of costs are associated with using BWS as a defense. Although it goes beyond insanity and self-defense claims to help women who kill their abusers, it perpetuates stereotypical images of women. Ferraro (2003, 110) appropriately criticizes pathologizing these women by calling it a syndrome and asks: "Is it so difficult to understand why battered women fear for their lives without relying on a dubious psychological malady?" Defining this as a syndrome, a psychological shortcoming or malady on the abused woman's part, diverts attention from the rational and deliberate strategies of survival that women employ when they are in violent situations (ibid., 112).

The most prominent feature of the syndrome in BWS is learned helplessness, most severely criticized by feminists because it perpetuates images of women as passive and weak. An adoption of this view stereotypes women who kill their abusers as abnormal, although their responses are quite normal compared to victims in similar situations (see Sheehy, Reinberg, and Krichway, 1991). Moreover, the guilt, low self-esteem, self-blame, and depression these women report might be a result of the failure of family, police, judges, and physicians to provide help (Gondolf and Fisher, 1988). Some women's justifiable anger at being abused and not being protected by the criminal legal system at least partially explains why they kill their abusers. By definition, this anger fails to fit the learned helplessness model (see Allard, 1991; Mahoney, 1991). In fact, it has been noted that BWS is less likely to work for African American women because they are more likely to be viewed as angry by judges and juries (Allard, 1991), and more recent research documents the lack of attempts to apply BWS to African American women who have killed abusers in self-defense (Ferraro, 2003). Another cost of the BWS defense is that when women are viewed as abnormal, irrational, weak, mentally ill, or angry, they are at increased risk of losing custody of their children (Stark, 1992). A 1996 report on BWS commissioned by federal departments of the U.S. Government concluded that BWS was neither appropriate nor useful and recommended substituting BWS with battering and its effects (Dutton, 1996, as described in Ferraro, 2003). Unfortunately, this has not occurred (Ferraro, 2003).

In similar ways that Jill Davies and her colleagues (Davies, Lyon, and Monti-Catania, 1998) outlined the manner that the battered woman was portrayed in the 1970s to gain public support, sympathy, and change, Ferraro (2003) elaborates on how BWS was used to get information on these women's abusive victimizations and garner public and criminal legal system support. In both cases, the depictions failed to account for many, many women abused by intimate partners. As stated earlier, many women were not the "pure victim" portrayed by activists in the 1970s (Davies, Lyon, and Monti-Catania, 1998). Similarly, many, likely most, abused women who kill their batterers in self-defense do not fit the rather limiting boiler-plate image drawn by BWS (Ferraro, 2003). Expert testimony on the dynamics of IPA can still benefit jurors' awareness and fairness for victims without having to strictly address BWS but rather explaining to jurors why some women stay and other phenomena not clearly understood by most of the public (and criminal legal professionals) (Dodge and Greene, 1991).

To address the lack of response to IPA, many scholars and activists have pushed for a more community-oriented and comprehensive approach to handling this violence. Currently, the police, courts, and corrections often have conflicting goals. The police are often frustrated by judges' dismissal of the often-dangerous cases they diligently pursued. Judges sometimes fail to grant restraining/protection orders in an effort to protect abusers' rights, and even when these orders are granted, they are often not enforced (McCann 1985). Therefore, there is a need to coordinate the police, judiciary, and social services in order to respond effectively to IPA (Gamache, Edleson, and Schock, 1988). Battered women who prosecute frequently report that criminal justice system personnel appear to consider them "unworthy victims" who are clogging up the courts with unimportant family matters (Hart, 1993, 626).

IPA AND HEALTH PROFESSIONALS

Although health professionals are not direct operators in the criminal legal system, they have key interactions with victims. Women's health is very much related to IPA (for an excellent overview, see Stark and Flitcraft, 1996). Historically, the training on IPA that physicians, welfare and mental health professionals, and the clergy traditionally received "reflects a bias toward keeping the family together at all costs" (Goolkasian, 1986, 3). Because of the severe injuries battered women frequently receive, it is not unusual for them to require help from their private physicians or emergency medical personnel. Although the potential for the medical field to deter IPA is great, the response has been "slow and sporadic" (Kurz and Stark, 1988, 249). When workers in the health care professions—physicians, nurses, and social workers—fail to ask the cause of battered women's injuries, they perpetuate the invisibility of IPA and contribute to the women's rationalization that they are not really victims (Campbell, 1991; Dobash and Dobash, 1979). Additionally, mental health clinicians and counselors frequently deal with battered women as their clients. It is important for all of these actors to label the act for what it is—violence.

Although physicians, particularly emergency room physicians, may be acutely aware that the woman they are treating is an IPA victim, they are unlikely to address the cause of the injury (Star et al., 1979). Research in nursing journals claims a lack of sensitivity and appropriate action on the part of nurses as well as doctors in treating abused women (Drake, 1982). One study of emergency department staff workers found three responses to battered women: 11 percent had positive reactions, where they showed concern for the battered woman's safety as well as providing medical care; 49 percent provided a partial response where medical provisions were brief and routine and had low priority; and 40 percent of the staff did not respond to the IPA aspect of the case (Kurz, 1987). This exemplifies how medical professionals maintain the invisibility of abused women. If one goal of medicine is prevention, then failure to address the cause is particularly problematic. Just as police officers should act professionally in response to IPA calls, health care workers also have professional responsibilities to determine the cause of the injury and to plan for prevention of further injury. Responding in similar ways as many law enforcement officials, many health care workers lose their patience with victims who leave the hospitals with their abusers or have returned to the hospital with injuries, presumably from the same abuser. That health care professionals are fed up with abused women is not a legitimate excuse for ignoring their injuries.

Medicalization is a process by which medical professionals define an emerging social problem as belonging within their professional expertise (Kurz, 1987). Medical professionals are reluctant to medicalize IPA and often view responding to IPA as detracting from their proper role (ibid.). (This is similar to police officers who view the appropriate response to IPA as "peace keeping" and who resent peace keeping because it is not considered "real" police work.) It is unusual for emergency room physicians to take detailed histories of women who are obviously victims of IPA, even when serious wounds or injuries are present. These physicians rarely open up a discussion for such crucial questions as how the abuse occurred and who did it, often reinforcing some abused women's efforts to minimize the reality and severity of their abuse (Warshaw, 1993). One example of how negatively emergency room professionals view abused women is that "battered women who attempted suicide were significantly more likely than nonbattered women to be sent home and/or to receive no referral of any kind after a suicide attempt" (Kurz and Stark, 1988, 253). More recent research reports that, not surprisingly, intimate partner abuse, particularly marital rape, increases a woman' likelihood of severe depression (Campbell and Soeken, 1999; Campbell et al., 1997; Forte et al., 1996). Furthermore, one study found that abused women "who are able to retain a strong interest in their own welfare in spite of abuse will be more resistant to depression" (Campbell et al., 1997, 288). This is an important finding in that the availability of resources and support for abused women likely increases their ability to retain an interest in their own welfare. Notably, leaving an abusive relationship is not necessarily the end of the depression for the victim (Herbert, Silver, and Ellard, 1991), suggesting the impacts of IPA can be long term. One study found that upon immediate exit from a women's shelter, 83 percent of the battered women experienced depression, but ten weeks later this proportion had decreased to one-half of the women (Campbell, Sullivan, and Davidson, 1995). Significantly, women who reported higher levels of social support in their lives were less likely to report depression, indicating the importance of adequate institutional responses to abused women (ibid.). Relative to the rest of the population, it is not uncommon for abused women or abusive men to attempt suicide. Both the abuser and the victim in these cases believe (and it would seem logically so) that the violence is not going to stop until one of them dies.

In sum, both criminal legal and health professionals tend not only to keep IPA hidden but also to condone it through their own failure to respond adequately. Any other phenomenon that occurred as frequently and caused the degree of injury that IPA does would likely result in a national outrage and an effort to treat the victim or control the cause (Star et al., 1979).

SUMMARY

Many of the myths and problems surrounding IPA are discussed in this chapter. IPA may take place in many forms, but its results are always devastating. When exploring the causes of IPA, it is not enough to simply examine abusers or the family system; rather, IPA must be viewed in a sociohistorical context. IPA must be deterred not only by reacting to individuals but also by building a political, economic, and social system more equitable to women and a criminal legal and health system more responsive to IPA. The current situation leaves abused women with little recourse to escape abusive relationships safely. Additionally, the culture provides an environment that accepts male violence as normal. Not until gender equality and male violence are confronted on a more global and pervasive level will IPA be viewed as unacceptable and indeed criminal.

NOTES

1.   I placed "elder" in quotation marks because many advocates for older people find the term "elder" offensive, particularly when referring to persons in their 60s.
2.   Consistently throughout this chapter I refer to the children as her/their because the batterer/abuser is not always the father of all or any of the children the battered woman is raising.

REFERENCES

Abraham, Margaret. 1999. Sexual Abuse in South Asian Immigrant Marriages. *Violence Against Women* 5:591–618.

Allard, Sharon A. 1991. Rethinking Battered Woman Syndrome: A Black Feminist Perspective. *UCLA Women's Law Journal* 1:191–207.

Allen, C., and B. Leventhal. 1999. History, Culture, and Identity: What Makes GLBT Battering Different. Pp. 73–82 in *Same-Sex Domestic Violence*, edited by B. Leventhal and S. E. Lundy. Thousand Oaks, CA: Sage.

Ames, Lynda J., and Katherine T. Dunham. 2002. Asymptotic Justice: Probation as a Criminal Justice Response to Intimate Partner Violence. *Violence Against Women* 8:6–34.

Apsler, Robert, Michele R. Cummins, and Steven Carl. 2003. Perceptions of the Police by Female Victims of Domestic Partner Violence. *Violence Against Women* 9:1318–1335.

Astin, Millie C., Kathy J. Lawrence, and David W. Foy. 1993. Posttraumatic Stress Disorder among Battered Women. *Violence and Victims* 8:17–29.

Attorney General's Task Force on Family Violence. 1984. Final Report, September, 157pp.

Avakame, Edem F., and James J. Fyfe. 2001. Differential Police Treatment of Male-on-Female Spousal Violence: Additional Evidence on the Leniency Thesis. *Violence Against Women* 7:22–45.

Bachman, Ronet, and Ann L. Coker. 1995. Police Involvement in Domestic Violence. *Violence and Victims* 10:98–106.

Balos, Beverly, and Katie Trotzky. 1988. Enforcement of the Domestic Abuse Act in Minnesota: A Preliminary Study. *Law and Inequality* 6:83–125.

Banks, M. E. 2003. Women with Visible and Invisible Disabilities: Multiple Intersections, Multiple Issues, Multiple Therapies—Part Preface. *Women & Therapy* 26:xxiii–xli.

Barnett, Ola W., Cheok Y. Lee, and Rose E. Thelen. 1997. Gender Differences in Attributions of Self-Defense and Control in Interpartner Aggression. *Violence Against Women* 3:462–481.

Barnett, Ola W., Tomas E. Martinez, and Brendon W. Bluestein. 1995. Jealousy and Romantic Attachment in Maritally Violent and Nonviolent Men. *Journal of Interpersonal Violence* 10:473–486.

Belknap, Joanne, Dee Graham, P. Gail Allen, Jennifer Hartman, Victoria Lippen, and Jennifer Sutherland. 1999. Predicting Court Outcomes in Intimate Partner Violence Cases: Preliminary Finding. *Domestic Violence Report, 1999* 5:1–10.

Belknap, Joanne, and Heather Melton. (2005). *Are Heterosexual Men Also*

Victims of Intimate Partner Abuse? Harrisburg, PA: National Electronic Network on Violence Against Women, Pennsylvania Coalition Against Domestic Violence, 13 pp. http://www.vawnet.org/ DomesticViolence/Research/ VAWnetDocs/AR_MaleVictims.pdf.

Bell, Daniel J., and Sandra L. Bell. 1991. The Victim-Offender Relationship as a Determinant Factor in Police Dispositions of Family Violence Incidents. *Policing and Society* 1:225–234.

Bennett, Lauren, Lisa Goodman, and Mary Ann Dutton. 1999. Systemic Obstacles to the Criminal Prosecution of a Battering Partner. *Journal of Interpersonal Violence* 14:761–772.

Berk, Richard A., Sarah F. Berk, Donileen R. Loseke, and David Rauma. 1983. Combat and Other Family Violence Myths. Pp. 197–212 in *The Dark Side of Families: Current Family Violence Research*, edited by D. Finkelhor, R. J. Gelles, G. T. Hotaling, and M. A. Straus. Beverly Hills, CA: Sage.

Berk, Richard A., and Phyllis J. Newton. 1985. Does Arrest Really Deter Wife Battery? An Effort to Replicate the Findings of the Minneapolis Spouse Abuse Experiment. *American Sociological Review* 50:253–262.

Berk, Sarah F., and Donileen R. Loseke. 1981. "Handling" Family Violence: Situational Determinants of Police Arrest in Domestic Disturbance. *Law and Society* 15:317–346.

Berkowitz, Leonard. 1983. The Goals of Aggression. Pp. 166–181 in *The Dark Side of Families: Current Family Violence Research*, edited by D. Finkelhor, R. J. Gelles, G. T. Hotaling, and M. A. Straus. Beverly Hills, CA: Sage.

Bogal-Allbritten, Rosemarie, and William L. Allbritten. 1985. The Hidden Victims: Courtship Violence among College Students. *Journal of College Student Personnel* 26:201–204.

Bograd, Michele. 1988. Feminist Perspectives on Wife Abuse: An Introduction. Pp. 11–27 in *Feminist Perspectives on Wife Abuse*, edited by K. Yllo and M. Bograd. Newbury Park, CA: Sage.

Bohannon, Judy R., David A. Dosser, and S. Eugene Lindley. 1995. Using Couple Data to Determine Domestic Violence Rates. *Violence and Victims* 10:133–141.

Bowker, Lee H. 1982. Police Services to Battered Women. *Criminal Justice and Behavior* 9:476–494.

Bowker, Lee H., Michelle Arbitell, and J. Richard McFerron. 1988. On the Relationship between Wife Beating and Child Abuse. Pp. 158–174 in *Feminist Perspectives on Wife Abuse*, edited by K. Yllo and M. Bograd. Newbury Park, CA: Sage.

Boye-Beaman, Joni, Kenneth E. Leonard, and Marilyn Senchak. 1993. Male Premarital Aggression and Gender Identity among Black and White Newlywed Couples. *Journal of Marriage and the Family* 55:303–313.

Breines, Wini, and Linda Gordon. 1983. The New Scholarship on Family Violence. *Signs: Journal of Women in Culture and Society* 18:490–531.

Brewster, M. P. 2000. Stalking by Former Intimates: Verbal Threats and Other Predictors of Physical Violence. *Violence and Victims* 15:41–54.

Brisson, Norman J. 1981. Battering Husbands: A Survey of Abusive Men. *Victimology* 6:338–344.

Brown, Stephen E. 1984. Police Responses to Wife Beating. *Journal of Criminal Justice* 12:277–288.

Browne, Angela. 1987. *When Battered Women Kill*. New York: Free Press.

Browne, Angela, Amy Salomon, and Shari S. Bassuk. 1999. The Impact of Recent Partner Violence on Poor Women's Capacity to Maintain

Work. *Violence Against Women* 5:393–426.

Browne, Angela, and Kirk R. Williams. 1993. Gender, Intimacy, and Lethal Violence: Trends from 1976 through 1987. *Gender and Society* 7:78–98.

Bui, Hoan N. 2001. Domestic Violence Victims' Behavior in Favor of Prosecution. *Women & Criminal Justice* 12:41–76.

Bui, Hoan N., and Merry Morash. 1999. Domestic Violence in the Vietnamese Immigrant Community. *Violence Against Women* 5:769–795.

Burch, Rebecca L., and Gordon G. Gallup. 2004. Pregnancy as a Stimulus for Domestic Violence. *Journal of Family Violence* 19:243–247.

Butler, Anne M. 1997. *Gendered Justice in the American West*. Urbana: University of Illinois Press.

Buzawa, Eve S., and Thomas Austin. 1993. Determining Police Response to Domestic Violence Victims. *American Behavioral Scientist* 36:610–623.

Cahn, N. R. 1992. Innovative Approaches to the Prosecution of Domestic Crimes. Pp. 161–180 in *The Changing Criminal Justice Response*, edited by E. S. Buzawa and C. G. Buzawa. Westport, CT: Auburn House.

Campbell, Jacquelyn C. 1991. Public-Health Conceptions of Family Abuse. Pp. 35–48 in *Abused and Battered*, edited by D. D. Knudsen and J. L. Miller. New York: Aldine De Gruyter.

———. 1992. If I Can't Have You, No One Can. Pp. 99–113 in *Femicide: The Politics of Woman Killing*, edited by Jill Radford and Diana E. Russell. New York: Twayne Publishers.

Campbell, Jacquelyn C., Joan Kub, Ruth Ann Belknap, and Thomas N. Templin. 1997. Predictors of Depression in Battered Women. *Violence Against Women* 3:271–293.

Campbell, Jacquelyn C., and Karen L. Soeken. 1999. Forced Sex and Intimate Partner Violence. *Violence Against Women* 5:1017–1035.

Campbell, Rebecca, Cris M. Sullivan, and William S. Davidson. 1995. Women Who Use Domestic Violence Shelters. *Psychology of Women Quarterly* 19:237–255.

Cappell, Charles, and R. Heiner. 1990. The Intergenerational Transmission of Family Violence. *Journal of Family Violence* 5:135–152.

Cate, Rodney M., June M. Henton, James Koval, F. Scott Christopher, and Sally Lloyd. 1982. Premarital Abuse: A Social Psychological Perspective. *Journal of Family Issues* 3:79–90.

Chaudhuri, Molly, and Kathleen Daly. 1992. Do Restraining Orders Help? Battered Women's Experience with Male Violence and Legal Process. Pp. 227–252 in *Domestic Violence: The Changing Criminal Justice Response*, edited by Eve S. Buzawa and Carl G. Buzawa. Westport, CT: Auburn House.

Corsilles, Angela. 1994. No-Drop Policies in the Prosecution of Domestic Violence Cases: Guarantee to Action or Dangerous Solution? *Fordham Law Review* 63:853–881.

Craven, Diane. 1996. *Female Victims of Violent Crime*. Annapolis, MD: U.S. Department of Justice, Bureau of Justice Statistics.

Crites, Laura L. 1987. Wife Abuse: The Judicial Record. Pp. 38–53 in *Women, the Courts, and Equality*, edited by L. L. Crites and W. L. Hepperle. Newbury Park, CA: Sage.

Dasgupta, Shamita D. 2001. *Towards an Understanding of Women's Use of Nonlethal Violence in Intimate Heterosexual Relationships*. http://www.vawnet.org/DomesticViolence/Research/VAWnetDocs/AR_womviol.php

Dasgupta, Shamita Das. 2002. A Framework for Understanding Women's Use of Nonlethal Violence in Intimate Heterosexual Relationships. *Violence Against Women* 8:1364–1389.

———. 2003. *Safety and Justice for All: Examining the Relationship between the Women's Anti-Violence Movement and the Criminal Legal System.* New York: Ms. Foundation. http://www.ms. foundation.org/user-assets/PDF/ program/safety_justice.pdf.

Dasgupta, Shamita Das, and Sujata Warrier. 1996. In the Footsteps of "Arundhati": Asian American Women's Experience of Domestic Violence in the U.S. *Violence Against Women* 2:238–259.

Davies, Jill, Eleanor Lyon, and Diane Monti-Catania. 1998. *Safety Planning with Battered Women.* Thousand Oaks, CA: Sage.

DeKeseredy, W., and M. Schwartz. 1998. *Measuring the Extent of Woman Abuse in Intimate Heterosexual Relationships: A Critique of the Conflict Tactics Scales.* http://www.vawnet.org/ DomesticViolence/Research/ VAWnetDocs/AR_ctscrit.php.

DeKeseredy, Walter S. 1995. Enhancing the Quality of Survey Data on Woman Abuse. *Violence Against Women* 1:139–157.

Dobash, R. Emerson, and Russell Dobash. 1979. *Violence against Wives.* New York: Free Press.

———. 1988. Research as Social Action: The Struggle for Battered Women. Pp. 51–74 in *Feminist Perspectives on Wife Abuse*, edited by K. Yllo and M. Bograd. Newbury Park, CA: Sage.

Dobash, R. Emerson, Russell P. Dobash, Kate Cavanagh, and Ruth Lewis. 2004. Not an Ordinary Killer—Just an Ordinary Guy: When Men Murder an Intimate Woman Partner. *Violence Against Women* 10:577–605.

Dobash, Russell P., and Rebecca E. Dobash. 1981. Community Response to Violence against Wives. *Social Problems* 28:563–581.

———. 1983. The Context-Specific Approach. Pp. 261–276 in *The Dark Side of Families: Current Family Violence Research*, edited by D. Finkelhor, R. J. Gelles, G. T. Hotaling, and M. A. Straus. Beverly Hills, CA: Sage.

Dobash, Russell P., R. Emerson Dobash, Kate Cavanagh, and Ruth Lewis. 1998. Separate and Intersecting Realities: A Comparison of Men's and Women's Accounts of Violence against Women. *Violence Against Women* 4:382–414.

Dobash, Russell P., R. Emerson Dobash, Margo Wilson, and Martin Daly. 1992. The Myth of Sexual Symmetry in Marital Violence. *Social Problems* 39:71–91.

Dodge, Mary, and Edith Greene. 1991. Juror and Expert Conceptions of Battered Women. *Violence & Victims* 6:271–282.

Dolon, Ronald, James Hendricks, and M. Steven Meagher. 1986. Police Practices and Attitudes toward Domestic Violence. *Journal of Police Science and Administration* 14:187–192.

Douglas, Kevin S., and Donald G. Dutton. 2001. Assessing the Link between Stalking and Domestic Violence. *Aggression and Violent Behavior* 6: 519–546.

Drake, Virginia K. 1982. Battered Women: A Health Care Problem in Disguise. *Image* 24:40–47.

Dunford, Franklyn W. 1992. The Measurement of Recidivism in Cases of Spouse Assault. *Journal of Criminal Law and Criminology* 83:120–136.

Dunford, Franklyn W., David Huizinga, and Delbert S. Elliott. 1990. The Role of Arrest in Domestic Assault: The Omaha Police Experiment. *Criminology* 28:183–206.

Dutton, Donald G. 1988. *The Domestic Assault of Women.* Boston: Allyn and Bacon.

Dutton, Donald G., and Susan L. Painter. 1981. Traumatic Bonding: The Development of Emotional Attachments in Battered Women and Other Relationships of Intermittent Abuse. *Victimology* 6:139–155.

Dutton, M. A. 1996. Impact of Evidence Concerning Battering and Its Effects in Criminal Trials Involving Battered Women. Section 1 in *The Validity and Use of Evidence Concerning Battering and Its Effects in Criminal Trials.* Washington, DC: DOJ, NIJ, USDHHS, and NIMH. http://www.ncjrs.org/pdffiles/batter.pdf.

Edleson, Jeffrey L., A. C. Eisikovits, E. Guttman, and M. Sela-Amit, 1991. Cognitive and Interpersonal Factors in Woman Abuse. *Journal of Family Violence* 6:167–182.

Edwards, Susan S. M. 1989. *Policing Domestic Violence: Women, the Law and the State.* London: Sage.

Eigenberg, Helen M., K. E. Scarborough, and Victor E. Kappeler. 1996. Contributory Factors Affecting Arrest in Domestic and Non-Domestic Assaults. *American Journal of Police* 15:27–54.

Ellis, Desmond. 1987. Post-Separation Woman Abuse. *International Journal of Sociology of the Family* 19:67–87.

Ellis, Desmond, and Walter D. DeKeseredy. 1989. Marital Status and Woman Abuse. *International Journal of Law and Psychiatry* 10:401–410.

Enarson, Elaine. 1999. Violence against Women in Disasters. *Violence Against Women* 5:742–768.

Eppler, Amy. 1986. Battered Women and the Equal Protection Clause: Will the Constitution Help Them When the Police Won't? *Yale Law Review* 95:788–809.

Erez, Edna. 1986. Intimacy, Violence, and the Police. *Human Relations* 39:265–281.

Erez, Edna, and Joanne Belknap. 1998. In Their Own Words: Battered Women's Assessment of Systemic Responses. *Violence and Victims* 13: 3–20.

Ewing, Charles P. 1987. *Battered Women Who Kill.* Lexington, MA: Lexington Books.

Fagan, Jeffrey A., Douglas K. Stewart, and Karen V. Hansen. 1983. Violent Men or Violent Husbands? Background Factors and Situational Correlates. Pp. 49–68 in *The Dark Side of Families: Current Family Violence Research,* edited by D. Finkelhor, R. J. Gelles, G. T. Hotaling, and M. A. Straus. Beverly Hills, CA: Sage.

Fernandez, Marilyn, Kichi Iwamoto, and Bernadette Muscat. 1997. Dependency and Severity of Abuse. *Women & Criminal Justice* 9:39–63.

Ferraro, Kathleen J. 1989a. The Legal Response to Woman Battering in the United States. Pp. 155–184 in *Women, Policing, and Male Violence,* edited by J. Hanmer, J. Radford, and E. A. Stanko. London: Routledge.

———. 1989b. Policing Woman Battering. *Social Problems* 36:61–74.

———. 1993. Cops, Courts, and Woman Battering. Pp. 165–176 in *Violence against Women: The Bloody Footprints,* edited by P. B. Bart and E. G. Moran. Newbury Park, CA: Sage.

———. 2003. The Words Change, But the Melody Lingers: The Persistence of the Battered Woman Syndrome in Criminal Cases Involving Battered Women. *Violence Against Women* 9:110–129.

Ferraro, Kathleen J., and John M. Johnson. 1983. How Women Experience Battering. *Social Problems* 30: 325–339.

Few, April L., and Patricia Bell-Scott. 2002. Grounding Our Feet and Hearts. Pp. 59–78 in *Violence in the Lives of Black Women*, edited by C. M. West. New York: Haworth Press.

Finesmith, Barbara K. 1983. Police Responses to Battered Women: A Critique and Proposals for Reform. *Seton Hall Law Review* 14:74–109.

Finkelhor, David. 1983. Common Features of Family Abuse. Pp. 17–28 in *The Dark Side of Families: Current Family Violence Research*, edited by D. Finkelhor, R. J. Gelles, G. T. Hotaling, and M. A. Straus. Beverly Hills, CA: Sage.

Finn, Mary A., Brenda Sims Blackwell, Loretta J. Stalans, Sheila Studdard, and Laura Duggan. 2004. Dual Arrest Decisions in Domestic Violence Cases. *Crime & Delinquency* 50: 565–589.

Fischer, Korla, and Mary Rose. 1995. When "Enough is Enough." *Crime and Delinquency* 41:414–429.

Flanakin, Nancy, and Christina Walsh. 2005. Letter to the Editor. *Violence Against Women* 11:822–827.

Fleury, Ruth E., Cris M. Sullivan, and Deborah I. Bybee. 2000. When Ending the Relationship Does Not End the Violence: Women's Experiences of Violence by Former Partners. *Violence Against Women* 6: 1363–1383.

Flynn, Clifton P. 1990. Sex Roles and Women's Response to Courtship Violence. *Journal of Family Violence* 5:83–94.

Flynn, Clifton P. 2000. Woman's Best Friend: Pet Abuse and the Role of Companion Animals in the Lives of Battered Women. *Violence Against Women* 6:162–177.

Flynn, John P. 1977. Recent Findings Related to Wife Abuse. *Social Casework* (January):13–20.

Ford, David A. 1991. Prosecution as a Victim Power Resource: A Note on Empowering Women in Violent Conjugal Relationships. *Law and Society Review* 25:313–334.

———. 2003. Coercing Victim Participation in Domestic Violence Prosecutions. *Journal of Interpersonal Violence* 18:669–684.

Forte, James A., David D. Franks, Janett A. Forte, and Daniel Rigsby. 1996. Asymmetrical Role-Taking: Comparing Battered and Nonbattered Women. *Social Work* 41:59–73.

Fothergill, Alice. 1999. An Exploratory Study of Woman Battering in the Grand Forks Flood Disaster. *International Journal of Mass Emergencies and Disasters* 17:79–98.

Gamache, D. J., J. L. Edleson, and M. D. Schock. 1988. Coordinating Police, Judicial, and Social Service Response to Woman Battering. Pp. 193–209 in *Coping with Family Violence*, edited by G. T. Hotaling, D. Finkelhor, J. T. Kirkpatrick, and M. A. Straus. Beverly Hills, CA: Sage.

Garcia, Crystal A. 2003. Digital Photographic Evidence and the Adjudication of Domestic Violence Cases. *Journal of Criminal Justice* 31:579–587.

Gauthier, DeAnn K., and William B. Bankston. 1997. Gender Equality and the Sex Ratio of Intimate Killing. *Criminology* 35:577–600.

Gee, Pauline W. 1983. Ensuring Police Protection for Battered Women: The Scott v. Hart Suit. *Signs: Journal of Women in Culture and Society* 8:554–567.

Gelles, Richard J. 1976. Abused Wives: Why Do They Stay? *Journal of Marriage and the Family* (November): 659–668.

———. 1980. Violence in the Family: A Review of Research in the Seventies. *Journal of Marriage and the Family* (November):873–885.

Gillespie, Cynthia K. 1989. *Justifiable Homicide: Battered Women, Self-Defense, and the Law.* Columbus: Ohio State University Press.

Giorgio, G. 2002. Speaking Silence: Definitional Dialogues in Abusive Lesbian Relationships. *Violence Against Women* 8:1233–1259.

Glass, Nancy, Jane Koziol-McLain, Jacquelyn Campbell, and Caorlyn Rebecca Block. 2004. Female-Perpetrated Femicide and Attempted Femicide. *Violence Against Women* 10:606–625.

Gondolf, Edward W., with Ellen R. Fisher. 1988. *Battered Women as Survivors.* New York: Lexington Books.

Goode, W. J. 1971. Force and Violence in the Family. *Journal of Marriage and the Family* (November):624–636.

Goodrum, S., D. Umberson, and K. L. Anderson. (2001). The Batterer's View of the Self and Others in Domestic Violence. *Sociological Inquiry* 71(2):221–240.

Goolkasian, Gail A. 1986. *Confronting Domestic Violence: The Role of Criminal Court Judges.* National Institute in Justice/ Research in Brief (November): 1–8.

Gorshick, Lori B. 2002. *Woman-to-Woman Sexual Violence.* Boston: Northeastern University Press.

Grau, Janice, Jeffrey Fagan, and Sandra Wexler. 1985. Restraining Orders for Battered Women: Issues of Access and Efficacy. Pp. 13–20 in *Criminal Justice Politics and Women: The Aftermath of Legally Mandated Change,* edited by C. Schweber and C. Feinman. New York: Haworth Press.

Greenblat, Cathy S. 1983. A Hit Is a Hit Is a Hit . . . Or Is It? Pp. 235–260 in *The Dark Side of Families: Current Family Violence Research,* edited by D. Finkelhor, R. J. Gelles, G. T. Hotaling, and M. A. Straus. Beverly Hills, CA: Sage.

Greenfeld, Lawrence A., and Tracy L. Snell. 1999. *Women Offenders.* Bureau of Justice Statistics: Special Report. U.S. Department of Justice, December, 14pp.

Haj-Yahia, Muhammad M. 1998. Beliefs about Wife Beating among Palestinian Women. *Violence Against Women* 4:533–558.

Hamberger, L. Kevin., and C. E. Guse. 2002. Men's and Women's Use of Intimate Partner Violence in Clinical Samples. *Violence Against Women* 8:1301–1331.

Hamberger, L. Kevin, Jeffrey M. Lohr, Dennis Bonge, and David F. Tolin. 1997. An Empirical Classification of Motivations for Domestic Violence. *Violence Against Women* 3:401–423.

Hanmer, Jalna, Jill Radford, and Elizabeth A. Stanko. 1989. Policing, Men's Violence: An Introduction. Pp. 1–12 in *Women, Policing, and Male Violence: International Perspectives,* edited by J. Hanmer, J. Radford, and E. A. Stanko. London: Routledge and Kegan Paul.

Hardesty, Jennifer L. 2002. Separation Assault in the Context of Postdivorce Parenting. *Violence Against Women* 8:597–625.

Hart, Barbara. 1993. Battered Women and the Criminal Justice System. *American Behavioral Scientist* 36: 624–638.

Hartman, Jennifer L., and Joanne Belknap. 2003. Beyond the Gatekeepers: Court Professionals' Self-Reported Attitudes about and Experiences with Misdemeanor Domestic Violence Cases. *Criminal Justice & Behavior* 30:349–373.

Hatty, Suzanne E. 1989. Policing Male Violence in Australia. Pp. 70–89 in *Women, Policing, and Male Violence,* edited by J. Hanmer, J. Radford, and E. A. Stanko. London: Routledge.

Heckert, D. A., and E. W. Gondolf. 2000. Predictors of Underreporting of Male Violence by Batterer Program Participants and Their Partners. *Journal of Family Violence* 15(4):423–443.

Herbert, Tracy B., Roxane C. Silver, and John H. Ellard. 1991. Coping with an Abusive Relationship: How and Why Do Women Stay? *Journal of Marriage and the Family* 53:311–325.

Hirschel, David, and Eve Buzawa. 2002. Understanding the Context of Dual Arrest with Directions for Future Research. *Violence Against Women* 8:1449–1473.

Hirschel, J. David, and Ira W. Hutchison III. 1992. Female Spouse Abuse and the Police Response: The Charlotte, North Carolina, Experiment. *Journal of Criminal Law and Criminology* 83:73–119.

———. 2001. The Relative Effects of Offense, Offender, and Victim Variables on the Decision to Prosecute Domestic Violence Cases. *Violence Against Women* 7:46–59.

———. 2003. The Voices of Domestic Violence Victims. *Crime & Delinquency* 49:313–336.

Hirschel, J. David, Ira W. Hutchison III, and Charles W. Dean. 1991. The Charlotte Spouse Abuse Study. *Popular Government* (Summer):11–16.

———. 1992. The Failure of Arrest to Deter Spouse Abuse. *Journal of Research in Crime and Delinquency* 29:7–33.

Hoff, Lee Ann. 1990. *Battered Women as Survivors*. London: Routledge and Kegan Paul.

Holtzworth-Munroe, Amy, Natalie Smutzler, and Leonard Bates. 1997. A Brief Review of the Research on Husband Violence. Part III. *Aggression and Violent Behavior* 2: 285–307.

Jaffe, Peter G., David A. Wolfe, Anne Telford, and Gary Austin. 1986. The Impact of Police Charges in Incidents of Wife Abuse. *Journal of Family Violence* 1:37–49.

Jaffe, Peter G., David A. Wolfe, and Susan Kaye Wilson. 1990. *Children of Battered Women*. Newbury Park, CA: Sage.

Johnson, Holly. 1995. Risk Factors Associated with Non-Lethal Violence against Women by Marital Partners. Pp. 151–168 in *Trends, Risks, and Interventions in Lethal Violence*. National Institute of Justice: Research Report.

Johnson, Holly, and Valerie Pottie Bunge. 2001. Prevalence and Consequences of Spousal Assault in Canada. *Canadian Journal of Criminology* 43:27–45.

Jolin, Annette. 1983. Domestic Violence Legislation: An Impact Assessment. *Journal of Police Science and Administration* 11:451–456.

Jones, Ann. 1994. *Next Time, She'll Be Dead: Battering and How to Stop It.* Boston: Beacon Press.

Jones, Dana A., and Joanne Belknap. 1999. Police Responses to Battering in a Pro-Arrest Jurisdiction. *Justice Quarterly* 16:249–273.

Kantor, Glenda K., and Murray A. Straus. 1987. The "Drunken Bum" Theory of Wife Beating. *Social Problems* 3:213–230.

Kanuha, V. 1996. Domestic Violence, Racism, and the Battered Women's Movement in the United States. Pp. 34–50 in *Future Interventions with Battered Women and their Families*, edited by J. Edleson and Z. Eisikovits. Thousand Oaks, CA: Sage.

Kaplan, A. 1997. Domestic Violence and Welfare Reform. *Welfare Information Network: Issue Notes* 1:1–9.

Kemp, Anita, Bonnie L. Green, Christine Hovanitz, and Edna I. Rawlings. 1995. Incidence and Correlates of Postraumatic Stress Disorder in

Battered Women. *Journal of Interpersonal Violence* 10:43–55.

Kernic, Mary A., Daphne J. Monary-Ernsdorff, Jennifer K. Koepsell, and Victoria L. Holt. 2005. Children in the Crossfire: Child Custody Determinations among Couples with a History of Intimate Partner Violence. *Violence Against Women* 11:991–1021.

Klein, Dorie. 1981. Violence against Women: Some Considerations Regarding Its Causes and Its Elimination. *Crime and Delinquency* 27:64–80.

Knutson, J. F., and J. G. Mehm. 1986. Transgenerational Patterns of Coercion in Families and Intimate Relationships. Pp. 67–90 in *Violence in Intimate Relationships*, edited by G. Russell. New York: PMA Publishing Corporation.

Kurz, Demie. 1987. Emergency Department Responses to Battered Women: Resistance to Medicalization. *Social Problems* 34:69–81.

———. 1993. Social Science Perspectives on Wife Abuse: Current Debates and Future Directions. Pp. 252–269 in *Violence against Women*, edited by P. B. Bart and E. G. Moran. Newbury Park, CA: Sage.

———. 1996. Separation, Divorce, and Woman Abuse. *Violence Against Women* 2:63–81.

Kurz, Demie, and Evan Stark. 1988. Not-So-Benign Neglect: The Medical Response to Battering. Pp. 249–268 in *Feminist Perspectives on Wife Abuse*, edited by K. Yllo and M. Bograd. Newbury Park, CA: Sage.

Lane, K. E., and P. A. Gwartney-Gibbs. 1985. Violence in the Context of Dating and Sex. *Journal of Family Issues* 6:45–59.

Langan, Patrick A., and Christopher A. Innes. 1986. *Preventing Domestic Violence against Women*. Bureau of Justice Statistics Special Report, August.

Langhinrichsen-Rohling, J., R. E. Palarea, J. Cohen, and M. L. Rohling. 2000. Breaking Up Is Hard to Do: Unwanted Pursuit Behaviors Following the Dissolution of a Romantic Relationship. *Violence and Victims* 15:73–90.

Lawrenz, Frances, James F. Lembo, and Thomas Schade. 1988. Time Series Analysis of the Effect of a Domestic Violence Directive on the Number of Arrests per Day. *Journal of Criminal Justice* 16:493–498.

Levendosky, Alytia A., Shannon M. Lynch, and Sandra A. Graham-Bermann. 2000. Mothers' Perceptions of the Impact of Woman Abuse on Their Parenting. *Violence Against Women* 6:247–271.

Lloyd, Susan, and Nina Taluc. 1999. The Effects of Male Violence on Female Employment. *Violence Against Women* 5:370–392.

Logan T. K., Lisa Shannon, and Robert Walker. 2005. Protective Orders in Rural and Urban Areas: A Multiple Perspective Study. *Violence Against Women* 11:876–911.

Loseke, Donileen R., and Spencer E. Cahill. 1984. The Social Construction of Deviance: Experts on Battered Women. *Social Problems* 31:296–309.

Loving, N. 1980. *Responding to Spouse Abuse and Wife Beating: A Guide for Police*. Washington, DC: Police Executive Research Forum.

Lyon, Andrea D., Emily Hughes, and Juanita Thomas. 2001. The People v. Juanita Thomas: A Battered Woman's Journey to Freedom. *Women & Criminal Justice* 13:27–63.

Mahoney, Martha. 1991. Legal Images of Battered Women: Redefining the Issue of Separation. *Michigan Law Review* 90:2–94.

Makepeace, J. M. 1981. Courtship Violence among College Students. *Family Relations* 30:97–102.

————. 1986. Gender Differences in Courtship Violence Victimization. *Family Relations* 35:383–388.

Manning, Peter K. 1992. Screening Calls. Pp. 41–48 in *Domestic Violence: The Changing Criminal Justice Response*, edited by Eve S. Buzawa and Carl G. Buzawa. Westport, CT: Auburn House.

Marcus, M. L. 1981. Conjugal Violence: The Law of Force and the Force of the Law. *California Law Review* 69:1657–1733.

Martin, Del. 1976. *Battered Wives*. San Francisco: Glide.

Martin, Margaret E. 1997. Double Your Trouble: Dual Arrest in Family Violence. *Journal of Family Violence* 12:139–157.

Matthews, William J. 1984. Violence in College Couples. *College Student Journal* 18:150–158.

Maxwell, C. D., J. H. Garner, and J. A. Fagan. 2001. *The Effects of Arrest on Intimate Partner Violence: New Evidence from the Spouse Assault Replication Program*. Washington, DC: Department of Justice.

McCann, Kathryn. 1985. Battered Women and the Law: The Limits of Legislation. Pp. 71–96 in *Women-in-Law: Exploration in Law, Family and Sexuality*, edited by J. Brophy and C. Smart. London: Routledge and Kegan Paul.

McDermott, M. Joan, and James Garofalo. 2004. When Advocacy for Domestic Violence Victims Backfires: Types and Sources of Victim Disempowerment. *Violence Against Women* 10:1245–1266.

Meloy, J. Reid. 1996. Stalking (Obsessional Following): A Review of Some Preliminary Studies. *Aggression and Violent Behavior* 1:147–162.

Melton, Heather C. 2004. Stalking in the Context of Domestic Violence. *Women & Criminal Justice* 15:33–58.

Melton, Heather C., and Joanne Belknap. 2003. He Hits, She Hits: Assessing Gender Differences and Similarities in Officially Reported Intimate Partner Violence. *Criminal Justice and Behavior* 30(3):328–348.

Meyer, Shannon-Lee, Dina Vivian, and K. Daneil O'Leary. 1998. Men's Sexual Aggression in Marriage. *Violence Against Women* 4:415–435.

Miller, Susan L. 1989. Unintended Side Effects of Pro-Arrest Policies and Their Race and Class Implications for Battered Women: A Cautionary Note. *Criminal Justice Policy Review* 3:299–317.

————. 2001. The Paradox of Women Arrested for Domestic Violence. *Violence Against Women* 7:1339–1376.

————. 2005. *Victims as Offenders: The Paradox of Women's Violence in Relationships*. New Brunswick, NJ: Rutgers University Press.

Miller, Susan L., and Sally S. Simpson. 1991. Courtship Violence and Social Control: Does Gender Matter? *Law and Society Review* 25:335–365.

Mills, Billy G., and Mary L. McNamar. 1981. California's Response to Domestic Violence. *Santa Clara Law Review* 21:1–19.

Mills, Linda G. 1999. Killing Her Softly: Intimate Abuse and the Violence of State Intervention. *Harvard Law Review* 113:550–613.

————. 2003. *Insult to Injury: Rethinking Our Responses to Intimate Abuse*. Princeton, NJ: Princeton University Press.

Mills, Trudy. 1984. Victimization and Self-Esteem: On Equating Husband Abuse and Wife Abuse. *Victimology* 9:254–261.

Molidor, Christian, and Richard M. Tolman. 1998. Gender and Contextual Factors in Adolescent Dating Violence. *Violence Against Women* 4:180–194.

Morse, B. J. 1995. Beyond the Conflict Tactics Scale: Assessing Gender Differences in Partner Violence. *Violence and Victims* 10(4):251–272.

Mrsevic, Zorica, and Donna M. Hughes. 1997. Violence against Women in Belgrade, Serbia. *Violence Against Women* 3:101–128.

Mustaine, Elizabeth, and Richard Tewksbury. 1999. A Routine Activity Theory Explanation for Women's Stalking. *Violence Against Women* 5:43–62.

Neidig, Peter H., Harold E. Russell, and Albert F. Seng. 1992. Interpersonal Aggression in Law Enforcement Families. *Police Studies* 15:30–38.

O'Keefe, Maura. 1997. Incarcerated Battered Women. *Journal of Family Violence* 12:1–19.

O'Keefe, Maura, and Laura Treister. 1998. Victims of Dating Violence among High School Students. *Violence Against Women* 4:195–223.

Olson, David E., and Loretta J. Stalans. 2001. Violent Offenders on Probation: Profile, Sentence, and Outcome Differences among Domestic Violence and Other Violent Probationers. *Violence Against Women* 7:1164–1185.

O'Neill, Damian. 1998. A Post-Structuralist Review of the Theoretical Literature Surrounding Wife Abuse. *Violence Against Women* 4:457–490.

Oppenlander, Nan. 1982. Coping or Copping Out. *Criminology* 20: 449–465.

Pagelow, Mildred D. 1981. *Woman-Battering.* Beverly Hills: Sage.

———. 1993. Justice for Victims of Spouse Abuse in Divorce and Child Custody Cases. *Violence and Victims* 8:69–83.

Parker, Linda S. 1997. A "Brutal Case" or (Only a Family Jar)?: Violence against Women in San Diego County,

1880–1900. *Violence Against Women* 3:294–318.

Pate, Antony M., and Edwin E. Hamilton. 1992. Formal and Informal Deterrents to Domestic Violence: The Dade County Spouse Assault Experiment. *American Sociological Review* 57:691–697.

Paternoster, Raymond, and Ronet Bachman. 1997. Do Fair Procedures Matter? *Law & Society Review* 31: 163–204.

Pearson, Jessica, Nancy Thoennes, and Esther Ann Girswold. 1999. Child Support and Domestic Violence. *Violence Against Women* 5:427–448.

Perilla, J. L., K. Frndak, D. Lillard, and C. East. 2003. A Working Analysis of Women's Use of Violence in the Context of Learning, Opportunity, and Choice. *Violence Against Women* 9:10–46.

Piispa, Minna. 2002. Complexity of Patterns of Violence against Women in Heterosexual Partnerships. *Violence Against Women* 8:873–900.

Pirog-Good, Maureen A., and Jan E. Stets. 1989. The Help-Seeking Behavior of Physically and Sexually Abused College Students. Pp. 108–125 in *Violence And Dating Relationships,* edited by Maureen A. Pirog-Good and Jan E. Stets. New York: Praeger.

Pizzey, Erin. 1974. *Scream Quietly or the Neighbors Will Hear.* Middlesex, England: Penguin.

Pleck, Elizabeth. 1983. Feminist Responses to "Crimes against Women," 1868–1896. *Signs: Journal of Women Culture and Society* 8:451–470.

———. 1989. Criminal Approaches to Family Violence, 1640–1980. Pp. 19–58 in *Family Violence,* edited by L. Ohlin and M. Tonry. Chicago: University of Chicago Press.

Potoczniak, M. J., J. E. Mourot, M. Crosbie-Burnett, and D. J. Potoczniak. 2003. Legal and Psychological Perspectives on Same-Sex Domestic Violence: A Multisystemic Approach. *Journal of Family Psychology* 17:252–259.

Ptacek, James. 1988. Why Do Men Batter Their Wives? Pp. 133–75 in *Feminist Perspectives on Wife Abuse*, edited by K. Yllo and M. Bograd. Newbury Park, CA: Sage.

———. 1999. *Battered Women in the Courtroom*. Boston: Northeastern University Press.

Quarm, Daisy, and Martin D. Schwartz. 1985. Domestic Violence in Criminal Court: An Examination of New Legislation in Ohio. Pp. 29–46 in *Criminal Justice Politics and Women: The Aftermath of Legally Mandated Change*, edited by C. Schweber and C. Feinman. New York: Haworth Press.

Rennison, Callie Marie, and Sarah Welchans. 2000. *Intimate Partner Violence*. Bureau of Justice Statistics. Department of Justice. Special Report, May, 11pp.

Renzetti, Claire M. 1992. Violent Betrayal: Partner Abuse in Lesbian Relationships. Newbury Park, CA: Sage.

Rigakos, George S. 1997. Situational Determinants of Police Responses to Civil and Criminal Injunctions for Battered Women. *Violence Against Women* 3:204–216.

Robbins, Kalyani. 1999. No-Drop Prosecution of Domestic Violence. *Stanford Law Review* 52:205–233.

Roberts, Karl A. 2002. Stalking Following the Break-up of Romantic Relationships: Characteristics of Stalking Former Partners. *Journal of Forensic Sciences* 47:1070–1078.

———. 2005. Women's Experience of Violence during Stalking by Former Romantic Partners: Factors Predictive of Stalking Violence. *Violence Against Women* 11:89–114.

Robinson, Amanda L., and Meghan S. Chandek. 2000. Differential Police Response to Black Battered Women. *Women & Criminal Justice* 12:29–62.

Robinson, Amorie. 2002. There's a Stranger in This House. Pp. 125–132 in *Violence in the Lives of Black Women*, edited by C.M. West. New York: Haworth Press.

Rosen, Leora N., and Chris S. O'Sullivan. 2005. Outcomes of Custody and Visitation Petitions When Fathers Are Restrained by Protection Orders: The Case of the New York Family Courts. *Violence Against Women* 11:1054–1075.

Rosewater, Lynne B. 1988. Battered or Schizophrenic? Psychological Tests Can't Tell. Pp. 200–216 in *Feminist Perspectives on Wife Abuse*, edited by K. Yllo and M. Bograd. Newbury Park, CA: Sage.

Rowe, Kelly. 1985. The Limits of the Neighborhood Justice Center: Why Domestic Violence Cases Should Not Be Mediated. *Emory Law Journal* 34:855–910.

Russo, A. 2003. Intimate Betrayal: Domestic Violence in Lesbian Relationships. *Psychology of Women Quarterly* 27:86–88.

Schechter, Susan. 1982. *Women and Male Violence: The Visions and Struggles of the Battered Women's Movement*. Boston: South End Press.

Schwartz, Martin D. 1987. Gender and Injury in Spousal Assault. *Sociological Focus* 20:61–75.

Schwartz, Martin D., and Walter S. DeKeseredy. 1997. *Sexual Assault on the College Campus*. Thousand Oaks, CA: Sage.

Sebastian, Richard J. 1983. Social Psychological Determinants. Pp. 182–191 in *The Dark Side of*

Families: Current Family Violence Research, edited by D. Finkelhor, R. J. Gelles, G. T. Hotaling, and M. A. Straus. Beverly Hills, CA: Sage.

Sev'er, Aysan. 1997. Recent or Imminent Separation and Intimate Violence against Women. *Violence Against Women* 3:566–589.

Sheehy, Lisa, Melissa Reinberg, and Deborah Krichway. 1991. *Commutation for Women Who Defended Themselves against Abusive Partners: An Advocacy Manual and Guide to Legal Issues*. Philidelphia: National Clearinghouse for the Defense of Battered Women.

Sherman, Lawrence W., and Richard A. Berk. 1984. The Specific Deterrent Effects of Arrest for Domestic Assault. *American Sociological Review* 49:261–272.

Sherman, Lawrence W., Janell D. Schmidt, Dennis P. Rogan, Douglas A. Smith, Patrick R. Gartin, Ellen G. Cohn, Dean J. Collins, and Anthony R. Bacich. 1992. The Variable Effects of Arrest on Criminal Careers: The Milwaukee Domestic Violence Experiment. *Journal of Criminal Law and Criminology* 83:137–169.

Silva, J. A., D. V. Derecho, G. B. Leong, and M. M. Ferrari. 2000. Stalking Behavior in Delusional Jealousy. *Journal of Forensic Sciences* 45:77–82.

Silverman, Jay G., Anita Raj, Lorelei A. Mucci, and Jeanne E. Hathaway. 2001. Dating Violence against Adolescent Girls and Associated Substance Use, Unhealthy Weight Control, Sexual Risk Behavior, Pregnancy, and Suicidality. *Journal of the American Medical Association* 286:572–579.

Slote, Kim, and Carrie Cuthbert. 1997. Women's Rights Network (WRN). *Violence Against Women* 3:76–80.

Smith, Douglas A., and Jody R. Klein. 1984. Police Control of Inter-personal Disputes. *Social Problems* 31:469–481.

Smith, Michael D. 1994. Enhancing the Quality of Survey Data on Violence against Women. *Gender & Society* 8:109–127.

Sorenson, Susan B., and Haikang Shen. 2005. Restraining Orders in California: A Look at Statewide Data. *Violence Against Women* 11:912–933.

Stanko, Elizabeth A. 1985. *Intimate Intrusions*. London: Routledge and Kegan Paul.

————. 1989. Missing the Mark? Policing Battering. Pp. 46–69 in *Women, Policing, and Male Violence: International Perspectives*, edited by J. Hanmer, J. Radford, and E. A. Stanko. London: Routledge and Kegan Paul.

Star, B., C. G. Clark, K. M. Goetz, and L. O'Malia. 1979. Psychological Aspects of Wife Battering. *Social Casework: The Journal of Contemporary Social Work* (October):479–487.

Stark, Evan. 1992. Framing and Reframing Battered Women. Pp. 271–292 in *Domestic Violence: The Changing Criminal Justice Response*, edited by Eve S. Buzawa and Carl G. Buzawa. Westport, CT: Auburn House.

————. 2003. Race, Gender and Woman Battering. Pp. 171–197 in *Violent Crime: Assessing Race and Ethnic Differences*, edited by D. Hawkins. New York: Cambridge University Press.

————. 2004. Insults, Injury, and Injustice: Rethinking State Intervention in Domestic Violence Cases. *Violence Against Women* 10:1302–1330.

Stark, Evan, and Anne Flitcraft. 1983. Social Knowledge, Social Policy, and the Abuse of Women: The Case against Patriarchal Benevolence. Pp. 330–348 in *The Dark Side of Families: Current Family Violence Research*, edited by D. Finkelhor,

R. J. Gelles, G. T. Hotaling, and M. A. Straus. Beverly Hills, CA: Sage.

———. 1996. *Women at Risk: Domestic Violence and Women's Health.* Thousand Oaks, CA: Sage.

Steinmetz, Suzanne. 1977/1978. The Battered Husband Syndrome. *Victimology* 2:499–509.

Stets, Jan E., and Maureen A. Pirog-Good. 1987. Violence in Dating Relationships. *Social Psychology Quarterly* 50:237–246.

Stets, Jan E., and Murray A. Straus. 1990. Gender Differences in Reporting Marital Violence and Its Medical and Psychological Consequences. Pp. 151–165 in *Physical Violence in American Families*, edited by M. A. Straus and R. J. Gelles. New Brunswick, NJ: Transaction Press.

Stith, Sandra M. 1990. Police Response to Domestic Violence. *Violence and Victims* 5:37–49.

Straus, Murray A. 1990. *Physical Violence in American Families.* New Brunswick, NJ: Transaction Publishers.

———. 1991. Physical Violence in American Families. Pp. 17–34 in *Abused and Battered*, edited by D. D. Knudsen and J. L. Miller. New York: Aldine De Gruyter.

Straus, Murray A., and Richard J. Gelles. 1986. Societal Change and Change in Family Violence from 1975 to 1985 as Revealed by Two Surveys. *Journal of Marriage and the Family* 48:465–479.

Straus, Murray A., Richard J. Gelles, and Suzanne Steinmetz. 1980. *Behind Closed Doors: Violence in the American Family.* New York: Anchor Books.

Strube, M. J., and L. S. Barbour. 1984. Factors Related to the Decision to Leave an Abusive Relationship. *Journal of Marriage and the Family* (November): 837–844.

Taylor, Janette Y. 2002. The Straw That Broke the Camel's Back. Pp. 79–94

in *Violence in the Lives of Black Women*, edited by C. M. West. New York: Haworth Press.

Tierney, Kathleen J. 1983. The Battered Women Movement and the Creation of the Wife Beating Problem. *Social Problems* 29:207–220.

Thompson, Martie P., Linda E. Saltzman, and Holly Johnson. 2003. A Comparison of Risk Factors for Intimate Partner Violence-Related Injury across Two National Surveys on Violence against Women. *Violence Against Women* 9:438–457.

Tjaden, Patricia, and Nancy Thoennes. 1998a. *Prevalence, Incidence, and Consequences of Violence against Women.* U.S. Department of Justice. Research in Brief. November, 16pp.

———. 1998b. *Stalking in America.* U.S. Department of Justice. Research in Brief. April, 20pp.

———. 2000. Prevalence and Consequences of Male-to-Female and Female-to-Male Partner Violence as Measured by the National Violence against Women Survey. *Violence Against Women* 6:142–161.

Tong, Rosemarie. 1984. *Women, Sex, and the Law.* Totowa, NJ: Rowman and Allanheld.

Ventura, Lois A., and Gabrielle Davis. 2005. Domestic Violence: Court Case Conviction and Recidivism. *Violence Against Women* 11:255–277.

Walker, Lenore E. 1979. *The Battered Woman.* New York: Harper and Row.

———. 1983a. The Battered Woman Syndrome Study. Pp. 31–49 in *The Dark Side of Families: Current Family Violence Research*, edited by D. Finkelhor, R. J. Gelles, G. T. Hotaling, and M. A. Straus. Beverly Hills, CA: Sage.

———. 1983b. Victimology and the Psychological Perspectives of

Battered Women. *Victimology* 1–2:82–104.

———. 1989. *Terrifying Love: Why Battered Women Kill and How Society Responds.* New York: HarperPerennial.

Wardell, Laurie, Dair L. Gillespie, and Ann Leffler. 1983. Science and Violence against Wives, Pp. 69–84 in *The Dark Side of Families: Current Family Violence Research*, edited by D. Finkelhor, R. J. Gelles, G. T. Hotaling, and M. A. Straus. Beverly Hills, CA: Sage.

Warshaw, Carole. 1993. Limitations of the Medical Model in the Care of Battered Women. Pp. 134–146 in *Violence against Women: The Bloody Footprints*, edited by P. B. Bart and E. G. Moran. Newbury Park, CA: Sage.

Websdale, N. 1995. Rural Woman Abuse: The Voices of Kentucky Women. *Violence Against Women* 1:309–388.

Websdale, N., and B. Johnson. 1997. The Policing of Domestic Violence in Rural and Urban Areas: The Voices of Battered Women. *Policing and Society* 6:297–317.

West, Carolyn M., and Suzanna Rose. 2000. Dating Aggression among Low-Income African American Youth: An Examination of Gender Differences and Antagonistic Beliefs. *Violence Against Women* 6:470–494.

Wiist, William H., and Judith McFarlane. 1998. Utilization of Police by Abused Pregnant Hispanic Women. *Violence Against Women* 4:677–693.

Wilson, Margo, and Martin Daly. 1993. Spousal Homicide Risk and Estrangement. *Violence and Victims* 8:3–15.

Worden, Robert E., and Alissa A. Pollitz. 1984. Police Arrests in Domestic Disturbances: A Further Look. *Law and Society Review* 18:105–119.

Yllo, Kersti. 1983. Using a Feminist Approach in Quantitative Research: A Case Study. Pp. 277–288 in *The Dark Side of Families: Current Family Violence Research*, edited by D. Finkelhor, R. J. Gelles, G. T. Hotaling, and M. A. Straus. Beverly Hills, CA: Sage.

———. 1988. Political and Methodological Debates in Wife Abuse Research. Pp. 28–50 in *Feminist Perspectives on Wife Abuse*, edited by K. Yllo and M. Bograd. Newbury Park, CA: Sage.

———. 1999. Domestic Violence against Women of Japanese Descent in Los Angeles. *Violence Against Women* 5:869–897.

Yoshihama, Mieko. 1999. Domestic Violence against Women of Japanese Descent in Los Angeles: Two Methods of Estimating Prevalence. *Violence Against Women* 5:869–897.

Zoomer, Olga J. 1989. Policing Battered Women in the Netherlands. Pp. 125–154 in *Women, Policing, and Male Violence*, edited by J. Hanmer, J. Redford, and E. A. Stanko. London: Routledge.

Zorza, Joan. 1992. The Criminal Law of Misdemeanor Domestic Violence, 1970–1990. *Journal of Criminal Law and Criminology* 83:46–72.

9

❖

Women Working in Prisons and Jails

> While there have always been women criminals and women victims,
> until a quarter-century ago, there was a paucity of women working in
> criminal justice occupations.
>
> BRITTON, 2000, 69

Part IV of this book examines women working in the criminal legal system. Restriction of women's employment is usually most extreme in women's entrance into what have traditionally been considered "men's" jobs, and there are few jobs more associated with masculinity than jobs poised to control offenders. Positions as prison guards, police officers, lawyers, judges, and even jury members have historically, and sometimes currently, been considered primarily "men's" jobs. Throughout the next three chapters, it is worth taking time to stop and think, "What difference could it have made to exclude women from these decision-making jobs in our justice system?" How did restricting these jobs not only affect women who wanted to work them but how did male-only decision-makers at the court, arrest, and prison levels also affect the handing down of justice? How does male-dominance in these professions today affect justice?

In Chapter 5 I avoided the word *corrections* to discuss the jail and prison system, given that there is little evidence that the system emphasizes treatment to correct behavior and rehabilitate prisoners. Similarly, the term *correctional officer* is not used in this book to describe persons working with prisoners (consistent with Zimmer [1986]). Given that U.S. prisons and jails do not train their employees in rehabilitation, nor do they hire significant numbers of employees with rehabilitative expertise, it seems inappropriate to call such workers "correctional officers." Therefore, the terms *prison and jail workers, prison officers*, and *guards* are used in place of the term *correctional officers* in this book.

This chapter, the first of three on women working in the criminal legal system, begins with an overview of societal and legal expectations concerning women's access to and need for paid work in the labor force. Although the steps involved do not apply just to women working in the criminal legal system, it is useful to have an understanding of the reluctance to admit women as equals into the paid labor force both societally and legally, and how this has had unique and more far reaching negative effects on women of color (due to the additional race discrimination they face) and poorer White women who are more dependent on these jobs. Thus, the roles of classism and/or racism combined with sexism hold profound potential for discriminating against women aspiring to work in the criminal legal system.

A BRIEF HISTORY ON SEX DISCRIMINATION IN WOMEN'S WORK OUTSIDE THE HOME

Before discussing women breaking into work in the criminal legal system, it is necessary to understand a history fraught with devaluing the role of women's work in the home (particularly raising children) and how women's expected roles as wives and mothers, as well as being considered "the weaker sex," have been used to discriminate against women in the paid work force (except as low-paid servants consistent with race, class, and gender roles). Various excuses have been given to restrict women from job opportunities and equality in general. These excuses often fall under the rubric of protection—protecting women "for their own good." Such a paternalistic attitude may "protect" women from certain physically grueling and dangerous jobs, but it often excludes women from many occupations and limits their ability to earn high wages and pursue career dreams. It was not until the 1970s, as a result of the second wave of the women's movement, that the U.S. Supreme Court agenda included sex discrimination cases. It has been stated that the legal status of U.S. women changed more during the 1970s and 1980s than in the two centuries preceding the 1970s (Hoff, 1991, 229).

Atkins and Hoggett (1984) discuss three ways the legal system has attempted to justify limiting women's job opportunities. First is a belief in women's *"natural" inferiority*. This view suggests that women are too emotionally, intellectually, and physically weak to endure certain jobs, most of which are outside the home and often relatively lucrative. *Maternity* is Atkins and Hoggett's (ibid.) second justification used to restrict women's work. This excuse was first posed in the 1847 House of Commons Factory Bill in England. The bill claimed that there was a danger to young infants whose mothers were working outside the home. If we combine the supposed inherent "weakness" of women with the idea that women are destined to stay home (because infants' well-being is supposedly dependent on their mothers not leaving the house), a bleak picture for women confronts us—women are trapped into staying home because society depends on them to do so. Until the mid-1970s, pregnant women workers were routinely "dismissed" (fired) and frequently were denied requests for reinstatement after giving birth. Additionally, most state unemployment and insurance programs excluded pregnant women (Rhode, 1989). *Marriage* is Atkins and Hoggett's (1984, 18) third and final justification used to limit women's employment opportunities. This justification assumes that all women (should) marry and that the man's job should be in the public sphere and the woman should remain in the private sphere (the home). William Blackstone's eighteenth-century legal treatise on wives was based on the Bible, where husband and wife were regarded as "one person in the law," where "the 'one' was the husband" (Rhode, 1989, 10). At the beginning of the nineteenth century in England, single women had more legal abilities than married women did, especially regarding property ownership (Fergus, 1988). Similarly, in the United States, regardless of marital status, all women were barred from many professions and trades. However, married women fared much worse than unmarried women because they were viewed as their husbands' property (Kirp, Yudof, and Franks, 1986, 31). In fact, most nineteenth- and early twentieth-century women had to choose between marriage and employment in the paid labor force, which is probably why as late as 1920, four in five women in the paid work force were unmarried (Rhode, 1989, 13).

There is a history of viewing women pursuing work outside the home (whether they have to in order to support their families financially or they want to have careers) as dismantling a healthy society. As noted in Chapter 2, there are still efforts to claim that women's equality in the labor force will have a negative impact on society as a whole, including efforts by some criminologists claiming women's work outside the home is related to juvenile delinquency (of their children), although research establishes no such connection (Vander Ven, 2003). Even if a woman's family could survive on income from her spouse, it is unfair to suggest that women carry the burden of society falling apart simply because they pursue a career outside of the home. This implies that careers are only, or are more important, for men. Given the high rates of female, single-head-of-household families, this argument is outdated as well as unfair.

The belief that women should marry and raise children and let men have careers results in obvious discrimination against women. If men can be married (and have children) and have careers, why can't women? Furthermore, the number of dependents should not be a criterion in assigning jobs. Even if the number of dependents were a legitimate criterion, there is a need to acknowledge the vast and growing number of single-parent mothers. Also, male workers vary by need and number of dependents. It is highly doubtful that males would want jobs assigned on the basis of the number of dependents.

U.S. Census Bureau data indicate that the female-to-male median earnings ratio of full-time, year-round workers 15 years old and older improved from about 61:100 in 1959 to about 76:100 in 2004 (U.S. Census Bureau, 2005; Fronczek, 2005). (This ratio indicates women make between 61 and 76 cents on the dollar that men make.) Thus, although the wage gap between women and men has closed some in the last five decades, there is still room for improvement in women's pay. Also, recent research examining a number of fields documents women's wages as significantly lower than comparable men's in current times in the professions of lawyers, professors, physicians, and social workers (Gibelman, 2003).

RATES OF WOMEN WORKING IN PRISONS AND JAILS

In the 1996 edition of this book, I reported that women constituted 11.5 percent of prison guards (U.S. Federal Bureau of Prisons, 1993). The 1996 data from the U.S. Bureau of Justice Statistics indicates that of the custodial and security staff in U.S. prisons, women constitute 19 percent of the staff in both state and federal institutions, 14 percent of the staff in federal institutions, and 24 percent of the staff in state institutions (U.S. Bureau of Justice Statistics, 1997, 87). In April 2000, 27.4 percent ($n = 8,573$) of the U.S. prison staff were women (U.S. Federal Bureau of Prisons, 2000). In 2003, 28.3 percent ($n = 9,663$) of U.S. prison staff were women (U.S. Bureau of Justice Statistics, 2005). In October 2005, 27.6 percent ($n = 9,504$) of prison staff were women (U.S. Federal Bureau of Prisons, 2005). Thus, since the mid-1990s women's representation as prison staff increased from about one in ten to over one in four today. The representation of women guards in jails is even higher. In 2003, women constituted 34.0 percent of guards in government-run jails and 40.8 percent of guards in privately operated jails (U.S. Bureau of Justice Statistics, 2005, Tables 1.100 and Tables 1.105, respectively).

Unfortunately, these reports do not distinguish by rank or race of the staff at the institution in terms of their gender/sex. Thus, it is impossible to determine the racial/ethnic breakdown of women working in prisons and jails. Nor do these national statistics distinguish between males' and females' prisons regarding the representation of women staff. This is important because other research indicates that women tend to constitute the highest percentage of staff in women's prisons (about half in one study of a Western state) and the lowest percentage in men's maximum security prisons (about 10 percent in the same state) (Hemmens et al., 2002).

COMPARING RACIAL AND GENDER WORKPLACE DISCRIMINATION

Comparisons and analogies are frequently made between political activism to promote racial equality and political activism to promote gender equality. Some people resist comparing gender to racial oppression, believing that because women do not constitute a minority in the population, they should not require special legislative appeals used by African Americans and other people of color. Nonetheless, women are a disadvantaged group despite their numerical dominance; they have limited access to rewards and opportunities in a system where the male is viewed as "normal" and the female is often viewed as deviant (Laws, 1975). At the same time, it is important to acknowledge the varying ways racial and gender oppression are perpetrated and experienced and how they intersect among women of color. This is important in the discussion of women working in the criminal legal system given that women of color present unique roles in breaking into criminal legal professions and have experienced additional discrimination. Furthermore, in the United States, women of color constitute many of the workers in policing and prison, and, as will be explained in Chapter 11, the first women of color lawyers were some of the most significant leaders in challenging racist discrimination.

Comparing gender and racial oppression is complex. We need to keep in mind that the lynching of African Americans, the genocide of American Indians, and the military conquest of Latino/as are not identical to the physical abuse, discrimination, and cultural denigration experienced by women of all races and ethnicities (King, 1988, 15). However, both racial minority members and women experience "shared subordinate treatment on the basis of ascribed attributes and have internalized the social values that perpetuate such subordination" (Rhode, 1987, 20–21). While members of an oppressed group usually understand and are frustrated by this oppression, it is also evident that oppression can affect members' self-esteem, self-confidence, and sense of self-worth.

A major distinction between racism and sexism is that people of color do not tend to share the private sphere as intimately with the empowered (that is, White men), whereas White women often benefit, particularly financially, from the advantages accrued to their White fathers and White husbands. Furthermore, racial and sex discrimination have been distinguished by motivation: Racial discrimination is more often motivated by the intent to degrade and disempower, while discrimination against women is more often motivated by paternalism (ibid., 21). Similarly, although the law has traditionally treated African Americans with "unremitting antagonism" and women as "frail" and "nobler" than men and thus in need of men's protection, the impact on women and African Americans has been the same: "a constraint on the choices open to individual blacks or individual women" (Kirp, Yudof, and Franks, 1986). Although the paternalism and protectionism supposedly guiding laws that restrict women are viewed more positively than the degrading laws restricting African Americans and other people of color, both paternalistic and degrading laws have extremely negative consequences. In some ways, the paternalistically motivated laws may be more difficult to fight because there is some element claiming to be helpful. Unfortunately, these laws usually serve to restrict women's rights (to employment, jury duty, and so on) and help to perpetuate stereotypes of women as weaker than or less than men.

In short, despite their proportion in the population, women have been considered "minorities" in some legislation and policies. This is a recognition of women's "deviant" status when they try to obtain rights ranging from educational and job opportunities to opportunities to play on athletic teams. Legislation and court decisions overturning sex discrimination acknowledge that society is not gender neutral, that boys and girls are raised with different attitudes about and access to rights and opportunities, and that males and females have different experiences. It is not surprising that one of the first successful sex discrimination cases in the United States, *Frontiero v. Richardson* (1973), compared the classification of sex to that of race. This case established sex as a "suspect class," similar to race, in that excuses unrelated to a group's abilities had been used historically to discriminate against members of the group (Hoff, 1991; Lucie, 1988). The *Frontiero* decision overturned regulations that denied female Air Force military officers the same dependents' rights as the male officers had.

The impact of holding more than one stigmatized status at once can be more than cumulative. Occupying a subordinate status in both sex and race has been referred to as "double marginality," "double jeopardy," and "intersectionality." Similarly, poor women of color experience "triple jeopardy," based on sex, race, and class (King, 1988). Examining the effects of racism or sexism fails to acknowledge that some individuals in society experience race discrimination and sex discrimination. For instance, the abysmally low wages earned by White single working women in the early decades of the 1900s were lower still for African American single working women (Meyerowitz, 1988). African American women who were leaders and key organizers in the civil rights movement remain, for the most part, unrecognized and invisible (Barnett, 1993).

The "intersectional experience" of being both African American and female "is greater than the sum of racism and sexism" (Crenshaw, 1989, 140). The history of tension between the African American and White feminist movements was discussed earlier. More recently, most White feminists have increased their attempts to acknowledge and address racism as well as sexism. Although many African American women have traditionally viewed racism as a more powerful cause of their subordination than sexism, since the mid 1970s, both African American and White women are becoming more integrated in unified feminist and antiracist activities and goals (Lewis, 1977).

Analysis of African Americans' progress toward economic equality notes that not only is employment outside the home necessary for single-women heads of households (who are predominantly African American) but such employment is also often necessary for women (and their families) who are married to African American men, given the economic and social discrimination faced by African American men (Geschwender and Carroll-Seguin, 1990). African American women's economic contributions to their families are relatively much greater than those of White women. The pressure of paid employment for married African American women, then, is usually greater than for married White women, given the reduced earning capacity of African American men. The decline in real income in recent years, combined with the lack of available educational and economic opportunities for African Americans, has not only loosened their precarious hold on the middle class acquired during the 1960s and 1970s but has also increased the proportion of African Americans living in poverty (ibid.).

In conclusion, despite feminist attempts to widen women's working opportunities, there remains a stubborn adherence to sex-segregated jobs, with women's jobs being the lowest paid. This has the most severe impact on women of color and their families.

THE MATRON ROLE: WOMEN'S BREAKING INTO CRIMINAL LEGAL SYSTEM JOBS THROUGH SEXIST STEREOTYPICAL POSITIONS

A clear pattern of women's breaking into the "men's" jobs in the criminal legal system is that they typically did so in serving roles more consistent with "mothering" than in professional roles. That is, these "pioneer" women did so mostly by maintaining a gender-specific role within these male-dominated jobs. For instance, the first women police, typically called "police matrons," worked with juveniles and "wayward women," the first female prison and jail workers were "matrons" for female offenders, and the first women lawyers and judges tended to work in juvenile courts and were often married to male lawyers. The term *matron*, lacking in a professional image, is certainly consistent with the nurturing and caretaking responsibilities these women were expected to perform. It is also consistent with the gendered expectations in physical and emotional caretaking referred to by Petersen (1996) as "obligations to care and conflicts about care." Indeed "matrons" are credited with bringing social service into police stations (Schulz, 1995, 17). Notably, the matrons in the prison work preceded the police matrons, and indeed the same group was responsible for the emergence of both police and prison matrons: prominent, upper-middle-class, well-connected, socially prominent women of native-born families who were reformers (ibid., 2). For example, activists for women in policing "drew on middle-class gender stereotypes," claiming "that women's inherently compassionate nature would make them better than men at performing some police duties, such as preventing crime, handling female and juvenile cases, and protecting the moral and physical safety of women and girls in public" (Appier, 1998, 3).

Undoubtedly, these token women were allowed to enter the male bastions of prison and policing work due not only to the work of these reformers but also to the fact that "matron" was likely the least-threatening role possible that a woman could hold in police and prison work. Pollock-Byrne (1995, 97–98) reports that "the attendant term of matron instead of guard or correctional officer remained virtually unchanged until the 1960s, when women began to push for enlarged opportunities."

The first women working in the criminal legal system were White and predominantly social reformers from wealthier homes, and their work in the system tended to be volunteer (Appier, 1998; Feinman, 1986; Martin and Jurik, 1996; Morris, 1987; Schulz, 1995). There is a strong link between women's advancement into policing jobs and their advancement into prison and jail employment. Women prison reformers, however, "paved the way" for women to work in policing, as well as advanced women's roles from volunteer to paid/professional services (Schulz, 1989). The first woman hired as a jail matron was in 1822, and in 1832, the first women were hired as prison guards (Pollock-Byrne, 1995; Zupan, 1992). Significantly, these "first" women were hired for their presumed maternal abilities and "were admitted as women and not as professionals" (Morris, 1987, 139). The separate institutions designed for women prisoners in the late nineteenth and early twentieth centuries not only provided women prisoners with more attention but also provided women with more opportunities to work with offenders (Zupan, 1992).

It is also important to document the profound impact of some of the earliest women working in prisons, jails, and juvenile institutions. For example, criminologist and penologist Katharine Bement Davis (1860–1935) is truly remarkable in her attempts in the 1800s (and early 1900s) to provide better understanding about race, gender, and sexuality, particularly women's sexuality including homosexuality (Deegan, 2003). Davis worked as a Superintendent of New York State Reform for women at Bedford Hills (1901–1914), was the first female Commissioner of New York City Corrections (1914–1916), and was Chair of the first NYC parole panel (1916–1917) (ibid.). Kate Barnard, born in the late 1870s or early 1880s, worked as a stenographer in the Oklahoma legislature in 1903 where she came to know most of the politicians and became known for her spirited speaking and her effectiveness in organizing women and men to support society's "unfortunates" (Bryant, 1969). Barnard successfully organized around women's labor unions and the prohibition of child labor and child abuse (ibid.). In 1907, she was elected the first Commissioner of Oklahoma Charities and Corrections for all of Kansas and Oklahoma, even though women did not have the right to vote (Holley and Brewster, 1998). In addition to great success in an all-male sexist political world with her advocacy against child labor and abuses, she was highly successful in improving the treatment of adult prisoners, male and female (Bryant, 1969; Holley and Brewster, 1998).

Mary Belle Harris (1874–1957), musically talented and with a Ph.D. in Sanskrit and Indo-European Linguistics from the University of Chicago, was the first Superintendent of the Federal Institution for Women in Alderson, Virginia (Rogers, 2000). She entered a career in prison work after a chance meeting where then–NYC Commissioner of Corrections Katharine Bement Davis "found" her on the dock to the Blackwell Island Workhouse in 1914 (ibid.):

> On July 1, 1914, the pair boarded a ferry for Blackwell's Island, a short trip which became the first leg of an extended journey in corrections for Mary Belle Harris, then age 39. That journey would embrace a career, incorporating such positions as these: Superintendent, State Reformatory for Women at Clinton, New Jersey; Assistant Director of the Section on Reformatories and Detention Homes for the U.S. War Department; Superintendent, Federal Institution for Women at Alderson, West Virginia; and Member of the Pennsylvania Board of Parole. (ibid., 8)

Estelle B. Freedman's (1996) biography of Miriam Van Waters (1887–1994) provides a powerful account of a woman who received a Ph.D., was one of the first to push for recognizing "juvenile delinquency," started and ran an institution for delinquent girls, and published about youths and justice. From 1932 to 1957, with a brief exception, Waters was the Superintendent of the Massachusetts Reformatory for Women; she retired at the age of 70. The brief exception was due to when she was fired, allegedly for mismanaging the reformatory. Freedman (ibid.) documents how the firing was really due to concerns about Waters's "deviant sexuality," that she was lesbian and allowing a lesbian "racket" in the institution. She successfully fought the firing, which was extremely courageous given her huge concerns (particularly dangerous at that time) about her lesbian identity being publicized, but recognizing the inherent unfairness for her and the women she was charged to oversee (ibid.). Waters served as a mentor to Edna Mahan (1900–1968), the Superintendent of the New Jersey Reformatory for women from 1928 to 1968. Waters and Mahan both worked tirelessly to advocate for rehabilitation for delinquent girls and incarcerated women, to treat female offenders with dignity, and to provide adequate care for new mothers and their babies and to find good homes for the babies (Freedman, 1996; Hawkes, 1998).

Margaret Moore, born in 1948 in Mississippi, is the first woman to be (1) superintendent of a male prison in Pennsylvania, (2) Deputy Commissioner (overseeing seven prisons and about 10,000 prisoners) in Pennsylvania, and (3) Director of the District of Columbia Department of Corrections (Yates, 2002). In addition to sexism, as an African American and a 16-year-old single mother, Moore faced significant oppression. Through now-noted author Barbara Neely, Moore was introduced to working with offenders, for which she developed a huge passion and commitment (ibid.). She also served as the director of a women's center in Pittsburgh, and began honing her "consciousness for racism and sexism in corrections" (ibid., 14). Moore has been highly successful in paving the way for many women and people of color to work with offenders (ibid.).

African American women's experiences working in prisons have mirrored the racism and sexism outside the prisons. Before the Supreme Court decision in *Brown v. the Board of Education* (1954), "racial segregation existed as institutional policy and practice, de jure in the South and de facto in the North" (Feinman, 1986, 141). Most superintendents and officers in the prisons were White, and when African Americans were hired, it was usually to guard African American prisoners, who were typically segregated and housed in the worst parts of prisons. Since the 1950s, African American women's (and men's) employment in penal institutions has significantly increased. It has also been noted that as more nonprison jobs opened for White women, more African American women moved into the vacuum created by their absence in prison employment (Feinman, 1986).

L. Mara Dodge's (2002, 242–243) powerful book on the history of women's prisons in Illinois describes how in the 1960s some women workers at the Dwight Reformatory were disheartened with the conditions for some of the women (including chamber pots for "toilets" as recently as 1967) and with the replacement of the therapeutic ideal of programming with harsh discipline for "vulgarity and unladylike behavior." Unlike the early progressive and compassionate women superintendents just discussed, Dodge (ibid.) illustrates Margaret D. Morrisey, superintendent of Dwight from 1962 to 1972, as an overly strict, rigid, and unreasonable force, whose priorities were security and custodial, not treatment. Dodge (ibid., 245) states this "lack of commitment to treatment goals" was consistent in women's prisons across the United States in the 1960s. Morrissey was obsessed with monitoring the prisoners' friendships for the possibility of homosexuality. Dodge (ibid., 256) concludes that in the 1990s most women prisoners in the United States "were primarily guarded by male staff."

Finally, it is inspiring and significant to trace the "herstories" of some of the important women scholars who helped shape the current understanding of female offenders, the links between victimization and offending, and female victimization. It is impossible to list and document all of these "pioneer" feminist criminologists, so I am mentioning three. Two of the first women with doctorates in criminology, Dr. Coramae Richey Mann and Dr. Vernetta Young, effectively "jump-started" the conversations on the intersections of gender, race, and class with crime, emphasizing the need for understanding what we now refer to as the intersectionalities of gender, race, and class (see Adams-Fuller, 2003; Mars, 2001). Both women are African American. Dr. Meda Chesney-Lind began documenting the forced vaginal exams of girls charged with offenses when collecting data for her master's degree in the early 1970s and has been highly influential in shaping feminist criminology (see Belknap, 2004).

Part of the remarkable pattern of the women listed here is the strong overlap in their lives. In particular, many of these women were childless and never married, and all devoted an incomprehensible amount of time and passion to improving the rights of women and girls charged with offenses. Moreover, they all held strong convictions in the power of rehabilitation.

THE POWERFUL ROLE OF LEGISLATIVE AND COURT RULINGS ON WOMEN'S WORK IN THE CRIMINAL LEGAL SYSTEM

Legislative and Supreme Court rulings have been important avenues for effecting social change. Virtually all of the movement of women into the areas of law enforcement, the courts, and prison and jail work has been because of lawsuits (initiated by women). The initial opportunities, as well as some current ones, were the result of court decisions, not genuine opportunity or goodwill on the part of the dominant group (wealthy, White males). Nonetheless, the courts have been less understanding of "more subtle sex-based classifications that affect opportunities for and social views about women" (Bartlett, 1991, 372).

Unfortunately, although legal changes are usually necessary, they are not always sufficient to bring about actual change. Many citizens are unaware of their own legal rights, and some institutions that discriminate may be unaware they are breaking the law (or even discriminating). However, even when some employers are aware of the laws they are breaking, they use various forms of direct or indirect coercion to override the law. For instance, even though a prison, jail, or police department may have a policy against sexual harassment, a woman employee may decide it is less costly emotionally and financially to "put up" with it or to change jobs than to take on the male-dominated police or prison and court system. In the same vein, workers who know they are being discriminated against may justifiably decide that to keep the job they have or even to maintain a good record for a future job, it is important not to "rock the boat." This is particularly crucial when the victims of discrimination or harassment have no other means of supporting themselves (and perhaps their dependents) during the time-consuming and costly experience of a trial. These are examples of how laws may be necessary but not sufficient to effect change. As Chamallas (1999, 18) points out, most institutions (be they governments or private businesses) "follow practices and policies saturated with implicit male bias. Simply to follow these 'neutral' rules and ignore gender reproduces patterns of exclusion and paradoxically assures that gender will continue to matter in the world." Alternatively stated: "Clearly the gender neutral terms of the federal constitution do not protect the rights of women to the same extent as they protect the rights of men" (Thomas, 1991, 116).

Feminist legal scholar Martha Chamallas (1999) identified three separate stages of feminist legal theory pertaining to the last three decades of the twentieth century. First, Chamallas characterizes the 1970s as the *equality stage*, where the goal was to establish gender equality through eliminating sex-based classifications and by obtaining equal access to education and jobs and promoting equality in the family. Next, Chamallas labeled the 1980s the *difference stage*, where feminist legal scholarship and activism attempted to respond to the inadequacies of liberal feminism and to highlight how women's inclusion "into male-dominated sites was not the exclusive meaning of equality" (ibid., 47). Simply hiring women into male-dominated jobs does not guarantee that they will be treated and paid as equals. The "difference" era of the 1980s was particularly motivated by the pregnancy discrimination rulings and ensuing debates. Finally, Chamallas identified the 1990s as the *diversity stage*, an attempt to redress the previous feminist activist and scholarship shortcoming of lumping all women together. More specifically, the goal of this stage was to be more inclusive of all women rather than to focus on middle-class and wealthy White women and their primary issues in sexism.

Significantly, legal pressure has been identified as the major impetus allowing equal entry of women into prison and jail employment (Jurik, 1985). The most important ruling regarding women's access to policing and prison work, and women's work across other professions as well, is Title VII. Title VII, a 1972 amendment of the 1964 Civil Rights Act, states that is illegal to base any terms of employment (conditions, compensation, firing, hiring, and so on) on a person's sex, race, religion, or national origin. The refusal to hire women to work in men's prisons was "unquestioned and unchallenged" until 1972 (Zimmer, 1986, 1). Title VII is viewed as the greatest motivation for hiring women into non-gendered jobs in prisons (Flynn, 1982; Jurik, 1985; Morton, 1981; Zimmer, 1989).

Ironically, although most employment sex-discrimination suits have been brought via Title VII, "sex" was added to the list of nondiscriminatory characteristics listed in the amendment (after race, religion, and natural origin) at the last minute before its passage, as an attempt to derail the entire amendment; that is, antiwoman sentiment was used to try to deny racial equality (Deitch, 1993). In fact, when the inclusion of sex was read to Congress, it was met with laughter, and all but one of the men who had voted for including "sex" in the amendment voted against the entire bill (ibid.).

Title VII allowed the Equal Employment Opportunity Commission (EEOC), a federal agency established in 1964, "the power to prosecute Title VII violators in the federal courts, a power it quickly utilized" (Zimmer, 1986, 4). In fact, most employment-discrimination suits have been brought pursuant to this amendment (Berger, 1980). However, it has also been stated that it took ten years for Title VII to get some "teeth" and be effective (Hoff, 1991, 234).

Despite its positive influence, Title VII has five important limitations. First, Title VII is problematic in that it is costly to litigate; the cost of discovery (proof of differential employee treatment) and the need for expensive experts prohibit most workers from charging these suits on their own (Berger, 1980, 39). Although Title VII's positive influence cannot be underestimated, there is concern that Justice Department and Supreme Court reinterpretations of Title VII in the 1980s had a "chilling effect on potential plaintiffs, making it more costly and difficult to win subsequent employment discrimination cases in the 1990s" (Martin, 1992, 285).

The second limitation of Title VII concerns the bona fide occupational qualification (BFOQ) safety net, which has been broadened so much as to make Title VII meaningless in some cases brought to court. Decided on a case-by-case basis, the BFOQ is a defense part of Title VII, designed for exceptions where it would be considered rational to prefer the employment of one sex, religion, and so on over another. (Notably, race never qualifies as a BFOQ [Blankenship, 1993].) Primarily, BFOQs are used in sex discrimination cases. In these cases, the employer typically agrees that one sex was hired over another but claims it was rational to do so. Some claim the only rational BFOQs regarding sex are sperm donors and wet nurses. BFOQs, however, have been legally used to exclude women's employment from a variety of occupations, including prison chaplain, prison guard, and international oil executive (Epstein, 1988).

A third problem with Title VII is that its bifurcation of race and sex has served to decrease the employment protection for women of color. The wording of Title VII separates race and sex, giving people of color, as a group, access to challenging employment discrimination that is different from what it provides for women as a group. In essence, the legislative history of Title VII suggests that women of color are not to be its beneficiaries (Blankenship, 1993). For example, *DeFraffenreid v. General Motors* (1976) was brought by five African American women employees because of the hiring and laying-off practices of General Motors (GM). The court sided with GM because they showed that White women and African American men had not been discriminated against in hiring and laying off. Thus, African American women may be protected only insofar as their discrimination experiences coincide with those of African American men or White women (Crenshaw, 1989).

The fourth limitation is that Title VII has been biased in ensuring *men's* gender equality. Perhaps the greatest irony of the first fifteen years of sex discrimination Supreme Court rulings is that males have been more successful than females both in their access to the courts and in obtaining favorable decisions (Rhode, 1987). The majority of cases recognizing sex discrimination overturned the few instances where the legal or social system favored women (the men in these cases claimed to have been the victim of "reverse discrimination"). "When one looks at the actual holdings [of Supreme Court triumphs on sex discrimination], the constant thread that runs through these 'women's rights' cases is that most of the winners have been men, and that women have won only when it was not at the expense of a man" (Berger, 1980, 19).

The final limitation of Title VII is that, although EEOC and affirmative action programs resulted in women being hired as police officers on patrol and to work with male prisoners, these programs do not guarantee women's employment in large numbers in these fields (Morton, 1981). Hiring women for police and prison work is still not the norm. Additionally, women police and prison workers have fallen victim to "last-hired, first-fired (or laid-off)" practices. Presumably, the longevity of male workers' employment overrode the commitment to having female officers. Thus, while women have their foot in the proverbial door, they are frequently still only represented in token status in many criminal-processing institutions.

In summary, Title VII legislation resulted in women gaining access to and improving their standard of work in many jobs previously limited to men, including women's work in policing and prisons. The courts heard many cases brought through Title VII, but although the courts acknowledged discrimination based on sex, the most successful cases in court are those that further advance males. Or, put more simply, sex discrimination is more likely to be considered unconstitutional in instances where males are discriminated against than in situations where females are discriminated against. Unfortunately, of course, the vast amount of sex discrimination is against females, and apparently that is the least likely to be rectified. Additionally, Title VII, legislation proposing to help discrimination against working women, was written and applied in a manner that provides significantly less coverage for women of color. Thus, Title VII is a mixed blessing. It resulted in the unprecedented hiring of women into policing and corrections, but it has bifurcated discrimination of women of color, often leaving them legally "uncovered" for discrimination, *and* Title VII has proven to be a better avenue to fight men's than women's job discrimination. Still, its impact on breaking the gates for women's access to jobs in the criminal legal system cannot be understated. Unfortunately, although legislation has helped in many ways to improve women's opportunities, it has not provided clear guidelines allowing women equal opportunities. That is, while supporters of women working with male offenders have been somewhat successful in overturning height and weight requirements used to systematically deny women policing and prison employment, other blocks to women's equality in working with male offenders still exist.

POST TITLE VII: WOMEN AS TOKENS IN THE HISTORY OF WOMEN'S ENTRY INTO WORKING AS PRISON AND JAIL GUARDS

Before examining the entry of women as tokens working in the criminal legal system, it is useful to briefly address the research on *tokenism*. Hughes (1944, 358) claims that exceptions to jobs previously employing only White males (or only males or only Whites) do so through "some elaboration of social segregation." Kanter (1977a, 968) identifies tokens as "people identified by ascribed characteristics (master statuses such as sex, race, religion, ethnic group, age, etc.) or other characteristics that carry with them a set of assumptions about culture status, and behavior highly salient for majority category members."

Kanter (ibid., 969) also argues that a person's token status is heightened when (1) her or his social category is obvious (such as sex); and (2) her or his social category is new to the setting, which is certainly true of the women breaking into criminal legal system jobs. Zimmer (1988) criticizes Kanter's (1977b) tokenism approach as overly simplified. She warns against perceiving male entrance into female-dominated jobs as identical to female entrance into male-dominated jobs. Tokenism alone will not account for problems women "pioneers" face as they advance into male jobs. For instance, Zimmer (1988) found that women integrated as guards in men's prisons faced substantial opposition from male coworkers. On the other hand, men recently hired in women's prisons reported no opposition from female staff or supervisors. In fact, the women's prison staff displayed appreciation for their addition. This may be because traditionally male jobs could be perceived as losing status by hiring more women, while tradition-ally female jobs may gain status by hiring more men (Yoder, 1991). Further evidence suggests that men more rigorously exclude token women from "their domain" in traditionally male jobs than women exclude token men in tradition-ally female jobs (Epstein, 1988). Given these hypotheses, it is not surprising that a study comparing male nurses and women police officers found that women police officers faced more sex stereotyping, were less accepted, experienced more sexual harassment, and felt more visible than the male nurses (Ott, 1989).

A related phenomenon is the "glass-ceiling effect," which symbolizes a promotion block experienced by many women and people of color in jobs traditionally unavailable to them. Put another way, women and people of color may have gotten a foot in the door, but they are still unlikely to be police captains or prison wardens (especially in men's prisons) and less likely than men to become judges and partners in law firms. On the other hand, a study of men in the predominately female professions of nursing, elementary education teaching, librarianship, and social work found that, unlike token women, most of the prejudice the token men faced was from people outside of their professions. Furthermore, instead of the "glass ceiling" that women tokens usually experience, this study found that token men in female-dominated jobs experienced a "glass escalator": Token men were given fair and often preferential treatment that enhanced their positions relative to their female coworkers (Williams, 1992).

Tokenism, then, must be examined in conjunction with sexism in order to understand women's experiences of entering male-dominated jobs. It is evident that it is not enough simply to increase women's proportions in male-dominated jobs—more importantly, gender-based attitudes on women's abilities and appropriateness in male-dominated jobs need to be changed. Clearly, this is not an easy feat. While increasing the number of women in male-dominated jobs may help men to view women as competent, Zimmer (1988) fears a backlash with increased opposition to women and cites evidence where women are more intimidated and discriminated against when they enter in larger numbers. For whatever reasons, some males feel threatened to realize women can adequately perform jobs previously available to males only. Simply being "allowed," legally or otherwise, to have the opportunity to work in the criminal legal system has clearly not been the last battle for women in these jobs. Although women's presence and range of jobs in the criminal legal system increased dramatically in the 1970s, they have faced significant roadblocks, largely from male professionals and to a lesser degree from their clients.

Baunach and Rafter (1982) identified four problem areas for women professionals in the male-dominated criminal legal system jobs. It is likely these applied more to the women hired shortly after Title VII, but there are still abundant examples of this pattern today. The first problem is the so-called "preferential" treatment women get when male coworkers and supervisors shield them from "real" work, such as female police officers and guards handling violent men (or even violent women), or women lawyers handling high-stress cases (including cases with violent men). Notably, similar to how studies reported (in Chapter 4) that chivalry and paternalism for offending women were more available to White women, a study on gender, race, and policing found that the preferential and protective treatment by coworkers and supervisors was more available to White women police officers than to African American women officers (Martin 1990). A second problem area is that women tokens often face higher expectations than their male colleagues encounter, including the pressure of representing all women by any of their actions. For example, women lawyers and judges "have had to be smarter, work harder, and be better at what they do than their male colleagues" in order to succeed (Feinman, 1986, 126).

Lack of access to the "old boy" network, Baunach and Rafter's (1982) third problem area, presents the "damned-if-you-do, damned-if-you-don't" dilemma of "fraternizing" with male colleagues. If women socialize with male coworkers, they are often assumed to be having sex with them, which results in negative assessments about the woman's, but not the man's, professionalism. Women who do not socialize with their male colleagues risk not receiving important information about the job or promotions, as well as being labeled "cold" or "lesbians." Some male supervisors report consciously spending less time with female supervisees so that people will not think they are sexually involved. This has an obvious cost to women employees. The final problem area identified by Baunach and Rafter (ibid.) is sex stereotyping in the job assignment. For example, women prison and jail workers were often restricted to working with juveniles and incarcerated women.

It is also important to recognize the additional token status burden and impact for those "new" workers who hold more than one token identity. More specifically, for women of color, women from a country other than the one they are working in, women with disabilities, lesbians, and so on, these women are often fighting oppression on more than one front or, stated another way, a wider range of forms of discrimination. Martin and Jurik (1996, 28) discuss how women breaking into criminal legal system jobs encounter gender as "an ongoing social production," where race and class interact with gender subordination, which also interact with "domination in other social institutions and sites (e.g., the state, family)." Greene's (1997) first-hand account of being one of the pioneer African American women law professors, starting in 1978, describes intense hostility she faced from students and colleagues alike. She states: "Tokenism masks racism and sexism by committing a small number of previously excluded individuals to institutions. At the same time, a system of tokenism maintains barriers of entry to others. Tokenism is therefore a symbolic equality" (ibid., 89).

Women were not hired to work as officers with male prisoners until the 1970s and Title VII. However, even when women worked in the "custodial institutions" for women prisoners (described in Chapter 5), they "tended to be subordinate to the male wardens at nearby men's prisons and were typically paid lower wages than their male counterparts" (Maschke, 1996, 34). Working in male prisons, however, provides important opportunities for women aspiring to a career in "corrections" for four reasons: (1) There are better posts and shifts, (2) there are more promotional opportunities, (3) there are more locations to work in prisons, and (4) working in a men's prison appears to be necessary for advancement into administration (Zimmer, 1986). The first three reasons are largely due to the fact that there are many more men's prisons than women's prisons (often there is only one woman's prison per state), and the men's prisons are more highly populated, allowing for more positions in each rank, shift, and post. Significantly, the wardens of women's institutions have typically been men.

PRISONER PRIVACY AND PRISON SAFETY: ROADBLOCKS FOR WOMEN GUARDS IN MALE PRISONS

The issue of prisoner privacy as a means to restrict women's employment in men's prisons easily fits under the previous heading regarding organizational barriers. However, the debate around this has been so significant that it deserves its own section in this chapter. Although some legislation has proven to be powerful in dismantling restrictions on women workers in men's prisons, other legislation has been instrumental in emphasizing why differential assignments of female and male officers should be considered bona fide occupational qualifications (BFOQs as described previously in this chapter). Chapter 5 addressed the gendered nature of prisoners' utilization of lawsuits for better and fairer conditions, reporting that male prisoners are far more likely than their female counterparts to use the court system. This holds true even regarding lawsuits about cross-sex prisoner supervision, even though female prisoners are far more likely than male prisoners to be leered at and sexually abused by opposite-sex guards (Maschke, 1996). Maschke (ibid., 35) reports that when comparing the judges' processing of lawsuits brought by male as opposed to female prisoners' regarding cross-sex supervision privacy claims, the seriousness of the gender differences is profound: "Although male inmates may have objected to cross-gender supervision because they were unaccustomed to being objects of the 'female gaze,' female prisoners may have been resisting more than the gaze of male correctional officers," that is, physical sexual abuse.

There appear to be two major issues used in legislation defending women's restrictions in working with male prisoners: (1) male prisoners' rights to privacy, and (2) the impact of women officers on prison security. This section first addresses the issue of prisoners' rights to privacy and then briefly discusses the impact of women on prison security.

Over time, male prisoners' rights have been increasingly prioritized (over prison security) as a BFOQ (or legitimate legal reason) to exclude women from working in men's prisons (Morton, 1981). In fact, questions about whether guards of the opposite sex are invading a prisoner's right to privacy in showers and bathrooms never occurred until women were employed in men's prisons—when women moved into the dominant sphere. Subsequently, the concern for prisoner privacy in legislation appears to be far more prevalent regarding male prisoners with female guards than for female prisoners with male guards (ibid.). Moreover, state guidelines developed to protect prisoner privacy have resulted in women officers being excluded from posts that have high contact with male prisoners (Zimmer, 1986, 9).

However, two points are worth making here. First, reviews of 1970s and 1980s court cases on prisoners' rights to privacy from guards of the opposite sex shows that the courts have tended to favor the officers' right to employment over the prisoners' right to privacy, regardless of the sex of the prisoner or the officer (see Bernat and Zupan, 1989; Lawrence and Mahan, 1998; Martin and Jurik, 1996). Second, a 1993 court case found that while the use of male guards to perform body searches of female prisoners does not violate their right to privacy (the Fourth Amendment), such actions do violate women prisoners' rights to freedom from cruel and unusual punishment (the Eighth Amendment), given the high rate of women prisoners who have survived physical and sexual violence at the hands of men. It was found that such searches could exacerbate preexisting mental conditions resulting from prior victimizations (*Jordan v. Gardner*, 1993).

No set guidelines have been established to confront the problem of balancing prisoners' privacy with the employment of officers of either sex (Zimmer, 1986). It is significant that most of the focus on this problem has centered on women working in men's prisons, despite the history (including recent documentations) of the stronger likelihood of male officers violating women prisoners' privacy than of women officers violating men prisoners' privacy. Finally, research on women working in male penal facilities has found that the job is often structured to deny women and men equal assignments, to the disadvantage of women workers (Belknap, 1991; Zimmer, 1986).

In addressing prisoners' rights to privacy and balancing this with women's rights to work in men's prisons (where there are the most job, shift, and promotional opportunities), we must ask a few questions. First, how is this different from having a doctor or nurse of the opposite sex? The appropriateness and right to privacy of this "intimate" professional interaction is rarely questioned. Second, is it really different or more degrading for men to have women, rather than other men, see them shower, undress, and so on? Presumably, if a doctor, nurse, or prison guard acts professionally and discreetly, the sex combination of the prisoner/patient and the professional should be irrelevant. Third, it might be argued that when one is imprisoned, certain rights and privileges are lost, including the privilege to choose the sex of the prison staff. (Obviously, it is important that prisoners have access to grievance procedures that seriously look into and provide enforcement when a staff person of either sex behaves inappropriately.) Despite all the fuss made over male prisoners' rights to privacy, research reports that the majority of male prisoners do not report that women officers violate their privacy (Kissel and Katsampes, 1980; Zimmer, 1986).

Maschke's (1996, 37) careful legal analysis of the court cases prisoners have brought regarding privacy rights concludes that the court decisions have permitted prisoner employers "to discriminate against women without having to provide objective evidence of the need for the policies they had implemented." Moreover, given that there are far more male prisoners and men's prisons than female prisoners and women's prisons, limiting cross-sex supervising in any manner has a far greater impact on women's than men's potential prison guard jobs (Maschke, 1996). Denying women equal access to a career in "corrections" does not seem to be the answer to the prisoner privacy issue, especially given some of the advantages women officers might bring to these institutions (which are discussed later in this chapter). It has also been pointed out that opaque shower doors or partial barriers (where the prisoner's feet and head can be seen) could help balance prisoners' privacy with the employment of officers of either sex (Zimmer, 1986).

Regarding the security aspect of women working in men's prisons, although *Dothard v. Rawlinson* (1977) eliminated minimum height and weight requirements for officers in men's prisons, it upheld that under at least some circumstances, men's prisons qualified for a BFOQ exception. This exemption was given because of the belief that the presence of even one woman officer might threaten the security of the prison, although there was no evidence to support this (ibid.). In fact, recent research on men and women working in male prisons found that women guards perceive the prisons to be less dangerous than male guards do (Lawrence and Mahan, 1998; Wright and Saylor, 1991). Additionally, a study of guards in Minnesota found that male guards (37 percent) were more than twice as likely as women guards (16 percent) to believe that male guards' safety was endangered when they worked with women guards. Additionally, this same study, in reviewing the prisons' records on prisoner-on-guard assaults and injuries found that female guards were no more likely than male guards to be assaulted or injured by the prisoners (Lawrence and Mahan, 1998). Ironically, *Dothard v. Rawlinson* has not been successfully used in subsequent cases to deny women "guard" jobs (Bernat and Zupan, 1989; Zimmer, 1986). However, "[t]he privacy issue was raised again and left unresolved" in *Gunther v. Iowa*, which ruled that men's prisons must make the necessary arrangements so that women employees' right to promotion is not superseded by male prisoners' rights to privacy but that women guards should not be placed in direct confrontation with male prisoners' privacy (Flowers, 1987).

> In effect, these two cases [*Dothard* and *Gunther*], determined that although women will still be able to move up the promotional ladder based on seniority and capability, they have yet to achieve full equality with men in the prison system. Instead, Title VII's sexual integration provisions has mandated a system of legally permitted "near equality" among male and female correctional officers. This has proved detrimental to women's momentum in corrections as well as their relationship with male guards with whom they have to compete and work at something less than full status while receiving full benefits. Equally affected are the prison administrators, whose job it is to implement and design integration policies effectively. (Flowers, 1987, 175)

Lawsuits about prison workers and sex discrimination in areas other than prisoners' rights to privacy and prison security have focused on discrimination in individual hiring, firing, and promotional decisions. These have routinely been decided in favor of men or against women (see Bernat and Zupan, 1989). It is hoped that in the future, prison security and prisoners' rights to privacy will not be misused to keep women from exploring careers working with offenders. Flynn (1982, 331) stresses that "[n]ot only should qualified women be given the opportunity to work in any potentially dangerous situation if they want to, but their work assignments should not differ, to any degree, from the assignments of their male counterparts."

GENDER SIMILARITIES AND DIFFERENCES IN THE JOB PERFORMANCES OF PRISON WORKERS

While there have been few attempts to evaluate women prison officers and to compare them to male officers, most of these evaluations portray these women favorably. Further, despite women officers' facing strong resistance from fellow officers, most male prisoners support women officers (Zimmer, 1986). "Overall, the presence of female officers in men's institutions seems to have normalized the environment, relaxed tension, and led to improvements in the inmates' behavior, dress and language" (Morris, 1987, 157).

Two explanatory models, the *gender model* and the *job model*, have been suggested to guide the research as to why there are gender differences in how guards perform their jobs (Jurik and Halemba, 1984; Zimmer, 1986). According to the *gender model*, gender differences in guards' occupational experiences are shaped by what they bring to the job in terms of attitudes, prior experiences, and preferred modes of interaction (Zimmer, 1986, 12). For example, "gender models suggest that women place greater importance than do men on relationships with others in their work environment" (Jurik and Halemba, 1984, 554). Alternatively, according to the *job model*, the organizational structure of the occupation and the institution are what impact guards' gender differences. For example, male coworkers' believe that women are unable to guard prisoners effectively simply because they are not allowed to guard males (in those cases where they were restricted to guarding women offenders). To some degree it is likely that both models operate simultaneously to promote gender differences among prison and jail staff members (Jurik, 1985, 376; Jurik and Halemba, 1984, 552; Zimmer, 1986, 13). Jurik and Halemba's (1984) study was more supportive of the job model than the gender model as influencing women guards' gender differences. Belknap's (1991) study of women guards in a jail found that these women workers reported support for both the job and gender models; however, they believed the gender model was a better explanation of why they did the job differently (e.g., used less force) than the male guards, attributing it to their life experiences, skills, and abilities as women.

Britton's (1997a, 802) study of women and men working in both men's and women's prisons as guards reports on "gendered organizational logic," or ways in which policies and practices within an organization are "explicitly and implicitly gendered." Britton (1997a) identified two ways in which the application of so-called gender-neutral policies and practices resulted in gender differences. First, the training for both the women and men guards presumed a male recruit. Second, the notions that administrators and the male and female officers themselves held about the "natures of male and female officers" superseded the gender-neutral policies. This was most apparent in the officers' assignments to various posts, which were strongly gendered by perceptions of women officers' (in)abilities to deal with violent prisoners, particularly in the men's (as opposed to the women's) prison (ibid., 808). Thus, Britton (ibid., 812, 814) concludes that the "organizational logic" is "deeply gendered" and that understanding it would likely be aided by applying a theory of "masculinized" organizations.

More recent research in this area included women and men guards in two medium-security men's prisons and found both female and male guards view gender differences in how the prisoners are supervised/guarded (Frakas, 1999). The male guards typically described the female guards as less assertive and authoritative than male guards and too "soft," "friendly," and "nice," applying words like "mother" and "social worker" disparagingly toward their female coworkers (ibid.). Notably, the women guards viewed these gender differences "in a more positive light": The women viewed female guards, relative to male guards, as more human-service oriented and more appropriately drawing on interpersonal skills. Similar to Belknap (1991), the women in this study were more supportive of the gender than the job model as the better explanation of gender differences in guarding (Frakas, 1999). Frakas (ibid., 37) notes the intersection of racism and sexism as reported by an African American woman guard:

I have to show I can cut it. I am Black and I am a woman—two strikes against me. Because I am Black, I might feel sorry for inmates. Because I am female, I will be afraid of inmates. When I first started, I got very little help from men I worked with. I had to ask things. I was finally placed on a unit with a Black male officer and he showed me what I was supposed to do.

Other researchers suggest that women prison and jail workers have a less-aggressive style than male penal workers, that the women are better at deescalating potentially violent situations (Belknap, 1991; Gates, 1976; Kissel and Katsampes, 1980), and that women guards tend to be more supportive of a human services and rehabilitative role than men (Belknap, 1991; Griffin, 2002; Jurik, 1985; Jurik and Halemba, 1984; Kissel and Katsampes, 1980; Walters, 1992; Zimmer, 1986; Zupan, 1986). Moreover, two studies reported that male guards are more likely than female guards to "talk out" or "reason with" defiant prisoners (Frakas, 1999; Jenne and Kersting, 1996). However, women guards were more likely than men guards to issue conduct reports (Frakas, 1999). This was likely due to the women officers' fears of being "tested" by the prisoners and failing some test of respect with them (ibid.). Men and women guards report similar rates in their likelihood of calling for backup from other officers in a dispute (Frakas, 1999; Jenne and Kersting, 1996). Another study reported that while women officers were more rehabilitative in *orientation* than men officers were, there were no gender differences concerning their rehabilitation/custodial *views*, punitiveness, and readiness to use force orientations and attitudes (Griffin, 2002).

CLASSIFICATIONS OF WOMEN PRISON WORKERS

Rosabeth Moss Kanter's (1977b) research on women tokens in corporations found that the men tended to place women coworkers in female roles that were familiar to them because "female coworker" was not a familiar role. The types of familiar female roles included "mother," "pet," "seductress," and "iron maiden." The "mother" is expected to attend to everyone's emotional needs in the office, and the "seductress" attends to the sexual stereotypes about women. The "pets" were the resident "cheerleaders," whose priority seemed to be to support male coworkers and build up their egos. The "iron maidens," on the other hand, were women who did not fit into any of the other categories, possibly resisting them by choice. In sum, Kanter (1977a) found these women tokens in corporations as falling or being "forced" into these sexist categories by society and their male coworkers and supervisors. This is relevant for subsequent research on women working in the criminal legal system.

Zimmer (1986) has identified three roles women working in men's prisons are likely to fall into, which she labels "adjustment strategies" (and which she compares to Martin's [1979] roles reported in the next chapter). The adjustment strategies were institutional role officers, modified role officers, and inventive role officers. The *institutional role officers* are rule and policy followers that tend to downplay their female status (and comparable to Martin's [1979] POLICE-women reported in the following chapter). They expect to do the same job as the male officers and are invested in maintaining professional relationships with everyone they work with in the prison. Zimmer's (1986) *modified role officers* do not view themselves as being as capable as men of performing the job and prefer safe assignments where they have no contact with the prisoners (and are analogous to Martin's [1979] policeWOMEN category reported in the next chapter). They often rely on male officers to back them up. Zimmer's (1986) third role for women prison workers is the *inventive role*. Women in this role do not view themselves as equal to or less capable than male officers, like the *institutional* and *modified* officers do. Instead, they see women officers as advantageous to the prison system. These women see their physical weakness (relative to men's) as overcompensated for by their communication skills and respect for prisoners. They believe in the importance of seeing the prisoners as individuals and count on backing from the prisoners. These officers receive the most hostility from male coworkers and are the most openly resentful of this hostility.

Drawing on Kanter's (1997b) work, Jurik (1988) studied women prison workers' entry into guarding male prisoners and found they had to address negative stereotyping by "striking a balance" between competing negative stereotypes. "Avoiding the role traps of incompetent pet and seductress often leaves female officers with a third iron-maiden-like stereotypic role. Female officers who work hard to demonstrate competence are alternatively described as 'climbers,' 'dykes,' or 'cold'; they are isolated and distrusted by their colleagues" (ibid., 295). In fact, some of the strategies women prison workers developed to combat this oppression included emphasizing humor, professionalism, a team approach, and sponsorship (Jurik, 1988).

RESISTANCE TO WOMAN WORKERS

Despite the legal and societal advancements in women's entry into the criminal legal system jobs, many still face considerable resentment and resistance, and this is most typically at the hands of their male coworkers, supervisors, and administrators. Moreover, women's upward mobility into the higher positions appears to be blocked. As expected, the accounts of women of color's employment experiences in policing, prison work, and legal careers (including work as law professors and law students) suggest that the effects of racism and sexism are more than cumulative (Banks, 1997; Cho, 1997; Christopher et al., 1991; Dreifus, 1982; Felkenes and Schroedel, 1993; Greene, 1997; Martin, 1994; Moran, 1990–1991; Russell, 1997; Townsey, 1982). That is, combining racism with sexism seems to result in more than twice the oppression.

Research on the early women entering work as guards in men's prisons reported male coworkers' confusion and hostility directed toward these women because the male workers often perceive the job as "masculine" and are thus confused and threatened when they see women capably performing the job

(Martin and Jurik, 1996; Zimmer, 1986). A study of some of the first women working in a men's prison found that this masculinity confusion by the male officers is a no-win situation for the female officers: Male officers may reject competent female officers because they are threatened by the fact that a woman can do "their" job; at the same time, they believe that incompetent women officers are "better women"—but unacceptable officers (Zimmer, 1986). The male coworkers' assessment also reported the women as "unsuitable" for guard work (ibid.). The women prison officers also reported that their male coworkers frequently ignored them (acting as if they were not present), assigned them the worst posts, and wrote them up for actions against prison policies that the male officers regularly violated and were not sanctioned for (ibid.). In the same study, the male officers believed that (1) women workers impair prison security because they are both physically and emotionally weaker; (2) women officers need male officers' protection; (3) women officers can do only some of the job; and (4) it is unfair for women officers to be placed only in those parts of the jobs that they are "suited" for (ibid.). Given this agenda, the only logical solution was to have no women working in the prison, according to many of the men (ibid.). Further, "rather than questioning the necessity of masculinity, most male guards question the ability of women to perform the job without it" (ibid., 57). If a woman can do the job, her "feminine" identity is questioned, and she is seen as abnormal or lesbian. Clearly these stereotypes are damaging for women who want to be taken seriously as guards (most if not all of the women guards). Thus, formal policies allowing the first women to work guarding male prisoners did not guarantee their cultural or professional integration into these jobs (e.g., Morris, 1987, 145).

A more recent study of prison guards also reported that men's resistance to their female coworkers inhibits the women's job performance (Frakas, 1999, 43):

> Instead of trying to find an approach that works for them, women COs [guards] may feel compelled to adopt a stricter, more punitive approach toward inmates in order to satisfy their male colleagues. Women COs are also reluctant to intervene in situations involving altercations with male coworkers and inmates because of fear of rejection or making a mistake.

Another more recent assessment of gender differences in prison guards' perceptions of women officers indicates that while male guards are becoming more accepting of their female coworkers than more dated research suggests, the women still face a considerable amount of sexism by these men (Lawrence and Mahan, 1998). For example, although most male guards believed that women should be hired as guards in men's prisons, one-fifth did not. Although the men typically reported that women could adequately perform various job requirements, the women rated themselves as significantly more able to perform the job tasks than the men did. The gender differences were greatest regarding officers' assessments of women's ability to use sufficient force to control prisoners, backing up a partner in a dangerous situation and during incidents and other emergencies. Thus, while the male guards' evaluations of the female guards' abilities and job performance were generally favorable, the notable exceptions had to do with the men's assessments of the female guards' use of physical force (ibid.). Significantly, men with more years of experience on the job rated the women less favorably than they rated newer male employees. The authors conclude: "The resistance to women that persists among some men officers is likely to provide an obstacle for women seeking opportunities for advancement and promotion in male prisons" (ibid., 63).

Thus, it is important to remember that even legislation supporting women's rights to equal employment cannot guarantee their acceptance by coworkers, clients, or the general public. Additionally, consent decrees aimed at having women hired in more than token status have not been effective. It is likely this is no more frequent or serious resistance to women working in the criminal legal system than the form of *sexual harassment* experienced on the job (e.g., Bartol et al., 1992; Cho, 1997; Gratch, 1995; Greene, 1997; Hagan and Kay, 1995; Jurik, 1985; Martin, 1980; McMahon, 1999; Morash and Haarr, 1995; Pierce, 1995; Pogrebin and Poole, 1997; Pollock-Byrne, 1986; Pollock-Byrne and Ramirez, 1995; Rosenberg et al., 1993; Sommerlad and Sanderson, 1998; Stohr et al., 1998). For example, a recent study of women guards in Canada reported that in addition to the most extreme forms of sexual harassment, aggressive physically sexual attacks, the women reported sexual insults and teasing, offensive sexual comments, rumors about their sexuality, sexual propositions, and unwanted sexual touching by their male colleagues (McMahon, 1999).

The organizational structures of prisons and jails have also managed to restrict women's roles in numerous ways. Organizational barriers include gender differences (discrimination) in training, work assignments, and performance evaluations (Jurik, 1985). Women guards often face barriers of gender stereotyping in treatment and job assignments (e.g., Belknap, 1991; Britton, 1997a; Flynn, 1982), in addition to bias from the veterans' preference system, physical requirements, safety considerations, and prisoners' privacy rights (Belknap, 1991; Flynn, 1982). Indeed, in organizations such as policing and prisons, which are highly patriarchal, women are operating in repressive systems (Heidensohn, 1992, 26). A recent Canadian study of women working in a jail reported three major forms of gender discrimination that are organizational/structural in nature: limiting the work hours available to women guards, differential allocation of tasks to women guards, and exclusion of women guards from some assignments (McMahon, 1999).

Despite these negative views that male supervisors and coworkers report of women guards, it appears from more recent publications that women prison/jail workers' acceptance by male coworkers may be better (e.g., Dowden and Tellier, 2004; Hemmens et al., 2002; Lawrence and Mahan, 1998). The token status is likely at issue. A recent study found that women guards employed in exclusively women's jails reported lower levels of sexual harassment than that reported in studies where the institutions were solely for male prisoners (Stohr et al., 1998). Thus, as more women are hired into these traditionally male jobs, along with increased training and policies on harassment, it is hoped that women's work environment will be less hostile.

In the same vein, the security level of the prison appears to influence the acceptance of/resistance to female officers: The more secure the prison (e.g., maximum security is highest), the more resistance exhibited by male guards to female guards (Lawrence and Mahan, 1998; Simpson and White, 1985). "Moreover, the longer one has been employed in corrections, the less liberal his/her attitude toward women guards" (ibid., 291).

Considering their reported experiences of dealing with male coworkers' hostility, it is not surprising that most research reports that women prison and jail workers, particularly in the earlier studies after Title VII was passed, report higher stress levels than men do in these professions (Van Voorhis et al., 1991; Wright and Saylor, 1991; Zupan, 1986). This is at least partially attributed to the constant pressure to prove competence and being worthy of the job to male coworkers and supervisors (McMahon, 1999).

However, more recent studies on jail and prison workers indicate job stress and satisfaction levels are improving for women and resistance from male coworkers is decreasing. A recent study reported that male jail and prison staff generally "had a positive opinion regarding females in the workforce" (Hemmens et al., 2002, 6). Although evaluations of female coworkers did not vary depending on whether the institution was a jail or prison, in this study the respondents' gender, security level of the prison/percent of female staff, and whether the respondent had prior military service had the greatest impact on the evaluation of female officers. The institutions with higher security levels also had the lowest rates of female guards and evaluated women officers less favorably, women tended to evaluate women more positively, and staff with prior military experience rated women less positively (Hemmer et al., 2002).

In another recent study, not only did women and men guards report similar levels of emotional exhaustion and depersonalization on the job but the women also reported *higher* levels of job-related personal achievement and accomplishment than the male guards did (Carlson, Anson, and Thomas, 2003). Notably, for both women and men, stress-training programs decreased the levels of reported job exhaustion and stress (ibid.). In another study, satisfaction was more related to officers' race than gender, but intersections between gender and race/ethnicity were important: African American officers of both sexes were generally less satisfied than their White counterparts with their work, regardless of the racial make-up of the prisoners or guards in the institution, and White women reported higher job satisfaction than White men did (Britton, 1997b). White women's higher rating of job satisfaction was associated with their higher evaluations of the supervision they experience on the job. African American women reported the lowest levels of job satisfaction compared with all other officers, and African American males and females and Latino males reported less job stress and more efficacy in working with prisoners, regardless of the prisoners' races/ethnicities (ibid.). Finally, the race and sex differences did not appear to change over time, that is, with longevity at the job.

Women working prison/jails as guards are generally pessimistic about the likelihood of their own and other women's advancements and promotions (Belknap, 1991; Chapman et al., 1980; Martin and Jurik, 1996; McMahon,

1999; Nallin, 1981). Similarly, a Canadian study of women working in men's prisons and jails reported that the sexist climate of these institutions made these women employees' advancement unlikely and their turnover particularly high (McMahon, 1999).

SUMMARY

It has been noted that the concept "citizenship" is so fraught with male privilege and access that women are routinely excluded, and when included, they stand out as "gendered beings" (Jones, 1990). This chapter is an introduction to understanding women working in the criminal legal system, with a focus on women working in prisons and jails. Perhaps nowhere has resistance to women workers been more heated than women attempting to work with male offenders; perhaps no jobs threaten men's sense of masculinity more than those of arresting, deterring, and incapacitating offenders, particularly male offenders.

Women have struggled with various societal restrictions, as well as legislation and court rulings, in attempts to work in the criminal legal system in the same fields and on equal footing with men. Ironically, while their female status and the presumed characteristics associated with it (e.g., weakness and deep emotions) were what kept women from access to prison and policing work, their initial entry into these fields was for their presumed "maternal" nature and strengths. Women's battle to overcome the barriers to work with male offenders has been grueling and continues to progress slowly. The resistance to change did not end simply by "allowing" women to work with male offenders. Indeed, it is a mistake to assume that legislation and communities committed to equality will in and of themselves remove all discrimination (McLean, 1988, 3). The more recent research indicates some progress in women's stature in the job of guarding prisoners, but the findings are somewhat split as to the degree of success in gender equity concerning the amount of sexism women guards still face and the amount of racism that women of color guards encounter.

REFERENCES

Adams-Fuller, Terri Marie. 2003. Living Up to Her Convictions: A View into the Life of Vernetta D. Young. *Women & Criminal Justice* 15:19–32.

Appier, Janis. 1998. *Policing Women: The Sexual Politics of Law Enforcement in the LAPD*. Philadelphia: Temple University Press.

Atkins, Susan, and Brenda Hoggett. 1984. *Women and the Law*. New York: Basil Blackwell.

Banks, Taunya Lovell. 1997. Two Life Stories: Reflections of One Black Woman Law Professor. Pp. 96–100 in *Critical Race Feminism*, edited by A. K. Wing. New York: New York University Press.

Barnett, Bernice M. 1993. Invisible Southern Black Women Leaders in the Civil Rights Movement. *Gender and Society* 7:16–82.

Bartlett, Katherine T. 1991. Feminist Legal Methods. Pp. 370–403 in *Feminist Legal Theory: Readings in Law and Gender*, edited by K. T. Bartlett and R. Kennedy. Boulder, CO: Westview Press.

Bartol, Curt R., George T. Bergen, Julie Seager Volckens, and Kathleen M. Knoras. 1992. Women in Small-Town Policing: Job Performance and Stress. *Criminal Justice and Behavior* 19:240–259.

Baunach, Phyllis J., and Nicole H. Rafter. 1982. Sex-Role Operations: Strategies for Women Working in the Criminal Justice System. Pp. 341–358 in *Judge, Lawyer, Victim, Thief*, edited by N. H. Rafter and E. A. Stanko. Stoughton, MA: Northeastern University Press.

Belknap, Joanne. 1991. Women in Conflict: An Analysis of Women Correctional Officers. *Women & Criminal Justice* 2:89–115.

———. 2004. Meda Chesney-Lind: The Mother of Feminist Criminology. *Women & Criminal Justice* 15:1–23.

Berger, Margaret A. 1980. *Litigation on Behalf of Women: A Review for the Ford Foundation*. New York: Ford Foundation Publication.

Bernat, Frances P., and Linda Z. Zupan. 1989. Assessment of Personnel Processes Pertaining to Women in a Traditionally Male Dominated Occupation: Affirmative Action Policies and Practices in Prisons and Jails. *The Prison Journal* 9:64–72.

Blankenship, Kim M. 1993. Bringing Gender and Race In: U.S. Employment Discrimination Policy. *Gender and Society* 7:204–226.

Britton, Dana M. 1997a. Gendered Organizational Logic: Policy and Practice in Men's and Women's Prisons. *Gender and Society* 11:796–818.

———. 1997b. Perceptions of the Work Environment among Correctional Officers: Do Race and Sex Matter? *Criminology* 35:85–106.

———. 2000. Feminism in Criminology. *Annals of the American Academy of Political and Social Science* 571:57–76.

Bryant, Keith L. Jr. 1969. Kate Barnard, Organized Labor, and Social Justice in Oklahoma during the Progressive Era. *The Journal of Southern History* 35:145–164.

Carlson, Joseph R., Richard H. Anson, and George Thomas. 2003. Correctional Officer Burnout and Stress: Does Gender Matter. *Prison Journal* 83:277–288.

Chamallas, Martha. 1999. *Introduction to Feminist Legal Theory*. Gaithersburg, NY: Aspen Publishers.

Chapman, J. R., E. K. Minor, P. Ricker, T. L. Mills, and M. Bottum. 1980. *Women Employed in Corrections*. Washington, DC: Center for Women Policy Studies.

Cho, Sumi K. 1997. Converging Stereotypes in Racialized Sexual Harassment. Pp. 203–220 in *Critical Race Feminism*, edited by A. K. Wing. New York: New York University Press.

Christopher, W., J. A. Arguelles, R. Anderson, W. R. Barnes, L. F. Estrada, M. Kantor, R. M. Mosk, A. S. Ordin, J. B. Slaughter, and R. E. Tranquada. 1991. Report of the Independent Commission on the Los Angeles Police Department.

Crenshaw, Kimberle. 1989. Demarginalizing the Intersection of Race and Sex: A Black Feminist Critique of Anti-Discrimination Doctrine, Feminist Theory and Anti-Racist Politics. *University of Chicago Legal Forum* 14:139–167.

Deegan, Mary Jo. 2003. Katharine Bement Davis (1860–1935). *Women & Criminal Justice* 14:15–40.

DeFraffenreid v. General Motors, 413 F. Supp. (E. D. M. 1976).

Deitch, Cynthia. 1993. Gender, Race, and Class Politics and the Inclusion of Women in Title VII of the 1964 Civil Rights Act. *Gender and Society* 7:183–203.

Dodge, L. Mara. 2002. *"Whores and Thieves of the Worst Kind": A Study of Women, Crime, and Prisons, 1835–2000*. Dekalb: Northern Illinois University Press.

Dothard v. Rawlinson, 433 U.S. 321 (1977).

Dowden, Craig, and Claude Tellier. 2004. Predicting Work-Related Stress in Correctional Officers: A Meta-Analysis. *Journal of Criminal Justice* 32:31–47.

Dreifus, Claudia. 1982. Why Two Women Cops Were Convicted of Cowardice. Pp. 427–436 in *The Criminal Justice System and Women*, edited by B. R. Price and N. J. Sokoloff. New York: Clark Boardman.

Epstein, Cynthia F. 1988. *Deceptive Distinctions: Sex, Gender, and Social Order*. New Haven, CT: Yale University Press.

Feinman, Clarice. 1986. *Women in the Criminal Justice System*. New York: Praeger.

Felkenes, George T., and Jean Reith Schroedel. 1993. A Case Study of Minority Women in Policing. *Women & Criminal Justice* 4: 65–90.

Fergus, T. D. 1988. Women and the Parliamentary Franchise in Great Britain. Pp. 80–101 in *The Legal Relevance of Gender*, edited by S. McLean and N. Burrows. Atlantic Highlands, NJ: Humanities International.

Flowers, Ronald Barri. 1987. *Women and Criminality: The Woman as Victim, Offender, and Practitioner*. Westport, CT: Greenwood Press.

Flynn, Edith E.. 1982. Women as Criminal Justice Professionals: A Challenge to Tradition. Pp. 305–340 in *Judge, Lawyer, Victim, Thief*, edited by N. H. Rafter and E. A. Stanko. Stoughton, MA: Northeastern University Press.

Frakas, Mary Ann. 1999. Inmate Supervisory Style: Does Gender Make a Difference? *Women & Criminal Justice* 10:25–45.

Freedman, Estelle B. 1996. *Maternal Justice: Miriam Van Waters and the Female Reform Tradition*. Chicago: University of Chicago Press.

Fronczek, Peter. 2005. *Income, Earnings and Poverty from the 2004 American Community Survey*. U.S. Department of Commerce, U.S. Census Bureau. http://www.census.gov/prod/2005pubs/acs-01.pdf.

Frontiero v. Richardson, 411 U.S. 677 (1973).

Gates, Margaret J. 1976. Occupational Segregation and the Law. Pp. 61–74 in *Women and the Workplace: The Implications of Occupational Segregation*, edited by M. Blaxall and B. Reagan. Chicago: University of Chicago Press.

Geschwender, James A., and Rita Carroll-Seguin. 1990. "Exploding the Myth of African-American Progress." Signs: Journal of Women in Culture and Society 15:285–299.

Gibelman, Margaret. 2003. So How Far Have We Come? Pestilent and Persistent Gender Gap in Pay. *Social Work* 48:22–32.

Gratch, Linda. 1995. Sexual Harassment among Police Officers. Pp. 55–77 in *Women, Law, and Social Control*, edited by A.V. Merlo and J. M. Pollock. Boston: Allyn and Bacon.

Greene, Linda S. 1997. Tokens, Role Models, and Pedagogical Politics: Lamentations of an African American. Pp. 88–95 in *Critical Race Feminism*, edited by A. K. Wing. New York: New York University Press.

Griffin, Marie L. 2002. The Influence of Professional Orientation on Detention Officers' Attitudes toward the Use of Force. *Criminal Justice & Behavior* 29:250–277.

Hagan, John, and Fiona Kay. 1995. *Gender in Practice: A Study of Lawyers' Lives*. New York: Oxford University Press.

Hawkes, Mary Q. 1998. Edna Mahan: Sustaining the Reformatory Tradition. *Women & Criminal Justice* 9:1–23.

Heidensohn, Frances. 1992. *Women in Control?: The Role of Women in Law Enforcement*. Oxford, England: Clarendon Press.

Hemmens, Craig, Mary K. Stohr, Mary Schoeler, and Bona Miller. 2002. One Step Up, Two Steps Back: The Progression of Perceptions of Women's Work in Prisons and Jails. *Journal of Criminal Justice* 523:1–17.

Hoff, Joan. 1991. *Law, Gender, and Injustice: A Legal History of U.S. Women*. New York: New York University Press.

Holley, Phillip D., and Dennis Brewster. 1998. A Brief History of Women in Oklahoma Corrections. *Journal of the Oklahoma Criminal Justice Research Consortium* 4:1–8.

Hughes, Everett C. 1944. Dilemmas and Contradictions of Status. *American Journal of Sociology* 50:353–359.

Jenne, Denise L., and Robert C. Kersting. 1996. Aggression and Women Correctional Officers in Male Prisons. *Prison Journal* 76:442–460.

Jones, Kathleen B. 1990. Citizenship in a Woman-Friendly Polity. *Signs: Journal of Women in Culture and Society* 15:781–812.

Jordan v. Gardner. 1986 F. 2d 1521 (U.S. App. 1993).

Jurik, Nancy C. 1985. An Officer and a Lady: Organizational Barriers to Women Working as Correctional Officers in Men's Prisons. *Social Problems* 32:375–388.

———. 1988. Striking a Balance: Female Correctional Officers, Gender Role Stereotypes, and Male Prisoners. *Sociological Inquiry* 58: 291–304.

Jurik, Nancy C., and G. J. Halemba. 1984. Gender, Working Conditions and the Job Satisfaction of Women in a Non-Traditional Occupation: Female Correctional Officers in Men's Prisons. *Sociological Quarterly* 25:551–566.

Kanter, Rosabeth M. 1977a. *Men and Women of the Corporation*. New York: Basic Books.

———. 1977b. Some Effects of Proportions on Group Life: Skewed Sex Ratios and Responses to Token Women. *American Journal of Sociology* 82:965–990.

King, Deborah K. 1988. Multiple Jeopardy, Multiple Consciousness: The Context of a Black Feminist Ideology. *Signs: Journal of Women in Culture and Society* 14:12–72.

Kirp, David L., Mark G. Yudof, and Marlene S. Franks. 1986. *Gender Justice*. Chicago: University of Chicago Press.

Kissel, Peter J., and Paul L. Katsampes. 1980. The Impact of Women Corrections Officers on the Functioning of Institutions Housing Male Inmates. *Journal of Offender Counseling, Services and Rehabilitation* 4:213–231.

Lawrence, Richard, and Sue Mahan. 1998. Women Corrections Officers in Men Prisons. *Women & Criminal Justice* 9:23–62.

Laws, Judith L. 1975. The Psychology of Tokenism: An Analysis. *Sex Roles* 1:51–67.

Lewis, Diane. 1977. A Response to Inequality: Black Women, Racism, and Sexism. *Signs: Journal of Women in Culture and Society* 3:339–361.

Lucie, Patricia. 1988. Discrimination against Males in the USA. Pp. 216–243 in *The Legal Relevance of Gender*, edited by S. McLean and N. Burrows. Atlantic Highlands, NJ: Humanities International.

Mars, Joan Rosemary. 2001. Coramae Richey Mann on Women, Crime and the Color of American Justice. *Women & Criminal Justice* 13:1–26.

Martin, Susan E. 1980. *Breaking and Entering: Policewomen on Patrol*. Berkeley: University of California Press.

———. 1990. *On the Move: The Status of Women in Policing*. Washington, DC The Police Foundation.

———. 1992. The Changing Status of Women Officers. Pp. 281–305 in *The Changing Roles of Women in the Criminal Justice System*, 2nd ed., edited by I. L. Moyer. Prospect Heights, IL: Waveland Press.

———. 1994. "Outsider within" the Station House: The Impact of Race and Gender on Black Women Police. *Social Problems* 41:383–400.

Martin, Susan E., and Nancy C. Jurik. 1996. *Doing Justice, Doing Gender: Women in Law and Criminal Justice Occupations*. Thousand Oaks, CA: Sage.

Maschke, Karen J. 1996. Gender in the Prison Setting: The Privacy-Equal Employment Dilemma. *Women & Criminal Justice* 7(2):23–42.

McLean, Sheila A. M. 1988. The Legal Relevance of Gender: Some Aspects of Sex-Based Discrimination. Pp. 1–15 in *The Legal Relevance of Gender*, edited by S. McLean and N. Burrows. Atlantic Highlands, NJ: Humanities International.

McMahon, Maeve. 1999. *Women on Guard: Discrimination and Harassment in Corrections*. Toronto: University of Toronto Press.

Meyerowitz, Joanne J. 1988. *Women Adrift: Independent Wage Earners in Chicago, 1880–1930*. Chicago: University of Chicago Press.

Moran, Beverly I. 1990–1991. Quantum Leap: A Black Woman Uses Legal Education to Obtain Her Honorary White Pass. *Berkeley Women's Law Journal* 6:118–121.

Morash, Merry, and Robin N. Haarr. 1995. Gender, Workplace Problems, and Stress in Policing. *Justice Quarterly* 12:113–140.

Morris, Allison. 1987. *Women, Crime, and Criminal Justice*. Oxford, England: Basil Blackwell.

Morton, Joann B. 1981. Women in Correctional Employment: Where Are They Now and Where Are They Headed? Pp. 7–16 in *Women in Corrections*, edited by B. H. Olsson. College Park, MD: American Correctional Association.

Nallin, J. A. 1981. Female Correctional Administrators: Sugar and Spice Are Nice but a Backbone of Steel Is Essential. Pp. 17–26 in *Women in Corrections*, edited by B. H. Olsson. College Park, MD: American Correctional Association.

Ott, E. M. 1989. Effects of the Male–Female Ratio at Work: Policewomen and Male Nurses. *Psychology of Women Quarterly* 13:41–58.

Petersen, Hanne. 1996. *Home Knitted Law: Norms and Values in Gendered Rule-Making*. Aldershot, England: Dartmouth Publishing.

Pierce, Jennifer L. 1995. *Gender Trials*. Berkeley: University of California Press.

Pogrebin, Mark R., and Eric D. Poole. 1997. The Sexualized Work

Environment: A Look at Women Jail Officers. *The Prison Journal* 77:41–57.

Pollock-Byrne, Joycelyn M. 1986. *Sex and Supervision: Guarding Male and Female Inmates.* New York: Greenwood.

———. 1995. Women in Corrections: Custody and the Caring Ethic. Pp. 97–116 in *Women, Law, and Social Control*, edited by A. V. Merlo and J. M. Pollock. Boston: Allyn and Bacon.

Pollock-Byrne, Joycelyn M., and Barbara Ramirez. 1995. Women in the Legal Profession. Pp. 79–95 in *Women, Law, and Social Control*, edited by A. V. Merlo and J. M. Pollock. Boston: Allyn and Bacon.

Rhode, Deborah L. 1987. Justice, Gender, and the Justices. Pp. 13–34 in *Women, the Courts, and Equality*, edited by L. L. Crites and W. L. Hepperle. Newbury Park, CA: Sage.

———. 1989. *Justice and Gender: Sex Discrimination and the Law.* Cambridge, MA: Harvard University Press.

Rogers, Joseph W. 2000. Mary Belle Harris: Warden and Rehabilitation Pioneer. *Women & Criminal Justice* 11:5–28.

Rosenberg, Janet, Harry Perstadt, and William R. Phillips. 1993. Now That We Are Here: Discrimination, Disparagement, and Harassment of Work and the Experience of Women Lawyers. *Gender and Society* 7:415–433.

Russell, Jennifer M. 1997. On Being a Gorilla in Your Midst, or The Life of One Black Woman in the Legal Academy. Pp. 110–112 in *Critical Race Feminism*, edited by A. K. Wing. New York: New York University Press.

Schulz, Dorothy M. 1989. The Police Matron Movement. *Police Studies* 12:115–124.

———. 1993. Policewomen in the 1950s. *Women & Criminal Justice* 4:5–30.

———. 1995. *From Social Worker to Crimefighter: Women in United States Municipal Policing.* Westport, CT: Praeger.

Simpson, Sally, and Mervin F. White. 1985. The Female Guard in the All-Male Prison. Pp. 276–300 in *The Changing Roles of Women in the Criminal Justice System*, edited by I. L. Moyer. Prospect Heights, IL: Waveland Press.

Sommerlad, Hilary, and Peter Sanderson. 1998. *Gender, Choice and Commitment: Women Solicitors in England and Wales and the Struggle for Equal Status.* Aldershot, England: Ashgate Publishing Company.

Stohr, Mary K., G. Larry Mays, Ann C. Beck, and Tammy Kelley. 1998. Sexual Harassment in Women's Jails. *Journal of Contemporary Criminal Justice* 14:135–155.

Thomas, Claire S. 1991. *Sex Discrimination in a Nutshell.* St. Paul, MN: West.

Townsey, Roi D. 1982. Black Women in American Policing: An Advancement Display. *Journal of Criminal Justice* 10:455–468.

U.S. Bureau of Justice Statistics. 1997. *Sourcebook of Criminal Justice Statistics 1996.* Washington, DC: U.S. Government Printing Office.

———. 2005. *Sourcebook of Criminal Justice Statistics On-Line*, 31st ed. edition. http://www.albany.edu/sourcebook/tost_1.html#1_d

U.S. Census Bureau. 2005. Current Population Survey, 1961–2005 Annual Social and Economic Supplements. Washington, DC: Government Publishing Office.

U.S. Federal Bureau of Prisons. 1993. Federal Bureau of Prisons Annual Statistical Report Calendar Year 1992. Washington, DC: Government Publishing Office.

————. 2000. Federal Bureau of Prisons Quick Facts, April 2000. Washington, DC: Government Publishing Office. http://www.bop.gov/fact0598.html.

————. 2005. Federal Bureau of Prisons Quick Facts, October 2005. Washington, DC: Government Publishing Office. http://www.gov.bop/news/quick.jsp#5.

Van Voorhis, Patricia, Francis T. Cullen, Bruce G. Link, and Nancy T. Wolfe. 1991. The Impact of Race and Gender on Correctional Officers' Orientation to the Integrated Environment. *Journal of Research in Crime and Delinquency* 28:472–500.

Vander Ven, Thomas. 2003. *Working Mothers and Juvenile Delinquency*. New York: LFB Scholarly Publishing.

Walters, S. 1992. Attitudinal and Demographic Differences between Male and Female Corrections Officers. *Journal of Offender Rehabilitation* 18:173–189.

Williams, Christine L. 1992. The Glass Escalator: Hidden Advantages for Men in the "Female" Professions. *Social Problems* 39:253–267.

Wright, Kevin N., and W. G. Saylor. 1991. Male and Female Employees' Perceptions of Prison Work: Is There a Difference? *Justice Quarterly* 8:505–524.

Yates, Heather M. 2002. Margaret Moore: African American Feminist Leader in Corrections. *Women & Criminal Justice* 13:9–26.

Yoder, Janice D. 1991. Rethinking Tokenism: Looking beyond Numbers. *Gender and Society* 5:178–192.

Zimmer, Lynn. 1986. *Women Guarding Men*. Chicago: University of Chicago Press.

————. 1987. How Women Re-Shape the Prison Guard Role. *Gender and Society* 1:415–431.

————. 1988. Tokenism and Women in the Workplace: The Limits of Gender-Neutral Theory. *Social Problems* 35:64–73.

————. 1989. Solving Women's Employment Problems in Corrections: Shifting the Burden to Administrators. *Women & Criminal Justice* 1:55–80.

Zupan, Linda Z. 1986. Gender-Related Differences in Correctional Officers' Perceptions and Attitudes. *Journal of Criminal Justice* 14:349–361.

————. 1992. The Progress of Women Correctional Officers in All-Male Prisons. Pp. 232–244 in *The Changing Roles of Women in the Criminal Justice System*, 2nd ed., edited by I. L. Moyer. Prospect Heights, IL: Waveland Press.

❖

10

Women Working in Policing and Law Enforcement

The marginalization of policewomen is well documented,
but generally ignored within law enforcement agencies.
POGREBIN, DODGE, AND CHATMAN 2000, 312

This chapter is on women who work as police officers or patrol sheriffs. I avoid the terms *policewoman* and *policewomen*, opting for the bulkier phrasing *woman police officer* or *women police officers*, given that regardless of sex, present-day police and law enforcement officers are expected to perform the same job. This is to deny neither the sexism still operating in job assignments and expectations in many departments nor the sexist treatment many women police officers experience on the job. Rather it is a recognition of the power of language and labels and an effort not to imply in any way that women and men should have different responsibilities, and thus, different titles, in policing and law enforcement jobs.

In the last chapter, I discussed the importance of asking: What difference could it have made to exclude women from these decision-making jobs in our justice system? As we learn about women's restriction in law enforcement jobs, it is useful to question whether responses to intimate partner abuse, stalking, and sexual victimizations may have been taken more seriously by the police if women had been allowed to work as officers (and been promoted up into the ranks) since the inception of these agencies.

THE HISTORY OF WOMEN IN POLICING

As stated in the last chapter, there are significant parallels regarding women's entry into jobs as prison and jail guards and those in policing. Both roles have long histories of stereotypical roles (such as working in clerical roles or with juveniles or women offenders); both still represent small percentages of overall employees in their departments (particularly in administration); both attained their current status through court challenges and despite strong male resistance; and substantial evidence suggests that both are as successful as their male counterparts (Pollock-Byrne, 1986, 5). Women prison reformers gained legitimacy for women professionals in public agencies caring for women, which "paved the way for the first police matrons and then women police officers to follow in establishing their own legitimacy in the criminal justice field" (Schulz, 1989, 117). The entrance of women into U.S. police work began in the late 1800s, spurred by increased problems with women and girls that male police officers seemed uninterested in or unable to confront, particularly prostitution (Appier, 1998; Feinman, 1986). Mrs. J. K. Barney, an executive officer of the Women's Christian Temperance Union (WCTU), spent some twenty years agitating in New York City for the appointment of police matrons, whom she described as ideally middle-aged, "scrupulously clean in person and dress, with a face to commend her and a manner to compel respect; quiet, calm, observant, with faith in God and hope for humanity" (as cited in Segrave, 1995, 7). WCTU, "probably the most powerful women's group of the era," has been identified as spearheading the demand for police matrons in the United States for the last quarter of the 1800s (Schulz, 1995, 12). Although New York State passed legislation in 1888 allowing New York City to appoint two such matrons to each station, they did not provide the funding for the positions, so no matrons were hired. Notably, the press played a significant role in the ensuing years, often arguing for the need of matrons in New York City (Segrave, 1995). "The first four matrons started work in New York City police stations on October 5, 1891, much later than in many other cities, and by 1899 the city employed sixty-one police matrons" (ibid., 10). In 1905, Lola Baldwin was hired as a safety worker in Portland, Oregon, to protect women and girls from male miners, lumberjacks, and laborers (Feinman, 1986).

During World War I in England, women conducted voluntary police patrol work to control other women such as prostitutes (Morris, 1987). Drawing on Martin's work in distinguishing phases in the early history of women police in the United States, Heidensohn's comparison of British and U.S. women police officers' historical phases adds another phase, a preliminary one. Specifically, Heidensohn (1992, 41) describes the first phase of women's entry into policing as *moral reform, rescue,* and *matrons* (1840–1910 in the United States and 1915 in England), the second phase as specialists and pioneers (1910 in the United States and 1915–1930 in England), and the third phase as latency and depression (1930–1945 in both countries). Heidensohn (1992) has also noted an expansion phase as a fourth phase occurring in the late 1960s and 1970s, when both England and the United States saw an unprecedented number of women police officers hired. (Martin and Jurik [1996] report similar phases.)

Regarding the *moral reform, rescue, and matron phase* in policing, many of the first women police officers identified more as social workers than as "cops" and saw

---

Comparative Perspectives: Women Police Stations in São Paulo, Brazil

In the early 1980s, Brazilian feminist activists helped elect the Partido do Movimento Democrático Brasileiro, an opposition party that gained control in many state governments, including São Paulo, Brazil (Santos, 2004). The newly elected governor of São Paulo, Franco Montoro, established Conselho Estadual da Condição Feminina (the State Council on the Feminine Condition) in 1983, staffed primarily by intellectual and middle-class feminists (ibid.). Concerned with intimate partner abuse and sexual victimization, these women helped implement Delegacia da Muher (DdM), the world's first all-women police station, in 1985, designed to respond to violent crimes against women (ibid.).

Notably, many of the women officers (*delegacias*) were transferred (unwillingly) from the regular police departments to DdM and did *not* identify themselves as feminists. They viewed feminists as "against men," particularly against male police officers (ibid.). Even the first head of DdM, Rosemary Corrêa, was not pleased about her appointment because she perceived that this would ruin her career in policing, she did not view violence against women as a "real" crime that should be addressed by the police instead of social workers, and she believed the regular police departments did not discriminate against women clients (ibid., 38). Thus, her belief that the DdM was unnecessary was severely challenged when 500 women lined up to file complaints the first day the DdM opened. Corrêa not only changed her idea that the DdM was unnecessary but she also grew to see her job and the DdM as extremely important, to "love" her work, and to understand feminism as "a movement struggling for women's rights" rather than being "against men," and she began to publicly identify herself as a feminist (ibid.).

Corrêa served as a great director/chief (*delegada)* of the DdM partly because she understood so well how the *delegacias* (women police) working under her were reluctant to work in the DdM for the same reasons she had been reluctant to head it (e.g., felt like their new job was not true policing and viewed responding to women victims of male violence as unimportant policing work). Similar to Corrêa, many of the women she supervised changed their views about women victims of male violence, the need for the DdM, and their lack of power compared to male officers (although none of them adopted the identity of "feminist" for themselves (ibid.).

SOURCE: Cecília M. Santos. 2004. En-Gendering the Police: Women's Police Stations and Feminism in São Paulo. *Latin American Research Review* 39:29–55.

---

their role as helping women and children. Indeed, between 1880 and 1930 in the United States, "many women activists devoted their entire careers in social work and social science to identifying the welfare needs of working-class women and children and pressing for the establishment of government programs and institutions to meet those needs" (Appier, 1998, 13). Importantly, the few African American women police officers were even further segregated—very much a minority within a minority. Hired to work specifically with African American women and juveniles, they shared many of the characteristics of their White sisters. They, too, were usually better educated than the average African American man or woman, and they were often teachers, social workers, or ministers' wives with status in their communities (Schulz, 2004a, 486). But it is important to remember that these stereotyped roles "were not forced on them [the African American and White women police] by the male police establishment but were the roles they sought" (ibid.).

The first two decades of the 1900s in the United States were important in advancing women into police departments, albeit in stereotypical roles. Hence, the phase after the preliminary entrance phase for women (the moral reform, rescue, and matron phase) has been identified as the *specialist phase* (Heidensohn, 1992; Martin and Jurik, 1996). Between 1910 and 1930, women police officers largely worked in specialist roles within the police departments, usually confined to traditionally female skills (Garcia, 2003; Martin, 1980). Martin and Jurik (1996, 49), however, state that the specialist phase in the United States lasted from the designation of the first woman police officer in 1910 through Title VII in 1972. However, it appears the 1910 to 1930 era had some unique characteristics as well. Although women were hired as women police officers in more cities from 1918 to 1929, "in absolute terms their number remained small" (Segrave, 1995, 44). "In 1930 there were reportedly 600 women police officers employed in 289 communities in the United States" (ibid., 85). Overall, policing itself did not change much between 1920 and the 1940s, including the hiring and roles of women police officers (Schulz, 1993).

The first woman in the United States to hold the title "policewoman" was Alice Stebbins Wells, in Los Angeles, California, in 1910 (Feinman, 1986; Hale and Bennett, 1995; Segrave, 1995). The first African American woman in the United States appointed to policing was Georgia Robinson, appointed as a matron to the Los Angeles Police department in 1916, and in 1919 she became a woman police officer in this department (Schulz, 1995). In Toronto, two women police officers were appointed in 1913 (Segrave, 1995), and the first woman to be sworn in and given arrest powers in England occurred in 1915 in Grantham, England (Heidensohn, 1992, 29). It has been noted that England's struggle for women police officers, relative to the United States, required far more organizing and lobbying, and the battle to achieve the first hires were more prolonged (ibid.). However, in both of these countries, these initial hires did not guarantee the security of women in policing: Instead, their entry was every bit as precarious as their initial hiring (ibid.). The phenomenon described in Heidensohn's (ibid., 54) third phase in women's policing, *latency and depression*, where stagnation in hiring women occurred between 1930 and 1945, was partly due to the Depression but even more so was a result of women's insecure entry into policing, which made a poor basis for expansion. Evidence of this is that in 1925, the City Council in Los Angeles considered reclassifying women officers from members of the LAPD police force to civilian employees (Appier, 1998). After intensive lobbying, the women officers won the right to continue to be classified as policewomen.

Making an international comparison of the first women police is difficult. Specifically, it is sometimes difficult to distinguish who qualifies as a woman police officer. Many of the early women gaining access to policing jobs across the globe, similar to those in the United States, were volunteers or, if paid, were still considered civilians. Thus, semantics makes it difficult to establish a clear time line. In England, there was friction between different groups of women advocating for women police officers on the British police departments, particularly in London. In 1918, the Metropolitan Police Women Patrols was announced, but it was a blow to some organizers because these women had fewer powers, such as

T A B L E 10.1 Different Countries' Adoption
of Women into Policing Roles

Canada[a]	1913
China[a]	1933
England[c]	1915
Germany[a]	1903
India[b]	1939
Japan[a]	1946
Nigeria[a]	1955
Poland[a]	1925
Sweden[a]	1949
United States[a]	1910

Compiled from data reported in the text in [a]Segrave (1995),
[b]Natarajan (1996), (1995), [c]Heidensohn (1992).

no power to arrest, than were available to the few women police officers elsewhere in the country (Douglas, 1999, 72). Natarajan (1996, 2) notes that women
play more minor roles in policing in the more traditional societies, and "the
willingness of various societies and their criminal justice systems to deploy
women as line officers in their police forces varies with the stage of social and
economic development in a given society and in relation to the strength of a
resistive or supportive culture." A 1961 report from a commission on hiring
women into policing in India supported hiring women, but only if they were
unmarried (Natarajan, 1996). At any rate, keeping in mind the disjuncture about
what counts as a woman police officer, Table 10.1 is an attempt to identify the
reported dates that various countries adopted some type of woman police officer
onto the police force (albeit in very stereotypical roles).

Alice Stebbins Wells, the first "policewoman" in the United States, was a
social worker and theologian who believed she could accomplish more to help
women and girls through police work than through volunteer work (Feinman,
1986). When asked why she wanted to enter policing, she answered that women
were more suited than men for some aspects of policing, such as comforting and
guiding wayward or abused children and preventing the victimization and
offending of women and children (Appier, 1998). Although the press negatively
characterized Wells as "unfeminine" and "muscular," she also received some
support (Feinman, 1986). (This is an example of Rafter and Stanko's [1982] image
of the "active woman as masculine," discussed in Chapter 1.) When she addressed
the International Associate of Chiefs of Police in 1914, she was treated extremely
rudely by the audience, including a heckler who yelled, "Call the patrol wagon,
another nut gone wrong" (Segrave, 1995, 15). It is unknown how long she stayed
on the force, but it is evident she had retired at least by 1934. Soon after
becoming the first "policewoman," Wells engaged in a heavy speaking tour

across the United States and Canada and was influential in mobilizing to bring about change in the hiring practices in many places (Appier, 1998).

There is considerable evidence that various women's groups in large cities across the United States advocated for the hiring of "matrons" and "police-women" around 1910, with many women willing to have these jobs. The pressure from these women's groups was significant regarding women's appointments to police departments in the United States between 1910 and 1970 (Segrave, 1995, 24). However, it is important to keep in mind that "[b]efore the 1970s, nearly all police officers in the United States were [W]hite men" (Martin and Jurik, 1996, 48).

Alice Stebbins Wells, along with other women police officers, is credited with helping to form the International Association of Policewomen (IAP). This professional organization lasted from 1915 to 1932. Unfortunately, this and other women's groups declined along with other reformist and temperance groups (e.g., the WCTU), especially given the IAP leadership's lack of recognition from men's policing groups, particularly the International Association of Chiefs of Police (IACP) (Schulz, 1995). Schulz (ibid., 55) maintains that the demise of the IAP was partly due to the leaders' inability to anticipate societal shifts but that such a focus "fails to recognize that even though the early women police officers were greatly expanding women's sphere by entering the police environment, they continued to accept the view of different roles for men and women." Indeed, their approach helped fuel an extremely sexist approach to hiring police.

> In 1917, the U.S. Civil Service Commission established a minimum standard for women police officers, consisting of a high school education and at least two years' practical experience in social casework or its equivalent in technical training and business experience. These standards were endorsed by the IACP and by the IAP and were then being implemented gradually in most areas. Male police had to meet a much lower standard, with high school graduation not being required in many areas until the 1960s (Segrave, 1995, 28).

Notably, the longevity of the sense of women as inherently nurturing and of the appropriateness of assigning women to specialized tasks commensurate with their nurturing is evidenced by the Los Angeles City Mothers' Bureau. This institution, a branch of the LAPD, lasted from 1914 to 1964 and was staffed completely by women police officers to work in crime prevention and give advice and aid on such matters as "disobedient children, spousal support, abusive husbands, alcoholism, immigration and citizenship, neighborhood quarrels, adultery, unem-ployment, and adoptions" (Appier, 1998, 73). During the postwar period of the 1950s and 1960s, the number of women police officers increased, but increased variation in roles was not commensurate (Schulz, 1993). Women police officers during this time, however, were actively attempting to broaden their roles. Title VII, therefore, did not create women police officers' desire for equality but rather provided legal support for changes that began in the 1950s (Schulz, 1993). None-theless, prior to 1968, "no women were assigned to the backbone of policing, patrol duty" (Martin, 1980, 48), and until 1972, women police officers' roles typically evolved around assisting male police officers (Hale, 1992).

In 1968, when the Indianapolis Police Department assigned Betty Blankenship and Elizabeth Coffal to patrol, they became the first women police officers to wear uniforms, strap gun belts to their waists, drive a marked patrol car, and answer general-purpose police calls on an equal basis with men police officers. Although they eventually left patrol and returned to traditional women police officers' duties, they broke the link to the mothering concept that had been the basis of women's roles in policing. Once this link was severed, the stage was set for the beginning of the modern women-on-patrol era (Schulz, 1995, 5).

Thus, the culture of policing remained virtually the same for women from the late nineteenth-century to the 1960s (Hale and Bennett, 1995). Indeed, until the 1970s in the United States, the history of the woman police officer reveals duties that were custodial and directed toward females and juveniles, whereas the man police officer's duties involved punitive and arrest powers (Garcia, 2003, 134). Women's entry into policing, then, has been hard won and is certainly not over. A major part of women's roles in both policing and prison work is appearing to be "man" enough for the job. Segrave notes the following regarding the first woman police officer killed in the line of duty:

> The first policewoman killed in the line of duty was 24-year old Gail Cobb of the Washington, DC, force, who was fatally shot in September 1974 while chasing a shotgun-toting fugitive. It was even suggested in some quarters that this incident would help ease the way for female entry into policing; that it would be a sort of baptism under fire and show that females were made of the right stuff. Needless to say, it had no such effect; discrimination and harassment continued apace. (1995, 115)

RATES OF WOMEN IN POLICING

In 1971, there were only seven women police officers on patrol in the United States (Gates, 1976). With the implementation of Title VII, the number of women officers on patrol exploded. Martin (1990, xi) notes, "Women's representation in municipal police departments serving populations over 50,000 has grown from 4.2 percent of all officers in 1978 to nearly 9 percent of officers at the end of 1986." In 1998, women constituted 10.5 percent of law enforcement personnel in the United States. In the United States in 2000, women constituted 16.3 percent of full-time sworn personnel in large city departments, 12.5 percent of full-time sworn personnel in sheriff departments, and 10.6 percent of full-time sworn personnel in local police departments (U.S. Bureau of Justice Statistics, 2005). Another government report stated the following statistics for 2000:

> Fourteen percent of the officers in larger municipal police departments and sheriffs' officers were women, as were 12 percent of county police officers [sheriffs]. Women accounted for 6 percent of the officers in State agencies.

From 1990 to 2000, the average percentage of female officers increased for each type of agency except sheriffs' offices. (Reaves and Hickman, 2004, v)

In U.S. local police departments, 6.5 percent of sworn officers are White women, 2.7 percent are African American women, and 1.1 percent are Latina. In U.S. sheriffs' departments, 9.1 percent of sworn officers are White women, 2.3 percent are African American women, and 0.8 percent are Latina (U.S. Bureau of Justice Statistics, 2005). In Canada, women's representation in law enforcement grew from 0.6 percent in 1965 to 15.3 percent in 2002 (Statistics Canada, 2002, as cited in Tougas et al., 2005).

A study evaluating political factors related to hiring women police officers in urban departments found that departments experiencing budget reductions hired significantly fewer women police officers (Warner, Steel, and Lovrich, 1989). Nonetheless, a growth in the number of available policing positions did not result in a corresponding increase in the hiring of women. Notably, the more women on city council, the more women hired onto the police department. Furthermore, although verbal affirmative action commitments were unrelated to the rate of women police officers hired, court-imposed and formal voluntary programs were effective in increasing the number of women police officers (ibid.). These findings suggest the importance of having women in political leadership roles and of formal policies to increase the rate of women in policing. However, a Florida study examined the effect of the local labor market on women's representations in local law enforcement jobs and reported that "[n]either the degree of parity between men and women in local economic conditions nor the availability of a qualified female applicant pool affected the percentage of women in individual departments" (Poulos and Doerner, 1996, 19).

A study on the racial and gender make-up of law enforcement officers in Southern California reported that different factors are related to "who is hired" (Schroedel et al., 1996). Notably, while similar factors resulted in hiring both African American women and African American men, there were gender differences among the hiring of White officers and among the hiring of Latino/a officers. (1) A higher percentage of African American population in the jurisdiction served increases the likelihood of both African American women and African American men being hired as officers. (2) When the police chief is a person of color, there is a greater likelihood for both African American women and African American men to be hired. (3) Affirmative action policies increased the likelihood of hiring African American women but not African American men. (4) The greater the Latino/a population, the greater the likelihood of Latino men but *not* Latina women being hired onto the police department. (5) When the police chief was a person of color, this increased the likelihood of Latino men but *not* Latina women hired. (6) The higher the violent crime rate, the less likely Latino men would be hired, but this variable was unrelated to the hiring of Latina women. (7) The greater the unemployment rate, the greater the likelihood of Latina women but not Latino men being hired. (8) Affirmative action policies increased the likelihood of Latina women but not Latino men being hired. (9) The greater the White population, the more the likelihood of White women but not White men being hired. (10) A police chief of color decreased the likelihood of hiring White women but had no effect on hiring White men. (11) The higher the unemployment and the presence of affirmative action policies, the less White men were represented, with no effect on White women. In sum, different factors appear to influence the likelihood of the hiring of various racial–gender groups (ibid.).

In 1973, Fanchon Blake, a twenty-five-year police force veteran, and some of her female coworkers brought a sex discrimination lawsuit against the city, chief, and police department in Los Angeles two years after the police chief, Ed Davis, announced that women were no longer wanted or needed by the LAPD (*Blake v. City of Los Angeles*, as cited in Felkenes, Peretz, and Schroedel, 1993). Davis reorganized the department not only to stop the hiring of women police officers but also to relegate the existing female officers into receptionist and secretarial roles. The plaintiffs won the suit in an appeals court in 1979, and in 1981, a "mutually agreed–upon 'Consent Decree' was signed" requiring better representation of women of all races as well as African American and Latino men (Felkenes, Peretz, and Schroedel, 1993, 34). Although the decision resulted in an increase in the hiring of women, it was not up to the required number, and little was done to alleviate the daily hostility the women police officers experienced afterward.

Mangai Natarajan (2001, 212) proposes four reasons for the slow integration of women into police forces, which she identifies as male dominated and possibly resulting in permanent barriers to (women's) full integration: (1) prejudice by male officers who view women as unable to perform the job; (2) societal attitudes that women are unable to police; (3) inherent physical differences between women and men; and (4) a lack of women who find the job of policing compatible with personal goals of raising a family. Feminists advocating for women's rights and abilities to be police officers would dispute the last two reasons, claiming there are many strong and physically capable women and many women who currently balance a policing career with raising a family. Or, stated another way, neither the desire or ability to police is biological. Thus, the first two reasons are likely the best explanations for women's low representation in even desiring policing (recruitment) and, once there, wanting to stay when they are discriminated against (retention).

Jennifer Brown's (1997) evaluation of women police officers in European countries suggests a six-stage process by which women become integrated into police forces. The first stage, *entry*, is often the result of a shortage of men to serve as police officers (e.g., World War I in Europe). The second stage, *separated restricted development*, is a departmental structure that limits women officers to working solely with women and children. This sexist restriction leads to legislation requiring the third stage, *integration*. Integration, mandated by legislation, is often met with resistance by male police officers, which results in litigation by women officers. This litigation leads to the fourth phase, *takes off*, where the number of women increases substantially, which leads to further backlash, including sexual harassment of women officers by men officers (ibid.). Research conducted to document this resistance by male officers and poor treatment of female officers has resulted in the fifth phase, *reform*, where there is increased inspection by outsiders, a clearer grievance process, and improved training. The final phase is *tip-over*, where the number of women increases from a small minority to more equal representation (about 25 percent). Brown (ibid.) suggests that this model helps explain the varying rates of women officers across countries due to varying rates of progress through these stages.

Natarajan (2001, 213) believes that Brown's six-stage model may work for Western countries but questions its applicability to traditional societies with very different expectations about the roles and duties of women. In a long-term and cross-national study of women police officers, Natarajan (2001) collected data from hundreds of women officers during three time periods (1988, 1994, 2000) and from a variety of police departments (all-women, sex/gender integrated, experienced professional women officers, and new-recruit women) in Tamil Nadu in India, as well as 1988 data on women officers in New Jersey in the United States. Two data collection points were from all-women units implemented in Tamil Nadu in the early 1990s to provide an entirely female force to respond primarily to women victims of male violence. Her questionnaire included items assessing the respondents' preferred roles for women officers: *traditional* (women officers' jobs are different from men officers' jobs, typically restricted to responding to women and children); *modified* (women take on similar duties as men, except they are restricted if violence is likely); and *integrated* (women and men have identical policing responsibilities). Her first finding was that women in the all-women units were more likely in 2000 than in 1994 to desire to be in integrated departments. She speculates that this might be due to disenchantment with the units, "but it may also be a result of improved confidence gained as a result of working successfully in the [all-woman] units" (ibid., 228). Second, new recruits (a younger generation) were more likely than the more experienced/older women officers and the women in the all-woman units to prefer an integrated role. Third, despite these changes indicating Indian women's desires for more integrated policing roles, the new recruits in India in 2002 (76 percent) were significantly less likely than the new recruits in New Jersey in 1988 (93 percent) to prefer an integrated role (ibid.). Natarajan (ibid., 229) concludes that Brown's (1997) integration model may not be limited to Western democracies but that integration of women into policing roles equal to men's in traditional countries is likely slower and subject to more reversals than in Western countries.

Natarajan (2001) described the all-woman departments in Tamil Nadu, India, implemented in the early 1990s, and she favorably evaluates their effect on intimate partner abuse cases (Natarajan, 2005). Others have written about (all) women's police stations implemented in São Paulo, Brazil, in 1985 (Hautzinger, 2002; Santos, 2004). Indeed, São Paulo is the site of the first women's police station in the world (Santos, 2004). Its inception is described in the Comparative Perspectives box for this chapter, but it is useful to point out some of the flaws with the implementation of the all-women unit in São Paulo. There were two primary flaws. First, there was a significant race and class difference between the women designing the department and the *delegacias* (women officers), *delegadas* (chiefs/magistrates of the departments), and the victims to which the *delegacias* responded (Hautzinger, 2002, 243):

Thus, poor black women predominated among the *delegacia's* complainants; lighter-skinned, better educated women worked as police officers, and mostly White, university-educated women led the stations as *delegadas*, or magistrate-police chiefs. In class and color terms, then, the *delegacia* reflected, in micro-cosm, the distribution of status, power, and dependency of the broader society.

The distance between the designers and the women officers produced inappro-priate expectations of women police officers (ibid.). Furthermore, and related to this first flaw, many of the *delegacias* (women officers) working in the department identified their job as more of a requirement of what we might call in this book "doing masculinity." That is, many saw their job as trying to achieve doing the identical work that male officers did. Thus, the feminists designing the program seriously erred in their assumptions that the *delegadas* and *delegacias* were feminists who wanted to help women victims of male violence (Hautzinger, 2002; Santos, 2004). This strong identification women police officers felt as *police*, or as potentially violent, somewhat masculinized workers, complicated their ability to identify with the female victims they attended (Hautzinger, 2002, 246). In sum, the idea was exciting, but the implementation was seriously hampered by a failure to understand the lives and experiences of the *delegacias, delegadas,* and the clients they served.

Women were not appointed to the Secret Service and the Federal Bureau of Investigation as agents until 1972, and in 1993, almost 10 percent of the U.S. Secret Service agents were women (Segrave, 1995, 111–112). As Schulz (1995, 6) states, "exceedingly few women have reached the top of all but small police agencies." Penny E. Harrington served as the chief of the Portland (Oregon) police department from 1984 to 1986. "As of 1994, only two additional women had served as chiefs in major cities, and fewer than 100 of the more than 17,000 municipal law enforcement agencies were led by women" (ibid., 6). In 2004, there were about 200 women chiefs of police and 30 women sheriffs in the United States, about 1 percent of these law enforcement leadership positions (Schulz, 2004b). Two recent books have been published on women in leadership positions in policing, one on the United States (ibid.) and one on England (Silvestri, 2003). Both docu-ment the varying ways these women climbed to the top and the many obstacles they faced, and both discuss the potential for women at the top to change policing.

WHY DO WOMEN WANT TO BE POLICE OFFICERS?

The research investigating why women want to be police officers mirrors the same reasons why men want to be police officers. Primarily, both women and men give the reason that they want to help people or to give back to their communities (Schulz, 2004b). A study of women police chiefs found that many of them began their policing careers after careers in teaching or nursing, careers that help others (ibid.). However, women also choose policing because of the salary and benefits or the potential for excitement, or simply out of curiosity (ibid.). Notably, most helping professions for women do not pay as well as work in law enforcement or firefighting: In all but a very few cities, police officers and firefighters earn higher salaries and can retire at younger ages than teachers and social workers (ibid., 18). Somewhat similar to what we will learn about women's advancement into the field of law in the following chapter, women chiefs of police often have/had husbands who were in the police department (Schulz, 2004b).

GENDER DIFFERENCES IN JOB PERFORMANCE

One of the major arguments against women on patrol centered on whether women were physically strong enough to be patrol officers (Townsey, 1982a). The vast majority of studies examining gender differences in the criminal legal system job performances have centered on policing and were conducted shortly after Title VII resulted in hiring women in larger numbers on patrol. For the most part, these studies reported that the women were as capable as men (Bartlett and Rosenblum, 1977; Bartol et al., 1992; Bloch and Anderson, 1974; Grennan, 1987; Sherman, 1975; Sichel et al., 1978). This is particularly impressive given a study on the evaluations of women on patrol, which found that the studies themselves were sexist, valuing typically male traits and devaluing typically female traits—most of which were not shown to be meaningfully related to policing (Morash and Greene, 1986). In sum, then, most of the evaluations of women on patrol in some manner assumed that *male* police officers do the job right in order to judge whether women police officers measure up. In fact, even with these sexist presuppositions, they measured up quite well. Progress in acceptance of women officers is evident in a 1990 study:

> [T]he salience of the physical differences [between women and men officers] has decreased because women officers have proven their ability to defend themselves and their partners. In addition, defensive tactics courses have been developed to overcome many of the disadvantages of smaller stature, and departmental policies (often designed to avoid law-suits) have curbed officers' physical aggressiveness. (Martin, 1990, xiii)

Researchers evaluating women police officers often report that, generally, they bring positive aspects to the policing role. For example, some research found that women police officers tend to have more support from and improved relations with citizens than do male police officers (Bloch and Anderson, 1974; Felkenes and Trostle, 1990; Marshall, 1973; Sichel et al., 1978). Other researchers suggest that women police officers are better at de-escalating potentially violent situations than are male officers (Belknap and Shelley, 1993; Bell, 1982; Gates, 1976; Grennan, 1987). Research has also indicated that women police officers may be more likely to have traits that should be associated with "good policing," such as having empathy for rape victims and battered women and possessing a broader and more creative outlook on policing (Feinman, 1986; Homant and Kennedy, 1985; Kennedy and Homant, 1983; Price, 1974). Research on community-oriented policing (C-O-P) stresses the importance of strong ties between officers and the beats they work and that in many ways this officer–citizen relationship strived for in C-O-P is consistent with early women in policing and even some current-day gendered differences women officers exhibit (Miller, 1999). Moreover, police departments, which are masculinist agencies, are charged with social control (ibid.). At the same time, C-O-P is often negatively stigmatized as social work instead of true crime fighting, even within departments that have C-O-P programs (Garcia, 2005). A study on citizen complaints of police misconduct found that while males are overrepresented among those officers complained about (men comprised 88 percent of the department and received 95 percent of the complaints), of those complained about, there were no gender differences in the types of citizen complaints, including the likelihood of accusations of misuse of force (Lersch, 1998). A similar study of Indianapolis police officers found *no* gender differences in officers' use of either physical or verbal coercion of citizens (Paoline and Terrill, 2004). The only gender difference was that male police officers were more likely to use higher levels of force against male suspects, while levels of force used by females were statistically independent of suspect gender (ibid., 114).

Recent research on African American women police officers details how most were raised in the African American community and how, due to their experiences as African American women, they offer a more compassionate view for the plight of minority people and overall view themselves as more effective in most police–minority encounters (Dodge and Pogrebin, 2001, 556). Clearly, this is consistent with C-O-P guidelines, yet police officers report C-O-P as significantly lacking in departmental support and resulting in ridicule and report being challenged as to whether they are real police officers (Garcia, 2005).

As stated, Title VII resulted in the hiring of many women on police patrol duties for the first time in U.S. history. Even after Title VII, sex segregation was maintained to some degree, which not only marginalized women officers but also provided excuses for gender pay discrimination and limited promotions. For example, in policing, promotions and advancement are directly tied to patrol, detective, and investigative work, yet women were historically barred from these jobs. Also, because these women have remained in such small numbers overall (token status at about 14 percent in 2000) and been in the lower strata of police departments (officers), it has been difficult for them to shape policing in a nonmale manner. Additionally, using the established law to fight discrimination can be hazardous; a backlash of countersuits and hostility—sometimes even violence—is often unleashed against oppressed groups and individuals who sue for basic rights (Smart, 1989, 138).

The question, as Barbara R. Price (1989) pointed out, is how much can women change policing, *or* does policing change women? Is it so hazardous to fight the status quo that women *become* the status quo (do policing by being like men)? Or do women really do the job differently than men? If there were no gender discrimination and sexual harassment, would women do the job differently? Similarly, Schulz (2004a) addresses a debate among feminist criminologists: Should the goal be for gender-neutral policing, where women and men perform the job similarly (i.e., women adapt to men's policing styles), or should the goal be to allow gendered-policing, where women and men perform the job differently? Or perhaps the goal should be commensurate with the women guards in

Zimmer's (1986) study who believed they did the job better than men and the goal should be for men to police more like women police. To some degree this is tongue-in-cheek, but future research needs to establish whether, and if so how, police recruits' ideals of doing policing are gendered. Perhaps there is no longer much in the way of gender differences in what those entering policing expect and how they conduct themselves on the job, especially given research cited in this chapter indicating women may be more like men in policing than originally thought in terms of using coercion, force, and comfort with citizens, or at least are when they first enter into patrol work (e.g., De Jong, 2004; Lersch, 1998; Paoline and Terrill, 2004).

One recent study documents the gendered way that emotional labor is conducted among police (Martin, 1999). On the one hand, the crime-fighting aspect of the job is highly masculinized, but on the other hand, appropriate, and at least compassionate, responses to victims and witnesses who are often highly distraught is more associated with femininity and nurturing/mothering. Martin (ibid.) describes the various gender expectations of how police officers respond to citizens regarding both the officers' and the citizens' genders (i.e., how male officers communicate with male versus female citizens and how female officers communicate with male versus female citizens). Furthermore, in addition to the gender expectations of officers in their responses to citizens is the gendered responses to their coworkers and supervisors, including sexist societal perceptions of the appropriate means to vent, show fear, and use humor (ibid.). In short, police must respond to people in a variety of circumstances (including as victims and offenders) and must fill the tall order of controlling crime (associated with masculinity) and communication skills (associated with femininity) (ibid.).

A test of this gendered labor was conducted by DeJong (2004) to examine how officer gender and citizen gender were related to police officers' likelihood of providing comfort to citizens. Surprisingly, officers' attitudes and behaviors in using comfort were *not* gendered. Rather, officers, female *and* male, are simply more likely to provide comfort when citizens most need it (e.g., they are injured, depressed, or victimized). However, a study of university students found they have gendered expectations about police officers' appropriate responses, which likely reflects a negative impact on women officers' policing work (Grant, 2000). For example, if they are good with victims, as they are expected to be, they may be required to do more of this work whether or not they want to. The stereotyped determination of appropriate response was further complicated by the type of offense. For example, women's perceived inability to handle calls that could result in death penalty charges is likely transformed into their real evaluations at their jobs (ibid.).

CLASSIFICATIONS OF WOMEN POLICE OFFICERS

The last chapter identified Kanter's labels of roles the first women working in corporations in the 1970s encountered (i.e., pet, mother, seductress, and iron maiden). Research on similar roles available to women in policing forced by male coworkers has been conducted. Similar to the male-focused view of work in prisons, male police officers' understanding of police work is often culturally centered on masculinity, particularly with the stressed importance of physical strength and aggressiveness. This view by male coworkers and supervisors appears to have influenced both the males' views of females as coworkers and, in some cases, the women's views of themselves in these crime-fighting roles.

Consistent with some of Kanter's roles, a study on women police officers found that one-third of the women did not feel supported by male police officers, while the two-thirds who reported feeling close to male police officers expressed being viewed as "mothers," "sisters," and "women" but not as police officers (Jacobs, 1987). A study of the first women police officers on patrol found that the *men* police officers fell into three categories in their views of women police officers: traditionals, moderns, and moderates (Martin, 1980). *Traditionals* believed that women police officers do not belong on patrol and if present should be protected and treated as junior partners. *Moderns* were willing to work with women police officers as equals. Finally, *moderates* were neither supportive nor negative toward women police officers; they tended to be ambivalent. Consistent with other research on token women, African American male coworkers were more supportive than White male coworkers of women police officers as equals (ibid.).

Jennifer Hunt's (1984) participant observation research on gender and policing reported that male coworkers frequently "tested" the women officers (including showing them pornography and taking them to topless bars). Hunt (ibid.) reported the male officers in her study tended to simply dichotomize women police officers as "dykes" or "whores." She learned that the women officers walked a fine line when they attempted to combine elements of both masculinity and femininity in order to gain acceptance. If a woman acts "too feminine," she is criticized for not being suitable for the job. However, if she acts "too masculine," she is criticized for not acting like a woman (Garcia, 2003, 341). Hunt's (1990) study reported that male police officers uncomfortable with women police officers' presence resolved their own confusion by placing women into such stereotypical categories as "seductress," "mother," or "lesbian." Another study found that the White male officers were often "protective" of the White women officers whom they could reduce to "pets," "mothers," and "seductresses," but when African American women acquiesced to these same roles, they did not receive the benefit of White male officers' protection and indeed were seen as "lazy" (Martin, 1994, 391).

While this section reported on some of the ways male coworkers and supervisors categorized women police officers, some research also addressed how the women coped. As already noted, some male police and prison officers are threatened by the idea that a woman can perform their job; they believe it is impossible that a person can be a woman and an officer when everything about the job is so strongly linked with masculinity. Thus, it is probably not surprising that the earliest research on women police officers on patrol found a tendency for these officers to emphasize either the police (POLICEwomen) or the woman (policeWOMEN) aspect of being a police officer (Martin, 1979). Susan E. Martin classified those women who emphasized their *job* over their female status through professionalism, assertiveness, occupational achievement, and departmental loyalty while downplaying their female status as POLICEwomen. On the other hand, Martin's (ibid.) policeWOMEN were women police officers who emphasized their *female* identity, often acquiescing to ascribed female roles (for example, "little girl"), and who were isolated from "real" police work. Notably, the male police officers did not appear to value either POLICEwomen or policeWOMEN. POLICEwomen were seen as strange women, while policeWOMEN were viewed as incompetent officers. Thus, male police officers seemed threatened by evidence that women could do the job, as well as by evidence that they could not. Zimmer's (1986) later work, identifying adjustment strategy roles for women working in prisons and jails, compared her *institutional role* to Martin's (1979) POLICEwomen role and her *modified role* to Martin's (ibid.) policeWOMEN role. (Martin [ibid.] identified two roles, while Zimmer [1986] identified three.)

Martin (1994, 395), similar to Hunt (1984), found that many women police officers struggle "to negotiate an identity that allows them to maintain their femininity, succeed as officers, and gain individual acceptance as 'just me'." In their attempts to do so, they are often critical of other women officers whom they perceive as role-playing the other extremes by acting either too masculine or too feminine (e.g., "sluts," "clinging vines," or making their way around the department on "knee pads") (Martin, 1994, 395). They perceive these too-masculine or too-feminine women coworkers as confirming stereotypes that "rub off" on all women police, including those who have managed a compromise between masculine and feminine.

These categories of women officers are important concerning the various ways that women do gender (see Chapter 1). For some women (including in prison work), a manner of coping is maintaining a strong tie and image to the traditional gender role (e.g., Martin's policeWOMAN). Southgate (1981) collected surveys from almost 700 of the first women in England assigned to do the same policing job as the male officers. In the survey, he distinguished three roles: The *traditional role* is characterized by women's specialized and gender "appropriate" and unique job assignments, such as working with minors and women as both victims and offenders. The *integrated role* is where women are expected to do the same job as the male officers. Finally, the *modified role* is characterized as a cross between the traditional and integrated roles, where women were provided with a wider range of duties than the traditional role but "could take account of differences between the sexes" (ibid., 163). Almost half (49 percent) of these first women assigned to policing identical to their male counterparts preferred a modified role, while over one-third (36 percent) preferred the integrated role, and only 15 percent favored the specialized or traditional role (Southgate, 1981). Of course, it is important to remember that many women are ordered to stereotypical work assignments, such as a recent study of women officers in the Philippines found (de Guzman and Frank, 2004).

Dodge and Pogrebin's (2001) study of African American women police officers found the women reported that most of the White male officers had few interactions with African Americans as children and as adults viewed them as an unknown entity, and a combination of the small numbers of both male and female African American officers and lack of repercussions appeared to allow or even encourage the White officers to use racist slurs when referring to citizens. These women had varying reports on the levels of support from fellow African American male officers. Many believed their presence on the force improved the African American male officers' status with White male officers, but some of the African American women officers reported that some African American male officers were deliberately unsupportive of them because of the African American men's own precarious status in the (racist) department (ibid.). Finally, the African American women officers viewed themselves as needing less protection from the other (mostly male) officers than the White women needed, and they prided themselves on their ability to do the policing job well (Dodge and Pogrebin, 2001; Pogrebin, Dodge, and Chatman, 2000).

Natarajan's (1996) more recent survey of women in India similarly situated to those in Southgate's (1981) British study (because they were new to patrol work) found that a significant proportion of the women reported that men were better suited/more competent for the job of policing for a variety of policing activities, including foot patrol, traffic offenses and accidents, surveillance, motor patrol, lethal weapon situations, and crowds of males. However, many of the women officers believed they were more able than men to deal with some other situations, such as interviewing female suspects, writing reports, domestic violence calls, and juvenile situations. Clearly, the demarcation between these activities the women officers saw as men and women doing better/worse are very gendered. Drawing on Southgate's (ibid.) categories, Natarajan (1996, 9) asked the women which of the roles and styles of police departments they preferred. She found that almost half of the women officers (46 percent) preferred a traditional role, one-third (33 percent) an integrated role, and almost one-quarter (24 percent) a modified role. However, she also found that "only a minority of the women had experience in most of the listed duties" and that women who had experienced the wider range of policing duties, particularly the primary line functions such as patrol and crime prevention, were the most likely to favor nontraditional roles for women.

RESISTANCE TO WOMEN POLICE OFFICERS

Struggles for the First Women on Patrol

The positive research evaluations of women police officers on patrol have not sheltered them from considerable hostility from their fellow officers and sometimes from administration (e.g., Balkin, 1988; Belknap and Shelley, 1993; Bloch and Anderson, 1974; Christopher et al., 1991; Gratch, 1995; Heidensohn, 1992; Jacobs, 1987; Marshall, 1973; Martin, 1983; Martin, 1980, 1990, 1994; Martin and Jurik, 1996; Pogrebin and Pool, 1997; Pope and Pope, 1986; Remmington, 1983; Rivlin, 1981; Segrave, 1995; Sherman, 1973; Timmins and Hainsworth, 1989; Wexler and Logan, 1983). Some male police officers believe many stereotypes about women in general and about women police officers in particular. For example, earlier research indicated that some male police officers believe that women police officers are emotionally and physically weak, that they are more likely to use deadly force, and that they get sick every month when they menstruate (Balkin, 1988; Koenig, 1978). Similar to research on female prison guards, research on women police officers has found that their male coworkers often perceive the job as masculine and are thus confused and threatened when they see women capably performing the job (Balkin, 1988; Gross, 1984; Martin, 1980; Martin and Jurik, 1996; Sherman, 1973; Wexler and Logan, 1983). Stated alternatively, Martin and Jurik (1996) report that the danger, power, and social control aspects of policing make it a highly masculine job. Thus, the men opposing women's integration into their ranks did so because when they saw women could do the job too, it took away their "fringe benefit" of policing making them feel more masculine (ibid., 67). The end result is these men's hostility directed at their coworkers and supervisees (ibid., 175).

Consistent with research by Hunt (1990), for women police officers to survive, they may need to balance extreme femininity and extreme masculinity. An autobiography of the first Los Angeles woman on police patrol, who served twenty years starting in 1969, suggests the ways that women officers are more accepted when they are able to both flirt and be "sexy" *and* act masculine in terms of using foul language, catching criminals, and so on (Hays and Moloney, 1992). (Incidentally, her badge identified her as Policewoman #1, an obvious way to distinguish her from the "real" officers, the policemen.) This officer, Gayleen Hays, describes how she was asked in 1972 to enter a Miss Fuzz beauty contest for women officers in the LAPD in order to promote an (apparently sexist policing) film entitled *Fuzz* that was soon to be released:

> The day of the contest about twenty policewomen showed up to compete, everyone in hot pants and go-go boots. Unlike the Miss America pageant, the Miss Fuzz contest didn't have a "talent" competition, and there was no one asking us questions to determine whether we were smart or had a good personality (however, I think they should have had a marksmanship competition). All we did was march slowly around a swimming pool and let the judges take a good look at us. Their decision would be final. (ibid., 22)

Evaluations of Women Police by Their Supervisors, Their Supervisees, and Citizens

A study on women police officers found that their token status affected their experiences on the job (Belknap and Shelley, 1993). For example, women from departments with 10 percent or fewer women police officers were more likely to report being seen as women first and police officers second. Although the increase in the numbers of women officers has been gradual, perhaps a combination of their increased numbers and the fact that they are no longer "new" to patrol work (citizens and coworkers have greater acceptance of their legitimate role on police forces) is the reason more research indicates that the acceptance of these women by their male coworkers has improved some in more recent years (Martin, 1990; Pogrebin and Pool, 1997). Of course, this is not to say that they do not still face considerable challenges, resistance, and hostility, but the situation does appear to be improving. Even some citizens balk at a woman officer's police authority, particularly if she is African American (Martin, 1994, 391). And male college students' assessments of women officers, although improving over the past couple of decades, still report a somewhat negative appraisal of women police officers, while female college students remain quite positive about them (Austin and Hummer, 1999, 18).

When examining women officers' formal evaluations on the job, there is evidence that some sex/gender discrimination starts in the police training academy, where all new recruits learn how to be officers (Harrington and Lonsway, 2004). An analysis of the Los Angeles police department, drawing on data from 1990 to 1999, found that women (19 percent) were twice as likely as men (9 percent) to be fired from or choose to leave the academy (ibid.). The next step, field training, is where successful graduates of the training academy are assigned to work with a field-training officer (FTO) who is responsible for on-the-job training and evaluating the new officer's performance before she or he becomes a full-fledged police officer. Some male FTOs have used this authority position to coerce sex from their female trainees by threatening them with unfavorable evaluations if they do not comply (ibid.).

A study evaluating the field-training evaluations of new police officers reported that women were rated significantly more harshly than men by their FTOs (Pelkey and DeGrange, 1996). Obviously, bias in evaluations at this point in a new officer's career could have serious implications. The last chapter discussed the higher expectations and scrutiny that women face when they are tokens and among the first women in criminal legal jobs. One example of this can be seen in a recent study of recruits and FTOs in a department where a woman in the recruit academy accidentally shot another recruit at the academy during firearms training (Lonsway and Welch, 2004). This accidental shooting by one woman recruit out of thirty new recruit women in the department resulted in skepticism about the abilities of women in law enforcement that remained for at least a year following the incident (ibid., 73). Additional examples of sex discrimination and gender stereotyping of women police officers include an early study that found competent women police officers were rated more negatively than competent male police officers (Deaux and Taynor, 1973).

GENDER AND STRESS

Similar to studies on women working as guards in men's prisons, the first studies of women on patrol report higher stress levels for women than for men in these professions (Martin, 1983; Rivlin, 1981; Wertsch, 1998; Wexler and Logan, 1983). This stress appeared to be largely due to experiencing male coworkers' and supervisors' hostility, but it may also be attributed to the constant pressure to prove competence (Martin, 1983; Rivlin, 1981; Timmins and Hainsworth, 1989; Wexler and Logan, 1983). Research in the 1990s indicates that the women officers' stress is highly related to the pressures related to their token status in a male-dominated institution (Bartol et al., 1992; Wertsch, 1998). This was manifested by decreasing their job satisfaction, motivation, and organizational commitment. One study found that despite their high stress levels, the women officers still reported high levels of job commitment and a strong commitment to policing, although they reported a weak attachment to the police department (Wertsch, 1998). An Australian study of women police officers evaluated how the women's work stress had a spillover effect onto their family environments in terms of increased personal emotional exhaustion and reduced family cohesion (Thompson, Kirk, and Brown, 2005). Notably, supervisors, but not coworkers, were effective in reducing the women's role stressors (ibid.).

A significant aspect of women police officers' stress is likely due to the numerous studies of these women documenting sexual harassment (e.g., Bartol et al., 1992; Brown, 1998; de Guzman and Frank, 2004; Gratch, 1995; Martin, 1980; McMahon, 1999; Morash and Haarr, 1995). Brown's (1998) research on women officers in England and Wales documents the more minor but still offensive everyday types of offensive comments, to medium-level sexual harassment, and also to actual sexual assaults of women police perpetrated by their male coworkers and male supervisors. Seventy percent of the women in her study reported sexual harassment on the job (ibid.).

Since women entered the policing force, there is also evidence of the added burden of racism on top of sexism (Dreifus, 1982). A U.S. study examined African American and White police officers and their levels of reported stress and the ways they coped with job stress (Haarr and Morash, 1999). This study found that when men and women were compared overall, women reported slightly higher stress levels than men. However, when examining just White officers, there were no gender differences in reported stress levels, and when examining just African American officers, "the African American women reported significantly higher stress levels than did African American men" (ibid., 318). Although this study found numerous *racial* differences in how the officers coped with stress, the only significant gender difference in coping was that women reported higher levels of *escape* (e.g., avoiding superiors and coworkers and ignoring situations) than men. However, both men and women who reported high levels of job stress also reported significantly higher levels of using escape to cope with the job.

A comprehensive study on policing and stress surveyed over 1,000 officers in twenty-five police departments in the United States (Morash and Haarr, 1995). Unlike previous studies, although women reported higher levels of stress than men, as a whole, the difference was slight, and the same factors that cause stress to men officers were found to generally cause stress to women officers. In particular, for both female and male police officers, the greatest stressor is their sense of a lack of influence over day-to-day operations, or how "policing gets done" (ibid., 127). However, there were some gendered predictors of stress for officers. For example, sexist jokes and language harassment were significant predictors of women's but not men's stress. "An increase in women's stress is related to their spending time and energy dealing with sex, age, race, or ethnic group bias directed against others and themselves" (ibid., 132). Notably, being "set up" in dangerous situations and ridiculed by coworkers was a predictor of only men's stress, and this was particularly acute for Latino men. A comparison of gender differences within races found no significant differences among Whites and among Latino/as; however, African American women reported significantly greater stress than did African American men (Morash and Haarr, 1995).

Another study conducted on gender and police stress drew on small-town departments in Vermont (Bartol et al., 1992). The authors divided potential stressors into four categories. *External stressors* were primarily frustrations with the courts and the processing of their cases. *Organizational stressors* included departmental politics, lack of recognizing good work, insufficient personnel, and inadequate retirement plans. *Task-related stressors* were the day-to-day routines of policing, and *personal stressors* included their family lives. Similar to the findings by Morash and Haar (1995), this study found that, *overall,* the stressors for the male and female officers were similar. Specifically, there were no gender differences in police officers' reported organizational, external, and personal stressors. However, also similar to Morash and Haarr (1995), those gender differences that existed were significant: (1) Women officers reported the frequent exposure to tragedy as more stressful than did their male counterparts; (2) women officers reported the sense of constant danger to themselves and their coworkers as more stressful than did their male counterparts; (3) women officers reported the responsibility of the lives and safety of others as more stressful than did the men; (4) consistent with other research, women officers reported the departmental rumors about themselves and their coworkers as more stressful than the men did; and (5) women officers reported their relationships with their coworkers, the size of the department, and the lack of proper training all as less stressful than did the male officers (Bartol et al., 1992).

A large-scale study of women police in Canada reported the intricacies of the effects of personal discrimination on two forms of psychological disengagement from the job: discounting and devaluing (Tougas et al., 2005). The study found that the more personal discrimination experienced, the more the women discounted work evaluations, which in turn led to devaluing the importance of police work (ibid., 790). Also, the more discounting the women did, the lower their self-esteem fell. And finally, lower self-esteem was associated with higher stress levels (ibid.). This study, more than any other on women police officers, substantiates the complicated means by which discrimination alienates women and the costs to the department and public when sex discrimination is allowed in law enforcement departments.

THE INTERSECTION OF RACISM AND SEXUAL IDENTITY WITH SEXISM FOR WOMEN POLICE

Martin (1994, 2004) conducted intensive interviews with police officers in an attempt to better understand the intersection of racism with sexism and some of the unique experiences of African American women police. She found that although White women officers reported more sex discrimination than African American women officers reported, the African American women still reported serious levels of sex discrimination. Moreover, although many of the African

American women reported experiencing both sexism and racism, (1) they reported experiencing racism at higher levels than they reported experiencing sexism, *and* (2) they reported higher levels of experiencing racism than the African American male officers reported (ibid.). This study also found that court orders and affirmative action plans in particular departments worked to African American women officers' disadvantage. Similar to discrimination highlighted in the first chapter of this book, African American women were left out of the decisions/promotions in terms that benefited African American men and White women. Indeed, when the few coveted promotional places earmarked for women or for African Americans became available, there was a sense that the former were for White women and the latter for African American men. Thus, some African American male officers were more hostile to African American women officers than White women officers with whom they had to compete for the African American positions (ibid.). Martin (1994, 396) concludes: "Men of each race control women's on-duty behavior by threatening them with social isolation."

More recent research, including intensive interviews with all twenty-one African American women officers in a large urban police department found that the women reported significant gender discrimination, racial discrimination, police subculture exclusion, and prejudicial assumptions about their hiring and promotions (Pogrebin, Dodge, and Chatman, 2000). The racial and gender discrimination often intersected, and the racism committed by the younger White officers appeared to be worse than that by the older White officers, indicating it might be getting worse. Exclusion for the department culture not only meant being blatantly or subtly told that no matter what they did on the job they would never be considered equals, but also the dangerous practice of not backing them up on a risky call (ibid.). Regarding their hiring and promotions, it was typically assumed by others that they were hired or promoted simply due to their race and gender, not that they deserved the appointments (ibid.).

Martin (1994) identified the token nature of African American men in police departments as an organizational structure that further impacts African American women. For example, White male officers were protective of White, but not of African American, female officers. Although the African American male officers were generally protective of the African American female officers, they were fewer in number and, therefore, less available when needed. In addition, African American men faced pressures from the White men (or their shared resistance to women on patrol) not to back the women up (ibid., 392). Another form of organizational impact regarding gender (and often, racism) was Martin's (ibid.) finding that as women (particularly African American women) advanced to some of the station house administrative jobs, their better clerical abilities (compared to the male administrators who worked there) actually backfired. Martin (ibid.) found that these first women advancing to administration had far better typing skills and thus were able to more quickly and effectively complete paperwork. The result was that these jobs became organizationally redefined as feminine, resulting in less prestige and authority. Finally, Martin (ibid.) documents the difficulty of women officers to unite against sexism across race. She notes that this is due not only to the effectiveness of White males' divide-and-conquer strategy but also to the fact that many of the African American women found the White female officers to be every bit as racist as the White male officers (ibid.).

On a more promising note, a review of policing and gender in the United States reported that formal organizational policy changes, such as in seniority rules, the degree of civilianization, criteria for obtaining specialized assignment, and compliance with equal opportunity policies, have resulted in an improved integration of women into the policing jobs, serving a greater number of assignments, including in administration (Martin, 1990).

The only study specifically examining lesbians in law enforcement had somewhat surprising findings (Miller, Forest, and Jurik, 2004). The women in the study reported varying degrees of being "closeted" and "out" at the jobs; some were quite closeted and others were out from the time they started the police academy. The women's "outness" seemed, understandably, to be highly influenced by the department climate. As expected, departments that valued sexual diversity, had training and verbal and written support respecting lesbian/gay identities, and saw this as plus for their interaction with the citizens housed lesbians who were more likely to be out (ibid.). Importantly, lesbians of color were more reluctant to be out because they already felt overly high visibility as women and women of color. Additionally, being closeted was related to higher job stress (ibid.).

SOME STEPS FORWARD FOR WOMEN, SOME STEPS BACK

Similarly, patterns of sexism on the job for women police officers, such as hostility, insufficient instruction, and alienation, were most visible for the first generation of women police (post–Title VII), suggesting that overall the women's situation is improving (Martin, 1994). The improvement in women officers' situation is not only a result of organizational changes but is also due to the widening of individual women's preferences and skills and informal influence networks. Unfortunately, although the informal networks have improved for women police officers they are

> ... often excluded from the informal networks that are essential for success. They are less likely than their male counterparts to have mentors, are more likely than men to adopt a supervisory style that others regard as too unassertive or too bossy, and tend to be challenged by male subordinates who resent a woman telling them what to do. (Martin, 1990, xv)

Remarkably, interviews with twenty-seven women police officers indicated that two-thirds ($n = 17$) reported any sex discrimination (Gossett and Williams, 1998). This is remarkable in that a third of the women reported *no* sex discrimination. One respondent reported that for a woman police officer to think she had never been discriminated against, she would have to be in a dream world (ibid., 62). This study indicates that most of the sex discrimination by fellow officers, supervisors, and administration is less frequent and less severe (ibid.). A common complaint was that of not being taken seriously or treated the same as men who had gone through the same training. Certainly, some still reported serious sexually discriminating statements by coworkers, and some women reported discrimination for being pregnant (ibid.). Although the actual rates were not reported, the majority of the sample also reported sex discrimination from citizens. Unlike other studies, there were no racial or ethnic differences among the women officers concerning their reports of sex discrimination (ibid.).

Similar to women working in prisons and jails, however, women in policing are generally pessimistic about the likelihood of their own and other women's advancements and promotions (Harrington and Lonsway, 2004; Martin and Jurik, 1996; Poole and Pogrebin, 1988). This is particularly acute for African American women (Dodge and Pogrebin, 2001; Harrington and Lonsway, 2004; Martin, 1994; Pogrebin, Dodge, and Chatman, 2000; Townsey, 1982b), other women of color, and lesbians (Harrington and Lonsway, 2004). Ironically, male police officers view women police officers as receiving unfair advantages in their promotional climbs and assignments; this view is at least partly due to the male police officers' negative attitudes about affirmative action (Weisheit, 1987). Despite the positive influence affirmative action has had on hiring and promoting women in the field of policing, women still have greater turnover rates and shorter policing careers than their male counterparts, which has been attributed to "an unrealistic view of police work when they enter policing and to rotating shifts and uncertain hours that are particularly problematic for women with child-care responsibilities" (Martin, 1990, xvi).

SUMMARY

It is clear that while sex stereotyping in policing and prison work for women professionals has improved over the past three decades, it is still in existence. However, some of the war stories from the pioneering women post–Title VII are valuable. Notably, as is evident in the classifications of women police officers (Martin, 1980) and of women guards (Zimmer, 1986) of these post-Title VII women, we cannot assume all these path-breaking workers were feminists. Indeed, their tenure with their male coworkers is likely much easier when they are not viewed as feminists. For women to work as true equals, then, legislation must be far reaching, and even then it cannot guarantee that everyone's behavior will be open and nonsexist. Although more-recent research indicates improved tolerance and even acceptance of women police officers by the male administration and male coworkers, a comparative study of the United States and England stresses the importance of understanding that women officers have varied and complex experiences (Heidensohn, 1992, 129). More specifically, some reported more extreme experiences with sexism and sexual harassment than did others. Whatever their experience, however hard they had tried to be just "one of the boys," all had had to face questions about their role and status, simply because they were women (ibid.). But women police officers are still viewed as different, and such a view sometimes makes it difficult for women police officers to "do gender" in difficult job situations where they are subordinated and where resistance to the subordination results in conflict (Garcia, 2003). And, unfortunately, sexual harassment is still an all-too-frequent occurrence for women police officers (Brown, 1998). Moreover, the most current research highlights the unique and additional stress faced by African American women police officers, who report considerable alienation on the job (e.g., Dodge and Pogrebin, 2001; Martin, 1994, 2004; Pogrebin, Dodge, and Chatman, 2000).

REFERENCES

Appier, Janis. 1998. *Policing Women: The Sexual Politics of Law Enforcement in the LAPD*. Philadelphia: Temple University Press.

Austin, Thomas L., and Don Hummer. 1999. What Do College Students Think of Policewomen? *Women & Criminal Justice* 10:1–24.

Balkin, Joseph. 1988. Why Policemen Don't Like Policewomen. *Journal of Police Science and Administration* 16:29–38.

Bartlett, Harold W., and Arthur Rosenblum. 1977. *Policewoman Effectiveness*. Denver: Civil Service Commission and Denver Police Department.

Bartol, Curt R., George T. Bergen, Julie Seager Volckens, and Kathleen M. Knoras. 1992. Women in Small-Town Policing: Job Performance and Stress. *Criminal Justice and Behavior* 19: 240–259.

Belknap, Joanne, and Jill Kastens Shelley. 1993. The New Lone Ranger: Policewomen on Patrol. *American Journal of Police* 12:47–75.

Bell, Daniel. 1982. Policewomen: Myths and Reality. *Journal of Police Science and Administration* 10:112–120.

Bloch, Peter B., and Deborah Anderson. 1974. *Policewomen on Patrol*. Washington, DC: The Police Foundation.

Brown, Jennifer. 1997. European Policewomen. *International Journal of Sociology of Law* 25:1–19.

———. 1998. Aspects of Discriminatory Treatment of Women Police Officers Serving in Forces in England and Wales. *British Journal of Criminology* 38:265–283.

Christopher, W., J. A. Arguelles, R. Anderson, W. R. Barnes, L. F. Estrada, M. Kantor, R. M. Mosk, A. S. Ordin, J. B. Slaughter, and R. E. Tranquada. 1991. Report of the Independent Commission on the Los Angeles Police Department.

Deaux, K., and J. Taynor. 1973. Evaluation of Male and Female Ability: Bias Works Two Ways. *Psychological Reports* 32:261–262.

de Guzman, Melchor C. and James Frank. 2004. Policewomen and Their Problems: The Philippine Context. *Policing* 27:396–412.

DeJong, Christina. 2004. Gender Differences in Officer Attitude and Behavior. *Women & Criminal Justice* 15:1–32.

Dodge, Mary, and Mark Pogrebin. 2001. African-American Policewomen. *Policing* 24:550–562.

Douglas, R. M. 1999. *Feminist Freikorps: The British Voluntary Women Police, 1914–1940*. Westport, CT: Praeger.

Dreifus, Claudia. 1982. Why Two Women Cops Were Convicted of Cowardice. Pp. 427–436 in *The Criminal Justice System and Women,* edited by B. R. Price and N. J. Sokoloff. New York: Clark Boardman

Feinman, Clarice. 1986. *Women in the Criminal Justice System.* New York: Praeger.

Felkenes, George T., Paul Peretz, and Jean Reith Schroedel. 1993. An Analysis of the Mandatory Hiring of Females: The Los Angeles Police Department Experience. *Women & Criminal Justice* 4:31–64.

Felkenes, George T., and L. Trostle. 1990, July. *The Impact of Fanchon Blake v. City of Los Angeles.* The Claremont Graduate School.

Garcia, Vanessa. 2003. Difference in the Police Department: Women, Policing and Doing Gender. *Journal of Contemporary Criminal Justice* 19: 330–344.

———. 2005. Constructing the Other within Police Culture. *Police Practice and Research* 6:65–80.

Gates, Margaret J. 1976. Occupational Segregation and the Law. Pp. 61–74 in *Women and the Workplace,* edited by M. Blaxall and B. Reagan. Chicago: University of Chicago Press.

Gossett, Jennifer Lynn, and Joyce E. Williams. 1998. Perceived Discrimination among Women in Law Enforcement. *Women & Criminal Justice* 10:53–74.

Grant, Diana R. 2000. Perceived Gender Differences in Policing. *Women & Criminal Justice* 12:53–74.

Gratch, Linda. 1995. Sexual Harassment among Police Officers. Pp. 55–77 in *Women, Law, and Social Control,* edited by A.V. Merlo and J. M. Pollock. Boston: Allyn and Bacon.

Grennan, Sean A. 1987. Findings on the Role of Officer Gender in Violent Encounters with Citizens. *Journal of Police Science and Administration* 15:78–85.

Gross, Sally. 1984. Women Becoming Cops: Developmental Issues and Solutions. *Police Chief* (January): 32–35.

Haarr, Robin N., and Merry Morash. 1999. Gender, Race, and Strategies of Coping with Occupational Stress in Policing. *Justice Quarterly* 16: 303–336.

Hale, Donna C. 1992. Women in Policing. Pp. 125–142 in *What Works in Policing? Operations and Administrations Examined,* edited by G. W. Cordner and D. C. Hale. Cincinnati: Anderson.

Hale, Donna C., and C. Lee Bennett. 1995. Realities of Women in Policing: An Organizational Cultural Perspective. Pp. 41–54 in *Women, Law, and Social Control,* edited by A. V. Merlo and J. M. Pollock. Boston: Allyn and Bacon.

Harrington, Penny, and Kimberly A. Lonsway. 2004. Current Barriers and Future Promise for Women in Policing. Pp. 495–510 in *The Criminal Justice System and Women,* 3rd ed., edited by B. R. Price and N. J. Sokoloff. Boston: McGraw-Hill.

Hautzinger, Sarah. 2002. Criminalising Male Violence in Brazil's Women's Police Stations. *Journal of Gender Studies* 11:243–251.

Hays, Gayleen, with Kathleen Moloney. 1992. *Policewoman One: My Twenty Years on the LAPD.* New York: Villard Books.

Heidensohn, Frances. 1992. *Women in Control? The Role of Women in Law Enforcement.* Oxford: Clarendon Press.

Homant, Robert J., and Daniel B. Kennedy. 1985. Police Perceptions of Spouse Abuse: A Comparison of Male and Female Officers. *Journal of Criminal Justice* 13:29–47.

Hunt, Jennifer C. 1984. The Development of Rapport through the Negotiation of Gender in Field Work among Police. *Human Organization* 43:283–296.

———. 1990. The Logic of Sexism among Police. *Women & Criminal Justice* 1:3–30.

Jacobs, P. 1987. How Female Police Officers Cope with a Traditionally Male Position. *Social Science Review* 72:4–6.

Kennedy, Daniel B., and Robert J. Homant. 1983. Attitudes of Abused Women toward Male and Female Police Officers. *Criminal Justice and Behavior* 10:391–405.

Koenig, Esther J. 1978. An Overview of Attitudes toward Women in Law Enforcement. *Public Administration Review* 38:267–275.

Lersch, Kim Michelle. 1998. Exploring Gender Differences in Citizen Allegations of Misconduct. *Women & Criminal Justice* 9:69–80.

Lonsway, Kimberly A., and Susan Welch. 2004. Witnessing an Accidental Shooting at the Police Training Academy. *Women & Criminal Justice* 15:59–80.

Marshall, Patricia 1973. Policewomen on Patrol. *Manpower* (October):15–20.

Martin, C. A. 1983. Women Police and Stress. *Police Chief* 50:106–109.

Martin, Susan E. 1979. Policewomen and Policewomen: Occupational Role Dilemmas and Choices of Female Officers. *Journal of Police Science and Administration* 7:314–323.

———. 1980. *Breaking and Entering: Policewomen on Patrol.* Berkeley: University of California Press.

———. 1989, May. *Women on the Move? A Report on the Status of Women in Policing.* Washington, DC: The Police Foundation.

———. 1990. *On the Move: The Status of Women in Policing.* Washington, DC: The Police Foundation.

———. 1994. "Outsider within" the Station House: The Impact of Race and Gender on Black Women Police. *Social Problems* 41:383–400.

———. 1999. Police Force or Police Service? Gender and Emotional Labor. *The Annals of the American Academy of Political and Social Sciences* 561:111–126

———. 2004. The Interactive Effects of Race and Sex on Women Police Officers. Pp. 527–541 in *The Criminal Justice System and Women*, 3rd ed., edited by B. R. Price and N. J. Sokoloff. Boston: McGraw-Hill.

Martin, Susan E., and Nancy C. Jurik. 1996. *Doing Justice, Doing Gender: Women in Law and Criminal Justice Occupations.* Thousand Oaks, CA: Sage.

McMahon, Maeve. 1999. *Women on Guard: Discrimination and Harassment in Corrections.* Toronto: University of Toronto Press.

Miller, Susan L. 1999. *Gender and Community Policing.* Boston, MA: Northeastern University Press.

Miller, Susan L., Kay B. Forest, and Nancy C. Jurik. 2004. Lesbians in Policing. Pp. 511–526 in *The Criminal Justice System and Women*, 3rd ed., edited by B. R. Price and N. J. Sokoloff. Boston: McGraw-Hill.

Morash, Merry, and Jack R. Greene. 1986. Evaluating Women on Patrol: A Critique of Contemporary Wisdom. *Evaluation Review* 10: 230–255.

Morash, Merry, and Robin N. Haarr. 1995. Gender, Workplace Problems, and Stress in Policing. *Justice Quarterly* 12:113–140.

Morris, Allison. 1987. *Women, Crime and Criminal Justice*. Oxford, England: Basil Blackwell.

Natarajan, Mangai. 1996. Towards Equality: Women Police in India. *Women & Criminal Justice* 8:1–18.

———. 2001. Women Police in a Traditional Society. *International Journal of Comparative Sociology* 42:211–233.

———. 2005. Women Police Stations as a Dispute Processing System. *Women & Criminal Justice* 16:87–106.

Officers for Justice et al. v. Civil Service Commission of the City and County of San Francisco, C-73-0657 RFP (N.D. Cal. 1975).

Paoline, Eugene A., III, and William Terrill. 2004. Women Police Officers and the Use of Coercion. *Women & Criminal Justice* 15:97–120.

Pelkey, William L., and Michele L. DeGrange. 1996. Gender Bias in Field Training Evaluation Programs: An Exploratory Analysis. *Women & Criminal Justice* 8:79–90.

Pogrebin, Mark, Mary Dodge, and Harold Chatman. 2000. Reflections of African American Women on their Careers in Urban Policing. *International Journal of the Sociology of Law* 28:311–326.

Pogrebin, Mark R., and Eric D. Poole. 1997. The Sexualized Work Environment: A Look at Women Jail Officers. *The Prison Journal* 77:41–57.

Pollock-Byrne, Joycelyn M. 1986. *Sex and Supervision: Guarding Male and Female Inmates*. New York: Greenwood.

Poole, Eric D., and Mark R. Pogrebin. 1988. Factors Affecting the Decision to Remain in Policing: A Study of Women Officers. *Journal of Police Science and Administration* 16:49–55.

Pope, K. E., and D. W. Pope. 1986. Attitudes of Male Police Officers toward Their Female Counterparts. *The Police Journal* 59:242–250.

Poulos, Tammy Meredith, and William G. Doerner. 1996. Women in Law Enforcement: The Distribution of Females in Florida Police Agencies. *Women & Criminal Justice* 8:19–33.

Price, Barbara R. 1974. A Study of Leadership Strength of Female Police Executives. *Journal of Police Science and Administration* 2:219–226.

———. 1989. Is Police Work Changing as a Result of Women's Contribution? A paper presented at The International Conference for Policewomen. The Netherlands, March 19–23, 1989. Published in the *Report of the International Conference for Policewomen, 1989*.

Rafter, Nicole H., and Elizabeth A. Stanko. 1982. Introduction. Pp. 1–28 in *Judge, Lawyer, Victim, Thief: Women, Gender Roles and Criminal Justice*, edited by N. H. Rafter and E. A. Stanko. Stoughton, MA: Northeastern University Press.

Reaves, Brian A., and Matthew J. Hickman. *Law Enforcement Management and Administrative Statics, 2000. Data for Individual State and Local Agencies with 100 or More Officers*. Department of Justice: U.S. Bureau of Justice Statistics. http://www.ojp.usdoj.gov/bjs/pub/pdf/lemas00.pdf.

Remmington, P. W. 1983. Women in Police: Integration or Separation? *Qualitative Sociology* 6:118–133.

Rivlin, G. 1981. The Last Bastion of Macho: Policewomen. *Update on Law-Related Education* 5: 22–24, 65–67.

Santos, Cecília M. 2004. En-Gendering the Police: Women's Police Stations and Feminism in São Paulo. *Latin American Research Review* 39:29–55.

Schroedel, Jean Reith, Scott Frisch, Nancy Hallamore, Julie Peterson, and

Nicole Vanderhost. 1996. The Joint Impact of Race and Gender on Police Department Employment Practices. *Women & Criminal Justice* 8:59–77.

Schulz, Dorothy M. 1989. The Police Matron Movement: Paving the Way for Policewomen. *Police Studies* 12:115–124.

———. 1993. Policewomen in the 1950s: Paving the Way for Patrol. *Women & Criminal Justice* 4:5–30.

———. 1995. *From Social Worker to Crimefighter: Women in United States Municipal Policing.* Westport, CT: Praeger.

———. 2004a. Invisible No More: A Social History of Women in Policing. Pp. 483–494 in *The Criminal Justice System and Women*, 3rd ed., edited by B. R. Price and N. J. Sokoloff. Boston: McGraw-Hill.

———. 2004b. *Breaking the Brass Ceiling.* Westport, CT: Praeger.

Segrave, Kerry. 1995. *Policewomen: A History.* Jefferson, NC: McFarland and Company.

Sherman, Lewis J. 1973. A Psychological View of Women in Policing. *Journal of Police Science and Administration* 1:383–394.

———. 1975. Evaluation of Policewomen on Patrol in a Suburban Police Department. *Journal of Police Science and Administration* 3: 434–438.

Sichel, Joyce, Lucy Friedman, Janet Quint, and Michael Smith. 1978. *Women on Patrol: A Pilot Study of Police Performance in New York City.* Washington, DC: National Institute of Law Enforcement and Criminal Justice.

Silvestri, Marisa. 2003. *Women in Charge: Policing, Gender and Leadership.* Cullompton, Devon: Willan Publishing.

Smart, Carol. 1989. *Feminism and the Power of Law.* London: Routledge and Kegan Paul.

Southgate, Peter. 1981. Women in the Police. *The Police Journal* 54:157–167.

Thompson, B. M., A. Kirk, and D. F. Brown. 2005. Work Based Support, Emotional Exhaustion, and Spillover of Work Stress to the Family Environment: A Study of Policewomen. *Stress & Health* 21: 199–207.

Timmins, William M., and Brad E. Hainsworth. 1989. Attracting and Retaining Females in Law Enforcement. *International Journal of Offender Therapy and Comparative Criminology* 33:197–205.

Tougas, Francine, Ann M. Beaton, Natalie Rinfret, and Roxane de la Sablonniere. 2005. Policewomen Acting in Self-Defense: Can Psychological Disengagement Protect Self-Esteem from the Negative Outcomes of Relative Deprivation? *Journal of Personality and Social Psychology* 88:790–800.

Townsey, Roi D. 1982a. Female Patrol Officers: A Review of the Physical Capability Issue. Pp. 413–426 in *The Criminal Justice System and Women*, 3rd ed., edited by B. R. Price and N. J. Sokoloff. New York: Clark Boardman.

———. 1982b. Black Women in American Policing: An Advancement Display. *Journal of Criminal Justice* 10:455–468.

U.S. Bureau of Justice Statistics. 2005. *Sourcebook of Criminal Justice Statistics On-Line*, 31st ed. http://www.albany.edu/sourcebook/tost_1.html#1_d.

Warner, Rebecca L., Brent S. Steel, and Nicholas P. Lovrich. 1989. Conditions Associated with the Advent of

Representative Bureaucracy. *Social Science Quarterly* 70:562–578.

Weisheit, Ralph A. 1987. Women in the State Police: Concerns of Male and Female Officers. *Journal of Police Science and Administration* 15: 137–143.

Wertsch, Teresa L. 1998. Walking the Thin Blue Line: Policewomen and Tokenism Today. *Women & Criminal Justice* 9:52–61.

Wexler, Judi G., and D. D. Logan. 1983. Sources of Stress among Women Police Officers. *Journal of Police Science and Administration* 11:46–53.

Zimmer, Lynn E. 1986. *Women Guarding Men*. Chicago: University of Chicago Press.

11

❖

Women Working in the Courts

The question here is not simply whether there is room in the law
for women's voices, but whether the law allows room for any voice
that has not been woven into its fabric.

BERNS, 1999, 13

Men have debated, legislated, taught and interpreted the law. The virtual
exclusion of women from lawmaking and legal policy-making
permitted, over time, the incorporation within the law of values and
perspectives belonging to men. This inherently biased perspective,
moreover, has been subtly masked by the pervasive assumption that our
system of justice, together with its defining first principles and values,
is necessarily just and impartial.

DURHAM, 1998, 217

This book started with theories related to crime, followed with information
on girls' and women's offending; this is the final chapter of the section on
workers within the criminal legal system. In Chapter 9, I requested that,
throughout these chapters on women working in the criminal legal system,
the reader ask: "How might justice have been served differently if women had
been key decision makers?" Durham (1998, 223) appropriately questions how
judicial decisions may have been different had women been at the judicial helm
earlier:

> It takes very little effort to identify countless ways in which the law . . .
> incorporates subtle and profound assumptions about the meaning of
> gender. What does it say about sex roles in marriage to enforce a rape
> statute that makes it legally impossible for a husband to rape his wife? . . .
> Why do girls experience far more incarceration for juvenile-status
> offenses than do boys? Why do juries in civil suits award only a small
> percentage of the damages for loss of female life or services as opposed to
> male?

Women's access to becoming police officers and prison and jail guards had significant overlap. Women's access to the courts is quite different, and it is useful to examine this transition of women into the most prestigious jobs in the criminal legal system, those of lawyers and judges. Before addressing women as lawyers and judges, however, it is valuable to understand the history of women on juries in the United States Thus, this chapter begins with the resistance to women on juries before addressing women as professionals in the roles of lawyers and judges.

THE HISTORY OF WOMEN ON JURIES

Serving on juries is an area in which women have been short-changed historically and sometimes continue to experience discrimination. Although many people view jury duty as annoying or inconvenient, it is a fundamental form of citizenship. Linda K. Kerber's (1997, 834) discussion on "the meaning of citizenship" identifies the word "citizen" "as an equalizing word. It carries with it the activism of Aristotle's definition: "a citizen is one who rules and is ruled in return." It has been argued that excluding women from jury duty and the military draft in fact excludes women from full citizenship and feeds stereotypes about women's weakness and dependency on men (Eastwood, 1975; Lucie, 1988). We are thus forced to ask, "When is an advantage discrimination?" (Lucie, 1988). For example, courts' restrictions of women from military service and some other occupations has "transformed biological distinctions into cultural imperatives" where biology becomes destiny (Rhode, 1990, 121). Jury duty is an important service, and jury selection should not systematically disallow members of the population. When laws or *voir dire* policies exclude women from jury duty, "they limit both the woman's right to participate in the judicial process and the plaintiff's and defendant's right to a representative jury" (Mahoney, 1987, 209).

Kerber (1997, 835) states that "an emphasis on rights is the most progressive characteristic of American legal traditions, the aspect of American law and social practices that is most admired abroad." (This is more than a little ironic given the current Patriot Act, anti-immigration laws, and other limiting policies enacted in the United States since George W. Bush became president.) Kerber (ibid.) makes this powerful statement about juries: "In liberal tradition, rights are implicitly paired with obligations. The right to enjoy a trial by jury is mirrored by an obligation to serve on juries if called." She goes on to claim that ignoring obligations "has camouflaged some of the complexities of the meanings of citizenship" (ibid., 836). In her treatise of citizenship, Kerber carefully reports the ways that citizenship has not been given or acquired equally or neutrally, through tracing the U.S. government sanctioned murders of American Indians, removal of Latino/as from the United States to Mexico, and forced internment of Asian Americans in camps. Thus, she concludes that "the dream of an unranked citizenship has always been in tension with the waking knowledge of a citizenship to which people came by different routes, bounded by gender, race, and class identities" (ibid., 846).

Comparative Perspectives: Women's Advocacy Changing Justice and Power through International Criminal Courts

- **The Women's Caucus for Gender Justice in the International Criminal Court (ICC):** In 1997, women advocates and activists from across the globe formed this group to work together to design, create, and mainstream gender into the Coalition for an International Criminal Court. This group helped ensure this court's independence from the United Nations Security Council so that it would not end up as led or unfairly influenced by this organization.

- **The 1998 Rome Statute:** This treaty formed the basis of the future International Criminla Court (ICC). The Rome Statute "explicitly codifies for the first time many crimes of sexual and gender violence as war crimes and crimes against humanity" (Spees, 2003, 1234). The jurisdiction for the ICC covers cases when a country is "unwilling or unable to genuinely investigate and/or prosecute" a violation (ibid., 1235).

- **The ICC:** The International Criminal Court, which began operating in 2003, is a major step toward an international human rights law. The ICC "is the world's first permanent international criminal tribunal set up to prosecute individuals for genocide, war crimes, crimes against humanity, and, eventually, aggression" (ibid., 1234).

- **The Specification of Human Rights Violations Typically or Always Unique to Women and Girls:** Due to the Women's Caucus for Gender Justice in the ICC, the Rome Statute emphasizes the prosecution of sexual and gender violence (ibid., 1238). Specifically, this includes the following war crimes against humanity:
  - Rape
  - Sexual slavery
  - Enforced prostitution
  - Forced pregnancy
  - Enforced sterilization
  - Sexual violence

- **Women and Gender Experts on the Court:** The Rome Statute requires not only that the court have an adequate representation of women serving as judges, but also that experts on gender and violence against women serve on the court.

Conclusion: "The ICC will be a critical component of an international framework of accountability aimed at closing the political, practical, and jurisdictional gaps that have long fostered a culture of impunity. It is to be hoped that the Rome Statute will have the more positive effect of ensuring adherence to international law among civilian and military officials and encouraging the pursuit of justice, rather than war, as a response to future acts of genocide, war crimes and the crimes against humanity" (ibid., 1248).

SOURCE: Pam Spees. 2003. Women's Advocacy in the Creation of the International Criminal Court: Changing the Landscapes of Justice and Power. *Signs: Journal of Women in Culture and Society* 28:1233–1254.

Jury duty is an excellent example of how gaining access was a hard-fought battle. Although at least some (propertied) women had the right to serve on juries in feudal England (Sommerlad and Sanderson, 1998, 59), it appears that this may have been a short-lived opportunity. In the United States, the 1957 Civil Rights Act permitted women to serve on federal court juries but had nothing to say about state courts (Mahoney, 1987, 210). It was common during this period for states to have *automatic exemptions* for women. This meant that women could avoid jury duty simply because they were women (an example of sex-specific legislation). This automatic exemption may strike some people as an advantage for women, but it had two unfortunate results: (1) Juries were not representative (which may be unfair to both complainants *and* defendants), and (2) in states where women had automatic exemption, clerks routinely and deliberately did not call women for jury duty because they assumed the women would want their exemption (Mahoney, 1987). Thus, even women who wanted or were indifferent to serving on juries were not aware of this opportunity, a practice that structured juries as almost completely or exclusively male.

An all-male jury convicted Gwendolyn Hoyt of the second-degree murder of her husband. Her counsel appealed this decision to the U.S. Supreme Court, charging in *Hoyt v. Florida* (1961) that requiring women to register for jury duty at the courthouse had denied Hoyt equal protection and a jury of her peers (Thomas, 1991). The U.S. Supreme Court decided that despite the "advent of 'TV' dinners," women's domestic burdens were more important than their civil obligations; that is, women's "rightful" place in the home justified deterring them from jury duty. "The court found no suspicion of denial of equal protection when only 10 out of 10,000 jurors were women" (Mahoney, 1987, 211). It was not until *Taylor v. Louisiana* (1975) that women could no longer be exempt from jury service based simply on their sex. Interestingly, in this case with a male defendant accused of aggravated kidnapping and rape, the Supreme Court decided an all-male jury was not equal protection. Thus, sexism in jury selection was not considered problematic for a woman defendant (*Hoyt v. Florida*), but it was viewed as unacceptable for a male defendant (*Taylor v. Louisiana*).

Another sexist legal standard in jury selection was the process of *voir dire*—the practice of lawyers questioning potential jurors before a trial. Thus, even if women made it as far as the jury pool, they were often easily dismissed from actual jury service due to stereotypic assumptions and questions by lawyers during the voir dire process. This practice was legally challenged for the first time in 1983, when attorney Carolyn Bobb, called for jury duty, "refused to answer questions regarding her marital status and spouse's occupation" given that the lawyers were not asking this of the men but routinely asked it of the women in the jury pool (Mahoney, 1987, 212). For her refusal to answer, she was "held in contempt of court and taken into custody . . . sentenced to one day in jail with credit for time served" (ibid.).

But even making it past step one (being called for jury duty) and step two (being selected during voir dire to serve on a jury) does not mean the sexism has ended. One study found that women serving on juries tend to be deferential to male jurists and more easily persuaded by other jury members' opinions (Constantini, Mallery, and Yapundich, 1983). Contrary to popular opinion, however, women jury members are not inherent enemies of *or* overly harsh to the women they are judging (Mahoney, 1987).

More recent research indicates significant gender differences in jurors' perceptions and decisions (Hahn and Clayton, 1996). "Male jurors found the defendant significantly more guilty when the attorney was aggressive, but female jurors found the defendant just as guilty when the attorney was aggressive as when the attorney was passive" (ibid., 549). Moreover, male jurors are more influenced than women jurors by attorneys' speech style, whereas women jurors are more likely than male jurors to consider the evidence (Hahn and Clayton, 1996). Another recent study found an added benefit to more gender balance of juries: The more a jury approaches gender balance, the greater the likelihood that jury deliberations are reported by the jurors as less hostile and more supportive, more thorough, and more satisfying (Marder, 2002). At the same time, the gender representation of the jury has no impact on the jury's ability to reach a verdict (ibid.).

THE HISTORY OF WOMEN'S ACCESS TO LEGAL EDUCATION AND TRAINING

Although the status of attorney is much higher than that of police officer and jail or prison guard, women have been more successful at breaking into the occupation of law than into policing or "corrections." Perhaps this is because in law there is less actual physical contact with male offenders than is likely with policing and prison jobs. Arresting, deterring, and guarding male offenders are perhaps the ultimate in masculinity, while lawyers have more physical distance from offenders. At any rate, women have practiced law in the United States since colonial times, despite active efforts to keep them out of the law field. Another characteristic of women's entry into law that differs from their entry to policing and prison work is a much higher focus on these women's marital status. Throughout this chapter, evidence is offered on the numerous ways historically, and even today, that women's marital status influences their right to practice law and to "make" partner.

Historically, objections offered to restrict women from practicing law included accusations that women had inferior minds and bodies, an inability to be discreet, and a role conflict between career and wife and motherhood (Weisberg, 1982). (These are consistent with the images of women discussed in Chapter 1.) Women were traditionally barred from entering law schools and practicing law based on the assumption that females were inherently unable to perform the job and were best suited to their "natural" environment: the home. In their efforts to keep women out of law, "bar associations claimed women lacked the physical strength to handle heavy case loads, and newspapers charged that attractive women would unfairly sway juries" (Morello, 1986, xi). In fact, until 1971, women and men taking the bar exam in New York had to sit separately because of assumptions that the women would "excite the men" and distract them from taking their exams (DeCrow, 1974).

The first woman to practice law in the United States arrived in the "New World" in 1638 and acquired considerable real estate holdings. She was addressed as "Gentleman Margaret Brent" in person and in court records (Morello, 1986).

Brent was a highly successful attorney, particularly regarding land deals, and was consistently employed by the governor. Little is known about women practicing law from colonial times until the mid-1800s except that they were denied acceptance to law schools and admission to the state bar. In the rare cases where women conducted litigation in court, they were usually there on their own behalf (Bernat, 1992). Although men could receive legal training either through clerkship with an attorney or by attending law school, both of these avenues were routinely closed to women unless a brother or husband "allowed" his sister or wife to clerk with him. "Males who oversaw the entrance of persons into law (judges, lawyers, law school professors, and bar admission boards) argued that law was a hard-nosed, 'male' profession which could impugn the 'delicacy' of a female's biological character" (ibid., 310–311). Thus, it was lawyer "brothers, fathers, or husbands that gave many women, [married and unmarried,] the opportunity to learn law" (Barteau, 1997, 53).

Although at least some women were allowed to be lawyers centuries before they were allowed to work as police officers or as guards in men's prisons, it is interesting that similar to the pioneering women in policing and guard work, women lawyers' most significant resistors were their male colleagues. An assessment of women lawyers in the 1800s in the United States noted: "Opposition to women lawyers came from male lawyers who perceived women as innately unsuited to practice law because of their emotional and sentimental nature" (Pollock-Byrne and Ramirez, 1995, 80). One of the first women law students, Lemma Barkaloo, left her native New York to attend law school in Missouri after being denied admittance to Harvard and Columbia law schools. A diary entry of one of the (all-male) faculty at Columbia at the time was about "saving women from practicing law" and how "women's rights women" were loud and offensive (Barteau, 1997).

In the 1800s, married women were unable to receive professional educations, hold elective offices, enter into contracts, obtain custody of their children, and control their own money—even when they had earned it (Morello, 1986, 9). Not surprisingly then, once admitted, women members of the legal profession "have used their expertise in courts and legislatures to gain the right to be admitted to law schools and state and federal bars, and to be permitted to plead cases before state and federal courts" (Feinman, 1986, 104). Laws forbidding women to enter into contracts also stymied their ability to practice law. According to the U.S. Census in 1870, there were five women lawyers in the United States. One of them was Myra Bradwell, who passed the bar in 1869 after apprenticing with her husband, a judge. However, the Illinois Bar denied her a license to practice *because she was married*. She argued to the courts that she was a citizen and her marital status did not matter. Unfortunately, all but one of the (all-male) judges disagreed, so *Bradwell v. Illinois* (1873) legally barred married women from practicing the law. Justice Bradley, concurring with the opinion of the court, was not concerned with discrimination against married or unmarried women. He wrote:

> It is true that many women are unmarried and not affected by any of the duties, complications, and incapacities arising out of the married state, but these are exceptions to the general rule. The paramount destiny and

mission of woman are to fulfill the noble and benign offices of wife and mother. This is the law of the Creator. And the rules of civil society must be adapted to the general constitution of things, and cannot be based upon exceptional cases. (Justice Bradley, in *Bradwell v. Illinois*, 1873)

Unfortunately, Bradwell's experiences are similar to what many other aspiring women attorneys had to endure until most states amended their statutes and dropped the word "male" for practicing attorneys (Barteau, 1997). The Illinois Supreme Court reversed *Bradwell v. Illinois* in 1985.

Historical accounts of women's aspirations to practice law in many other countries suggest similar sentiments. An analysis of women breaking into the field of law in Canada states that the process was similar to women's experiences in the United States, with the first woman "finally admitted as a barrister in [Ontario in] 1897" (Hagan and Kay, 1995, 7). In the United Kingdom, a successful challenge to women's exclusion from medical school in 1873 at the University of Edinburgh at least partially opened the door for women's entry into law school in the 1880s (Sommerlad and Sanderson, 1998, 60). Although a number of women consequently completed law degrees, their applications to the bar were denied with no stated reason. A bill to allow women to be barristers and solicitors first introduced in 1912, again in 1914, and again in 1917 failed after significant opposition citing the importance of "separate spheres" (ibid., 60–68). Finally, in 1919, obstacles to women's entry to the legal profession in England were removed. Carrie Morrison, in 1922, was the first woman admitted to the Law Society in England, and eight women followed the next year. Unfortunately, their attire was considered more significant than the remarkable academic characteristics of these women (Sommerlad and Sanderson, 1998). Also unfortunate was that likely due to the elite class of many of the first women in the legal profession in England, most were invested in maintaining and not challenging the male-dominated legal profession (ibid., 81–82).

As might be expected, many of the first women practicing law in the United States were dedicated to fighting different aspects of discrimination, including women's issues (such as suffrage, birth control, and equal rights) and advocating for the poor, American Indians, African Americans, and immigrants (Morello, 1986). In the late 1800s, after countless refusals allowing her to practice before the federal courts, solely because she was a woman, Belva Lockwood was finally granted the opportunity to be the first woman lawyer to argue a case before the U.S. Supreme Court (Barteau, 1997). She obtained a $5 million settlement for the Cherokee nation from the U.S. government (Morello, 1986). This is particularly remarkable given that Lockwood was also denied acceptance to numerous law schools on the basis that she would distract the young men. When she was finally accepted to a law school, her all-male classmates threatened to boycott graduation if she were given a law degree (Barteau, 1997).

Two historical events relate to legal training becoming accessible to women and to less wealthy men in the 1830s and 1840s (Morello, 1986). First, as Whites increasingly populated the western part of the United States, more women became lawyers. In fact, the first law schools open to women were in the West (Feinman, 1986). The westward movement of Whites gave European–American women increasing amounts of freedom: The farther away women were from the staid northeastern society, the greater their independence (Morello, 1986). The corresponding decrease in the prestige of legal practice, predictably, opened the door to women. The second historical event that increased women's access to legal training was the Civil War. With men off fighting in the war, women had the opportunity to fill the vacant clerkship and law school positions.

The link between women's right to vote (suffrage) and women's entry into legal professions is significant, as battling the law was necessary both for the right to vote and for women's greater equality. "The history of women's efforts to gain legal identity and citizenship status therefore reveals the interconnections between the common law as a crystallization of existing power relations, and the legal profession as both enforcers of those relations and a social nexus" (Sommerlad and Sanderson, 1998, 70). The first woman formally admitted to the bar and licensed to practice in the United States, Arabelle Mansfield, passed the Iowa bar in 1869 (Feinman, 1986). In 1879, she helped found the Iowan Suffrage Association. Again, it was particularly difficult for married women to become lawyers unless they were married to a lawyer who was willing to train them. In fact, more than one in six women lawyers in 1890 were married to lawyers (Weisberg, 1982). Still, even many married women who were legally permitted to practice law were restricted by society and their own husbands and families who did not believe women could have both marriages and careers (Drachman, 1989). In addition to the strong likelihood of having husbands and family members who were lawyers, another characteristic that the first women lawyers shared was their tendency to come from wealthy families (Weisberg, 1982). In England between 1912 and 1919, the fight for women's suffrage was closely tied to women's fight to become barristers and solicitors (Sommerlad and Sanderson, 1998).

The first African American women lawyers were caught in the double marginalization discussed previously. White feminist activists focused on White women's rights, and African American male activists focused on African Amer-ican men's rights. Thus, African American women activists often felt ignored and forced to divide their loyalties between their race and their gender (Morello, 1986). Even Howard University, a traditionally African American university, resisted admitting women to the law school. In the 1880s, Charlotte E. Ray, the first African American woman lawyer in the United States, gained entry to Howard Law School by using only her initials for her first and second names in her application. Although Morello (ibid., 52) claims Ray was never allowed to practice law, Barteau (1997) identifies her as the first woman lawyer in the District of Columbia.

The Ivy League law schools were the last to accept women students. One letter directed to Yale Law School in 1872 suggested that perhaps "ugly women" should be allowed to enroll because they would not distract the male students (ibid.). Harvard Law School was one of the last law schools to accept women when it did so in 1950. Even relatively recent research found that women law students at the University of Pennsylvania Law School were more likely than male law students to report feeling alienated, and women received lower grades and were selected for fewer honors and awards than their male law student peers (Guinier et al., 1994). Some of the other major findings from this study of these women law students included:

> Although there were no gender differences in the law school entry-level credentials, by the end of the first year of law school "men are *three times more* likely than women to be in the top 10 percent of their law school class." The women in the first year class are far more critical of the social status quo, their legal education, and themselves than the first year men, but by the third year have become less critical than their third year male peers and the first year female law students.
>
> The women in the first year are far more likely than the first year male law students to be dedicated to social justice issues, but by their third year often switch to corporate law and have increased mental health distress. (ibid., 3, italics in original)

Many of the women lawyers reported that being trained in law school meant "learning to think and act like a man," which was distressing to them (ibid., 5).

Surveys of over 200 African American women lawyers found 87 percent reported being personally discriminated against in law school, reporting such actions as professors who repeatedly ignored their raised hands in class (Simpson, 1996). Ninety percent said they had been excluded from study groups organized by fellow students (ibid.).

WOMEN ATTORNEYS

The Number of Women Attorneys

In 1890, there were 135 women lawyers in the United States, mostly trained by brothers, fathers, or husbands (Barteau, 1997). In 1910, women were 1.0 percent of U.S. lawyers and by 1930, they were 2.1 percent (Berkson, 1981–82). But by 1963, they were still only 2.7 percent and by 1970, only 2.8 percent. In 1980, women constituted 13 percent of lawyers, or almost 59,000 women lawyers (ibid.). Between 1973 and 1983, the number of African American women lawyers in the United States increased from 446 to 4,272 (Simpson, 1996). By the mid-1990s, women represented "nearly half of the new entrants" (Gorman, 2005, 710), and 2001 was "the first time more than half of the entering class of law students" in the United States were women (Schafran, 2004). In 2003, women constituted nearly or, in some cases, more than half of the graduating classes in the most prestigious law schools' graduating classes (depending on the law school) (Noonan and Corcoran, 2004). Indeed, in the last three decades in the United States and Canada, "the gender and racial composition of the legal profession" has changed "dramatically" (Krakauer and Chen, 2003, 66).

A historical overview of women lawyers in the United States and Canada in the first half of the 1900s reported that in both countries (1) the number of lawyers about doubled in the first half of the 1900s, (2) the ratio of lawyers to the general population remained about the same from 1900 to 1961 (0.7 per 1,000 population in Canada and 1.25 per 1,000 in the United States), and (3) the ratio of men to women lawyers was declining (Hagan and Kay, 1995, 8). These authors report that "the addition of just a few women lawyers quickly reduced the size of the ratios"; however, "small but steady gains occurred for women in both countries through most of this century, with the most profound gains . . . since 1971" (ibid.). Similarly slow growth in the number of women lawyers was reported for the early years of women's admittance to this profession in England (Sommerlad and Sanderson, 1998, 80). In their review of Canada and the United States in the 1960s and 1970s, Hagan and Kay (1995, 10) report that the number of women increased from 3 percent to 14 percent of lawyers in the United States and from 3 percent to 15 percent in Canada. Similarly, in England, women represented less than 2 percent admitted to the profession in the 1920s, 3 percent in the 1940s, and 10 percent in 1971 and by the end of the 1980s were entering in equal proportions to men (Sommerlad and Sanderson, 1998, 89 and 106). "Although in 1911 there were only 7 women lawyers in all of Canada, by 1986 there were nearly 10,000" (Hagan and Kay, 1995, 11).

The percent of women law students increased from 8.5 percent to 33.5 percent between 1970 and 1980, yet the percent of women lawyers increased only from 4.7 percent to 12.0 percent for the same time period (Epstein, 1983). Regarding law school attendees, Bernat (1992) stated that half of the law students in the United States are women. Women's representation on law school faculty and in law firms, however, is more dismal. Pollock–Byrne and Ramirez (1995) report that women are only 8 percent of deans and about 16 percent of full professors in U.S. law schools. Consistent with other fields, in the field of law, women are more predominant in the lower status, lower-paid positions (ibid.). Moreover, women faculty have more trouble getting tenure than their male counterparts, particularly when they specialize in feminist jurisprudence (see ibid.). A 1998 publication reports that women make up 26 percent of lawyers and 11 percent of partners in the top 251 firms in the United States, reported as a significant improvement (Epstein, 1998, 109). A recent account reports that nationwide in the United States in law firms, women are 17 percent of partners and 48 percent of associates (and people of color are 4 percent and 15 percent, respectively of partners and associates in these firms) (National Association for Legal Career Professionals [NALP], 2005a). Moreover, about a tenth of U.S. law firms report no women partners, and 41 percent report no partners of color (ibid.). It is useful to note that there were huge variations across cities and regions of the United States in terms of the representation of women (of any race/ethnicity) and men of color (ibid.).

Classifications of Women Attorneys

Relative to the studies on women in policing and working in prisons and jails, little research effort has been conducted to determine categories of women lawyers. A notable exception, taking a somewhat different approach from those of the policing and guarding studies reported in the next section, is a study by Pierce (1995), who portrays male attorneys as "Rambo litigators." Additionally, she carefully analyzes the gendered nature of the roles available to and expected of attorneys, describing them in terms of "gamesmanship":

> I described the two main components of the gamesmanship required of litigators—intimidation and strategic friendliness. Unlike male attorneys, women encounter a double bind in the aggressive component of the emotional labor.... [In her study] women attorneys were criticized for being "too nice to the witnesses," "not forceful enough," "too bashful," and "unaggressive," at the same time that they were admonished for being "too aggressive." Men, on the other hand, were sometimes criticized for being "too aggressive" and not listening carefully to the witness but were more likely to be praised for their ruthlessness. This double bind emerged not only in the aggressive component of games-manship, but in its less confrontational—though equally manipulative—form, strategic friendliness. For example, when male attorneys used cajoling and placating strategies to achieve an instrumental end, they received support and encouragement from their colleagues. Women who adopted similar tactics were accused of using their "feminine wiles" to get their way with the witness or opposing counsel. (ibid., 113)

Another study examining the experiences of women attorneys classified the women by professional role orientation into two groups (Rosenberg, Perstadt, and Phillips, 1993). *Feminists* displayed strong support for feminist positions, were members of women's organizations, and viewed the position of women in the legal system from a feminist base. *Careerists*, on the other hand, while supporting basic economic rights for women, rejected feminist labels. They were also less likely to conduct pro bono work for women's rights, support feminist candidates, or view the subordinate status of women lawyers as political. Instead they believed refining their legal skills was the best avenue for improving the position of women lawyers. Unexpectedly, the careerists were more likely than the feminists to report experiencing sexual harassment and gender-disparaging comments (ibid.).

The Experiences of Women Attorneys

Women in the legal professions have generally fared much better with regard to their representation than women in policing and guard work. However, research on attorneys suggests ways in which the profession still disproportionately restricts women and rewards men.

Two steps are useful to begin this discussion on gender in legal professions. First, it is useful to understand the rankings of positions, from most to least prestigious: (1) firms, (2) corporations, (3) federal government, (4) state government, and finally, (5) private practice (Heinz and Lauman, 1982). Overall, the most recent U.S. statistics report that about three-fifths (58 percent) of the graduating law school classes of 2001 accepted jobs in law firms (NALP,

2005b). The next step is far more complex: determining whether women's differential placements in these prestigious rankings is due more to what they "want" or what they "get." For example, are women more prevalent in nonfirm jobs because that is what they want, or is it because they are not hired into the more prestigious and higher paying firm jobs? Or is it some institutionalized combination; for example, are women more likely than men to resist firm/partner jobs because they are more likely than male lawyers to want to be actively involved in parenting children they have or plan to have and recognize this is not valued in most firms? These are not easy distinctions to determine with the current research. Just as policing scholar Barbara R. Price (1989) asked whether women change policing or policing changes women, it is useful to pay attention in discussions on women in legal professions as to whether these women change these jobs or these jobs are so static that women must simply fit into a "male model" to be successful. Would the jobs be better for everyone, including men, if they allowed individuals (women and men) to spend sufficient time parenting and with their families *and* to also be considered worthy colleagues? Would these jobs be better if they allowed women *and* men to be more well rounded (not just in parenting and intimate relationships, but doing hobbies, volunteer work, etc.) and still be able to succeed?

Once again, in assessments of women's opportunities and restrictions, it is important to recognize the unique hurdles faced by women of color lawyers. An overview of research on lawyers in the United States and Canada claims that these women "have reported facing barriers to success while in law school, lower levels of career satisfaction on entry into the profession, and greater incidence of discrimination through their careers" (Krakauer and Chen, 2003, 67).

The Gendered Implications of Marital and Family Status for Lawyers

Even in the new millennium, women pursuing elite careers (e.g., in law and medicine) encounter "gendered expectations about homemaking and breadwinning" that influence their "opportunities for professional advancement and individual decisions to marry, have children, regulate employment hours, or use 'family-friendly' programs" (Coltrane, 2004, 596). In short, in legal careers, women are more governed than men by decisions to have children (Epstein, 1998; Graham, 1986; Sommerlad and Sanderson, 1998), and women newly out of law school attempting to find jobs are more routinely questioned about and evaluated based on their plans to have children (see Hagan and Kay, 1995).

Sommerlad and Sanderson (1998, 3), however, argue that the idea of lawyers' "commitment to work" is "itself gendered. It is predicated on a naturalized view of the independence of the public and private spheres, and the role of men and women in each. Thus studies of commitment . . . rarely if ever use the data to illuminate the question of men's commitment to their home lives, and the distinct work which is undertaken in the private sphere." Thus, Sommerlad and Sanderson (1998) call into question the whole focus and bias in the analysis of women's commitment to work versus family (focusing on attorneys), asking why we do not ask about *men's* commitments to their families when we ask about women's commitment to both work and family. In a study of lawyers who had graduated from the University of Michigan law school, 1 percent of fathers and 42 percent of mothers took a leave from work to care for children (Noonan and Corcoran, 2004). Given these assumptions about caretaking and the differences between mothering and fathering, it is hardly surprising to find that female lawyers are less likely than male lawyers to be married (Epstein, 1998; Noonan and Corcoran, 2004). Moreover, among women lawyers, those with children reported more conflict between their work and personal lives (Wallace, 2001). A Canadian study found that women lawyers are more likely than their male counterparts to believe that they must put their careers before their families/ personal life to advance in firms (Catalyst, 2005). A study comparing men and women lawyers of color beginning their first post–law school job found that while no gender differences existed in their likelihood of being married or having children, the women were far more likely than the men to be part of a "dual career" marriage (Merritt and Reskin, 1992).

Cunningham (2001, 997) effectively demonstrates the gendered nature of lawyers requesting family leave from their firms: "Thus for a woman, the double-bind is external and obvious; if she is a good lawyer, she must be a bad mother, or vice versa. She can only be a successful lawyer at the expense of her children, and she is often seen as failing on both fronts." Cunningham also describes the growing generation of male attorneys who are fathers and would prefer to spend more time with their children but who understand, like women lawyers, how such requests will label them as not sufficiently committed to their law firms. He describes Kevin Knussman's request for twelve weeks of paternity leave from his law firm when his wife was suffering from medical complications from childbirth. Indeed, Knussman became the first man to win a gender bias claim under the 1993 Family and Medical Leave Act (a federal bill that entitles twelve weeks of paid leave for family childbirth, adoption, illness, or elder care) (ibid.). The national press presented Knussman as a "poster" parent and "folk hero" (ibid.), something for which women professionals are never lauded when they prioritize family over work. After successfully suing, however, Knussman's firm required him to take a psychiatric exam before he could return to work, giving the retributive message that "any man who goes to such lengths to put family above work must have some sort of mental defect" (ibid., 968).

Managing Sexist Images

Key to the acceptance of women lawyers is their perceived *credibility*, which affects women as plaintiffs and defendants as well: "Women are denied collective credibility because as a group they are perceived as less believable than men" (Schafran, 2004, 459). Related to this, Kay and Hagan (2003, 486) argue that "[t]he basis of the modern law firm is rooted in the trading relationships that exist between junior and senior lawyers," and crucial to this is the level of trust attorneys have regarding the sharing of assets and opportunities. In a longitudinal study of lawyers in Ontario, Canada, they found that the denial of women lawyers' full access to social networks and professional rewards undermined their trust in the firm, and this distrust and exclusion "prompt women to contemplate leaving their respective firms."

Women lawyers are also likely to struggle with whether they should appear "feminine" or "masculine" in order to be most effective (Blodgett, 1986; Sommerlad and Sanderson, 1998). This is similar to Martin's finding of women emphasizing the femininity in women police officers' roles and trying to negate femininity in the roles. A study of "mock" jurors, liberal arts college students, found that although lawyers were perceived as better and getting the verdict they desired when they were more "aggressive," this was a double-edged sword for women lawyers who were less likely to obtain guilty verdicts when their manners were aggressive (Hahn and Clayton, 1996).

A large-scale study evaluating the gendered nature of U.S. law firms' hiring practices found that, as expected, when selection characteristics include stereotypically masculine traits, "women constitute a smaller portion of new hires," and when selection criteria stress feminine characteristics, "women are better represented among new hires" (Gorman, 2005, 702). This study also found that law firm decision makers tend to select candidates of their same gender: "Female decision makers also fill more vacancies with women than do male decision makers, but among entry-level hires, this effect diminishes as women's share of high-ranking positions increases toward gender balance" (ibid.).

The Gendered Placement of Lawyers

Women and men do not have equal access to the same practices and ranks; women and lawyers of color are more likely to end up in the least prestigious lawyer jobs (Epstein, 1998). Research indicates that women continue to be overrepresented in family law and underrepresented in other types of law, such as corporate, commercial, and civil litigation (e.g., Hagan, 1990; Hagan and Kay, 1995; Martin and Jurik, 1996; Sommerlad and Sanderson, 1998). An important organizational aspect of sexism in legal professions is the distinction between governmental attorney jobs and private practice jobs. "In brief, women are proportionally underrepresented in private practice and overrepresented in government and corporate work; within each of these organizational hierarchies, they are concentrated on the bottom rungs of prestige and income" (Martin and Jurik, 1996, 115). In a study of over 200 African American women lawyers, about half were employed in government service, 17 percent in private practice, 12 percent in firms, and 12 percent in nonlegal administrative positions (Simpson, 1996). Nine-tenths of the women reported that they were in different practice settings than what they had aspired to during law school (ibid.).

Pierce (1995, 1999) addresses the sex segregation in most law firms in the United States, where most attorneys are still men and most support staff (e.g., paralegals and legal secretaries) are still women. The work is highly gendered, and the gendered nature of it is related to vast differences in men's and women's pay in the firms. Specifically, the women workers do the vast majority of the clerical work and most of the emotional work, particularly the "mothering" in the firm (ibid.). Pierce's (1999, 127) study of paralegals documents the gendered nature of lawyers versus paralegals:

These legal workers function to support and maintain the emotional stability of the lawyers for whom they work through deferential treatment and caretaking. By affirming the status of lawyers, paralegals also reproduce gender relations in the law firm. Most attorneys who receive caretaking and support are men, and the majority of the legal assistant who provide these emotional services are women.

Meanwhile, the men are primarily the trial lawyers, who exercise hyper-masculinity and are what Pierce refers to as "Rambo litigators" (1999). This is congruent with assumptions about women's expected role as emotional and physical caretakers (Petersen, 1996). Gender is played out in other significant ways as well because "gender is not simply a social category but a signifier for power relations" (Pierce, 1995, 9). For example, Pierce's (1995) study found that men occupy more of the office space than women do, the few males in paralegal positions have greater chances at upward mobility and are encouraged more by the male attorneys, and the male paralegals are given "more latitude to resist or ignore the feminized socio-emotional requirements" than are the female paralegals.

The most comprehensive exploration of the distinction between what women lawyers *want* and what they *have* is a study by Hull and Nelson (2000) on almost 800 lawyers in the Chicago area. They found women lawyers were "somewhat" underrepresented in small/medium firms and heavily overrepresented in government, public-interest law, and legal education in the early stages of their careers, and this gender gap grows over the course of their careers (ibid.). Notably, there was no gender difference in women and men lawyers starting their careers in large law firms. Although job preferences were strong predictors of the lawyers' first jobs, "controlling for preferences does not eliminate the effect of gender" (ibid., 244). Stated alternatively, a gender difference in what women *wanted* for their first jobs explained some of the gendered variations in lawyers' first jobs out of law school, but it did not explain all of it, which was likely due to sexism. Across statistical models, women were significantly less likely than men to make partners in their firms (ibid., 250). Moreover, while the work–family constraint reduces women's chances of partnerships, it does not reduce men's (ibid.). The findings suggest that women choose to leave law firms to take the less prestigious and well-paying job of "inside counsels" because the latter offers "a better resolution of the competing demands of practice and family" (ibid., 252). But Hull and Nelson (2000) claim that they are unable to determine from their data whether these women were "discouraged from staying in these firms" as partners or fired from being partners because the firms "would not accommodate the flexible work schedules mothers and young children often require."

Treatment by Male Coworkers and Supervisors

Research on the courts indicates that even when ignoring sexism, racism, and so on, civil litigation is anything but civil (e.g., Cortina et al., 2002; Pierce, 1995). That is, that the process encourages a sort of combat mentality (Cortina et al., 2002). Thus, it is not surprising that this can be acted out in ways that include both sexism (and other forms of discrimination and offensive behaviors and words, such as racism) and unilaterally poor behavior.

The research on women lawyers' experience with sexism suggests that while it is "getting better," sexism, as well as racism, classism, anti-Semitism, and homophobia, is alive and well in most legal jobs (as well as in other jobs and in the private sphere). Given the more stringent hiring, firing, and promotion guidelines in the public than in the private sector, it is not surprising to find that sexism is more prevalent in private law firms than in the public sector (see, for example, Katz, 1998; Rosenberg, Perstadt, and Phillips, 1993). Historically, public jobs were often the only lawyer jobs open to women, and they tend to be far better about issues such as maternity leave, child care, and flexible schedules (Katz, 1998). Notably, public sector law jobs do not pay nearly as well as private sector lawyer jobs (Beinish, 1998), and this gap in income widens significantly over time (Hull and Nelson, 2000; Krakauer and Chen, 2003).

The limited research conducted on the experiences of women attorneys suggests that they also face a considerable amount of male hostility. This is most likely to be perpetrated by male lawyers, followed by clients, judges, and other legal staff, respectively (Rosenberg, Perstadt, and Phillips, 1993). Similar to women working in prisons and policing, sexual harassment by coworkers and supervisors is a major issue for many women attorneys (e.g., Hagan and Kay, 1995; Pierce, 1995; Pollock-Byrne and Ramirez, 1995; Rosenberg, Perstadt, and Phillips, 1993; Sommerlad and Sanderson, 1998). In one study, one in four of the women attorneys reported being sexually harassed in a professional situation, and this rate was significantly higher for women in private firms and in token positions in their practice (Rosenberg, Perstadt, and Phillips, 1993). Sexual harassment is effective in maintaining the gendered power differences: "Another means of [male lawyer's] heightening the boundaries between male and female attorneys is through sexual harassment. The sexualization of women is perhaps the most blatant way to exaggerate differences between the sexes" (Pierce, 1995, 108). One study reported that sports talk and play was a way the men bonded, and sexist and racist banter by the White male attorneys not only undermined women and people of color in general but was also a form of bonding and camaraderie for the White men regardless of age and rank (Sommerlad and Sanderson, 1998, 147).

A study of the climate for attorneys in Mississippi reported that two-thirds of lawyers and three-fifths of judges reported unfairness toward women lawyers in court (Winkle and Wedeking, 2003). Whereas 6 percent of the men attorneys thought bias against women attorneys in the courts was widespread, 44 percent of women attorneys thought so. Similarly, 3 percent of men judges and more than a third of women judges thought unfairness to women lawyers was widespread in the courts (ibid.). A recent large study of interpersonal mistreatment during federal litigation completed by female and male lawyers found that 60 percent of women and 15 percent of men reported gender-related incivility in the context of federal litigation in the previous five years, and 8 percent of women and less than 1 percent of men reported "unwanted sexual attention in the context of federal litigation" (Cortina et al., 2002, 244). Furthermore, when women lawyers experience incivility, only in 17 percent of the cases is it unrelated to gender (e.g., sexual attention or sexist comments), while for men 67 percent of the incivility they experience in federal litigation is unrelated to gender (ibid.). Notably, many of the women attorneys reported derogatory remarks about their pregnancies (ibid.). Needless to say, for both women and men, interpersonal mistreatment resulted in higher stress, which resulted in lower job satisfaction and a greater likelihood of considering leaving federal law practice (ibid., 252). This study concludes:

> [W]omen's social and occupational advances threaten the status quo of male dominance and female subordination, inspiring hostility toward women as a means of maintaining control. This seemingly trivial incivility can thus perpetuate the relegation of women to the margins of professional society. (ibid., 256)

A study of the legal profession in England found some women reporting that their sexuality was viewed as a commodity to advance in some firms, with more attractive women advancing to the top to "show off the firm" (Sommerlad and Sanderson, 1998, 176–177). Male judges are also known to have reinforced sexist stereotypes of women lawyers. In July 1986, U.S. Circuit Court judge Arthur Ceislik said to attorney Susan Tone Pierce in a pretrial conference on a rape case:

> I am going to hear the young lady's case first. They say I'm a male chauvinist. I don't think that ladies should be lawyers. I believe that you belong at home raising a family. Ladies do not belong down here. Are you married? (quoted in Blodgett 1986, 48)

A study of lawyers and judges in Illinois reported that although some portion of both male and female lawyers and judges agreed that there was the presence of gender bias/discrimination in courts, as expected, women lawyers and judges were far more likely than male lawyers and judges to report this sexism in the courtrooms (Riger et al., 1995). However, there was optimism that "things were getting better" for women law students and lawyers and judges, such as one woman who wrote on her survey: "Things have improved *vastly* over the last two years. Before that I was pinched, patted, and asked for dates, dismissed as incompetent and harassed by judges and attorneys alike" (ibid., 471).

The Gendered Nature of Income, "Making Partner," and Other Rewards for Lawyers

The potential for women's (and other oppressed groups', such as people of color's) promotional status to be evaluated is through terms such as *glass ceilings*. Baker (2003, 694) describes the glass ceiling as "an invisible barrier, erected by third parties, that blocks women (and minorities) from reaching the income elite. The alternative model is that the glass ceiling is really a 'sticky floor' that results from self-imposed limitations by female law graduates regarding employment."

Thus, analyses of women's promotional abilities as lawyers (as well as many other types of jobs) are assessed by looking at the women's mobility in the ranks. Legal scholar Cynthia Fuchs Epstein (1998, 106) identifies women as "one of the newest groups—and certainly the largest—whose talents, training and achievements qualify them to compete for places at the top of the [legal] profession." However, she also states that while ceilings exist in all fields, "they are strongest and most impenetrable in those in which wealth and power are located," where the dominant groups "typically defend their privileged access by obvious and subtle means, excluding contenders who hope to share their positions in society" (ibid.).

Simpson's (1996, 180) study of African American women lawyers found that 18 percent reported that being promoted at their jobs required "fitting in" or "being a White male." Additionally, once in their legal jobs, they "felt that their race (36 percent), sex (35 percent) or a combination of both (45 percent), limited their mobility in the organization in which they worked and nearly half (49 percent) felt that they had not been assigned the types of prestigious cases that lead to promotion" (ibid.). Simpson (ibid.) concludes that African American women lawyers face a *plexiglass ceiling*, due to their options "to practice in high status, powerful, and financially remunerative sectors of the [legal] profession" being seriously limited by their race *and* gender.

On a brighter note, Epstein (1998, 109) reports that women constitute a larger share of partners in large firms than they ever have, "although still at a slower rate than men," with women constituting 11 percent of partners in the top 251 firms in the United States. However, a study of gender trends in the upward mobility of lawyers during the last quarter of the 1900s in Canada reported that while both women and men encountered a "ceiling" effect in upward mobility and a "shrinking partnership class" during this period, the impact was greater on women (Hagan and Kay, 1995).

Also concerning firms, a recent study of about two decades of University of Michigan Law School graduates found that men are more likely than women to become partners and less likely than women to leave private practice (Noonan and Corcoran, 2004). Moreover, among partners, men earn more than women, even when controlling for the number of years in practice and other relevant variables (ibid.). Furthermore, "lawyers who have taken time out of the labor force to attend to child care responsibilities are less likely to become partners and earn less if they do become partners." These findings document indirect evidence that "women lawyers face multiple glass ceilings" (ibid., 130). However, Baker's (2003) analysis found more evidence for a "sticky floor" than for a "glass ceiling." More specifically, he claims that women lawyers, lawyers of color, and lawyers with disabilities are *not* discriminated against in terms of obtaining the top quintile (20 percent) of elite firm jobs but rather that there is more evidence of the "sticky floor," whereby these lawyers *prefer* and/or are "crowded into" the lower-paying firm jobs (ibid.).

On the other hand, women are making some advances in large firms in corporate settings (Hagan, 1990) and in the 1970s went from "virtual invisibility" in Wall Street corporate firms to "significant numbers" (Epstein, 1982). This is due in part to corporate firm members' fears of and experiences with sex-discrimination lawsuits, and a recent report on attorneys' income states that "women in the same kinds of practice as men, and at the same ranks, are now making 90 percent or more of male salaries" (Epstein 1998, 110). Furthermore, while experience increased the earnings for both women and men in a Canadian study, women gained "an annual average of about $3,000, compared to nearly $4,400 for men. The cumulative effect across careers is substantial" (Hagan, 1990, 845). This study concludes that, although there has been a "tremendous growth" in women entering the profession, "areas of law are still highly sex typed and gender cross-cuts other cleavages that stratify legal practice" (ibid., 849).

A Canadian study found that "although women and men lawyers report working about the same number of hours overall, men report docketing and billing larger numbers of hours than women," and based on the number of hours billed, "[m]en gain nearly twice the return in earnings as women for each hour they work" (Hagan and Kay, 1995, 152). In one study, however, women attorneys believed that if they were treated differently from men during the hiring process, it was to their own advantage. "In contrast, once the women lawyers were on the job, in salary, promotion, or task allocation, very few (from 1.5 percent to 10.2 percent) said they benefited from different treatment based on gender" (Rosenberg, Perstadt, and Phillips, 1993, 422).

A survey of women lawyers in large firms in the United States reported that while the women believed their salaries and bonuses were comparable to those of male lawyers, they also reported "they have fewer chances for top job assignments, litigation experience and promotions and that they are underrepresented in firm management" (Epstein, 1998, 114). Women lawyers are still less likely than their male colleagues to be made partners (Epstein, 1998; Graham, 1986; Hagan and Kay, 1995; Hagan et al., 1991; Sommerlad and Sanderson, 1998). In fact, a study on the effects of centralization and concentration of law partnerships found that the reduction of female partners was far greater than the corresponding decrease in male partners; this was most acute in small firms (Hagan et al., 1991). Title VII was effective in a 1984 case, *Hishon v. King & Spalding*, in which Elizabeth Hishon brought a case against a prestigious law firm in Atlanta where she had been denied partnership after working there for seven years (Epstein, 1998). The court found that partnership decisions in law firms must be fair and are applicable to Title VII.

Finally, a discussion of promotion, pay, and other perks for attorneys would be remiss in leaving out the role of *mentoring*. Some of the research on the gendered nature of advancement in the legal profession contributes the lack of women's success in the legal profession to the gendered nature of mentoring by more senior attorneys. More specifically, male attorneys are mentored better than female attorneys are (e.g., Hagan and Kay, 1995; Sommerlad and Sanderson, 1998). In Simpson's (1996) study of African American women lawyers, some of the women also reported lack of mentors and lack of cases to develop a specialty, something that was necessary to make partner in most firms. Notably, one study found that although women lawyers mentored by men earned more money than women lawyers mentored by women, the women lawyers mentored by women reported "more career satisfaction, more intent to continue practicing law, professional expectations that were met to a greater degree, and less work–nonwork conflict than those women who were mentored by men" (Wallace, 2001, 366).

The Gendered Nature of Sanctions against Lawyers

One recent study assessed the 325 disciplinary cases involving lawyers practicing law in the Commonwealth of Virginia from 1999 through 2002 (Payne, Time, and Raper, 2004). Notably, 90 percent of the sanctioned lawyers were men. In this sample of charged attorneys, women attorneys (11 percent) were less likely than men attorneys (22 percent) to be accused of "failing to maintain the integrity of the profession" (ibid., 90). Men attorneys were more likely than women attorneys "to be sanctioned for being convicted of a crime" (ibid.), while women attorneys were more likely than men attorneys "to be sanctioned for failing to comply with previous bar decisions and for failing to show fairness to opposing party and counsel" (ibid., 91). Whereas there were no gender differences in the sanctions given to the charged attorneys, women were suspended for far more time (average 808 days) than men (average 456 days) (ibid.).

WOMEN JUDGES

> The integration of women into the federal judiciary has been achingly
> slow ... [but] real changes in the law have been, and will continue to
> be, the result of the hard work done by women in the American judiciary.
> PALMER, 2001, 95

Women's Entry into Judgeships

Not surprisingly, women's advancement into judicial roles was far slower than their roles as attorneys and lawyers practicing law. Women lawyers were not eligible for elective judgeships in most states in the United States until the Nineteenth Amendment (women's suffrage) was passed in 1920 (Cook, 1978; Flowers, 1987). Thus, women judges were a rarity prior to 1920 (Flowers, 1987). The first woman judge in the United States, Esther Morris, was appointed justice of the peace in South Pass Mining Camp in Wyoming in 1870 (Berkson, 1981–1982), and fifty years later, in 1922, Florence Allen was the first woman elected to a state supreme court (Abrahamson, 1998). But only a "sprinkling" of women judges were appointed by various states in the following century (Epstein, 1983, 239). The first women judges, however, did not preside over a criminal court (Feinman, 1985; Flowers, 1987). Predictably, when women were first elected or appointed judges, it was frequently to judgeship roles consistent with stereotyped gender roles, especially "family law," divorce courts, juvenile courts, and the lower municipal courts. The first woman appointed to sit on the federal bench, Burnita Shelton Matthews, was appointed by President Truman in 1949.

Fewer than 200 women served on state courts in the United States in 1971 (Berkson, 1981–1982), and only 19 women were on the federal bench by 1976, when Jimmy Carter was elected president. Women judges made up only 1 percent of federal judges (Epstein, 1983) until President Carter made "a concerted effort to diversify the bench by seeking out and appointing women and members of ethnic minorities" (Abrahamson, 1998, 197), although he was never given an opportunity to nominate a judge to the U.S. Supreme Court. Remarkably, it was not until 1979 that all states had at least one woman serving in some judicial capacity (ibid.).

Indeed, Carter appointed more women to the federal bench in his four years in office than Reagan and Bush did together in their twelve years in office (Abrahamson, 1998). The first woman and 102nd justice appointed to the U.S. Supreme Court, Justice Sandra Day O'Connor, was appointed by President Ronald Reagan in 1981. At that time, women made up about 5 percent of both state and federal court judges (Morello, 1986). Notably, despite graduating at the top of her class at Stanford Law School (and finishing law school in just two years) at the age of 20, O'Connor was unable to find a job after graduation other than working as a law clerk or secretary. Though a Republican and conservative, she surprised many liberals and conservatives with flashes of independent voting, inconsistent with many conservatives. O'Connor served twenty-four years as a U.S. Supreme Court justice until she stepped down in 2005 to retire.

In the 1940s, Constance Baker Motley, the second African American woman to attend Columbia University, was active in many important civil rights cases, working with Thurgood Marshall and serving as counsel to the Reverend Martin Luther King Jr. Ms. Motley worked as a politician and a judge, as well. A brief biography of Motley states: "Three separate incidents of racial discrimination while in high school were probably the cause of her active participation in civil rights groups at an early age" (Alpha Kappa Alpha Sorority, 1968, 19). Her recently published autobiography is not only an important historical account of civil rights litigation but is also a portrayal of the intersection of sexism with racism in Ms. Motley's personal and professional life. Further, it is a carefully written account of the current state of racism, classism, and sexism in the United States (see Motley, 1998). A 1968 publication, *Negro Women in the Judiciary*, briefly highlights the contributions and lives of ten early African American judges (including Motley) (Alpha Kappa Alpha Sorority, 1968). Similar to what has been written about Motley, over their lives many of these African American women lawyers dedicated to social justice and equality experienced considerable economic hardship, racism, and sexism. Additionally, these publications on the first African American women on the judiciary not only are a tribute to them but also underline the continuing need for attorneys who challenge the racist, sexist, and classist status quo.

Although the following overview is written in an upbeat and positive manner, it is somewhat distressing when one considers that women constitute slightly over half of the population. In 1991, twenty-five of the fifty states had one woman on their highest court, and often she was the first woman to sit on that court; twenty-one states had no woman on the highest court. Four states and the District of Columbia had more than one Supreme Court justice who was a woman. In 1991, Minnesota became the first state with a female majority on its highest court, with four women among the seven justices of the court (Abrahamson, 1998, 196).

Even still, women are not nearly as highly represented in judge positions as they are in the attorney pool as a whole. Abrahamson (ibid., 196–197), drawing on various publications, estimates that women constituted about 10 percent of federal district court judges and 13 percent of federal circuit court judges at the time of the writing. "At the end of the Clinton administration [2001], only 14.5 percent of district court judges and 14.9 percent of circuit court judges were women" (Palmer, 2001, 95). In terms of tokenism, once a state has one woman on its supreme court, "the chance that another woman would be selected substantially drops," and this is more pronounced when judges are appointed (instead of elected) (ibid., 94). Thus, "the numbers of women and minority judges continue to be much lower than the number of [W]hite male judges" (Solberg and Bratton, 2005, 120). A study of federal district court judges (appointed by U.S. Presidents) concluded that White women and people of color are most likely to be appointed when the courts are (1) very large in number and (2) very homogenous (ibid.). In so doing, these appointments "may offer an opportunity to diversify with relatively few trade-offs in representation of other groups or interests" (ibid., 119). Or stated alternatively, placing a token White woman or person of color on large courts has a minimal change in the power base (White men) of the court.

Characteristics of Women Judges and Their Experiences as Judges

It has been noted that given the nature of the law and how it is structured, based heavily on precedent (previous rulings), Anglo-Saxon law is inevitably sexist, racist, and classist (e.g., Berns, 1999). Stated another way, elite White men were the designers of the Constitution and early laws, on which subsequent laws have been based, and historically attendees of law schools were almost exclusively wealthy White men. Consequently, it is no easy task for a White male or a woman of any race or men of color who become judges to "buck" the status quo, no matter how unfair, given that legal precedence drives judicial decision making in Anglo-Saxon culture.

A gender comparison of judges appointed by President Carter reported that although gender does not play a significant role in distinguishing judges' responses regarding a conflict between their careers and their roles as spouses, strong spousal support is "a major prerequisite to women's [but not men's] decisions to seek office" (Martin, 1990). Furthermore, although both male and female judges report greater conflict in balancing parental roles with "judging" than in balancing their spousal roles, male judges report far less conflict than female judges regarding balancing their career roles with their parenting roles (ibid.). Another study found male judges (84 percent) were more likely than female judges (64 percent) to be married (Steffensmeier and Hebert, 1999, 1172). Yet another study reported that women judges who are "single" are viewed as not only "odd" but as more "appropriate" for sexual harassment, including requests for sexual acts by male judges (Schafran and Winkler, 1989).

Also of importance is that those not of the White male elite are likely to better understand the variety of clients who come into their courtrooms than are the elite who have contact with a more restricted section of the population. It has been noted that women judges are more likely than male judges to do their own housework and that Supreme Court Justice O'Connor's pushing her own cart in the grocery store might make her more in touch with the average citizen (Morello, 1986). Another study found, in a comparison of female and male judges, overall gender similarities in hiring someone else to do the actual house-cleaning; however, women were more likely than men to be responsible for "running the house" (Martin, 1990). Research comparing female and male judges finds "that women judges tend to be younger, more liberal, less interested in politics, less wealthy . . . , and that they possess a higher degree of scholarship and academic talent on the average than the men" (Morello, 1986, 246).

Not surprisingly, a comparison of male and female judges found significant gender differences when the judges were asked to describe their major problems as "a woman or a man" in the law (Martin, 1990). The problem most frequently listed by women (81 percent) was sex discrimination, while the most frequently listed problem of men was "professional challenges or time pressure" (ibid., 207). Given that the women in this study reported greater parenting and household-running duties and stresses, it is likely that their "professional challenges and time pressures" were greater than the men's; however, compared to the other forms of sex discrimination they experienced, it was not ranked first. Notably, about one-fifth of these male, Carter-appointed judges reported racial or class discrimination as their major problem as men lawyers (Martin, 1990).

Surprisingly, a recent study of judges in Australia suggests that these "pioneering" women, the first of their kind appointed to the bench, face less sexism and discrimination than women attorneys who are not judges (Laster and Douglas, 1995). Laster and Douglas (ibid., 192) attribute women's acceptance into the judicial circle by their male colleagues, at least in part, to judges' isolation "from the mainstream of the profession" where they "cannot rely on assistance from the outside," and thus "organizational culture values mutual aid and tolerance." Additionally, women's relatively smooth acceptance to the bench by their male colleagues was also attributed to the more recent belief "that 'female' attributes are now consistent with the requirements of the job" for both women and men (ibid., 184). Thus, the authors conclude that women's entry to the bench "is a consequence rather than a cause of a significant paradigm shift already taking part in the courts" (ibid., 185), namely that more "feminine" qualities are needed in the legal culture. Finally, through their interviews with female and male judges, this study reported that they "do judging" similarly; they report weighing evidence and determining sentences in the same way. The one gender difference here was in the degree to which women were less comfortable with the adversarial approach. Upon closer examination, however, it appeared this was not a gender difference so much as a difference in longevity on the bench: Those with less experience on the bench, both women and men, were less comfortable with the adversarial approach (Laster and Douglas, 1995).

LOOKING FOR GENDER DIFFERENCES IN JUDGES' DECISION MAKING

In short, the American judiciary has often professed objectivity and neutrality while practicing a general subjectivity and differentialism toward women.
Thus, as women move toward equal representation on the bench, the question of the different voice becomes one of potentially great significance.
FOX AND VAN SICKEL, 2000, 263

Finally, turning to whether judges' gender influences their decision making, except in cases of sexual harassment and sex discrimination, the research is somewhat inconclusive. An early study comparing male and female trial judges in over 30,000 felony cases found that overall the only gender differences in judges' convicting and sentencing of male and female defendants were that women judges are less likely to find defendants guilty and more likely than male judges to send women defendants to prison (Gruhl, Spohn, and Welch, 1981). Perhaps the women judges felt more pressure than male judges to appear to be not "siding" with defendants of their own sex.

Recent research on gender and judicial sentences indicates women may be increasingly harsh and even harsher than male judges, particularly regarding female defendants and African American repeat offenders. One study found the higher the proportion of female judges in a district, the less the disparity (chivalrous sentencing) between women and men defendants' sentences (Schanzenbach, 2005). Stated alternatively, "the greater the proportion of female judges on the district's bench, the longer the sentences received by female offenders" (ibid., 74). A study of Pennsylvania sentencing from 1991 to 1993 found that while both women and men judges are highly influenced by the prior record and sentence severity of the charged defendants, women judges are about 10 percent more likely than men judges to incarcerate defendants, and they impose sentences about five months longer (Steffensmeier and Hebert, 1999). This difference in incarceration and sentence length was most pronounced for property offenders, confirming the authors' contention that women judges will be harsher than male judges regarding offenses that are less serious challenges to norms and laws (ibid., 1182). Perhaps most surprising in this study was the finding that although there were no gender differences in judges' decisions when the defendants were White women, women judges were harsher than men judges when the defendants were African American women, African American men, and White men. And women judges were particularly harsher than men judges when the defendants were repeat African American offenders (ibid.).

Another recent study on gender and judicial decision making reported that women judges are more likely than men judges to "side" with the prosecution/district attorney, while male judges are more likely to "side" with the defense

(Fox and Van Sickel, 2000). This study also found that both female and male judges employed both masculine and feminine "voice" in responding to various persons during court cases. More specifically, both used stern (masculine) and compassionate (feminine) words and tones in processing cases. This study identified four judicial styles from previous research and attempted to determine whether these styles were gendered. Two of the four styles were identified as "masculine" styles by the authors (the *procedural* and *authoritarian* styles), and two were deemed "feminine" (the *consensual* and *inclusive* styles) (ibid.). The "feminine" *inclusive style*, characterized by soliciting input from all parties and ensuring that everyone is heard, was exhibited more often by women than men judges (ibid., 268). It is difficult to distinguish from the "feminine" *consensus style*, where the judge solicits information from everyone to try to find a "middle ground," which was exhibited more by the men judges (ibid.). The male judges were also more likely to employ the "masculine" *authoritarian style*, where the judge dictates the courtroom without input from all parties, typically quickly disposing of cases and using a "patronizing or belittling tone" (ibid., 268). However, the female judges were more likely to employ the "masculine" *procedural style*, characterized by strict adherence to laws and procedures, often rejecting options suggested by attorneys (ibid.).

However, in a study of the sexual harassment and sex discrimination Title VII cases decided by U.S. federal courts of appeals from 1999 to 2001, although the plaintiffs lost in almost three-quarters of the cases, "the presence of a female judge significantly increased the probability that the plaintiff would prevail" (Peresie, 2005, 1768–1769). Controlling for such factors as judges' ages, prior employment, political ideology, and so on, if the judges in these cases were women, the probability of siding with the plaintiff increased by 86 percent in sexual harassment cases and by 65 percent in sex discrimination cases (ibid., 1776). Moreover, the data indicated that "male judges decided with their female colleagues rather than against them" (ibid., 1769) and that "male judges were more likely to find for plaintiffs when at least one female judge was on the panel" (ibid., 1778). Indeed, "serving with a female judge had more than 1.5 times the effect on a male judge of being appointed by a Democrat" (ibid., 1778). Thus, this study concludes "that female judges mattered to outcomes on Title VII sexual harassment and sex discrimination cases" (ibid., 1786).

An overview of the research on gender differences in judicial decision making summarizes that the trend is clear and consistent regarding the impact of women judges on sex discrimination cases: "[W]omen judges are more supportive of women's claims than men judges, regardless of their ideology" (Palmer, 2001, 89). However, there is not a clear pattern regarding a gendered difference in methods of reasoning (ibid.).

Another study examined the impact of judicial gender in 170 police brutality dispositions in 47 state courts from 1990 to 2000 (McCall, 2005). The dependent variable was whether the judge voted "liberal" (a vote for the person brutalized by the police or a department suspending an officer for police brutality) or "conservative" (a vote for the police officer charged with excessive force/brutality). In addition to gender, the study examined whether the judges were elected or appointed (ibid.). Regardless of whether elected or appointed, women judges were more likely than men judges to vote "liberal." And regardless of gender, elected judges were more likely to vote "liberal" (ibid.).

WOMEN LAW PROFESSORS

Although little has been written about women law professors, they too are still often represented in token status on law school faculties. Indeed, their barriers to faculty positions in law schools have been even greater than the barriers they faced in practicing law (Martin and Jurik, 1996). However, Martin and Jurik's (ibid., 122) review of various studies and data indicate that by the late 1980s, women constituted about one-quarter of full-time law faculty. Unfortunately, they are still more predominant in the lower-paying, less prestigious, and non-tenure-track faculty jobs. Driven by the finding that women of color face even more significant barriers than men of color in being hired and then retained on law school faculties, Merritt and Reskin (1992) attempted to understand the phenomenon through in-depth data collection. They found that the double marginalization of being a woman of color faculty member has resulted in what has been referred to as a "triple penalty" compared to men of color as faculty in law schools: Compared to men of color and law school faculties, women of color "enter teaching at lower ranks, teach at less prestigious schools, and are more likely to teach low-status courses" (ibid., 2322). This was despite controlling for differences in credentials and personal constraints (such as needing to stay in a particular geographical region). "These results suggest that law schools, especially the most prestigious schools, could hire more minority women if they were willing to hire them on the same basis as they hire minority men" (ibid., 2356).

Consistent with a "no-win" situation many marginalized people face, recent research in the field of law suggests ways that women in the legal profession are further stigmatized if they are *not* married. For example, a study comparing women and men lawyers of color found that women of color tend to advance more if they are married (while men of color do not); for example, it increases their chances of obtaining a tenure-track faculty position in a law school (Merritt and Reskin, 1992).

One African American law professor notes that African American women need to be hired not just because they serve as role models for African American women law students but because they hold the potential for a significant contribution to the study of law (Allen, 1997). Another African American woman law professor points out how African American women professors' experiences as African American women in a White-male-dominated society provide a necessary perspective in law classes and legal academics (Banks, 1997). Yet another African American woman describes the shock of acquiring an "honorary White pass" immediately after she began her job as a law professor:

White students of the type who had been repulsed by me in law school (their own status threatened by the presence of African Americans in their classes) now curried my favor. Secretaries who had once made me wait at the photocopying machine for hours now let me know I was too important to make a single copy myself. Restaurateurs wanted my business so badly that they shouted "Professor" as I came through the door (the better for the patrons to hear). Partners in law firms who made more in a year than my parents had made in their entire lifetimes sought me out at cocktail parties. (Moran, 1990–1991, 119)

This section noted a number of minor but mostly serious ways that women are discriminated against in "the bar." Given the breadth and seriousness of the hostility and discrimination women lawyers continue to face, perhaps it is not surprising that one study found that women are more than twice as likely as men to not practice law after passing the bar (Hagan and Kay, 1995, 115). Even an overview of women students in law school reports that although they typically constitute half of the class, they often face a highly gendered environment and report more dissatisfaction and alienation during their education (Martin and Jurik, 1996, 131). Moreover, law students who are women of color often report marginalization in their education and mentoring in terms of both their sex and race (e.g., Guinier, 1997).

SUMMARY

This chapter is an overview of women working in the field of law. Although women's entry into legal practice differed in many respects from their entry into the less prestigious work of prison and jail guards and policing and law enforcement, there are also similarities. Specifically, women have faced significant sexist hurdles in their efforts to become lawyers, practice law, serve as judges, and work as law professors. And these hurdles have been seriously compounded for women of color. The history of women in legal professions underscores the resistance they encountered to being apprenticed to be lawyers in colonial times, the resistance to allow them into law schools, the resistance to allow women who apprenticed or went to law school to actually practice law, the resistance to accept women into firms as partners, the resistance to appointing and electing women judges, and the resistance to appointing women to law school faculty. The theme of women's marital status has been significant over time (since women apprenticed and applied to law schools) and across the various legal jobs (e.g., law professor, judge, and partner in a law firm). Despite the battles women have faced to practice and teach law, they have been highly successful, particularly in terms of advocating for gender, race, and immigrant equality. The impact of women judges is less clear, whether they are harsher or more lenient than men and in what contexts, although it is clear that women judges are far more likely than men judges to side with the plaintiffs in sexual harassment and sex discrimination cases.

REFERENCES

Abrahamson, Shirley S. 1998. Do Women Judges Really Make a Difference? The American Experience. Pp. 75–82 in *Women in Law*, edited by S. Shetreet. London: Kluwer Law International.

Allen, Anita L. 1997. On Being a Role Model. Pp. 81–87 in *Critical Race Feminism*, edited by A. K. Wing. New York: New York University Press.

Alpha Kappa Alpha Sorority. 1968. Negro Women in the Judiciary. *Heritage Series Number 1*, August, 1968, 24 pp., Chigaco: IL.

Baker, Joe G. 2003. Glass Ceilings or Sticky Floors?: A Model of High-Income Law Graduates. *Journal of Labor Research* 24:695–711.

Banks, Taunya Lovell. 1997. Two Life Stories: Reflections of One Black Woman Law Professor. Pp. 96–100 in *Critical Race Feminism*, edited by A. K. Wing. New York: New York University Press.

Barteau, Betty. 1997. Thirty Years of the Journey of Indiana Women Judges: 1964–1994. *Indiana Law Review* 30:43–202.

Beinish, Dorit. 1998. Are Women More Successful in the Public Service than in Private Practice? Pp. 99–104 in *Women in Law*, edited by S. Shetreet. London: Kluwer Law International.

Berkson, Larry. 1981–1982. Women on the Bench. *Judicature* 65:286–293.

Bernat, Frances P. 1992. Women in the Legal Profession. Pp. 307–322 in *The Changing Roles of Women in the Criminal Justice System*, 2nd edition, edited by I. L. Moyer. Prospect Heights, IL: Waveland Press.

Berns, Sandra. 1999. *To Speak as a Judge*. Aldershot, England: Ashgate Publishing.

Blodgett, Nancy. 1986. I Don't Think that Ladies Should Be Lawyers. *ABA Journal* (December 1):48–53.

Bobb v. Municipal Court, 143 Cal. App. 3d 849, 192 Cal. Rptr. 260 (1983).

Bradwell v. Illinois, 83. U.S. (16 Wall.) 130 (1873).

Catalyst. 2005. *Beyond a Reasonable Doubt: Creating Better Opportunities*. http://www.catalystwomen.org/files/exe/Canadian%20Flex%20in%20Law%202.pdf.

Coltrane, Scott. 2004. Elite Careers and Family Commitment: It's (Still) about Gender? *Annals of the American Academy of Political and Social Science* 596:214–220.

Constantini, E. M., M. Mallery, and D. M. Yapundich. 1983. Gender and Jury Partiality: Are Women More Likely to Prejudge Guilt? *Judicature* 67:124.

Cook, Beverly B. 1978. Women Judges: The End of Tokenism. Pp. 84–105 in *Women in the Courts*, edited by W. L. Hepperle and L. L. Crites. Williamsburg, VA: National Center for State Courts.

Cortina, Lilia M., Kimberly A. Lonsway, Vicki J. Magley, Leslie V. Freeman, Linda L. Collinsworth, Mary Hunger, and Louise F. Fitzgerald. 2002. What's Gender Got to Do with It?: Incivility in the Federal Courts. *Law & Social Inquiry* 36:234–270.

Cunningham, Keith. 2001. Father Time: Flexible Work Arrangements and the Law Firm's Failure of the Family. *Stanford Law Review* 53:967–1008.

DeCrow, Karen. 1974. *Sexist Justice*. New York: Random House.

Dothard v. Rawlinson, 433 U.S. 321 (1977).

Drachman, Virginia G. 1989. My "Partner" in Law and Life: Marriage in the

Lives of Women Lawyers in Late 19th and Early 20th Century America. *Law and Social Inquiry* 14: 221–250.

Durham, Christine M. 1998. Thoughtful and Worldly Women: Women Judges and the Law. Pp. 217–234 in *Women in Law*, edited by S. Shetreet. London: Kluwer Law International.

Eastwood, M. 1975. Feminism and the Law. Pp. 325–334 in *Women: A Feminist Perspective*, edited by J. Freeman. Palo Alto, CA: Mayfield.

Epstein, Cynthia F. 1982. Women's Entry into Corporate Law Firms. Pp. 283–306 in *Women and the Law*, Vol. 2, edited by D. Kelly Weisberg. New York: Schenkman.

———. 1983. *Women in Law*. Garden City, New York: Anchor Books.

———. 1998. Reaching for the Top: "The Glass Ceiling" and Women in the Law. Pp. 105–130 in *Women in Law*, edited by S. Shetreet. London: Kluwer Law International.

Feinman, Clarice. 1985. Women Lawyers and Judges in the Criminal Courts. Pp. 271–275 in *The Changing Roles of Women in the Criminal Justice System*. Prospect Heights, IL: Waveland Press.

———. 1986. *Women in the Criminal Justice System*. New York: Praeger.

Flowers, Ronald Barri. 1987. *Women and Criminality: The Woman as Victim, Offender, and Practitioner*. Westport, CT: Greenwood Press.

Fox, Richard, and Robert Van Sickel. 2000. Gender Dynamics and Judicial Behavior in Criminal Trial Courts. *The Justice System Journal* 21:261–280.

Gorman, Elizabeth H. 2005. Gender Stereotypes, Same-Gender Preferences, and Organizational Variation in the Hiring of Women: Evidence from Law Firms. *American Sociological Review* 70:702–728.

Graham, Deborah. 1986. It's Getting Better, Slowly. *ABA Journal* (December 1):54–58.

Gruhl, John, Cassia Spohn, and Susan Welch. 1981. Women as Policy-makers: The Case of Trial Judges. *American Journal of Political Science* 25:308–322.

Guinier, Lani, 1997. Of Gentlemen and Role Models. Pp. 73–80 in *Critical Race Feminism*, edited by A. K. Wing. New York: New York University Press.

Guinier, Lani, Michelle Fine, Jane Balin, Ann Bartow, and Deborah Lee Stachel. 1994. Becoming Gentlemen: Women's Experiences at One Ivy League Law School. *University of Pennsylvania Law Review* 143:1–110.

Hagan, John. 1990. The Gender Stratification of Income Inequality among Lawyers. *Social Forces* 68:835–855.

Hagan, John, and Fiona Kay. 1995. *Gender in Practice: A Study of Lawyers' Lives*. New York: Oxford University Press.

Hagan, John., Marjorie Zatz, Bruce Arnold, and Fiona Kay. 1991. Cultural, Capital, Gender, and the Structural Transformation of Legal Practice. *Law and Society Review* 25:239–262.

Hahn, Peter W., and Susan D. Clayton. 1996. The Effects of Attorney Presentation Style, Attorney Gender, and Juror Gender on Juror Decisions. *Law & Human Behavior* 20:533–555.

Heinz, John P., and Edward O. Lauman. 1982. *Chicago Lawyers*. New York: Russell Sage Foundation.

Hishon v. King and Spalding, 467 US 69, 73 (1984).

Hoyt v. Florida, 368 U.S. 57 (1961).

Hull, Kathleen E., and Robert L. Nelson. 2000. Assimilation, Choice, or Constraining? Testing Theories of Gender Differences in the Careers of Lawyers. *Social Forces* 79:229–264.

Katz, Deborah S. 1998. Perspectives on Women in Public-Sector Law. Pp. 75–82 in *Women in Law*, edited by S. Shetreet. London: Kluwer Law International.

Kay, Fiona M., and John Hagan. 2003. Building Trust: Social Capital, Distributive Justice, and Loyalty to the Firm. *Law and Social Inquiry* 28: 483–519.

Kerber, Linda K. 1997. The Meanings of Citizenship. *Journal of American History* 84:833–854.

Krakauer, Lianne, and Charles P. Chen. 2003. Gender Barriers in the Legal Profession. *Journal of Employment Counseling* 40:65–79.

Laster, Kathy, and Roger Douglas. 1995. Feminized Justice: The Impact of Women Decision-Makers in the Lower Courts in Australia. *Justice Quarterly* 12:177–206.

Lucie, Patricia. 1988. Discrimination against Males in the USA. Pp. 216–243 in The *Legal Relevance of Gender*, edited by S. McLean and N. Burrows. Atlantic Highlands, NJ: Humanities International.

Mahoney, Anne R. 1987. Women Jurors: Sexism in Jury Selection. Pp. 208–224 in *Women, the Courts, and Equality*, edited by L. L. Crites and W. L. Hepperle. Newbury Park, CA: Sage.

Marder, Nancy S. 2002. Juries, Justice, and Multiculturalism. *Southern California Law Review* 75:659–726.

Martin, Elaine. 1990. Men and Women on the Bench: Vive La Difference? *Judicature* 73:204–208.

Martin, Susan E., and Nancy C. Jurik. 1996. *Doing Justice, Doing Gender: Women in Law and Criminal Justice Occupations*. Thousand Oaks, CA: Sage.

McCall, Madhavi. 2005. Court Decision Making in Police Brutality Cases,

1990–2000. *American Politics Research* 33:56–80.

Merrit, Deoborah J., and Barbara F. Reskin. 1992. The Double Minority: Empirical Evidence of a Double Standard in Law School Hiring of Minority Women. *Southern California Law Review* 65:2299–2359.

Moran, Beverly I. 1990–1991. Quantum Leap: A Black Woman Uses Legal Education to Obtain Her Honorary White Pass. *Berkeley Women's Law Journal* 6:118–121.

Morello, Karen B. 1986. *The Invisible Bar: The Woman Lawyer in America, 1638 to the Present*. Boston: Beacon Press.

Morris, Allison. 1987. *Women, Crime and Criminal Justice*. Oxford, England: Basil Blackwell.

Motley, Constance Baker. 1998. *Equal Justice under Law*. New York: Farrar, Straus and Giroux.

NALP. 2005b. *Diversity & Demographics*. http://www.nalp.org/content/index.php?pid=143.

National Association for Legal Career Professionals (NALP). 2005a. *Women and Attorneys of Color at Law Firms— 2004*. http://www.nalp.org/content/index.php?pid=253.

Noonan, Mary C., and Mary E. Corcoran. 2004. The Mommy Track and Partnership: Temporary Delay or Dead End? *Annals of the American Academy of Political and Social Science* 596: 130–150.

Officers for Justice et al. v. Civil Service Commission of the City and County of San Francisco, C-73-0657 RFP (N.D. Cal. 1975).

Palmer, Barbara. 2001. Women in the American Judiciary. *Women & Politics* 23:89–99.

Payne, Brian K., Victoria Time, and Sarah Raper. 2004. Regulating Legal Misconduct in the Commonwealth of

Virgina. *Women & Criminal Justice* 15:81–95.

Peresie, Jennifer L. 2005. Female Judges Matter. *Yale Law Journal* 114:1759–1790.

Pierce, Jennifer L. 1995. *Gender Trials.* Berkeley: University of California Press.

———. 1999. Emotional Labor among Paralegals. *Annals of the American Academy of Political and Social Science* 561:127–142.

Pollock-Byrne, Joycelyn M., and Barbara Ramirez. 1995. Women in the Legal Profession. Pp. 79–95 in *Women, Law, and Social Control*, edited by A.V. Merlo and J. M. Pollock. Boston: Allyn and Bacon.

Price, Barbara R. 1989. Is Police Work Changing as a Result of Women's Contribution? A paper presented at The International Conference for Policewomen. The Netherlands, March 19–23, 1989. Published in the *Report of the International Conference for Policewomen*, 1989.

Rhode, Deborah L. 1990. Gender Differences and Gender Disadvantage. Pp. 121–136 in *Women, Politics and the Constitution*, edited by N. B. Lynn. New York: Harrington Park Press.

Riger, Stephanie, Pennie Foster-Fishman, Julie Nelson, and Barbara Curran. 1995. Gender Bias in Courtroom Dynamics. *Law and Human Behavior* 19:465–480.

Rosenberg, Janet, Harry Perstadt, and William R. Phillips. 1993. Now That We Are Here: Discrimination, Disparagement, and Harassment of Work and the Experience of Women Lawyers. *Gender and Society* 7:415–433.

Schafran, Lynn Hecht. 2004. Overwhelming Evidence: Gender and Race Bias in the Courts. Pp. 457–472 in *The Criminal Justice System and Women*, 3rd edition, edited by B. R. Price and N. J. Sokoloff. Boston: McGraw-Hill.

Schafran, Lynn Hecht, and Norma Wikler. 1989. Integration of Women and Minority Judges into the American Judiciary. Pp. 43–56 in *The Judge's Book*. Chicago: American Bar Association.

Schanzenbach, Max. 2005. Racial and Sex Disparities in Prison Sentences. *Journal of Legal Studies* 34:57–92.

Simpson, Gwyned. 1996. The Plexiglass Ceiling: The Careers of Black Women Lawyers. *Career Development Quarterly* 45:173–188.

Solberg, Rorie L. Spill, and Kathleen A. Bratton. 2005. Diversifying the Federal Bench. *Justice System Journal* 26:119–133.

Sommerlad, Hilary, and Peter Sanderson. 1998. *Gender, Choice and Commitment: Women Solicitors in England and Wales and the Struggle for Equal Status.* Aldershot, England: Ashgate Publishing Company.

Steffensmeier, Darrell, and Chris Hebert. 1999. Women Policy Makers: Does the Judge's Gender Affect the Sentencing of Criminal Defendants? *Social Forces* 77:1163–1196.

Taylor v. Louisiana, 419 U.S. 522 (1975).

Thomas, Claire S. 1991. *Sex Discrimination in a Nutshell*. St. Paul, MN: West.

Wallace, Jean E. 2001. The Benefits of Mentoring for Female Lawyers. *Journal of Vocational Behavior* 58:366–391.

Warner, Rebecca L., Brent S. Steel, and Nicholas P. Lovrich. 1989. Conditions Associated with the Advent of Representative Bureaucracy. *Social Science Quarterly* 70:562–578.

Weisberg, D. Kelly. 1982. Barred from the Bar: Women and Legal Education in the U.S., 1870–1890. Pp. 231–258 in *Women and the Law*, Vol. 2, edited by D. Kelly Weisberg. New York: Schenkman.

Winkle, John W., and Justin Wedeking. 2003. Perceptions and Experiences of Gender Fairness in Mississippi Courts. *Judicature* 87:126–134.

12

❖

Effecting Change

Sexual assault programs do more than counsel victims of rape. They
document sexual violence in the community, keep it on the public
agenda, and work toward lasting social change.
O'SULLIVAN, 2002, 191

This book describes the state of women and girls as victims and offenders in the
criminal legal system and the experiences of women working in the criminal legal
system. It also discusses how laws have differentially affected women, particularly in
terms of employment outside of the home. Chapters 1 through 11 portray the invisibility
and negative state of women and girls in crime processing, whether they are workers,
offenders, or victims. This concluding chapter summarizes and describes recent advances
in the visibility of females in criminological theories and the crime-processing system.
Additionally, it offers some hope of solutions to the existing problems.

NEW THEORIES

Chapter 2 provides a discussion on various criminological theories and how women
and girls were routinely excluded from most studies and theories or, if included, were
done so in gender-stereotypical ways. Since the 1970s, feminist researchers have
worked to make female offenders and victims visible (Morris and Gelsthorpe, 1991).

Given that Chapter 2 provided a careful overview of the numerous feminist and
pro-feminist research additions to the field of offending since the late 1970s, this
chapter will not rehash these theories. However, *the most significant contributions to
understanding why people offend in recent years are the "pathways" and similarly designed
studies that incorporate a more inclusive "whole-life" experience.* Feminists, in particular, have
identified the importance of examining childhood traumas, such as various forms of
abuse (e.g., physical and sexual) and neglect, and how these place youth at risk of
offending. At the same time, feminists have identified ways that intimate partner abuse

places women at risk of offending (e.g., Browne, 1987; Lake, 1993; Richie, 1996). Moreover, the feminist approach to include child and adult sexual and physical abuse appears to also be useful for understanding *males'* risk of offending (e.g., Belknap and Holsinger, 2006; Dembo et al., 1992; Dodge, Bates, and Pettit, 1990; Widom, 1989a, 1989b). Additionally, it is important to understand the roles of acute poverty, classism, and racism to understand risks for offending (e.g., Arnold, 1990; Richie, 1996; Sommers and Baskin, 1994). The gendered and "raced" nature of sexuality and masculinity/femininity are also paramount in understanding not only the commission of crimes but, like race and poverty, the differential (read: discriminatory) processing of offenses. This new approach to studying crime causation is appealing in that it accounts for both males and females, as well as the impact of gender, race, class, and sexuality. Furthermore, it explains crime and its formal processing within the important social structures that shape society and the individuals in it.

CHANGING THE TREATMENT OF FEMALE OFFENDERS

A number of solutions to the problems facing delinquent girls and adult women offenders have been offered in the form of recommendations, some of which have been implemented in some jurisdictions. First, women's prisons need to provide programs and opportunities to maintain contact between incarcerated women and their children (American Correctional Association, 1990; Baunach, 1992; Bloom, 1993; Bloom and Steinhart, 1993; Collins, 1997; Luke, 2002; McCarthy, 1980; McGowan and Blumenthal, 1981; Pollock, 1998; Sharp and Marcus-Mendoza, 2001; Stanton, 1980). Second, appropriate, adequate, and continuous child-care/temporary custody alternatives should be made for the children of incarcerated women (Brodsky, 1975; Collins, 1997; McGowan and Blumenthal, 1981; Sharp and Marcus-Mendoza, 2001), including housing for infants or even small children within the prison structure (American Correctional Association, 1990; Baunach, 1992; Bloom, 1993; Bloom and Steinhart, 1993; Haley, 1980; Knight, 1992; McCarthy, 1980; McGowan and Blumenthal, 1981; Schupak, 1986).

Third, improved medical services should be provided, including the needs of special populations such as HIV-positive and pregnant women (Acoca, 1998; American Correctional Association, 1990; Anderson, 2003; Barry, 1991; Clark and Boudin, 1990; Collins, 1997; Daane, 2003; Greenfeld and Snell, 1999; Hankins et al., 1994; Knight, 1992; Lawson and Fawkes, 1993; McGowan and Blumenthal, 1981; McHugh, 1980; Ross and Fabiano, 1986; Schupak, 1986; Wooldredge and Masters, 1993; Zaitzow and West, 2003). Many of the supporters of pregnant prisoners advocate that they should not be in prison for part or all of their pregnancy and for some period thereafter. (This recommendation is congruent with the following one.) On a positive note, some progressive programs have been developed and implemented, including for pregnant offenders

(Daane, 2003), for women offenders with HIV/AIDS (Zaitzow and West, 2003), and for incarcerated women with substance abuse problems (Kelley, 2003).

The fourth recommendation of women prisoner advocates is to stop the building of maximum-security prisons and provide alternative housing, particularly for the majority of women prisoners who are nonviolent, nonserious offenders with dependent children (American Correctional Association, 1990; Baunach, 1992; Chesney-Lind, 1991; Collins, 1997; Immarigeon, 1987a, 1987b; Immarigeon and Chesney-Lind, 1992; Owen, 1998; Rafter, 1985; Richie, 1996; Von Cleve and Weis, 1993). The fifth recommendation is to improve drug/alcohol treatment programs (American Correctional Association, 1990; Belknap, 2000; Greenfeld and Snell, 1999; McGowan and Blumenthal, 1981; Pollock, 1998); the sixth is to improve legal services available to incarcerated women (Collins, 1997; McGowan and Blumenthal, 1981; Pendergrass, 1975); and the seventh is to improve vocational and educational programs, particularly literacy programs and training in traditionally male labor skills (American Correctional Association, 1990; Collins, 1997; Feinman, 1984; Knight, 1992; McGowan and Blumenthal, 1981; Ross and Fabiano, 1986; Stanton, 1980).

The next three recommendations regarding the incarceration of women are somewhat related. The eighth recommendation is to improve therapy and counseling (Acoca, 1998; Haley, 1980; McGowan and Blumenthal, 1981; Pollock 1998); the ninth recommendation is to provide empowerment programs (for example, participatory management in the prison system and peer counseling) (Baunach, 1992; Hardesty, Hardwick, and Thompson, 1993; Kendall, 1994; Pendergrass, 1975; Pollack, 1994; Pollock, 1998); and the tenth recommendation is to provide post-release services to help women reincorporate themselves into non-prison life (American Correctional Association, 1990; Belknap, 2000; McGowan and Blumenthal, 1981; Richie, 2001). However, caution must be taken regarding incarcerated women's empowerment programs. Hannah-Moffat (2000) reports on the incongruence of the idea that a system that contains and punishes can in any way empower. Moreover, her findings on incarcerated Canadian women noted that the "corrections" system (1) expected the women to discipline themselves to take the offered "empowerment" programs (e.g., anger management, life skills, parenting, substance abuse) that were not particularly empowering, and (2) punished the women if they did not conform. Furthermore, the Correctional Services of Canada expect women to take responsibility for their actions "irrespective of victimizations and structural impediments" (ibid., 525). Thus, the state has twisted feminist empowerment dicta to further punish and disempower incarcerated women.

Most of these recommendations have been tried in some women's prisons in the United States. Unfortunately, budget constraints and the lack of power of incarcerated women often keep innovative programs from being funded or from being maintained once implemented. Also, there is little in the way of evaluative research and analysis to rate the effectiveness of these programs. For example, Acoca (1998, 56) states: "There are no consistently applied policies regarding contraception, abortion, and general reproductive education and counseling for incarcerated women. When these services are available, they are rarely provided in a comprehensive or consistent manner" (ibid.). Thus, for prison treatment to be effective, it needs to be high quality, available, exhaustive, and comprehensive.

Notably, many of the preceding recommendations exist in a women's prison in Mexico. Jennifer Pearson (1993) studied Centro Feminil and reported positive, supportive conditions: Children can live inside the facilities with their mothers, a sense of respect and caring exists between the prisoners and the guards, visits and communication with family members are facilitated, and human rights are emphasized and based on the needs of the collective unit.

> The Mexican prison system I observed appeals to the strengths, rather than the weaknesses, of the inmates and their families. Imprisonment deprives a prisoner of her liberty. However, it seeks to do so as little as possible. Not only is it more humane, its costs—both social and economic—to society as a whole are far less. Deviants who can be reincorporated back into the community through their primary networks are not incarcerated, a much less costly alternative. (ibid., 89–90)

Additionally, Canadian feminists have worked tirelessly for change in women's sentencing and incarceration. In 1939 in Vancouver, the first Canadian Elizabeth Fry Society was established, followed by the conception of the Canadian Association of Elizabeth Fry Societies (CAEFS) in 1969 and the incorporation of this group as a nonprofit in 1978. Today the CAEF includes twenty-five Elizabeth Fry Societies across Canada, providing significant support and advocacy for individual women and girls charged with offenses and working to implement changes in sentencing, treatment, and confinement. Additionally, The Task Force on Federally Sentenced Women formed in 1989 in Canada was comprised not only of academic and legal experts but also of former women prisoners and Aboriginal and other racial/ethnic minority women (see Shaw, 1993). Their recommended plan included regional facilities closer to the sentenced women's homes in their own provinces (instead of the central Canadian prison for women in Kingston), a Healing Lodge for Aboriginal women, and a community release strategy (ibid.).

Many feminist prison activists focus on practices to allow women to "do" their time with their children. One "woman-centered" approach that has been offered is the use of electronic monitoring devices (EM), as made popular by Martha Stewart when she was released from prison recently and had to wear an EM ankle "bracelet." To date, only one study has been conducted on the gendered nature of EM, and it found that while mothers of dependent children felt it was "worth it" to wear the EMs to be home with their children, most of the women experienced sexist repercussions (Maidment, 2002). This study found the women more likely than the men with EMs to be convicted of property crimes, which were often motivated by survival (e.g., one woman stole a check to pay for her child's hospital bill when welfare refused to do so), while the men's offenses were "most closely related to their pursuit of recreational activities and/or substance addictions" (ibid., 36). Moreover, women with EMs experienced greater tension in their homes if they had partners, due to changes in role expectations such as her not being able to transport children, buy groceries, bank, and so on. Their husbands/boyfriends were resentful of suddenly having to do this work. For single mothers, this was compounded because they often had no one else to ask to do these essential errands. Family members tended to be far more supportive of male relatives' restrictions due to their EMs than they were of female relatives with EMs. Thus, if it were not for daily contact with their children, some of these women stated that it was more stressful to be on EMs, with all the responsibilities but limited resources and numerous restrictions, than a prison sentence would have been (ibid.).

A particularly progressive women's prison is the Minnesota Correctional Facility–Shakopee, near Minneapolis (Luke, 2002; Command, n.d.). In addition to no bars or fences and its location within the community, it offers extensive parenting education and child visitation programs. Children under 12 are allowed for overnight and weekend visits, and a program for children over 11 is based on an empowerment model, allowing for support-group meetings for the mothers of teenagers and for the teenagers themselves (Luke, 2002).

Thus far, this chapter has focused on *women's* offending. More exciting changes have occurred regarding treating and responding to delinquent *girls*. Girls are being processed through the system at alarming rates, particularly if one controls for how many of these girls are victims and not offenders or became offenders in response to their victimization. The bright light in all of this is that the Office of Juvenile Justice and Delinquency Prevention (OJJDP) has recently given unprecedented attention to research and evaluation of policies and treatment regarding delinquent girls.

In 1992, there was a reauthorization of the Juvenile Justice and Delinquency Prevention Act of 1974 (JJDPA) (the 1974 act was designed to deinstitutionalize status offenders). A significant aspect of this reauthorization was that the U.S. Congress heard and understood some of the concerns raised by some professionals who work with delinquent girls, who reported that the existing program was insufficient for delinquent girls' needs. These professionals were convincing in their presentation of the existing programs as designed for boys, and even then, being often unavailable for girls. Hence, the 1992 Reauthorization of the 1974 JJDPA birthed the current focus on identifying and implementing the "gender-specific needs" of delinquent girls. The 1992 Reauthorization legislation provided that each state should (1) determine the need for and assessment of existing services and treatment for delinquent girls, (2) develop a plan to provide needed gender-specific services for the prevention and treatment of juvenile delinquency, and (3) provide assurance that youths in the juvenile system are treated fairly regarding their mental, physical, and emotional capabilities, as well as on the basis of their gender, race, and family income (Belknap, Dunn, and Holsinger, 1997). To this end, states across the United States have been receiving federal monies in attempts to attend to the three provisions outlined in the 1992 Reauthorization of the JJDPA. Most of this work is in progress, so it is too early to draw any conclusions.

Another significant outcome of this is that OJJDP funded Greene, Peters, and Associates (1998) to identify the most promising programming available for delinquent girls across the United States. This "inventory of best practices" not

E X H I B I T 12.1 **Girls' Needs for Healthy Development and the Challenges They Face to Obtain These Needs that Place Them at Risk for Delinquency**

- *Need for physical safety and healthy physical development*
  challenged by poverty, homelessness, violence, inadequate health care, inadequate nutrition, substance abuse

- *Need for trust, love, respect, validation from caring adults to foster healthy emotional development and form positive relationships*
  challenged by abandonment, family dysfunction, poor communication

- *Need for positive female role models to develop healthy identity as a woman*
  challenged by sexist, racist, homophobic messages, lack of community support

- *Need for safety to explore sexuality at own pace for healthy sexual development*
  challenged by sexual abuse, exploitation, negative messages about female sexuality

- *Need to belong, to feel competent and worthy*
  challenged by weakened family ties, negative peer influences, academic failure, low self-esteem

SOURCE: Cited verbatim from Greene, Peters, and Associates. 1998. *Guiding Principles for Promising Female Programming: An Inventory of Best Practices*. The Office of Juvenile Justice and Delinquency Prevention. Nashville, TN, p. 8.

only highlights the best programs but also identifies what good programming for delinquent girls should look like. In order to further understanding of the challenges in girls' necessary pathways for healthy development, Greene, Peters, and Associates (1998, 8) identify not only the needs but also what may challenge these needs and place a girl at risk of becoming delinquent (see Exhibit 12.1).

Similar to Acoca's (1998) claim that programming for imprisoned women must be comprehensive, Greene, Peters, and Associates make the same claim about delinquent girls' programming:

> [Gender–specific programming] represents a concentrated effort to assist all girls (not only those involved in the justice system) in positive female development. It takes into account the developmental needs of girls at adolescence, a critical stage for gender identity formation. It nurtures and reinforces "femaleness" as a positive identity with inherent strengths. (1998, 33)

Greene, Peters, and Associates (1998, 36) also state that for a treatment to be truly comprehensive for delinquent girls, it must address all of the following risks: poverty, ethnic membership, poor academic performance, teen pregnancy, substance abuse, victimization, health and mental health concerns, and gang membership. Exhibit 12.2 presents the elements identified by Greene, Peters, and Associates (1998) as most promising for effective programming for delinquent girls. One promising approach was reported in a study of multiple sites of Boys and Girls Clubs of America (BGSA) in predominantly African American or predominantly Latino/a communities that had high rates of poverty and violent crime (Hirsch et al., 2000). This study found that these organizations helped girls by empowering them and improving their self-esteem. Many of the girls referred to the organizations as

E X H I B I T   12.2   Elements and Features of Promising Programs for Delinquent Girls

Organization and Management: Creating an environment of teamwork, where girls can make positive life choices, good communication within the environment, consistency in care

Staffing Pattern: Charismatic and authentic staff, who have "been there" and "walk the talk" (Not all staff have to be female.)

Staff Training: Must include gender-specific training on adolescent female development, risks and resiliency of girls, cultural sensitivity, ability to assess a girl's needs

Intake Process: Individualizing each girl's needs at intake, assessing her personal background and contact with the system

Education: Addresses the needs of the whole person, including academic, life, and social skills. This includes education on and appreciation of women's history and ethnic histories, physical development, sexual behavior, and art, in addition to academic education in math and so on

Skills Training: Designed to help girls discover their strengths and adopt pro-social skills (e.g., self-defense and physical training and self-esteem training)

Promote Positive Development: Teach girls that development is a life process, and even if they've gotten "off track," they can get back on

Relationship Building: "Effective programs don't attempt to compete with girls' need for relationships. Instead, programs address girls' behavior in context by focusing on the choices they have made (both positive and negative) as a result of relationships" (1997, 49)

Culturally Relevant Activities: Programming must value diversity in race and culture to counter-act the negative stereotypes the girls may have internalized about themselves and others

Career Opportunities: Programming to help girls explore and prepare for careers

Health Services: Effective programming includes comprehensive physical and mental health promotion and treatment

Recreational Activities: Providing a variety of recreational activities including art, sports, volunteer and extracurricular activities

Responsive Services: Programs may need access to outside services and support, particularly if a girl has a unique culture or health or family needs

Mentoring: Allowing girls a chance to interact with capable women and girls who have "mastered life challenges of their own" (1997, p. 53)

Peer Activities: How to promote and have positive peer interactions and relationships in and out of treatment

Full Family Involvement: Building positive family support for girls, includes involving parents in the treatment plan via home visits, discussion groups, etc.

Community Involvement: Involving girls in their communities in positive ways; girls see themselves as contributing members of their communities

Specific Treatment Concerns: Based on an individual's needs, a girl may need treatment for a specific problem, such as substance abuse, prenatal or postpartum care, and well baby and day care

Re-entry into Community: Assess and develop resources to assist girls with reentry so that they may best avoid behaviors that place them at risk of reoffending

Evaluation: Evaluate through research various approaches to determine which are best for which types of girls

SOURCE: Greene, Peters, and Associates. 1998. *Guiding Principles for Promising Female Programming: An Inventory of Best Practices*. The Office of Juvenile Justice and Delinquency Prevention. Nashville, TN, pp. 43–57.

"homes" where they received encouragement from (paid and volunteer) adults and the other peers who participated. The BGSAs provided them not just a place to feel nurtured but also a place to nurture others, particularly those younger than them, and where their opinions were listened to and valued. The one negative report was that sports programs were predominantly available for boys (ibid.).

CHANGING RESPONSES TO MALE VIOLENCE AGAINST WOMEN

Women and girls do not cause their sexual, stalking, and intimate partner abuse victimizations. For abusive men to discontinue their violent and violating behaviors, the socialization of men and boys must change, as well as the criminal legal system's reactions to these abusers and the victims. Finally, we must also empower women and girls to resist these victimizations.

Sexual Victimization

During the 1970s and 1980s, every state repealed or modified traditional rape laws and enacted evidentiary reforms (Spohn and Horney, 1992):

> The most common changes were (1) redefining rape and replacing the single crime of rape with a series of graded offenses defined by the presence or absence of aggravating conditions; (2) changing the consent standard by eliminating the requirement that the victim physically resist her attacker; (3) eliminating the requirement that the victim's testimony be corroborated; and (4) placing restrictions on the introduction of evidence of the victim's prior sexual conduct. (ibid., 21).

Many states have enacted rape law reforms to help victims prosecute, to broaden the definition of rape to include forms other than penile–vaginal, and to assert that rapes are actual assaults rather than crimes "of passion" (as they are commonly portrayed in the media and in rape trials). Unfortunately, at present, rape law reform appears to be more symbolic than productive. That is, although rape law reform is necessary to address the complex issues surrounding sexual victimizations, the reforms are not sufficient to ensure that changes are actually practiced (Berger, Serles, and Neuman, 1988; Caringella-MacDonald, 1988; Horney and Spohn, 1991; Spohn and Horney, 1991, 1992, 1993). Therefore, although the first step has been taken—to change the rape laws—it is now important that these laws be used to protect all rape victims, regardless of the victim–offender relationship, the victim's prior sexual history, and the form the abuse takes.

It should be noted that while rape reform has been significant, there are still major shortcomings to law reforms, including the fact that some states exempt marital rape. A recent analysis of rapes reported to the police found that "a rape that occurred in the modern reform era (1990–1996) was significantly more likely

E X H I B I T 12.3 Community Rape Prevention Strategies

- Challenge societal beliefs and cultural values that promote and condone sexual violence.

- Educate potential victims about risk, risk avoidance, and self-defense.

- Reduce the emotional and physical trauma of rape by early and appropriate attention to the needs of individual rape victims.

- Prevent recurrent instances of rape by offender incarceration and treatment.

SOURCE: Mary P. Koss and Mary R. Harvey. 1991. *The Rape Victim: Clinical and Community Intervention,* 2nd ed. Newbury Park, CA: Sage, p. 246.

to be reported than one that occurred in the pre-reform period (before 1975)" (Clay-Warner and Burt, 2005, 167). Unfortunately, however, across time periods the gap between aggravated and "simple" rapes remains unchanged. Aggravated rapes are those committed by strangers, gang rapes, where weapons were used, or where serious injuries result.

Exhibit 12.3 summarizes the changes that need to occur within communities in order to deter sexual victimization (Koss and Harvey, 1991). The remainder of this section discusses these issues.

Given that women cannot count on rape law reform or individual violent men to stop raping, it is necessary to recognize and foster empowering behaviors and actions in women and girls. The research on sexual victimization points to the importance of instilling in women the confidence to identify and escape potentially threatening situations, as well as to physically fight back, where this is possible. Although sexually threatening situations may and often do develop to the point where it is impossible for the woman to escape, Parrot (1986) claims it is often possible to watch for danger signs in order to avoid sexual victimization. Specifically, women should trust their "gut feelings" when they feel that a situation or person is potentially dangerous. Women need to feel strong enough to say "no" or to leave situations in which they are uncomfortable (see Glavin, 1986; Parrot, 1986). Some women worry that they are "rude," "ungrateful," or even "prudish" if they do not go along with unwanted attention; however, men's offensive behavior is frequently a prelude to sexual victimizations.

Clearly, both women and men need to be educated that women and girls are to be respected, that women are to be believed when they say "no" or "stop," and that women should be able to leave potentially dangerous situations, however they are perceived, without feeling guilty about hurting someone's feelings. Research on both high school and college students has shown that rape awareness programs in the educational environment are effective in dispelling rape myths (Fonow, Richardson, and Wemmerus, 1992; Proto-Campise, Belknap, and Wooldredge, 1998). Therefore, such programs need to be implemented in all educational environments. This is particularly important given the wide range of positive and negative responses rape victims report hearing when they disclose their victimizations. Given the extremely negative reactions rape victims receive, including from loved ones, the results of a study of rape survivors explained "the critical importance of the social context in which survivors discuss sexual victimization and why, at times, silence may be the most logical response" (Sudderth, 1998, 572).

Verbal, physical, and legal resistance to sexual victimization may all prove fruitful in deterrence. It is important to note that confronting sexual harassment has effectively raised awareness about it. Three years before the Anita Hill/Clarence Thomas hearings, it was pointed out that African American women have been "at the forefront of the fight against sexual harassment," which has resulted in the legal definitions of sexual harassment, the identification of sexual harassment as sex discrimination, the Title VII prohibition against sexual harassment, and liability for employers who engage in sexual harassment (Eason, 1988, 140).

One study found that women college students base their decision to report sexual harassment on (1) severity of the harassment, (2) fear of being accused of lying, (3) perceived effectiveness of reporting, and (4) fear of the reporting procedure itself (Sullivan and Bybee, 1987). This implies the importance of universities and other institutions creating and maintaining policies and an environment that facilitate the reporting of and adequate response to sexual harassment charges. Another more recent study reported that most sexual harassment victims in college settings still do not report their victimizations to campus officials, largely due to their concerns about safety (Grauerholz, Stohl, and Gabin, 1999). Thus, special networks must be implemented to create a safer environment both for sexual harassment victims to report and for those complaint-receivers to act on the reports (ibid.).

A comprehensive overview of the ways in which the media, the courts, the public, and even some feminist organizations have discounted some of those few women who have had the courage to protest their sexual harassment victimizations legally, identified ways to improve sexual harassment responses for all women but particularly the most marginalized: (1) stronger enforcement of sexual harassment laws; (2) amendment of welfare, food stamps, and unemployment insurance policies to identify sexual harassment as a "good cause" for leaving jobs; (3) amendment of policies that suspend penalties and time limits for welfare mothers who leave word due to sexual harassment; (4) guarantee by states of Title VII safeguards "to all workforce participants" and "require[ment of] strict Title VII compliance of private employers who hire welfare recipients" (Mink, 2000, 140).

Research evaluating the best way to resist rape once an actual assault has begun consistently finds that in most cases it is best for victims to fight back. Victims who fight back are much less likely to experience "completed" rapes than those who do not resist (Bart and O'Brien, 1985; Kleck and Sayles, 1990; Ullman and Knight, 1992). Of utmost importance is to act immediately to the assault and to combine resistance strategies. The most effective combination of two strategies is physical force and yelling, the single most effective strategy is fleeing, and pleading and begging appear to have a negative effect, increasing the chance of a completed rape (Bart and O'Brien, 1985; Ullman and Knight, 1992). There is no evidence that resisting an attacker will lead to further injuries in addition to the rape in most cases—resistance rarely precedes injury (Bart and O'Brien, 1985; Kleck and Sayles, 1990; Ullman and Knight, 1992). Moreover, victims who fight back tend to have fewer psychological injuries after the attack, even if the rape was completed (Bart and O'Brien, 1985). It is also important to remember that not all rapes are escapable—some women (and men) are simply overpowered despite active resistance. Furthermore, victims who do not resist should not be blamed for their victimizations. As a whole, however, physical resistance appears to be the most powerful hindrance of sexual attacks.

Finally, the criminal legal system must become more responsive to both victims and offenders in an effort to stop sexual victimization. In Chapter 7, the numerous problems associated with the official criminal legal responses are discussed. Exhibit 12.3 summarizes factors important to enhancing victims' likelihood to report sexual assaults to the police and follow through with the courts. Special care must also be taken in crime processing of child sexual abuse, not only to protect the child from further abuse but also to understand the victims' reluctance to answer police questions (Kirkwood and Mihaila, 1979).

Although most of the criticism of the criminal legal system is focused on the police, it is also important that the courts adequately address victims' needs and offenders' responsibility (see Klein, 1981; Smart, 1989; Spohn and Horney, 1992). Recent research indicates that a restorative justice model in Australia was positively evaluated overall by rape survivors (Curtis-Fawley and Daly, 2005). Previous research indicates that one of the most significant frustrations for rape survivors in the traditional court process is their lack of opportunity to face their assailants, speak to them, and question them (Konradi and Burger, 2000). The restorative justice model allows victims and offenders (who admit their guilt) to meet face-to-face in the presence of others (e.g., judges, counselors, victim advocates, etc.), sometimes in lieu of the formal traditional courts but often, alongside the courts. Interviews with rape victim advocates in Australia posed support for the restorative justice model, as it offers victims more voice and agency in their own cases and likely encourages rapists to take more responsibility for their violence (Curtis-Fawley and Daly, 2005).

Regarding legal reform for the processing of child sexual abuse cases, the following goals have been proposed: (1) expedite the case; (2) provide advocates and guardians for the victims; (3) reduce unnecessary contact of the child with the crime-processing system; (4) institute "child-friendly" procedures; and (5) enhance case development through exceptions to hearsay rules and use of expert witnesses (Whitcomb, 1991).

In conclusion, important advances have been made in legal reforms and the general crime processing of sexual abuse cases. It is necessary, however, that the implementation of legal reforms occur, as well as evaluations and improvements of individual crime-processing professionals' responses to victims and offenders. Rape crisis centers and abused women's shelters offer ways the community can impact awareness and education about abuse at the same time they support survivors in the criminal legal system and their everyday lives (e.g., work, child care, education, etc.) (see, for example, O'Sullivan, 2002). The Copenhagen Center for Victims of Sexual Assault at Denmark, offering a 24-hour medical treatment and psychosocial follow-up regardless of whether the offense is reported to the police, provides a model example of a commitment to aid these survivors. Given that the need for medical treatment did not differ between those survivors who subsequently reported to the police and those who did not, a study on this center concluded the importance of a 24-hour facility that responds to all sexual abuse survivors (Schei et al., 2003).

Intimate Partner Abuse

Since the 1970s, the battered women's movement has increased public awareness of intimate partner abuse (IPA) through a wide range of services, agencies, laws, and community organizations (Tierney, 1982, Davies, Lyon, and Monti-Calania, 1998). A lack of shelters or available space in existing shelters and an often unresponsive criminal legal system continue to be problems. Nonetheless, progress has been made. For example, despite an effort since the early 1990s to withdraw support from pro-arrest policies for intimate partner abusers (see Sherman, 1992), current research offers support for the crime-processing system's proactive responses against these offenders. Some scholars have criticized the current attempt to withdraw pro-arrest policies as a narrowly focused view of effectiveness—solely examining arrest and recidivism (Bowman, 1992; Frisch, 1992; Gondolf and Fisher, 1988; Lerman, 1992; Stanko, 1989). Such a focus ignores that arrest may provide positive outcomes unrelated to recidivism—such as an escape opportunity for victims and their children—and may communicate to all involved parties (the batterer, the victim, the children, and other witnesses) that battering is unacceptable and illegal behavior.

The focus on the arrest decision regarding the system's response to battering ignores the importance of court action (and inaction) in IPA cases. For example, one study found that for cases where the prosecutor decided to proceed through the initial hearing, the batterer was less likely to recidivate (Ford and Regoli, 1992). In addition, two studies have shown how arrest empowers some abused women. In one study intimate partner abusers perceived arrest as increasing both the visibility and the risks of their behavior—including a greater likelihood of going to jail and having their abused partner leave them. The abused women perceived arrest as an opportunity to speak out to the authorities and others against the abuse and to exercise their power (Dutton et al., 1992). Moreover, results from another study (Ford, 1991b) suggest that the dropping of charges by abused women does not necessarily negate the usefulness of filing the charges. Rather, abused women can use the threat of prosecution to influence the batterer to change (ibid.). Perceived this way, dropping charges may be an indication that the system does work for some women.

Critics of pro-arrest policies also raise concerns that arresting intimate partner abusers may place victims at increased risk of violence by retaliation of the offender. Research examining this issue, however, found the majority of abused women are not at risk of increased violence following the offender's arrest (Ford, 1991a; Jaffe et al., 1986; Maxwell, Garner, and Fagan, 2001). For those few women who are more at risk of violence, the police should expand their protection (Stark, 1993). It is difficult to state definitively that jailing intimate partner abusers is an effective deterrent due to insufficient research on this response; however, there are a variety of alternative sanctions that need to be evaluated that might also, or more effectively, hold intimate partner abusers accountable and address victims' needs (e.g., Tolman, 1996). At any rate, it is important to allow individual abused women a voice in the decision making of their own cases through discussions with police and court officials (Davies, Lyon, and Monti-Calania, 1998; Ferraro and Pope, 1993). It may be necessary to allow the victim to unilaterally veto the arrest or prosecution decision, as she knows her situation and risks better than anyone else. It is crucial for prosecution decision making to understand victim reluctance; such understanding increases the likelihood of victim cooperation and a successful disposition in court (Hart, 1993).

For effective and meaningful responses to abused women to exist, the many arms of the crime-processing system and other health and helping agencies must work together—from the police and the emergency room personnel to the social workers, prosecutors, and judges (see Belknap and McCall, 1994; Cahn, 1992; Gamache, Edleson, and Schock, 1988). For example, one study found that the most promising site for the "public health screening for victims of family or intimate assault and possibly for perpetrators" was the county hospital (Saltzman et al., 1997, 326). To date, most of the criminal legal policy implementation geared at addressing woman battering focuses on changes in policing. In addition to police departments, courts must have stated policies and goals that recognize woman battering as a crime and force intimate partner abusers to take responsibility for their behaviors. "They [the courts] can then support police in their efforts, help break the cycle of violence, and control the abuser" (Cahn, 1992, 177).

It is not sufficient simply to have laws and policies in place to protect women (and girls) abused by their current or former intimate partners—they must also be enforced (Ferraro, 1989; McCann, 1985). In fact, although policy reforms resulting from feminist activism finally criminalized woman battering, they also effectively moved control of this problem from feminists and abused women's advocates to crime-processing professionals, the press, mental health professionals, and academics who often fail to account for gender inequality in the family (Bush, 1993).

Therefore, programs in which abused women's groups are actively involved with the criminal legal professionals are the best hope for effective crime-processing responses to woman battering (Kurz, 1992; Pence and Shepard, 1988). Pro-arrest policies and other formal actions against intimate partner abusers may prove fruitless without a systems approach that includes a feminist perspective from abused women's groups (Kurz, 1992). Research shows that most abused women make "multiple efforts" to "seek help," and married women are those most likely to seek such help (Hutchison and Hirschel, 1998). Seeking help by identifying themselves and their needs provides the community and criminal legal system an entry to helping them. Too often, these women report unfavorable responses from those from whom they have requested help. However, interaction between abused women's groups and the crime-processing system has provided productive models for change in the system in Denver, San Francisco, and Minneapolis (Kurz, 1992).

An important contribution to understanding the "best responses" to abused women is the recently published book *Safety Planning with Battered Women* (Davies, Lyon, and Monti-Calania, 1998). Two of the most important points of information in response about how best to be effective with responses to abused women are identical to what Greene, Peters, and Associates (1998) reported as "best practices" for delinquent girls. Specifically, abused women need a *comprehensive program* and an *individualized program*. Furthermore, Davies, Lyon, and Monti-Calania (1998, 3) stress that the response be a woman-defined advocacy, defined as an "approach to advocacy that builds a partnership between advocates and battered women, and ultimately has each battered woman defining the advocacy and help she needs." Too often, according to Davies and colleagues (ibid.), abused women are not consulted about their needs and a service-defined program is used, where women are simply expected to find and use available programming, regardless of whether it fits their needs. Needless to say, these practices often alienate abused women from the criminal legal system, making them less likely to recontact shelters or the police or to seek assistance in the future.

Another important contribution that Davies and colleagues (ibid.) provide in *Safety Planning with Battered Women* is identifying the distinctions between life-*generated* and *batterer-generated* risks in an abused woman's life, given that both must be addressed. Life-generated risks are the environmental and social risks a woman must consider in her decisions to leave or report her abusive partner, including financial limitations, racism, a woman's disability status, and sexual orientation (in same-sex battering cases). The batterer-generated risks involve the risks related to a batterer's control of the victim, such as physical and psychological harm and threats to the victim, her/their children, and her friends and family. Again, similar to what Greene, Peters, and Associates (1998) stressed about delinquent girls, Davies and others (1998) stress about abused women: Their lives are often complex, and these women vary on a wide variety of risk and life conditions (e.g., income, education, race/ethnicity, motherhood status, levels of abuse experienced, access to agencies and aid); thus, it is necessary that responses to them be individualized to meet each woman's particular and varied needs. Davies, Lyon, and Monti-Calania (ibid.) and others, such as Kanuha (1996), highlight the racism that abused women of color encounter not only in the police and courts but sometimes within victim advocacy agencies, such as shelters. Vinton (1998) addresses the unique needs of older women (aged 60 and older) who are victims of intimate partner battering. Finally, Davies and colleagues (1998) effectively show how many of the risks women face if they stay in abusive relationships are identical to those they face if they leave these relationships (e.g., increased abuse, loss of child custody, and so on), pointing out the problem with blaming women for staying.

It is important in evaluating programs for IPA or the individual survivors of IPA not to fall into the trap of measuring a successful outcome only in terms of whether a woman leaves her abuser. Indeed, too much community chest and other funding for shelters and victim advocacy agencies require this outcome measure for continued funding. Many women, including women who have been in shelters, return to their abusers. They still may eventually leave, but some stay "forever." "In addition, a woman may have made critically important changes without having left the abuser. Staying in the relationship does not mean the abused woman is inactive or that an intervention has had no effect on her" (Brown,

1997, 6). Brown (ibid.) states that for responses to abused women to be effective, they must address the "stage of change" the woman is in. The *precontemplation phase* refers to a woman either being unaware of the abuse she is subjected to or simply accepting it with no desire for change. The second stage, *contemplation*, involves thinking about intentions to change. Next, in the *preparation stage*, the woman actively plans change; this is followed by the *action stage*, where she actually makes some changes. The final stage, the *maintenance stage*, is where change is solidified and temptations to relapse are overcome. Brown (ibid., 10) points out that progression through the stages "is not usually linear. It is cyclical, with people progressing from precontemplation to contemplation and then action, usually relapsing, and then recycling back to another stage before moving forward again." Obviously, we must be careful in examining this approach not to slip into the assumption that she stays because she is not "self-actualized" yet. As noted repeatedly in this book, many women do not have the choice of leaving because it is too dangerous for them and/or their children.

One study examined the victims of intimate partner abusers who were court-ordered to treatment (Gondolf, 1998). This study found that these women were disproportionately from lower economic and educational levels than women whose abusers were not court-ordered to treatment and that they were more likely than other survivors of battering to seek help primarily through the courts. Gondolf (ibid.) attempts to explain this court focus as (1) it may be considered sufficient by these women; (2) they may be seeking the short-term immediate results expected with treatment; and (3) they may be caught in the abuser-imposed isolation, not have ready access to services, or may not believe the services will work. "Consequently, they may feel that they have to fend for themselves, as suggested in the high percentage of women who use informal strategies, such as threatening to leave the abuser or responding aggressively toward their batterer" (ibid., 673). Finally, although these women were optimistic about their abusers' discontinued use of abuse against them (which may be another reason that they are likely to limit their help-seeking to the courts and court-ordered treatment), only about half of the abusers completed the court-ordered treatment.

Just as the restorative justice (RJ) model was identified in the last section as a potentially meaningful manner of processing sexual assault cases, feminists have also identified restorative justice as an important consideration for intimate abuse cases (Presser and Gaarder, 2000). Similar to how the last section discussed the importance of survivors' ability to verbally confront their assailants in a safe and formal practice (RJ) for rape survivors, the same can be said for survivors of intimate partner abuse. Additionally, the RJ model discontinues the formal court practice of isolating the survivors from their communities, but RJ "generalizes ownership of the battering problem beyond victims and offenders and beyond government to communities," thus allowing for more actual change in deterring IPA (ibid., 188). Similarly, recent research emphasizes the need for flexible, woman-centered, easily accessible centers and policies to address the unique and varied needs across survivors of IPA (e.g., Dasgupta, 2003; Goodman and Epstein, 2005; Mills, 2003).

One of the more recent changes in responses to woman battering is the increasingly *globalized* response. Quite literally, advocates from across the world are working together not only to raise awareness about the problem and frequency of woman battering but also to unite in determining "best responses" (e.g., Edleson and Eisikovits, 1996; Heise, 1996; Roche, Biron, and Reilly, 1995; Slote and Cuthbert, 1997; Zabelina, 1995). From an international perspective, a key component of this is to get violence against women (e.g., rape and IPA) acknowledged as a *human rights violation*. Regarding global issues at home, a significant contribution of the 1994 (the first) Violence against Women Act (in addition to funding research and programming on sexual harassment, rape, stalking, and battering) is allowing "battered immigrant women to obtain lawful permanent resident status through self-petitioning or suspension of deportation" (Orloff and Kelly, 1995, 381). Although this is a huge step forward, abused women who are not legal immigrants to the United States still face incredible hardship in reporting their abuses and risking deportation. Similarly, a study of South Asian community-based responses to non-English-speaking women in Toronto found that these feminist victim-advocacy organizations had to curb their criticisms of patriarchal society to obtain state funding (Agnew, 1998, 153): "Consequently, they give priority to ensuring access to social services for non-English-speaking, working-class, immigrant women. But helping women with their problems does not expose the systemic power relations underlying wife abuse and, although some political and social change does occur, it is slow and moderate." Moreover, policies need to be designed and implemented with understanding the unique needs of immigrant women who have been abused (Abraham, 2000; Bui, 2004) and recognizing "that immigrant culture and context offer resiliency factors through which programs and policy can be used to better serve" these women (Raj and Silverman, 2002, 367). Additionally, policies and programs to respond to abused women who are also disabled must address their unique experiences and circumstances (Gilson, Cramer, and DePoy, 2001).

Chapter 8 includes a discussion of court problems for victims of IPA who kill their abusers in self-defense. Current self-defense laws are insufficient to account for the resistance that abused women must use to protect themselves (and often their children). Moreover, acquittal by reason of insanity has obvious negative repercussions for victims who were likely behaving quite sanely; for example, it may be difficult to find employment and retain custody of children. Therefore, some advocates for abused women who have killed abusive mates suggest that an entrapment defense be employed, including a psychological self-defense (Ewing, 1987; Stark, 1992). Such a defense proposes that women may have to use more force than men in similar situations and that abused women may be entrapped by a combination of social and psychological factors, making it impossible or seemingly impossible to escape (as discussed in Chapter 8).

Finally, the importance of IPA women's shelters cannot be overemphasized. Shelters save the lives of abused women, their children, and even the abusers; an increase in shelters is correlated with a decrease in intimate partner homicides of both women *and* men (Browne, 1992; Steffensmeier, 1993; Walker, 1989). In addition to providing a safe haven for women and children and decreasing the likelihood of homicides, shelters advocate for and enable women to escape abusive relationships and to view themselves as worthy of respect (Ferraro and

Johnson, 1983; Pence and Shepard, 1988). An evaluation of a shelter found that residents positively evaluated "the supportive nature of the staff, safety, relationships with other residents, and the child care. Residents expressed some concerns about the availability of counseling from busy staff and the appropriateness of some shelter residents. Generally, the women endorse the shelters as resources that save lives" (Tutty, Weaver, and Rothery, 1999, 898).

CHANGES FOR WOMEN WORKING IN THE CRIMINAL LEGAL SYSTEM

The experiences of women working in crime-processing jobs are described in Chapters 9 through 11. As a result of the women's movement, Title VII of the Civil Rights Act, and affirmative action, women have been accepted into law schools and employed in men's prisons and on police patrol in unprecedented numbers since the 1970s. For example, the percentage of women law students has grown from 4.2 percent in 1965 to 42.5 percent in 1991, and the percentage of women in the total lawyer population has grown from 2.5 percent in 1950 to 8.1 percent in 1980, 22 percent in 1990, and 27 percent in 1998 (American Bar Association, 1992; U.S. Census Bureau, 1999). Women have also been elected and appointed judges in larger numbers than ever before. While the rate of women as police officers and women working with prisoners (especially male prisoners) has not grown as significantly, there have been important advancements in terms of these women's promotions to sergeants, captains, lieutenants, and (rarely) chiefs and wardens (only in women's prisons).

Nonetheless, there is still considerable room for improvement. Many law school programs provide no training and coursework on feminist issues, such as IPA victims (including those who have killed their abusers), stalking victims, rape victims, and women discriminated against in hiring, firings, and promotions. Women still make up about 10 percent of officers in most police departments and men's prisons. And the research summarized in this book, Chapters 9–11, suggests that women in these nontraditional, male-dominated jobs continue to face considerable hostility from some of their male coworkers and supervisors. Although the research on gender comparisons of the stress levels of police officers and guards suggests that the gap is closing (women's higher rates of stress are less obvious), where there are gender differences, they have to do with women's increased stress due to their token status (e.g., Bartol et al., 1992; Wertsch, 1998), sexist differences in job assignments (e.g., Britton, 1997), and the hostility and harassment from their male coworkers (e.g., Morash and Haarr, 1995; Pogrebin and Poole, 1997). Although women's representation in the field of law has increased significantly, women's representation as partners in law firms remains disappointingly low (Epstein, 1998; Hagan and Kay, 1995; Hagan et al., 1991; Sommerlad and Sanderson, 1998).

Research contributes the higher turnover rate in women's versus men's employment in policing to unpleasant working environments for women,

E X H I B I T 12.4 **Policies and Practices to Accelerate the Integration of Women into Policing**

- Departments implement a voluntary affirmative action plan with women and people of color on the advisory group for its design and implementation.

- Clear policies prohibiting sexual harassment should be adopted and vigorously enforced.

- Recruit training should include physical fitness, self-defense, verbal and nonverbal communication, and gender and cultural differences training.

- Outstanding women officers should be part of academy training to indicate women's effectiveness to officers.

- Probationary officers' assignments should be monitored to ensure that all officers have similar opportunities in assignments needed for success and promotion.

- Departments should periodically audit assignments to ensure that officers are tracked similarly (e.g., women are not disproportionately tracked into clerical work).

- Departments should create and maintain an open system of merit for promotion and encourage women to apply for promotions.

- Soon-to-be-promoted-to-sergeant officers should spend some time apprenticing with an existing sergeant.

- Women need to be given more responsibility for operations via increased promotions to command staff positions.

- Departments need to implement ways to decrease family stresses, disproportionately experienced by women, in order to reduce burnout and high turnovers of women officers.

- Departments should implement pregnancy policies that allow women officers to stay on the job in noncontact positions and improve opportunities for taking parental leaves for all parents (male and female) with newborn babies.

- Equipment, facilities, uniforms, and language in the department should not be male-centered.

- Specific job-related performance evaluations and measures need to be designed and routinely audited to ensure they do not stereotype women and are not biased against them.

- Research on the status of women in policing needs to be continued.

SOURCE: Susan E. Martin, 1990. *On the Move: The Status of Women in Policing.* Washington, DC: The Police Foundation.

problems mixing policing with family responsibilities (especially for single parents on rotating shifts), inadequate pregnancy leave and light–duty pregnancy policies, exaggerated views of police work portrayed on television and by police recruiters, and problems associated with being "tokens" (Martin, 1989; Martin and Jurik, 1996) These factors are probably equally applicable to women working in men's prisons. (Chapter 11 presents similar hostility and career blocks that women lawyers face.) Thus, policies must be implemented and followed to address conditions that make females' working environments more difficult than those of their male counterparts. To this end (Martin, 1990, xvii) identified a number of recommendations to "accelerate the integration of women into policing" (see Exhibit 12.4).

Furthermore, the influence of tokenism is crucial. As long as women are hired as tokens—whether in policing, prison work, or law firms, or as elected or appointed attorneys and judges—they are unlikely to be able to perform their duties as "just another professional" on the job. Research has shown that token status in these positions is likely to limit how much women can bring change to these jobs (see Belknap and Shelley, 1993). Additionally, the socialization in the training and on the job is so powerful that positive aspects women may bring to the job—such as empathy for rape victims—may be negated (see Spohn, 1990). For example, some women may be interested in becoming police officers, judges, or lawyers because they want to change conditions for victims of IPA or rape victims. However, they may be heavily inundated with victim-blaming messages during their "education" or formal and informal training. Thus, we must ask, can women change the way criminal legal jobs are done, or do these jobs change the women who are hired? The latter is far more likely as long as women continue to be hired in token status.

Administrators in the criminal legal professions (policing, prisons/jails, and courts), therefore, need to actively recruit and appoint more women and determine methods of keeping existing women employees in the field and promoting them. Regardless of whether women will, in fact, bring positive changes to these jobs, hiring, firing, and promotional decisions should not be made simply on the basis of sex/gender.

SUMMARY

Considerable research is presented in this book describing the invisibility of and injustices experienced by female victims, offenders, and workers in society and the criminal legal system. Important advances in terms of legal reforms and employment practices and policies have been made since the 1970s. Nonetheless, female victims of male violence, female offenders, and women working as criminal legal professionals continue to face damaging stereotypes and discrimination.

The feminist movement has advanced legal reforms and changes in hiring practices; however, further legal and policy reform is still necessary. Moreover, the implementation of policies and laws to improve the recognition and treatment of women and girls as victims, offenders, and workers must be carefully examined and evaluated to ensure gender equality and justice. However, women have made important strides in both their representation in sheer numbers and advancement in promotions. Although it is not nearly to the point of being "equal," it is significant progress. Moreover, women's increased representation is likely having an effect on how they experience the job, given the more recent studies reported in this book indicating that women's stress as tokens and due to hostility from their male coworkers is decreasing. Thus, there appears to be growing acceptance of women as professionals in the criminal legal system, and it is likely that they are more able than ever before to do their jobs in the manner they want to, rather than as merely token women.

REFERENCES

Abraham, Margaret. 2000. *Speaking the Unspeakable: Marital Violence among South Asian Immigrants in the United States*. New Brunswick, NJ: Rutgers University Press.

Acoca, Leslie. 1998. Defusing the Time Bomb: Understanding and Meeting the Growing Health Care Needs of Incarcerated Women in America. *Crime and Delinquency* 44(1):32–48.

Agnew, Vijay. 1998. Tensions in Providing Services to South Asian Victims of Wife Abuse in Toronto. *Violence Against Women* 4(2):153–179.

American Bar Association. 1992. *Legal Education and Professional Development and Education Continuum*. Chicago: Report of the Task Force on Law Schools and the Profession: Narrowing the Gender Gap.

American Correctional Association. 1990. *The Female Offender: What Does the Future Hold?* Arlington, VA: Kirby Lithographic Company.

Anderson, Tammy L. 2003. Issues in the Availability of Health Care for Women Prisoners. Pp. 49–60 in *The Incarcerated Woman*, edited by S. F. Sharp. Upper Saddle River, NJ: Prentice Hall.

Arnold, Regina. 1990. Processes of Victimization and Criminalization of Black Women. *Social Justice* 17:153–166.

Barry, Ellen M. 1991. Jail Litigation Concerning Women Prisoners. *The Prison Journal* 71:44–50.

Bart, Pauline B., and Patricia H. O'Brien. 1985. *Stopping Rape: Successful Survival Strategies*. New York: Pergamon Press.

Bartol, Curt R., George T. Bergen, Julie Seager Volckens, and Kathleen M. Knoras. 1992. Women in Small-Town Policing: Job Performance and Stress. *Criminal Justice and Behavior* 19(3):240–259.

Baunach, Phyllis Jo. 1992. Critical Problems of Women in Prison. Pp. 99–112 in *The Changing Roles of Women in the Criminal Justice System*, 2nd ed., edited by I. L. Moyers. Prospect Heights, IL: Waveland Press.

Belknap, Joanne. 2000. Programming and Health Care Responsibility for Incarcerated Women. Pp. 109–123 in *States of Confinement: Policing, Detention, and Prisons*, edited by Joy James. New York: St. Martin's Press.

Belknap, Joanne, Melissa Dunn, and Kristi Holsinger. 1997. *Moving toward Juvenile Justice and Youth-Serving Systems That Address the Distinct Experience of the Adolescent Female*. Gender Specific Services Work Group Report to the Governor. Office of Criminal Justice Services, Columbus, OH. February, 36 pp.

Belknap, Joanne, and Kristi Holsinger. 2006. The Gendered Nature of Risk Factors for Delinquency. *Feminist Criminology* 1:48–71.

Belknap, Joanne, and K. Douglas McCall. 1994. Woman Battering and Police Referrals. *Journal of Criminal Justice* 22:223–236.

Belknap, Joanne, and Jill K. Shelley. 1993. The New Lone Ranger: Policewomen on Patrol. *American Journal of Police* 12:47–75.

Berger, Ronald J., Patricia Searles, and W. Lawrence Neuman. 1988. The Dimensions of Rape Law Reform Legislation. *Law and Society Review* 22:329–357.

Bloom, Barbara. 1993. Incarcerated Mothers and Their Children: Maintaining Family Ties. Pp. 60–68 in *Female Offenders: Meeting the Needs of a Neglected Population*. Laurel, MD: American Correctional Association.

Bloom, Barbara, and D. Steinhart. 1993. *Why Punish the Children?* San Francisco: National Council on Crime and Delinquency.

Bowman, Cynthia G. 1992. The Arrest Experiments: A Feminist Critique. *Journal of Criminal Law and Criminology* 83:201–209.

Britton, Dana M. 1997. Gendered Organizational Logic: Policy and Practice in Men's and Women's Prisons. *Gender and Society* 11(6):796–818.

Brodsky, Annette M. 1975. Planning for the Female Offender: Directions for the Future. Pp. 100–108 in *The Female Offender*, edited by A. M. Brodsky. Beverly Hills, CA: Sage.

Brown, Jody. 1997. Working toward Freedom from Violence: The Process of Change in Battered Women. *Violence Against Women* 3(1):5–26.

Browne, Angela. 1987. *When Battered Women Kill*. New York: Free Press.

———. 1992. Violence against Women: Relevance for Medical Practitioners. *JAMA* 267:3184–3189.

Bui, Hoan H. 2004. *In the Adopted Land: Abused Immigrant Women and the Criminal Justice System*. Westport, CT: Greenwood.

Bush, Diane M. 1993. Women's Movements and State Policy Reform Aimed at Domestic Violence against Women. *Gender and Society* 6:587–608.

Cahn, Naomi R. 1992. Innovative Approaches to the Prosecution of Domestic Crimes. Pp. 161–180 in *Domestic Violence: The Changing Criminal Justice Response*, edited by E. S. Buzawa and C. G. Buzawa. Westport, CT: Auburn House.

Caringella-MacDonald, Susan. 1988. Marxist and Feminist Interpretations on the Aftermath of Rape Reforms. *Contemporary Crises* 12:125–144.

Chesney-Lind, Meda. 1991. Patriarchy, Prisons, and Jails: A Critical Look at Trends in Women's Incarceration. *Prison Journal* 71:51–67.

Clark, Judy, and Kathy Boudin. 1990. Community of Women Organize Themselves to Cope with the AIDS Crisis: A Case Study from Bedford Hills Correctional Facility. *Social Justice* 17:90–109.

Clay-Warner, Jody, and Callie Harbin Burt. 2005. Rape Reporting After Reforms: Have Times Really Changed? *Violence Against Women* 11:150–176.

Collins, Catherine Fisher. 1997. *The Imprisonment of African American Women*. Jefferson, NC: MacFarland & Co.

Command, Janice. n.d. *Women of Shakopee Prison*. http://www.dickshovel.com/shak.html.

Curtis-Fawley, Sarah, and Kathleen Daly. 2005. Gendered Violence and Restorative Justice: The Views of Victim Advocates. *Violence Against Women* 11:603–638.

Daane, Diane M. 2003. Pregnant Prisoners. Pp. 61–72 in *The Incarcerated Woman*, edited by S. F. Sharp. Upper Saddle River, NJ: Prentice Hall.

Dasgupta, Shamita Das. 2003. *Safety and Justice for All: Examining the Relationship between the Women's Anti-Violence Movement and the Criminal Legal System*. New York: Ms. Foundation. http://www.ms.foundation.org/user-assets/PDF/program/safety_justice.pdf.

Davies, Jill, Eleanor Lyon, and Diane Monti-Catania. 1998. *Safety Planning with Battered Women*. Thousand Oaks, CA: Sage.

Dembo, R., L. Williams, W. Wothke, J. Schmeidler, and C. H. Bronn. 1992. The Role of Family Factors,

Physical Abuse, and Sexual Victimization Experiences in High-risk Youths' Alcohol and Other Drug Use and Delinquency: A Longitudinal Model. *Violence and Victims* 7(3):245–266.

Dodge, Kenneth A., John E. Bates, and Gregory S. Pettit. 1990. Mechanisms in the Cycle of Violence. *Science* 250:1678–1683.

Dutton, Donald G., Stephen D. Hart, Les W. Kennedy, and Kirk R. Williams. 1992. Arrest and the Reduction of Repeat Wife Assault. Pp. 111–127 in *Domestic Violence: The Changing Criminal Justice Response*, edited by E. S. Buzawa and C. G. Buzawa. Westport, CT: Auburn House.

Eason, Yla. 1988. When the Boss Wants Sex. Pp. 139–147 in *Racism and Sexism*, edited by P. S. Rothenberg. New York: St. Martin's Press.

Edleson, Jeffrey L., and Zvi C. Eisikovits. 1996. Visions of Continued Change. Pp. 1–4 in *Future Interventions with Battered Women and Their Families*, edited by J. L. Edleson and Z. C. Eisikovits. Thousand Oaks, CA: Sage Publications.

Epstein, Cynthia F. 1982. Women's Entry into Corporate Law Firms. Pp. 283–306 in *Women and the Law*, Vol. 2, edited by D. Kelly Weisberg. New York: Schenkman.

———. 1998. Reaching for the Top: "The Glass Ceiling" and Women in the Law. Pp. 105–130 in *Women in Law*, edited by S. Shetreet. London: Kluwer Law International.

Ewing, Charles P. 1987. *Battered Women Who Kill*. Lexington, MA: Lexington Books.

Feinman, Clarice. 1984. A Historical Overview of the Treatment of Incarcerated Women: Myths and Realities of Rehabilitation. *The Prison Journal* 63:12–26.

Ferraro, Kathleen J. 1989. Policing Woman Battering. *Social Problems* 36:61–74.

Ferraro, Kathleen J., and John M. Johnson. 1983. How Women Experience Battering: The Process of Victimization. *Social Problems* 30:325–339.

Ferraro, Kathleen J., and Lucille Pope. 1993. Irreconcilable Differences: Battered Women, Police, and the Law. Pp. 96–126 in *Legal Responses to Wife Assault*, edited by N. Zoe Hilton. Newbury Park, CA: Sage.

Fonow, Mary M., Laurel Richardson, and Virginia A. Wemmerus. 1992. Feminist Rape Education: Does It Work? *Gender and Society* 6:108–122.

Ford, David A. 1991a. Preventing and Provoking Wife Battery through Criminal Sanctioning: A Look at the Risks. Pp. 191–209 in *Abused and Battered: Social and Legal Responses to Family Violence*, edited by D. D. Knudsen and J. L. Miller. New York: Aldine De Gruyter.

———. 1991b. Prosecution as a Victim Power Resource: A Note on Empowering Women in Violent Conjugal Relationships. *Law and Society Review* 25:313–334.

Ford, David A., and Mary Jean Regoli. 1992. The Preventive Impacts of Policies for Prosecuting Wife Batterers. Pp. 181–207 in *Domestic Violence: The Changing Criminal Justice Response*, edited by E. S. Buzawa and C. G. Buzawa. Westport, CT: Auburn House.

Frisch, Lisa A. 1992. Research That Succeeds, Policies That Fail. *Journal of Criminal Law and Criminology* 83:209–217.

Gamache, D. J., J. L. Edleson, and M. D. Schock. 1988. Coordinated Police, Judicial, and Social Service Response to Woman Battering. Pp. 193–209 in *Coping with Family Violence*, edited by G. T. Hotaling, D. Finkelhor, J. T. Kirkpatrick, and M. A. Straus. Beverly Hills, CA: Sage.

Gilson, Stephen French, Elizabeth P. Cramer, and Elizabeth DePoy. 2001. Linking the Assessment of Self-Reported Functional Capacity with Abuse Experiences of Women with Disabilities. *Affilia* 16:220–235.

Glavin, Anne P. 1986. *Acquaintance Rape: The Silent Epidemic*. Massachusetts Institute of Technology: Campus Police Department.

Gondolf, Edward W. 1998. The Victims of Court-Ordered Batterers. *Violence and Victims* 4(6):659–676.

Gondolf, Edward W., with Ellen R. Fisher. 1988. *Battered Women as Survivors*. New York: Lexington Books.

Goodman, Lisa, and Deborah Epstein. 2005. Refocusing on Women: A New Direction for Policy and Research on Intimate Partner Violence. *Journal of Interpersonal Violence* 20:479–487.

Grauerholz, Gottfried, Cynthia Stohl, and Nancy Gabin. 1999. There's Safety in Numbers: Creating a Campus Advisers' Network to Help Complaints of Sexual Harassment and Complaint Receivers. *Violence Against Women* 5(8):950–977.

Greene, Peters, and Associates. 1998. *Guiding Principles for Promising Female Programming: An Inventory of Best Practices*. The Office of Juvenile Justice and Delinquency Prevention. Nashville, TN, 93pp.

Greenfeld, Lawrence A., and Tracy L. Snell. 1999. *Women Offenders*. Bureau of Justice Statistics: Special Report. U.S. Department of Justice, December, 14pp.

Hagan, John, and Fiona Kay. 1995. *Gender in Practice: A Study of Lawyers' Lives*. New York: Oxford University Press.

Hagan, John., Marjorie Zatz, Bruce Arnold, and Fiona Kay. 1991. Cultural, Capital, Gender, and the Structural Transformation of Legal Practice. *Law and Society Review* 25:239–262.

Haley, Kathleen. 1980. Mothers behind Bars. Pp. 339–354 in *Women, Crime and Justice*, edited by S. K. Datesman and F. R. Scarpitti. New York: Oxford Press.

Hankins, Catherine A., Sylvie Gendron, Margaret A. Handley, Christiane Richard, Marie Therese Lai Tung, and Michael O'Shaughnessy. 1994. HIV Infection among Women in Prison. *American Journal of Public Health* 84(10):1637–1640.

Hannah-Moffat, Kelly. 2000. Prisons that Empower: Neo-Liberal Governance in Canadian Women's Prisons. *British Journal of Criminology* 40:510–531.

Hardesty, Constance, Paula G. Hardwick, and Ruby J. Thompson. 1993. Self-Esteem and the Woman Prisoner. Pp. 27–44 in *Women Prisoners: A Forgotten Population*, edited by B. R. Fletcher, L. D. Shaver, and D. G. Moon. Westport, CT: Praeger.

Hart, Barbara. 1993. Battered Women and the Criminal Justice System. *American Behavioral Scientist* 36:624–638.

Heise, Lor L. 1996. Violence against Women: Global Organizing for Change. Pp. 7–33 in *Future Interventions with Battered Women and Their Families*, edited by J. L. Edleson and Z. C. Eisikovits. Thousand Oaks, CA: Sage Publications.

Hirsch, Barton J., Jennifer G. Roffman, Nancy L. Deutsh, Cathy A. Flynn, Tondra L. Loder, and Maria E. Pagano. 2000. Inner-City Youth Development Organizations: Strengthening Programs for Adolescent Girls. *Journal of Early Adolescence* 20:210–230.

Horney, Julie, and Cassia Spohn. 1991. Rape Law Reform and Instrumental Change in Six Urban Jurisdictions. *Law and Society Review* 25:117–153.

Hutchison, Ira W., and J. David Hirschel. 1998. Abused Women: Help-Seeking Strategies and Police Utilization. *Violence Against Women* 4(4):436–456.

Immarigeon, Russ, 1987a. Few Diversion Programs Are Offered Female Offenders. *Journal of the National Prison Project* 12:9–11.

———. 1987b. Women in Prison. *Journal of the National Prison Project* 11:1–5.

Immarigeon, Russ, and Meda Chesney-Lind. 1992. *Women's Prisons: Overcrowded and Overused.* San Francisco: National Council on Crime and Delinquency.

Jaffe, Peter, D. A. Wolfe, A. Telford, and G. Austin. 1986. The Impact of Police Charges in Incidents of Wife Abuse. *Journal of Family Violence* 1:37–49.

Kanuha, Valli. 1996. Domestic Violence, Racism, and the Battered Women's Movement in the United States. Pp. 34–52 in *Future Interventions with Battered Women and Their Families*, edited by J. L. Edleson and Z. C. Eisikovits. Thousand Oaks, CA: Sage Publications.

Kelley, Margaret S. 2003. The State-of-the-Art in Substance Abuse Programs for Women in Prison. Pp. 119–148 in *The Incarcerated Woman*, edited by S. F. Sharp. Upper Saddle River, NJ: Prentice Hall.

Kendall, Kathleen. 1994. Creating Real Choices: A Program Evaluation of Therapeutic Services at the Prison for Women. *Forum on Corrections Research* 6:19–21.

Kirkwood, Laurie J., and Marcelle E. Mihaila. 1979. Incest and the Legal System. *University of California–Davis Law Review* 12:673–699.

Kleck, Gary, and Susan Sayles. 1990. Rape and Resistance. *Social Problems* 37:149–162.

Klein, Dorie. 1981. Violence against Women: Some Considerations regarding Its Causes and Elimination. *Crime and Delinquency* (January):64–80.

Knight, Barbara B. 1992. Women in Prison as Litigants: Prospects for Post Prison Futures. *Women & Criminal Justice* 4:91–116.

Konradi, Amanda, and Tina Burger. 2000. Having the Last Word: An Examination of Rape Survivors' Participation in Sentencing. *Violence Against Women* 6:351–395.

Koss, Mary P., and Mary R. Harvey. 1991. *The Rape Victim: Clinical and Community Interventions*, 2nd ed. Newbury Park, CA: Sage.

Kurz, Demie. 1992. Battering and the Criminal Justice System: A Feminist View. Pp. 21–40 in *Domestic Violence: The Changing Criminal Justice Response*, edited by E. S. Buzawa and C. G. Buzawa. Westport, CT: Auburn House.

Lake, E. S. 1993. An Exploration of the Violent Victim Experiences of Female Offenders. *Violence and Victims* 8(1):41–51.

Lawson, W. Travis, and Lena Sue Fawkes. 1993. HIV, AIDS, and the Female Offender. Pp. 43–48 in *Female Offenders*, edited by The American Correctional Association. Laurel, MD: American Correctional Association.

Lerman, Lisa G. 1992. The Decontextualization of Domestic Violence. *Journal of Criminal Law and Criminology* 83:217–240.

Luke, Katherine P. 2002. Mitigating the Ill Effects of Maternal Incarceration on Women in Prison and Their Children. *Child Welfare* 81:929–948.

Maidment, MaDonna R. 2002. Toward a "Woman-Centered" Approach to Community-Based Corrections: A Gendered Analysis of Electronic

Monitoring (EM) in Eastern Canada. *Women & Criminal Justice* 13:47–68.

Martin, Susan E. 1989. Women on the Move? A Report on the Status of Women in Policing. *Police Foundation Reports* (May):1–7.

———. 1990. *On the Move: The Status of Women in Policing*. Washington, DC: The Police Foundation.

Martin, Susan E., and Nancy C. Jurik. 1996. *Doing Justice, Doing Gender: Women in Law and Criminal Justice Occupations*. Thousand Oaks, CA: Sage.

Maxwell, C. D., J. H. Garner, and J. A. Fagan. 2001. *The Effects of Arrest on Intimate Partner Violence: New Evidence from the Spouse Assault Replication Program*. Washington, DC: Department of Justice.

McCann, Kathryn. 1985. Battered Women and the Law: The Limits of the Legislation. Pp. 71–96 in *Women-in-Law: Explorations in Law, Family and Sexuality*, edited by J. Brophy and C. Smart. London: Routledge and Kegan Paul.

McCarthy, Belinda R. 1980. Inmate Mothers: The Problems of Separation and Reintegration. *Journal of Offender Counseling, Services and Rehabilitation* 4:199–212.

McGowan, Brenda G., and Karen L. Blumenthal. 1981. Imprisoned Women and Their Children. Pp. 392–408 in *Women and Crime in America*, edited by L. H. Bowker. New York: Macmillan.

McHugh, Gerald A. 1980. Protection of the Rights of Pregnant Women in Prisons and Detention Facilities. *New England Journal on Prison and Law* 6:231–263.

Mills, Linda G. 2003. Insult to Injury: *Rethinking Our Responses to Intimate Abuse*. Princeton, NJ: Princeton University Press.

Mink, Gwendolyn, 2000. *Hostile Environment: The Political Betrayal of Sexually Harassed Women*. Ithaca, NY: Cornell University Press.

Morash, Merry, and Robin N. Haarr. 1995. Gender, Workplace Problems, and Stress in Policing. *Justice Quarterly* 12(1):113–140.

Morris, Allison, and Loraine Gelsthorpe. 1991. Feminist Perspectives in Criminology: Transforming and Transgressing. *Women & Criminal Justice* 2:3–26.

National Victim Center. 1992, April 23. *Rape in America: A Report to the Nation*. Arlington, VA.

Orloff, Leslye E., and Nancy Kelly. 1995. A Look at the Violence against Women Act and Gender-Related Political Asylum. *Violence Against Women* 1(4):380–400.

O'Sullivan, Elizabethann. 2002. Assessing the Role of Sexual Assault Programs in Communities. Pp. 191–204 in *Sexual Violence*, edited by J. F. Hodgson and D. S. Kelley. Westport, CT: Praeger.

Owen, Barbara. 1998. *In the Mix: Struggle and Survival in a Women's Prison*. State University of New York Press.

Parrot, Andrea. 1986. *Acquaintance Rape and Sexual Assault Prevention Training Manual*. Department of Human Services Studies. Ithaca, NY: Cornell University.

Pearson, Jennifer M. 1993. Centro Feminil: A Women's Prison in Mexico. *Social Justice* 20:85–128.

Pence, Ellen, and Melanie Shepard. 1988. Integrating Feminist Theory and Practice: The Challenge of the Battered Women's Movement. Pp. 282–298 in *Feminist Perspectives on Wife Abuse*, edited by K. Yllo and M. Bograd. Newbury Park, CA: Sage.

Pendergrass, Virginia E. 1975. Innovative Programs for Women in Jail and Prison: Trick or Treatment. Pp. 67–76 in *The Female Offender*, edited by A. M. Brodsky. Beverly Hills, CA: Sage.

Pogrebin, Mark R., and Eric D. Poole. 1997. The Sexualized Work Environment: A Look at Women Jail Officers. *The Prison Journal* 77(1): 41–57.

Pollack, Shoshana. 1994. Opening the Window in a Very Dark Day: A Program Evaluation of the Peer Support Team at the Kingston Prison for Women. *Forum on Corrections Research* 6:7–10.

Pollock, Joycelyn M. 1998. *Counseling Women in Prison*. Thousand Oaks, CA: Sage.

Presser, Lois, and Emily Gaarder. 2000. Can Restorative Justice Reduce Battering? *Social Justice* 27:175–195.

Proto-Campise, Laura, Joanne Belknap, and John Wooldredge. 1998. High School Students' Adherence to Rape Myths and the Effectiveness of High School Rape-Awareness Programs. *Violence Against Women* 4(3):308–328.

Rafter, Nicole H. 1985. *Partial Justice: Women in State Prisons, 1800–1935*. Boston: Northeastern University Press.

Raj, Anita, and Jay Silverman. 2002. Violence against Immigrant Women. *Violence Against Women* 8:367–398.

Richie, Beth E. 1996. *Compelled to Crime: The Gender Entrapment of Black Battered Women*. New York: Routledge.

———. 2001. Challenges Incarcerated Women Face as They Return to Their Communities. *Crime & Delinquency* 47:368–389.

Roche, Susan E., Katy Biron, and Niamh Reilly. 1995. Sixteen Days of Activism against Gender Violence. *Violence Against Women* 1(3):272–282.

Ross, Robert R., and Elizabeth A. Fabiano. 1986. *Female Offenders: Correctional Afterthoughts*. Jefferson, NC: McFarland.

Saltzman, Linda E., L. Rachid Salmi, Christine M. Branche, and Julie C. Bolen. 1997. Public Health Screening for Intimate Violence. *Violence Against Women* 3(3):319–331.

Schei, B., K. Sidenius, L. Lundvall, and G. L. Ottesen. 2003. Adult Victims of Sexual Assault: Acute Medical Response and Police Reporting among Women Consulting a Center for Victims of Sexual Assault. *Acta Obstetricia et Gynecologica Scandinavica* 82:750–755.

Schupak, Terri L. 1986. Comment: Women and Children First: An Examination of the Unique Needs of Women in Prison. *Golden Gate University Law Review* 16: 455–474.

Sharp, Susan F., and Susan T. Marcus-Mendoza. 2001. It's a Family Affair: Incarcerated Women and Their Families. *Women & Criminal Justice* 12:21–49.

Shaw, Margaret. 1993. Reforming Federal Women's Imprisonment. Pp. 50–75 in *Conflict with the Law: Women and the Canadian Justice System*, edited by E. Edelberg and C. Currie. Vancouver, Canada: Press Gang Publishers.

Sherman, Lawrence W. 1992. *Policing Domestic Violence: Experiments and Dilemma*. New York: Free Press.

Slote, Kim, and Carrie Cuthbert. 1997. Women's Rights Network (WRN). *Violence Against Women* 3(1):76–80.

Smart, Carol. 1989. *Feminism and the Power of Law*. London: Routledge and Kegan Paul.

Sommerlad, Hilary, and Peter Sanderson. 1998. *Gender, Choice and Commitment: Women Solicitors in England and Wales and the Struggle for Equal Status*. Aldershot, England: Ashgate Publishing Company.

Sommers, Ira, and Deborah R. Baskin. 1994. Factors Related to Female Adolescent Initiation into Violent Street Crime. *Youth & Society* 25(4):468–489.

Spohn, Cassia. 1990. Decision Making in Sexual Assault Cases: Do Black and Female Judges Make a Difference? *Women & Criminal Justice* 2:83–106.

Spohn, Cassia, and Julie Horney. 1991. The Law's the Law, But Fair Is Fair: Rape Shield Laws and Officials' Assessment of Sexual History Evidence. *Criminology* 29:137–161.

———. 1992. *Rape Law Reform: A Grassroots Revolution and Its Impact.* New York: Plenum Press.

———. 1993. Rape Law Reform and the Effect of Victim Characteristics on Case Processing. *Journal of Quantitative Criminology* 9:383–409.

Stanko, Elizabeth A. 1989. Missing the Mark? Policing Battering. Pp. 46–69 in *Women, Policing, and Male Violence: International Perspectives*, edited by J. Hanmer, J. Radford, and E. A. Stanko. London: Routledge and Kegan Paul.

Stanton, Ann M. 1980. *When Mothers Go to Jail*. Lexington, MA: Lexington Books.

Stark, Evan. 1992. Framing and Reframing Battered Women. Pp. 271–292 in *Domestic Violence: The Changing Criminal Justice Response*, edited by E. S. Buzawa and C. G. Buzawa. Westport, CT: Auburn House.

———. 1993. Mandatory Arrest of Batterers: A Reply to Its Critics. *American Behavioral Scientist* 36: 651–680.

Steffensmeier, Darrell. 1993. National Trends in Female Arrests, 1960–1990. *Journal of Quantitative Criminology* 9:411–441.

Sudderth, Lori K. 1998. It'll Come Right Back at Me: The Interactional Context of Discussing Rape with Others. *Violence and Victims* 4(5):572–594.

Sullivan, Mary, and Deborah I. Bybee. 1987. Female Students and Sexual Harassment: What Factors Predict Reporting Behavior? *Journal of the National Association for Women Deans, Administrators and Counselors* 50: 11–16.

Tierney, Kathleen J. 1982. The Battered Women Movement and the Creation of the Wife Beating Problem. *Social Problems* 29:207–220.

Tolman, Richard M. 1996. Expanding Sanctions for Batterers: What Can We Do besides Jailing and Counseling Them? Pp. 170–185 in *Future Interventions with Battered Women and Their Families*, edited by J. L. Edleson and Z. C. Eisikovits. Thousand Oaks: Sage Publications.

Tutty, Leslie M., Gillian Weaver, and Michael A. Rothery. 1999. Residents' Views of the Efficacy of Shelter Services for Assaulted Women. *Violence and Victims* 5(8):898–925.

Ullman, Sarah E., and Raymond A. Knight. 1992. Fighting Back: Women's Resistance to Rape. *Journal of Interpersonal Violence* 7:31–43.

U.S. Census Bureau. 1999. *Statistical Abstract of the U.S. 1998*. Washington, DC: U.S. Government Printing Office.

Vinton, Linda. 1998. A Nationwide Survey of Domestic Violence Shelters' Programming for Older Women. *Violence and Victims* 4(5):559–571.

Von Cleve, Elizabeth, and Joseph G. Weis. 1993. Sentencing Alternatives for Female Offenders. Pp. 94–100 in *Female Offenders: Meeting Needs of a Neglected Population*, edited by the American Correctional Association, Laurel, MD.

Walker, Lenore E. 1989. *Terrifying Love: Why Battered Women Kill and How Society Responds.* New York: Harper Perennial.

Wertsch, Teresa L. 1998. Walking the Thin Blue Line: Policewomen and Tokenism Today. *Women & Criminal Justice* 9(3):52–61.

Whitcomb, Debra. 1991. Improving the Investigation and Prosecution of Child Sexual-Abuse Cases. Pp. 181–190 in *Abused and Battered: Social and Legal Responses to Family Violence,* edited by D. D. Knudsen and J. L. Miller. New York: Aldine de Gruyter.

Widom, Cathy S. 1989a. The Cycle of Violence. *Science* 244:160–166.

———. 1989b. Child Abuse, Neglect, and Adult Behavior: Research Design and Findings on Criminality, Violence, and Child Abuse. *American Journal of Orthopsychiatry* 59(3):355–367.

Wooldredge, John D., and Kimberly Masters. 1993. Confronting Problems Faced by Pregnant Inmates in State Prisons. *Crime and Delinquency* 39:195–203.

Zabelina, Tatiana. 1995. Syostri (Sisters): The Moscow Sexual Assault Recovery Center. *Violence Against Women* 1(3):266–271.

Zaitzow, Barbara H., and Angela D. West. 2003. Doing Time in the Shadow of Death: Women Prisoners and HIV/AIDS. Pp. 73–90 in *The Incarcerated Woman,* edited by S. F. Sharp. Upper Saddle River, NJ: Prentice Hall.

Name Index

Subject Index